THIRD EDITION

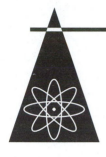

THE NUCLEAR PREDICAMENT: NUCLEAR WEAPONS IN THE TWENTY-FIRST CENTURY

D0149003

Peter R. Beckman

Hobart and William Smith Colleges

Paul W. Crumlish

Hobart and William Smith Colleges

Michael N. Dobkowski

Hobart and William Smith Colleges

Steven P. Lee

Hobart and William Smith Colleges

PRENTICE HALL, UPPER SADDLE RIVER, NEW JERSEY 07458

The Library of Congress Catalog Card Number 99-47280

Editorial director: Charlyce Jones Owen
Editor in chief: Nancy Roberts
Senior acquisitions editor: Beth Gillett Mejia
Editorial assistant: Brian Prybella
Marketing manager: Christopher DeJohn
Editorial/production supervision: Kari Callaghan Mazzola
Electronic page makeup: Kari Callaghan Mazzola and John P. Mazzola
Interior design: John P. Mazzola
Cover director: Jayne Conte
Cover design: Bruce Kenselaar
Buyer: Ben Smith

To our children and all children

This book was set in 10/11 Goudy by Big Sky Composition
and was printed and bound by Courier Companies, Inc.
The cover was printed by Phoenix Color Corp.

Printed in the United States of America
10   9   8   7   6   5   4   3   2   1

ISBN 0-13-680638-4

PRENTICE-HALL INTERNATIONAL (UK) LIMITED, *London*
PRENTICE-HALL OF AUSTRALIA PTY. LIMITED, *Sydney*
PRENTICE-HALL CANADA INC., *Toronto*
PRENTICE-HALL HISPANOAMERICANA, S.A., *Mexico*
PRENTICE-HALL OF INDIA PRIVATE LIMITED, *New Delhi*
PRENTICE-HALL OF JAPAN, INC., *Tokyo*
PEARSON EDUCATION ASIA PTE. LTD., *Singapore*
EDITORA PRENTICE-HALL DO BRASIL, LTDA., *Rio de Janeiro*

CONTENTS

PREFACE

In 1995, the world reached a new milestone. It had learned to live with nuclear weapons through a difficult and costly fifty-year effort. The fact that it had managed not to destroy itself in the process was something at which to marvel, for it was never obvious that the world could in fact avoid nuclear war. By 1995, the threat of a catastrophic nuclear war had receded as the Cold War between two superpowers ended. The first nuclear age was over.

Now we are entering a second nuclear age, an age whose properties are largely unknown to us. Will what we learned during the first nuclear age be applicable here, or will we have to learn anew how to manage our affairs to make our collective future possible? How did we get here? Where are we going? Where do we want to go? How do we get where we want to go, knowing that the potential for nuclear catastrophe exists and *will always* exist? This book is a look to the future—our nuclear future.

More than fifty years of experience with nuclear weapons have provided some tentative lessons that underpin this book:

- The real secret of nuclear weapons is that they can be made. Getting rid of nuclear weapons can never blot out that critical knowledge; they cannot be "uninvented." In a fundamental way, the nuclear age will never end.
- Nuclear weapons, even in relatively small numbers, can produce catastrophic damage, and there is no adequate defense against such damage.
- The existence of sovereign nation-states, which embody and protect cherished values, increases the likelihood of conflicts that may lead to the use of such weapons, which would destroy those very values.

The first nuclear age produced this conclusion: A nuclear war must never be fought. Yet sovereign nation-states in possession of nuclear weapons make such a war possible. No nation has given up the right to wage war to protect itself and its values. This is one crucial part of the nuclear predicament. A predicament is a dangerous situation from which there seems no escape. Our situation is dangerous because the nuclear arsenals of the United States, Russia, Britain, France, China, Israel, India, and Pakistan threaten our global civilization. A predicament exists because it is hard to see how to move away from this threat without making the danger of war greater or putting at risk other things that a nation values highly. Put another way, nations have made decisions based on goals that seemed both reasonable and responsible. Yet when a number of these decisions are put together in the shadow of nuclear weapons, they create a situation in which the nations are at mortal risk.

In the first nuclear age, the predicament appeared in various forms. It appeared, for instance, in the implications of the old adage, "To keep the peace, prepare for war." In a nonnuclear world, preparation for war might keep the peace, and if it failed to do so, war might be an acceptable outcome. Although this adage seems so well-grounded in experience, applying it to nuclear weapons raises paradoxes. If nuclear war must never be fought—a position endorsed by the leaders of the United States and the Soviet Union during the Cold War—then how could a nation prepare to wage such a war? Or how can nuclear deterrence—the threat to use such weapons—be effective? If no adequate defense is possible against such weapons—which is our condition today and for years into the future—how can we hope to use such weapons to defend ourselves?

The second nuclear age has brought with it its own contributions to the predicament. First, the end of the Cold War has reduced the urgency with which people consider the nuclear threat that hangs over us all. Yet without a sense of urgency, we will have less incentive to think carefully and creatively about what this new era demands of us, or to mobilize the political will to bring about change. What we do—or fail to do—today shapes our nuclear future. Second, as we move further from the Cold War, now ten years behind us, we tend to forget how threatening it was. It becomes easier to equate nuclear weapons with peace and prestige. To the degree that the current crop of nuclear and nonnuclear states accepts this equation, the greater will be the pressure on nuclear weapons states to retain the weapons or on nonnuclear states to acquire them (a process labeled nuclear proliferation). India's and Pakistan's open entries into the nuclear weapons club in 1998 may prove to be the unhappy theme of the second nuclear age.

Nuclear proliferation would perpetuate and deepen the nuclear predicament. Will the new nuclear states be able to absorb the lessons of the two superpowers and preserve the nuclear peace? Or do they have to relive the nuclear experience, with all its potential for disaster, in order to come to the conclusion reached by the superpowers—nuclear weapons exist not to be used? Or—and here the predicament becomes particularly harsh—will some of the newly nuclearized states find that the use of nuclear weapons pays off? After all, they seemed to have worked the only time they were used. As we shall discuss in Chapter 2, the United States used two nuclear weapons to compel the surrender of Japan in 1945.

This book is an attempt to think about the various faces of the predicament inherent in our evolving nuclear world. Perhaps the real difficulty that we face rests in our inability to think through our nuclear problems. As Albert Einstein pointed out years ago, "The unleashed power of the atom has changed everything save our modes of thinking, and we thus drift toward unparalleled catastrophe."* That we avoided the catastrophe for over fifty years is no guarantee that we will continue to do so. Perhaps the nuclear predicament—past, present, and future—results from our inability to

---

*Quoted in Otto Nathan and Heinz Norden, eds., *Einstein on Peace* (New York: Schocken, 1968), p. 376.

Albert Einstein at Princeton, September 1943. *National Archives*

recognize how our thinking must change in a world changed by nuclear weapons and in a changing nuclear world. This book is written in that spirit. This third edition has changed from the previous editions in the following ways:

- *The future awaits us.* We have made a concerted effort to imagine what the next twenty-five years might look like. We say that we are living in a second nuclear age—an age that is different from the first in that the older nuclear weapons states do not contemplate nuclear war with each other (whereas in the Cold War, both the United States and the Soviet Union pledged to reduce each other to a ruin of radioactive rubble), there is only one superpower (whereas in the past, the Soviet Union was accorded that status, today its successor state of Russia is barely holding on to a great power status), and a host of current nonnuclear states will be able to produce nuclear weapons and delivery systems relatively cheaply (whereas in the past, cost considerations and pressure from other states dampened interest). It is difficult to say what this future might look like; indeed, it would be better to think of *several possible futures* before us, not only because we cannot see clearly what the future will look like, but also because it reminds us that there is a future to be shaped. We do suspect, however, that we know one way in which the second nuclear age may end and a third begin: when a nuclear weapon is detonated against an opponent. Sadly, we think it is not improbable that such a use will happen in the next twenty-five years.

- ■ *The future is more complex.* For much of the first nuclear age, nuclear weapons were bound into the Cold War between the United States and Soviet Union. The use of nuclear weapons in that age would always have run the risk of escalation to a massive exchange between the two superpowers. Today, those linkages have been broken. While it is still possible that there may be a massive exchange between nuclear armed states that brings the planet close to ruin, we are now confronted with the possibility that we will see in the next twenty-five years the use of one or several nuclear weapons or a regional nuclear conflict that, for all its costs to humans, is not planet-threatening. How can we create measures of control that deal with these possibilities? Is it reasonable to expect that we can keep the next twenty-five years free of any nuclear use?

- ■ *The past is still the prologue to the future, but the prologue is ambiguous.* We present some of the history of the nuclear past so that the reader will understand how individuals came to create the nuclear world and how they fashioned policies to attempt to live in it. Those decisions set the context and the initial direction for our future. But the closer one looks at some aspects of the past, the more uncertain its lessons become. For instance, our nuclear experience has historically been bound up in the Cold War. Are its lessons applicable for the post-cold war situation we are now in? Do we even know what the Cold War's specific lessons were? For instance, is it the case that the threat of mutual destruction kept the peace between the United States and the Soviet Union? While we do attempt to discern lessons from the first nuclear age, perhaps the main lesson is that we have little sure knowledge about how the nuclear world operates.

Some things do remain the same, however. This edition of the book is, like the earlier editions, a collaborative effort of four individuals who approach the nuclear predicament from different perspectives. Our hope remains that those differences give the reader a greater purchase on the issues of the nuclear future. Also, we continue to suggest what might be done to shape the nuclear future. We fear the emergence of a third nuclear age ushered in by the use of nuclear weapons, for we see little benefit for the globe's inhabitants. On the other hand, we welcome and hope to encourage an alternative third nuclear age, one where nuclear weapons are reduced to insignificance.

The book itself is organized into four sections. The first section (Chapters 1–3) focuses on the lessons of the early stages of the first nuclear era; it begins with the dawn of the atomic age in 1945 with the American decision to use its new invention against the Japanese. We look at this event from three perspectives: At ground zero, when a nuclear device detonates; within the councils of government when leaders decide to use such weapons; and in the scientific labs, where resources and human understanding of how the world works are brought together with a political will to create new weapons. While each of these three perspectives does describe the American war-time effort, we broaden our analysis to bring the story to the present and try our hand at imagining the future.

The book's second section (Chapters 4–6) begins with the post-Hiroshima world, and asks how the national leadership and defense bureaucracies attempted to bend the technology to suit their national purposes once nuclear capability was in the hands of several states. From the start, nuclear weapons became a part of the arsenal that was dedicated to defending the nation in time of war. Also from the start, leaders strove to find ways to make nuclear weapons a part of their peacetime diplomacy. The result historically was a changing pattern of defense policies and international relations that made nuclear weapons prominent elements. Drawing on this history, we attempt to sketch the possible contours of defense and foreign policy for the next twenty-five years.

The third section of the book (Chapters 7 and 8) emphasizes the contemporary world, but does not forget the historical roots. It concentrates on the pressures that states and other actors will be under to acquire nuclear weapons. We suspect that proliferation is not a settled issue. In particular, any use of nuclear weapons in the future will have important ramifications for proliferation. Presently, nuclear and non-nuclear states have fashioned a number of agreements and understandings seeking some form of control over nuclear weapons and potential crises that would bring nuclear weapons to the forefront. Ironically, our contemporary nuclear world, in its state of nuclear complacency, sees less compelling need to expand the agreements that have been already reached, yet this may be the very time that such agreements can, in fact, be reached.

The fourth section (Chapters 9–11) returns us to Einstein's exhortation: Can we change our way of thinking about nuclear weapons? Here we try to move beyond the prudence that has characterized most of our thinking about nuclear weapons and suggest important moral criteria that should play a role in our attempt to shape the future. We provide a set of prescriptions for the future. This is our contribution to a needed public debate. We believe that it is important for teachers to take a reasoned position in the classroom. We acknowledge that other perspectives provide other prescriptions and other interpretations of our past and present. We hope that our analysis will receive thoughtful scrutiny by the reader; any solution to the nuclear predicament will depend upon actions by all of us. But this section also acknowledges that nuclear weapons create a difficulty for us in trying to think about what should be done—we are prisoners of the terrifying power of the weapons.

The heart of the past and present nuclear age is that history consists of humans making decisions. The predicament is the result of the choices they have made. The future is the result of the choices we make. Therefore, our basic questions are as follows: (1) Can we live another fifty years without nuclear war? (2) How might that be accomplished?

This book represents a collaborative effort of more than a decade of discussion and debate, facilitated by Hobart and William Smith Colleges' emphasis on interdisciplinary study. We are grateful for Larry Campbell's willingness to allow us to use his materials on the physics of nuclear weapons that appeared in the first two editions. We also want to acknowledge Harmon Dunathan's encouragement at the beginning of this project, Rene Schoen-Rene's aid in drafting the first edition of the book, and Louise Bond's patient support of a four-author effort that never seemed to end. We benefited from reviewers whose extensive comments helped shape the previous editions of the book: Among them are Larry Elowitz, Georgia College; Donald S. Will, Chapman College; Mark Reader, Arizona State University; George Hunsinger, Bangor Theological; and John F. Stack Jr., Florida International University. We must, of course, lay claim to the errors that remain.

Peter R. Beckman, Paul W. Crumlish,
Michael N. Dobkowski, Steven P. Lee

1

HIROSHIMA
AND THE NUCLEAR PREDICAMENT

Before dawn on August 6, 1945, the B-29 bomber "Enola Gay," piloted by Colonel Paul Tibbets, took off from Tinian in the Mariana Islands in the Central Pacific and headed for southern Japan. On board was a single atomic bomb nicknamed "Little Boy" (see Figure 1-1 on page 3). At 8:16 A.M., the bomb, armed during the flight, was released over Hiroshima. It exploded forty-three seconds later, 1,900 feet above the city, as it had been set to do, to increase the area of destruction. "I had a definite job to do," Colonel Tibbets later remarked. "I did it. I had orders to carry out.... When I passed through the town wiped out by the atomic bomb, my only reaction was: good job, well done! That is, I had done my job thoroughly."[1] On target, on time—the mission was technically a perfect success.

By present standards the bomb, with an explosive yield of 12,500 tons of TNT, was a small one, equivalent to a battlefield weapon in today's nuclear arsenals. Yet it was powerful enough to transform a city of some 340,000 people into a plain of devastation in a matter of seconds.

Although the inhabitants of Hiroshima had expected American conventional bombing because an air base and military factories were located in the area and they had not yet been extensively bombed, the surprise and shock were absolute. The citizens of this densely populated urban sprawl on wide river plains had prepared shelters and cleared fire lanes in anticipation of an American air raid. But they were totally unprepared for what was to occur. About 7 A.M. on August 6, Japanese radar detected a group of approaching planes (the lead weather reconnaissance plane and the Enola Gay, accompanied by two observation planes), and officials sounded an air raid alert for the area. But only the single weather plane circled at high altitude over the city. Most people believed the all-clear signal issued at 7:31 A.M. when the weather plane left the area, and they emerged from shelters to set about their daily tasks. The authorities and general population assumed that the three planes that appeared shortly before 8:15 A.M. were on a routine reconnaissance mission and hardly anyone went to the shelters. Instead, fathers set off to work, children to school, and soldiers to their appointed jobs.

Their world suddenly disintegrated. A blinding flash of white light, like an exploding sun, was instantly followed by a searing heat and tremendous blast. A huge fireball of several million degrees centigrade vaporized people and poured radiation in all directions. Debris and smoke sucked up by the ascending fire ball spread a dark pall over the city and fell for hours in a radioactive "black rain." Fires erupted everywhere and, fanned by the swirling winds set up by the explosion, burned for six hours and consumed 3.8 square miles of homes and offices. In a few seconds, 13 square miles of city had been flattened or set aflame. Of 76,000 buildings in Hiroshima, 70,000 had been damaged or destroyed, 48,000 totally. Up to 130,000 people had been killed or doomed by wounds and radiation burns. Among the casualties were tens of thousands of children. Most of the survivors who emerged from the holocaust believed that they had survived a direct hit. As one survivor recalled: "Then it happened. It came very suddenly.... It felt something like an electric short—a bluish sparkling light.... There was a noise, and I felt great heat—even inside the house. When I came to, I was underneath the destroyed home.... I thought the bomb had fallen directly upon me."[2] But, of course, he was wrong.

Gradually the extent of the devastation came into focus. As a survivor noted: "Hiroshima was no longer a city, but a burnt-over prairie. To the east and to the west everything was flattened. The distant mountains seemed nearer than I would ever remember.... How small Hiroshima was with its houses gone."[3] Another said: "I climbed Hijiyama Hill and looked down. I saw that Hiroshima had disappeared.... I was shocked by the sight.... What I felt then and still feel now I just can't explain with words."[4] The survivors encountered massive suffering and horror wherever they looked. "I and mother crawled out from under the house. There we found a world such as I had never seen before, a world I'd never even heard of before ...," a world that another survivor called "an uncanny world of the dead."[5]

On August 8, the Soviet Union declared war on Japan, and one day later the United States dropped another atomic bomb, this one of plutonium, nicknamed "Fat Man" (see Figure 1-1), on Nagasaki, killing or injuring 100,000 people. Japan surrendered five days later. World War II was over at last, after nearly six years of total war and 40 million deaths.

The survivors of Hiroshima and Nagasaki are the only people in the world who have endured the wartime use of atomic weapons. Damage done to them and to their cities has been exhaustively studied by scholars and governments. The number of deaths that occurred, both immediately and over a period of some months, will probably never be fully known, but is variously estimated from 180,000 to 300,000 or more. In addition to those killed immediately, tens of thousands of people began (within hours and days after the explosions) to manifest the ill-effects of toxic radiation—vomiting, diarrhea, bloody stools, fever, inflammation, ulcerations, bleeding from body cavities, loss of hair, low white blood cell counts—and many died. In subsequent years, increased incidences of leukemia, other types of cancer, and birth defects were noticed and documented among the *hibakusha*, or "explosion-affected persons." Additional debilitations have been either demonstrated or suspected to have been caused by exposure to the radiation—including various blood diseases, endocrine and skin disorders, damage to the central nervous system, premature aging, and general weakness. The *hibakusha* are still, psychologically, a group set apart. From this information on the results of two small bombs, we can extrapolate and even predict the effects of a nuclear war today, when

FIGURE 1-1

"Little Boy," a gun-assembly type atomic bomb utilizing U-235, was dropped on Hiroshima on August 6, 1945. It had never been tested. *Department of Defense/U.S. Air Force*

"Fat Man," an implosion-type bomb utilizing Pu-239, was dropped on Nagasaki on August 9, 1945. Its prototype had been tested at Trinity. *Department of Defense/U.S. Air Force*

the power of nuclear arsenals is measured in units of millions of tons of TNT. As Robert Jay Lifton has argued, Hiroshima is our text. It is the template of the first nuclear age. Although the world today is very different, with a diminished threat of global nuclear conflict since the dismantling of the Soviet Union, it is not without risk and volatility. What are some of the potential new "hiroshimas" we face?

POST-COLD WAR NUCLEAR RISKS

On Friday morning, August 7, 1998, two powerful truck bombs exploded within minutes of each other, targeting the American embassies in Nairobi, Kenya, and Dar es Salaam, Tanzania, killing 257 innocents and wounding more than 5,000. On June 25, 1996, a fuel truck packed with thousands of pounds of explosives detonated at the King Abdul Aziz Air Base near Dhahran, Saudi Arabia, killing 19 Americans and injuring hundreds. On April 19, 1995, Oklahoma City's Alfred P. Murrah Federal Office Building was demolished by a fertilizer-based truck bomb, killing 168 men, women, and children, making it the worst domestic terrorist attack in American history. For weeks the press projected images of the scoured-out office building, of bleeding babies and shocked survivors and relatives, their faces drained of hope and color. The same news photograph of a firefighter carrying the limp body of a dead child from the collapsed day-care center on the building's first floor appeared on the covers of *Time* and *Newsweek*. These images are reminiscent of some of the early photographs of Hiroshima and its survivors, days after the August 1945 attack. On March 20, 1995, the deadly nerve gas *sarin* was released into the Tokyo subway system by a group known as *Aum Shinri Kyo*, or the Supreme Truth Sect, killing twelve people and hurting hundreds more. On the morning of February 26, 1993, international terrorists attacked New York City's 110-story World Trade Center, killing six and injuring over a thousand. Had that explosion succeeded in undermining the structural foundation of that building as intended, thousands of people might have died.

Terrorism is back. After being subdued internationally and within most Western countries in the late 1980s, it has returned in fearful and pernicious new forms. What the bombing of the World Trade Center in Manhattan and the federal building in Oklahoma City demonstrated to Americans is that terrorism can now strike in downtown New York City, the center of international finance and banking, or in a southwestern city far removed from the locus of national or international politics. The shock, the fear, the anxiety produced by these deadly incidents only suggest what the impact of the explosion of a nuclear device in the United States by terrorists would have on the fabric of American society. In the days and weeks after Oklahoma City, one could sense an almost palpable anxiety during panel discussions and phone-in talk shows. The panicky aftermath is still with us.

Terrorism in the 1990s has been accompanied by a steady escalation in the means of violence, from automatic weapons, to suicide bombers, to truck bombs capable of bringing down entire buildings, to lethal gas that can threaten entire cities. The very real possibility that terrorist organizations and states unwilling to comply with international norms (often called "rogue" states) may soon acquire nuclear weapons and use them to escalate terrorism beyond anything ever thought of is not beyond imagination. With shaky control of nuclear fissile material in Russia, with increased numbers of countries able and perhaps willing to sell components needed to develop nuclear capability to countries that lack them, fear has grown that terrorists or rogue states may obtain nuclear explosives and a means of delivering them to targets they choose. In September, 1998, North Korea tested a new two-stage missile, the Taepo Dong-1, with a range of up to 1,240 miles capable of reaching Japan. The missile also raised new threats, since North Korea has sold its missiles to clients like Libya and Iran. Also disturbing has been evidence of a massive excavation northeast of Pyongyang that suggests the North Koreans have been attempting to revive a nuclear weapons project they had agreed to shelve. The worry is real.

Let us examine the following scenario. The expansion of militant Islam and its ability to intimidate the West would be greatly enhanced if the Islamic Republic of Iran succeeded in acquiring or building nuclear weapons. There are estimates in 1999 that place Iran between three and five years away from being able to produce its own nuclear weapons without the importation of materials or technology from abroad. How could Iran use such nuclear weapons? It might threaten the West or any of its neighbors outright, just as Saddam Hussein of Iraq would probably have done had his nuclear program born fruit before his invasion of Kuwait in 1990. One shudders to think of the consequences had patience been one of his virtues. He could have threatened to strike neighboring capitals like Riyadh or cities like Tel Aviv or to destroy oil-loading facilities in the Persian Gulf, if he did not get his way. How would Israel have responded to such threats or imminent attacks? It is generally assumed that Israel has an impressive nuclear capability of some one hundred weapons. Would it have deployed these weapons if sufficiently threatened? Would it have used them? What impact would either deployment or use have on the stability of the region and even global stability, given that the United States, Russia, England, and France have such a stake in the area? If Iran maintains its commitment to fundamentalist Islam and follows a course of nuclear arms development or procurement, would Israel consider a preemptive strike as it did against the Iraqi nuclear facility in June of 1981?

A nuclear-armed Iran would have additional options. It could avoid a direct threat to the United States or Israel and the attendant consequences of horrible retaliation by resorting to indirect intimidation of nuclear holocaust by using any number of Islamic terrorist groups such as Hizballah and Islamic Jihad, with which it has influence. Such groups nullify in large measure the need to have air power or missiles as delivery systems. They will be the delivery system. In the worst of such scenarios, the consequences may not be a fertilizer bomb but a nuclear device in front of a building in a yet-to-be-targeted American or Israeli city. This is unlikely, surely, but not impossible. We can only speculate on what impact the exploding of a nuclear terrorist device would have. The sheer scope of the ensuing tragic loss of life, the random arbitrariness of the deaths of those unlucky enough to be the victims, the surprise and shock of the event, would undoubtedly undermine confidence in the government. Fear of nuclear terror arises from the assumption that if terrorists can get nuclear weapons they *will* get them, and would consider using them. This is comparable to assuming that if weak or relatively unstable states or regional powers such as India and Pakistan are locked in historic competition and have nuclear weapons, they would be more likely than the superpowers to use them. This is a credible assumption. That is why India's testing of nuclear devices in the summer of 1998 and Pakistan's following suit is such a concern.

It is easy to imagine what the consequences of this nuclear terrorism would be. Suppose that instead of the trucks filled with hundreds of pounds of crude explosives used in Oklahoma City and New York, terrorists had acquired a suitcase carrying one hundred pounds of highly enriched uranium, smaller in size than a soccer ball. Using a simple, well-known design to build a weapon from this material, terrorists could have produced a nuclear blast equivalent to 10,000 to 15,000 tons of TNT, about the size of the Hiroshima bomb. Under normal conditions, this would devastate a three- to four-square-mile urban area. Much of Oklahoma City would have disappeared, leaving hundreds of thousands dead and seriously injured. Within a fraction of a second of the explosion, intense heat from expanding gases could have set fires in buildings up to a mile away. The tip of Manhattan, including all of Wall Street reaching up to Grammercy Park, would have been destroyed, with over a million casualties. Within seconds of detonation, radioactive debris would have begun spreading out over the area. In the next minutes and hours, this radioactive cloud would be carried by prevailing winds and fall to the ground, creating a highly lethal radioactive area many miles from the point of detonation, reaching portions of New Jersey, upstate New York, and Connecticut.

The goal of terrorism is to instill fear in a society for political ends and to undermine confidence in the ability of that society to protect its citizens and to function normally. That is why terrorism purposefully targets innocent civilians. In fact, the more removed the target of the attack from any connection to the grievance of the terrorists, the greater the terror. The idea soon spreads that everyone is a potential target and no one is safe. What possible connection is there between the day-care children savaged in Oklahoma and the conspiracy theories of militia and patriot groups in Arizona? What do the bloodied and maimed clerks and shoppers in the World Trade Center have to do with the Islamic Jihad? What do the thousands of innocent Africans in Nairobi and Dar es Salaam have to do with Osama bin Laden and his network? Nothing, and that is precisely the point.

We can only speculate on what impact the exploding of a nuclear terrorist device would have on a society so victimized. Would Libya or Iran or their surrogates try to destroy Israel through the use of terror, nuclear or conventional, at the risk of nuclear retaliation directed at Tripoli, Benghazi, or Teheran? And what would be left of Israel if Tel Aviv or Haifa were destroyed? And what would the American response be? The sheer scope of the tragic loss of life, property, and economic infrastructure; the random arbitrariness of those tens of thousands victimized; the surprise and shock of the event, would undoubtedly undermine confidence in the government, increase feelings of vulnerability, and lead to pervasive fear and anxiety. The targeted city would eventually be rebuilt, like Hiroshima and Nagasaki, but there would be deep psychological, emotional, and "political" scars left over that would take much longer to repair.

There are, of course, other reasons to be concerned. If nuclear proliferation continues, there are some potential nuclear states that may not be politically strong and stable enough to ensure control of the weapons and control of the decision to use them. If neighboring, hostile, perhaps politically unstable states, such as India and Pakistan, have them, the temptation to strike against traditional rivals may be too hard to resist. When the weak fear the strong, the weaker party often does what it can to maintain its security. Pakistan has fought three wars with its larger and more powerful neighbor, India. If it feels threatened, it might be tempted in the future to act preemptively. Many fear that states that are radical at home, say a Libya, will recklessly use their nuclear weapons in pursuit of revolutionary ends abroad. In some of the new nuclear states, civil control of the military may be weak. Nuclear weapons may fall into the hands of military officers more inclined to use them.

We are clearly living in a different nuclear world than existed during the Cold War.

With the fall of the Berlin Wall in 1989 and the disintegration of the former Soviet Union in the early 1990s, the chances of unlimited thermonuclear exchanges between major nuclear powers have diminished to the point that remarkably few even worry about them anymore. The conventional wisdom suggests that the world is a much safer place now that communism has expired and with it the expansionist Soviet adversary that served as the fixed point for the American foreign policy compass for four decades of Cold War. The threat of nuclear war is over or greatly diminished, people say.

We believe that conclusion to be a bit premature, even a case of wishful thinking. A certain form of the nuclear threat, namely, a global nuclear conflagration initiated by the superpowers, may have been lessened by recent events, but not the threat itself in other guises. It can be a fundamental and analytically mischievous error to confuse the end of the Cold War with tranquility or predictability. Peace is quite compatible with trouble, conflict, racism, inequality, injustice, xenophobia, genocide—and therefore with chaos, uncertainty, and unpredictability. We have seen extraordinary changes in the former Soviet Union and in Eastern Europe, in South Africa, and in the Middle East. What is equally extraordinary is that no one foresaw these changes. All the statesmen and the experts were caught unaware. History has an abiding capacity to undermine our certitudes. We should approach predicting the future, therefore, with some caution and humility.

As a result of the dramatic political transformations of the 1990s, has the likelihood that a nuclear weapon will explode somewhere in the world decreased? Probably not. Even as the probability of large-scale nuclear war between the United States and Russia has decreased dramatically, the probability that a nuclear weapon will detonate in Russia, or Asia, or the Middle East, or even the United States, may have increased. But because this new threat comes in a form so different from prior experience, and because the instruments and policies needed to address it are so unlike the familiar Cold War approaches, Americans have had difficulty awakening to this new reality.

The winding-down of the superpower nuclear arms race may, ironically, produce two distinct types of threat in the twenty-first century: the more traditional problems of proliferation and of how to prevent former Soviet warheads and missiles from falling into the "wrong" hands; and the newer, perhaps more daunting task of dealing with large quantities of loosely controlled fissile material from which nuclear weapons can be made, material that is a profound security and ecological hazard. The collapse of Soviet power and the failure of totalitarian institutions certainly open up long-term possibilities of democratic transformation. But in the short term, the prospects may be for more political upheavals, dislocation, and economic distress, an environment that may allow some of this material to be purchased by those interested in a quick nuclear "fix." The periodic economic and political crises Russia has faced since 1991 are an indication of how unstable the situation can become. The news is not entirely grim. But as long as Russia continues to be buffeted by turbulence, economic collapse, and disorder, the threat of nuclear leakage will persist.

This situation is complicated by the possibility of future breakdowns in Arab-Israeli relations; the growth of Moslem fundamentalism and the use of terror; ethnic conflict in the Balkans and Africa; volatile and aggressive regimes in Libya, Iraq, and North Korea; the emergence of regional nuclear powers like India and Pakistan; technological advances in the Chinese nuclear arsenal; and the proliferation of sophisticated and deadly weaponry, including chemical, biological, and nuclear weaponry, around the globe.

The United States has obviously emerged as the only superpower after the Cold War. However, there are a number of countries—Pakistan, India, Israel, Argentina, and Brazil, to name a few—that are now capable of equipping themselves with nuclear armaments and of constructing or purchasing sophisticated long-range missiles. When we add the so-called "rogue" nations like Iran, Iraq, Syria, Libya, Sudan, North Korea, and Afghanistan, for instance, some of whom have actively pursued nuclear capability, we have a growing list of nations that could pose a real threat to the security of their neighbors, not to mention the interests of the major powers. What is more, it may be premature to envision a new era of permanent cooperation and peace between the United States and Russia. The political, ethnic, and economic volatility of that region is still troubling. It remains to be seen if Russia's challenge to the West is truly over, or for that matter the challenges raised by Marxism or some other brand of authoritarianism. German reunification is a fact and it is unlikely that Russia will regain its influence over Poland, Hungary, or the Czech Republic. The situation in the Balkans, however, is less stable or predictable. It is possible that at some time in the future the struggle between different national or ethnic groups might lead to regional conflict. It is possible that such a struggle might encourage the Russians or the Germans to extend their influence in the Balkans. Turmoil in Albania and conflict in Serbia's Kosovo province in late 1998, is a concern, as are the irredentist populations in some of the former Soviet republics.

So we now face a wider range of contingencies. There is the possibility that nuclear weapons will proliferate to rogue states and terrorists. There remains the risk of accidental or unauthorized use by nuclear states. This threat increases if more states or groups have access to the weapons. Finally, there is the possibility of deliberate use of nuclear weapons by existing states and threshold states; Israel could believe itself sufficiently threatened to resort to a nuclear strike; Russia could feel itself threatened by neighboring states or China; an India-Pakistan war could erupt. One suspects that political and military leaders are scrambling to think through the implications of these new threats, and only the most sanguine observer can assume that they will get it right on every occasion. But what would "getting it wrong" mean?

Let us consider for a moment what the impact of an India-Pakistan war that involved nuclear weapons would have on the region and globally. These nations fought three wars (1962, 1965, 1971) partially over the disputed Kashmir region, and partially over questions of power and prestige. There are strong indications that in May 1990 the Pakistan air force went on nuclear alert during a crisis over Kashmir. The tensions there are real. The temptation may be to assume that such a conflict, albeit tragic and horrific, because it is in a remote part of the world, could be contained. We believe such a conclusion to be unwarranted and dangerous. Nuclear weapons used again, anywhere in the world, would shake confidence and stability, threaten the environment, send shock waves through the world economy, threaten other nations in the region, and actually encourage states on the nuclear "fence" to consider acquiring these weapons for their own defensive or political purposes. The nuclear genie released again would be hard to contain.

The use of several small nuclear weapons in the Hiroshima range or slightly larger in such a conflict would be devastating. They would virtually destroy the cities or areas targeted. Local or regional governments would have difficulty getting into the areas affected to direct recovery efforts. The contamination from even one small bomb could displace hundreds of thousands of people and lead to panic and anarchy. With the death of several hundreds of thousands of people, maybe up to a million over a period of several weeks, the toll on the survivors would be psychologically traumatic. Radiation sickness would continue to claim additional victims. Given global communications, much of this horror would be broadcast to the world through searing images of death and destruction. Contamination of food supplies in rumor or fact would test order and civility. The fear of contamination would quickly spill over the affected borders and have regional, even global repercussions. Fires could rage out of control for days and weeks, spreading dark, radioactive clouds of smoke throughout the area. Medical and emergency services would be inadequate to treat the hundreds of thousands of people injured. Burying the dead would also create major logistical and psychological nightmares. The overall psychological impact could be so significant that a victimized nation or region might not have the will or the capability to pull itself back to some level of normality for many years. And as indicated earlier, it would be difficult to contain these social, political, and psychological effects to the nations involved.

If the nuclear attacks are very limited and only on one or two cities, eventually there would be recovery. The Japanese reconstructed Hiroshima and Nagasaki relatively quickly and they are now normal, functioning cities. The issue of global impact and ultimate recovery arises if there are additional weapons used and of significantly larger power. For example, the recovery of the Japanese cities was largely dependent on outside assistance. Comparable Indian or Pakistani cities, such as Madras, Pondicherry, or Karachi, could expect outside assistance if it were available. If the detonations, however, were more numerous, widespread, and potent, then sufficient sources of outside help would be more difficult to enlist. That certainly is the case as we contemplate the prospects of a more global conflagration, however unlikely that may be.

At present, the combined arsenals of the United States and Russia and the other major nuclear powers contain over twenty-five thousand nuclear warheads. If even a small portion of these weapons, most of which are far more powerful than the weapons that destroyed Hiroshima and devastated Nagasaki, were actually used in nuclear war, the ensuing holocaust would dwarf the worst human tragedies in history.[6] A recent World Health Organization study estimated that a nuclear war fought with about one-half of the present arsenals would cause one billion immediate deaths and seriously injure an equal number, most of whom would eventually die due to the effects of radiation exposure, lack of food and uncontaminated water, shortages of medicine and medical care, and the general collapse of the social, economic, and political infrastructures of society.[7] To these findings must be added the possible climatic and long-term environmental and biological consequences of nuclear war, including the possibility of a "nuclear winter." The spreading blanket of darkness from smoke and other atmospheric debris generated by fires ignited by the nuclear explosions could reduce light intensities dramatically, thereby causing world temperature to plummet tens of degrees.[8]

We have briefly described the possible consequences of nuclear terrorism or the use of nuclear weapons in a regional conflict. We have also stated that the initiation of a nuclear war between the superpowers is less likely today than at the height of the Cold War. But it is not an impossibility. What would the effects of such a war be? What is it that has made nuclear weapons so feared—feared in the profound sense that in them we see the possible death of civilization as we know it? What would be the effects of a major nuclear exchange between weaker nuclear states? Or the effects of a nuclear attack against a nonnuclear state? The prospects are fearsome, but we need to be aware of them to better prepare ourselves for the future.

THE EFFECTS OF NUCLEAR WEAPONS

Our only experience with nuclear war was the attacks on Hiroshima and Nagasaki, two unprepared urban targets. The American government was intensely interested in discovering the effect of nuclear weapons; in 1953 and 1955 it conducted extensive tests against a variety of objects: houses and buildings, vehicles, electrical and communications transmission systems, and animals. From the theoretical understanding of the bomb, its use against Japan, and this postwar curiosity came the most concrete knowledge we have about nuclear weapons as weapons of destruction.

Assume that nuclear war comes to pass, and the urban area where you live or are near to is a target of a nuclear weapon. As that weapon detonates, there would be a brilliant flash of light as the release of nuclear energy through fission and fusion occurred. (See Chapter 3 for a discussion of these phenomena.) Temperatures on the order of tens of millions of degrees would heat the air around the blast to create a glowing fireball, expanding and rising into the sky, creating the familiar mushroom-shaped cloud.

The energy released by the weapons would take three forms. At the instant of detonation, 5 percent of the energy would be radiation (in the form of neutrons and gamma rays), which would travel out for a relatively short distance from the point of blast.[9] The flash would be thermal (or heat) radiation, accounting for 35 percent of the bomb's energy. Another 50 percent of the energy would be converted into a shock wave of air created by the superheated air in the vicinity of the detonation. (A detonation close to the ground would also create a shock wave of lesser strength transmitted through the ground.) And finally, 10 percent of the energy would be in the form of radioactive fission fragments. If the blast occurred close enough to the ground surface, small pieces of earth would be sucked up by the fireball as it rose, and the radioactive particles would fuse to those pieces of dust and debris. Carried aloft, and then pushed away from the blast site by prevailing winds, these radioactive particles would eventually fall out of the atmosphere. The result—radioactive fallout.

How does this differ from a chemical explosive found in a conventional bomb? The conventional explosive produces no nuclear radiation and very little thermal effect compared to nuclear weapons because the heat of its explosion is much less (no more than 9,000° F). There is a blast or shock effect, but it is of short duration and does not reach very far. Such weapons can, of course, kill and destroy, but not with the range and relentless efficiency of nuclear weapons.

The effects of a single nuclear blast do not end with atomic and thermal radiation and blast (shock) effects. Unlike conventional weapons, a nuclear device multiplies its destructiveness. The initial shock wave from an airburst, for instance, can "echo" off the ground and combine with the shock wave as it travels outward to produce a more powerful wall of pressure. Moreover, behind the shock waves are intense winds, that exert a dynamic, relatively long-lasting pressure on structures and that can topple them as a hurricane can. The air will fill with flying debris and the destruction of structures is likely to dump tons of building materials into streets, making passage difficult, if not impossible. While the thermal radiation effects are strong enough to start fires, the main source of fires after a nuclear attack in an urban area is more likely to be the ruptured natural gas lines in buildings. Such fires are likely to spread, creating a blazing inferno as they move outward as conflagrations. Or, if the heat in a particular area is strong enough, it may pull in oxygen from surrounding areas. The inrushing wind creates a firestorm, totally consuming everything in the area.

One other effect, which seems minor compared to the physical damage of a nuclear blast, is EMP, or electromagnetic pulse. As a nuclear weapon detonates, it creates an intense, brief surge of electrical energy. Such energy is likely to disrupt or destroy communications systems and devices with unshielded electronic components.

What happens at ground zero, the point directly underneath an exploding nuclear device? Thermal and atomic radiation and the shock wave radiate outward in all directions from this point. As they move outward, they diminish in strength or destructiveness. Therefore, we can image a series of concentric circles of destructiveness ranging from ground zero out for some distance. Figure 1-2 (on page 12) illustrates the effects of a one megaton warhead.

One rough index of destructiveness is the pounds per square inch index (known as *psi*). At the earth's surface, the atmosphere puts approximately fifteen pounds of pressure on each square inch of surface. The shock wave of a nuclear blast creates its own pressure, called "overpressure." One conventional reference point is 5 psi of overpressure. Within the circle with this much overpressure, it is expected that 50 percent of the individuals will die and that "lightly constructed commercial buildings and typical residences are destroyed; heavier construction is severely damaged."[10] It is not the blast (or overpressure) itself that accounts for all the destruction of human lives or property, although that will contribute. Rather, the 5 psi ring indicates where falling buildings, fires, wind-driven debris, and other effects will cause such devastation to those people and things unfortunate enough to be within that circle. Farther out from the ground zero, the casualties from the blast itself will decrease.

Other casualties will come from radiation. Those close to ground zero, if they survive the effects of blast and thermal radiation, will immediately receive lethal doses of nuclear radiation. The range of nuclear radiation, however, is limited; the range of thermal radiation is greater but still limited. For instance, a one-megaton explosion can produce third-degree burns up to five miles; death is likely if such burns cover more than a quarter of the body's surface. These, then, are the "prompt" effects of a nuclear blast.

To this point, we have looked at the impact of a single nuclear weapon on an urban area. The range of nuclear explosiveness is quite varied, from several kilotons to many megatons. The W33 artillery shell can deliver from 1 to 12 kilotons against a target; the Lance short-range missile could deliver 1 to 100 kilotons. The example in the preceding paragraphs spoke of a one-megaton weapon. The evolving nuclear predicament means that we must consider what a range of nuclear use might produce. Of course, the damage effects of a single weapon would be different if used against a rural area, perhaps against a concentration of military forces: The debris would be minimized, but all the other effects would obtain. As the explosion would be an airburst (to maximize the area covered by the blast), the amount of fallout would be decreased due to less debris in the mushroom cloud.

It would be misleading, however, to concentrate on a single nuclear weapon's effects. During the Cold War, the superpowers' plans for waging nuclear war envisioned extensive use of nuclear weapons. Even today, when such war is unlikely (although not impossible), we need to understand where we may be headed if other nations acquire nuclear weapons and engage in an extensive exchange with each other. So once again, we need to examine the calculations made about the superpowers during the Cold War. What would be the effects of nuclear attacks against a great number of targets with powerful warheads within a short period of time?

The superpowers considered such attacks because they assumed that it would be

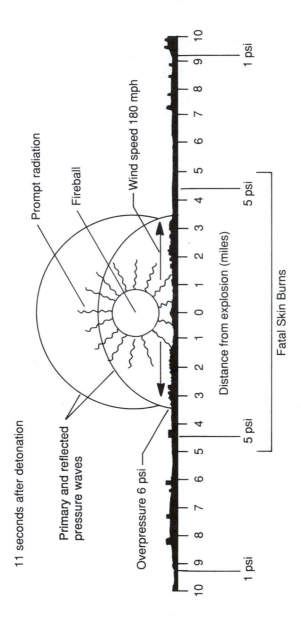

FIGURE 1-2

This figure shows a one megaton explosion eleven seconds after detonation. *Adapted from K. Lewis, "The Prompt and Delayed Effects of Nuclear War," Scientific American 241 (July 1979): 36.*

important to destroy an opponent's military forces (especially its nuclear forces) quickly, which would necessitate using a large number of warheads. For instance, to destroy 1,000 American land-based missiles in their underground silos, it is likely that Russia would need to use at least two warheads per silo; assuming a modest failure rate of 20 percent, 1,600 warheads would detonate. As they would need to be ground-burst to maximize the damage to hardened silos, there would be large-scale fallout as well as enormous amounts of dust put into the atmosphere. Attacks of a more limited nature—designed, for example, only to reduce American oil refinery capability by two-thirds—might involve ten Russian SS18s with eight warheads each, yet such an attack would be a major one. Five million fatalities, for instance, would be expected.[11] The casualty figures would grow astronomically if targets were urban areas: possibly 155 million *deaths* if there was no time for precautionary actions such as evacuation or extensive sheltering.

In the near future, nuclear exchanges between lesser nuclear-weapons states would likely produce fewer casualties and less physical destruction, but even a modest arsenal of 100 warheads of 25 kilotons each would wreak unparalleled devastation.

The detonation of large numbers of warheads would produce local effects identical to those described above. But multiple detonations would also have more general systemic effects. Such systemic effects have been observed in some cases, but for most, all we have are plausible hypotheses.

One class of systemic effects concerns probable physical changes. Fallout is perhaps the effect that we know most about because extensive above-ground nuclear tests by both superpowers produced measurable fallout patterns. Multiple detonations with a significant proportion of ground bursts would likely produce extensive fallout over populated areas and farming areas. As the radioactive fission fragments decay (that is, as they emit particles to move toward stable, nonradioactive elements), they release doses of radiation that may be lethal for unsheltered people and animals. Even in shelters, unless the shelter is well-shielded and closed off from air-transported radioactive dust, radiation will be a problem. In areas far removed from the blast sites and not in the central plume of fallout it might be safe to emerge in the open after two to three weeks. The amount of radioactivity would still greatly exceed what we now consider to be safe, but would not produce short-term deaths. In the direct plume areas, depending on the distance from ground zero, two to ten years would be required for the radiation to return to levels considered safe.

Fallout itself can produce death or sickness that so weakens the body that it falls prey to other diseases. In the long run, those individuals who survive radiation deaths will most likely suffer greatly increased cancer rates and pass on genetic defects to their offspring.

Such effects, of course, are not confined to humans. Indeed, as most animals, domestic or wild, will not be sheltered, we can expect extensive deaths of livestock and game, depriving humans of food, power, and transportation. The killing off of birds may prove quite serious, as birds are natural controls for insect populations. Ironically, insects are the most immune to radiologic effects. They would become a serious threat to food crops.

There is a second systemic effect that has broader and more deadly implications. Nuclear weapons are likely to put into the atmosphere a large volume of dust particles and soot from fires. These could block a large proportion of the sun's light (depending on the amount of dust and soot in the upper atmosphere, which in turn depends on the targets and megatonnage used). The initial work done by Carl Sagan and others[12] suggested that the dust and soot from even a light nuclear exchange between the superpowers would likely produce at least a 15° C decrease in temperature, lasting for three months. In more severe attacks, the decline might be greater than 40° C, which would mean that, even in summer, the surface temperature would be far below freezing (O° C or 32° F) for more than three months. The earth would become cold and, for an abnormally long period, dark. A "nuclear winter" would prevail.

Since the publication of what came to be known as the TAPS study (after the initials of the authors), others have challenged the conclusions. They have pointed to critical limitations in the computer model used in the analysis, such as not including the effects of oceans or wind. Revised models portray less dramatic temperature drops (perhaps 10 to 15° C for a major attack). As Stephen Schneider points out, however, such modeling must always be imprecise, and we are now aware that "the earth's biota can be highly sensitive even to small climatic disturbances."[13]

The studies raise the possibility of a massive disruption of the growth, reproduction, and survival patterns of green plants. A spring or summer nuclear exchange of significant proportions might mean, in the Northern Hemisphere, the loss of the crops for that year. In addition, animals dependent upon the plants would die. A fall or winter exchange would not destroy the harvest, but would probably delay or make impossible agricultural growth the following year. Modern farming in both cases would be disrupted or halted completely; not only would the ecological systems not sustain such agriculture, but fertilizers and gasoline for farm machinery would probably not be available.[14]

Massive interference with plant life would severely erode the basis for human life. The cold and the dark of a nuclear winter would make survival more difficult for humans who escaped death in the initial attack. Food stocks in communities (perhaps three weeks' worth) would deplete, and the promise of more food in the future would become less credible as the collapse of the agriculture environment became clear. Hunger, now adding to the weakened condition of many humans and compounded by almost continuous cold, would contribute to more casualties.

Hunger on a scale unknown to most American or Russian citizens would be one likely consequence of a superpower nuclear war. But there are likely to be even more profound changes. For the individual, the postattack environment would be radically different. Humans would have to cope with physical and psychological damage. Studies of disasters show that people have the capacity to recover and to repair the physical damage. Yet there is a fundamental difference: Disasters such as hurricanes and flooding occur in relatively well-defined areas. Outside such areas, there is no physical loss, and there are individuals and organizations able and willing to help those afflicted. Such outside sources of aid are likely to be scarce in a nuclear environment.

Furthermore, the assumption that aid is available from outside the damaged area encourages those within it to look to the future. At Hiroshima, for instance, in the evening following the atomic attack, a Japanese naval launch moved up and down the rivers flowing through Hiroshima.

> The sight of the shipshape launch against the background of havoc across the river; the unruffled young man in his neat uniform; above all, the promise of medical help—the first word of possible succor anyone had heard in nearly twelve awful hours—cheered the people in the park tremendously.[15]

Without such a sustaining belief, individuals are likely to succumb to wounds, disease, or a destructive apathy.

The central question may well be what people expect their individual futures to look like. Their ability to deal with the shock of death and destruction, to cope with a disrupted life, may depend strongly upon a sense of the purpose of living. Interest in the future will be close to breaking at many points. For those in shelters during the first two to three weeks, the interest in the future may erode as sanitation breaks down (where will human waste go?), food decreases, and some in the shelter begin to show the first signs of illness. An individual's willingness to cope with adversity may be compromised by the uncertainty of surviving the adversity. Consider one key measure of one's future—vomiting: "Someone who vomited would not know if he had received a moderate, severe, or lethal dose of radiation; if he had severe psychological shock; if he had vomited because of contagion [seeing others vomit]; or if he had some other illness."[16] Vomiting—which will affect many, but for different reasons—may come to have one psychological meaning: no future.

SURVIVING A MAJOR NUCLEAR WAR

The *interest* in survival may be the thing most at risk for the survivors of the effects of a nuclear war. If there are undamaged areas that can offer both aid and the prospect of a future different from that surrounding the survivors, then they may have a general willingness to deal with the damage. More likely, the message day after day will be one that brings no hope. While radiation levels will, within several weeks, fall below lethal levels in many areas, deaths will continue to mount from those with radiation sickness and other illnesses that attack bodies weakened by radiation damage, foul water, hunger, and cold. The medical profession and its support facilities—hospitals, drug manufacturing and distributing operations—are likely to be greatly reduced in number by a major attack. The reassuring, healing hand of the physician may not be available. Food, or its absence, will be another continuing reminder that the future is precarious. Even if food is available for a while in some areas, disruption of transportation systems will keep it out of the mouths of many.

Scattered among the many who have lost interest in survival are likely to be a number of optimists. Their number will depend on the nature of the attack—the less damaging the attack, the more optimists. Political leaders and governmental bureaucrats, habituated to dealing with problems, are likely to be numerous among the optimists. Those who made their living organizing economic activities are also likely to contribute a disproportionate share of optimists. Can a postattack society be rebuilt on their efforts? Could they manage the societies they inherit, let alone provide some tangible hope for the future?

Modern economies are generally resilient, finding ways to cope with shocks, creating new solutions to problems as they emerge. But the strength of such economies also points to a key problem: the interdependence of a large number of individuals on each other for their continued economic well-being. A catastrophic disturbance in one area of the economy is likely to ripple through the entire economy. More traditional economies are not as interdependent; significant disruption in one area does not necessarily imperil the rest. Yet traditional economies often operate close to the boundary between economic sufficiency and extreme scarcity. Widespread nuclear attacks are likely to plunge the entire society into monumental privation.

The Office of Technology Assessment's judgment of the economic impact of a nuclear strike limited to an attack on just 66 percent of American petroleum refinery capacity is illustrative.[17] Numerous industries would be crippled. Automobile production, for instance, would decrease precipitously; consumers would not be interested in cars for which there was no gasoline. Orders for steel, glass, plastics, and other materials for automobiles would drop as well. A vast array of workers would be laid off. Rationing of gasoline would cripple businesses dependent upon the automobile—retailers in malls, restaurants, and travel services such as motels, for instance. A cascading number of individuals would become unemployed. Their number would likely overwhelm government funds reserved for unemployment compensation and welfare. As the unemployed lost their purchasing ability, the declining demand for goods and services would throw others out of work.

We would expect that, over time, the political leadership and the economic system would be able to meet the crisis created by an attack on American refinery capability. We might also expect that the public at large would "learn" to live with five million fatalities. This, however, was a relatively limited attack. The bulk of the society suffered no direct effects. The study contemplated a total of some 80 megatons used in the attack, but the detonations were in the air, thus minimizing fallout. However, the location of the refineries near cities would raise the probabilities that smoke particles from fires might trigger major atmospheric changes. Finally, the study assumed that no further nuclear attacks took place.

Imagine, now, that the attack was not just on refineries, but other economically important installations as well (for example, an attack on natural gas wells and pipe lines, coal mines, and electric power-generating stations). We would expect that the economic dislocation would increase exponentially—that is, if twice the number of targets were struck, the result would not be twice the dislocation of the refinery scenario, but that degree of dislocation squared. In hypothetical terms, if the petroleum scenario created, say, 25 units of dislocation, an attack twice that size would produce 625 units of dislocation. And because the attacks created more devastation, the critical interest in the future would be more in peril and the possibility of nuclear winter that much closer.

At some point, therefore, a nuclear attack would likely move the economy past the point where it could regenerate itself. Even with government efforts, it could not produce enough to sustain the survivors at a subsistence level. Every day would be a losing struggle to keep warm, dry, and fed enough to prevent death through starvation and disease; an interest in the future would be an early victim.

Similarly, at some point a nuclear attack will push the political system beyond recovery, even if the nation is said to be the "victor" in the nuclear exchange. Most attack strategies are likely to target the enemy's top leadership; "decapitation" appears to be one way to win. Indeed, as we will discuss later in the book, the war-fighting strategies of the superpowers during the Cold War made not only the leadership of the nation but the political apparatus and channels of communication targets for attack.

Even if the political structure survived relatively intact, it would be overwhelmed with immense problems. The political process would be expected to put together the shattered economy. If this were not challenge enough, the traditional governmental functions themselves would be under challenge. Who would have the right to issue orders? Who would be willing to obey? Public order would be precarious. Parts of the nation would be awash with refugees from devastated areas, who would fall upon areas ill-prepared to receive them, and animosities would grow as shortages increased and demands grew that resources held by undamaged areas and individuals ought to be redistributed.

At least initially, the most active political system would likely be found at the local level. There, surviving officials would be joined by others seeking to define effective political authority. These political leaders would be under intense pressure to define the community that they served in a very parochial way. Their loyalty and interest would extend to the range of their personal contacts. Such leaders would promote the survival prospects of the community by protecting it from demands or appeals made by others. Conversely, they would insist that other, less damaged communities owed assistance to theirs.

If a significant number of individuals in a community no longer accepted the claim of the surviving political leadership to rule, then the right to rule would be contested by force. Establishing who had enough power and legitimacy to rule might be a protracted process. The economic disruption of the community would not give the political system time to decide. Was the currency, be it a piece of paper called a dollar or a rupee, worth anything? Would it secure what was needed to sustain life? People would demand immediate answers from the political process. And given the number of people in need, there would be incessant demands for a reallocation of resources. Thus, mixed in with the claims about who should rule would be claims about who could best provide for the living. In a condition of scarcity, some individuals or groups would see the possibility of not acquiring what they needed and therefore be tempted to listen to claimants for political power who promised them a share.

In sum, at the local level, there would be pressure for the emergence of competing systems of plunder. Those who were able to effectively organize themselves and their firepower (or other instruments of coercion and defense) would likely become the leaders of the community. At least in the United States, with its fragmentation of police forces (local, county, and state police) and with its tradition of an armed citizenry, not to mention the local National Guard or Reserve Units in the area, the ability to organize competing centers of plunder would be great.

Would such conflict affect the individual's interest in survival? For those who saw the desirable future in terms of cooperation, such conflict would likely encourage them to have little interest in the future. For others, the presence of active contention might serve as a sign of hope—politics, even of a violent sort, occurs when there is an expectation that the future can be different. Not only does conflict suggest one way to meet an individual's needs, it becomes an affirmation that a significant number of individuals see a better tomorrow.

Would a national government be able to constrain the various local conflicts? It, too, would be damaged, even beyond the loss of key leaders and the disruption of its channels of communication. The very fact that nuclear war had occurred might lead many to reject a national government's demands for obedience. Successors to dead presidents might need something more than statute or custom to keep a hold on the reins of government. Collecting the revenues to finance the government might prove extremely difficult.

The nation does have one resource not available locally as a rule: the armed forces of the nation. They could be the instrument to compel order and obedience. In fact, the declaration of martial law would likely be one of the earliest responses of the national government. The question would be, however, whether the national military establishment would be in any condition to report on conditions and execute the orders of national authorities. If counterforce targeting (attacking an opponent's forces) was central to the attack, most of the major military installations in the nation would be crippled. Moreover, we might imagine that after a severe attack, many military personnel would demand to return to their homes, rather than to use force against their fellow citizens.

The image we present here is one of chaos and despair as the probable aftermath of a modest nuclear exchange. There are, of course, much more horrendous outcomes, depending on the level at which the war was conducted. Our more optimistic example allows us to reach the same kind of conclusion that the more terrifying projections lead to. Even if nuclear winter did not come to pass or were less severe than projected, we do not see the effective functioning of political and economic systems. While some forms of prewar social interaction would continue (especially within the family), we would expect many individuals to look with bitterness and hostility on others outside a small circle of contacts. To speak of a return to the Dark Ages is misleading. Life would be precarious for many and learning and culture would wither. But this would be a new age, a broken age, where the future did not exist. It would be an age, as former Soviet leader Nikita Khrushchev once remarked, where the living would envy the dead.

The next use of nuclear weapons need not, however, push many of the world's peoples into chaos and despair. We began this chapter with a discussion of a limited use of nuclear weapons by the United States. Those who felt the effects of such weapons (including friendly forces or populations who were contaminated by fallout) would be living in a blackened world, as did the hibakusha of Japan's two nuclear cities. One might feel, as the American administration did in 1945, that to use such weapons to achieve important policy goals was to risk little. And indeed, in the emerging world, the immediate nuclear risk may be minimal. "Little" nuclear wars have contained nuclear effects. But the political fallout is fundamental here. All nations would be forced to consider whether having and using nuclear weapons would significantly enhance their security and their ability to achieve their policy objectives. A successful "little" war would have dire implications for nuclear proliferation.

THE NUCLEAR PREDICAMENT

The predicament we face as we enter the new millennium, simply put, is that even with the relaxation of tensions between the superpowers, the United States, Russia, Great Britain, France, and China still possess nuclear weapons of awesome destructive capability. Furthermore, India, Pakistan, Israel, and a growing list of countries including Iran, Libya, North Korea, and Iraq possess or may soon possess weapons that, if ever used, could precipitate a regional nuclear exchange that could destroy millions of lives.

There is also the specter of nuclear terrorism. It is unclear, as well, whether the revolutions of the late 1980s in Eastern Europe and the Balkans will be stabilizing in the long-term, given the emergence of long-suppressed nationalisms and ethnic rivalries. A reunified Germany is also a potential concern. So, although humans created this awesome technology of death, they have not yet been able to devise a method of ensuring that it will never be used again in an attempt to achieve military or political objectives, deliberately or accidentally. Simply put, the predicament is that nuclear weapons exist, but we have not found unambiguous and universally accepted ways of controlling them, and most proposed solutions have embedded within them potential or actual risks and problems. Whether means will be found to force nation-states armed with weapons of mass destruction to change before they destroy themselves remains to be seen. That nuclear powers have not engaged each other in war since 1945 is some consolation, but it is no guarantee that accident or miscalculation could not at any time draw them into a conflagration. The deployment of and particularly the decision to use the atomic bomb against the Japanese (discussed in the next chapter) reveal many of the features of the nuclear age in which we live, and begin to form the questions we need to ask for today and tomorrow. We are in the nuclear predicament largely because our modes of thought and our nuclear weapons policies are based on pre-Hiroshima categories of thought. Because of Hiroshima, we must recognize the truth in Albert Einstein's insight that although reality has been transformed, our ways of thinking about reality have been relatively unaffected. "The unleashed power of the atom has changed everything save our modes of thinking, and we thus drift toward unparalleled catastrophe."[18] By relying on assumptions, values, methods, objectives, and policies rooted in the prenuclear age, we run the risk of missing or misconstruing the singular nature of the nuclear threat. Unless we overcome the conceptual and psychological problems of comprehension and action, we may not be in a position to fashion an appropriate and imaginative nuclear weapons policy consistent with the uniqueness of the nuclear predicament.

SUMMARY

On the morning of August 6, 1945, Hiroshima was destroyed by a single atomic bomb (See Figure 1-3 on page 20). On August 9, a second bomb was dropped on Nagasaki. Japan surrendered five days later. Many see the decision to drop these bombs as being consistent with the blurring of the distinction between military and civilian targets that had characterized the waging of World War II as a total war. Others see the use of nuclear weapons as morally distinctive and reprehensible because they are indiscriminate in their destruction and their effects are long lasting. Some support their use because they may have helped shorten the war; others claim that Japan would have surrendered anyway before the proposed invasion and that an alternative motive was the forestalling of Soviet entry into the Pacific war. The debate continues and will be further analyzed in the next chapter.

The stakes of living in the nuclear age are obviously high. What we have tried to do in this chapter is to focus on the continuing nuclear dangers of the post-Cold War world, including the threat of nuclear terrorism, and to describe the horrific consequences that can be expected if nuclear weapons are ever used again. By focusing on these issues, we prefigure the problems and questions that will occupy our attention for the remainder of the book, including the role of science and the scientific imagination in bringing us to where we are.

NOTES

1. Quoted in Fernand Gignon, *The Bomb* (New York: Pyramid Books, 1958), p. 13.
2. Quoted in Robert Jay Lifton, *Death in Life: Survivors of Hiroshima* (New York: Random House, 1967), p. 21.
3. Michihiko Hachiya, *Hiroshima Diary* (Chapel Hill, NC: University of North Carolina Press, 1955), p. 8.

FIGURE 1-3
Hiroshima in October 1945. *National Archives*

4. Lifton, *Death in Life*, p. 23.
5. Quoted in Richard Rhodes, *The Making of the Atomic Bomb* (New York: Simon & Schuster, 1986), pp. 723–724.
6. *SIPRI Yearbook 1989, World Armaments and Disarmament* (New York: Oxford University Press, 1989), pp. 3–18.
7. International Committee on Experts on Medical Sciences and Public Health. *Effects of Nuclear War on Health and Health Services* (Geneva: World Health Organization, 1984), p. 5. See also Eric Markusen, "Genocide and Total War," in *Genocide and the Modern Age*, ed. Isidor Wallimann and Michael Dobkowski (Westport, CT: Greenwood Press, 1987), p. 99.
8. R. P. Turco et al., "Nuclear Winter: Global Consequences of Multiple Nuclear Explosions," *Science* 222 (December 23, 1983): 1283–1291. See also Stephen H. Schneider, "Climate Modeling," *Scientific American* (May 1987): 72–80; and Markusen, "Genocide and Total War," p. 99.
9. These are approximations for an airburst of a fission device. Samuel Glasstone and Philip Dolan, ed. *The Effects of Nuclear Weapons*, 3d ed. (Washington, D.C.: U.S. Government Printing Office, 1977), pp. 7–8. This is the single most important source of effects.
10. Office of Technology Assessment, U.S. Congress, *The Effects of Nuclear War* (Washington, D.C.: U.S. Government Printing Office, 1979), pp. 18–19.
11. Ibid., pp. 64–75.
12. Paul Ehrlich, Carl Sagan, Donald Kennedy, and Walter Orr Roberts, *The Cold and the Dark* (New York: W. W. Norton, 1984); Paul Ehrlich et al., "Long-Term Biological Consequences of Nuclear War," *Science* 222 (December, 23 1983): 1293–1300.
13. Stephen Schneider, "Climate Modeling," *Scientific American* 256 (May 1987): 80.
14. Ehrlich, *Cold and Dark*, pp. 50–51.
15. John Hersey, *Hiroshima* (New York: Bantam Books, 1946, 1973), p. 55.
16. Office of Technology Assessment, *Effects*, p. 87.
17. Ibid., pp. 64–75.
18. Otto Nathan and Heinz Norden, eds., *Einstein on Peace* (New York: Schocken, 1986), p. 376.

2

THE DECISION
TO USE NUCLEAR WEAPONS

Secretary of War Henry Stimson returned to Washington, D.C. on April 12, 1945, after inspecting a top-secret nuclear facility in rural Tennessee. Stunned to learn that President Franklin Roosevelt had just died, Stimson went to the White House where Harry Truman waited to be sworn in as president. Once that had been done, Truman spoke briefly to Stimson and the other hastily assembled cabinet members, telling them that he would continue Roosevelt's policies and would look to them for advice, but that "all final policy decisions would be mine."[1]

Truman recalled that the cabinet members then

> rose and silently made their way from the room—except for Secretary Stimson. He asked to speak to me about a most urgent matter. Stimson told me that he wanted me to know about an immense project that was under way—a project looking to the development of a new explosive of almost unbelievable destructive power. That was all he felt free to say at the time, and his statement left me puzzled. It was the first bit of information that had come to me about the atomic bomb, but he gave me no details.[2]

Stimson was a very knowledgeable cabinet officer, as he stood at the top of the military-scientific-bureaucratic complex known as the Manhattan Project that was rushing to produce the atomic bomb. (We describe the process of bomb-building in the next chapter.) On April 25, he and General Leslie Groves, who directly oversaw the Project, met with Truman. In a way, it was an anticlimactic meeting. Others had spoken to Truman about the bomb and its potential. For instance, the day after Stimson had first broached the subject, Truman had spoken with James Byrnes (whom Truman planned to appoint as secretary of state). Byrnes had told him "that the weapon might be so powerful as to be potentially capable of wiping out entire cities and killing people on an unprecedented scale. And he added that in his belief the bomb might well put us in a position to dictate our own terms at the end of the war."[3]

Secretary Stimson confirmed the bomb's extraordinary power and indicated that "in all probability" it would be available within four months. But what he really wanted to talk about was what should be done *after* the bomb was used. As he saw it, other nations would very likely develop their own atomic devices and possibly use them "suddenly and effectively with devastating power." For Stimson, the most pressing issue for the United States in the soon-to-be atomic world was the *control* of atomic weapons.[4] This was the same argument Stimson had made in his last meeting with Franklin Roosevelt, and Roosevelt seemed to agree.[5] Stimson hoped Truman would also adopt his perspective.

Henry Stimson looked to the future precisely because he assumed that the decision to use the bomb was a foregone conclusion. The bomb would be just another weapon to bring the war against the Japanese to a successful and speedy conclusion. Would the new president see matters the same way?

We know that Truman ultimately did decide to use the bomb against Japan. How and why did he come to that decision? How and why might future leaders decide that they, too, must use nuclear weapons? In the last chapter, we took you into the firestorm of nuclear war, both real (as at Hiroshima and Nagasaki) as well as imagined. In this chapter, we step back and ask: How did that happen? In the following chapter, we take one further step back and ask: How did such enormous power came into the hands of leaders in the middle of the twentieth century, a power that will continue to be available to the leaders of many nations—and possibly other individuals—for all time to come?

MAKING CHOICES

In war—as in politics—things happen because individuals make decisions. Sometimes, of course, individuals believe that they have no choice; they are simply implementing decisions made by others. The personnel in command of nuclear-tipped missiles, for instance, may believe that if they receive authenticated orders to launch their missiles, they have no choice but to comply.[6] But they, in fact, do have a choice not to comply, although they may not be aware that that choice exists. Similarly, leaders of nations may believe at times that they have no choice available to them. Roosevelt and his advisors felt that once the Japanese attacked Pearl Harbor on December 7, 1941, they had no choice but to wage war against Japan. There were, however, other choices open to them, such as attempting to negotiate with Japan or simply retiring to the West Coast and building a "Fortress America."[7]

Similarly, the use of nuclear weapons will always constitute a choice for leaders to make. The key question is: Will they recognize that they indeed have a choice and give serious consideration to the options? Did Truman in the summer of 1945?

To say that choice always exists does not mean that all options would be equally attractive or possible. On the contrary, leaders often face pressures that narrow the range of choice to what political leaders think will be politically viable. However, even though they see themselves as constrained by circumstance to make a particular choice, leaders may still recognize that a choice exists. Indeed, they might even wish to make a choice different from the one they feel pressured into making. Will leaders in the future use those weapons because they feel constrained to do so, in spite of being aware that there are other—perhaps more desirable—options? Was this the case for Harry Truman?

Some choices, of course, seem so fraught with risk that they encourage a careful examination of the options. Given our contemporary understanding of nuclear weapons, we might imagine that their possible use would create a great deal of debate among the decision makers. Debate tells us that people perceive a range of choices (though they, in the end, may feel constrained to use the weapon). Was there debate? We have seen that Henry Stimson did not suggest that a real choice lay before the president;

Stimson had concluded that the bomb should be used. Neither he nor those who spoke with Truman in the days just after the swearing-in appear to have suggested that there was something to debate about the use of the weapon. A president might ask questions of his advisors, questions that would expose the existence of different options, or at least engender a debate that would make the options more apparent. Indeed, a newly installed leader might be just the person to ask such questions. Did Truman?

Harry Truman was in a difficult position. Vice-president for only three months and essentially a stranger to Roosevelt, Truman had had little involvement in policy making. What he knew about Roosevelt's foreign and military policy he had learned from the newspapers. His sudden accession to the presidency meant that he had a lot to learn quickly, as Stimson's mysterious comments after the swearing-in suggested.

Moreover, leadership is more than just holding title to an office; it is the ability to command respect and loyalty from one's subordinates. Truman's statement at the swearing-in about "making all the final policy decisions" was both an attempt to ensure that the room full of Roosevelt appointees understood that he was president in more than just name, and to assure them that he would, in fact, make decisions—that he would be a leader.

In such circumstances, new leaders in the short run are likely to adopt the perspectives and preferences of their predecessor and of the predecessor's advisors. As the people around Truman were like Stimson in his belief that the bomb was a legitimate and very effective means of waging war, we would expect Truman to be quite disposed to adopt this view because this was the received wisdom of his advisors. If there were no debate among them, a new, untried, and uninformed leader might be quite reluctant to raise questions that would spark such a debate and thus create dissension among the advisors, or create suspicions in their minds about her or his soundness on the issue or about her or his capacity to lead. Finally, even if the new leader had some personal reservations, he or she is likely to feel pressured to use the bomb for these reasons as well.

It is important to realize that, except for the suddenness of his acquisition of power and his lack of specific knowledge about nuclear weapons, the relationship between Truman and his advisors is typical of the interaction between leaders and advisors. Those individuals around the key decision maker are important actors who help shape the decision maker's choice—even when the decision maker insists that "all final policy decisions would be mine." They do so in four key ways:

1. They *provide information* about the world in which the decision maker works. For instance, Stimson revealed to Truman the existence of the bomb-making project.
2. They help *create the agenda*—the issues that are deemed important enough for the leaders to pay attention to. Stimson wanted Truman to think about what should be done after the bomb was used, rather than whether the bomb should be used.
3. They help *frame the options* that a decision maker considers. For Stimson, that meant looking for ways to create international control over nuclear weapons.
4. They often *advocate a particular course of action and politick* to bring it about. Stimson wanted Truman to adopt the control option and he used his access to Truman to push his point.

Of course, the leader brings some information and beliefs to any situation, as well as a sense of what the agenda should be, and a set of preferences for particular options. And in an open political system, where there is a dispersion of power among various individuals and groups, the leader often must engage in politicking to set the agenda, create the options, and get her or his perspectives and preferences accepted by others. In open systems, therefore, the leaders help shape national policy. Rarely do they dictate it. Democracies are usually very open political systems, but even the imperial Japan that attacked the United States in 1941 had a degree of openness. There were powerful factions in the Japanese political and military elite whose consent was usually necessary in order to reach decisions.

Thus, to the question "How and why might the leadership of a nation choose to use nuclear weapons?" our approach says that we must examine who the decision makers and advisors are, and how they interact with each other to produce that choice. In more formal terms, we need to look at both the *actors* and the *process* by which they create decisions. In addition, we need to know the *context* in which decisions are made. For instance, if leaders are contemplating the use of nuclear weapons, we need to know if the decision comes in the midst of a war (as it did for Truman in 1945), or if it comes in a period of intense crisis when war is feared but has not yet broken out. Another aspect of the context concerns the size of the state's nuclear arsenal. Does the state contemplating the use of nuclear weapons have many nuclear weapons or just a few?

Our model for understanding the decision to use nuclear weapons can be depicted in this fashion:

$$\frac{\text{Context}}{\text{Actors} \ + \ \text{Process}} \ \rightarrow \ \text{The Decision to Use}$$

TRUMAN AND HIS ADVISORS

How can this model add additional richness to our understanding of how the United States came to attack Japan with two atomic bombs? We begin with the *context* of the decision. By the spring of 1945, the United States had been at war against Japan for three and one-half years. Japan's ally, Nazi Germany, was collapsing and would surrender unconditionally to the United States, Britain, and the Soviet Union on May 7. American forces had gradually carried the Pacific war closer to Japan. By April 1945, when they invaded the island of Okinawa, 300 miles off Japan, they essentially commanded the seas around the Japanese home islands. In March 1945, the new bomber commander in the Pacific, Curtis LeMay, had ordered his B-29s to stage low-level fire-bomb attacks against Japanese cities, causing extensive death and destruction. There were, however, large Japanese armies in the home islands and in China and Manchuria. In every engagement with the Japanese army, American forces suffered heavy casualties as the Japanese chose to die rather than surrender.

A second important part of the context was the American government's January 1943 pledge to force Japan to surrender unconditionally—to submit itself to any and every American demand. Behind this goal of complete victory over Japan were elements of racism,[8] a desire for revenge for being humiliated at Pearl Harbor, and an American conviction (created in the aftermath of World War I) that unless an enemy were thoroughly defeated and reorganized according to the winner's dictates, that enemy state would rise again to threaten the survival of the United States (as had Germany after World War I). American decision makers felt they had little choice but to force the Japanese to surrender unconditionally. Their military successes to that point had reinforced the goal. To impose unconditional surrender (which was also imposed on the

Germans), American planners prepared a series of invasions of the Japanese home islands, the first scheduled for late fall 1945.

Surrounding this context of immediate events was the larger context of how Americans (and many others) thought about war. While we examine this point in more detail in Chapter 4, we can note here that since the First World War, political and military leaders have confronted a very vexing question: How could a nation achieve a decisive victory over the enemy at a reasonable cost to itself? (Achieving an unconditional surrender would take a decisive victory.) The First World War (1914–1918) seemed to suggest that states could *not* achieve victory at a reasonable cost—too many men would die in a stalemated war that would end only when one side collapsed. The "winning" side would then be too exhausted to make victory complete, thus breeding future wars as the losers sought to rewrite the outcome, or other states took advantage of the weakened condition of the warring states. This problem seemed compounded for democracies. Their publics would reject leaders who thrust their nations into another bloody stalemate.

In the period between 1919 and 1939, two types of answers to the threat of bloody stalemate seemed to predominate: The first was to stay out of war (which the United States had initially adopted). The second was to discover "the winning weapon" that would produce victory at a reasonable cost. The United States, anxious to end the Second World War at as low a cost as possible, had mounted a vast effort to harness technology to provide winning weapons. Ironically, atomic bomb research had been spurred initially by fears that the Germans might develop that technology first, which would leave the Allies with some very hard choices. But now, by the spring of 1945, American scientists felt they were close to being able to produce atomic bombs, and those bombs seemed to be a potential war-winning weapon.

Thus, the context of events and the context of thinking about waging war came together in the spring of 1945. The context would exert a great pressure on the people around Truman who had been involved in perfecting nuclear weapons (as well as the military establishment charged with waging war) to use *any* perfected weapon (nuclear or otherwise) *unless* (1) some compelling reason not to use it emerged in the minds of powerful actors, and (2) those actors could find a way to enter their objections into the decision-making process.

Turning now to the *actors*, we find that Truman's immediate advisors who knew of the bomb project were of one mind: If it worked, it should be used. Other innovations such as the firebombing of cities had become a staple of war. Truman appears to have shared their general orientation about the application of modern weapons to the American war effort. The new president saw no problems. The choice now seemed inevitable because there were no other options and no concerns about the use of such weapons— that is, there was no debate.

If there were to be challenges to the momentum pushing the leaders toward the bomb's use, those challenges might come during the process of resolving important *implementation questions* such as "What would be the target of the bomb?" and "How long would an atomic campaign go on against Japan?" Wars (and peacetime politics) always involve a number of such implementation choices. The process of making choices on those matters provides additional opportunities to raise questions and provoke debate and thus reveal a broader range of choice open to the leaders.

The targets, for instance, had been identified by Air Force planners—the major Japanese cities that had yet to be extensively attacked by conventional bombing raids and that had some military significance (generally as points with large numbers of troops or with war industries). But they were to be cities, and hence civilian casualties would be great. Target identification had occasioned the one instance when top civilian leaders interfered with those implementing decisions. Secretary of War Stimson insisted over strong opposition from the American military that Kyoto, a religious site as well as the old capital, be removed from the list. Truman backed him up, noting that "even if the Japs are savages, ruthless, merciless and fanatic, we as the leader of the world for the common welfare cannot drop this terrible bomb on the old capital or the new [Tokyo]."[9] But the debate about specific targets had not been enough to raise the basic question of whether the bomb should be used or not. In seeing America's opponents as "savages, ruthless, merciless, and fanatic," Truman was less inclined to think about them either as humans (Should one use such a "terrible weapon" against fellow humans?) or as people who might respond rationally to their worsening military situation by suing for peace without the use of the bomb.

While the top American leadership seemed to have moved easily to a decision to drop the bomb, at the middle levels of the government there were individuals with different perceptions. What options did they have in mind, and why did their perceptions not become those of the top leadership? Recall that Secretary of War Stimson was convinced that the basic issue was the future of an atomic world. He also recognized that the Congress would have to create legislation regarding nuclear policy. In early May 1945 he created an Interim Committee to consider what kind of policy the United States wanted to promote in the atomic world, and, with that in mind, what it would say about the bomb when it was first used and how much information it would release about the weapon. Stimson chaired the committee composed of representatives of the various departments, including James Byrnes as Truman's personal representative. He also created a Scientific Advisory Panel to provide the technical information that might be needed.

At lunch in late May 1945, Byrnes asked one of the scientists on the Advisory Panel, then meeting with the Interim Committee, to amplify a remark that he had made that morning about demonstrating the power of the bomb to the Japanese before using it against a real target. Such an approach might involve informing the Japanese of the existence of a very powerful weapon and announcing that it would be dropped on a deserted location where the Japanese could observe its effects. The discussion spilled over into the afternoon session of the Interim Committee, but after looking at the various options, the Committee endorsed anew its recommendation that the bomb be used as soon as possible, without warning, against a real target. A subsequent letter from James Franck, a scientist at the University of Chicago involved in the research on the bomb, prompted further discussion among the scientists on the Advisory Panel. Their conclusion in mid-June was the same: "We can propose no technical demonstration likely to bring an end to the war; we see no acceptable alternative to direct military use."[10] That remained the Interim Committee's general view as well, and no further consideration of these kinds of options occurred.

Truman did come to hear of the "warning option" in talking with a member of the Interim Committee who had gradually come to endorse this option but was now leaving the committee, and in a brief exposition by a War Department official during a high-level strategy session planning the invasion of Japan. But Truman displayed little interest except to endorse a consensus among his advisors in late June that Japan be warned of dire consequences if it did not surrender. That imprecise warning was issued as part of the Potsdam Declaration, a call by the United States, Britain, and China for

Japan to surrender unconditionally and accept the military occupation of Japan. The Japanese government rejected the terms.

The "demonstration option" had made it to the top in an indirect manner, and without the cachet of a committee's recommendation. The top leaders dismissed the warning option without much reflection They did, however, feel that they had to offer the weak substitute of a warning in the Potsdam Declaration. To our knowledge, no broader consideration of whether to use the weapon or not ensued.

TRUMAN'S DECISION

Thus in July 1945, when Truman learned of the Manhattan Project's successful test of the technologically complex implosion device at Alamogordo, New Mexico (which we describe in the next chapter), the stage was set for a decision about which the president would not likely perceive any meaningful choice. Military planners told him that a similar bomb and a second type of bomb (untested, but judged highly reliable) would be ready for use in early August and a third by late August. Moreover, the U.S. Air Force had successfully modified its B-29 bomber to carry the new weapons and trained its crews to deliver the device on target.

Truman therefore authorized the Air Force to "deliver after about 3 August" the available bombs on four cities: Hiroshima, Kokura, Nagasaki, and Niigata.[11] Actual target selection was left up to the Air Force—and in fact to the aircrews themselves: Kokura was spared on August 9th because it was obscured by smoke; the B-29 pilot elected to try the second target on his list, Nagasaki, even though his plane was running low on fuel and clouds initially covered that site.[12]

After the Hiroshima attack, the administration waited for the Japanese to capitulate. As they did not, the execute order remained in force, and the second bomb struck Nagasaki. Between these two attacks, the Truman administration might have decided to suspend the attacks in order to give the Japanese more time to accept the idea of unconditional surrender. It appears not to have thought about the issue. After the second bomb, the Japanese emperor personally intervened and compelled the Japanese government to accept the surrender terms.

Thus the first two uses of nuclear weapons did not, at the top levels, occasion much of the process that we often associate with critical decisions. The top leadership did not struggle with the basic question, "Should we use the bomb or not?" They did not examine the costs and benefits of those two options. This is not to say that Truman or his advisors such as Stimson treated the matter lightly. All the top leadership were concerned with the costs of the impending invasion of Japan, which they saw as the only other way to bring about the unconditional surrender of the Japanese. Any weapon that offered to reduce that cost dramatically would, without much thinking, recommend itself. Context, actors, and process had merged smoothly to produce the first (and, to this point, the only) decision to use nuclear weapons.

THE DEBATE ABOUT THE USE OF THE BOMB

After the war a debate arose about the use of the bomb on Japan and continues to this day.[13] It centers around three intertwined questions: (1) Was dropping the bomb necessary? (2) Were there other, hidden motives that lay behind Truman's decision other than to win the war as quickly as possible with the least number of American casualties? (3) Did Truman and his advisors violate important moral or ethical principles in deciding to use the bomb? We need to look at this debate, not only to understand the nuclear past, but also because this debate, to one degree or another, established a *context for future decisions* about the use of nuclear weapons in the Cold War and beyond. Decision makers who contemplate using nuclear weapons are likely to find that these questions become prominent in their decisions, as will the competing answers.

Critics of the decision to use the bomb against Japan answer the three questions in these ways:

1. The use of the bomb was not necessary because Japan was on the verge of surrender. By the summer of 1945, the Japanese had no effective navy and the United States had cut off the home islands from Japan's sources of raw materials, particularly oil. American bombers were devastating Japanese cities. It was only a matter of time before the Japanese war machine ground to a halt, forcing capitulation. The Japanese had already advanced peace feelers. Moreover, when the Soviet Union entered the Pacific war on August 8—as Stalin had promised in response to American entreaties that he do so—the Japanese were stunned. This set of circumstances, the critics argue, would have produced a quick decision for surrender. The bomb was unnecessary; the loss of life was therefore unacceptable.

    The critics bolster their case by pointing out that the key issue preventing the Japanese from accepting American demands for surrender was the ambiguity in the American position regarding the future of the Japanese Emperor. The Japanese elites were committed to preserving the emperor's position. The long-standing American goal seemed to be to remove the emperor from the Japanese political system. While the Truman administration had begun to move toward accepting a figure-head Emperor under American control (which is indeed what eventually emerged), it never communicated this clearly to Japan prior to the dropping of the Hiroshima bomb. If it had done so, the critics charge, the situation would have been ripe for a surrender without the bomb.

    Other critics modify this argument by saying that perhaps the bomb was necessary, but that the demonstration option was the correct choice. Japanese national pride, which allowed the war to continue in spite of an unrelenting string of losses, would have been overcome by the demonstration of a powerful weapon that the Japanese did not have. Realism would have overcome national pride—even a prideful nation can legitimately give in to such unanswerable power.

2. While the Truman administration did want to end the war quickly, some critics allege that there was another key motivation: to get the Japanese to surrender before the Soviet Union became actively involved in the war and therefore able to make demands for full participation in settling Japan's future. Given what appeared to be Soviet obstructionism in occupied Europe, Truman wanted to keep control of a defeated Japan in American hands. And perhaps the bomb might also make the Soviets more tractable in the growing conflict over the future of Eastern Europe. Thus, say the critics, the bomb was directed more at Joseph Stalin and his challenge to the American definition of a desirable postwar order than at a crumbling Japan whose new order for Asia had been irrevocably smashed.

3. Finally, some critics condemn the Truman administration's lack of moral vision. For the first time weapons were used that were inherently indiscriminate in their terror and destructiveness. Even accepting the premise that dropping the atomic bomb on Hiroshima and Nagasaki saved tens of thousands of American lives and countless Japanese lives by obviating the need for an invasion, the invasion would at least have been a legitimate form of warfare. Dropping the bomb, on the other

hand, without fully understanding all the possible scientific, medical, ecological, and political consequences, was to break with accepted practice and unleash the destructive genie.

Moreover, the critics charge, Truman and his advisors lost sight of what this war was all about. The war was a struggle between the Hitlerites, on the one hand, who claimed that only the brutal survived and therefore anything a state did to ensure its survival was legitimate, and the democrats, on the other hand, who argued that democracy and humane values could not survive in the world of the brutal. Decent human beings, therefore, had to ask if the means one chose—even in the cause of defending democratic moral values—were so repugnant as to make one indistinguishable from a Hitler. To condemn children to die—and massive bombings of cities by conventional or nuclear weapons ensured that thousands would die—was to allow the Hitlerites to win the war. It was Hitlerite morality that had triumphed, not the democrats' vision that said that moral people simply could *not* do all that was possible to do in war.

The members of the Truman administration rejected these allegations, claiming that the critics were factually wrong, or were working from hindsight, which is (nearly) always perfect and misunderstands the conditions in which leaders actually make decisions. The administration and scholars supporting it assert that the better answers are these:

1. In July and August, 1945, most American policymakers believed that the Japanese were not about to surrender on terms acceptable to the United States. Though clearly losing the war, the Japanese continued to fight on. The symbol of their resoluteness was the *kamikaze*, the Japanese aviator who willingly piloted his explosive-laden plane into an American ship. Their appearance in large numbers in defense of the Japanese island of Okinawa, along with a stubborn and effective ground resistance that produced 75,000 American casualties, seemed to indicate that the Japanese were developing a potent form of resistance. It seemed clear that it would take a devastating blow to compel Japan's surrender. No one could predict in advance how the Japanese would react to a Soviet declaration of war. No one could predict in advance whether the Japanese would quickly surrender once a land invasion began. Thinking it prudent to assume the worst case, the administration saw the bomb as the reasonable alternative to a prolonged, bloody invasion. From all the information that the administration had at the time, say its defenders, the bomb was necessary if one wanted to get the war over—completely over—as soon as possible, with the smallest possible cost.

2. There were no other primary motives that led to the bomb's use. The administration, the defenders acknowledge, was wrestling with a variety of issues as the war came to its climax. One of those problems was how to deal with what Washington perceived to be Russian demands and obstructionism. The bomb might have useful consequences for dealing with the Russians, but that was never a prominent feature of the top leadership's thinking. Their focus then, as it had been for more than three years, was the defeat of Japan.

    There was, of course, a more basic political motive. If the administration had not used the bomb, large numbers of Americans, after surveying the casualty lists created by the invasion of Japan, might have turned on the administration, condemning it for withholding the one weapon that would have minimized the loss of American life. But acting like political animals is the price, so to speak, of governing a democracy; political leaders must give weight to what the public wants (or to their best estimates of those wants).

3. War always threatens the ethical standards of a society, the defenders of the administration would argue. The key question is, in the face of competing moral standards, which standard outweighs the others. The Truman administration viewed the bomb as another weapon, horrible like other weapons, but used for clearly moral purposes: to end a brutal Japanese imperialism and to bring the suffering of war to an end as quickly as possible. Civilians would die in large numbers— and no one denied that fact, even though one might try to soften its reality by thinking of the Japanese cities as *military* targets. But that was the price one had to pay to wage war successfully in the middle of the twentieth century, argued some defenders. Without success in this war, the world would likely be left with a monstrous tyranny in Europe and Asia dedicated to the extirpation of the very values the critics sought to protect. What moral condemnation would then fall on the administration? These moral dilemmas continue unresolved to this day, as we shall see in Chapter 9.

This postwar debate about the appropriateness of the use of the bomb cannot be definitively resolved. We cannot replay history to see what might have happened if the bomb were not dropped. Nor can we watch over the shoulders of decision makers as they thought their way through all the issues surrounding nuclear weapons. We might fault them for not asking the questions that would have led to a full-scale review of the alternatives or to a more careful examination of what would cause the Japanese to surrender. But we can also recognize that our criticism comes from having lived in the nuclear world, an experience denied Truman and his advisors. And we can recognize that unlike the abundance of time we have to formulate our criticisms, they were continuously engaged in waging a world war.

THE IMPLICATIONS OF HIROSHIMA AND NAGASAKI FOR THE FUTURE

After Hiroshima and Nagasaki, after the months and years of living in a new nuclear age, how did decision makers respond to the new context in which they found themselves? We suggest that the use of the bomb, a knowledge of its effects, and the controversy surrounding its use have influenced—and will continue to influence—leaders of all nuclear-armed states. Using the bomb has become stigmatized as an immoral act.[14] Leaders contemplating its use may first have to overcome their own moral scruples or those of powerful people around them. There would likely be a debate among the decision makers about the wisdom of any use of nuclear weapons. Leaders might have to be convinced that the use of such weapons would achieve the nation's goals and that incurring the opprobrium of the international community and of their own societies was politically bearable. President Dwight Eisenhower's comment when a member of his staff presented a report recommending use of nuclear weapons in Vietnam reflects the restraint that the past imposes on leaders: "You boys must be crazy. We can't use those awful things against Asians for the second time in less than ten years. My God."[15]

The citizenry of nuclear-armed states may also have serious reservations about using nuclear weapons. For instance, on the fortieth anniversary of dropping the bomb, 43 percent of American respondents told pollsters that if the decision had been theirs to make, they would have ordered the bombs dropped on Japan, but 50 percent said they would have tried some other way.[16] Fifty-nine percent approved using the atomic bomb on Japanese cities, while 35 percent disapproved.[17] Leaders contemplating the use of nuclear weapons might have to consider (and debate) what a divided public might mean for the use of nuclear weapons and how the public might be brought to accept the use of such weapons.

There is, of course, another feature of today's nuclear world that is very likely to encourage intense debate among the leadership of a nation: the possibility of devastating nuclear retaliation by the target of the attack or by its nuclear-armed ally. In the Truman administration's case, there was no concern about Japanese retaliation. Today, however, the leadership will have to consider whether it recklessly and irresponsibly risks the nation's existence in using nuclear weapons. The damage that nuclear weapons can inflict makes some form of debate within the leadership all but certain when use becomes an option.

We suggest also that, in the future, decision makers should consider two additional questions that arise from the attacks on Japan: (1) Did nuclear weapons in fact compel Japan's surrender? (2) How did they do so? One image of Hiroshima and Nagasaki is that they must have compelled the Japanese leadership to accept the inevitable. But that is not quite the case. The Japanese government in the summer of 1945 was deeply divided between those who wanted to fight until the Americans offered far better terms and those who wanted to end the war as quickly as possible. The stalemate between these factions perpetuated the status quo—the continuation of the war. Only after two bombs had dropped did the Emperor feel compelled to intervene, confident that the die-hards in the military would not challenge his request to accept the American terms. But there were still important Japanese military leaders who wanted to continue to resist *in spite of* the bombs. (And, as it happened, a small group of renegade military officers did stage an unsuccessful coup against the Emperor to prevent the surrender.)

The bombs changed the political dynamics within the Japanese elite. The Emperor, who until that point did not feel he could impose his wishes if important members of the elite were opposed (particularly the military), now stepped forward to make the decision for surrender. In the future, the use of nuclear weapons may change the influence and initiative of those in the government, but there is no guarantee that the internal balance of power will change, or that those willing to concede or surrender will gain the upper hand. Indeed, if history had been slightly different—if there were a more timid Emperor who could not find the political will to intervene, or if the process of decision-making within the Japanese government had been more prolonged—we might have drawn quite different lessons about what the bomb can do. Indeed, it is possible that the Japanese die-hards might have recovered their power if days slipped by without a further attack and then the subsequent attacks were few and far between.[18]

It is also possible that in the only case we have of nuclear use, the bombs themselves were not enough. They may have been a culmination to a series of losses that the United States had inflicted on Japan since the carrier battle at Midway in June 1942. If atomic bombing made the difference, it was only because all the other defeats had come before. Alternatively, we might see the bombs as part of a combination of defeats occurring at roughly the same time: the loss of Okinawa, the devastating air raids, the Soviet entry, the bombs. Without the force of all those roughly simultaneous blows, the two bombs might not have had the kind of impact they appear to have had on the Japanese leadership. (After all, LeMay's fire raids were causing even more casualties and devastation in some Japanese cities than the two atomic bombs caused.)

Thus, the usefulness of nuclear weapons might be quite limited. Their use alone may be insufficient to compel others to behave in desired ways. These caveats notwithstanding, we suspect that leaders and their citizens have understood the history of the atomic war against Japan in this way: In 1945, nuclear weapons were the war-winning weapon (even when used in small numbers). The historical experience suggested that nuclear weapons can resolve important but seemingly intractable political issues between states. The historical experience would seem to encourage leaders to make nuclear weapons available as an option in spite of their moral stigma.

NEAR USES OF NUCLEAR WEAPONS

Since 1945, no leaders of any nuclear-armed state have decided to use nuclear weapons. Was one use enough, and thereafter, for a variety of reasons, the use of nuclear weapons never appeared as an attractive option? We look at this question from two perspectives. First, we ask if there were *historical* occasions when leaders seriously considered using nuclear weapons. Second, we ask if the Cold War created *compelling images* of situations in which leaders would choose to use nuclear weapons or might be compelled to do so. After looking at these two questions, we turn to the future. Are future decisions to use nuclear weapons likely to mimic these patterns, or do we need to envision new ways in which leaders come to make such fearful decisions?

The American use of nuclear weapons in 1945 involved particular actors, following a particular process, in a particular context. As the first-ever use of nuclear weapons, we might say that it was a unique case, one that is unlikely to occur again for these reasons. We all now have a sense of what nuclear weapons can do (which the Truman administration did not). Moreover, we tend to see nuclear weapons in negative terms (which the Truman administration did not). Third, we are not likely to find ourselves in another global world war (the occasion for the first use).

But we can also suggest that the American decision in 1945 might be an example of one type of choice that we may find recurring in the future: Nuclear weapons might be used when a state is engaged in a protracted major war that begins with conventional weapons, proves to be costly, and spurs one or both combatants to seek a rapid and victorious end to the war. We might refine this generalization to take into account one other aspect of the circumstances of the American decision: Nuclear weapons are likely to be used if the weapon becomes available during that war. In the post-Hiroshima age, there was one such circumstance that met most of these characteristics. From 1980 to 1988, Iran and Iraq fought a very costly war, and both sides had nuclear weapons programs. Neither side, however, achieved a nuclear weapons capability before a truce ended the fighting.[19]

In our quest for an understanding of how future leaders might decide to use nuclear weapons, the historical record is limited to just one case. We can partially get around this problem by asking a different question: Have there been occasions when states have stood on the verge of a decision to use nuclear weapons? We call this the *near use* of nuclear weapons. It occurs when the top leadership of a nation accepts the use of nuclear weapons as a meaningful option in dealing with another state, and the top leaders give serious consideration to the use option.[20] We know, of course, that historically the leadership in all such possible cases ultimately decided against using the weapons, but near-use considerations provide clues about when states might move to the point of using such weapons in the future.

Finding evidence of near-use decisions, however, is difficult. After a decision, leaders usually do not say what other options they contemplated but rejected, and the stigma attached to nuclear weapons makes it unlikely that most leaders would admit to having considered their use.[21] But what we can do is hypothesize that there are moments when a state's leaders will be most likely to consider nuclear weapons as an option and look intensively at the historical record for that time period. Such moments likely come when nuclear-armed states are involved in war, or involved in crises that threaten to escalate into warfare.

You might imagine that nuclear weapons are so central that in time of war or crisis they would automatically become an option. That is possible, of course, but there is little evidence for it. It is also possible that the use of nuclear weapons will enter an individual leader's mind during a war or crisis. For instance, Richard Nixon told an interviewer that he thought about nuclear weapons as an option for ending the Vietnam war, although he decided against doing so.[22] We treat this as a near use only when the leader is willing to articulate that option before other top leaders and the leadership collectively discusses the option. We need to take this approach as it is usually impossible to determine in any systematic fashion what goes on in the minds of leaders.

Outside of crisis and warfare, are there other situations in which we should look for near-use decisions? The literature on nuclear issues does suggest that when a state attempts to become a nuclear power, its nuclear-armed rival might attack the emerging nuclear production and storage facilities with its own nuclear weapons. We looked for near-use deliberations on these occasions. In addition, we considered occasions when political leaders discuss the nation's general military strategy. They might, as the Eisenhower administration did in October 1953, adopt the following kind of orientation: "In the event of hostilities, the United States will consider nuclear weapons to be available for use as other munitions."[23] Such an orientation creates a context that might encourage a decision to use such weapons in the next crisis or conflict. This kind of planning is not, however, what we will consider to be near use. We need to examine the crises themselves to detect the actual near-use decision.

There is, however, another way in which the top leadership's consideration of military plans could be considered a near-use decision: when that leadership contemplates *preventive war*. Nowhere is this better expressed than in President Eisenhower's formulation to his secretary of state. There might be, Eisenhower said, certain conditions in which "we would be forced to consider whether or not our duty to future generations did not require us to *initiate* war at the most propitious moment that we could designate."[24] Apparently, Eisenhower and his top advisors did discuss the question at several points during 1953 and 1954 and collectively rejected a preventive war policy. Was this a near use? We treat this as a form of a near-use decision *if* it is accompanied by *a discussion of whether the then-prevailing conditions made preventive war necessary*. Otherwise, such a discussion should be treated as part of the planning of possible military operations.

Indeed, military planning is a governmental process in which nuclear use considerations are prominent, as the military establishments of nuclear-armed states make plans and preparations for using their nuclear weapons. (We consider such plans and preparation in Chapters 4 and 5.) However, we will say that while military establishments may make the nuclear option available to the top leadership, unless the top leadership actively considers using the capability provided by the military, we do not have a near-use decision.

There are other governmental processes in which the nuclear option might appear in the debate over policy. For instance, a policymaker may raise the nuclear option as a way of convincing others to adopt a different, nonnuclear, option. That is, by raising the specter of nuclear use, other options seem much more reasonable.[25] Similarly, a leader might argue for a greatly expanded nuclear option to make the original proposal to use nuclear weapons even more unpalatable to those proposing it. In June of 1954, for instance, President Eisenhower's key advisors proposed that nuclear weapons be used against China if it intervened in the Indochina war. Eisenhower replied that if the United States struck China, it would also have to wage nuclear war against Russia, China's ally, and even if it devastated Russia, it would be a hollow victory because of the loss to civilization.[26] Was Eisenhower talking seriously about the nuclear option, or did he want to *end* the consideration of the nuclear use option? It is hard to say. We have chosen to err on the side of over-reporting near-use decisions by including all cases where the top leadership spoke about using weapons, even though some of those instances might in fact have been political maneuvers to head off any further discussion of nuclear use.

Another way in which leaders might discuss the nuclear option occurs when they consider the option of *threatening* to use nuclear weapons to secure certain policy goals (which we examine in Chapter 6). For instance, in 1953, the United States warned the People's Republic of China that the United States would use atomic weapons against Chinese forces if the Chinese did not agree to armistice terms to end the Korean War. In these cases, however, the leadership considered the option of making the threat, not the option of using such weapons. Indeed, in cases of nuclear threat-making, the top leadership usually did not want to have to use the weapons. We do not include such cases of threat-making except where the top leadership actively discussed the use of nuclear weapons.[27]

Finally, there are the cases in which the leadership feels that it has to present an *image* of having considered nuclear use for public relations purposes. The classic case of this came in November 1950, when Chinese intervention in the Korean War threatened to bring defeat to U.S. and South Korean forces. A reporter asked President Truman at a news conference if the atom bomb was under consideration as a means to deal with the worsening military situation.

> TRUMAN: That includes every weapon that we have.
>
> REPORTER: Mr. President, you said "every weapon we have." Does that mean that there is active consideration of the use of the atomic bomb?
>
> TRUMAN: There has always been active consideration of its use. I don't want to see it used. It is a terrible weapon, and it should not be used on innocent men, women, and children who have nothing whatever to do with this military aggression. That happens when it is used.[28]

There is no evidence that the bomb was, in fact, under active consideration by Truman or his top advisors, but Truman may have felt that, politically, he could not say otherwise. After all, American lives were on the line. McGeorge Bundy suggests that Truman's concluding sentences showed his unwillingness to think of such weapons as meaningful options.[29] Perhaps the destruction of Hiroshima and Nagasaki made Truman the least likely leader to entertain that option again.

With these points in mind, we have examined the historical record to identify near-use decisions. As Table 2-1 (on pages 36–37) indicates, we have identified twenty-five occasions when considerations of nuclear use *would be most likely*—if it occurred at all. We find evidence of only ten cases in which the use of nuclear weapons was actively considered, although a lack of evidence in some of the cases could simply mean that near-use decisions occurred but we have not found the evidence for them.[30]

TABLE 2-1 POTENTIAL NEAR-USE OCCASIONS AND CASES OF ACTIVE CONSIDERATION OF THE NUCLEAR OPTION

CATEGORY	EVENT[1]	NUCLEAR ACTORS	EVIDENCE FROM THE HISTORICAL RECORD
Wars in Which Nuclear Actors Were Direct Participants	Korean War (1950–1953)	United States	Case 1: Eisenhower administration considers nuclear weapons in conduct of the war and to force an end to the stalemate.[2]
	Suez War (1956)	Great Britain	Nuclear weapons were not considered as an option by military planners or top leadership.[3]
	Algerian War (1960–1962)	France	No evidence of consideration of nuclear weapons.
	Vietnam War (1965–1973)	United States	Johnson and Nixon administrations probably did not consider using nuclear weapons in Vietnam War.[4]
	Egypt-Israel War (1970)	Israel	No evidence of consideration of nuclear weapons.
	Yom Kippur/Ramadan War (1973)	Israel	Case 2: Probable consideration after Israeli counterattack initially failed.[5]
	Sino-Vietnamese War (1979)	China	No evidence of consideration of nuclear weapons.
	Afghan War (1979–1989)	Soviet Union	No evidence of consideration of nuclear weapons.[6]
	Falkland/Malvinas War (1981)	Great Britain	No evidence of consideration of nuclear weapons.
	Gulf War (1990–1991)	United States, Great Britain, France	No evidence of consideration of nuclear weapons.
Crises Directly Involving Nuclear Armed States	Berlin Blockade (1948–1949)	United States	No evidence of consideration of nuclear weapons.
	Indochina War (1946–1954)	United States	Case 3: Eisenhower administration considers using nuclear weapons to prevent French defeat by Vietminh (April/May 1954).[7] Case 4: Eisenhower administration considers using nuclear weapons if Chinese intervene in Indochina war.[8]
	Quemoy Crisis (1954–1955)	United States	Case 5: Eisenhower administration considers likelihood of using nuclear weapons if Chinese attack two small islands on China's coast.[9]
	Quemoy Crisis (1958)	United States	Case 6: Eisenhower administration again considers nuclear weapons to defend the off-shore islands.
	Berlin Crisis (1961)	United States, USSR	Case 7: Kennedy administration reviews plans for nuclear use.
	Lao Civil War (1959–1962)	United States	No evidence of consideration of nuclear weapons.
	Cuban Missile Crisis (1962)	United States, USSR	Case 8: Kennedy administration pledges to use nuclear weapons against USSR if any Cuban-based missile is launched.
	Vietnam (1961–1965)	United States	No evidence of consideration of nuclear weapons.

Arab-Israeli War (1973)	United States, USSR	No evidence of consideration of nuclear weapons.
India-Pakistan Crisis (1990)	India, Pakistan (?)	Rumors of possible Pakistani consideration but no credible evidence.
Chinese Nuclear Program (1955–1970)	United States, USSR	Case 9: Kennedy administration considers a nuclear attack on Chinese facilities and asks for Soviet view (May 1963).[10] Case 10: Johnson administration considers a nuclear attack on Chinese facilities (September 1964).[11] Case 11: Brezhnev Politburo considers a nuclear attack on Chinese facilities (spring/summer 1969).[12]
Pre-emptive Strike against Nuclear Facilities by Current Nuclear States		
Indian Nuclear Program (1960s–1980)	China	No evidence of consideration of nuclear weapons.
Iraqi Nuclear Program (1960s–1991)	Israel	No evidence that Israeli government considered nuclear weapons; it did successfully attack the Iraqi facility with conventional bombs (1981).
Pakistani Nuclear Program (1970s–present)	India	No evidence that India considered using nuclear weapons; there was a flurry of press reports in 1984 that India might attack conventionally.[13]
Iranian Nuclear Program	United States	No evidence of consideration of nuclear weapons.

1. Dates are for the time when the participants had nuclear weapons. In the case of attacks on nuclear weapons facilities, the dates are from the inception of the program to approximately 5–6 years after a test or the estimated time of joining the nuclear club. After that time, the new nuclear state probably had a meaningful retaliatory force (warheads and delivery systems).

2. See evidence cited in this chapter.

3. British military planners "… assumed that … nuclear weapons would not be used," according to Keith Kyle, Suez (New York: St. Martin's), p. 168. Kyle reports no further discussion of nuclear weapons in top civilian or military circles.

4. McGeorge Bundy reports that "in seven years of warfare, from 1965 to 1972, not one of three American presidents ever came close to using a nuclear weapon." He notes that "once, when American forces at Khe Sanh were thought by some to be in danger of suffering the fate that overtook the French at Dien Bien Phu, General Westmoreland did want contingency planning for a nuclear strike to save them, but Johnson made it plain that he wanted no such proposal, and when Westmoreland 'established a small secret group to study the subject,' he was 'told to desist.'" McGeorge Bundy, Danger and Survival: Choices about the Bomb in the First Fifty Years (New York: Random House, 1988), p. 536. Bundy quotes from William Westmoreland, A Soldier Reports, p. 338.

5. Seymour Hersh argues that the Israeli cabinet on October 8, 1973 agreed to arm its weapons and target them, with use depending on the state of the battlefield (The Samson Option [New York: Random House, 1991]). Yair Evron believes that Defense Minister Moshe Dayan raised the issue of nuclear weapons, which apparently provoked heated remonstrances from powerful cabinet members, and Prime Minister Golda Meir "ruled against Dayan's tentative proposals." (Israel's Nuclear Dilemma [Ithaca, NY: Cornell, 1994]). p. 72.

6. Diego Cordovez and Selig Harrison, Out of Afghanistan (New York: Oxford University Press, 1995), which has some details about Soviet decision making, reports nothing suggested at a top-level consideration of nuclear weapons.

7. See McGeorge Bundy, Danger, pp. 260–270.

8. Stephen E. Ambrose, Eisenhower, Vol. 2. The President (New York: Simon & Schuster, 1984), pp. 205–206.

9. Bundy, Danger and Survival, p. 274.

10. See the Kennedy to Averill Harriman message of 1963 quoted by Gordon H. Chang, Friends and Enemies: The United States, China, and the Soviet Union, 1948–1972 (Stanford, CA: Stanford University Press, 1990), p. 243. See also Chang, p. 245.

11. McGeorge Bundy memo of September 15, 1964; quoted in Chang, Friends and Enemies, p. 250.

12. Arkady Shevchenko, Breaking with Moscow (New York: Knopf, 1985), p. 166. Henry Kissinger, White House Years (Boston, MA: Little, Brown, 1979), p. 183.

13. P. R. Chari, Indo-Pak Nuclear Standoff (New Delhi, Manohar, 1995), pp. 128–129.

Consider the following two examples as illustrations of what near-use decisions look like (and what kind of evidence is available):

KOREA 1953 NEAR USE

Dwight Eisenhower came to office in January 1953, having pledged to end the stalemated war in Korea. Top secret summaries of the discussions in the National Security Council[31] indicate that Eisenhower himself suggested "the use of tactical atomic weapons on [Chinese forces in] the Kaesong [Korea] area, which provided a good target for this type of weapon."[32] He pressed the point again three months later at an NSC meeting when the chairman of the Joint Chiefs indicated that the Chinese and North Koreans were trying to reactivate airfields in North Korea. Eisenhower "inquired whether these airfields might not prove a target which would test the effectiveness of an atomic bomb. At any rate, said the President, he had reached the point of being convinced that we have got to consider the atomic bomb as simply another weapon in our arsenal."[33]

Eisenhower's military commanders generally opposed using nuclear weapons, believing them to be ineffective for the purposes the president had in mind (and likely to alienate American allies and prolong the war). Under the president's prodding, however, the military commanders drew up plans for an extensive nuclear campaign against China if he decided to expand the war. Eisenhower continued to challenge their view that atomic weapons could not be used effectively against the Chinese dug into the Korean hills; certainly, he said, they would be cheaper than using conventional ammunition. On May 20, 1953, the NSC endorsed this approach "if conditions arise requiring more positive action in Korea."[34]

In July 1953 the Chinese and North Koreans ended the fighting in Korea by signing the armistice, bringing further discussion of nuclear use to an end in the American government. Eisenhower, however, had appeared willing to see the bomb as another weapon to be used against a nonnuclear foe (even though that foe was supported by a nuclear-armed Soviet Union), and had forced his subordinates to consider and discuss the option.[35] In the end, the top leadership decided against immediate use, but agreed in principle that the bomb would be used if the war were escalated—which the leadership agreed would be necessary if the Communist states rejected an armistice.

NEAR USES IN RESPONSE TO THE CHINESE NUCLEAR WEAPONS PROGRAM

Declassified secret messages show that in July 1963, President Kennedy instructed Averell Harriman to "try to elicit [Soviet leader] Khrushchev's view of means of limiting or preventing Chinese nuclear development and his willingness either to take Soviet action or to accept U.S. action aimed in this direction."[36] Apparently there had been some discussion in Washington about the use of nuclear weapons to accomplish this, but it is not clear if Kennedy actively considered them (although it is hard to imagine how an attack with conventional weapons or sabotage could be thought to be effective).[37] Neither the Soviets or the Americans took further action at the time.

According to a secret memorandum summarizing decisions made at the top level in September 1964—a month before the first Chinese nuclear test—President Johnson and his top advisors reviewed their options to keep China from going nuclear, and concluded that "we are not in favor of unprovoked unilateral U.S. military action against Chinese nuclear installations at this time."[38]

Five years later, it was the Soviets' turn to take up the issue, although China was now a nuclear-weapons state. According to the account of a Kremlin insider, the Politburo (the top Soviet policymaking council) discussed a proposal by Defense Minister Andrei Grechko to use nuclear weapons to destroy the Chinese nuclear facilities. (This came at a time when the Chinese had dramatically escalated the tension along their common border.) The Politburo could only agree to sound out the United States.[39] In August 1969, a Soviet embassy official asked an official of the U.S. State Department "out of the blue ... what the U.S. reaction would be to a Soviet attack on Chinese nuclear facilities."[40] The Americans quickly replied that the United States would be strongly opposed (and the Chinese soon appeared willing to negotiate to reduce the conflict along the frontier). The matter apparently went no further.

Looking at Table 2-1 as a whole, the following conclusions emerge, conclusions that may be guideposts for the future:

1. A "young" nuclear power (such as the United States in the Eisenhower administration), caught up in a stalemated war, will consider using nuclear weapons against a nonnuclear foe (even if the foe has a nuclear patron). A "mature nuclear" power (the United States in 1970, the Soviet Union in 1985) will not consider nuclear weapons against a similar opponent (North Vietnam, Afghanistan respectively).

2. A young nuclear power will consider contingent nuclear weapons use in times of a crisis with a nonnuclear power. (Cases 3–6 during the Eisenhower administration.) Mature nuclear powers will not.

3. Nuclear powers will not consider nuclear use against other nuclear weapons states in times of a crisis. The Berlin 1961 and Cuban crises are models of caution in this regard, although they came as both powers began to enter their maturity as nuclear powers. (Chapter 6 explores both crises in greater detail.)

4. Nuclear powers will consider nuclear weapons as an option to keep another state from going nuclear or to destroy a small nuclear arsenal.

We need to recall that in all but one case (Japan, 1945), the active consideration of nuclear weapons has never led to their use. In the next several chapters, we will explore some of the reasons that the top leadership of nuclear armed societies has been ultimately unwilling to use the power at its disposal. But it is clear that nuclear use has been actively contemplated. Given the right kind of situation (wartime, crisis, or unsettling nuclear proliferation), top policymakers have seen the merits of nuclear use, especially in the "youth" of a nuclear weapons state.

THE COLD WAR'S VISIONS OF NUCLEAR USE

We indicated that in addition to an examination of the historical record, thinking done during the Cold War also offers us clues about nuclear use in the future. The Cold War (1947–1989) was a period of tension between the United States and the Soviet Union and China. Academics and strategists considered how that tension might lead to the use of nuclear weapons and developed the following five standard scenarios:

SCENARIO I: NUCLEAR ESCALATION TO ACHIEVE GOALS

This scenario argued that decision makers might, at some point, use nuclear weapons to achieve goals that were being thwarted by the opponent. The several cases of near use in the Eisenhower administration are the closest historical counterparts to this scenario, contemplating as they did nuclear escalation against a nonnuclear power (China or the Vietnamese insurgents) to achieve a goal such as ending the Korean war or preventing the fall of territory to the Communists. In Europe, the United States and several of its NATO allies planned to use nuclear weapons first if Soviet-led Warsaw Pact forces initiated conventional war in Europe. NATO planners feared that Pact tank forces might be able to break through NATO's forward defenses in West Germany and set the stage for a massive Western defeat, which would nullify the American goal of keeping Europe free of Soviet control. Such planning affected how individuals were trained to respond to situations, and it conditioned leaders to think in particular ways. If war did break out in Europe, the leaders of the NATO nations would likely have been called upon to make a decision to use such weapons (or to give local commanders the power to do so on their own volition). We might imagine that the pressure to approve at least a limited number of battlefield strikes against Warsaw Pact forces would have been immense.

This escalation from conventional to nuclear weapons on the battlefield raises the issue of *thresholds* on the *escalation ladder*.[41] (See Figure 2-1.) In a crisis or war, there will be pressure on leaders to escalate the severity, the location, or the nature of their actions in order to achieve their goals. At some point, the next step in escalation would involve behavior quite different in character from previous actions. Taking that next step is said to be the crossing of a threshold (or firebreak). The idea of threshold implies that leaders will be forced to think long and hard before making such a move because they recognize and fear that a different kind of conflict lies across the threshold,

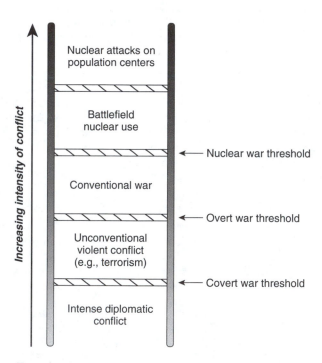

FIGURE 2-1   THRESHOLDS ON THE ESCALATION LADDER

a conflict in which the risks might be much greater and the likelihood of success more in doubt. Thresholds, therefore, would keep conflict at a lower level, and may give leaders a greater incentive to seek some other method to resolve the conflict than to cross the threshold.

Scholars and decision makers have suggested that there is a significant threshold between the use of conventional and nuclear weapons on the battlefield. Leaders might be very reluctant to cross that threshold if they had reason to believe that (1) their nation would not benefit from the increased destruction (as the enemy might retaliate with its nuclear weapon or other weapons of mass destruction such as chemical or biological weapons), or (2) once the battlefield threshold had been crossed, there would be a great temptation to cross the next threshold—the use of nuclear weapons against the homeland of the other state (particularly its cities). Crossing the threshold from conventional to nuclear weapons on the battlefield may also be unattractive because of the ambiguity of what would in fact constitute battlefield use. To the extent that NATO first-use plans included attacking Warsaw Pact transportation systems and supply areas in Poland and Czechoslovakia, or even similar targets in the western border areas of the Soviet Union, the clarity of the threshold between nuclear battlefield use and attacks against homelands begins to break down; Soviet leaders might reasonably have concluded that NATO had in fact crossed the threshold separating local from homeland nuclear war, and have decided to retaliate in kind against cities in Western Europe or in the continental United States.

Crossing the threshold between conventional and nuclear war thus seemed to offer a possibility of securing one's goals in war, but with the very great risk that the cost of doing so would be catastrophic. On the other hand, to the degree that leaders felt that there was a strong threshold between *battlefield* and *homeland* use, they might be tempted to use nuclear weapons on the battlefield. They might, of course, seriously misjudge the strength (or weakness) of a particular threshold and face catastrophe for that misjudgment, but their decision to use nuclear weapons would be based on the assessment of the strength of the threshold to prevent further escalation.

One thing should be apparent from our discussion: In this scenario, rational leaders in the pursuit of seemingly rational goals (such as the defense of West Germany) could contemplate—and plan for—the use of nuclear weapons in order to achieve their goals. Put another way, using nuclear weapons—even against an opponent with the capability to retaliate—was not judged to be a sign of madness, even when it came to be recognized that a full-scale nuclear war could achieve no meaningful political purpose. Therefore, we should not be terribly surprised if, in the future, leaders of other nuclear-armed countries decide that they, too, must use nuclear weapons in order to achieve their goals.

SCENARIO II: BOLT FROM THE BLUE

In this scenario, the leadership of one state simply decides that it is time to strike an opponent a crushing blow, typically when the relations between the two states are relatively peaceful. The scenario presumes that the leadership believes that war with the opponent is likely at some point in the future and, therefore, it is better to attack at the most favorable moment for oneself—presumably when the opponent lowers its guard. This is the scenario of *preventive war*.

Both the Soviet Union and the United States had been struck by such bolts from the blue. Although the Germans and Soviets were de facto allies in 1941, both sides recognized the alliance was temporary and did not change the deep hostility between the two. The timing of Hitler's attack caught Stalin by surprise. The Japanese and Americans were exploring the possibility of a diplomatic settlement in the Pacific in 1941, although neither was willing to make a meaningful concession to make it happen. While the American leadership expected some dramatic Japanese move, the attack at Pearl Harbor against the American Pacific fleet was entirely unexpected.

During the Cold War, apparently individuals in both the Soviet and American governments did feel that the leadership of the other side was, in fact, thinking such thoughts. We have no evidence, however, that either side in fact seriously contemplated launching such a bolt. We do have a tantalizing piece of evidence, however, that it might have crossed their minds. President Kennedy reportedly said to a confidant during the height of the Cuban Missile Crisis, "You know, if it wasn't for the children, you could easily say the hell with it and push the button. But I can't do that. Not for just Caroline and John, but for all the children all over the world—not only for those that are alive who will suffer and die, but all those who will have never lived."[42]

Kennedy's statement suggests that launching nuclear bolts from the blue would be constrained by fears of retaliation (although in the Cuban missile crisis the United States held a decided nuclear superiority, a superiority likely to be effectively enhanced by an unexpected nuclear strike). They would also be restrained by a leader's sense of propriety (one does not willingly harm the world's children). The implication is, of course, that a different leader might feel far less constrained. How likely is it that the leadership of nuclear nations—the individuals with the power to commit the society to the use of such weapons—would be vested in the hands of individuals who, far from fearing retaliation and condemnation for their nuclear acts, might see a bolt from the blue as exactly what should be done?

Would a Hitler, for instance, be just such a leader? Historically, even Hitler exercised restraint in the use of certain weapons. For instance, he did not begin the air attacks on urban populations far removed from the battlefield in World War II; that was initiated by Great Britain. And even when the war turned against Germany, he refrained from ordering the use of poison gas against his enemies (including the detested Russians). His fear of retaliation held in check some features of his violent nature.

Moreover, nuclear-armed states have taken great precautions to make sure that those who can launch nuclear weapons are under tight supervision. Such individuals in turn are likely to have internalized a strong sense of personal responsibility. If an order to use nuclear weapons came when there appeared no reason to launch (precisely the context envisioned by a bolt from the blue) we might expect that up and down the chain of command, from the military elite to the individuals who would actually send the weapons toward detonation, there might be challenges to the order and outright disobedience. Indeed, an order to stage a bolt from the blue may be the very thing that leads to a military coup against the political leadership.

Finally, the leadership selection processes in the nuclear-armed states have tended to weed out the individuals who seemed unstable or willing to take bizarre, high risk political actions. This has held true for Western democracies as well as communist systems; the leadership that emerged might have been quite Machiavellian, but it was also a leadership that was cautious.

Will such restraining conditions continue to hold in the future? There is reason for some worry. Democratic political systems do not guarantee stable leaders; after all, Hitler came to power legally in a democratic political system. The collapse of Communist party control in Russia and the novelty of democracy there increases the likelihood that new parties or factions, led by individuals only recently thrust into positions of leadership and therefore not sifted by any process of selection, might find themselves with their fingers near the nuclear "button." A highly demoralized Russian military apparatus might not provide the bulwark against a bolt from the blue. Indeed, the more the military itself becomes swept up into the political process, the more likely that individuals who might look favorably on nuclear use will begin to populate the nuclear chain of command. The "what-the-hell" syndrome that Kennedy mentioned might well be more pervasive.

Such characteristics of unstable political systems, demoralized military establishments, and political leaders of varying degrees of rationality and intelligence are rather widespread among the states of the international system. While fingers are often pointed at Third World states, no state is proof against such characteristics. It may well be, however, that the ability to insulate nuclear weapons from these kinds of destabilizing features will be most under stress in the Third World nations with nuclear weapons.

Just to reinforce the point that all nations might be tempted to stage a bolt from the blue, consider the narrower version of this scenario: a preemptive strike against the nuclear facilities of an emerging nuclear power. We found three such cases of near-use of nuclear weapons—all by developed states (the United States and the Soviet Union). Such a strike would likely come without warning, and be predicated on the assumption that it would be better to face an embittered state deprived of its nuclear potential today than a nuclear-armed rival tomorrow.

SCENARIO III: FEAR-INDUCED PREEMPTION

Fear-induced preemption may occur in any number of ways, but its central feature is a crisis worsening to the point that one side fears that it is about to be struck with nuclear weapons and decides therefore to strike first. Historically, there have been no near-use decisions that have the earmarks of preemption. Looking retrospectively at the Soviet-American relationship, however, there were any number of conflicts that might have spiraled upward in intensity to reach that point. Consider the Cuban missile crisis. The United States was poised to invade Cuba and was within two days of doing so when the United States and the Soviet Union reached agreement. Suppose that the two sides had not been able to reach agreement in that time, and the Kennedy administration, in despair, had ordered the invasion. Soviet commanders in Cuba had tactical (battlefield) nuclear weapons, and urged Moscow to permit their use on the commanders' volition. Suppose that Khrushchev, fearing the loss of Cuba, the missiles, and his personal standing, gave permission. Further suppose that a Soviet commander, about to have an American invasion force overrun his unit, ordered a single atomic device used against that force. Kennedy had pledged to retaliate against the Soviet Union if any Cuban-based missile were launched against any target in the Western hemisphere. So finally suppose that Khrushchev and his advisors, on hearing the news that their own commander had crossed the nuclear threshold in Cuba, and fearing Kennedy might order that retaliatory strike against the Soviet Union, order a preemptive attack against the United States in the hope of blunting an American attack that the Soviet leadership was convinced would come.

The Cuban missile crisis is replete with other departure points for fear-induced preemption. During the crisis, the American leadership had agreed that any attack against its reconnaissance aircraft over Cuba would bring a strike against the offending Soviet air defense system in Cuba. A Soviet surface-to-air missile did down such an aircraft (fired, incidentally, on the orders of Soviet commanders in Cuba). Kennedy put off implementing the agreed retaliatory strike over the stiff objections of American commanders. Suppose that Kennedy had ordered such a strike. Imagine that just as fragmentary, excited radio messages come in from Cuba reporting the American attack and predicting the start of an American invasion, an American reconnaissance aircraft inadvertently penetrates Soviet airspace, creating consternation in Moscow. Further suppose that instead of anxiously waiting (as the Soviet leadership did when the latter event actually happened), the Soviet leadership erroneously read the intrusion as the lead aircraft of an incoming nuclear bomber attack on the Soviet Union and ordered Soviet nuclear systems to attack the United States before they were destroyed.

What characterizes fear-induced preemption scenarios is the assumption that, as the likelihood of war increases, the fear of being the victim of the first blow increases. The remedy is to strike first. Such a decision can be rationalized in a number of ways:

- The nation that strikes first at the military assets of the opponent may lessen the damage the opponent can deliver through retaliation.
- A quick strike might so disrupt the opponent's government and military command system that enemy retaliation would be insignificant.
- The enemy government would be so anxious to save what was left that it would not launch a retaliatory strike.
- If one does not strike first, one's own weapons are likely to be destroyed by the opponent's attack, thus leaving one at the mercy of the opponent.
- And, given the emotions likely among the leadership (the enemy has, after all, seemingly ordered the destruction of much of one's society), it is easy to see the enemy as so monstrous as to deserve such punishment.

Thus fear leads to a decision to act, and that action is buttressed by what sounds to fearful men and women like compellingly rational arguments for action.

Fear, of course, is internal. It may rest directly on what others are doing or on what one *believes* others are doing. The rush to war because of fear is nothing new—it seems to have been a critical ingredient in the beginning of World War I. If the leadership of a nation believes that nuclear war is to come, a first strike is a reasonable option under the circumstances. Even a leadership loath to go to war may decide on war.

SCENARIO IV: INSENSATE NUCLEAR WAR

Insensate nuclear war is the initiation of nuclear war in a blind act of rage, a lashing out at one's enemies. The typical scenario is one in which a small but nuclear-armed nation is about to be overrun by its mortal enemy. That small nation, faced with subjugation, decides that having lost all, it might as well destroy the victor. Nuclear weapons allow such retribution even in losing causes. There has been no historical case of a near-use decision that fits this scenario. The Israeli consideration of nuclear weapons in the 1973 war centered on a battlefield use in a war that was not lost (although proving costly to Israel in terms of lives).

It is tempting to think that only small states and parochial leaders would behave so irresponsibly, but the superpowers pledged to do something similar under a nuclear policy of assured destruction (which we discuss in Chapter 5). Even if it were not policy, many citizens of a nation attacked by nuclear weapons might expect their leaders to order massive retaliation, simply as a matter of punishment. The situations are fundamentally different, however. In the case of the superpowers, emotional reaction comes as *retaliation* for a nuclear first strike. In the insensate scenario, the small state leadership orders the *initiation* of nuclear war out of revenge. Small states may, in fact, be more prone to this. Lacking extensive territory, they run the risk of being overrun quickly by their opponents' conventional armies. In addition, their nuclear weapons are likely to be relatively few, thus removing the restraints that a concern for the rest of the world might exercise.

SCENARIO V: INADVERTENT NUCLEAR WAR

Inadvertent nuclear war is war thrust upon the leadership of a nation, a war begun by mistake. All accidents can be explained. Some are the result of unintended error. Others are the result of unauthorized actions. An example of *unintended error* is the monitoring service of a nation that interprets radar signals incorrectly and reports that an attack is coming. During the Cuban missile crisis, "U.S. radar operators mistakenly warned that a missile had been launched from Cuba and was about to hit Tampa. Only after the expected detonation failed to occur was it discovered that an operator had inserted a training tape into the system."[43] Similarly, what might be *innocuous behavior* at one time might be perceived by others as anything but at another time. During the Cuban missile crisis, "the Strategic Air Command deployed nuclear warheads in nine of ten test silos at Vandenberg Air Force Base and then launched the tenth missile in a previously scheduled test, oblivious to the possibility that the Soviets might have been aware of the warhead deployments and could have confused the test for a nuclear attack."[44] If leaders launch their weapons in response to such false information or innocuous behavior, we have an accidental nuclear war. (The nation actually striking first can, in fact, be seen as acting as the fear-induced preemption scenario stipulates; the nation receiving the "retaliation" might react as if this were a bolt from the blue.) The key aspect of this scenario is that decision makers erroneously assume that nuclear war has already begun and they are only acting in response to the decision of the other, whereas, in reality, their own actions initiate nuclear war.

Historically, the superpowers have experienced these kinds of accidents, but built-in safeguards and a measure of luck have prevented accidental war. Even the demise of the Cold War has not reduced the risk. In 1995, a meteorological rocket launched by Norway was misread by Russian monitoring systems. According to press reports, for the first time the top Russian leadership was warned that it was about to be struck by a nuclear warhead.[45] (Fortunately, the leadership discovered the truth, but the press reports indicated that President Yeltsin felt that he had very few minutes in which to make a decision—and this when the terrors of the Cold War had presumably dissipated.)

An inadvertent war may also begin with the *unauthorized* use of nuclear weapons by subordinates. A common scenario depicts subordinates' attempting to force the national leadership into a full-scale war. In the movie *Dr. Strangelove*, renegade Air Force General Jack D. Ripper ordered his bomber wing to attack the Soviet Union. He calculated that the American government would order a follow-on attack in order to blunt Soviet retaliation.

Are such forms of inadvertent nuclear war likely? Although there is always the possibility that erroneous information might bring on nuclear war, the experience of the last fifty years suggests that decision makers are reluctant to react to warnings that an attack is about to happen until further checks are made on the reliability of the information. This may be especially true if the information has an element of strangeness to it—such as the launch of a single missile. Indeed, it is likely that decision makers may be prepared to accept a single such launch as a mistake, and negotiate the next stage of the ensuing crisis rather than respond in kind. Moreover, in well-maintained monitoring systems, the chance of erroneous reporting is likely to be low. As such systems degrade (for instance, as personnel go unpaid, morale drops, and training decreases, as in Russia today), the leadership may see the system as unreliable and therefore put less credibility in its reporting (which reduces the likelihood of erroneous messages having an impact). *In a crisis*, however, a leadership faced with a erratically operating monitoring system may be more likely to treat seriously any warning such a system produces.

As to "rogue" elements in a nation's military establishment using nuclear weapons to force the hand of the leadership, well-ordered military establishments that are responsive to civilian oversight are not likely to go astray in such ways. An out-of-control military system or a decaying military system—and the Russian system currently seems to have such a character—may have less ability to control its subordinates, who may decide that they will rewrite the nation's foreign policy using the weapons at their disposal. Elements of the Japanese military, for instance, in 1931 seized the Chinese province of Manchuria to force the Japanese government to begin the conversion of China into part of the Japanese empire. Unfortunately, even in well-ordered military systems there does seem to be the possibility that military personnel will seek to circumvent controls on their capabilities in the belief that they are acting responsibly. During the Cuban missile crisis, "officers at Malmstrom Air Force Base jerry-rigged the launch system to give themselves the ability to launch their Minuteman missiles without higher authorization."[46]

A variant of inadvertent nuclear war has been called a *catalytic* war. A nation or a group detonates a nuclear device on the territory of a second nuclear-armed nation in a way that makes the attack appear to be staged by a third nuclear-armed nation. The intention is to provoke the victim into retaliating in kind against the presumed guilty party, thus initiating nuclear war.

How likely is this pathway to nuclear war? First recognize that we are not talking about *nuclear terrorism*—the detonation of a device to advance a group's or nation's political agenda in which the intention is not, as a rule, to provoke nuclear retaliation but to create enough havoc to lead to concessions to the terrorists' demands. We discuss nuclear terrorism in later chapters. Here we are asking whether a detonation designed to provoke a nuclear response against an innocent third party will in fact accomplish its aim. We suspect that a nuclear-armed state is not likely to respond in a hair-trigger fashion to such an incident, nor is it likely to retaliate against the innocent third party without compelling evidence that the third party was involved, and the third party is likely to make strenuous efforts to convince the victim that it was not to blame.

These five scenarios came out of the Cold War era, and concentrated on the ways in which nuclear war might begin between the two nuclear-armed superpowers. Though the Cold War is history, these scenarios captured some of the basic dynamics of the nuclear age and will continue to have some relevance in the future. Table 2-2 speculates on how the five scenarios might be applicable in the next twenty-five years.

TABLE 2-2 CLASSIC COLD WAR SCENARIOS OF NUCLEAR USE
APPLIED TO THE SECOND NUCLEAR AGE

SCENARIO I: NUCLEAR ESCALATION TO ACHIEVE GOALS	Chronic tension between India and Pakistan produces a conventional shooting war along the border of the two nations. An Indian offensive overwhelms Pakistani forces in the south, threatening Karachi. Pakistan uses several nuclear weapons to blunt the offensive (and to force the great powers to restrain the Indians before the situation spirals out of control).
SCENARIO II: BOLT FROM THE BLUE	The tensions between a nuclear-armed Iran and the Islamic movement that controls most of Afghanistan have eased in recent months, but the Iranian leadership worries that the large number of Afghan units on its border constitutes a continuing threat. If Iran stationed similar-sized Iranian units opposite the Afghan forces—as well as along the frontiers Iran shares with five other states—the treasury would soon be depleted. Seeing the Kabul government as inherently hostile, and likely to revive the conflict in the future, the Iranian government decides to strike unexpectedly at the Afghan units with small-sized nuclear weapons.
SCENARIO III: FEAR-INDUCED PREEMPTION	A nuclear North Korea enters a profound internal crisis, threatening Communist Party control. Factions within the North Korean military establishment now appear to be independent; those officers in command of nuclear weapons units call for an all-out war to reunite the two Koreas. The American government, fearing that nuclear strikes are about to occur against American forces in South Korea, orders nuclear preemption (as it judges conventional weapons incapable of destroying the North Korean nuclear arsenal).
SCENARIO IV: INSENSATE NUCLEAR WAR	A regional rebel movement has been at war against Moscow for years, gradually building its control over a swath of territory, and purchasing a number of nuclear devices and short-range delivery systems from the ineffectively guarded Russian stockpile. A skillful Russian commander now begins an offensive into the rebel enclave and rebel control quickly collapses. As a last act of defiance, the rebel commander launches the missiles into a nearby Russian city, devastating it.
SCENARIO V: INADVERTENT NUCLEAR WAR	Tension mounts in the Formosa Straits as the new president of Taiwan announces that Taiwan will seek international recognition as an independent state. The Chinese begin a new round of test-firings of missiles into the waters around Taiwan as a warning against seeking independence. American warnings that it will not permit a Chinese offensive against Taiwan are met with a Chinese order to assemble an invasion fleet in Chinese ports opposite Taiwan. At this point, a malfunction in the Chinese radar system erroneously detects a massive launch of cruise missiles from the American fleet operating in the Straits. The Chinese order a limited nuclear missile strike against the American fleet.

DECISIONS TO USE NUCLEAR WEAPONS IN THE SECOND NUCLEAR ERA

Our speculations in Table 2-2 do not mean that the first nuclear era "discovered" the only pathways to nuclear use. Indeed, the end of the first nuclear era forces us to consider what new pathways might be emerging. The Cold War came to an abrupt and unexpected end between 1989 and 1991. The end of the Soviet Union's control over Eastern Europe, the collapse of Communist Party control within the USSR, and finally the breakup of the Union itself into weaker and disorganized states ushered in a new age of world politics. The United States became the sole global superpower. The United States and the successor states to the Soviet Union, particularly Russia, no longer saw each other as mortal enemies (although it would take some time for the defense bureaucracies to acknowledge that fact in the procedures they had created to prepare for war with the other). It became almost inconceivable that these nations would consider nuclear use against the other.

The 1990s demonstrated that all the traditional nuclear weapons states (the United States, Russia, Britain, France, and China) had redefined their relations with each other. The Cold War scenarios no longer seemed plausible for the five; the probability of nuclear use by one of the five against another member of the group dropped quite close to zero. The dramatic emergence of India and Pakistan, however, as full-fledged nuclear weapons states in May 1998 helped to redefine and refocus the nuclear predicament.[47] Such open proliferation was a strong possibility in the years after the demise of the Cold War and its occurrence completed the emergence of the second nuclear era. This new era did not make the experiences of the young nuclear weapons states or the Cold War scenarios obsolete. They remain as possible pathways to a decision to use nuclear weapons. But the new era poses two new questions for us: Are there *new* pathways to the use of nuclear weapons in the next twenty-five years? What is the probability that the next quarter-century will see any use of nuclear weapons?

Can we imagine the conditions that might bring about the use of nuclear weapons in the future? Or can we imagine the conditions that increase the number of times that decision makers contemplate the use of the weapons, thus increasing the probability that such scenario dynamics as fear-induced preemption or escalation to achieve goals dictate the course of events? While the actors and circumstances are likely to change, the pressures for use and the scenarios developed during the Cold War will continue to have applicability. In addition, the second nuclear age may give new importance to four other pathways to nuclear use:

1. *"The shot across the bow"*: As you will recall, in 1945 the Interim Committee discussed demonstrating the bomb against a relatively uninhabited area in Japan. Such a demonstration would communicate two messages. First, the United States possessed a terrible weapon against which the Japanese nation would be virtually defenseless (a demonstration of power). Second, the United States stood ready to use it against a more meaningful target unless Japan surrendered (a demonstration of resolve to achieve an announced goal). We imagine that, in the future, more leaders of nuclear states will come to see this kind of detonation of a nuclear weapon as a means of demonstrating their power and resolve to an opponent, particularly one that is a nonnuclear state or possesses only a small nuclear arsenal.

   In the second nuclear era, a nuclear demonstration is now a "safer" use of a nuclear weapon. Its use does not necessarily initiate nuclear war per se—although that might occur as a consequence of the demonstration—and it may force a successful resolution of a political conflict. Granted, such a temptation existed in the Cold War period. What is different now is that such a nuclear use will not engage the delicate balance of terror that existed between the United States and Soviet Union during the Cold War. Today the consequences of a demonstration are fewer, thereby making a demonstration far more attractive than it would have been during the Cold War. Secondly, any use is likely to energize the other current nuclear powers to bring about a diplomatic solution to the crisis. Thus, we expect that in the future leaders will be more likely to perform this calculation: "Will our use of a nuclear weapon as a shot across the bow lead other nuclear powers, particularly the United States, to act to head off further use by persuading our opponent to make the desired concession?" To the degree that the answer is "Yes," the probability of use increases.

2. *Internal politics*: Governments have, from time to time, employed their military's weapons in political crises within their states, ranging from conventional high explosives to more exotic weapons, as Iraq's Saddam Hussein's use of chemical weapons against dissident Kurds within Iraq. In the future, governments may see their nuclear arsenals as "another weapon of *internal* war," to be used to destroy or subdue internal opponents. Alternatively, the use of nuclear weapons may come as part of a military establishment's coup d'etat, or as part of the jockeying for power among a highly factionalized military. Moreover, if a society breaks up and nuclear-armed warlords come to dominate regions of a nation, one warlord may attempt to use nuclear weapons to dominate the others. Finally, we can imagine that in intense ethnic or ideological conflict, groups who acquire nuclear weapons may be tempted to use them for political purposes, including genocide.

3. *Terrorism*: As we discussed in the last chapter and will see in the next, we are rapidly moving to the point at which nuclear weapons can come into the possession of organizations other than central governments. Such groups might detonate such weapons as part of their campaign to force a nation to meet their political demands, or to extort money or other things of value from governments, corporations, or wealthy individuals. We discuss terrorism extensively in Chapter 7.

4. *Reprisal*: Inflicting injury in retaliation for an action by another nation has long been a practice in world politics. To this point in history, nuclear weapons have remained outside the range of acceptable means of reprisal, but we suspect that this may be changing. In the Gulf crisis of 1990–91, for instance, President Bush threatened to retaliate with nuclear weapons if the Iraqis used chemical or biological weapons against coalition forces. Chemical and biological weapons have been judged unacceptable by many societies, and their use proscribed by more than 130 nations who ratified the conventions of 1972 and 1993 outlawing them.

   President Bush's threat suggests a day when nuclear weapons might be used to punish another nation for violating international rules. Such punishment is not war-waging (i.e., designed to affect the outcome of a particular conflict), nor necessarily to force the violator back into compliance (though no one would object if that occurred). Rather, the use is purely punishment—to exact some cost for a transgression of the rules. Initially, the violation must be relatively monstrous, but we can imagine that once a successful reprisal occurs, there will be a temptation to sanction for other violations, thus stretching nuclear use to cover a broader set of activities.

THE LIKELIHOOD OF NUCLEAR USE IN THE NEXT TWENTY-FIVE YEARS

How likely is it that we will see a hostile nuclear use in the next twenty-five years? As we write these words, it seems hardly conceivable that the United States, Russia, or China would use nuclear weapons against each other. Does that mean that, overall, the chances for the use of nuclear weapons in next twenty-five years are next to zero? Recall that the presence of nuclear weapons in the arsenals of any state gives decision makers the *option* to use such weapons. In the next twenty-five years, there are likely to be as many nuclear-capable states as there are now, if not more. Use, therefore, remains possible. Also recall that the historical record reveals that young nuclear nations are more likely to consider using such weapons. As states join the nuclear club, they will need to pass through a period of maturation in which there will be such temptation. 1998 marked only the beginning of India and Pakistan's nuclear youth.

The Cold War scenarios that emerged in the nuclear youth period of the United States and the Soviet Union seemed real because the opponent was judged capable and willing to use nuclear weapons. The scenarios provided the intellectual and emotional justifications for why a nation—itself loath to consider using nuclear weapons—might have to do so, even to the point of actually striking first. New nuclear weapons states are likely to see their opponent(s) in similar terms.

Thus, history suggests that basically rational leaders might decide to use nuclear weapons. This is not to deny that irrationality may play an important role. We might imagine, for instance, that in a circumstance such as panic, even rational leaders might respond instinctually rather than thoughtfully. Instinct or emotion, however, need not produce a decision to use nuclear weapons. A decision not to use them may be made on an emotional, nonrational basis. Indeed, as McGeorge Bundy argues, the fear of nuclear weapons may be what keeps leaders away from the decision to use them.[48] But rational calculations may impel them to do so in spite of their fears. We expect, therefore, that future use decisions will be made by men and women who think and behave in essentially rational ways.

No matter the pathway that leads to use, we estimate that the probability of the use of nuclear weapons in the next twenty-five years is relatively high. We define nuclear use as the intentional detonation of a nuclear weapon to affect an opponent's calculations or behavior. Nuclear tests can, of course, be intended to produce similar effects (Pakistan's 1998 tests were a clear warning to India) but what we mean by nuclear use is a detonation that is clearly outside a test site. There must be a great deal of uncertainty in making any prediction about the future, for there are many factors that will press leaders to decide for or against the use of nuclear weapons. Nonetheless, we believe that making predictions is essential if we are to cope intelligently with the nuclear predicament. The prediction must be a speculative effort, but a useful one nonetheless because it forces us to examine our assumptions about nuclear weapons and the behaviors that have emerged around them.

Our prediction is based on the following assumptions that, for the moment, seem reasonable:

1. For the next twenty-five years, world politics will remain essentially a self-help system: individual actors, particularly states, will have to provide for their own

security; there will be no general security system (provided, say, by the United Nations), although military alliances will provide some security to their members.

2. There will be contentious issues that divide nations—issues for which a state traditionally has been willing to contemplate war.

Our prediction is also based on the following propositions that we draw from the analysis in this chapter.

1. The more nuclear-armed states, the greater the likelihood of use.
2. The more nuclear-armed states are organized into hierarchical, rival blocs (as during the Cold War), the less likely the use (because any use is likely to engage the rival blocs). Stated conversely, the more autonomous the nuclear-weapons states, the more likely the use.
3. The greater the number of young nuclear weapons states in the international system, the more likely the use.
4. The more positive the imagery of nuclear weapons (that they are desirable, that their effects are just those of any powerful weapon, that they can produce positive outcomes in political or military conflicts), the more likely the use.[49]
5. The more conflictual the internal politics of nuclear weapons states, the more likely the use.

In the chapters that follow, we will assess the trends in these five areas. For instance, is the number of nuclear-armed states likely to grow in the next twenty-five years? Can states such as India and Pakistan navigate the nuclear maturation process without resort to the use of these weapons? That assessment will provide the argumentation for our prediction about the likelihood of use. For the moment, however, we must ask you to rest content with the following general prediction. The likelihood of nuclear use in the next twenty-five years is on the order of .2 to .3: There is a 20 to 30 percent chance that in the next twenty-five years you will witness the use of a nuclear device, not necessarily against your society, but some place in the world.[50] In comparison, the likelihood of earth's being struck by a asteroid or comet large enough to have a major regional or global impact is roughly one out of a thousand (.001) in the next seventy-five years,[51] of a top major league baseball player hitting safely is approximately .329 (or roughly three out of ten times),[52] and of a thirty-year old American citizen reaching eighty-five years of age is better than .6 (or better than six out of ten chances).[53] In other words, we are speaking of a relatively strong possibility of such an event. A batter doesn't get a hit every time up of course, and we may well pass the next twenty-five years without a nuclear use. But the risk is great that we won't be that lucky.

The hostile use of nuclear weapons, after more than fifty years of abstinence, will push us into a *third nuclear era*, one in which it will take dramatic if not heroic efforts to restabilize international political life. Failure to do that may bring more uses, and the calamities that we pointed out in Chapter 1 may come to pass, not just for the immediate victims of the detonation of a nuclear weapon, but for many of us in a more uncertain, more perilous world.

How is it that humankind launched itself down this road? Was it inevitable? Chapter 3 takes us back another step, to ask how nuclear power can into the hands of humans.

NOTES

1. Harry Truman, *Memoirs*, Vol. 1: *Year of Decisions* (Garden City, NY: Doubleday, 1955), p. 10.
2. Ibid., p. 10.
3. Ibid., p. 87. Franklin Roosevelt had told Byrnes of the Project, possibly as early as 1943, and Byrnes, as director of War Mobilization, had to intervene in a labor dispute in December of 1944 that threatened to reveal the existence of the project.
4. Godfrey Hodgson, *The Colonel: The Life and Wars of Henry Stimson 1867–1950* (New York: Knopf, 1990), pp. 316–317.
5. Henry L. Stimson and McGeorge Bundy, *On Active Service in Peace and War* (New York: Harper, 1948), pp. 615–616.
6. Military training, in fact, recognizes that subordinates might be tempted to make choices under pressure, and tries to ensure that the subordinates make only certain choices that advance the military establishment's mission.
7. Geoffrey Blainey, *The Causes of War* (New York: Free Press, 1973) ably argues for the existence of choice. Congresswoman Jeannette Rankin of Montana was the only vote in the Congress against the declaration of war against Japan, but she, along with forty-nine other members of the House members, had also voted against American entry into World War I. She and they had recognized a choice. See Hannah Josephson, *Jeannette Rankin: First Lady in Congress* (Indianapolis, IN: Bobbs-Merrill, 1974).
8. John W. Dower, *War Without Mercy: Race and Power in the Pacific War* (New York: Pantheon Press, 1986).
9. Diary entry, Harry Truman, *Off the Record*, ed. Robert H. Ferrell (New York: Harper & Row, 1980), pp. 55–56, quoted by McGeorge Bundy, *Danger and Survival* (New York: Random House, 1988), p. 79.
10. Report of Compton, Fermi, Lawrence, and Oppenheimer, quoted by Bundy, *Danger*, p. 71.
11. Barton J. Bernstein, ed., *The Atomic Bomb* (Boston, MA: Little, Brown and Co., 1976), p. xi.
12. Frank Chinnock, *Nagasaki: The Forgotten Bomb* (New York: New American Library/World Publishing, 1969), pp. 65–69.
13. For an introduction to the debate, see Gar Alperovitz, *Atomic Diplomacy* (New York: Simon & Schuster, 1965); G. Alperovitz, *The Decision to Use the Atomic Bomb and the Architecture of an American Myth* (New York: Knopf, 1995); Bernstein, *Atomic Bomb*; Barton Bernstein, "The Atomic Bombings Reconsidered," *Foreign Affairs* 74 (January/February 1995): 135–152; McGeorge Bundy, *Danger and Survival*; Herbert Feis, *The Atomic Bomb and the End of World War II* (Princeton, NJ: Princeton University Press, 1966); Gregg Herkin, *The Winning Weapon* (New York: Knopf, 1980); John Ray Skates, *The Invasion of Japan* (Columbia, SC: University of South Carolina Press, 1994); Stewart L. Udall, *The Myths of August* (New York: Pantheon, 1994); Samuel Walker, "The Decision to Use the Bomb: A Historiographical Update," *Diplomatic History* 14 (winter 1990): 97–114; and Peter Wyden, *Day One* (New York: Simon & Schuster, 1984).
14. See Peter Gizewski, "From Winning Weapon to Destroyer of the World: The Nuclear Taboo in International Politics," *International Journal* 51 (summer 1996): 397–419; and T. V. Paul, "Nuclear Taboo and War: Initiation and Regional Conflicts," *Journal of Conflict Resolution* 39 (December 1995): 696–717.
15. Meeting of May 1, 1954, with Robert Cutler; quoted by Stephen E. Ambrose, *Eisenhower*, Vol. 2, *The President* (New York: Simon & Schuster, 1984), p. 184.
16. "If the decision about dropping the bomb had been yours to make, would you have ordered the bombs to be dropped, or would you have tried some other way to force the Japanese to surrender?" *The Gallup Poll Monthly*, no. 359 (August 1995): 3.
17. Ibid., p. 4. There were interesting variations: men approved but women were split; the younger the respondent, the more disapproving; whites approved, while nonwhites disapproved; Democrats were more likely to disapprove; the better educated were more likely to approve.

18. It is tempting to speculate what might have happened, for instance, if the U.S.S. *Indianapolis*, which delivered the uranium for the Hiroshima bomb to the bomber base, had been sunk before the delivery rather than after.
19. Of course, in the historical case, Truman did not confront the prospect of nuclear retaliation by the Japanese, or by a nuclear-armed ally of Japan. If such retaliation in kind were possible, would the state be as likely to use nuclear weapons as our generalization suggests? As we have no historical experience to draw on, we cannot know for sure, and Cold War theorizing seemed to say that nuclear use might occur—or it might not. The question of whether the fear of nuclear retaliation effectively removes the choice for decision makers is a critical question, one that we will discuss across several chapters.
20. In some cases, the top leadership may *agree in principle* that the use of nuclear weapons will be a meaningful option *if* certain events transpire. For our purposes, we consider these as near-use decisions if there is an active consideration of nuclear weapons at that point, although we acknowledge this to be an intermediate case.
21. James G. Blight claims that all American presidents shared a "revulsion against using nuclear weapons." He does note (in a footnote), however, that "Richard Nixon claims to be an exception. In a recent interview Nixon told Roger Rosenblatt that he gave the use of nuclear weapons serious consideration on four occasions: (1) during the Vietnam War, (2) during the 1973 Middle East War, (3) during the 1969 Soviet-Chinese border dispute, and (4) during the India-Pakistan War of 1971. See Rosenblatt, *Witness: The World Since Hiroshima* (Boston, MA: Little, Brown, 1985), pp. 78–79.... In subsequent interviews, however, Henry Kissinger gently suggested that when a president (in this case his former boss) says he 'considered' going to nuclear war, one must take it with a grain of salt." James G. Blight, *The Shattered Crystal Ball: Fear and Learning in the Cuban Missile Crisis* (Savage, MD: Rowman & Littlefield, 1990), pp. 107–108. Footnote 41 is on p. 187.
22. Reported in Roger Rosenblatt, *The World Since Hiroshima* (Boston, MA: Little, Brown, 1985), pp. 77–78.
23. NSC 162/2, October 23, 1953; quoted by Bundy, *Danger*, p. 246.
24. Quoted by Bundy, *Danger*, p. 251; Eisenhower's emphasis.
25. Often called the "option B" ploy, it has an official or government department presenting a range of options in the following manner: (A) cravenly give in to the other side's demands, (B) take action X, or (C) take some drastic action, such as use of nuclear weapons. Such policy advocacy strives to make option "B"—the one preferred by the official or department—seem the only reasonable one.
26. Reported in Stephen E. Ambrose, *Eisenhower*, Vol. 2, *The President* (New York: Simon & Schuster, 1984), pp. 205–206. Ambrose appears to interpret Eisenhower's discussion of nuclear options in this way.
27. Issuing nuclear threats does create a context in which nuclear use might later occur; thus this might be a particularly important place to look for use decisions.
28. Truman news conference of November 20, 1950; *Public Papers of the Presidents: Harry S. Truman, 1950* (Washington, D.C.: Government Printing Office, 1965), p. 727.
29. Bundy, *Danger*, pp. 231–232.
30. What constitutes a "case" does determine what our count of such near-use decisions will be. Generally, we say a separate case occurs when three conditions are met: there is some separation in terms of time between deliberations about the use of nuclear weapons, the goal sought (or problem being responded to) is different, and the participants have a sense that a decision has been reached (rather than a decision postponed). For this reason, we treat the series of discussions about nuclear use in Korea (reported in the text) as one case, but the two decisions in the spring of 1954 regarding French Indochina as two cases.
31. The people present at the February 11, 1953, NSC meeting were the president, vice president, secretaries of State and Defense, and the director of Mutual Security as top level participants; and the chairman of the Joint Chiefs of Staff, acting director of the CIA, the

secretary of the Treasury, the director of the Bureau of the Budget, and four NSC staffers attended as advisors.

32. Summary of February 11, 1953, NSC meeting; *Foreign Relations of the United States 1952–1954*, Vol. 15 (Korea), Part I (Washington, D.C.: Government Printing Office, 1984), p. 770.
33. Summary of NSC meeting of May 6, 1953; *FRUS*, Vol. 15, Part I, p. 977.
34. *FRUS*, Vol. 15, Part I, pp. 1012–1017, 1064–1068.
35. Stephen Ambrose would likely interpret Eisenhower's response differently, suggesting that the president was more likely to be either exploring ideas rather than advocating a position, or making sure that the members of the government were prepared to consider nuclear weapons in a serious way if an acceptable armistice could not be arranged.
36. Kennedy to Harriman, 15 July 1963, quoted by Gordon H. Chang, *Friends and Enemies: The United States, China, and the Soviet Union, 1948–1972* (Stanford, CA: Stanford University Press, 1990), p. 243.
37. Chang, *Friends and Enemies*, p. 245.
38. McGeorge Bundy memo, 15 September 1964, quoted in Chang, *Friends and Enemies*, p. 250.
39. Reported in Soviet defector Arkady N. Shevchenko's account, *Breaking With Moscow* (New York: Knopf, 1985), p. 166. This insider's account leads us to classify the action as a near-use rather than a nuclear threat, although we suspect that that is what the Politburo ultimately decided to do with Grechko's proposal.
40. The message was quickly relayed to the top American leadership; Henry Kissinger, then National Security Advisor, reports it in his memoirs, *White House Years* (Boston, MA: Little, Brown, 1979), p. 183.
41. For a discussion of thresholds and escalation, see Herman Kahn, *On Thermonuclear War* (Princeton, NJ: Princeton University Press, 1961).
42. 25 October 1962, John Kennedy to Dave Powers, quoted in Dino A. Brugioni (edited by Robert F. McCort), *Eyeball to Eyeball: The Inside Story of the Cuban Missile Crisis* (New York: Random House), p. 430.
43. Steve Fetter and Kevin T. Hagerty, "Nuclear Deterrence in the 1990 Indo-Pakistani Crisis," *International Security* 21 (summer 1996): 178.
44. Fetter and Hagerty, "Nuclear Deterrence," p. 178.
45. Bruce Nelan, "Nuclear Disarray," *Time*, May 19, 1997, p. 46.
46. Fetter and Hagerty, "Nuclear Deterrence," p. 178.
47. As we will see in the next chapter, these states had become all-but-nuclear-weapons states before 1998 (India in 1974, Pakistan probably by 1990).
48. McGeorge Bundy, *Danger and Survival*.
49. If there is a successful use of nuclear weapons in the future that resolves a conflict in favor of the user, there will likely be two pressures: (1) Other states will be tempted to emulate the success, if not by direct use, then by the threat of use, which will increase the odds of use. (2) Some states will make concerted efforts to build a firewall against further use. Outside of threats to retaliate in kind against users (the reprisal option, which itself may be another use of nuclear weapons), the only likely firewall is rapid denuclearization of all nations. We are dubious about the possibility of (2) in the next twenty-five years. Hence, our pessimistic prediction is that successful use will dramatically increase the probability of further use.
50. For another attempt to estimate the probabilities of nuclear use, see Ike Jeanes, www.nuke-fix.org.
51. NASA Ames Space Science Division, "Asteroid and Comet Impact Hazard," Executive Summary, 1995; www.impact.arc.nasa.gov/report/neoreport.
52. Average of the American League batting champion, 1980–1993; *The World Almanac 1995* (Mahwah, NJ: World Almanac, 1994), p. 944.
53. Interpolated from "How Long Will I Live?" *The Participant* (November 1997): 12–13.

3

BUILDING THE BOMB

The "Gadget" (see Figure 3-1 on page 56) stood fully assembled atop a hundred-foot steel tower in a remote section of the Alamogordo Air Base in New Mexico.[1] It was roughly spherical in shape with a diameter of about six feet, and electrical cables draped themselves crazily over its surface. Inside the metal casing, two and one-half tons of high explosives surrounded a thirteen and one-half pound plutonium core, no larger than a grapefruit. The final assembly had taken place under unusual and ominous weather conditions, amid heavy rains, thunder, and lightning. Code-named Trinity, this was to be the first full-scale test of the Manhattan Project's highly secret atomic bomb research.

On July 16 at 5:30 A.M., electrical signals ignited the explosives, which sent a powerful shockwave into the plutonium core, compressing it into a supercritical mass. In less than a millionth of a second the resulting chain reaction in the plutonium was over, the temperature of the core had risen to about 100 million degrees, and its pressure had risen to about 100 million atmospheres. Shining many times brighter than the noonday sun, the glowing core of hot plasma became a rapidly expanding fireball (see Figure 3-2 on page 56), vaporizing everything in its path, and lighting up the clouds and nearby mountain ranges with an eerie brilliance. Although the two and one-half tons of triggering explosives weighed 400 times as much as the plutonium core, the energy released by the fissioning core was 9,000 times greater. Pound for pound, the nuclear explosive yielded more than a million times as much energy as the chemical explosives. "Trinity" was a complete success, exceeding the expectations of most of its builders. The assembled scientists who were, or were to become, the luminaries of American physics were jubilant. The gray skies, however, bore silent testimony to a future more ominous than anyone there could have foreseen.

For thousands of years, we have used the chemical energy stored in the environment by burning wood, coal, petroleum, and gunpowder to satisfy our needs for warmth, power, and weapons. Suddenly, an energy source a million times greater had exploded on the scene—nuclear energy. What forces are responsible for this new source of power that carries with it so much potential for destruction? How have nuclear weapons

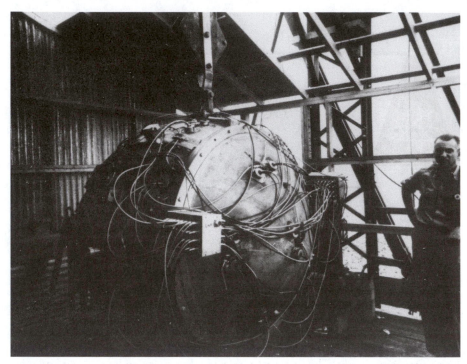

FIGURE 3-1
The "Gadget" in place at the top of the tower at the Trinity test site. *Los Alamos National Laboratory*

FIGURE 3-2
Trinity test site 0.016 seconds after the "Gadget" was fired. *Los Alamos National Laboratory*

evolved, and what makes them unique? The answers to these and many other important questions presuppose an understanding of the basic physics involved—an understanding that we hope this chapter will provide.

It is important to ask these questions for three basic reasons. First, as we understand the problems faced by the nuclear physicists and engineers, their ingenious solutions, and the extraordinary physical conditions created by nuclear explosions, we will be able to appreciate the fascination that this subject holds for them, a fascination that undoubtedly plays some role in the development of nuclear weapons. Nuclear weapons are part of a widespread human endeavor to know and control the physical world. Second, as we understand how nuclear weapons come to be built, we are able to appreciate the role that governments play in the process. Nuclear weapons represent political decisions made by humans. Third, as we make nuclear weapons more understandable, we are able to demystify them and change our thinking about them, from things over which we as citizens have no control (because they are too hard to understand) to seeing them as any other human artifact—often complex, but amenable to change given the human will to bring about change.[2]

In this chapter, we explore how scientists unlocked the power of the nucleus, how governments mobilized these skills to build two types of nuclear weapons—fission and fusion devices, and how extensive has been the effort by the nations of the world to build nuclear devices.

THE EARLY HISTORY OF ATOMIC AND NUCLEAR PHYSICS

Our understanding of the atom and its nucleus is as deeply rooted in Europe as was the great war that engulfed the Western world and gave impetus to the development of nuclear weapons. It will be useful for us to trace briefly these scientific roots that led to our understanding of the nature of the atom.[3]

A year after the discovery of x-rays in 1895, French scientist Henri Becquerel discovered that salts of uranium gave off strange rays that, like x-rays, could blacken photographic plates. Thus was discovered the phenomenon of *natural radioactivity*. Working in their Paris laboratory, Marie Curie and her husband Pierre took up the search for other radioactive elements and discovered the new elements radium and polonium. Further work with such naturally radioactive elements showed that they emitted radiation of three rather different kinds. Since the properties and nature of these emissions were poorly understood, they were simply designated by the first three letters of the Greek alphabet: *alpha*, *beta*, and *gamma* rays. Intrigued by these discoveries, scientists began to seek answers to the new questions that they raised: What was the nature of these mysterious rays, and what strange transformations were going on inside the atom to produce them?

Many of the answers were to come from a transplanted New Zealander, Ernest Rutherford. Working briefly in Canada with Frederick Soddy, he took up some experiments with natural radioactivity, which in 1902 led to the conclusion that upon emitting its radiation, a radioactive element transforms itself into a new chemical element. This does not seem strange to us now, but at that time it was revolutionary. Until then, the atom was generally considered to be the final, immutable, and indivisible unit of matter. (The word "atom" comes from the Greek word *atomos*, which means indivisible.) It was now clear that the atom had constituent parts that could be altered, and the race was on to find out what they were, how they were arranged, and what held them together.

Once again it was Ernest Rutherford who designed and carried out experiments crucial to answering these important questions. In 1907 Rutherford left Canada to assume the chair of Professor of Physics at the University of Manchester in England. There, working with his German assistant Hans Geiger, he bombarded metal foils with the alpha particles emitted by radium and observed that while most of them passed directly through the foil, some were strongly deflected, and a few even bounced back rather than passing through. This led him to conclude that each atom in the foil consisted of a very small, heavy, and positively charged central core that he called the nucleus, surrounded at relatively large distances by light, negatively charged electrons. The year was 1912.

Further experimental work by Rutherford led to the conclusion that hydrogen was the simplest atom and consisted of an electron somehow attached to a single proton nucleus. Niels Bohr, a young Danish theoretical physicist working at Rutherford's laboratory, took this simple physical image and developed it into a workable model of the hydrogen atom.

In Bohr's "planetary" model, a single electron moves about the proton in a circular orbit, held there by the electrostatic attraction between the proton and electron, much the way the gravitational attraction between the earth and the moon keep the moon in its orbit about the earth. Bohr's model was further extended and developed to allow for noncircular orbits and for atoms with more than one electron and nuclei with more than one proton. However, it was only with the later development of quantum mechanics by Werner Heisenberg and Erwin Schrödinger that a completely successful account of atoms was achieved, a development that replaced the "planetary" orbits of Bohr with something new called *quantum states*. The quantum state describes the probability of finding the electron at different locations about the nucleus, rather than describing the exact position of the electron at every instant of time, as would a classical orbital description. There are a great many different quantum states available to the electrons, just as there were many possible different orbits in the classical description.

The discovery of the neutron by the British scientist James Chadwick in 1932 seemed to provide the last missing piece to this remarkable new model of the atom and its nucleus. Neutrons have about the same mass as the proton, possess no electrical charge, and reside together with protons in all nuclei except those of ordinary hydrogen. Since protons and neutrons are about 1,800 times as massive as electrons, most of the mass or weight of an atom is due to its nucleus and is approximately equal to the sum of the numbers of protons and neutrons. This can be written as $A = Z + N$, where A is the *atomic mass number*, Z is the *atomic number* (the number of protons in the nucleus), and N is the number of neutrons in the nucleus. All atoms have the same number of electrons as protons (Z) and are therefore electrically neutral.

While the masses of atoms are primarily due to the protons and neutrons in their nuclei, the volume they occupy is primarily due to their electrons. This can be illustrated in the following way. If an oxygen atom were enlarged until the nucleus was the size of a baseball, the atomic electrons could be found as far as 0.9 miles away. However, 99.97 percent of the atom's mass would be confined to the nucleus.

The chemical properties of each element are unique and are determined by the number of electrons surrounding the nucleus, which must in turn equal the number of protons in the nucleus. However, the number of neutrons is somewhat arbitrary. This means that an element may exist in more than one form, differing only in the number of neutrons in the nucleus and therefore in the mass of the atom. Such different forms of a particular element are known as the isotopes of that element. Different isotopes of an element are chemically almost identical, despite their differences in weight. Any particular isotope is completely specified by giving its element name and its atomic mass number, as in uranium-235. All uranium atoms have 92 protons, which means that an atom of the isotope uranium-235 consists of a nucleus of 92 protons and 143 neutrons (235 − 92 = 143), surrounded by 92 electrons. By the same token, uranium-239 consists of a nucleus of 92 protons and 147 neutrons, surrounded by 92 electrons.

The development of a convincing theory of the atom has enabled us to understand why and how chemical energy is released when fossil fuels or gunpowder are burned. The source of the energy is the electrostatic force between the negatively charged electrons and the positively charged protons in the nucleus. This force is known as the *Coulomb force*, named after the man whose experimental studies led him to quantitatively describe it. The Coulomb force exists between all electrically charged objects, with opposite charges attracting each other and like charges repelling each other. Furthermore, the strength of the force increases rapidly with decreasing distance between the charges. (It is inversely proportional to the square of the distance between them.) Static electricity, frequently encountered when we comb our hair on a dry day, is a manifestation of the Coulomb force.

It takes energy to move an electron away from its nucleus, against the attractive Coulomb force. By the same token, energy is released when an electron is pulled closer to the nucleus by the Coulomb force. We say that the Coulomb force has done work on the electron, and the energy so produced is given up by the atom. Thus the energy possessed by an electron in an atom depends on how close its orbit is to the nucleus or, as we prefer to say today, on the quantum state in which it finds itself. A quantum state that keeps the electron relatively far from the nucleus possesses more energy than one that allows it to come closer, and when an electron leaves the former state to occupy the latter, it must give up the energy difference.

For example, when two atoms or molecules combine in a chemical reaction, the electrons will find themselves in the new quantum states characteristic of the new molecule. If the energy of the electrons in these new quantum states is less than the energy they possessed in the old ones, the difference will appear as the heat of chemical reaction. The source of the energy is the action of the Coulomb force between the electrons and the nuclei. Thus, the explosive force of TNT comes from the rearrangement of the electrons in the Coulomb force fields found inside trinitrotoluene (TNT) molecules.

The *electron volt* (eV) is the appropriate energy unit for describing the energies of electrons in molecules and atoms. It is a very small unit; it would take about 4×10^{23} of them to heat a cup of coffee.[4] Chemical reactions typically involve changes in electron energy of a few electron volts per participating molecule. The very large number of molecules that take part in any macroscopic chemical reaction multiplies this unit accordingly, so that chemical reactions are capable of supplying quite appreciable amounts of energy.

We saw earlier that the discovery of natural radioactivity provided an impetus and important tools (alpha, beta, and gamma rays) for exploring the inner structure of atoms. But what light does the atomic model just described shed on the nature of radioactivity? Rutherford and Soddy's discovery that naturally radioactive elements transformed themselves into other elements meant that the number of protons in the nucleus had changed and that radioactive emissions must come from the nucleus. Continuing the alpha particle bombardment experiments that led to the discovery of the atomic nucleus, Rutherford found that he could artificially induce stable elements to transform into other stable elements. His bombarding alpha particles had penetrated the atom, collided with a nucleus, and succeeded in changing its proton composition. Working together in a laboratory in Paris, Madame Curie's daughter Irene and her husband Frederick Joliot conducted similar experiments, and in 1934 were the first to produce new radioactive elements by means of alpha particle bombardment. Their work, and that of many others, resulted in the proliferation of such new *radioisotopes* and a greater understanding of the behavior of atomic nuclei.

Such work also succeeded in elucidating the nature of the mysterious alpha, beta, and gamma rays. An alpha ray (now called an alpha particle) is a small nucleus consisting of two protons and two neutrons bound tightly together. It is in fact the nucleus of the most common isotope of helium. Alpha particles are frequently emitted by very heavy nuclei that are unstable by virtue of their large size. Gamma rays were found to be very energetic photons of "light," a light with frequencies well beyond the visible and ultraviolet regions of the electromagnetic spectrum. Nuclei emit gamma rays in order to reduce their energy without changing their proton and neutron composition. Beta rays turned out to be electrons with either positive or negative electric charge. Thus was discovered the positive electron, or *positron.*

You may share the physicists' surprise at finding electrons being shot out of a nucleus. Where did they come from? Were they there all along? No, electrons do not reside in nuclei; however, protons can turn into neutrons and neutrons into protons, in the process creating positrons and electrons, respectively, which are then ejected from the nucleus. This provides one of the important ways in which a radioactive nucleus transmutes itself into a more stable one.

An important feature of these atomic transformations was the large amount of energy released in the process. The new products produced by alpha-particle bombardment emerged with extraordinarily high energies—energies a million times greater than those achieved by the electrons in an atom undergoing ordinary chemical reaction. The reason for this is that to transform one element into another, its atomic nucleus must be changed, and the force that holds the nucleus together is very much greater than the force that holds electrons in the atom. Consequently the rearrangement of the protons and neutrons (collectively called *nucleons*) in a nucleus involves much greater changes in energy than the rearrangement of electrons in an atom during a chemical reaction. As a consequence, if a sample of matter undergoes a *nuclear reaction* or change, the energy produced can be more than a million times greater than the energy it would yield if it were to undergo a chemical reaction. (The burning of gasoline and the explosive burning of TNT are examples of chemical reactions.) Hence, nuclear explosions may be conveniently measured in millions of tons of TNT equivalent, or megatons (Mt). Another convenient energy unit is the kiloton (Kt), or the energy that would be released by the explosion of a thousand tons of TNT. We will have more to say about this later.

It was Enrico Fermi, a young physicist at the University of Rome, who initiated a series of experiments that opened up the possibility of the large-scale release of the energy stored in nuclei. It occurred to him that atomic transformations might be produced more readily by bombarding elements with neutrons instead of alpha particles. An alpha particle has an electrical charge of $+2e$ (e is the magnitude of the electron's charge) and is repelled by the positive charge of the nuclei with which it is intended to collide. A neutron, on the other hand, has no electrical charge, and therefore is not repelled by the target atomic nucleus as it approaches. So Fermi began a series of experiments in which he bombarded most of the elements of the periodic table with neutrons.

He began with the light elements (those near the beginning of the periodic table), and at first was unsuccessful. But as he made his way further along the table to the heavier elements, neutron bombardment resulted in new nuclear transformations. In all cases, the element produced was very close to the target element in the periodic table, because the transformation process consisted of the nucleus absorbing the neutron and then emitting one or a few other protons and/or neutrons, resulting in only a small change in the nuclear constituents. In 1934, Fermi bombarded uranium with neutrons and something very peculiar occurred. At least four different radioactive substances were produced, *but none of them could be identified with an element near uranium in the periodic table*. Uranium was the heaviest known element at the time, and Fermi speculated that perhaps a new, heavier element had been created.

The work on uranium was taken up by Curie and Joliot in Paris and by Lise Meitner and Otto Hahn in Berlin. Between 1934 and 1939, all of the work on neutron-irradiated uranium was undertaken at these two laboratories. Many careful and difficult experiments were performed, and many new radioactive elements were produced, but a definite identification of these new substances eluded all efforts. During this time, Lise Meitner left Germany because of Nazi anti-Semitism and went to the Swedish Academy of Sciences in Stockholm. Her place in Berlin was taken by Fritz Strassmann.

Finally, decisive experiments were performed, and Hahn and Strassmann found products from the neutron bombardment of uranium that could only be associated with barium and lanthanum, elements near the middle of the periodic table. They found these results so surprising that their 1939 paper reporting their experiment avoided a definite interpretation. Hahn had communicated his findings to Meitner in Sweden late in 1938, and she in turn had discussed them with her nephew, an Austrian physicist named Otto Frisch. After two days of discussion they felt confident that they understood what was happening and together in 1939 published a short letter in the British journal *Nature* describing their conclusions.[5]

Surprising as it seemed, after absorbing a single neutron of rather modest energy, the *uranium nucleus had split into two smaller nuclei*. Taking the word *fission* from the biologists, who used it to describe the division of a cell, Frisch coined the phrase *nuclear fission*. Meitner and Frisch had discussed their conclusions with Niels Bohr just before his departure on a trip to the United States, and he immediately recognized the validity of their interpretation. Thus the news of nuclear fission was carried almost immediately to the United States, where Enrico Fermi (one of the many talented scientists who had fled fascist Europe) and others immediately recognized the importance of the discovery and confirmed this interpretation with experiments in their own laboratories. Very quickly nuclear physics became the focus of a great deal of scientific attention. Adding to the sense of excitement and urgency was the fact that nuclear fission had been discovered in Berlin, the capital of Hitler's Germany. This had a special significance for the many scientists who had only recently fled fascist governments in Europe.

THE PHYSICS OF THE NUCLEUS

Why did the discovery of nuclear fission create such a stir among the physicists? To appreciate the implications of this discovery, we must delve a bit deeper into the physics of nuclei.[6]

The nucleus consists of neutrons and protons, collectively called "nucleons," bound tightly together into a very small volume. What keeps them together? After all, the protons are all positively charged, and since the Coulomb force increases rapidly with decreasing distance between charges, they must repel each other very powerfully; in fact the Coulomb repulsion between protons in a nucleus is about one hundred million times (10^8) greater than the attraction of the nucleus for the surrounding electrons.[7] For this reason nuclear transformations involve millions of electron volts (MeV) of energy per atom as compared to chemical reactions that involve only a few electron volts (eV) per atom.

Clearly some hitherto unknown and very powerful attractive force holds the nucleus together. Now called the *strong nuclear force*, it consists of a very strong attraction between nucleons (neutrons and protons) when they are close together, but disappears altogether when they are a few nucleon radii or more apart. We say that the nuclear force is strong, but has a very short range. Do not imagine that when the nuclear force is operating, the electrical repulsion has disappeared. It is still there but has been overpowered by its stronger rival.

How many different atomic nuclei are there, and what are some of their properties? Since each element may exist in more than one isotopic form, there are far more different nuclei than there are elements in the periodic table of the elements. By way of illustration, Table 3-1 lists a few isotopes that will figure prominently in our later discussion of nuclear explosives.

Scientists have arranged all of the known isotopes on a chart called the *chart of the nuclides*. The complete chart is too large to be conveniently included here, but a schematic representation of it is shown in Figure 3-3. The atomic number Z is plotted along the vertical axis, and the neutron number N is plotted along the horizontal axis. Every point represented by a pair of integers on this chart is a conceivable isotope. However, nature does not produce all of the isotopes of which we can conceive. Rather, only certain combinations of Z and N will result in a stable nucleus.

Each small dark square in Figure 3-3 represents a stable nucleus or isotope. The stable isotopes occupy a fairly narrow region, called the line of stability, which runs up and across the graph and stops at about Z = 92. The upper dashed line on the graph

TABLE 3-1   ISOTOPES COMMONLY USED IN THE PRODUCTION OF NUCLEAR WEAPONS

Z	N	COMMON NAME	HALF-LIFE
1	0	H-1; hydrogen	stable
1	1	H-2 or D; deuterium or heavy hydrogen	stable
1	2	H-3 or T; tritium	12.3 yrs
2	1	He-3; helium-3	stable
2	2	He-4; helium-4; its nucleus is the alpha particle	stable
3	3	Li-6; lithium-6	stable
3	4	Li-7; lithium-7	stable
92	143	U-235; uranium-235; fissionable	7×10^8 yrs
92	146	U-238; uranium-238; comprises 99.3% of naturally occurring uranium; fissionable	4.5×10^9 yrs
94	145	PU-239; plutonium-239; fissionable	2.4×10^4 yrs

Note: Z is the number of protons; N is the number of neutrons.

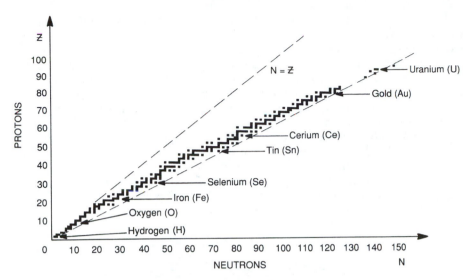

FIGURE 3-3   CHART OF THE NUCLIDES

Each dark square represents a stable isotope. A few familiar ones are identified. Unstable isotopes occupy positions along both sides of this "line of stability." Generally, the farther away from this line they lie, the more unstable they are and the more quickly they decay into isotopes lying near the line.

represents the location of all points where $Z = N$, that is, where the number of protons in the nucleus would equal the number of neutrons. Comparing this line with the points representing the stable isotopes, one quickly sees that although the number of protons approximately equals the number of neutrons for light nuclei, as one moves up the chart toward heavier nuclei, the number of neutrons becomes increasingly greater than the number of protons, and the line of stability bends below the $Z = N$ line. Table 3-1 illustrates the same effect. We will shortly see why this is so.

Only the stable isotopes are shown in Figure 3-3, but many other isotopes are possible. Lying on either side of the stable isotopes, these isotopes are unstable and radioactive, and sooner or later transform themselves into stable isotopes by emitting alpha or beta rays and in this way changing their N and Z values. Some of these unstable isotopes, for example those of radium, can be found in certain ores and give rise to the natural radioactivity discovered by Becquerel and studied intensively by Marie Curie. Others are produced artificially when stable isotopes are bombarded with alpha particles, protons, or neutrons. This occurs in "atom smashers," but it also goes on in nuclear reactors and nuclear explosions where nuclear fission occurs. It is the alpha, beta, and gamma rays from such unstable nuclei that can damage biological tissue and pose a serious threat to living organisms.

Why are some isotopes unstable (radioactive), spontaneously transforming themselves into more stable forms and giving off the radiation associated with radioactivity? One factor is size. Consider what happens when one tries to make larger and larger nuclei by adding neutrons and protons to a smaller nucleus. Each time another proton is added, it finds itself attracted to only the three or four nucleons in its immediate neighborhood (remember, the nuclear force is a short-range force) but repelled by all of the other protons already in the nucleus (the electrical force of repulsion can act over very large distances). So as nuclei grow larger, the attractive nuclear force experienced by the added proton remains relatively constant, while the repulsive electrical force it experiences grows greater. Eventually, the repulsive force dominates, and the nucleus cannot be made larger. This is why the line of stability stops at $Z = 92$ (uranium). This also accounts for the fact that as nuclei become heavier, the number of neutrons grows faster than the number of protons, giving rise to what is known as the neutron excess, and gradually pushing the line of stability below the $Z = N$ line on the chart of the nuclides. Additional neutrons added to the nucleus experience the strong nuclear force of attraction, but are not affected by the electrical repulsive force, and so up to a certain point it is advantageous to add neutrons rather than protons.

Nuclei that are unstable because of their excessive size can remedy the situation in two principal ways. The first is by means of *alpha decay*, in which the nucleus spontaneously ejects two protons and two neutrons together in the form of an alpha particle. For example,

$$U\text{-}238 \quad \rightarrow \quad Th\text{-}234 \quad + \quad alpha\ particle$$

In this way, the uranium nucleus quickly loses two destabilizing protons and four units of mass, becoming thorium in the process. The second process, and the one that lies at the heart of nuclear power and nuclear weapons, is the *neutron-induced fission* discovered by Hahn and Strassmann in Berlin after Fermi's pioneering work in Rome. The schematic diagram of Figure 3-4 will help to make this clearer.

In this process, a relatively unenergetic neutron collides with a U-235 nucleus and is absorbed, temporarily forming the isotope U-236. However, the energy and disruption that it brings with it is too great for this precariously unstable nucleus, and the nucleus spontaneously breaks into two main pieces and a few free neutrons. It is clear that it is the incipient instability of large, marginally stable nuclei like uranium that makes neutron-induced fission possible.

What are the important features of nuclear fission? First and foremost, the smaller nuclei and neutrons that emerge from the reaction come off with very great velocities and energies. It is this energy that is utilized in a nuclear reactor or explosion.

Second, the neutrons that emerge from the reaction may collide with other heavy nuclei, causing them to fission, thus leading to the possibility of a self-sustaining *chain reaction* and the release of macroscopic amounts of energy. Well before fission was

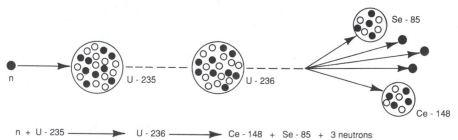

$$n + U\text{-}235 \longrightarrow U\text{-}236 \longrightarrow Ce\text{-}148 + Se\text{-}85 + 3\ neutrons$$

FIGURE 3-4   NEUTRON-INDUCED FISSION
Unstable U-236 breaks up into Se-85 and Ce-148, which can be located in Figure 3-3. This is only one of many possible sets of fission fragments.

discovered, it was well known that nuclear transformations released relatively large amounts of energy per nucleus. But as long as nuclei had to be individually transformed by laboratory-generated beams of bombarding particles, the numbers of nuclei that could be affected and therefore the amount of energy that could be produced was insignificant. Thus, the self-sustaining character of nuclear fission is absolutely essential for large-scale energy production.

Third, the two smaller nuclei into which the large nucleus divides, called *fission fragments*, are almost always unstable and radioactive. When heavy nuclei fission, they break into two different nuclei, but not always the same two. In fact, more than 300 different isotopes of 36 light elements have been found in the products of nuclear fission. It is the radioactivity of the fission fragments that creates much of the radioactive fallout from a nuclear explosion and the highly radioactive wastes characteristic of the nuclear power industry.

What is the source of the energy that is released when nuclei fission?[8] We are now in a position to understand the answer to that question. The immediate source is the electrostatic repulsion between the protons of a large nucleus. This can be clearly seen by considering the reverse of nuclear fission. Suppose you were trying to reassemble a large nucleus from its two fission fragments. It would be similar to compressing a spring. As the two pieces are brought together, the strong Coulomb repulsion must be overcome, and a considerable amount of work expended. If at any point you let go of them, they would immediately fly apart. The closer together they come, the greater the repulsion to be overcome. Finally, however, if you are successful in getting them sufficiently close to each other, the strong, attractive nuclear force takes over and relieves you of the job of keeping them together.

For large nuclei, however, the nuclear force is just barely strong enough to keep the protons together, and if a neutron enters, the delicate balance may be upset. If the neutron disturbs the nucleons in such a way that the nuclear attraction is briefly diminished, the repulsive Coulomb force will begin to drive the protons apart, thus further decreasing the attractive nuclear force. From this point, the fission process proceeds rapidly, and the repulsive Coulomb force drives the fission fragments apart with very large velocities, and consequently very high energies.

Before moving on to discuss the development of nuclear explosives, we need to look a little more closely at the process of fission and the problems associated with turning it into a self-sustaining chain reaction. As we have already seen, nuclear fission itself releases neutrons that may collide with other unstable nuclei and cause them to fission, producing yet more itinerant neutrons. If more than one neutron from each fission manages to produce a subsequent fission, the process will continue at an ever-increasing rate, until the fissionable material is sufficiently depleted. What conditions must be met in order to make this possible?

First each fission must produce, on the average, one or more free neutrons. For the two most commonly used fissionable isotopes, uranium-235 and plutonium-239, the average number of new neutrons per fission is about 2.5 and 3 respectively, and so this requirement is satisfied. Second, one or more of the neutrons from each fission must succeed in fissioning another nucleus before being lost to other potential fates. What other fates await an itinerant neutron?

1.   It may leave the sample of fissionable material entirely before causing another fission. There are several ways to reduce the likelihood of this happening: (a) Make

the sample of fissionable material larger. This provides the neutron with more chances of meeting a fissionable nucleus before it arrives at the boundary of the sample; (b) Surround the sample with a neutron reflector, like beryllium, so that neutrons are reflected back in as they try to escape; (c) Choose a shape for the sample that minimizes the surface area through which neutrons may escape. (A sphere has the minimum surface area for a given volume.); (d) Increase the density of the sample by judicious choice of its chemical form or by compressing it. If the atoms are packed closer together, the chance becomes greater that a neutron will run into a fissionable nucleus before escaping entirely.

2. The neutron may be absorbed by a nonfissioning nucleus before causing another fission. For example, there may be impurity atoms in the material whose nuclei absorb neutrons without fissioning. Thus materials designed for use in power plant fuel rods and nuclear weapon cores must be produced with great care to eliminate such neutron-absorbing impurities.

Even uranium itself forms part of the impurity problem when one tries to produce a self-sustaining nuclear chain reaction in it. Uranium-235 has a high probability of capturing a neutron and fissioning, but uranium-238 can capture a neutron without fissioning at all. Since naturally occurring uranium is 99.3 percent uranium-238 and only 0.7 percent uranium-235, a significant number of neutrons would be lost to the U-238 in a sample of natural uranium, and sustaining a chain reaction would be rendered more difficult. For this reason, natural uranium is usually processed and some or most of the U-238 removed in order to produce reactor-grade and weapons-grade uranium. Weapons-grade uranium is typically enriched to 95 percent U-235 whereas uranium enriched to 4 percent U-235 is adequate for most power reactors.

The ability of a given sample of fissionable material to sustain a fission reaction can be measured by a single number k called the *multiplication factor*. We can define it in the following way. Consider a piece of uranium of a certain size, density, shape, and isotopic composition and possibly surrounded by a certain configuration of neutron reflectors. Now imagine throwing 100 neutrons into it and waiting for the very small fraction of a second it takes to decide the fate of each of them. k is defined as the ratio of the number of free neutrons now to be found in the material, divided by the original number thrown in. For example, if there are now 67 free neutrons in the block, then $k = 0.67$. On the other hand, if there are now 123 free neutrons in the material, $k = 1.23$.

What is the meaning of k? If one calls the first 100 neutrons in our example the first generation and the neutrons they directly produce the second generation, and so on, then the number of neutrons present in any generation is k times the number of neutrons in the previous generation. Thus, if $k > 1$, the number of neutrons in successive generations will grow and the reaction will increase in intensity. If $k < 1$ the number of neutrons decreases from generation to generation, until there are none left and the reaction stops. If $k = 1$ the reaction is sustained at a constant power level, with a constant number of free neutrons traversing the sample.

Since $k = 1$ represents that critical transition point between a fission reaction that will grow and one that will die out, a mass of fissile material with $k \geq 1$ is called a *critical mass*. k is made as large as possible for nuclear explosives; it is made equal to 1 for a power reactor operating at constant power output; and it is made slightly greater than or less than 1 when bringing a power reactor up or down in power.

THE MANHATTAN PROJECT

Although Hahn and Strassmann's discovery of nuclear fission immediately suggested to physicists the possibility of an energy-releasing fission chain reaction, a great many questions such as the following had to be answered before one could turn this possibility into a reality. Which isotope of uranium had Hahn and Strassmann succeeded in fissioning? What other heavy nuclei might be fissionable? How many free neutrons are produced by the fission of each different fissionable nucleus? What is the probability of a neutron producing a fission in each of the fissionable nuclei? With what probabilities would free neutrons be absorbed by various impurity elements? Could materials be produced that were sufficiently free of neutron-absorbing materials? As it turned out, practical fission chain reactions could be achieved, but only with great difficulty. The effort and expense needed were so great that only a major national power could marshal the scientific, technical, and economic resources necessary.[9]

Niels Bohr arrived in Princeton on January 16, 1939, with the news that uranium nuclei had fissioned upon bombardment with neutrons. By February 15, 1939, four laboratories in the United States, one in Denmark, and one in Paris had published papers confirming this conclusion. In the spring of 1939, Leo Szilard, Eugene Wigner, Edward Teller, Victor Weisskopf, Enrico Femri, and Neils Bohr (all except Bohr were emigrés from Europe) tried to organize a voluntary halt to the publication of further papers on this subject, but papers continued to be published at a steady rate until April 1940, when a censorship committee was formed to control publication in American scientific journals. The results of fission-related research then ceased to appear in the open literature.

The first significant attempt to interest the U.S. government in nuclear fission was a March 1939 meeting between Enrico Fermi and representatives of the Navy Department. Despite expressed interest, no specific action was taken. In July 1939 Wigner and Szilard discussed the matter with Albert Einstein. Although Einstein was a consistent advocate of pacifism and world government, as a German emigré his fear that Hitler might obtain the atomic bomb was so great that he agreed to write a letter to President Roosevelt alerting him to the military potential of nuclear fission and urging him to provide government support for further research. This letter was delivered to President Roosevelt in the fall of 1939 asking him to support work in this field. A "Committee on Uranium" was formed, and the first funds ($6,000) were allotted on November 1, 1939. The following year contracts were issued to various laboratories to undertake research, which was becoming increasingly expensive.

As the research progressed it became clear that full-scale plants were needed, and on June 18, 1942, the Army Corps of Engineers was instructed to form a new "district," to be responsible for carrying on the bomb work. Established on August 13, 1942, this new unit was named the Manhattan District, and on September 17, 1942, General Leslie Groves was placed in complete charge of the district and all Army work related to nuclear weapons.

Many people associate the Manhattan Project with the bomb-design work carried on at Los Alamos, New Mexico. However, its scope was much greater. Large facilities were constructed in Hanford, Washington, and Oak Ridge, Tennessee, and important research was supported at the University of Chicago, University of California, Princeton University, and Columbia University, to name just a few. Two billion dollars were spent before this project was brought to a successful conclusion. What was going on at these various facilities, and how did they contribute to the final success?

As noted previously, naturally occurring uranium is 99.3 percent uranium 238 (U-238) and 0.7 percent uranium-235 (U-235). Shortly after Hahn and Strassmann's experiment it was ascertained that only the U-235 had undergone fission. Although U-238 can be fissioned by a neutron of the proper energy, the probability of its fissioning is much less than that for U-235. U-238 can absorb a neutron without fissioning at all. For this reason an explosive fission chain reaction cannot occur in U-235 if too much U-238 is present and so U-235 must be separated from natural uranium before it can be used in a bomb. But U-235 is chemically almost identical to U-238, and there was no practical chemical method to effect this separation. Several nonchemical methods were suggested, all of them difficult. The three principal ones were electromagnetic separation, ultracentrifuge separation, and gaseous diffusion separation.

The electromagnetic method consisted of producing a gas of uranium ions and accelerating them in a vacuum chamber into a large magnetic field. The trajectories of moving charged particles in a magnetic field are circles whose diameters depend on the mass of the particles. This means that U-235 and U-238 would follow different trajectories, and by placing a collector at the correct position in the magnetic field, U-235 ions could be collected ion by ion. The most important research on this method was carried on at the University of California by Ernest O. Lawrence, inventor of the cyclotron. Several technical problems were overcome, and milligram quantities of U-235 were produced. This proved to be an important early source of small amounts of U-235 for basic experiments. Large-scale versions of such separators, known as calutrons, were built at Oak Ridge and provided U-235 for the first uranium bomb. The ultracentrifuge method did not yield significant results at the time although it has been the object of increasing interest more recently.

Although the calutrons got there first, the gaseous diffusion method turned out to be the more practical, eventually producing much larger quantities of U-235-enriched uranium, and became the principal American method of production. This method utilizes the fact that when a gas of atoms is forced through a porous medium with very small pores, the lighter isotopes make their way through somewhat more easily, and so the gas emerging from the other side is slightly richer in the lighter isotopes. Since U-235 is fractionally only slightly lighter than U-238, the enrichment after a single pass through such a filter is very small. Therefore the gas must be passed repeatedly through such filters before a significant enrichment is achieved. The development of suitable filter materials was a technical problem of considerable difficulty, and a suitable gaseous form of uranium had to be found. Uranium hexafluoride, a very corrosive gas at elevated temperatures, was the only practical candidate.

An enormous gaseous diffusion plant was built at Oak Ridge, consisting of cascades of diffusion units each feeding a subsequent one (see Figure 3-5). Thousands of pumps were needed, specially designed to resist the highly corrosive effects of the uranium hexafluoride and possessing seals that were effective in keeping lubricants out of the gases and the gases from leaking out of the system. Thousands of kilowatts of electrical power were needed to run these pumps, and one of the largest steam power plants ever built was constructed at Oak Ridge to provide the necessary power. After the enriched gas leaves such a gaseous diffusion separator, it is chemically converted into uranium metal or an oxide of uranium suitable for use in a reactor or a weapon.

Soon after fission was discovered, there was speculation about other isotopes that might be fissionable. In particular, it was predicted on theoretical grounds that a hitherto unknown element with a fissionable isotope could be produced from U-238. This

FIGURE 3-5
Original K-25 gaseous diffusion plant at Oak Ridge, Tennessee. *Department of Energy*

69

new element, plutonium, can be produced in the reaction shown below. A nucleus of U-238 absorbs a neutron and becomes U-239. The U-239 is unstable and decays to neptunium-239, which in turn decays to plutonium-239, emitting an electron and a neutrino (a subatomic particle with rather unusual properties) in the process.

$$N + U\text{-}238 \rightarrow U\text{-}239 \rightarrow Np\text{-}239 + e^- + neutrino$$
$$\downarrow$$
$$Pu\text{-}239 + e^- + neutrino$$

Pu-239 is unstable, decaying by alpha decay to U-235 with a *half-life* of 24,000 years. This accounts for the fact that no Pu-239 is found occurring naturally on the earth. Any Pu-239 with which the solar system may have been endowed at its inception has long since vanished. This means that every single atom of plutonium used in the production of nuclear explosives has to be produced artificially.

What is needed for the production of Pu-239 is a copious supply of neutrons and U-238. U-238 is quite plentiful, of course, which leaves only the problem of producing neutrons in large quantities. Work on this problem was undertaken by a group at the University of Chicago under the direction of Enrico Fermi that set out to produce a *controlled* fission chain reaction in *natural* uranium. We emphasize natural uranium because it should be borne in mind that only the 0.7 percent of natural uranium that is U-235 is readily fissionable. However, if a self-sustaining fission reaction could be achieved in the U-235, enough superfluous neutrons might be produced to convert some of the abundant U-238 present into Pu-239. Fermi's work on controlled nuclear fission was important for yet another reason: It was crucial to ascertain whether or not a chain reaction in U-235 was possible at all, and then, if it were, to learn as much as possible about the characteristics of such reactions. This information would be vital to those engaged in the theoretical design of high-speed chain reactions (the bomb).

The story of Fermi and the first nuclear reactor is a famous one. A squash court under the stands of the University of Chicago's Stagg Field was chosen as the site of the first self-sustaining chain-reacting nuclear "pile." It was called a pile because that is literally what it was. Blocks of very pure graphite were assembled into a large pile with lumps of metallic uranium or uranium oxide arranged in a regular array inside. Also included in the pile were channels into which control rods of neutron-absorbing materials could be inserted. The insertion of these control rods would result in the absorption of neutrons, thus controlling or ending the chain reaction as necessary.

The graphite in the pile, known as a *moderator*, served to slow down the fission-produced neutrons. This increased the multiplication factor k for the pile, because slow neutrons are more likely to fission a U-235 nucleus than fast ones.

As the pile grew so did the multiplication factor k, gradually getting closer to 1. Finally, on December 2, 1942, Fermi calculated that the pile had reached critical size, the control rods were withdrawn, and the first human-made self-sustaining nuclear chain reaction was created at a power level of about ½ watt.

After this successful demonstration of the first nuclear reactor, plans went rapidly forward for the construction of larger reactors whose neutrons could be used to produce Pu-239. A pilot plant was built at Oak Ridge, a location soon judged insufficiently isolated in light of the hazards posed by such reactors, and so a site in Hanford, Washington, was chosen for the construction of large-scale plants. Reactor production of Pu-239 and its subsequent chemical separation from the other elements in which it was embedded was highly successful, as witnessed by the Trinity and Nagasaki explosions, which were plutonium devices. All of the weapons-grade plutonium used in current nuclear arsenals is made in nuclear reactors designed especially for this purpose. For this reason, fears about nuclear proliferation center on the widespread availability of nuclear power reactors and the possibility of their being used to produce weapons-grade materials. The principal difficulty in developing fission weapons lies in the procurement of the fissionable material, not in the assembly of the material into an explosive device.

The choice of the Los Alamos site for a bomb design laboratory in November 1942 provided a focus for the project. J. Robert Oppenheimer (see Figure 3-6), the director of the laboratory, arrived at the site in March 1943 and was soon followed by a stream of scientists, technicians, and support personnel. To Los Alamos came the U-235 and Pu-239 being produced at Oak Ridge and Hanford, at first in a trickle, and later in increasing amounts. To Los Alamos came the results of measurements at Chicago and elsewhere of neutron absorption probabilities, critical sizes, neutron reflectors, and a host of other matters. And from Los Alamos came the "Gadget" (Figure 3-1 on page 56), "Little Boy," and "Fat Man" (Figure 1-1 on page 3) that demonstrated so dramatically the feasibility of an explosive, self-sustaining nuclear fission reaction.

The Hanford Works and the immense facility at Oak Ridge continued for decades, as did the nuclear weapons design laboratory at Los Alamos. Edward Teller was instrumental in the establishment of a second weapons design laboratory at Livermore, near the Berkeley campus of the University of California. These two laboratories continue to do all the design work for new U.S. nuclear weapons.

After the war ended, many scientists went back to their previous scientific interests. Others, including Oppenheimer, remained at the laboratory doing further design work aimed at increasing the yields and efficiencies of nuclear weapons as well

FIGURE 3-6
J. Robert Oppenheimer, 1945. *Los Alamos Scientific Laboratory. Courtesy AIP Niels Bohr Library*

as reducing their size in order to make them more easily deliverable—that is, converting them from laboratory devices to off-the-shelf military hardware. When the decision was made to develop the H-bomb, a decision which Oppenheimer opposed, that work was carried out at Los Alamos as well.

We now turn to that most interesting of all questions: What were those deadly secrets unraveled by the Los Alamos scientists while working under the most stringent security precautions?

THE FISSION BOMB

To appreciate the nature of nuclear explosions[10] and the technical difficulties that must be overcome to produce them, we must first consider the speed with which a nuclear chain reaction proceeds. A fission-produced neutron in highly enriched fissionable material takes only about .01 microseconds (.01 millionths of a second) to be captured by a fissionable nucleus and to produce another fission. Let us suppose that, on the average, two neutrons from each fission survive to produce additional neutron-induced fissions (that is, the multiplication factor $k = 2$). It is easy to calculate exactly how much energy has been produced at any time after the chain reaction has begun.

A single trigger neutron, after .01 microseconds, will have caused one fission, released 180 MeV (180 million electron volts) of energy, and sent two neutrons flying through the material to fission more nuclei. After an additional .01 microsecond, two more nuclei will have fissioned, producing 360 MeV of prompt energy and four more neutrons. Each .01 microsecond results in a new generation of fissions and neutrons, and the number of fissions grows very rapidly. This is analogous to the population explosion that occurs when a birth rate is significantly greater than the death rate, though on a much shorter time scale. Because of the statistical nature of the process the numbers actually grow somewhat faster than in the simple doubling scheme just described above.

Table 3-2 gives values for the number of neutrons present (N) during each generation n, when $k = 2$. The N values are not cumulative. They give the number of free neutrons within the material at the end of the nth generation. The energy column is cumulative, however, and provides the sum of all the prompt energy produced up to that point.

From the table we see that it takes almost 57 generations to produce an amount of energy equivalent to that produced by the detonation of about 20 thousand tons of TNT (20 Kt), or about 0.57 microseconds! The energy produced by the first 50 generations is only about 0.1 percent of the final energy, which means that 99.9 percent of the total energy was produced in the last 0.07 microseconds by the last 7 generations. This poses a very serious problem for the weapon designer. During the first 50 generations, a significant amount of energy is produced—not enough to destroy a city, but certainly enough to cause considerable damage to the bomb material. Suppose that this energy, which is equivalent to about 15 tons of TNT, blows the fissionable material apart and thus stops the chain reaction. The bomb has only produced a "fizzle" (by nuclear standards). How does the weapon designer keep this from happening?

The trick to making a fission explosion is to take a mass of fissionable material that is not critical, suddenly turn it into a critical mass, and keep it critical long enough for the reaction to produce the desired energy. The simplest way to do this is to take two subcritical masses, each of which is too small to be critical, and rapidly bring them together to form a critical mass. The earliest design accomplishes this by the so-called gun

TABLE 3-2 GROWTH OF RELEASED ENERGY AND NUMBER
OF NEUTRONS IN AN EXPLOSIVE FISSION REACTION

N (GENERATION NUMBER)	TIME IN MICROSECONDS FROM ONSET OF FISSION	N (NEUTRONS IN THAT GENERATION)	TOTAL ENERGY IN MeV RELEASED TO THIS POINT
0th	0.00	1	0
1st	.01	2.7	245
2nd	.02	7.4	910
3rd	.03	20.0	2720
10th	.10	2.2×10^4	3.1×10^6
20th	.20	4.9×10^8	6.9×10^{10}
.			
.			
.			
50th	.50	5.2×10^{21}	7.4×10^{23}
56th	.56	2.1×10^{24}	3.0×10^{26}
57th	.57	5.7×10^{24}	8.1×10^{26}
			$1 \text{ Kt} = 2.6 \times 10^{25}$ MeV
			$20 \text{ Kt} = 5.2 \times 10^{26}$ MeV

assembly technique, in which a precisely shaped piece of uranium-235 is shot down a gun barrel into a larger piece of uranium-235 at the other end. The larger piece contains a hole to receive the smaller one. The speed of the driven slug must be sufficiently high to continue its progress into the other mass long enough after the reaction has begun to produce the desired energy yield. The weapons designers were so confident of this design that it was not tested before its use on the city of Hiroshima, where it produced a 12.5 Kt explosion.

The weapons tested at Trinity and dropped on Nagasaki employed a different design and produced explosions of about 22 Kt. In this design, a critical mass is achieved by taking a sphere of Pu-239 that is not critical, surrounding it with specially shaped conventional high explosives, and detonating all of the explosives simultaneously. This produces a powerful shock wave that drives inward and compresses the fissionable material until it has reached a density sufficient to make it critical. Figure 3-7 (on page 74) illustrates this and also introduces a few additional features. Most of the fission weapons in our current arsenals are of this type.

The detonators are placed at strategic positions around the shell of explosives and must be triggered simultaneously so that the implosion will be symmetrical and compress the core uniformly from all sides. Otherwise, the core may be blasted into a nonspherical, noncritical shape. The layer of uranium-238, which is very dense and heavy, is given a high inward velocity and acts as a driver. It is the inertia of this high-speed heavy metal that helps to keep the compression of the core proceeding, even after the nuclear chain reaction has begun, and thus keeps the core at a supercritical density long enough for the requisite number of generations to be born. The vacuum layer shown in the diagram allows the uranium to achieve full velocity before hitting the

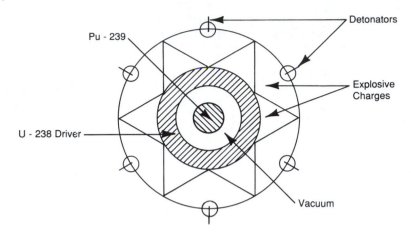

Pu - 239

Detonators

U - 238 Driver

Explosive
Charges

Vacuum

FIGURE 3-7
A schematic diagram of an implosion-type fission bomb. *Adapted from Howard Morland,* The
Secret That Exploded *(New York: Random House, 1981)*

core. The U-238 driver also acts as a neutron reflector and aids in making the compressed core supercritical.

The complete fission of 2.2 pounds of fissionable material would produce a 17.5 Kt explosion. Since fission explosions never succeed in fissioning all of their material, a typical 17.5 Kt bomb would require larger amounts of fissionable material, the exact amount depending on the efficiency of the bomb design.

THE OTHER NUCLEAR STATES

Once the bomb detonated over Hiroshima, the nuclear age had begun for everyone, for the basic secret was out: A nuclear bomb could be built. Given time and resources, any group of scientists and political leaders could retrace the steps taken by the United States to discover the means to create sufficient fissile material and package it in a way that would make a nuclear explosion possible. Indeed, the curiosity inherent in physics itself led physicists everywhere to learn more about the bomb, and the political and military potential would similarly attract the attention of many political and military leaders.

But even before Hiroshima, the news that fission had been discovered in Germany in late 1938 spread as quickly to Soviet scientists as it had to those in the West.[11] Warnings from Soviet physicists about the potential for nuclear weapons had little effect on the Soviet government until Germany invaded the Soviet Union in June 1941 and until Soviet intelligence provided evidence that the Germans, British, and Americans were engaged in research on such weapons. Joseph Stalin ordered a small pilot project begun in 1942. His intelligence system kept close track of American efforts, and its findings helped Soviet physicists choose between the alternative approaches to the creation of fissile materials and bomb design that they had developed on their own. The intelligence work took the surprise out of Truman's remark to Stalin at the Potsdam conference that the United States had a weapon of unusual strength. What Stalin probably failed to envision was the impact of nuclear weapons on the war or on postwar politics.

Then came Hiroshima and Nagasaki. The bomb worked. It had clear military relevance. It threatened to shift the balance of power decisively into American hands. And it was "a new and potent symbol of power."[12] In August 1945 Stalin spoke with officials of the Ministry of Munitions and Igor Kurchatov, the director of the Soviet nuclear project:

> A single demand of you, comrades. Provide us with atomic weapons in the shortest possible time. You know that Hiroshima has shaken the whole world. The balance has been destroyed. Provide the bomb—it will remove a great danger for us.[13]

The nuclear program was put under the direction of the secret police and given priority status, as were the development of radar, jet propulsion, and long-range rockets—all war-time developments in which the Soviet Union lagged behind. The new economic plan for the Soviet Union emphasized defense needs, and Stalin's personal intervention ensured that science and resources would be mobilized. Soviet scientists had told Stalin in August 1945 that it would take five years to produce the bomb. It took four. The successful Soviet test of a fission device came in August 1949.

Within the next fifteen years, three other nations joined the nuclear club: industrialized Britain in 1952 and France in 1960, and far less economically developed China in 1964. (See Table 3-3 on page 76.) Their experiences, added to the American and Soviet experiences, suggest the following factors are important for the development of nuclear weapons:

1. After 1945, the national leadership saw the bomb as critical for the security of the state in a threatening world, and believed it was better to possess the bomb oneself than to rely on a nuclear-armed ally.

2. The bomb was important to maintain the state's status in world politics. Britain and France saw the bomb as a way to arrest the decline of their status as world powers; China sought a way to reassert itself and clearly end a century and a half of domination by the West and Japan.

3. Only governments had the ability to assemble the resources needed for bomb construction, and they would do so only if there was a political will to begin and sustain a weapons program.

4. Acquiring the bomb required a cadre of skilled scientists, access to fissile materials, and a technological base that could convert fissile materials into the explosive component of the weapon and that could create the physical mechanisms of the bomb itself. Once this cadre is assembled and the initial bombs are produced, most states continue their development program, moving toward fusion devices (discussed below) and the development of missile delivery systems (discussed in Chapter 4). "These developments belie the popular notion that emerging nuclear weapons countries slacken their efforts after obtaining a few 'bombs in the basement.'"[14]

5. With all these factors in place, a well-endowed state might count on a working fission device after 4–5 years of a crash program, and 7–15 years in a normal but still costly program. The Chinese case suggested that even a less economically advanced state could, under the right circumstances, go nuclear.

6. A state could cut the time needed to produce a bomb or get around shortages of materials by drawing on others' resources. From 1955 to 1959, for instance, the Soviets actively helped China develop the capacity to make the bomb (and then thought better of it, abruptly ending all support). In addition, American and Russian support for peaceful uses of atomic energy (a point we discuss in more detail

TABLE 3-3   STATES WITH NUCLEAR WEAPONS PROGRAMS

THE NUCLEAR CLUB

United States	Tested in 1945 (program begun in early 1940s)
Soviet Union	Tested in 1949 (program begun in early 1940s)
United Kingdom	Tested in 1952 (program begun in early 1940s)
France	Tested in 1960 (program begun in late 1940s)
China	Tested in 1964 (program begun mid-1950s)
India	Tested in 1974, 1998 (program begun mid-1960s)
Pakistan	Tested in 1998 (program begun mid-1970s)

OPAQUE PROLIFERATORS

Israel	nuclear capable, 1968–1971; remains nuclear armed
South Africa	nuclear capable, 1979–1981; denuclearized by 1991

INHERITED NUCLEAR CAPABILITIES

Belarus, Ukraine, and Kazakhstan	1991 break-up of the USSR left former Soviet nuclear weapons within territory; all returned to Russia by middle 1990s

NUCLEAR ASPIRANTS

HISTORICAL (NO CURRENT NUCLEAR WEAPONS PROGRAM; NO WEAPONS PRODUCED)

Germany	Canada	Libya
Japan	Argentina	Syria
Sweden	Brazil	South Korea
Switzerland	Egypt	Taiwan

CURRENT (ON-GOING PROGRAM LIKELY; NO WEAPONS PRODUCED)

Iran	Iraq	North Korea

later) meant that they provided research reactors and energy-producing reactors to other states, as well as the theoretical knowledge on which they were based. Such facilities could become the seed-bed for a weapons program. Alternatively, a state could use espionage (as the Soviets did) or theft (as the Israelis did in acquisition of some fissile materials) or purchases on the open market (as Iraq did) to assemble the missing pieces of their nuclear weapons program.

Thus, it was no surprise that the United States, the Soviet Union, Britain, France, and China became nuclear powers by 1965. The first four were at the cutting edge of industrial/scientific knowledge (and China benefited from the Soviets' commitment to help them build the bomb). In the post-World War II period, each had a self-image of being world powers in a threatening world. *Nuclear proliferation*—the term given to the process whereby states join the nuclear club—was just a matter of time.

Did no one else consider joining the club during the first fifteen years after Hiroshima? Table 3-3 lists a large number of states that purposefully explored the feasibility of adding such weapons to their arsenals. The six factors we listed above came into play for them as well. Sweden, for instance, thought that nuclear weapons might make its neutrality secure. South Korea worried that in the aftermath of Vietnam the United States might not protect it. The Germans, barred by post-war agreements from making nuclear weapons, explored an arrangement of funding the French nuclear effort in return for access to some of the weapons; the German leadership saw nuclear weapons as security against a Russian threat and a mark of equality within the American-led NATO alliance.

In most cases, the nuclear programs did not lead to proliferation. The Swedish government, for instance, ended the program when it was near success; they apparently reached an understanding that American nuclear protection would extend to them in a crisis in spite of their neutrality. A return to civilian rule in both Brazil and Argentina led to a halt in the weapons program championed by the military, although it is not clear if the programs were completely terminated. American threats (and promises of protection) ended the nuclear programs in South Korea and Taiwan. Some nuclear ambitions remain on hold (as in North Korea) and others are yet to be realized (as in Iran).

Four states, however, did see their programs through to entry into the nuclear club, and a fifth, Iraq, would probably have done so in the mid-1990s if not for its defeat in the Gulf War of 1991. But the face of proliferation was changing in the period after 1965. The proliferators now came from the less developed world, from states that had not traditionally been world powers. And these new proliferators were cautious in actually demonstrating their nuclear status by conducting a test of the weapon.

Chronologically after China, Israel became the next nuclear state, doing so during the period 1968–1971. It has never tested a device, and has publically said that it would not be the first to introduce nuclear weapons in the region. There is every reason to believe, however, that Israel has at least 50–100 warheads, possibly 200, in its arsenal. The nonacknowledgment of being a nuclear power but with others believing the state to be a nuclear power has been called *opaque proliferation*. In 1974 India detonated a nuclear device, but claimed it was for peaceful purposes (such as in the excavation of large amounts of earth as conventional blasting does) and denied having a nuclear arsenal. Twenty-four years later it publicly tested several nuclear weapons. India may have some 75–200 nuclear devices. South Africa was the third proliferator, secretly building seven devices, and then, just before the white apartheid regime gave up power, destroying them and the nuclear production facilities. Its nuclear power remained opaque from 1979–1989. Pakistan became the latest proliferator in the early 1990s, publicly revealing its capabilities in May 1998, following the Indian tests, by conducting tests of its own. Pakistan probably has a dozen or more warheads, with the count likely to grow each year.

Thus, nine states had entered the nuclear club by the end of the 1990s, or a rate of a new nuclear state every five years. In 1991, there was another form of proliferation that temporarily expanded the membership in the nuclear club. This *proliferation by inheritance* came as the Soviet Union disintegrated and three of the newly independent republics—Belarus, Ukraine, and Kazakhstan—acquired parts of the Soviet nuclear arsenal. By the fall of 1996, however, all the warheads were back within Russia, completing the de-nuclearization of the three states. (It is not likely that any of the three governments actually had control over the warheads, as they remained under a military system controlled by the Russians.)

In Chapter 7 we explore why these nine states (and potentially others) were interested in proliferation. What we will discuss now is what made proliferation feasible. In some cases, it came with the cooperation of an existing nuclear weapons state, as China probably aided Pakistan in the development of its weapons. But a more common beginning—and one that will be with us into the future—is with power-generating nuclear reactors.

THE ROLE OF NUCLEAR POWER GENERATION IN PROLIFERATION

Without enriched uranium-235 or plutonium (itself the product of nuclear fission), there is no bomb. But both of these are natural parts of the nuclear power industry. Although the U.S. nuclear power industry is moribund, concerns about global warming from fossil fuels, the desire for independence from foreign oil imports, and the largely unmet need of less developed countries for energy have renewed general interest in nuclear power. Europe and Japan have committed themselves to nuclear-produced electricity to a much greater extent than the United States, and that trend is not likely to be reversed in the near future. Even if it turns out that the nuclear power industry does not return to a high-growth state for one reason or another, the currently existing reactors (about 430 worldwide) and the steady diffusion of technical expertise will continue to afford opportunities for proliferation.

Most civilian nuclear reactors are fueled with a mixture of U-235 and U-238, contained in long thin rods that are inserted into the reactor core in an array that leaves space for water to circulate between them. The U-235 slowly fissions, heating the water to produce steam, which in turn powers a turbine-driven electrical generator. (The water is also used as a coolant.) Unlike a nuclear explosive, the uranium in a power reactor need not be highly enriched in U-235. In fact, natural uranium, containing only 0.7 percent U-235, will do if heavy water is used.[15] Canadian nuclear reactors are generally heavy water reactors, employing natural, unenriched uranium as their fuel. Canada has exported this technology to other countries, enabling them to build and operate nuclear reactors without having to engage in the difficult uranium isotope separation process, although in this case they must obtain a significant quantity of heavy water in addition to the natural uranium.

If, on the other hand, one uses ordinary water, then the fuel rods must contain uranium enriched to 3–4 percent in U-235. The ability to separate the isotopes of uranium for enrichment purposes is the first step toward a nuclear weapons capability, where weapons-grade uranium calls for approximately 90 percent enrichment, although the bomb can be manufactured with far less U-235. On the other hand, research reactors (many of which have been supplied by the major nuclear powers) typically operate at the 80–90 percent enrichment level, but typically donor states do not permit large amounts of such highly enriched uranium to be in researchers' hands.

The second connection between nuclear power reactors and nuclear weapons is in the Pu-239 that nuclear reactors create. Since the fuel rods contain an abundance of U-238, a significant amount of U-238 is converted into Pu-239 as a part of the fissioning process we discussed earlier. In principle the Pu-239 can be chemically separated from spent fuel rods, but the extreme radioactivity of the rods makes such reprocessing a difficult technical matter. Furthermore, commercial power reactors are designed to be refueled infrequently, with the rods left in the reactor for about a year. This results in the build-up of Pu-240, another isotope produced when U-238 is bombarded with neutrons. The presence of Pu-240 mixed in with the Pu-239 (and these isotopes cannot be chemically separated) renders the product ill-suited for nuclear weapons use. It is for this reason that nuclear weapons states obtain their plutonium from reactors that are specially designed to produce plutonium and not power.

Plutonium reprocessing is a technology that is relatively well known. It was initially feared that the world's supply of uranium would run out; thus the reprocessing of plutonium was desirable because plutonium could be used in power reactors in place of uranium. Indeed, a properly designed reactor can produce more new nuclear fuel than it consumes—such reactors are known as breeder reactors. Even though the world's supply of uranium is nowhere near exhaustion, plutonium reprocessing continues (in part because it liberates the reprocessor from having to depend on imports of uranium).

The nuclear weapons states (and those that have sought nuclear weapons status) have pursued both uranium isotope separation strategies and the reprocessing of plutonium as the route to create nuclear weapons. Iraq, for instance, concentrated on electromagnetic isotope separation of uranium (one of the approaches the United States used in the Manhattan project). Using devices available on the open market, and incorporating "microprocessors, fiber optics, and computer-assisted manufacturing controls into the systems to achieve gains in reliability, precision, and availability,"[16] Iraqi engineers constructed a separation process that over time would have give them sufficient weapons-grade uranium. Plutonium reprocessing, on the other hand, seems to have been the Israeli choice. In South Asia, "India's route ... would be based on plutonium derived from its natural uranium fueled, heavy water cooled and moderated reactors, and separated in its established reprocessing facilities. By contrast, Pakistan's route would follow the uranium path, based on its centrifuge enrichment capabilities."[17]

THE HYDROGEN OR FUSION BOMB

We conclude our technical consideration of nuclear explosives with an account of the so-called "super," or hydrogen bomb. As we shall see in Chapter 4, after the successful development and testing of fission bombs, a debate arose in governmental, scientific, and military circles as to whether or not the United States should proceed with the development of yet more powerful nuclear explosives based on the fusion of light nuclei. Edward Teller, one of the physicists active in the nuclear weapons project from the beginning, had great interest in the possibilities of nuclear fusion. He had in fact wanted to begin work on that problem while others were still occupied with producing a fission chain reaction. Robert Oppenheimer, the wartime director of the Los Alamos Laboratory, strongly opposed the development of a fusion bomb, but the advice of Teller and others prevailed and the government authorized the project.

Just what is an H-bomb, and how does it differ from the fission bombs we have been considering? The H-bomb is a *fusion* device; it derives its energy from fusing small nuclei together to form larger ones rather than from splitting large nuclei to produce smaller ones. We can understand fusion energy in terms similar to those used to explain fission energy.

Consider two small nuclei, those of hydrogen, for example. Each consists of a single proton. Since the Coulomb repulsion of two protons is not very great compared to the strength of the attractive nuclear force, why does not the strong nuclear force pull them together to form a single nucleus? It is because the nuclear force has a short range and is not felt until the protons come very close together. Under ordinary circumstances, the Coulomb repulsion will keep nuclei from approaching each other that closely. However, if we succeed in bringing two nuclei sufficiently close together, the nuclear force will completely overwhelm the Coulomb repulsion, and they will come crashing together, releasing energy in the process.

Whereas fission occurs when a very powerful Coulomb repulsion in a large nucleus overwhelms the attractive nuclear force and drives parts of the nucleus apart at great speed, fusion occurs when a powerful attractive nuclear force overwhelms a much weaker Coulomb repulsion between two small nuclei and draws them powerfully together. In either case, the energy released is rapidly turned into heat energy, which produces the ultra-high temperatures characteristic of nuclear explosions.

Nuclear fusion brings light nuclei together to form heavier ones and in the process releases large amounts of energy. It is this process, going on in the interior of the sun and the stars, that both supplies the energy that keeps them radiating and has produced many of the naturally occurring heavier elements from primeval hydrogen.

Fusion sounds perfectly simple, but technically it is difficult to achieve. The problem lies in bringing the two nuclei close enough together for the nuclear force to act. Even though the repulsive force is much smaller for light nuclei than for heavy nuclei, it is still a considerable force to overcome. One way to accomplish this is to heat the light nuclei to a temperature high enough that they form a gas of particles with thermal velocities great enough to produce close encounters in spite of the Coulomb repulsion. It is for this reason that fusion weapons are also called *thermonuclear* weapons.

The temperatures needed are in the tens of millions of degrees, temperatures found ordinarily only in the interior of stars, and more recently in the initial fireball of a fission bomb explosion. The trick then is to detonate a fission device in the vicinity of some light nuclei, heat them to a very high temperature, and then allow the resulting fusion reaction to proceed. It was not easy to devise a way to heat the fusion material hot enough before the force of the explosion blew it away. The U.S. solution to this problem was devised by Teller and Ulam. It was one of those very "sweet" (meaning beautifully ingenious) technical ideas that so exhilarate scientists.

The technical details of nuclear weapons designs are highly classified secrets. However, there is much information in the public domain, which, when considered in the light of known principles of physics, can give rise to educated guesses that are probably not too far from the truth.[18] The H-bomb description that follows, including the diagram in Figure 3-8, is based largely on these sources, particularly Howard Morland's work.

Stage 1 of the device (the upper stage) consists of an ordinary fission bomb of the sort we have already considered. It provides the high temperatures needed to initiate fusion in the second stage. Stage 2 consists of a heavy U-238 tamper shell, which encloses the fusion material. A rod of fission material is imbedded at the center of the fusion fuel, and the space between the tamper shell and the outer casing is filled with a polystyrene-type foam. A heavy shield between stages 1 and 2 helps to protect stage 2 against the direct blast for a brief instant. X-rays from the stage 1 blast, traveling at the speed of light, are reflected from the casing walls onto the polystyrene-type foam that absorbs them, is converted into a hot plasma, and implodes on the stage 2 fusion material, simultaneously heating and compressing it.

The heavy U-238 tamper provides the inertia that keeps the implosion moving inward and the reaction contained long enough for it to proceed to completion. The

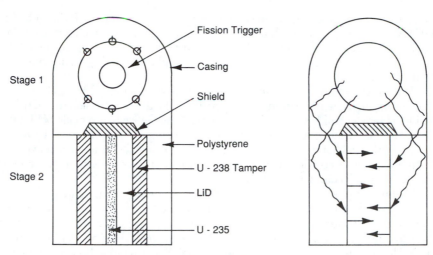

FIGURE 3-8
A schematic diagram of a possible configuration of a fusion (thermonuclear) bomb. *Adapted from Howard Morland,* The Secret That Exploded *(New York: Random House, 1981)*

fusion material, which consists of lithium deuteride (LiD), is an interesting feature of the device, and worthy of some explanation.

The most easily attained fusion reaction is

$$D \; + \; T \; \rightarrow \; He\text{-}4 \; + \; N \; + \; 17.6 \, \text{MeV}$$

D and T are shorthand names for two isotopes of hydrogen—deuterium (D) is hydrogen-2, and tritium (T) is hydrogen-3 (see Table 3-1); both are gases at ordinary temperatures and pressures. Gases have very low densities and so require large volumes if an appreciable mass is to be achieved. One way to achieve a large mass with a small volume for the hydrogen isotopes is to liquify them by cooling them to temperatures near absolute zero. The first successful U.S. fusion device utilized liquid hydrogen isotopes, weighed sixty-two tons, and included cryogenic equipment to keep the deuterium and tritium liquified. Obviously such a device is not suitable as a deliverable weapon. The Russians and the Americans, apparently independently, arrived at the same solution to this problem.

The solution consists of using an isotope for the fusion fuel that is stable and solid at ordinary temperatures and that is converted into tritium when it is bombarded with neutrons. Lithium-6 (Li-6) is such an isotope undergoing the following reaction upon neutron bombardment.

$$Li\text{-}6 \; + \; N \; \rightarrow \; Li\text{-}7 \; \rightarrow \; H\text{-}3 \, (tritium) \; + \; He\text{-}4$$

Where do the neutrons come from? This is where the rod of fissionable material buried within the fusion material comes into play. It is compressed to supercriticality and begins to fission, in the process providing neutrons to begin transforming lithium to tritium. As the fusion reaction progresses (D + T $\rightarrow$ He-4 + N) the neutrons that it produces continue the process of converting lithium-6 into tritium.

But where does the deuterium come from? This is quite simple. Lithium hydride (LiH) is a solid compound of lithium and hydrogen. If this compound is produced from the Li-6 isotope of lithium and the H-2 (deuterium) isotope of hydrogen, one has LiD that incorporates the necessary fusion fuel isotopes in close proximity and in convenient physical form.

There is yet a third stage to many thermonuclear devices. U-238 can be made to fission by the high energy neutrons that are produced by the D + T fusion reaction. Thus the U-238 tamper will fission, and if the casing of the device is also made of U-238, it too will fission.[19] In this way the energy of the fusion neutrons can be turned into blast energy and the yield of the weapon increased. Thus a typical thermonuclear explosion is a fission-fusion-fission device, in which about half of the energy comes from fusion and the other half comes from fission.

Fusion is also used to "boost" fission bombs. If some gaseous deuterium and tritium are introduced under pressure into a small volume in the center of an ordinary implosion-type fission device, the heat from the fission reaction will cause them to fuse, with the emission of characteristic 14.1 MeV neutrons. These neutrons in turn produce additional fissions in the fissionable material. What is more, because of the high energy of these neutrons, the fissions they produce give off more than the usual number of free neutrons, which enhances or "boosts" the subsequent chain reaction. The energy coming directly from the fusion process itself does not make a significant contribution to the boosted weapon's output. The fusion reaction simply makes the fission reaction more efficient, so that a greater fraction of the fissionable material actually undergoes fission before the reaction ends.

The yield of a fusion-boosted weapon is adjustable by varying the amount of tritium and deuterium in the core. This can be done in the field and makes possible the dial-a-yield weapons that are widely deployed today. Since tritium has a half-life of 12.3 years, the tritium in these weapons must be replaced from time to time.

SUMMARY

Here we bring the scientific story of nuclear explosives to a close. We have watched with interest as a relatively small group of European physicists, following their curiosities, began to make remarkable progress in understanding the basic building blocks of matter—what they consisted of and the forces that held them together. This was a golden age for physics. The names and the accomplishments are legendary. It is also a deeply human story: Marie Curie, winner of two Nobel Prizes, struggling to teach her classes, care for her children, and carry on her painstaking research; Albert Einstein, quietly working in a patent office by day and dreaming incredible ideas by night; Ernest Rutherford, transplanted New Zealander making one fundamental discovery after another. And all of them working under the rising shadow of totalitarian fascism.

It was this shadow that drove the center of nuclear science to the more tranquil shores of the United States, where European physics, American industrial might, Yankee ingenuity, and the looming war converged to produce the awesome weapons of destruction we have been studying. The end of the war coincided with the closing of one chapter of this remarkable scientific and technological story; nuclear fission had been turned into practical energy, but much more was yet to come. Scientists and engineers in other nations sought to duplicate the feats of the Manhattan Project, and American scientists turned their attention to warhead efficiencies, missile delivery systems, and harnessing nuclear fusion. Politicians, military planners, and the concerned public sought answers to the question: How should nuclear weapons be used and controlled? It is to these chapters in the nuclear story that we now turn.

NOTES

1. For extensive accounts of the Trinity Test and the scientific and technological developments that led to it, see the following references: Henry DeWolf Smyth, *Atomic Energy for Military Purposes: The Official Report on the Development of the Atomic Bomb under the Auspices of the U.S. Government, 1940–1945* (Princeton, NJ: Princeton University Press, 1945); Robert Jungk, *Brighter Than a Thousand Suns* (New York: Harcourt Brace, 1958); Lamont Lansing, *Day of Trinity* (New York: Atheneum, 1965); and Richard Rhodes, *The Making of the Atomic Bomb* (New York: Simon & Schuster, 1986).
2. Howard Morland captured this nicely in the subtitle of his article, "The H-Bomb Secret: To Know How Is to Ask Why." *The Progressive* (November 1979): 245.
3. The following books provide interesting accounts of the early development of modern atomic and nuclear physics: J. G. Feinberg, *The Story of Atomic Theory and Atomic Energy* (New York: Dover, 1960); Emilio Segre, *From X-rays to Quarks: Modern Physicists and Their Discoveries* (New York: W. H. Freeman, 1980); Laura Fermi, *Atoms in the Family* (Chicago, IL: University of Chicago, 1954); Eve Curie, *Madame Curie* (New York: Garden City Publishing Co., 1943); and Nuel Pharr Davis, *Lawrence and Oppenheimer* (New York: Simon & Schuster, 1968).
4. 4×10^{23} is scientific notation for 4 followed by 23 zeros.
5. Lise Meitner and O. R. Frisch, *Nature*, no. 3615 (February 11, 1939): 239.
6. For a more thorough account of the relevant nuclear physics, see David Rittenhouse Inglis, *Nuclear Energy: Its Physics and Its Social Challenge* (Reading, MA: Addison-Wesley, 1973).
7. The factor 10^8 is obtained in the following way: Since the average distance between the atomic electrons and the nucleus is about 10,000 times (10^4) greater than the distance between protons in a nucleus, and since the Coulomb force changes inversely with the *square* of the distance between the charges, the Coulomb repulsion must be $10^4 \times 10^4$, or 10^8 greater than the attraction of the nucleus for the electrons.
8. It is customary in talking about the bomb to invoke Albert Einstein's famous equation $E = mc^2$, and to say that mass converted into energy is the source of the bomb's extraordinary power. This is misleading in three respects. First, Einstein's theoretical work did not have a direct impact on the development of practical nuclear energy. Second, associating a loss of mass with nuclear energy leads one to believe that only nuclear energy involves such mass changes. In fact, any production of energy involves a corresponding change in mass. The only difference is that the energy released in nuclear explosions is much greater than in chemical explosions, and the corresponding mass loss is more noticeable. Third, to offer a loss of mass as an explanation is no explanation at all. The loss of mass is the result of the energy release, not its cause. In order to understand why and how the energy was produced, one must consider the balance and action of the microscopic, intra-atomic forces, as we have done.
9. For official accounts of the Manhattan Project, see Smyth, *Atomic Energy for Military Purposes*; and Vincent C. Jones, *Manhattan: The Army and the Atomic Bomb* (Washington, D.C.: U.S. Army Center of Military History, 1985).
10. For more extended treatments of the physics of nuclear weapons, the following books will be helpful: Samuel Glasstone and Philip J. Dolan, *The Effects of Nuclear Weapons* (Washington, D.C.: Department of Defense and Energy Research and Development Administration, 1977); Smyth, *Atomic Energy for Military Purposes*; Thomas B. Cochran, William M. Arkin, and Milton M. Hoenig, *Nuclear Weapons Databook Vol. I: U.S. Nuclear Forces and*

Capabilities (Cambridge, MA: Ballinger, 1984); Ground Zero, *Nuclear War: What's in It for You?* (New York: Pocket Books, 1982); Kosta Tsipis, *Arsenal: Understanding Weapons in the Nuclear Age* (New York: Simon & Schuster, 1985); MIT Faculty, *The Nuclear Almanac: Confronting the Atom in War and Peace* (Reading, MA: Addison-Wesley, 1984), pp. 195–204, 447–494; Inglis, *Nuclear Energy*; and David Hawkins, Edith Trulow, and Ralph Carlisle Smith, *Project Y: The Los Alamos Story*, Vol. II of *A Series in the History of Modern Physics 1800–1950* (Los Angeles, CA: Tomash Publishers, 1983).

11. The following comes from David Holloway, *The Soviet Union and the Arms Race* (New Haven, CT: Yale University Press, 1983); and David Holloway, *Stalin and the Bomb: The Soviet Union and Atomic Energy, 1939–1956* (New Haven, CT: Yale, 1994).

12. Holloway, *Stalin and the Bomb*, p. 133.

13. Quoted by Holloway, *The Soviet Union and the Arms Race*, p. 20. In 1979 or 1980, a close advisor to the Ayatollah Khomeini reportedly used very similar language in speaking with an Iranian official in charge of the Shah's nuclear program: "It is your duty to build the atomic bomb for the Islamic Republican Party.... Our civilization is in danger and we have to have it." Quoted in Leonard Spector and Jacqueline R. Smith, *Nuclear Ambitions: The Spread of Nuclear Weapons 1989–1990*, p. 208.

14. Spector, *Nuclear Ambitions*, p. 11.

15. Ordinary water (H_2O) has too great a probability of absorbing the neutrons needed to fission the U-235. Using "heavy water" (where the hydrogen atom already has a neutron, a form of hydrogen called deuterium) allows the fission process to proceed.

16. Jay C. Davis and David A. Kay, "Iraq's Secret Nuclear Weapons Program," *Physics Today* 45 (July 1992): 23.

17. P. R. Chari, *Indo-Pak Nuclear Standoff: The Role of the United States* (New Delhi, Manohar, 1995), p. 38.

18. Howard Morland, a former Air Force pilot who had taken some engineering courses while in college, engaged in this kind of sleuthing and published his conclusions in the November 1979 issue of *The Progressive*. The government sought unsuccessfully to obtain a court injunction to restrain its publication but did succeed in delaying publication for half a year. Morland has written an interesting book chronicling his pursuit of the secret and his efforts to see it published. Howard Morland, *The Secret That Exploded* (New York: Random House, 1981). This was followed by A. DeVolpi, G. E. Marsh, T. A. Postol, and G. S. Stanford's *Born Secret: The H-Bomb, the Progressive Case, and National Security* (New York: Pergamon, 1981). Written by four scientists, it provides an interesting technical and legal analysis of this attempt to penetrate government secrets.

19. To make a "clean" bomb, one makes the stage 1 fission trigger as small as possible and removes any uranium from stage 2. In this way, the fission fragment production is reduced to a minimum. The enhanced radiation weapon, popularly known as the "neutron bomb," is a device of this sort. Since the second stage is not surrounded by uranium, the neutrons produced by the fusion reaction can proceed without being absorbed, and it is this flood of neutrons that showers the blast region and beyond, incapacitating people in the vicinity by damaging their central nervous systems.

4

THE ROOTS
OF THE PREDICAMENT:
THE EMERGENCE OF TOTAL WAR

On the morning of August 7, 1945, Bernard Brodie, who at age thirty-five had a reputation as one of the nation's foremost writers on naval strategy, stopped in a drugstore to buy the *New York Times*. After reading just two paragraphs in the *Times* story on the bombing of Hiroshima, he turned to his wife and said, "Everything that I have written is now obsolete."[1]

Brodie saw that the atomic bomb had changed forever the nature of war. He observed that "everything about the atomic bomb is overshadowed by the twin facts that it exists and its destructive power is fantastically great."[2] Since it exists, it cannot be "disinvented." Even if every scientist and engineer who knew how to build a bomb were put to death, everyone knows the basic fact of the bomb—that it works. Because it is known that the bomb works, the bomb can be reinvented in time and with effort by any industrial nation willing to commit the resources and willing to pay the political price. Brodie looked ahead to the day when all the world's major powers would be armed with atomic weapons. Furthermore, because the bomb is so very, very powerful, any defense against the bomb would have to be perfect to be useful. During World War II, for instance, British defenses were able to stop, at best, 96 percent of the German V-1 guided missiles launched against England. If even 4 percent of a flight of nuclear weapons reached their targets, the resulting losses would be unacceptable. Brodie felt, therefore, that no defense was possible against an atomic attack. In the wars of the past, there had been time to develop defenses against new weapons. However, he realized that an atomic war would be too brief to allow time for developing countermeasures. All of those weapon systems and strategies heretofore useful in a long war would have little use in an atomic war of such brief duration.

In a paper published in 1945, Brodie set out his remarkably farsighted predictions about how life would differ in a nuclear age. He observed that in the future a nation

> must remain constantly prepared for war; there would be neither the time nor the surviving industrial machinery to mobilize once the atomic bombs start exploding. This constant readiness may encourage aggression, exacerbate world tension, or possibly even spark in some minds the luring temptation of a "preventive war"—that is to strike

first to destroy an adversary before it can grow powerful enough to be a threat. Then again the calamity that would certainly ensue if the other side struck back with its own atomic bombs would be so grimly devastating, its very anticipation might deter a potential aggressor from attacking in the first place.[3]

Jacob Viner told the conference at which Brodie presented his paper that "the atomic bomb makes surprise an unimportant element of warfare." As he later pointed out, it will make no difference "whether it was Country A which had its city destroyed at 9:00 A.M. and Country B which had its city destroyed at 12:00 A.M. or the other way around.... Retaliation in equal terms is unavoidable and in this sense the atomic bomb is a war deterrent, a peace making force."[4]

Brodie and Viner had glimpsed the new truths of the nuclear age. Nuclear weapons had made warfare between nuclear-armed states irrational. The central irony of the wars of the twentieth century was that "the very situations that bring about a modern war are destroyed in its wake."[5] World War I began as a conflict between Czarist Russia and the Austro-Hungarian Empire over Serbia; none of these states survived the war. Germany began World War II in Europe to expand its territory; it remained a divided nation for forty-five years after the end of the war and has not yet regained its 1939 borders. Nuclear weapons make this irony complete—a nuclear exchange involving only the smallest tactical nuclear weapons would devastate much of Europe, and an exchange of even a small fraction of the strategic arsenals of the United States and Russia would destroy both societies. Thus, while nuclear weapons might increase the tension between nations—and thereby increase the likelihood of war—nothing could be gained by such a war.

Yet in spite of these momentous changes in the nature of war, the nations of the postwar world have continued to act much as they have in the past and have continued to regard war, or at least the threat of war, as a useful instrument of policy to achieve national objectives. Why did Einstein's assertion that everything had changed except our ways of thinking seem most true when it came to critically important individuals—the political and military leaders of the nations of the world?

In this chapter and Chapter 5, we will examine the development of nuclear weapons in the arsenals of the world and the nations' efforts to find strategies for the use of these weapons. We explore the past in order to discover *how* the leaders of nuclear-armed nations made critical decisions about nuclear weapons and strategies and the *consequences* of those decisions. Since 1945, leaders and citizens have had to imagine the future of war with nuclear weapons and ask: How will war be an effective means of promoting the national interest? Will the patterns we discover in their answers continue to be the answers the nations of the world reach in the second nuclear age?

Before turning to how and why these decisions were made, consider the basic decision that both the United States and the Soviet Union made during the first nuclear age: Both would build more powerful and more numerous nuclear weapons, targeted in large measure on the civilian populations of its adversaries. The United States, like other nations of the otherwise civilized world, had come to regard the civilian population of its adversaries not only as legitimate targets but also as targets whose destruction would assure victory. How did this image of war come to be so widely accepted, and how did it influence the leaders' decisions about what weapons and weapons delivery systems to produce and deploy and their thinking about how these weapons might be used?

THE SEARCH FOR AFFORDABLE VICTORY

Interestingly, to think about war in the twentieth century meant using the theory and concepts of a nineteenth-century German military officer, Carl von Clausewitz, who fought against Napoleon and spent the rest of his short life developing a theory about war. For Clausewitz, the purpose of war was "to compel our opponent to do our will." But that act of force does not exist in isolation—it is a result of politics, and "war is a continuation of political activity by other means."[6] He said that "if you are to force the enemy, by making war on him, to do your bidding, you must either make him literally defenseless or put him in a position that makes this danger probable. It follows, then, that to overcome the enemy, or disarm him must always be the aim of warfare."[7] Clausewitz identified three objectives when seeking to disarm an adversary: the armed forces, the country, and the enemy's will. If the aim of the war was the complete overthrow of the enemy,

> the fighting forces must be destroyed: that is, they must be put in such a condition that they can no longer carry on the fight. The country must be occupied; otherwise the enemy could raise fresh military forces. Yet both these things may be done and the war cannot be considered to have ended so long as the enemy's will has not been broken.[8]

The notion that the will of the enemy is decisive, and therefore a justifiable, and in some cases, necessary target for attack, has become a basic assumption about warfare in the twentieth century.

The irony of the twentieth century has been that while war has become more absolute—employing all the resources of industrial states—it has become far more difficult to compel our opponent to do our will. World War I (1914–1918) revealed that irony, but at a staggering price—France alone lost about 640,000 men killed in battle between the first of August and the first of December 1914.[9] The battle lines in France and Belgium never fluctuated more than a few miles in the generals' quest for a decisive battle that would produce a victory, with the same terrain changing hands again and again, in spite of the loss of some four million lives. To the soldier in the field, the stalemate of trench warfare (see Figure 4-1 on page 88) appeared to be the direct result of recent innovations in the technics of war, most notably the machine gun and barbed wire.[10]

In fact, the stalemate was due less to the failure of prewar army staffs to devise tactics appropriate for the firepower of modern rifles, machine guns, and artillery—that happened quickly enough once the war began—than it was the inevitable consequence of the two great revolutions of the nineteenth century. These two revolutions—the democratic revolution, ushered in with the French Revolution, and the Industrial Revolution—transformed warfare as radically as they did other Western institutions. The democratic revolution unleashed the forces of nationalism, making wars not simply the business of kings, but the concern of every citizen. "National wars are fought by the people as a whole, and no longer by professional armies; the stakes are no longer dynastic interests or the fate of a province, but the future of the collective society or its ideals."[11]

The patriotism of ordinary citizens increased exponentially the will of a society to resist and provided a large pool of individuals willing to die in that resistance. States refined techniques to use these manpower resources with increasing effectiveness, creating large standing armies and quickly mobilizable reserves. Thus, over six million troops were hurled into battle within two weeks of the beginning of World War I.[12]

FIGURE 4-1

Canadian forces leaving their trench to attack the German trench line, World War I. *Corbis*

Even today, many states maintain large military establishments. The United States, for instance, has almost one-and-a-half million personnel on duty in its armed forces, with almost another million in the reserves and in national guard units that can be quickly called into national service.[13] Nationalism continues to make it possible to sustain large numbers of men (and, increasingly, women) in the world's armies.[14]

The Industrial Revolution provided ever more deadly weapons and the increasing deadliness of weapons in the nineteenth century increased the power of the defender to resist the attacker. In Napoleon's time, when the principal weapon was the smooth-bore musket, with a range of eighty yards and a rate of fire of two shots per minute, there was time for only one or two shots before an enemy's charge reached the defender's lines. Therefore, an attacker who could achieve a three-to-one superiority in numbers could be reasonably certain of success. However, with the adoption of the rifle in the 1850s, the effective range of the basic infantry weapon increased to over 500 yards. Thus, a defender could fire at least fifteen shots between the time an attacker came into range and the attacker reached the defender. The introduction of the breech-loading rifle, which could be reloaded while prone, and the repeating rifle made possible a sustained rate of fifteen shots per minute fired from a position of relative invulnerability—the firer sheltered in trenches. By the end of the U.S. Civil War, the shovel (to dig trenches) had become as indispensable to the soldier as his rifle.

But new weapons were only part of what Walter Millis called the industrialization of war. Modern production capacity, transportation, and communications profoundly influenced the manner in which war is conducted and armies sustained.[15] For instance, when the wars of the French Revolution began in 1792, it was estimated that 80 percent of French manpower was employed in the basic task of raising food to feed the nation.[16] However, at the beginning of the American Civil War in 1861, the first of the large-scale wars of the industrial age, only 52 percent of the work force was involved in the production of food.[17] Advances in agricultural technology had created a manpower surplus that could be used to maintain large armies.

But the most radical change brought by the Industrial Revolution was the transportation revolution of the mid-nineteenth century, in particular the railroad. During the American Civil War, the Union commander, General Grant, proved it possible to maintain indefinitely an army in constant contact with the enemy, even while being defeated on the battlefield with heavy losses. If served by either railroad or steam-powered water transport, an army could be fed, resupplied, and, most important, reinforced with newly raised troops as long as there were resources and a political will to continue. As Theodore Ropp said, "'it was the railway, in short, which made mass armies practical."[18]

To appreciate these changes in war-waging, consider this contrast. In 1815 Napoleon saw no choice but to gamble everything on one roll of the dice at Waterloo. His only hope was to defeat the British army before it joined with the Prussian army and then to capture the British supplies at Brussels. When that attempt failed, even with half of his army still intact, he had no alternative but to abandon his army and surrender to the British. Some hundred years later, on July 1, 1916, the British sustained sixty thousand casualties (twenty thousand of them fatal) on the first day of their attack against the Germans on the River Somme in northern France; their gain of territory that day was measured in yards. The British did not capitulate but continued their offensive for four more months and the war for over two more years. Thus, by the twentieth century, a single battle could no longer determine the outcome of a war. As long as a nation had the ability to mobilize its manpower and material resources and transport these resources, an army could be sustained in the field indefinitely, regardless of losses it might suffer.

And losses it would suffer. The effect of these revolutions was to strengthen the position of the defender to the point, that, by 1914, an attack had little prospect for success against a prepared and supplied defender unless the attacker had an overwhelming superiority in numbers; even then, the attacker would pay a high price in casualties. Thus, war had become a matter not of brilliant generalship, but of *attrition*, as the first nation to exhaust its manpower resources, or lose the will to continue the struggle, became the loser.

Therefore, the deadlock on the western front in World War I was implicit in the very nature of the war itself. It was a war between two groups of modern industrial nation-states, approximately equal in strength, qualitatively and quantitatively.[19] Both groups had the political means to make virtually unlimited demands on the resources, human and otherwise, of their nations, and both had a productive capacity sufficient to sustain their armies in the field indefinitely. Germany's fatal weakness was its land-locked position, which denied it access to the agricultural and manpower resources of an overseas empire; cut off from trade, Germany slowly strangled from want of raw materials. Russia's lack of a year-round port through which it could receive supplies from the Allies played a role in its defeat as well.

War had become a matter of attrition on the strategic level as well as the tactical—a slow grinding down of the opponent's ability, or will, to wage war. As a nation could make claims on the entire manpower resources of its population, it was necessary to destroy a substantial portion of the available manpower resources before a nation would consider surrender. France and Germany each lost 1.5 million men in World War I; the

British Empire nearly a million; Russia lost more than all the rest put together. As A. J. P. Taylor says, "the losses seemed staggering. Yet they left no permanent scar. No nation was permanently knocked out of the ranks of the Great Powers by these wartime losses, although France came near to being. Young males could be more easily spared than at any other time in the world's history, brutal as this sounds."[20]

World War I did, however, challenge the idea that war could serve the nation's interests. Who would want to pay these enormous costs again? As the British poet Robert Graves (who served in the trenches as an infantry officer) suggested, because of the suffering and eventual disillusionment, after World War I "you just couldn't get men to do that again." Both political and military leaders feared that, after World War I, their people no longer had the will to sustain a prolonged war.

The world's military establishments spent the ensuing three decades trying to ensure that there would be "no more Sommes." The search for alternatives to the stalemate of trench warfare ranged from the smallest scale to the grandest, from the tactical to the strategic.[21] One influential writer on military affairs in the interwar period, Basil Liddell Hart, suggested the internal-combustion engine would allow an attacker to break through the defenses and restore mobility to the battlefield. The tank would overcome the enemy's barbed wire and machine guns, and motor vehicles would carry infantry and supplies through the breaks in the enemy's defenses. Motor transport would allow an army to concentrate in one restricted area, attack with overwhelming force against the enemy at that particular point, and once having broken through the thin crust of the enemy's defenses, pour through this break in an "expanding torrent," isolating the enemy from his supplies. The enemy's field army, unable to receive reinforcements and supplies, could then be easily defeated piecemeal; battle would again be decisive.

Liddell Hart's writings found enthusiastic reception in certain military establishments. Although the *blitzkrieg* as practiced by the German Army was a potent tactic, World War II revealed its limitations. The blitzkrieg did not in the long run change profoundly the balance between offense and defense, as the German attack on the Soviet Union in 1941 showed. Typically armies would be virtually stationary for three or four months while gathering the supplies and material that would make such a breakthrough possible, and the breakthrough would be limited to the range of motor transport, usually not much over 100 miles. Then, the armies would have to halt while supply lines were built and supplies and reinforcements were brought forward, thus providing the enemy time to build a new line of defense. Therefore, warfare in World War II took on a rhythm of alternating periods of brief, sharp offensives and then months of relative inactivity, expensive in both time and lives. Against unprepared adversaries and where there was little room for maneuver, the blitzkrieg could be decisive, as in Poland in 1939 and again in France in 1940. However, in Eastern Europe where there was ample room to maneuver, the Russian Army traded distance for time, and a war of attrition ensued. Russia, with superior manpower resources and with material aid from the Western Allies, ground down the technically superior German Army.

A second alternative to avoid the prolonged attrition of trench warfare sought to strike directly at a nation's ability to sustain an army in the field. This grew in part from observations that Germany had surrendered in World War I with its armies in the field still undefeated, because it could no longer sustain these armies. The advocates of this approach after World War I, usually labeled "the strategic offensive," looked to the bombing airplane as the weapon to wage such a war. To these interwar planners, there could be no defense against a determined air bombardment of a nation's homeland.

This widely held fear was expressed by the British cabinet minister Stanley Baldwin in 1932: "I think it is well for the man in the street to realize that there is no power on earth that can keep him from being bombed. Whatever people may tell him, the bomber will always get through."[22]

Instead of first destroying the enemy's military forces and therefore his means to resist, the advocates of airpower sought to go over the heads of the adversary's army with their strategic bombers. Airpower would strike at an adversary's ability to sustain its armies in the field, and by striking directly at the enemy's population, destroy an adversary's very will to persist (see Figure 4-2). Thus the will of the people to fight a prolonged war was now seen as an adversary's most vulnerable point. Clausewitz himself had insisted that "the overthrow of the enemy should not be misunderstood as an emphasis laid upon mere physical killing. The main battle involves the killing of the enemy's courage rather than that of the enemy's soldier."[23]

Therefore, just as the democratic revolution of the nineteenth century had brought the entire nation to arms and the Industrial Revolution made the farmer in the field, the worker in the factory, and the engineer in the locomotive as important as the soldier in the ranks to success in war, the advocates of strategic air bombardment proposed attacking not just the will of the soldier in the field, but the will of the entire nation. As one particularly outspoken proponent of airpower, Douhet, prophesied:

> A complete breakdown of the social structure cannot but take place in a country being subjected to … merciless pounding from the air. The time would soon come when, to put an end to horror and suffering, the people themselves, driven by the instinct of self-preservation, would rise up and demand an end to the war.[24]

Thus, the ability to disrupt production and undermine the national will might be as important as battlefield success in weakening the enemy. Civilian suffering might be a cause of defeat—not just a consequence.

The experience of World War II, however, showed that strategic air bombardment had limitations, just as blitzkrieg did. The strategic bombing campaigns did impair the efficiency of the enemy's economy, forcing the dispersal of industries and producing raw material shortages and transportation bottlenecks. Continued bombing did require the nations under attack to divert considerable resources to defending themselves against air attack. By 1944 some two million German soldiers and civilians were employed in antiaircraft defense and some 30 percent of guns manufactured in 1944 were for antiaircraft use.[25] But a well-organized and resolute defender could mount a very effective defense against a strategic air offensive indeed. The Germans in 1940 were unable to achieve a decisive result from their air war against Great Britain, with British aircraft production actually increasing during the German air offensive. (The Royal Air Force emerged from the German attack with more fighter aircraft than it had when the battle began.) The Allied bombardment of Germany was hardly more effective in destroying the capacity of the German economy to produce war goods. In fact, the peak month for tank production by Germany was October 1944 and for aircraft production was November 1944, in spite of a protracted and intensive bombardment by Allied air forces. Although the Allied air forces attacked "panacea target" after "panacea target" (first ball-bearing plants, then petroleum production facilities, and then railroad rolling stock and bridges), the decisive target whose destruction would bring the enemy to its knees eluded the leaders of the air forces, just as it had the leaders of the ground armies in World War I.

FIGURE 4-2

Germany, 1945: The destruction shown here is typical of that suffered by cities across Europe during World War II. *Corbis*

Strategic bombing was no more effective in destroying the will of the German people to resist the Allied forces. The morale of civilian populations under continued air bombardment proved remarkably resilient. After the initial panic, bombing apparently stiffened the civilian will to resist and aided government efforts to mobilize civilians. Thus the attempt to force the surrender of an enemy by inflicting pain on its population may have had the opposite effect of strengthening an enemy's ability to persist. Even though the United States and Britain dropped some two million tons of bombs on Europe, "those who expected bombing to win the war on its own were frustrated by events."[26] The strategic bomber in World War II proved itself not to be "an instrument of a decisive early blow, but as another weapon of attrition."[27]

When World War II ended, the images of war and what it took to achieve victory were clearer than they were in 1918: The stalemate in the trenches could be avoided; men were still willing to die in the millions for their nations. But the price would continue to be enormous: There were at least 30 million killed in the part of the Allied nations waging war against Germany and Japan, fairly evenly divided between military and civilian deaths.[28] Moreover, the new technologies meant that vast areas, including cities, would come under devastating attack. The material and cultural losses from World War II were unprecedented. So the old question remained. How could one hope to achieve victory in war at a reasonable cost?

With the atomic bomb, however, proponents of strategic air bombardment felt they finally had the absolute weapon. Clausewitz had spoken of absolute war as an ideal or abstraction that could not be obtained in practice because of the friction of war. The commander could never achieve the ideal of absolute war because of the fog of war: imperfect intelligence, imperfect control of troops, and chance. The atomic bomb appeared to be an instrument that could finally make absolute war achievable. The conventional bombs dropped on Britain, Germany, and Japan, although causing immense damage, were dropped over several years and at widely scattered targets. The damage sustained could be repaired, factories and railroads restored to use, and resources from undamaged parts of a country used to aid the worst hit areas. However, an extensive atomic attack would be virtually instantaneous and would inflict damage simultaneously across the country, making recovery impossible, as we pointed out in Chapter 1. The atomic bomb would therefore shatter both the enemy's ability to wage war and its will to do so; to the proponents of strategic air bombardment this was at last the war-winning weapon.

THE ENVIRONMENT FOR AMERICAN NUCLEAR DECISIONS

In 1945 atomic bombs seemed for Americans to have all the requisites for the ideal weapon: The atomic bomb could win wars without paying the cost of another Somme, the atomic bomb could be produced relatively cheaply by American industrial capacity, and the atomic bomb was the monopoly of the United States. But ideal weapons do not automatically point the way to the ideal government policy. The American government found itself wrestling with a set of intriguing questions:

1. Was the bomb needed at all in peacetime or, like the army itself in past wars, should the United States wait to build the bombs if and when they were needed?
2. If the bomb were needed in peacetime, how many bombs did the United States need to have on hand and what should the characteristics of these bombs be?
3. What plans should be made for their use in the event of war?
4. What use did the bomb have in peacetime?

There have not yet been, nor are there likely to be, final answers to these questions. How did the United States and then, in turn, each of the new nuclear nations answer these questions? Each generation of leaders and each nation with the capability to build nuclear weapons has had to find the answers appropriate for its time and place. Examining in detail the course of the search for answers by the United States and the Soviet Union will provide insight into the process now underway in nations that have just recently acquired atomic weapons and those that may do so in the future. In the United States, the search for these answers has gone forward both in the context of its military traditions and in the light of the experience of fighting two world wars, as well as in its perception of the nature of the world.

World War II had ended the dominance of such traditional great powers as Britain, France, and Germany and had elevated the United States and the Soviet Union to the status of the key powers. The Soviets and Americans, however, had little experience in playing a dominant role in world politics, and what experience they did have in their relationship with each other had negative elements. The United States had briefly participated in the foreign intervention in the Russian Civil War (1918–1920) against the Bolsheviks and had refused diplomatic recognition of the Soviet Union until 1933. The Soviet Union had expressed hostility to all capitalist states and encouraged the subversion of those states by indigenous Communist parties, including the American Communist party, through the Communist International. The Soviet government, in turn, took for granted the hostility of the capitalist states, even though it might collaborate with capitalist countries for particular objectives that furthered its own interests.[29] But given the physical distance between the two states, a lack of historical confrontations, and the inability of each to challenge the security of the other, pre-World War II relations might be best described as cool but correct.

The experience of waging war as allies had increased contacts among various levels of American, Soviet, and British officialdom but the officials had one compelling, clearly defined objective—the defeat of Nazi Germany. The return of peace removed the reason for unity, although Britain in its weakened condition chose to attach itself to the United States. The absence of a history of Soviet-American relations meant that those two states would build their relationship through a process of trial and error.

While we might expect errors to create conflict, they need not create hostility unless the others' errors are seen as conscious, systematic attempts to injure. Soviet actions in different parts of the globe suggested to many in the United States that the Soviet Union sought to expand its political control at the expense of the Western democracies. In Europe, Stalin insisted on Soviet domination in Eastern Europe, an area that had been the historic invasion corridor into Russia. Many of these states had allied with Nazi Germany. Moreover, Stalin was not inclined to restore capitalist or monarchist governments in the areas liberated by the Red Army when he had the opportunity to install loyal (and thus docile) communists in power. Finally, and most critically, Stalin had no interest in reviving a powerful Germany.

From the American perspective, the defeat of the Nazis had ended the security threat to the Soviet Union, so heavy-handed Soviet actions in the East European states (including the arrest or murder of non-Communist leaders) seemed to signal a Soviet interest in expansion and control over all of Europe. Then, in 1947, the Soviets became more menacing as they indirectly supported an armed insurrection in Greece against a government the United States had labeled democratic. Although there had been tension between the United States and the Soviet Union early in 1946 over Russia's continued presence in Iran, the American orientation toward Europe made Soviet activities there far more threatening.

In March 1947, President Truman declared what came to be called the Truman Doctrine: The United States would provide weapons, advisors, and economic aid to friendly governments trying to cope with Communist insurgencies (Greece) or pressures (as in Turkey, where the Soviets were pressing the Turks to return former Russian territory to the Soviet Union). This was part of the emerging containment policy—the attempt to confine Soviet influence to its existing sphere of influence.

But containment could not solve the German problem. The Allies had agreed to divide Germany into four occupation zones. Berlin, in the middle of the Soviet zone, would be divided into four sectors. As long as there was no agreement on how Germany would be reunited, and who would rule the new state, the four sectors remained separate entities. The American government wanted to end financial support for Germans, especially in terms of food supplies and consumer necessities, and wanted at least economic reunification in the belief that Germans could take care of themselves if Germany were an economic unit. The Soviets balked (as did the French initially), as economic unification would set Germany on the road to economic recovery, which held enormous security implications for those two states.

American persistence convinced the French, but the Soviets continued to reject economic reintegration. When in the spring of 1948 the Western powers unilaterally began a currency reform in their sectors, the Soviets clamped a land blockade on the western sectors of Berlin. The blockade indicated that the Soviet Union was willing to risk war with the Western powers in order to promote its interests. To Truman and his advisors, this implied that the Soviet Union might try to expand its control by an invasion of Western Europe.

The blockade and the Communist coup in Czechoslovakia in February 1948 (which ended any form of political independence in Eastern Europe) prompted the nations of Western Europe to come together in a formal military alliance and to invite American participation. The process culminated in 1949 with the creation of the North Atlantic Treaty Organization (NATO). NATO was the tangible expression of an American commitment to containment. NATO had only one target—the Soviet Union. (The Soviet Union would follow six years later with the creation of its own alliance system, the Warsaw Treaty Organization, comprised of itself and the aptly named satellite nations of Eastern Europe.)

EXPLANATIONS OF NUCLEAR BEHAVIOR

Our brief overview of the emergence of the Cold War and the rival military blocs illustrates one of the patterns of relations between the two states that we want to highlight: a pattern of *action-reaction*. This pattern explains the behavior of a state as resulting from the behavior of another, salient state. We saw in the last chapter, for instance, how Stalin ordered a crash nuclear weapons program as a reaction to the dropping of the American bombs on Japan. Similarly, Soviet actions to protect its security in Eastern Europe (essentially defensive actions) struck the United States as provocative, aggressive actions, signaling a Soviet threat to Europe. The United States reacted defensively to protect its interests, but the reaction seemed to be aggressive to the Soviet leadership.

It is possible, of course, that either state might have had aggressive intentions (a possibility we discuss below). It is also possible that in an action-reaction pattern, states might cooperate with each other (cooperative actions are met with cooperative reactions). Our point here is that looking for action-reaction sequences is one way to explain the behavior of states. Will we find such a pattern when we consider the weapons that a state acquires and the strategies for their use?

A second explanation for the behavior of the state is what we can term the *bureaucratic interests* explanation. What states do in the nuclear field, this explanation says, comes as a result of bureaucracies pursuing their particular interests. In this view, once the Manhattan Project bureaucracy was created and had acquired large amounts of resources (personnel, funds, physical plant), it had a strong incentive to perfect nuclear weapons and, given the context of an on-going war, to see that those weapons were used. In general, this explanation expects bureaucracies to have an interest in at least perpetuating their existence and their current missions. Many bureaucracies will want to acquire more resources and more missions. Thus, our second explanation says that if we want to understand the decisions regarding nuclear weapons, we look for pressures emanating from bureaucracies.

A third basic explanation concentrates on *key individuals*, particularly policymakers, and their perceptions, goals, and persuasiveness within their political systems. Perceptions are much conditioned by ideology. Some argued, for instance, that communist ideology or the historical past of the Soviet state promoted outward expansion. Further, an individual's goal can promote the national interests or personal self-interest, or, more commonly, a mix of both. Expansionism, in this view, might be accounted for by

Stalin's need to eliminate all possible threats to his personal control of the USSR. Alternatively, a leader such as Nikita Khrushchev, faced with mounting agricultural problems at home, might adopt a more defensive posture internationally. Policymakers respond to three environments: their immediate colleagues and subordinates, other powerful actors in their political system, and the public at large. (Even in dictatorial systems, leaders are often quite concerned about what they think the public will tolerate.)

As you might expect, any decision regarding nuclear weapons and the plans for their use (what we will call strategy or doctrine) likely bears the imprint of all three of these explanations (and other factors). Our point, however, in isolating these three is to suggest (1) that at times, one type of pressure is more important than the others, and (2) that if we want to gauge the nuclear future, we need to understand how these pressures work. How did the key decisions about nuclear weapons come to be made in the Cold War?

From Atomic Scarcity to Plenty

During the period 1945 to 1948 the Soviet Union and the United States discovered the issues that would divide them bitterly. The result was a "Cold War": an *assumption* that the other state was hostile to one's own existence and would wage war to promote its interests. Thus, its actions had to be challenged in order to keep the peace. Both states experimented with policies to deal with the other, but the "war" was meant to remain cold—neither side wanted a shooting war. Whether it was possible to avoid shooting in the nuclear age remained to be seen.

Several weeks after President Truman announced his declaration of the Cold War in the Truman Doctrine, he assembled the commissioners of the Atomic Energy Commission, the newly created agency responsible for the production of the atomic bomb, to hear an assessment of the state of the nation's atomic arsenal. Not only was the president dismayed at how few bombs had been produced, but the chairman of the commission also reported to the president that "None of these bombs is assembled. The highly technical operation of assembly hitherto has been effected by civilian teams no longer organized as such. Training of military personnel to effect assembly is not complete." As reported by a commissioner who was present, the president blanched; he realized his atomic arsenal was empty—the United States had no deliverable atomic bombs.[30]

The United States's stockpile and delivery capability remained extremely limited for some time.

> There were only two weapons in the stockpile at the end of 1945, nine in July 1946, thirteen in July 1947, and fifty in July 1948. None of these weapons were assembled. They were all Mark 3 "Fat Man" implosion bombs which weighed ten thousand pounds, were relatively inefficient in their use of fissionable materials and took thirty-nine men over two days to assemble. Because the bombs were so large and heavy, they could only be loaded on their bombers by installing a special hoist in a 12 ft. x 14 ft. x 8 ft. deep pit, trundling the bomb into the pit, rolling the aircraft over it and then hoisting the weapon into the specially modified bomb bay.[31]

In 1948 the Strategic Air Command had only about thirty long-range bombers modified to drop atomic bombs, all World War II-era B-29s, similar to the aircraft shown in Figure 4-3, with a range of about 4,200 miles, and all based in Roswell, New Mexico.[32]

FIGURE 4-3
The B-29 bomber. *National Archives*

Lacking a nuclear opponent, however, the United States was allowed its traditional approach of peacetime unpreparedness. While the United States lacked nuclear weapons for emergency use (such as a sudden Soviet attempt to seize Berlin by force), if war were declared, the American government would remobilize its resources, assemble its bombs, deploy them and the bombers close to the Soviet Union, and then begin the strategy that it had inherited from World War II: an on-going nuclear attack against Soviet cities. The imprecision of bomb-aiming, the small numbers of bombs, and the conviction that nuclear weapons were war-winning weapons made this strategy seem plausible.

In the spring of 1948, following the Communist coup in Czechoslovakia and during a time of increasing concern over Soviet pressure against U.S., British, and French control of the divided Berlin, the military commanders of the U.S. armed forces, the Joint Chiefs of Staff,[33] began a reexamination of national security policy. It was now feared that the Soviet Union would risk war with the Western nations. In the words of one participant:

> Neither we nor the prostrate nations of Western Europe could match Russia's land army, man for man, or tank for tank, on D-Day without total peacetime mobilization which was practically out of the question. Given the military spending limits, we were forced to rely principally on our atomic monopoly.[34]

Thus began America's reliance on nuclear weapons as the primary safeguard of the nation's security. Nuclear weapons were more palatable politically than a large standing army equipped with conventional weapons, which would require substantial dislocation in the lives of the youth of America. And a large army would cost substantially more than a nuclear armed strategic bomber force. The American commitment to nuclear weapons was, in part, a way to "wage war on the cheap." As Walter Lippman pointed out at the time, atomic weapons appeared to be

> the perfect fulfillment of all wishful thinking on military matters: Here is war that requires no national effort, no draft, no training, no discipline, but only money and

engineering know-how of which we have plenty. Here is the panacea which enables us to be the greatest military power on earth without investing time, energy, sweat, blood and tears, and—as compared with the cost of a great Army, Navy and Air Force— not even much money.[35]

Just when the United States was coming to rely on nuclear weapons as the foundation of its military security, the age of nuclear scarcity in which nuclear weapons were limited in number and could be used only sparingly was ending. In April and May 1948, Operation Sandstone, the first weapons test whose purpose was to improve the design of the wartime atomic bomb, was being conducted at Eniwetok Atoll. These three test explosions ranged in yield from 18 to 49 kilotons (the Hiroshima explosion was 13 kilotons, the Nagasaki explosion was 21 kilotons). In the words of a leading atomic scientist, "these tests evidently did result in substantial improvements in the efficient use of fissile material. By making use of new designs based on these experiments, ... it would now be able to produce more weapons than had been required in the schedule which the Joint Chiefs of Staff prepared in late 1947."[36]

These discoveries proved to be more momentous than the discovery of the bomb itself. Think what the world would have been like if nuclear weapons could only be laboratory devices, laboriously assembled by teams of highly skilled scientists after years of work at astronomical expense. At best, only the superpowers would have the bomb and there would be no arsenals of tens of thousands of weapons poised in missile nose cones, as bombs on fighter aircraft and even packed into artillery shells. Consider the analogy with controlled fusion: Although controlled fission has been commonplace for over fifty years, lighting our streets and driving our submarines, sustained controlled fusion has continued to elude the scientific community. Controlled fusion experiments have produced only successes whose duration has been measured in microseconds and power outputs equivalent to a flashlight battery, while requiring power inputs sufficient for a small city and equipment costing tens of millions of dollars. Imagine what our world would be like if making nuclear weapons had proved to be as technically difficult as controlled fusion. Instead, the developments of these early years produced weapons very efficient in their use of fissile material, small enough to fit into a missile and rugged enough to withstand reentry into the earth's atmosphere, and methods to produce unlimited quantities of fissile material. The age of nuclear plenty was beginning, in which a nation could have as many nuclear weapons as it wished.

Thus by the end of 1948 two of the four questions that confronted the U.S. government had been answered. The United States had decided it was necessary, in view of the growing tension with the Soviet Union and in light of the assumption of inferiority to the Soviet Union in conventional arms, to maintain stocks of atomic bombs in peacetime, and to stockpile as many bombs as it was possible to produce.

NUCLEAR STRATEGY BEGINS

Having decided to rely on nuclear weapons to guarantee its security, the United States was the first nation to face the same pressing question that all nuclear states— including the most recent nuclear proliferators—face: developing a strategy for using nuclear weapons. A strategy, to be effective, must identify targets to be attacked, determine how these targets are to be attacked, and decide to what end those targets are being attacked. The first strategy adopted was to destroy the capability of the Soviet

Union to wage war against the United States and the responsibility for its execution in event of war was assigned to the Air Force Strategic Air Command. Based on World War II experience, primary emphasis in a series of war plans drafted from 1947 to 1949 was on identifying urban-industrial centers for attack. Subsequent plans increased the number of urban centers targeted from 24 to 104 as more nuclear weapons became available and as the Air Force's ability to deliver those weapons increased. The targets whose destruction would most disrupt the Soviet Union's war-making capability were considered to be the liquid fuel, electric power, and atomic energy industries—all located in Soviet cities.

Still unresolved was the debate over the basic aim of strategic bombing: Was the aim to destroy an enemy's *ability* to wage war or its *will* to wage war? In May 1949 a committee from all three services reviewed the ability of existing nuclear weapons to "bring about capitulation, destroy the roots of communism or critically weaken the power of the Soviet leadership to dominate the people"; in other words, to destroy the will of Soviet leaders to wage war against the United States, and the willingness of the Russian people to support such a war.[37] The report did concede that the bomb had the capability to inflict "serious damage to vital elements of the Soviet war-making capabilities." Rather than undermine the will of the Russian people, however, the committee suggested the bomb might have the opposite effect: "For the majority of Soviet people, atomic bombing would validate Soviet propaganda against foreign powers, stimulate resentment against the United States, unify these people and increase their will to fight."[38]

The Strategic Air Command (SAC) was assigned a second mission as the U.S. commitment to aid its allies in Western Europe grew with the signing of the North Atlantic Treaty in 1949. That mission was to retard Soviet advances in Western Europe in the event of a Soviet invasion. The North Atlantic Treaty was the first formal commitment by the United States to defend Western Europe and the treaty implied that American troops would be sent back to Europe (four divisions were, in fact, committed there by 1951). However, in 1949, "the nuclear stockpile was still too small and the weapons too large and unwieldy to be used against true tactical targets such as troops and transportation bottlenecks."[39]

STALIN AND THE AMERICAN MONOPOLY

In Stalin's time, Soviet nuclear policy decisions were his to make, but in the postwar period there were other issues demanding his attention. While Soviet scientists sought to develop their own atomic bomb, Stalin confronted the rebuilding of a shattered Soviet economy and the ensuring of his own undisputed control over the Soviet Union. At the same time he hoped to deter any future attacks on the Soviet Union by the West. How could this be accomplished in the face of an American nuclear monopoly?

Stalin saw little reason to modify the Leninist view of a hostile West and the inevitability of a major war. In the short run, however, some accommodation might be possible with the capitalists. Stalin had, after all, allied himself with Hitler in August 1939. He had been convinced that Hitler meant to attack the Soviet Union some day, but by then the USSR would be too strong to defeat. The German offensive of June 1941 was an unpleasant surprise. Stalin drew, however, several comforting conclusions from the experience. Surprise was not decisive. The Soviet Union, the victim of the surprise, had won the war. Therefore, Stalin argued, there were "permanent operating factors" that decided the outcome of any war, and those factors favored the USSR. Aided by these factors, the Soviet Union would wage any future war to victory, deploying armed forces whose quantity would overwhelm the enemy and whose operating principle would be the offensive.

It appeared to Stalin that these conditions and the evident desire in the West to enjoy the benefits of peace meant that immediate Western aggression was unlikely, although in the long run innate Western hostility would produce that aggression. He could, therefore, turn his attention to more immediate foreign policy problems. These problems, emerging in the day-to-day contact with the West, had the potential to bring on an unwanted war.

Stalin's foreign policy during the period of American nuclear monopoly has been interpreted in diverse ways.[40] To some, the policy seemed defensive—to push American power away from the Soviet Union and to prevent the reemergence of Germany as a mortal threat to the Soviet Union. Prewar Poland had flirted with the Nazis, the Czech government had capitulated without a fight, and Hungary, Romania, and Bulgaria had served Hitler. Equally important, these East European states served as a route of invasion into the Soviet Union three times in the preceding thirty years. For others, the policy was aggressive—to acquire influence or control outside Soviet borders (as in Eastern Europe) and to disrupt Western influence or control in its traditional spheres of influence. The Berlin blockade of 1948–49 illustrates this interpretive dilemma. Was this a provocative challenge to American, British, and French control of West Berlin, or was it a warning to the Western Powers not to try to recreate a powerful German state? In either case, it represented a risk that one might not have expected Stalin to run, given the American nuclear monopoly. Indeed, the whole confrontation with the West in the postwar period (the Cold War) seems unexpected in a period of decided nuclear inferiority, no matter whether the Soviets were defensive or offensive in their orientation.

While we cannot know for sure, the absence of nuclear weapons does not seem to have affected Soviet foreign policy to an appreciable degree. Stalin's military doctrine did allow for some risk taking. In his view, atomic weapons would not win wars. The large Soviet army could overrun Western Europe quickly, so that a war begun by the West would mean the loss of Europe (and the staging bases for the B-29). But on the whole, Stalin was cautious, although that caution was probably driven more by the need to rebuild the Soviet economy and to maintain his personal control. At the same time, Stalin could not allow the West to draw the conclusion that the Soviet Union would not defend its interests. Stalin had tried appeasement with Hitler; it had proven a costly mistake.

As we saw in Chapter 3, Stalin concluded in August 1945 that the Soviet Union needed the bomb because the Americans had acquired it. The available evidence suggests that Stalin's decisions on atomic weapons came essentially as *reactions* to the efforts of Germany and the United States. Stalin may actually have been quite reluctant to enter the atomic race with the United States. George Kennan, a longtime student of the Soviet Union, has argued that

> there is no reason to doubt that Stalin saw this weapon as he himself described it: as something with which one frightened people with weak nerves. Not only was he aware from the start of its potentially suicidal quality, but he will be sure to have recognized, as one in whose eyes wars were no good unless they served some political purpose, that for such purposes the nuclear weapon was ill suited: It was too primitive, too blindly destructive, too indiscriminate, too prone to destroy the useful with the useless.[41]

The Soviet decision to push for a bomb, in Kennan's view, was essentially a response to the American achievement.

When there are several powerful states, decisions by one state regarding what weapons to build, the doctrine for their use, or the linkage of such weapons to foreign policy may cause the other states to mimic that behavior or develop specific counter-measures. Those responses in turn provoke the first state into new decisions, and the cycle of action and reaction bounces along. Historically, the United States has generally been the leader in nuclear weapons technology. It has set the standards and the pace of de-velopment. What the leader has, the others must try to get. In a broader sense, a less pow-erful state must consistently respond to the powerful if it hopes to create some security. Clearly, Pakistan's quick response to India's open demonstration of a nuclear weapons capability in 1998 suggests how strong the action-reaction phenomenon can be.

THE IMPACT OF THE SOVIET BOMB

On September 23, 1949, the White House announced that it had confirmed evidence that the Soviet Union had detonated its first atomic test explosion. The intelligence reports had caught President Truman by surprise. American aircraft, flying between Alaska and Japan to sample the downwind from the most likely Soviet test sites, had detected increased levels of radiation during September 1949. The conclusion was in-escapable—the Soviet Union had a working nuclear device.[42] No one had doubted that the Soviets would obtain nuclear weapons. The surprise was in the timing. Ad-ministration officials made great efforts to exude an air of calm and confidence; there was no reason for alarm. Privately, however, there was a growing uneasiness. Senator Arthur Vandenberg noted in his diary, "This is now a different world. The new prob-lems are appalling. Where do we go from here and what do we do about it?"[43] Ameri-can military planners were less dismayed; they had expected Soviet nuclearization at some point, and it was obvious that some years would pass before the Soviet Union would have a sufficient stockpile of deliverable nuclear weapons and the means to de-liver those weapons against the United States. Nonetheless, the detonation did give ur-gency to policy debates that had been going on for some time within the U.S. government. One outcome was that the Strategic Air Command was assigned as its first priority destroying targets "affecting the Soviet capability to deliver atomic bombs."

The Soviet test foreshadowed the nuclear world we are familiar with—two states with the power to annihilate each other (and their neighbors). American and Soviet lead-ers now faced parallel problems: What would the opponent do with its nuclear weapons? Would they consider war? What strategy and what nuclear weapons would be necessary to wage a war successfully, a war thrust on it by the opponent? Much of what we know about how the United States wrestled with these questions comes from documents pre-pared for or by the National Security Council.[44] These documents, milestones in policy formation, provide a window into the thoughts and values of the times. One of the first of these policy documents to consider the circumstances under which nuclear weapons might be used was *U.S. Policy on Atomic Warfare* (NSC-30). (Previous plans had been contingency plans drawn up by military staffs.) Approved in September 1948 by Presi-dent Truman, NSC-30 recognized that the military "must be ready to utilize promptly and effectively all appropriate means available, including atomic weapons."

NSC-30 also stipulated that the decision to employ atomic weapons in the event of war rested with "the Chief Executive when he considers such a decision to be required."[45] This established the principle of presidential control of nuclear weapons. Moreover, the custody of the nuclear warheads themselves initially rested with a civilian agency, the Atomic Energy Commission, rather than with the military services, creating a bureaucratic safeguard against use unless authorized by the president. NSC-30 is still in force today, but as we shall see, the exact manner in which presidential control is exercised has changed over time. Beginning in 1951, custody of the weapons was gradually transferred to the services, until, in 1967, all nuclear weapons had been delivered to the military.[46] Nonetheless, nuclear states recognized early on that control over nuclear weapons—in terms of both command authority and custody—were key issues. Stalin's approach was similar: He would make any decision regarding use, and the secret police would be the custodians of the warheads.

The detonation of the Soviet atomic device forced a reexamination of U.S. strategy regarding the Soviet Union in general and atomic weapons in particular. In January 1950 President Truman directed the secretaries of State and Defense "to undertake a reexamination of our objectives in peace and war and the effect of these objectives on our strategic plans, in the light of the probable fission bomb capability and possible thermonuclear bomb capability of the Soviet Union."[47] The resulting document, titled "U.S. Objectives and Programs for National Security (NSC-68)," was submitted to the National Security Council in April 1950. One of the document's chief architects, Secretary of State Dean Acheson, frankly admits in his memoirs that the "purpose of NSC-68 was to so bludgeon the mass mind of top government that not only could the president make a decision, but that decision could be carried out,"[48] thus recognizing that senior officials can do much to delay and obstruct the implementation of presidential directives with which they do not agree.

While it is difficult to know how much influence such a policy statement actually has, NSC-68 certainly expressed the temper of the times and its rhetoric reflected the basic assumptions that fueled the Cold War for years to come. It portrayed the Soviet leadership as "inescapably militant ... because it possesses, or is possessed by a world wide revolutionary movement, because it is the inheritor of Russian imperialism and because it is a totalitarian dictatorship" which "requires a dynamic extension of authority and the ultimate elimination of any effective opposition." The United States, as "the principal center of power in the non-Soviet world," is "the principal enemy whose integrity and vitality must be subverted or destroyed ... if the Kremlin is to achieve its fundamental design." Thus the world is divided by "the underlying conflict" between the "free world" of the West and the "slave society" behind the Iron Curtain.[49]

NSC-68 foretold that when "the Kremlin calculates that it has sufficient atomic capability to make a surprise attack on the United States, nullifying our atomic superiority and creating a military situation decisively in its favor, the Kremlin might be tempted to strike swiftly and with stealth." NSC-68 even predicted that the year of maximum danger of a bolt from the blue would be 1954, when the Soviet Union would have amassed 200 atomic bombs and "an atomic bomber capability ... in excess of that needed to deliver the available bombs," thus giving the Soviet Union the capacity to damage seriously "the vital centers of the United States by surprise attack." Given the assumption of overwhelming Soviet superiority in conventional military forces, NSC-68 rejected a policy of no first use of nuclear weapons: "In our present situation of relative unpreparedness in conventional weapons, such a declaration would be interpreted by the USSR as an admission of great weakness and by our allies as a clear indication that we intended to abandon them."[50]

It is important to note some of the critical developments of nuclear thinking that came with NSC-68. American planners assumed that its nuclear opponent would be constantly calculating its nuclear strength and assessing the possibility of a successful bolt from the blue. That is, they expected that an opponent committed to "subverting or destroying" the United States would naturally consider nuclear weapons. They assumed that just 200 nuclear weapons would constitute the peril point. This is a small number. As a point of comparison, by 1960 the U.S. arsenal alone would reach over 12,000 nuclear weapons and the U.S. nuclear stockpile peaked in 1966 at an estimated 32,200 nuclear bombs and warheads; during fifty years of weapons production, the United States manufactured more than 70,000 warheads.[51] The planners calculated that such an arsenal (and its necessary delivery systems) would be available in five years, a relatively short time. Note that these nuclear-created fears emerged in the state that possessed a monopoly on nuclear weapons. Note also that this way of perceiving the world has a paranoia-like quality to it: Our opponent, who is out to get us, will some day be very powerful and will be tempted to use that power to destroy us. Felt strongly enough, such paranoia might push a state into a preventive war: We should attack now while our ruthless opponent is still relatively weak.

There is no evidence that the Soviet leadership did in fact make such calculations about the payoffs from a bolt from the blue. The American government did not completely succumb to nuclear paranoia (although there were mid-level officials who did suggest a preventive war). We do not know if in fact there is some magic threshold number that would embolden a nuclear state. But it is possible that nuclear-armed states in the future might act in ways implied by NSC-68. For example, the United States did, in response to its fears of the Soviet Union, plan a *conscious first use of nuclear weapons* in case of a Soviet conventional attack. The sort of planning that did occur is, we suspect, likely to be typical for one or both parties in a nuclear relationship. Pakistan, for instance, might conclude that it too faces an opponent with superior conventional capabilities and therefore must employ a strategic doctrine that emphasizes first use.

NSC-68's prescriptions to protect American security called for increased military spending, improved air and civil defense, and an increase in the U.S. atomic capability. Expansion is always expensive, and that provoked an intense debate in Washington, a debate that was ended by the invasion of South Korea by the North Korean Army in June 1950. The invasion of a state within the U.S. sphere of influence by a Soviet protégé seemed to signal a Soviet willingness to use force to extend the area under their domination. Following as it did the Communist victory on mainland China, President Truman felt he had no choice but to commit U.S. troops to the United Nation's effort to repel the North Korean invasion. As the Soviet Union had shown it was willing to use force to achieve its goals and had demonstrated its ability to build atomic weapons, a massive buildup of U.S. military forces was considered necessary to deter further Soviet attacks.

By 1953, because of high priority given to developing the Air Force's strategic nuclear weapons delivery capability, the Strategic Air Command, under General Curtis LeMay, had become a formidable force, matched by the growing sophistication and power of nuclear weapons. The 10,000 pound Mark III had been replaced by bombs weighing under 3,000 pounds, yet twenty-five times more powerful. Soon to be available was a 1,000 pound bomb, easily carried by most Air Force fighter-bombers and Navy attack planes and usable as a warhead on short-range guided missiles, in shells for long-range artillery (as shown in Figure 4-4 on page 104) and as atomic demolition

FIGURE 4-4
Test firing of the atomic cannon, 1953. *U.S. Department of Energy*

mines.[52] The U.S. stockpile of nuclear weapons has been estimated as 1,000 weapons by the summer of 1953,[53] virtually doubling again by 1955.[54]

THE "SUPER"

The detonation of the first Soviet nuclear device forced a reexamination of the U.S. atomic arsenal itself. Less than two months after evidence of the Soviet explosion reached the United States, the General Advisory Committee of the Atomic Energy Commission was asked to review all the proposals for responding to the Soviet detonation by increasing both the production and efficiency of fission weapons and by developing a "Super bomb" or a bomb based on nuclear fusion.[55] The committee recommended strongly against diverting effort from the fission bomb program, and they also made strategic and moral arguments for not proceeding with the development of the "Super." They pointed out that there would be no limit to the explosive power of a fusion bomb. It would be easy to conceive of a weapon that was deliverable with existing delivery systems that would have the explosive effect of hundreds of existing fission bombs. They felt that the "Super" would only be a weapon of genocide, beyond any military objectives, stating, "It is not a weapon which can be used exclusively for the destruction of material installations of military or semi-military purpose. Its use, therefore, carries much further than the atomic bomb itself the policy of exterminating civilian populations."[56]

The General Advisory Committee (GAC) instead recommended developing small atomic bombs for tactical or battlefield use against strictly military targets. The chairman of GAC, Robert Oppenheimer, continued to press for increased production of tactical nuclear weapons, in the hope that "battle could be brought back to the battlefield."[57]

The Joint Chiefs of Staff in their response to the report of the General Advisory Committee argued "that there is a possibility that such a weapon might be a decisive factor if properly used and (we) prefer that such a possibility be at the will and control of the United States rather than of an enemy." The Joint Chiefs warned "that the United States would be in an intolerable position if a possible enemy possessed the bomb and the United States did not." In response to the argument of the GAC that the "Super" was intrinsically immoral, the Joint Chiefs of Staff said that "in war it is folly to argue whether one weapon is more immoral than another. For, in the larger sense, it is war in itself which is immoral, and the stigma of such immorality must rest upon the nation which initiates hostilities."[58]

The step from fission to fusion bombs was at least as significant as the earlier step from the largest conventional bombs to fission. The standard "blockbuster" of World War II weighed one ton (2,000 pounds). The very largest conventional bombs of World War II, used only for very special tasks, weighed 11 tons, and not all that weight was explosive. The bomb that was dropped on Hiroshima had a force of 12½ kilotons, or 12,500 tons of TNT. Thus the Hiroshima bomb was more than one thousand times as powerful as the "blockbuster" bomb used in World War II. There were fusion bombs in the U.S. inventory of almost ten megatons, or about one thousand times as powerful as the Hiroshima bomb. To illustrate the difference between a fission and a fusion bomb: "A fission bomb of 15 Kilotons dropped on the Statue of Liberty in New York harbor would do little more than break windowpanes at the distance of Time Square (some seven miles away). A ten megaton hydrogen bomb dropped at the same place would utterly devastate all of Manhattan (shown in Figure 4-5) and indeed the entire New York City and harbor area."[59]

FIGURE 4-5
New York City as a target. A 10-megaton thermonuclear weapon would completely devastate the area shown. *Courtesy of the New York Historical Society, New York City*

President Truman was more strongly influenced by the arguments of the Joint Chiefs and authorized the development of the hydrogen, or thermonuclear, bombs as well as an increase in the production of fission weapons, including tactical battlefield weapons.[60] Thus when presented with divided counsel, the president chose both courses of action. As a result, the U.S. strategic retaliatory force is now armed with fusion weapons, and the United States eventually deployed over five thousand tactical nuclear weapons in Europe.

The "Super" came at the point when the U.S. monopoly on fission weapons had been broken. Now the United States had a new lead and as its production of nuclear weapons increased, the United States was entering an *age of nuclear plenty*—it had the ability to wage total war and the ability to destroy not only the enemy's capability to fight a war and the enemy's will to fight a war, but also to destroy the enemy itself.

DOCTRINES FOR AN AGE OF PLENTY

As more weapons became available, military leaders (and eventually civilian leaders as well) reevaluated how these weapons would be used in time of war. Nuclear war plans themselves have been a particularly perplexing problem. Everyone expected nuclear war to be relatively short. There is not time in the midst of a crisis to begin selecting targets and matching them to weapons, so in the United States the drafting of detailed plans for the use of nuclear weapons in the event of war had begun as early as 1947, and by the 1950s had become a full-time occupation for large staffs of officers in all three services, the Air Force, the Navy, and the Army. Planning is a labor-intensive and time-consuming process requiring identification of potential targets, determination of the exact location of the target, assignment of the appropriate weapon to the target (size of weapon, altitude of detonation, and so forth), determination of the method of delivery of the weapon (strategic bomber, carrier aircraft, missile, and so forth), mapping the exact route and timing for each bomber sortie to minimize the effectiveness of Soviet air defenses,[61] and finally the writing and distribution of detailed orders to each ship, aircraft, and missile launch control center.

Moreover, war plans guide the services in preparing their personnel for combat. Men and women need to be trained to perform the operations called for. The resources (the aircraft, the bombs, the fuel, the communications equipment, and so on) needed for the operations have to be acquired long in advance. War plans thus represent what the military services are prepared and able to do—they reflect and perpetuate the standard operating procedures of a large and complex organization.

Planning for future operations, training personnel, and assembling the needed resources are important and essential parts of military doctrine, but underpinning them is a set of expectations and goals that the services set for war-waging. When one stepped back from the details, what did one see as the over-arching strategy? Where does that strategy come from? In the American political system, National Security Council memoranda such as NSC-68 typically set general goals for the services. In most cases these documents were approved by the president. They provided guidance in drafting war plans and acquiring weapons. They do not, however, commit any president to a particular action in a crisis, nor, because of their secret nature, were they intended as public statements of declared policy.

American officials have made public statements about policy, which we call *declared national policy*, for they have judged it useful for the sake of deterrence to present to their citizens and to the leaders of foreign nations particular visions of how the United States might wage war. The U.S. government, for instance, has explicitly rejected *preventive war*—the destruction without provocation of a potential enemy for fear that someday the enemy might have sufficient power to threaten U.S. security. NSC-68 characterized preventive war as morally repugnant and contrary to the American tradition of not acting as an aggressor. There is no evidence that the top leaders of the United States ever seriously considered a preventive war against the Soviet Union, even when it had overwhelming nuclear superiority as it did from the late 1940s through the 1950s. (As we have seen, American leaders did consider using nuclear weapons against less powerful opponents.)

Beyond this public denial, which seems to be in line with actual strategy, the American government in the 1950s was ambiguous in its public pronouncements about war planning. When you look at the plans themselves—and the attitudes of some of the key military leadership—a more complex picture emerges. In 1960, Daniel Ellsberg was studying the Single Integrated Operational Plan (SIOP), the document that would direct the nation's nuclear forces in the event of war, as part of the review of national defense by the incoming Kennedy administration. At first he was baffled by the apparent illogic of the plan, but he came to the realization that the plan was based on the assumption that the United States would be the nation to strike first in a nuclear war.[62] It was apparent to Ellsberg that the American government had adopted a *strategy of preemption*: The United States would strike first when there was positive evidence an attack was about to be mounted against the United States or possibly even against its closest allies. This was recognized in NSC-68, which noted that "the military advantage of landing the first blow ... required the United States to be on the alert in order to strike with our full weight as soon as we are attacked, and, if possible, before the Soviet blow is actually delivered."[63] Preemption was therefore regarded as a defensive measure only to be employed when an attack against the United States appeared imminent. And a preemption doctrine obviously made war-planning before the war a crucial activity.

But to publicly declare that one would follow a preemption strategy had its own risks. Declared policy is intended in part to send signals to potential adversaries, warning them that certain of their actions could bring a nuclear response from the United States. One can imagine that to declare publicly a policy of preemption would make the United States seem excessively bellicose and might actually increase the risk of a surprise attack against the United States. On the other hand, starting with NSC-68 in 1950, the United States has consistently refused to declare that it would not be the first to use nuclear weapons in a conflict. Preemption, after all, requires first use. This ambiguity was intended to warn the Soviet Union and its Warsaw Pact allies that if they invaded Western Europe, they would risk a nuclear counterattack by the United States, even if they did not use nuclear weapons themselves. That does not mean, however, that an administration would necessarily have chosen to use nuclear weapons if Western Europe were invaded.

We have emphasized that when the moment came, the leadership of a nation might decide not to follow through on its plans and the threats it had issued. But who would make the decision to refrain from implementing a nuclear strategy—or to order the preemptive strike? Normally, we think of the American president as the individual who would do so, as he is the constitutionally designated commander in chief. However, who would have the finger on the metaphorical "button" has been a contentious issue. The military services and their leaders have some autonomy, and that autonomy gives those leaders some freedom of action.

Consider this example: In his book *The Wizards of Armageddon*, Fred Kaplan recounts a conversation in September 1957 at the headquarters of the U.S. Air Force Strategic Air Command (SAC). Robert Sprague, deputy head of the Security Resources Panel, appointed by President Eisenhower to examine national security in view of the Soviet Union's developing nuclear capability, had just observed a practice alert of the entire SAC bomber force. In six hours, not a single bomber had been able to take off. Sprague pointed out to General Curtis LeMay, at that time commanding general of SAC, that Strategic Air Command bombers were extremely vulnerable to a Soviet surprise attack. In the time it would take a Russian bomber to fly from the United States Distant Early Warning radar line in Canada to SAC bases in the United States, only a few of the SAC bombers could take off. Those bombers that did get away before their bases were destroyed would have only limited crew, limited fuel, and no atomic weapons on board. Therefore, even though some bombers might get off the ground, they probably could not reach the Soviet Union, and if they did, they wouldn't have anything to drop on Russia.

LeMay responded that "the United States had airplanes flying secret missions over the Soviet territory 24 hours a day picking up all sorts of intelligence information, mostly communication intelligence and Soviet military radio transmissions." LeMay went on to say, "If I see that the Russians are amassing their planes for an attack, I am going to knock the shit out of them before they take off the ground."[64]

LeMay's response was in line with the undeclared national policy of preemption. What shocked Sprague was that LeMay would *himself* order an attack on Soviet air bases; Sprague pointed out that was not national policy. Both knew that NSC-30 declared that the decision as to the employment of atomic weapons in the event of war was reserved to the president, not the head of SAC. Furthermore, NSC-30 did not say that electronic surveillance evidence in itself would automatically trigger a preemptive attack. LeMay replied that he did not care; "It is my policy—that is what I am going to do."[65]

LeMay's assertion raises the problem of exactly how much control a president can exercise over the military establishment, both in peacetime and in a crisis. Although direct defiance of orders has been rare in the U.S. military establishment, all three services have at one time or another seen the country's interests differently than the president and have delayed or obstructed changes a president wished made. The 1960s in particular saw occasions when subordinates did deliberately disregard policy directives, and, even at best, presidents have had difficulty monitoring compliance with their directives. Thus, in a crisis a president might find his options constrained by the weapons his subordinates, or subordinates of a previous president, had acquired and war plans they had drafted.

The conversation between LeMay and Sprague also points out a dilemma that has concerned leaders of all the nuclear states since the beginning of the atomic era—the problem of the *command and control* of nuclear weapons. Command and control are often lumped together with the problem of maintaining reliable communications and obtaining timely intelligence during a crisis or war as the "Command, Control, Communications and Intelligence" problem, abbreviated C^3I. Although control of a nation's armed forces has always concerned national leaders, until the advent of nuclear weapons there was a limit to the irreversible harm a military commander acting without authority could do. Armies could always be recalled, invaded territory evacuated, apologies made, and reparations paid. But because nuclear weapons are so very destructive, the commander of even a small unit—a missile squadron, for instance—has the power to do irreparable damage and even precipitate a full-scale nuclear war.

Thus, by the end of the 1950s, the American government had a large stockpile of bombs—over 12,000, a doctrine for war-waging that called for the obliteration of the Soviet Union in a massive, preemptive attack, and a president nominally in command of the nuclear establishment, but with enough service autonomy to suggest that in fact there were several fingers near the nuclear button. The doctrine had emerged from a number of sources: It reflected the recent historical tradition of the U.S. military (strategic bombardment as a means to victory, with nuclear weapons being the winning weapon), and the painful memory of Pearl Harbor—never again was the nation to be victim of the first blow if that could be avoided. It also reflected a long-standing American strategic tradition that set the annihilation of the enemy as the only legitimate war aim. The almost universal public acceptance of this doctrine of annihilation ill-prepared the United States for limited wars with limited objectives, such as the Korean War, whose aim became, after China's entrance, simply the maintenance of the South Korean state, and for a protracted Cold War in which there never could be a decisive conclusion. It also reflected a moral assumption that aggression had to be punished. The U.S. Air Force and its commanders (particularly of SAC) would have a strong institutional interest in having the maximum flexibility to safeguard the nation. The size and complexity of the strategic nuclear establishment meant that actual control over the execution of strategy would remain untested, but fraught with unsettling possibilities.

THE SOVIET EXPERIENCE

Our ability to predict the maturation process of new nuclear states would be enhanced if (1) we found that the Soviet experience paralleled the American, and (2) where it did not, we could identify the essential differences. In the main, we suggest that the Soviet experience has some close parallels. Moreover, we can make some informed judgments about the causes of Soviet nuclear behavior. We saw, for instance, that Stalin reacted to the American use of nuclear weapons against Japan by ordering a crash program to develop a Soviet bomb. Their internal scientific research indicated that fusion was an alternative means of developing nuclear power. In November 1949 the Soviets accelerated work on their fusion bomb, possibly in response to the American discovery of the August test and from a belief that the Americans themselves would move to produce the "Super."

This concentration on the H-bomb may have contributed to a rather slow production of fission devices by Soviet arsenals. Work progressed slowly as well on the development of the means to deliver such devices against the United States. This slow growth reinforced Stalin's basic strategic outlook. Without the means of direct attack on the United States, the Soviet Union still envisioned the seizure of Western Europe as its principal war-fighting strategy. Just the threat to do so might be enough to deter a Western attack. And to blunt American strategic attacks, the Soviets invested heavily in antiaircraft defenses.

Dictatorships increase the likelihood that individuals will have a disproportionate influence on policy decisions regarding the number and type of nuclear weapons and the strategies for their use. Conversely, when such a leader dies, major policy changes may become possible. Stalin's death in March 1953 prompted a vigorous debate on defense policy within the Politburo, the leadership group of the Soviet Communist Party (and hence of the Soviet state). This debate captures part of the central dilemma for states who choose to go nuclear and then must make decisions about numbers and types of weapons and strategies appropriate for them. Because this debate takes place within a political context, some of the debate will reflect the struggle for political power. Different individuals and factions may adopt different positions, not necessarily on their merits, but because the position seems to be a politically popular one (it advances the political fortunes of a particular individual or group).

This politicization of nuclear policy was not confined to the Soviet system. For instance, at the end of the 1970s, the Reagan Republicans found it politically useful to claim that the United States was in grave peril and called for a reorientation of nuclear strategy and weapons. Similarly, the Bharatiya Janata Party in India sought leverage at the polls by calling for India to add nuclear weapons to its arsenal.[66]

In addition to the impact of politics on nuclear issues, we need to be aware that in states with strong ideological backgrounds, those too will affect nuclear policy. The Soviet leadership, for instance, had to work within the context of a deeply rooted Marxist-Leninist ideological heritage, which meant that any position on nuclear weapons had to show that it was compatible with the ideology's basic tenents. That heritage was complex enough to allow many different positions to find support, but it meant that debate about policy would become a debate about who were in fact the true adherents to Leninist visions, making a resolution of the debate that much more difficult.

It would be a mistake, however, to see this defense debate as devoid of substance. Soviet leaders, for instance, like their American counterparts, were attempting to make sense of the unknown. The new Soviet premier, Georgi Malenkov, took the position that nuclear war would likely mean the death of civilization. Nuclear war, therefore, was both undesirable and—given rationality on both sides—unlikely. This challenged two fundamental ideological tenets that many Soviet leaders held: War with the capitalist system was inevitable, and a proletarian world community would arise from the ashes of such a war. As a corollary, Malenkov seemed unwilling to invest heavily in nuclear weapons. Malenkov's opponents, led by the new Communist Party General Secretary, Nikita Khrushchev, insisted that war was possible (because of the aggressiveness of the capitalist states) and that civilization would not be destroyed.

This opposition stemmed in part from a desire to supplant Malenkov, since once Khrushchev had done so, he would adopt Malenkov's position that war was not inevitable and that the need to prevent nuclear war was a prime goal of Soviet foreign policy. But there were other considerations as well. There was a fear that Malenkov's position would reduce a sense of vigilance and encourage a sense of defeatism in the Party and masses. After all, Malenkov's vision of nuclear weapons seemed to negate the future, which Marxism had reserved for the proletariat. And there was an uncertainty about American intentions. Contradictory signals came from the Eisenhower administration's threat in 1953 to use nuclear weapons to end the stalemate in the Korean War, the president's subsequent call for negotiations on nuclear weapons in December of that year, and Dulles's statements about massive retaliation in January 1954.

At the same time the political leadership debated the war issues, the Soviet military, now freed from the fear of Stalin's displeasure, began to debate the Stalinist military doctrine.[67] Some suggested that *surprise attack* now might decide the outcome of a war. If decisive outcomes could be achieved in a limited time, particularly in the opening stages of a war, then nuclear weapons would take on far more importance than Stalinist doctrine accorded them. The more traditional Soviet military leaders denied that surprise attack could determine the winner of a war. They did not reject nuclear weapons in the arsenal, but saw them in traditional ways: Nuclear weapons would function like conventional artillery—clearing the way for the ground forces by destroying enemy troop concentrations and rear supply and transportation facilities.

By February 1955 the Khrushchev-led faction won the political struggle. Nuclear weapons would be a key part of the future. The same year also marked the end to the military debate about the effect of surprise attack. Marshal Rotmistrov declared that "it must be plainly said that when atomic and hydrogen weapons are employed, surprise is one of the decisive conditions for the attainment of success not only in battles and operations, but also in war as a whole...." But a preventive war was unacceptable. These judgments led to this conclusion: "The duty of the Soviet armed forces is not to permit an enemy surprise attack on our country and, in the event of an attempt to establish one, not only to repel the attack successfully but also to deal the enemy counterblows, or even pre-emptive surprise blows, of terrible destructive force."[68]

Thus the Soviet Union, like the United States, had come to the conclusion that preemption (which necessarily meant first use) was the central doctrine for nuclear war. We suspect that this is likely to be the approach of many "young" nuclear powers. The underlying assumption is that nuclear wars can be waged, and waged successfully, as long as one is able to detect and successfully preempt the attack being readied by the opponent. Such a strategy would not make such a war cost-free to the "winner," just that its suffering would be less, and it would be able to impose its will on its opponent.

Unlike the Soviet Union, however, the United States had "solved" the problem of how to deliver a preemptive attack against its opponent. American technological developments had enhanced the effectiveness and reduced the vulnerability of the U.S. bomber force. The B-29 and its successor, the propeller-driven B-36, were quickly displaced by the B-52 jet bomber which for forty years would be a key nuclear delivery system. With a combat radius of over 3,000 miles, the B-52 made possible the basing of the U.S. retaliatory bomber force in the United States with airborne refueling where needed to permit the bombers to reach targets deep in the Soviet Union. By 1959, all of the B-36 bombers had been replaced with the B-52 (see Figure 4-6 on page 112), which required very little warm-up before takeoff, thus reducing the possibility of a surprise attack eliminating the American bomber force. One-third of the bomber force was maintained on ground alert in the United States and would take off at the first sign of a Soviet strike. They would then proceed along emergency war plan routes toward their targets, but their missions would be aborted at prespecified points unless they received a "go code" to continue.[69]

Recognizing the vulnerability of the U.S. bombers while on the ground, the United States began building distant early warning lines, chains of radar stations in Alaska, Canada, and Greenland, that would provide warning of a bomber attack against the United States. In addition there were continual improvements in the U.S. strategic intelligence-gathering capability, including overflights of the Soviet Union by U2 aircraft from 1956 through 1960, and finally the success of the Discoverer and Samos reconnaissance satellites in 1961.[70]

But the Soviet Union lacked a bomber force capable of reaching the United

FIGURE 4-6
A B-52 bomber lifts off from a SAC base near Rome, New York. *U.S. Air Force photo*

States in any strength, and had no allies close enough to the United States for forward-basing of its shorter-range strike aircraft. They did, however, have very public programs to build a strategic bomber fleet. The 1950s, in fact, were characterized by increasing American concern that the Soviet Union was acquiring the capability to destroy a large enough portion of the U.S. retaliatory capacity in a single bomber strike that it could initiate a nuclear war with relative impunity. This concern within the defense community was based in part on a Soviet ruse in 1955 when the Red Air Force flew a portion of the long-range bombers in its inventory over Moscow several times, leading the U.S. air attaché to report the Soviet Union had twenty-eight long-range bombers—twice the number they had the previous year—when in fact they had only eighteen. Using the inflated report of Soviet bomber production, U.S. Air Force Intelligence predicted that the Soviet Union would have 600 to 800 long-range bombers by 1960, a sufficient number to destroy all of the U.S. strategic bomber force on the ground.[71] (The Soviets, in fact, produced a small bomber force; they would come to rely on missiles as their primary delivery system, a development we explore in the next chapter.)

In sum, then, in the 1950s there was a decided strategic asymmetry: The United States had a growing stockpile of fusion bombs and a growing bomber force that could deliver the weapons against the Soviet Union. The Soviets had a growing fusion stockpile as well; in November 1955 the Soviets tested their first true "Super" of 1.6 megatons.[72] From that point on, the megatonnage of Soviet tests steadily increased to nearly fifty megatons before atmospheric testing ended. But they lacked the ability to deliver these warheads against the United States. The American nuclear monopoly still existed in practice.

NUCLEAR DOCTRINE IN PEACETIME

Acquiring weapons and planning for their use are traditional military activities directed toward providing for the security of the nation. From time to time, the power and symbolism of such weapons has influenced the *peacetime relations* of the nation. At the start of this century, the battleship, and in the 1930s, the airplane (particularly the bomber), became caught up in a nation's foreign policies and in the reactions of other states, especially those who were deficient in such weapons. The power of nuclear weapons, and therefore the announced doctrines for their use, mean that they will be part of the peacetime relations between states, especially states with traditions of rivalry or enmity. We have called this the *nuclear shadow effect*. Sometimes the shadow is quite consciously manipulated in the nation's foreign policy, a point we examine in Chapter 6. Here we concentrate on the military aspects of nuclear weapons in peacetime. In particular, we want to contrast two basic military postures: the short-lived "massive retaliation" motif of the United States, and the longer-lived "peaceful coexistence" theme of the Soviet Union.

As a state without the military ability to retaliate against its principal rival, and increasingly committed to the idea that nuclear war was too horrible to live through, the Soviet Union by the mid-1950s had enunciated a position that states with radically different social systems could keep the peace—though they might be intensely competitive in nonviolent ways. Nuclear weapons might be useful—perhaps essential—to ensure the peace, but there was no presumption that the future had to involve nuclear war. Moreover, if two different states could in principle coexist, the implication was that there was no issue so terribly divisive that could be "solved" only by recourse to war. Hence, nuclear weapons had no legitimate role in day-to-day politics. There was, of course, a great propaganda advantage to such a position (the Soviet Union seemed to be the champion of peace), but it did represent one path to pushing nuclear weapons into the background.

The American government, particularly during the middle 1950s, took the alternate approach and occasionally brought nuclear weapons into the foreground of its peacetime practices. At the height of the golden age of the American monopoly, the U.S. declared nuclear policy to cope with traditional forms of aggression was simple: massive retaliation. As defined by Eisenhower's secretary of state, John Foster Dulles, massive retaliation meant a capability to "retaliate, instantly, by means and at places of our own choosing."[73] Dulles was quick to explain that he did not mean that every aggression anywhere would be met with massive nuclear retaliation, but rather that the United States reserved the option of choosing the place and method of retaliation.

In part, the doctrine was a policy reaction to the frustrations the American public, and many political and military leaders, felt at the Korean War. Accustomed to total wars fought until the unconditional surrender of the enemy, the American people had little understanding of and less patience for a protracted limited war whose only realistic goal, once the Chinese had intervened, was the restoration of the conditions that existed before the war began. And worse, for the first time in memory, aggression was allowed to go unpunished. There was a substantial opinion in the country that the United States had permanently conceded the initiative to the Soviet Union as the U.S. goal of containment was defensive and the Communist goal of the spread of Communism was offensive. The Soviet Union, therefore, was able to choose the place and terms most favorable to itself for each confrontation. As the Soviets (or their Chinese allies) had unlimited manpower, they would of course choose a conventional war in the most difficult location for the United States. The Republican victory in the 1952 presidential election was due partly to widespread feeling that the Truman administrations had not been sufficiently vigorous in prosecuting the war in Korea. Dulles felt that the Chinese final acceptance of the armistice was the direct result of U.S.

threats to employ nuclear weapons to break the stalemate on the battlefield. Therefore, the doctrine of massive retaliation was an attempt to regain the strategic initiative and to use means most favorable to the United States to meet Soviet aggression. As the United States had an overwhelming superiority in nuclear weapons at the time, the choice would be obvious.

The doctrine of massive retaliation as held out by Dulles was, in some ways, simply a public statement of the implications of a military policy called the "New Look." When Eisenhower became president, in addition to liquidating the continued drain of the Korean War, he was very much concerned with the long-term effects of an arms race with the Soviet Union. He felt that it was unlikely that there would be an immediate resolution to the tension between the United States and the Soviet Union. He was therefore concerned about the erosion of the fundamental strength of the U.S. economy if a military buildup were to continue at the rate that it had since 1950. The "New Look" was set out in the National Security Council paper NSC-162/2 titled *The Basic National Security Policy*, and was approved in October 1953. It set as the objective of U.S. security policy meeting the Soviet threat while at the same time avoiding "seriously weakening the U.S. economy or undermining our fundamental values and institutions."[74]

It was again assumed that "the basic Soviet objectives continue to be consolidation and expansion of their own sphere of power and the eventual domination of the noncommunist world." Contrary to NSC-68, NSC-162/2 did not expect that the Soviet leadership would deliberately embark on a general war. "The uncertain prospects for Soviet victory in a general war, the change in leadership, satellite unrest and the U.S. capability to retaliate massively makes such a course improbable." Therefore, the basic outline of U.S. national security policy was to develop and maintain the following:

1. A strong military posture with emphasis on the capability for inflicting massive retaliatory damage by offensive striking power;
2. U.S. and allied forces in readiness to move rapidly initially to counter aggression by Soviet bloc forces and to hold vital areas and lines of communication;
3. A mobilization base, and its protection against crippling damage, adequate to ensure victory in the event of general war.[75]

With regard to nuclear weapons, NSC-162/2 continued the tradition of NSC-68 and NSC-30 in saying that "in the event of hostilities, the United States will consider nuclear weapons to be as available for use as other munitions." Left unanswered were the questions of what would constitute aggression by the Soviet bloc forces and at what level of hostilities would the use of nuclear weapons be appropriate.

Unlike NSC-68, NSC-162/2 did recognize that when the two major powers reached a stage of atomic plenty and ample means of delivery, the result could be a "stalemate with both sides reluctant to initiate general warfare."[76] While the ability to retaliate massively did not necessarily mean use of nuclear weapons, the reduction of U.S. conventional forces as President Eisenhower prepared the country for the long haul reduced the U.S. ability to respond with conventional forces to aggression. However, it was recognized that as the Soviet Union approached effective parity in its nuclear weapons capability, the U.S. ability to retaliate massively would be of less and less value in deterring the Soviet Union from aggression other than a general war. Once the Soviet Union had the ability to inflict unacceptable damage on the United States, the

United States would be very unwilling to risk a nuclear exchange with the Soviet Union over some "brush fire" war or local crisis.

ANTICIPATING THE END OF MONOPOLY

Therefore, the principal task of the American defense establishment in the 1950s was to prepare for a future in which the United States would no longer be the only nation with a sufficient stockpile of deliverable nuclear weapons to destroy an adversary's society. The United States was clearly committed to nuclear weapons as the principal guarantee of its national security, but exactly how could nuclear weapons be used to ensure the security of the United States? As early as 1946, General "Hap" Arnold, chief of staff of the Air Force, had realized that "our first line of defense is the ability to retaliate even after receiving the hardest blow an enemy can deliver."[77] It was becoming increasingly apparent that the only military use that could be made of nuclear weapons in a world in which the United States had lost its nuclear monopoly was retaliation in response to a nuclear attack or an overwhelming conventional attack on the United States or its Western European allies.

As planners began to look forward to the time when the Soviet Union would have both a significant number of nuclear weapons and the means to deliver them to the United States, systematic consideration was given to the elements of *deterrence*. Nuclear deterrence is the ability of a nation to prevent a nuclear or conventional attack on itself or its allies by the threat of nuclear retaliation. It was quickly recognized that the essential requirement of deterrence is credibility. For deterrence to prevent an attack on the United States, it is necessary that all potential attackers believe that the United States has the capability to inflict an unacceptable level of damage on any attacker, regardless of the effect of any attack the aggressor may have made on the United States. This means that an attacker must have very little hope that it could destroy enough of the U.S. nuclear arsenal in a disarming first strike to forestall nuclear retaliation by the United States. Any potential aggressor must also believe that the United States does in fact have the will to retaliate.

Thus, the ability to retaliate must be apparent, and this includes the ability of the U.S. retaliatory forces to survive a disarming first strike. Therefore the United States has taken pains to make public the size and power of the country's strategic nuclear forces and the measures taken to ensure their ability to survive an attack. The final irony of the nuclear age would be for an attacker to initiate a nuclear exchange that caused the destruction of its own society because it was unaware that the adversary had forces of such strength and survivability that the attack had no prospect for success.

SUMMARY

As the 1950s drew to a close, the two nuclear powers looked forward to the end of the American monopoly—the Soviets anticipating a way to make nuclear weapons the effective protector of their security, the United States preparing to cope with a true nuclear rival. The first fifteen years of their nuclear youth had been devoted to building stockpiles of nuclear weapons, the bomber delivery systems, and the doctrines for their use. In the main, both reached similar conclusions to the questions that all nuclear nations must confront: The bomb was essential; more nuclear weapons seemed better than fewer; if war came, preemption was the favored strategy. The difference was in the ability to preempt against the homeland of the other—the Soviets had to settle for a pale substitute: to attack Western Europe. As each nation began to anticipate that soon its opponent would have the ability to destroy it, regardless of any damage the opponent might suffer in an attack, both came to realize that the only use of nuclear weapons would be to prevent their use through the threat of retaliation.

How much of these conclusions came from the specific historical circumstances of these two nations, and how much from relatively permanently operating forces that will affect all nations in roughly the same fashion? The question for the future is: Will this same pattern be repeated by new nuclear nations that, like the United States and the Soviet Union, do not rest under the protective umbrella of another nuclear state?

We suggest the following possibilities to consider:

- "No more Sommes": That new nuclear nations will seek to lower costs of a military engagement and in particular avoid prolonged, expensive, and inconclusive stalemates. All nations will strive to avoid conflicts such as the eight-year Iran/Iraq war that cost the two sides three quarters of a million to one million lives, ending in a cease fire in 1988 with no victory for either combatant. If nuclear weapons are less costly than large armies and promise decisive results, the doctrine may be nuclear use and the preferred use may be the "Sunday punch" of the LeMay era.

- No more Pearl Harbors: Both the United States and the USSR suffered surprise attacks in the opening days of World War II though neither attack—given the weapons available—decided the war. Will new nuclear states be driven to get in the first blow if they fear war is inevitable?

- How dangerous were these doctrines? Preemption, and the reciprocal fear of an adversary's preemption puts the nuclear forces on a hair trigger: A strong suspicion that the other is massing its planes or preparing its missiles or dispersing its arsenal for an attack creates pressure to preempt. The chances for error are great, particularly in countries lacking a long tradition of strong, central decision making and firm control of their military establishment. Worse yet, preemption coupled with Sunday punch (probably an inevitable combination) means that if war comes, it will be horrific. But does this produce caution?

- Questions of scale: Do numbers matter? Are states with only a few nuclear weapons likely to act differently than states with large nuclear arsenals and robust delivery systems?

- Which of the three processes/explanatory factors—action-reaction, individuals, and institutions—examined in this chapter will be most useful in predicting the future? We can cite examples of all three at work today. Did China build nuclear weapons because the Soviet Union had them, and then India because China did, and then did Pakistan demonstrate their weapons because India had? Do we have most to fear from Saddam Hussein's apparently insatiable desire to make Iraq a nuclear state? Or do we have most to fear from a former Soviet—now Russian—defense establishment that will not give up its nuclear arsenal even though the economy and political structure of the country itself is showing increasing signs of strain?

NOTES

1. Fred Kaplan, *The Wizards of Armageddon* (New York: Simon & Schuster, 1983), pp. 9, 10.
2. Quoted in Lawrence Freedman, *The Evolution of Nuclear Strategy*, 2d ed. (New York: St. Martin's Press, 1989), p. 427.

3. Quoted in Kaplan, *Wizards of Armageddon*, p. 26.
4. Ibid., p. 27.
5. Raymond Aron, *The Century of Total War* (Garden City, NY: Doubleday and Company, 1954), p. 17.
6. Carl von Clausewitz, *On War*, ed. and trans. by Michael Howard and Peter Paret (Princeton, NJ: Princeton University Press, 1976), Bk. I, Chap. 1, pp. 75, 87. He further stated that "when whole communities go to war—the reason lies in some political situation, and the occasion is always due to some political objective; war, therefore, is an act of policy." "Policy then, will determine all military operations, and, insofar as their violent nature will admit, it will have a continuous influence on them. It is clear, consequently, that war is not a mere act of policy, but a true political instrument, a continuation of political activity by other means. What remains peculiar to war is simply the peculiar nature of its means." Clausewitz, *On War*, Bk. I, Chap. 1, pp. 86–87.
7. Clausewitz, *On War*, Bk. I, Chap. 1, p. 77.
8. Ibid., p. 90.
9. William H. McNeill, *The Pursuit of Power: Technology, Armed Force and Society since A.D. 1000* (Chicago, IL: University of Chicago Press, 1982), p. 318.
10. Correlli Barnett, *Swordbearers: Supreme Command in the World War* (Bloomington, IN: Indiana University Press, 1975, © 1963), p. 29.
11. Aron, *Century of Total War*, p. 19.
12. A. J. P. Taylor, *First World War: An Illustrated History* (New York: Putnam, 1963), p. 22.
13. U.S. Department of Defense, *Quadrennial Defense Review—May 1997*. Section V, p. 3.
14. Nationalism has proved to be a corrosive force as well; in multiethnic nations such as Yugoslavia, societies have fragmented into warring factions, each creating its own military force by drawing on the patriotism of its ethnic group.
15. Walter Millis, *Arms and Men: A Study in American Military History* (New York: Capricorn, 1987, © 1956).
16. Norman S. B. Gray, *A History of Agriculture in Europe and America* (New York: Crofts, 1929), p. 234.
17. U.S. Bureau of the Census, *Historical Statistics of the U.S., Colonial Times to 1970* (Washington, D.C.: U.S. Government Printing Office, 1975), p. 139.
18. Theodore Ropp, *War in the Modern World* (New York: Collier, 1962), p. 161.
19. Aron, *Century of Total War*, p. 21.
20. Taylor, *The First World War*, p. 279.
21. A pair of terms that is used in a very general sense in everyday conversation, but in a military context have very specific meanings: strategy and tactic. Traditionally "tactics" has been used to describe the handling of troops in contact with the enemy and "strategy" to mean the handling of troops not in contact with the enemy. More recently, strategy has been defined as "the art of distributing and applying military means to fulfill ends of policy." Basil H. Liddell Hart, *Strategy: The Indirect Approach* (London: Faber & Faber, 1968), p. 334.
22. Quoted in Freedman, *The Evolution of Nuclear Strategy*, p. 5.
23. Quoted in Edward Mead Earle, ed., *Makers of Modern Strategy: Military Thought from Machiavelli to Hitler* (Princeton, NJ: Princeton University Press, 1944), p. 112.
24. Although the Italian Guilo Douhet (1869–1930) is most quoted as the advocate of the development of strategic airpower, there is evidence that the same notion was occurring to many airmen and in many countries quite independently. Freedman, *Evolution of Nuclear Strategy*, p. 6.
25. R. J. Overy, *The Air War, 1939–1945* (New York: Stein and Day, 1980), p. 122.
26. Ibid., pp. 119–120.
27. Freedman, *The Evolution of Nuclear Strategy*, p. 12.
28. *The New Encyclopedia Britannica* (Chicago, IL: 1998) v. 29, p. 1023.
29. Anton W. DePorte, *Europe Between the Superpowers—The Enduring Balance*, 2d ed. (New Haven, CT: Yale University Press, 1984), p. 107.

30. Richard Pfau, *No Sacrifice Too Great: The Life of Lewis L. Strauss* (Charlottesville, VA: University Press of Virginia, 1984), pp. 94–95.
31. David Alan Rosenberg, "The Origins of Overkill: Nuclear Weapons and American Strategy, 1945 to 1960," *International Security* 7, no. 4 (spring 1983): 14–15.
32. Rosenberg, "The Origins of Overkill," pp. 14–15
33. The Joint Chiefs of Staff (JCS) is an organization within the Department of Defense under the supervision and control of the secretary of defense. The JCS are the primary military advisors to the president, the National Security Council, and the secretary of defense, and consist of the Chairman of the Joint Chiefs, the chief of staff of the Army, the chief of Naval Operations, and the chief of staff of the Air Force and on occasion the commandant of the Marine Corps. In addition, within the Department of Defense are the three military departments, the Department of the Army, the Navy (including the Marine Corps), and the Air Force, each of which has its own civilian secretary. B. Thomas Trout and James E. Harf, eds., *National Security Affairs: Theoretical Perspectives and Contemporary Issues* (New Brunswick, NJ: Transaction Books, 1982), pp. 169–170.
34. Omar N. Bradley and Clay Blair, *A General's Life: An Autobiography by General of the Army, Omar N. Bradley* (New York: Simon & Schuster, 1983), p. 490.
35. Quoted in Freedman, *The Evolution of Nuclear Strategy*, p. 48.
36. Herbert F. York, *The Advisors: Oppenheimer, Teller and the Superbomb* (San Francisco, CA: Freeman, 1976), p. 20.
37. Rosenberg, "Origins of Overkill," p. 16.
38. Quoted in Freedman, *The Evolution of Nuclear Strategy*, p. 55.
39. Rosenberg, "Origins of Overkill," p. 16.
40. See George Kennan, *Russia and the West under Lenin and Stalin* (Boston, MA: Little, Brown, 1961); Marshall Shulman, *Stalin's Foreign Policy Reappraised* (Cambridge, MA: Harvard University Press, 1963); and William Taubman, *Stalin's American Policy* (New York: W. W. Norton, 1982).
41. George Kennan, *The Nuclear Delusion: Soviet-American Relations in the Atomic Age* (New York: Pantheon, 1982), p. 32.
42. Lester Machta, "Finding the Site of the First Soviet Nuclear Test in 1919." *Bulletin of the American Meteorological Society*, 73, no. 11 (November 1992): 1797–1806.
43. Arthur Vandenberg, Jr., ed., *The Private Papers of Senator Vandenberg* (Boston, MA: Houghton Mifflin, 1952), p. 518.
44. Established by the National Security Act of 1947, the National Security Council (NSC) is the formal advisory body to the president on major national security issues. By law, the chairman of the NSC is the president and stated members include the vice-president and the secretaries of state and defense. In addition, there are a number of designated advisors to the NSC, including the director of Central Intelligence, the chairman of the Joint Chiefs of Staff, and the assistant to the president for National Security Affairs. Other members of the executive branch are invited to attend NSC meetings at the pleasure of the president. The staff of the NSC has varied in size and independence from time to time. Trout and Harf, *National Security Affairs*, p. 162.
45. U.S. Department of State. *Foreign Relations of the United States: 1948*, Part 2 (Washington, D.C.: U.S. Government Printing Office, 1976), pp. 624–628.
46. Robert S. Norris and William M. Arkin, "Nuclear Notebook: U.S. Weapons Secrets Revealed," *Bulletin of the Atomic Scientists*, March 1993, p. 48.
47. U.S. Department of State, *Foreign Relations of the United States: 1948*, Part 2 (Washington, D.C.: U.S. Government Printing Office, 1976), p. 236.
48. Dean Acheson, *Present at the Creation* (New York: W. W. Norton, 1969), p. 371.
49. U.S. Department of State, *Foreign Relations of the United States: 1950*, pp. 234–292.
50. Ibid.
51. Robert S. Norris and William M. Arkin, "Nuclear Notebook: U.S. Weapons Secrets Revealed," *Bulletin of the Atomic Scientists* (March 1993): 48. Robert S. Norris, Steven M.

Kosiak, and Stephen I. Schwartz, "Deploying the Bomb." In *Atomic Audit: The Costs and Consequences of U.S. Nuclear Weapons Since 1940*, ed. Stephen I. Schwartz (Washington, D.C.: Brookings Institution, 1998), pp. 189, 203–204.

52. Rosenberg, "Origins of Overkill," p. 30.
53. Ibid.
54. Gregg Herken, *Counsels of War* (New York: Knopf, 1985), p. 83.
55. Pfau, *No Sacrifice Too Great*, p. 114. Work on the theory of a fusion device had begun before the explosion of the first fission device at Los Alamos, but had not been given a very high priority and had not produced a workable device.
56. Quoted in Freedman, *The Evolution of Nuclear Strategy*, p. 66.
57. Ibid., p. 68.
58. U.S. Department of State, *Foreign Relations of the U.S. 1950*, pp. 506–511.
59. Richard Smoke, *National Security in the Nuclear Dilemma: Introduction to the American Experience* (New York: Random House, 1984), pp. 58–59.
60. Robert Oppenheimer was a major figure in the production of the first atomic bombs and although in future decisions regarding nuclear weapons developments the scientific community would be consulted and would have a major voice, it is interesting to note that by 1950 the scientific community no longer had the power to decide nuclear weapons policy.
61. In the 1950s and 1960s a considerable portion of the U.S. nuclear arsenal was committed to the destruction of Soviet air defenses to clear a path for aircraft on their way to attack strategic targets deep in Russia.
62. Herken, *Counsels of War*, p. 144.
63. U.S. Department of State, *Foreign Relations of the U.S.: 1950* (Washington, D.C.: U.S. Government Printing Office, 1977), pp. 281–283.
64. Kaplan, *The Wizards of Armageddon*, p. 139.
65. Ibid., p. 134.
66. Krishnan Guruswamy, "India Coalition Says Nuclear Weapons Are Part of Its Plan," *Boston Globe*, March 19, 1998, p. A2.
67. See Herbert Dinerstein, *War and the Soviet Union: Nuclear Weapons and the Revolution in Soviet Military and Political Thinking* (New York: Praeger, 1959).
68. Quoted in Dinerstein, *War and the Soviet Union*, pp. 127–128; emphasis supplied.
69. Rosenberg, "The Origins of Overkill," p. 49.
70. Walter A. McDougall, ... *The Heavens and the Earth: A Political History of the Space Age* (New York: Basic Books, 1985), p. 329; and William E. Burrows, *Deep Black: Space Espionage and National Security* (New York: Random House, 1986), pp. 110–111.
71. Burrows, *Deep Black*, pp. 67–68.
72. David Holloway, *Soviet Union and the Arms Race* (New Haven, CT: Yale University Press, 1983), pp. 23–24.
73. Lawrence Freedman, *The Evolution of Nuclear Strategy*, p. 86.
74. U.S. Department of State, *Foreign Relations of the United States: 1952–1954*, Part I (Washington, D.C.: U.S. Government Printing Office, 1984), p. 578.
75. Ibid., pp. 579–582.
76. Ibid., p. 581.
77. Freedman, *The Evolution of Nuclear Strategy*, p. 41.

5

SURVIVAL IN AN AGE OF NUCLEAR PLENTY

Imagine, Gentle Reader, that it is December 1960, John F. Kennedy has just been elected president of the United States and you, as a member of the Kennedy transition team, have been assigned the responsibility of briefing the president on the U.S. strategic nuclear arsenal and the options open to the president in a confrontation with the Soviet Union. Armed with a top secret clearance, you immerse yourself in the Air Force's nuclear war plans.

You learn that as the number of nuclear weapons in the American inventory increased through the 1950s, so did the number and size of the planning staffs, until finally in 1960 a Single Integrated Operational Plan (SIOP) integrating the strategic nuclear plans of all three services and their subordinate commands was created. The Strategic Air Command acted as agent of the Joint Chiefs of Staff in updating the plan each year, and so the first SIOP, SIOP-62 approved in December 1960, reflected the bias of SAC through the 1950s.

You are immediately aghast to discover that if the president ordered the use of the nation's strategic nuclear force, the SIOP committed the United States to launching the entire nuclear alert force at one time in a "Sunday Punch." There were no options open to the president for selective targeting or withholding attacks on Soviet allies, such as the People's Republic of China, that might not have joined in the Soviet action that provoked the U.S. strike.

You are equally dismayed to discover that three years ago a top-secret blue ribbon panel of the nation's top scientists, the Gaither Commission, had pointed out that the principal strategic nuclear delivery systems—the fleet of long-range bombers—is based on only a few bases in the United States and therefore is vulnerable to a Soviet first strike. In the ensuing three years, little progress had been made in replacing the bombers with missiles and the missiles that were in place, liquid-fueled missiles and the first short-ranged submarine-launched ballistic missiles, were of dubious reliability and themselves quite vulnerable.

You realize that the United States and the Soviet Union are like two scorpions in a bottle: Each can destroy the other in a moment but only at the cost of its own life.

The metaphor of two men, each hating the other, and both standing up to their waists in the same pool of gasoline and each with a package of matches comes to your mind. You realize the truth of the nuclear predicament: that because the bomb exists and because it is so very powerful, no real defense is possible. Because the United States has created a sizeable stockpile of nuclear weapons and delivery systems of reasonable effectiveness and because the Soviet Union was in the midst of doing the same, you realize that you are alive that morning only because the Soviet leadership had not chosen to annihilate the United States during the night. Your research showed you that there was nothing the United States could have done to prevent that annihilation.

You finally decide what you must tell the president:

- Given the vulnerability of the U.S. strategic force and the growing capability of the Soviet Union, very soon the president will find himself in a deadly dilemma: In any crisis that might end in war, the president will have to decide on very short notice and with very little hard information, whether to launch the U.S. nuclear striking force or risk losing it to a Soviet strike. Although the bombers can be recalled, the missiles, an increasingly important component of our strategic force, can not be—once launched, the United States would be irretrievably committed to nuclear Armageddon.
- Given the lack of nuclear options available to the president, the destructive power of even small-scale use of nuclear weapons, and the reduction in U.S. conventional arms, the United States would have difficulty defending itself and its allies against threats to their interests other than a full-scale attack. The United States was at risk of being sliced away, slice by slice like a salami, as the Soviet Union dismembered the United States and its allies through a series of attacks, each too small to justify a nuclear attack on the Soviet Union. And the United States also faced the risk that its allies would not believe the president would come to their aid in the event of a Soviet attack—that no U.S. president would risk a Soviet attack on Chicago to save Paris.

Thus you come to understand the central dilemmas of the first nuclear age:

- In a crisis, unless a nation's retaliatory force is absolutely indestructible, the nation's leadership will be faced with the *use it or lose it* dilemma—to delay attacking may permit an adversary to destroy the nation's nuclear arsenal and therefore disarm it.
- A nation would have difficulty preserving its or its allies interests in matters too small to risk a nuclear exchange.

In the previous chapters we traced the steps that led to the nuclear predicament: the invention of the bomb by U.S. and British scientists and engineers, aided by refugees from Hitler's Germany, driven by fear that Nazi Germany would build an atomic bomb first. And then, driven by reciprocal fears of each other's intentions, first the United States and then the Soviet Union had built large stockpiles of nuclear weapons of all sizes and characteristics and were investing considerable resources in developing delivery systems for those weapons. In this chapter, we will trace the search for immediate solutions to these dilemmas. We will see how the two superpowers learned to maintain the balance of terror so they could live with the bomb, and we will look at how states that have just acquired nuclear weapons may be confronting these same dilemmas.

The 1960s and 1970s were a time of increasing maturation in weapons systems, as both sides manufactured large inventories of weapons and developed increasingly numerous and accurate delivery systems. It was also a time of increasing sophistication in thinking about nuclear weapons, as both sides confronted the fact that a nuclear war between the two nations could mean the end of their societies, perhaps of human societies around the globe. An examination of the American and Soviet experiences with nuclear weapons will illuminate the issues we face in the second nuclear age, in which both the United States and Russia still possess vast arsenals of nuclear weapons, Britain, France, and China have potent arsenals of their own, and the other nuclear states, particularly India and Pakistan, are just beginning the journey toward their nuclear futures, to be joined perhaps by other states.

COMMAND AND CONTROL IN THE NUCLEAR AGE

Codifying the preparations for nuclear war into the American SIOP made clearer a dilemma that has concerned leaders of all the nuclear states since the dawn of the atomic era—the problem of the *command and control* of nuclear weapons. When the Sunday punch was *the* nuclear option, the president had an incentive to make sure that he and he alone could order such action. But giving the president a range of options also put a premium on control, for now there were expectations within the services that just some components of the military would be called upon to deliver a nuclear attack.

The American government has not relied solely on the expectation that subordinate officers would be unfailingly responsive to the chain of command. Today, most U.S. nuclear weapons are equipped with Permissive Action Links (PAL)—devices that require the use of a unique code to arm or to launch the weapons. Military personnel in possession of the weapons would be sent the code only when ordered to use the weapons. (Entering an incorrect code into the PAL automatically disables the weapon permanently.)

During the Cold War era, the famous locked briefcase, nicknamed the "Football," always accompanied the president—an omnipresent symbol of how close the world was then to Armageddon. This briefcase contained the *SIOP Decision Handbook*, which, along with the special codes carried by the president that positively identify him to the nuclear commanders who would actually disseminate the *Emergency Action Messages* ordering a nuclear strike, would enable the president to launch a nuclear strike. These authentication codes are still provided only to the president and his designated alternates or successors (known collectively as the National Command Authorities) and to certain specified senior military commanders.[1]

On the other hand, there are risks in concentrating control of nuclear weapons in too few hands, lest an enemy be tempted to try to eliminate the top command in a single strike (called *decapitation*) and thereby immobilize the nation's nuclear forces. Which senior commanders have the codes authorizing the launch of U.S. missiles has not been made public. Although the number is not large, it includes the SAC Airborne Command Post code-named "Looking Glass." "Looking Glass" is now only on runway alert, but for almost thirty years, from February 1961 to July 1990, one of a fleet of nine planes was always in the air with a battle staff aboard with the means to prepare and disseminate an Emergency Action Message, the coded orders to execute the nuclear war plan, and with the required authentication codes.[2] Therefore, even if the president were eliminated, a retaliatory strike could still be ordered by the surviving successor to the president or even by the commander of the Strategic Air Command.

By the end of the Cold War, a sizeable and expensive infrastructure had grown up to ensure, in the jargon of the nuclear age, "continuity of government." For example, by 1980, "there were reportedly more than seventy-five sites around" the United States, "all manned twenty-four hours a day."[3] During the Cold War years, captains of missile-carrying submarines (with the cooperation of their crews) had the capability to launch their missiles without the codes if all communication with their fleet commander were lost. Thus, any potential attacker would know that even if it eliminated the president and all his successors and the entire command structure of the military forces, it could still receive a retaliatory strike from the missiles on submarines.[4] (In March 1993 the secretary of defense directed that all submarine missiles would be equipped with Permissive Action Links by 1997;[5] in 1997 the missile submarine fleet was equipped with special safes containing a vital launch key that cannot be opened unless and until a combination unlocking code is received from a higher authority.[6])

The Soviet leadership recognized the same dilemma: how to ensure against unauthorized use of nuclear weapons but not prevent their use in a crisis. The Soviet Union kept notoriously tighter control of its weapons. Initially at least, the Soviet solution was even more extreme in safeguarding nuclear weapons against unauthorized use: The production and the custody of all nuclear devices was under control of the Committee for State Security (KGB) and the delivery vehicles (aircraft and missiles) were under military control. Over time, custody of the weapons was transferred to the Ministry of Defense, but even then, the weapons themselves remained under the direct control of the Soviet General Staff. Special nuclear security troops, perhaps under the control of the General Staff, were located at nuclear bases, and weapons deployed on launchers were fitted with coded use-control locks. The KGB and its successor in Russia, the FSB, provided security for nuclear storage installations and is the source of the use-control devices and their codes (just as the U.S. National Security Agency creates and distributes the codes for authenticating orders of the president and the codes for enabling use of nuclear weapons by the troops who have physical custody of the weapons).[7]

Equally well-recognized by Soviet leadership was the need to guarantee continuity of government; that is, the ability of the Soviet leadership to continue to control their armed forces and to order retaliatory nuclear strikes. The Soviet Union apparently invested hundreds of billions of dollars more than the United States in protecting its command and control network and the Russian government continues to spend money it really does not have on facilities the size of Washington, D.C. in the Yamantau Mountains and in the Urals, and on an underground subway network for rapid evacuation of military leaders from Moscow.[8]

The new nuclear states will have to confront these same dilemmas themselves: Without some sort of use-control devices, the government of India or Pakistan will have to (1) choose to keep the warheads themselves under separate custody, releasable only under authorization from a specific command authority, or (2) trust to the professionalism of the officers who have direct command over the warheads and the delivery systems. In Chapter 4, we saw that in the 1950s General LeMay, commander of the U.S. strategic bomber force, said that he would launch a preemptive strike against the Soviet Union if his intelligence told him the Soviets were massing for an attack against the United States. New nuclear states, such as Pakistan and India, will have to confront the same issues. It may be that the likelihood of commanders making such a decision on their own is fairly high *if* it appears that the opponent has the ability to cause massive devastation to one's society. On the other hand, if the opponent has few nuclear weapons, the incentive for the implementation of a "private doctrine of use" is likely to be low. But even more troubling are states such as Iran that aspire to acquire nuclear weapons but have substantial military establishments not under the effective control of the government. For example, the Iranian Pasdaran (Islamic Revolutionary Guard Corps) is independent of the military, acquires its own weapons, is in conflict with the Foreign Ministry, and is responsive to Iran's clerical leaders rather than the elected political leadership.[9]

And these states will have to face the other side of the dilemma as well: If control of all nuclear devices is vested in too few individuals, their adversaries may be tempted to attempt decapitation, that is, to try to eliminate the few leaders who do have control of the nuclear arsenal and thereby render the nuclear weapons useless.

MAINTAINING THE ABILITY TO RETALIATE

As the United States and the U.S.S.R. struggled with the dilemmas of ensuring command and control of their nuclear arsenals, they also faced a second issue: preserving their ability to retaliate after a nuclear attack.

When American strategists in the 1950s began to plan for the day when the Soviet Union acquired sufficient weapons and the necessary delivery systems to be able to stage a massive attack on the United States, they assumed that the Soviets would first attack American nuclear weapons and their delivery systems, destroying enough of them so that the United States could not wage nuclear war in retaliation; the Soviets would then be able to conduct, or threaten to conduct, a nuclear campaign against the United States (presumably its cities) and compel it to surrender. The key was the devastating first strike that would disarm the United States. The answer seemed to be to find ways to preserve the nuclear capabilities of the United States *even if* the Soviet Union were able to stage a first strike, and so preserve the ability to retaliate and carry the war to a successful conclusion.

In the decade of the 1950s, retaliation rested on the bomber fleet. The question then was how to ensure its survival. Fears of the Russian threat to U.S. retaliatory forces went in a new and more disturbing direction in October 1957 when the Soviet Union launched the first artificial earth satellite, Sputnik, with a second following a month later. The U.S. public quickly saw that a nation that had rockets powerful enough to put a satellite into orbit around the earth could use these same rockets to deliver nuclear weapons directly to the United States with no warning and no possibility of interception. Thus the Soviet Union had found a way to create nuclear symmetry with the United States—nuclear tipped missiles would make the United States defenseless.

A succession of public failures was to follow before the United States successfully placed a satellite into orbit three months later. This shock to the American public, long used to assuming U.S. scientific and technical superiority, surpassed even the shock felt in 1949 when the Soviet Union detonated their first nuclear device. The only question after Hiroshima was not whether but when the Soviet Union would have their own bomb, and the American public took some comfort from the revelation of Soviet spies in the U.S. and British atomic establishment. This allowed the public to believe that the Soviet Union simply stole the American bomb. The launching of a satellite into orbit around the earth before the United States was not so easily explained away. Even more frightening, if the Soviet Union could put a satellite in orbit before the United States, what other weapons might the Soviet Union have that the United States did not?

The worst fears of the American public, primed by years of portrayal of the Soviet Union bent on world domination, were suddenly realized. Eisenhower, aware of the gap between the successful launch of a single satellite and an intercontinental missile as a reliable weapon, publicly minimized the importance of the Soviet satellite. Sputnik was soon taken up as an issue by Democratic presidential aspirants, and so nuclear weapons policy became intertwined with U.S. domestic politics.[10]

Once the Soviets had demonstrated their missile capability with the orbiting of Sputnik, the American intelligence community pondered how soon the Soviets would have an operational missile force. They made the same sort of inflated prediction about Soviet strategic missile production that they had about Soviet bomber production. Air Force Intelligence predicted that the Soviet Union could build and deploy 500 intercontinental ballistic missiles (ICBMs) by 1961.[11]

What were the implications for the American retaliatory capability—the bomber fleet? SAC bombers were principally located on only forty-four bases, and two to six ICBMs would destroy the effectiveness of an air base.[12] It was therefore assumed by the most pessimistic (which of course included both Air Force and SAC Intelligence) that the Soviet Union could, and possibly would, launch a disarming first strike against the United States when it had some 250 operational missiles, completely destroying the U.S. strategic retaliatory capacity. The United States would then have no choice but to capitulate or be faced with the destruction of its cities by the remaining Soviet ICBMs and bombers.

This continual tendency to overstate Soviet capabilities was in some ways a legacy of Pearl Harbor and the adoption of "worst-case analysis" as a planning tool by the U.S. military after World War II. A legitimate methodology if responsibly used, worst-case analysis sought to establish as a baseline for planning the most damaging course of action that an enemy could take. Thus, in the 1950s the U.S. intelligence community sought to determine how many aircraft, missiles, or nuclear weapons the Soviet Union could build if they devoted the maximum possible resources and if their programs were perfectly successful. This worst case could then serve as an upper limit on U.S. measures to counter the enemy threat.

The problem arose with the second half of the task—risk assessment. Having once determined the worst possible case, it was then the task of the intelligence community to assess the probability of the worst case occurring and what the most likely case would be; political leadership could then make informed decisions about what resources the United States ought to commit to countering the threat. By confounding "worst case" with risk assessment, worst-case analysis became a tool for overstating the needs of a service or program in competition with other agencies. For example, the number of targets in the Soviet bloc whose destruction the Strategic Air Command claimed in 1950 was necessary to disrupt the Soviet ability to fight a war was 70 targets to be hit with 133 bombs. Ten years later, the number had been increased to 1,060 targets to be hit with 3,423 warheads, a tenfold increase in ten years.[13] And worst-case analysis became a tool for "covering your ass" for military staffs; no matter what calamity occurred, a resourceful staff could pull a memorandum out of their files predicting it.

How should the United States react? Just as news of Sputnik was reaching the public, the Gaither Commission presented their report to the president. Formally titled the "Security Resources Panel," the commission of scientists and industrialists had been appointed by President Eisenhower to examine the vulnerability of the United States to Soviet attack. Based on what they had seen of the SAC bomber force and Air Force Intelligence reports, they urged the building of a large offensive missile force, protected from attack by dispersal and hardened shelters.[14] For both sides, missiles now seemed to be the answer to the central question: How could one protect one's ability to retaliate?

BALLISTIC MISSILES

The guided missile revolutionized nuclear weaponry. Modern military rocketry emerged in Germany during World War II. The German Army and Air Force had independently (and competitively) developed two different guided missiles, the V-1 and V-2. Each employed a different approach to produce a strategic guided missile (a missile with sufficient range to reach beyond the battlefield to strike targets whose loss would impair an adversary's ability or its will to sustain the war effort).

The German Air Force's V-1 was essentially a pilotless aircraft that marked one path to a strategic missile that both the United States and Soviet Union explored immediately after World War II. After extensive experimentation, both cancelled their other programs to concentrate on the more promising but far more technologically demanding path blazed by the German Army's V-2. The V-2 was essentially a rocket-powered artillery shell that expended all of its energy in the initial part of its flight, reaching a great height above the earth and then falling to its target in a ballistic trajectory (a trajectory whose path is determined by the missile's initial velocity and the force of gravity). Attaining speeds as high as 15,000 miles per hour as it approached its target, the ballistic missile was at last a delivery system "that would always get through," as Stanley Baldwin had foretold twenty years earlier. (The V-1 could, like piloted craft, be shot down, and many were during the war.)

The German V-2 rocket did not have the range, accuracy, or payload capacity to constitute a decisive military weapon even though its successor, the A-10 transoceanic rocket, designed to reach New York from Germany, might have been operational by 1946.[15] Given the scarcity of atomic weapons and their great costs in the immediate postwar period, the judgment of Vannevar Bush that "one does not trust them to a highly complex, possibly erratic carrier of inherently low precision" was probably justified and therefore the early postwar decision to subordinate missiles to manned aircraft, most importantly jets, was probably appropriate at the time.[16] However, the justification became increasingly weak as technology advanced and the advantages of the ballistic missile became more obvious. As defensive measures such as radar-controlled surface-to-air antiaircraft missiles were improving in effectiveness, the ability of a manned conventional subsonic bomber to reach a defended target was becoming increasingly doubtful, while the ballistic missile was virtually invulnerable to enemy countermeasures.

The irony was that, in the United States, the Air Force had a monopoly over the strategic bombardment mission and showed great reluctance to develop the strategic missile. Air Force research on long-distance ballistic missiles was canceled in 1947 and was not to be revived until 1951, and then only at a minimal level,[17] principally because of resistance on the part of the Air Force leadership. The Air Force was committed to manned aircraft, particularly manned bombers, and refused to change. "Organizations that had been designed to advocate and maintain bombers continued to do so."[18]

Thus we see that bureaucratic interests help determine which weapons a nation has at its disposal. Organizations tend to pursue organizational goals, and policies are influenced to a greater or lesser degree by organizational and personal interests. "Before 1954, the Air Staff was interested in long-range strategic missiles only when they perceived a threat from an enemy or from a sister service. And of the two, threats from the Army or Navy seemed to motivate the Air Staff more."[19] The Air Staff had concluded that only manned bombers would be able to carry thermonuclear weapons, which were heavier than fission weapons, and only the Air Force was permitted to build bombers large enough for a strategic mission.

However, increasingly lighter and more powerful thermonuclear weapons proved successful in tests in 1954. These and other advances in weapons technology, as well as increasing intelligence evidence of Soviet missile development, made it impossible for the Air Staff to resist civilian pressure both to establish an organization outside normal Air Force channels to bring an operational ballistic missile to completion and to give this program a high enough priority to permit it to go ahead, in some cases at the cost of existing programs. By 1958 this effort produced an American ICBM, adding a missile component to the Strategic Air Command. But the bomber remained in the inventory as well.[20]

At the same time, in an attempt to gain a role in strategic weapons delivery, the Navy and the Army had joined together on the development of a liquid-fueled intermediate-range ballistic missile (1,500 mile range) for use on land or on board surface ships or submarines. The Navy realized that only submarines could approach close enough to the Soviet Union to launch their shorter-range missiles at strategic targets deep within the Soviet Union and quickly saw the unsuitability of liquid-fueled missiles on submarines. Therefore, in December 1956 the Navy severed its connection with the Army liquid-fuel project and began work on the solid-fueled Polaris, designed to be launched from submerged submarines.

Given the impetus of Sputnik, the Navy had no difficulty getting adequate funding to press development. As its development was not in competition with existing Navy weapon systems, there was little of the resistance within the Navy to the Polaris that ballistic missiles had engendered in the Air Force, where it threatened to make obsolete the hard-won skills, training, and experience of an entire officer corps of pilots, navigators, bombardiers, etc. On the contrary, the submarine-launched ballistic missile greatly enhanced the value of the Navy's other principal technological innovation of the post-World War II period—the nuclear-powered submarine. The nuclear-powered submarine could stay submerged at sea, practically limited only by the crew's psychological endurance. The solid-fueled Polaris missiles could be fired while the submarine remained submerged, aimed by an inertial navigation system that keeps very accurate track of the submarine's position. The combination of the two systems gave the United States (and later Russia, Britain, and France) what remains today virtually the absolute deterrent. There still is no way an attacker can be certain of simultaneously destroying a decisive number of the missile submarines that are deployed at sea, continually submerged and continually moving. (See Figure 5-1 on page 128.)

SHAPING THE NUCLEAR ARSENALS

As the previous history indicates, the present U.S. inventory of nuclear weapons was the result of the interplay of Soviet actions and U.S. service politics. Organizational politics have had much to do with determining the exact rate and sequence in which individual weapons systems have appeared and the precise form they have taken. It was

FIGURE 5-1
SLBM missile tubes along the back of an American Trident submarine, the USS Ohio. *Department of Defense*

clear through the late 1940s and into the mid-1950s that the military leadership of the Air Force had a very strong interest in preserving an Air Force based on manned aircraft, in whose use the Air Force leadership had considerable experience. The Navy had a very strong incentive to have a role in the delivery of strategic nuclear weapons during the period in which conventional forces were given very little support. Thus we see that these institutions in American society, the three military services and later the Department of Defense itself, were potent actors who were able to influence the nuclear future, and they remain so today.

The Soviet experience paralleled the American: Their response to U.S. weapons was conditioned by domestic politics. The existing service components of the Red Army wanted to fit nuclear weapons into their existing traditions. Communist party leader Nikita Khrushchev's answer was to create an entirely new military organization, Strategic Rocket Forces, to control the new technology. Thus a separate organization, whose leadership was carefully selected, was another means of exercising close political supervision over a very dangerous weapon.

The previous narrative also shows that there were a number of instances in which weapons innovations did not progress as rapidly or in all of the directions that were technologically and scientifically possible. Even though the "sweetness of technology" led scientists and engineers to define certain weapons innovations as possible and therefore generate pressure by the scientific community for their construction, the political environment finally is as important in determining what is accomplished as the scientific or technological environment. The Gaither Commission Report might have been another government report gathering dust on depository shelves had not Sputnik given the American public a dramatic demonstration of the Soviet Union's technological capability.

As the Cold War intensified, a war economy became a permanent feature in both countries. The defense establishments came to represent a major portion of government expenditures, and defense industries a significant segment of the total economy. For example, by 1985, U.S. expenditures for defense constituted 28 percent of its national budget and 7 percent of its Gross National Product.[21] This economy created special interests, both within and outside the military service, that had, and continue to have, a major stake in the continued development and procurement of more weapons. President Eisenhower in his farewell address in January 1961 warned the nation

> against the acquisition of unwarranted influence … by the military-industrial complex. The potential for the disastrous rise of misplaced power exists and will persist.… The conjunction of an immense military establishment and a large arms industry is new in the American experience. The total influence—economic, political and even spiritual—is felt in every city, every statehouse, every office of the federal government.[22]

In his memoirs, Eisenhower also warned against parochial political interests: "Each community in which a manufacturing plant or a military installation is located profits from the money spent and the jobs created in the area. This fact constantly presses on the community's political representatives—congressmen, senators, and others—to maintain the facility at maximum strength."[23]

The irony of the creation of a permanent war economy in the United States is that the continued buildup of U.S. military strength, particularly the development and acquisition of expensive and sophisticated weapons systems, also created an arms industry with considerable economic, and therefore political, power, able to exert considerable influence on decisions to acquire new weapons. Thus each purchase of new weapons by the U.S. government provided the arms industry with even more resources to influence future decisions to purchase more weapons. We see these forces continuing to work in the United States today as the aerospace industry continues its very effective lobbying campaign for missile defense funding, even though all previous missile defense programs have yielded nothing but expensive failures.[24]

The Soviet economy, even more so than the American economy, was geared toward the provision of military security. The Communist party leadership determined the spending priorities and the nature of the defense industry. Soviet missile systems were designed by a number of competing design bureaus, each of which had a strong stake in the adoption of its particular missile. By the early 1960s, there were four such bureaus touting their current wares, and each had attractive new missiles on the drawing boards. These design bureaus produced eleven different ICBMs, six of which became the mainstay of the Soviet strategic force, thus ensuring that all design bureaus stayed in business. The result was a Soviet missile force that included both very powerful missiles capable of carrying monstrously large warheads and missiles whose "throwweight" matched the standard American ground-based missile, the Minuteman. But there was an incentive to reward each of the competing design bureaus, and there was constant pressure on the political leadership to deploy something today—even inferior missiles—and to hope for something better tomorrow. The new organization, Strategic Rocket Forces, ensured that the other services could not reduce the importance of strategic missiles as long as the political leadership saw them as essential, but at the price of having an organization with a vested interest in more and better missiles.

Ironically, the missile era would begin on an uncertain note: only four SS-6s, the first Soviet ICBM, entered the Soviet arsenal in 1958.[25] Their deployment proved to be a mistake. This large, above-ground missile (with liquid propellants that could not be stored within the missile itself) could not be a viable deterrent to an American attack because of its vulnerability, nor could it execute a disarming strike aimed at the U.S. strategic forces because of its inaccuracy. But it could and certainly did help push the United States into a major missile-building program, which in three years would again create an imbalance in favor of the United States. The Soviets could not accept the imbalance. The nuclear arms race intensified, now centered around the delivery systems, and then in making the warheads more sophisticated—and numerous.

THE TRIAD EMERGES

By March 1958, both President Eisenhower and Congress had accepted ballistic missiles as the answer to the vulnerability of U.S. retaliatory forces, in spite of persistent opposition from the Air Force.[26] The issue became not whether but how soon and how many missiles would be built and deployed. The 1960 presidential campaign rang with Democratic party assertions that there was a missile gap that favored the Soviet Union. Kennedy would win the election in part on claims that the Republican administration had sacrificed national security on the altar of the balanced budget.[27] Eisenhower knew, from U-2 overflights over the Soviet Union and from radar observation of Soviet missile tests, that no missile gap existed, but that in fact the Soviet Union was deploying missiles at a considerably slower rate than the United States. Although the Eisenhower administration asserted that no missile gap existed, to reveal the evidence on which the assertion was based would have revealed to the Soviet Union the U.S. intelligence-gathering capability, and that was judged unwise.

By September 1961, according to CIA estimates, the Soviet Union had only 10 to 25 ICBMs deployed.[28] At that time, including intermediate range missiles in Europe and Turkey, the United States had some 223 missiles capable of reaching Soviet territory.[29] By the time of the Cuban missile crisis in October 1962, the Soviet Union had at most about 30 ICBMs, while the United States had about 200 ICBMs, including 20 solid-fuel Minuteman, deployed.[30] This count was somewhat misleading, as the reliability of these early missiles was woeful. For instance, only 4 percent to 20 percent of the U.S. first generation ICBMs were likely to reach their targets, or detonate if they did.[31]

When the Kennedy administration came into office, it discovered that the gap did not exist, and that there were plans to continue to increase the missile inventory. Thus the key questions became: How much is enough, and what is the optimum mix of strategic weapons or force structure? The mix adopted by the Kennedy administration created the U.S. strategic arsenal of today, known as the "Triad" (see Table 5-1 for the U.S. arsenal at its height). It is so named because it rests on three legs: land-based ICBMs buried in underground concrete silos to provide protection against attack, submarine-launched ballistic missiles (SLBMs), and manned bombers. The Soviets adopted a similar mix, although their bomber force was a smaller proportion.

The genesis of the American Triad may have been interservice rivalry. The Air Force, committed to the manned bomber, built the ICBM only to be sure the Army could not, and the Navy built the Polaris to ensure for itself a continued role in national defense at a time when all weapons but strategic nuclear weapons were being denigrated. Nonetheless, the virtues of having three different strategic nuclear weapons

TABLE 5-1 U.S. STRATEGIC FORCE STRUCTURE, 1990

TYPE	DESIGNATION	FIRST DEPLOYED	RANGE (MILES)	THROW WEIGHT (LB)	ACCURACY* (METERS)	LAUNCHERS DEPLOYED	WARHEADS PER LAUNCHER	WARHEADS DEPLOYED	YIELD PER WARHEAD
ICBM	Minuteman II	1966	7,000	1,600	370	450	1	450	1.2 Mt.
ICBM	Minuteman III	1970	9,200	2,200	220	200	3	600	170 Kt.
ICBM	MX	1986	7,000	7,000	100	50	10	500	300 or 400 Kt.
Subtotal						1,000		2,450	
SLBM	Poseidon C-3	1971	2,500	3,300	450	192	10	1,920	40 Kt.
SLBM	Trident C-4	1980	4,600	3,000+	450	384	8	3,072	100 Kt.
SLBM	Trident D-5	1989	6,500		200	48	8	384	300–475 Kt.
Subtotal						624		5,376	
Aircraft	B-52G/H	1959	7,500	45,000		39	Aircraft Weapons:		
	B-52G/H with cruise missiles	1981	7,500	45,000		172	ALCM	1,600	5–150 Kt.
	B-1B	1986	7,500	64,000		95	SRAM	1,100	170 Kt.
	FB-111	1969	3,000	37,500		32	BOMBS	1,800	LOW Kt.–9Mt.
Subtotal						338		4,500	
Total						1,962		12,326	

*Mean-missile distance: one-half of warheads will land within this distance of target.

Note: ALCM = Air-Launched Cruise Missile; SRAM = Short-Range (Air-Launched) Attack Missile

Sources: The Military Balance, 1990–91 (London: International Institute for Strategic Studies, 1990), pp. 216–217; World Armaments and Disarmament: SIPRI Yearbook 1990 (Oxford: Oxford University Press, 1990), p. 14.

delivery systems of very different characteristics came to be recognized. The Triad made the simultaneous destruction of all the U.S. retaliatory capability in a disarming first strike virtually impossible, and protected the country against any single technological breakthrough that would render the entire U.S. retaliatory force vulnerable.

In addition, each component of the Triad had particular advantages useful in certain situations. Land-based ICBMs were for decades the most accurate and the most quickly useable should the president require the option of a nuclear strike against a specific target. However, land-based ICBMs, in spite of increased "hardening" or reinforcing of the silos to withstand attack (Figure 5-2), would be increasingly vulnerable to a disarming first strike as an opponent developed its ICBM force, especially as missile accuracy improved. The submarine-launched ballistic missiles were an extremely invulnerable retaliatory force, as the possibility of an enemy simultaneously destroying all the missile-carrying submarines at sea was very remote: At the height of the Cold War, about twenty American subs were at sea at any one time, and perhaps ten Soviet subs. The submarines, however, were much more expensive to maintain, and submarine missiles were inherently less accurate than land-based missiles, and carried smaller warheads. In addition, communications with submarines are slower and less reliable than with land-based missile batteries.

Both long-range land-based bombers and, for the United States, short-ranged carrier-based naval aircraft could be assigned new targets in flight or even choose their own targets or they could be ordered to return to base without dropping their bombs. Once launched, ICBMs or SLBMs cannot be recalled or destroyed or rerouted in flight. Bombers could be kept on airborne alert during a crisis, a very invulnerable position for a brief time. On the other hand, manned bombers were becoming increasingly vulnerable to air defenses, to the point that their ability to penetrate the defended air space of a technologically sophisticated enemy was becoming very doubtful.

FIGURE 5-2
An MX ICBM emerges from its protected silo in a test firing. *Department of Defense*

This mix, offering flexibility and survivability, has become the standard—at least for relatively wealthy states. The triad, or its Soviet counterpart, served admirably both the United States and the Soviet Union, reassuring both in the recurring crises of the Cold War that each could wait to see events develop, secure in the knowledge that there was little risk that their nuclear arsenal could be destroyed by a single preemptive strike from the other. However, for new states now acquiring, or seeking to acquire, nuclear weapons, the Triad simply is not obtainable.

The seaborne leg of the Triad not only requires ready and secure access to the oceans but also demands a sophisticated naval establishment with long training in submarines. The Soviet Navy experienced considerable difficulty in maintaining its submarine fleet and the U.S. attempts to transfer even WWII-era diesel submarines to second-tier states such as Argentina and Turkey were a complete disaster.[32] Even the United Kingdom required substantial aid from the United States to develop its submarine-based nuclear retaliatory force and the history of the Soviet submarine force is marked with disaster after disaster.

Even maintaining an aircraft delivery system of sufficient robustness and reliability will challenge these aspiring states. And the paradox of the modern age for the newly acquiring states is that building nuclear weapons puts less demand on their industrial and technical infrastructure than does maintaining a reliable and secure delivery system. Even China and India, the most sophisticated industrial states of the recent nuclear arrivals, have had little success with their attempts to create an indigenous aviation or submarine building industry. China has repeatedly built unsuccessful submarines and India's indigenous aircraft industry has not been able to produce aircraft as capable as their regional rivals who rely on imported aircraft. For these reasons, land-based missiles, easily acquired from abroad and not requiring a large industrial base to maintain, are likely to be the delivery system new nuclear states would prefer.[33]

While missiles might be the preferred delivery system, the warheads manufactured by recent arrivals are neither compact enough to fit into a missile warhead nor rugged enough to survive launching on a missile. Years of testing and engineering development were needed before warheads reached the ruggedness and miniaturization needed for missile warheads—even after fifteen years of nuclear weapons development, only a quarter of the Polaris warheads were expected to detonate. Therefore, for the immediate future, recent nuclear states will most likely be forced to rely on aircraft for delivery, with their attendant problems.

Even the land-based leg of deterrence requires considerable land area to hide the launch vehicles, control facilities, storage bunkers, etc. Finally, the newest tier of nuclear states lacks the resources to support the elaborate edifice of delivery systems, sophisticated command and control mechanisms, and continuation of government structure that the triad requires.

Therefore, the newer nuclear weapons states are not likely to have the secure retaliatory capability that the triad provided. There is good reason to fear that in a crisis involving those states, the temptation to strike preemptively, rather than risk losing their entire arsenals, will be much greater than in U.S./Soviet crises of the past.[34]

If warheads can be made compact and rugged enough, there will be pressure in these states to go to missiles as the principal nuclear weapons delivery system as quickly as possible for cost-savings—the missiles themselves are easily obtainable from a host of willing arms suppliers and once in place, require substantially less upkeep than aircraft and, what may be even more important in third world economies, substantially less indigenous skilled manpower. But missiles in third world countries will bring with them the traditional host of problems:

- If based on fixed sites, missiles will be vulnerable, even though more accurate than mobile missiles. It is unlikely that the newly arrived nuclear states will have the resources to go as far as the United States and Soviets in hardening their missile sites, or to put in place effective communications and the remainder of the infrastructure missiles require.

- If mobile, then the missiles will be less vulnerable but less accurate—good for retaliation, less useful for a first strike. But this would perhaps make any nuclear exchange an exercise in purposeful destruction of cities and therefore very costly in civilian lives. However, it may be that major cities are far more central to the survival of the elites and government in the third world, even though destroying them is not likely to bring the people to their knees. Thus, threatened retaliation against cities may make deterrence work.

HOW RUGGED IS DETERRENCE?
VULNERABILITY AND DETERRENCE IN THE MISSILE AGE

It is well to keep in mind that, despite the accelerating arms race and the perception of the other as a mortal enemy, neither the United States nor the Soviet Union sought nuclear war with the other. Their wish to preserve the peace, however, had to reckon with the *fear* that the *other was* in fact willing to contemplate nuclear war. Thus both prepared to wage nuclear war if it were thrust on them by the other, yet at the time, each sought to persuade its opponent that there was no real likelihood that the opponent could benefit from starting a nuclear war. As indicated in Chapter 4, the condition of *deterrence* occurs when a state contemplating nuclear aggression determines that, even if it struck first, it would still suffer retaliation so devastating that there would be no possible gain to be had from initiating nuclear war.

Thus, for deterrence to work, the ability to retaliate must be apparent to any possible opponent, and this includes the ability of a nation's retaliatory forces to survive a disarming first strike. Some states, such as the United States, have intentionally made public the measures taken to ensure their ability to survive an attack. The key question that emerged in the 1950s concerning capability was how *vulnerable* was one's existing retaliatory force? As nuclear war was expected to be short, only the forces that were ready to retaliate at the time of the attack would be credible retaliatory threats. The watchword was this: Deterrence works if there is a credible retaliatory force—a retaliatory force that is certain to survive any attack.

In the American strategic debates of the 1950s, no one doubted that bombers were becoming increasingly vulnerable, but the question that was never resolved was whether this vulnerability made any difference—whether the vulnerability of the bombers significantly weakened deterrence. Behind these debates was the issue of whether or not one believed that the Soviet Union would ever deliberately initiate a nuclear war to achieve national purposes. There were those who could envision the Soviet Union's initiating a general nuclear war as a calculated act if the Soviet leadership felt that it could destroy a significant part of the U.S. retaliatory capacity. These individuals felt that deterrence was very delicate. In this light, effective deterrence depended on the continued increase of the U.S. nuclear striking force and continued efforts to increase the invulnerability of the U.S. retaliatory capacity.[35]

The other point of view was that no nation would ever deliberately initiate a general nuclear war as there was no possible end whose attainment would be worth the cost of the nuclear strike it could receive in retaliation even if the ability to retaliate were uncertain. This position held that deterrence *was* quite rugged and that only by miscalculation or in desperation could a general nuclear exchange ever occur. In this view, strenuous efforts to increase both force levels and invulnerability were wasted effort— or worse: Such efforts could be read by the opponent as a search to achieve a *first-strike capability*, that is the capability to destroy a rival's ability to retaliate.

We expect that this debate between those who see deterrence as delicate and those who see it as rugged will recur in the future. Deterrence rests on the perception that the other side has (or does not have) both the physical capability and the will to retaliate devastatingly against us. Perceptions are, by their nature, subjective, and so there can be no objective verification that deterrence is working. If the opponent is acting in a very restrained fashion, is this because deterrence is working, or because the opponent has no aggressive intentions? If the opponent is acting aggressively, is deterrence fragile, or is the opponent simply probing to determine what it can get away with, while having a deep respect for deterrence?

The debate is also fueled by differing interpretations of the role of uncertainty and risk in nuclear strategy. For instance, those who held that deterrence was quite rugged contended that unless an attacker could be positive it would destroy every bomber in the target's retaliatory force, it would not dare launch an attack. Because the bomb is so very powerful, if even a few bombers survived, they would do incalculable damage to the attacker's society. All that was necessary, therefore, to maintain deterrence was to create doubt in a potential attacker's mind that it could stage a surprise attack and emerge unscathed. That could be done with a modest nuclear arsenal. Meanwhile, the nation's foreign policy could seek to reduce tension with the rival and reach agreement on areas of mutual interest.

Those who held that deterrence was quite delicate contended that the opponent was controlled by leaders whose values differed so profoundly from their own leaders that the opponent's leaders must be absolutely convinced that they had no prospect of success for deterrence to be maintained. There were many in the United States who insisted Soviet leaders were just such—godless men who put no value on human life; there were many in the Soviet Union as well who contended that the western nations were unalterably committed to the destruction of the Soviet Union as a threat to capitalism everywhere. That meant an energetic build-up of nuclear weapons systems, and a continued demonstration of resoluteness to challenge the other. Tension was inevitable.

Watching the American debate from afar, the Soviet leadership saw an American elite divided into two camps: the sober-minded who recognized the military power of the Soviet Union and acted with circumspection, and the "mad" or reckless who seemed willing to march the world to the brink of a nuclear holocaust. The Soviet leadership prepared to cope with either type of leader, while hoping that the sober-minded would prevail. In any case, nuclear war was to be avoided; that was the fundamental requirement of the nuclear age. Washington, too, would come to have similar perceptions and hopes. Indeed, for much of the Cold War, these two nuclear states had similar views of each other and reacted in a similar manner.

Newly arrived nuclear states will have to confront this same question, but their dilemma is made more complicated by the radical disparity between opponents in the size of their respective nuclear arsenals and asymmetries in delivery systems. Consider the nuclear balance between India and China: Given India's substantial nuclear industry and strong technical base, India possesses or could quickly assemble from fissile material on hand at least 80 nuclear warheads. These warheads may not be small enough and sufficiently rugged to mount as a missile warhead, but the Indian Air Force has sufficient aircraft to deliver nuclear weapons to battle sites on India's borders, to enemy troops massing on its borders, or to any Pakistani city or into China's border regions. Given the size of China's nuclear arsenal—about 284 strategic warheads and about 150 tactical and theater weapons, China has little to fear from a disarming preemptive first strike from India and therefore has little incentive to preempt themselves. India, conversely, might fear a disarming strike from China in a crisis but given their limited delivery capability, could not launch a disarming strike; they would instead reserve their limited resources for use against Chinese troop concentrations near the India border or against a Chinese invasion force.

Pakistan, however, might look at a preemptive strike differently. The general assumption is that Pakistan has fissile material for 15 to 25 Hiroshima-style uranium fission bombs. Although Pakistan has been developing guided missiles with Chinese assistance, there is doubt that Pakistan's weapons would be small enough or robust enough to be delivered by missiles. However, the Pakistan Air Force does have aircraft capable of delivering weapons to targets in India, including many of India's major cities. Therefore, in a crisis, Pakistan might be tempted to launch a preemptive strike aimed at reducing their damage, if Pakistan thought an India strike was inevitable. In a crisis, it is not that one side benefits from striking first—rather that it fears it will be worse off if it does not strike.[36]

THE BALANCE OF TERROR

By the early 1960s, the leadership of the United States and the Soviet Union came to recognize that both countries were fast approaching a balance of terror in which the survival of each state completely depended on the leadership of the other state's forbearance, restraint, and—most vitally—perfect control of its nuclear forces. This condition was labeled *Mutual Assured Destruction*. Although coined by its critics, the new acronym of the age, MAD, captured the ambiguous relationship that existed between mature nuclear powers.

In the words of U.S. Secretary of Defense Robert McNamara, the basic objective of U.S. strategic military forces had become "to deter a deliberate nuclear attack upon the United States or its allies by maintaining at all times a clear and unmistakable ability to inflict an unacceptable degree of damage upon any aggressor, or combination of aggressors—even after absorbing a surprise first strike."[37] That ability would assure the destruction of any opponent; McNamara felt that assured destruction would be reached when surviving American forces could "destroy 20 percent to 33 percent of the Soviet population and 50 percent to 75 percent of the industrial capacity."[38]

At the same time, as the Soviet Union increased the survivability of its retaliatory forces by protecting its ICBMs in concrete underground silos and by dispersing its missiles in submarines at sea, McNamara's analysts realized that little could be done to protect the United States against intolerable damage. These analysts calculated that even if the Air Force was given the 10,000 Minuteman missiles they had lobbied for, a U.S. first strike aimed at the Soviet nuclear arsenal under the best of circumstances would leave the Soviet Union with roughly 100 ICBMs and 100 submarine-launched missiles. These 200 missiles could kill 50 million Americans, even if the United States embarked on building fallout shelters.[39] This number of dead was very close to the number of Russian dead that McNamara's analysts said would assure the destruction of Russia as a viable society.

With this realization, the leadership of the nuclear nations spent the remainder of the first nuclear age managing the mutual terror of MAD. They did this by managing the relations between the nuclear blocs with a range of confidence-building measures—unilateral or multilateral measures meant to reassure an opponent that its rival is not seeking an advantage by the sudden use of force—such as the hot line connecting Washington and Moscow, by a series of arms limitation treaties discussed in Chapter 8, and by managing very carefully their own arsenals. Not only did all the nuclear nations make sizeable investments in enhancing the survivability of their weapons and their delivery systems and ensuring continuity of government in the event of a nuclear exchange, but they also expended considerable effort in planning exactly how nuclear weapons might be used. Their argument was, paradoxically, that the readier they were to use nuclear weapons, the less likely an adversary would be to engage in acts of aggression that might lead to nuclear war. So the cost of living in a nuclear age was continual attention to controlling one's own weapons and in controlling, as far as possible, the behavior of other states.

In reviewing the range of diplomatic and military options available to the United States during the Berlin Crisis of 1961, Secretary of Defense McNamara informed the White House that existing military plans in case of trouble in Berlin assumed almost immediate resort to nuclear war. McGeorge Bundy, the president's national security advisor, had pointed out the dangerous rigidity of the strategic war plan of the time, calling for an all-out nuclear strike against the Soviet Union and its allies.[40] President Kennedy was aghast at the "nuclear option" he had—do nothing or commit mass murder, including the murder of innocent Soviet allies who might have chosen to stay out of the conflict. And, as the Soviets developed their own nuclear forces, America's policy meant its own inevitable suicide if it were to launch a nuclear attack on the Soviet Union. Kennedy insisted that he be provided with a range of options for the use of nuclear weapons as well. The Kennedy administration had sought "controlled responses and negotiating pauses." Four Major Attack Options (MAO) were added to the SIOP, as well as the options to withhold attacks from certain categories of targets, most notably Soviet cities. Even so, through the 1960s SAC consistently opposed providing options to the president, contending that multiple options would complicate their planning and introduce the risk of confusion and mistakes in the execution of their plans.[41]

HOW MUCH IS ENOUGH IN A BALANCE OF TERROR?

If the optimal mix of nuclear weapons seemed militarily as well as politically to have three components, the triad of land-based ballistic missiles, submarine-launched missiles, and manned bombers, the question then for the United States in the 1960s became one of numbers. The first task of Kennedy's new secretary of defense, Robert McNamara, was to determine exactly *how much was enough*. The numbers finally arrived at by McNamara were 1,000 land-based solid-fueled Minuteman, the 54 liquid-fueled Titan ICBMs previously deployed, 41 missile submarines, each carrying 16 missiles, and about 600 B-52s.[42] By 1967, the deployment of this force was more or less complete and these numbers remained largely unchanged throughout the Cold War.

As you might suspect, these numbers were in part a political decision negotiated between rival services and with an eye to an American public that had perceived the previous administration's program, about half as ambitious, as inadequate. But they were also based on the serious and systematic study of strategic doctrine for the employment of nuclear missiles that had been going on, both within and outside government, for some time. McNamara's staff had concluded that "beyond the level of around 400 1-megaton-equivalent delivered warheads would not significantly change the amount of damage inflicted." Doubling the number of delivered 1-megaton-equivalents would increase the destruction of Soviet industry by only 1 percent.[43]

The new nuclear states will face the same dilemmas but may solve them differently. China, a nuclear power now for over thirty years, has chosen to build far fewer weapons than it could have, given its resources, and, most significant, has chosen to build very few intercontinental delivery vehicles—only four to seven. This suggests that China's solution to the question "how much is enough" may be the solution often labeled "Minimum Deterrence": weapons enough to ensure that any state that launched a nuclear attack on China would suffer intolerable damage in return, but not enough weapons to provoke fear of a preemptive disarming Chinese attack on any major power. Other states, on the other hand, may have such severe resource constraints that they are simply unable to build more than a small number of weapons.

STRATEGIC DOCTRINE EMERGES

Strategic doctrine is not an empty set of theories about how war might be waged in some future, for, in fact, "strategies for possible wars are already inscribed in the guidance mechanisms of the missiles.... Nowadays nuclear warheads have names written on them: not of individuals ... but of cities and military targets for which they are intended.... The settings of all the missiles ... specify the latest theories about how the next big war is to be fought."[44] It is the choices made about doctrine that prescribe which weapons are to be acquired, how targets are to be selected, and how those targets are assigned to what weapons as part of what plan. And the adequacy of doctrine rests on the correctness of the assumptions that underlie it, many of which cannot be tested in advance—assumptions about what possible opponents will do in a crisis, about how weapons will actually perform in battle, and even about how one's own forces will behave under the stresses of a crisis or an actual nuclear exchange. So much of the preparations that nations have made to ensure nuclear peace rest on assumptions that must remain untested. As one critic observes "Relativity is almost as tricky as nuclear deterrence, but at least they don't roast your children alive if you flunk it."[45]

The strategic nuclear thinking that culminated under McNamara provided the first nuclear age with a vocabulary and a set of assertions about nuclear weapons that became the focal point of discussion, policy, and negotiation. While it is not clear if the second nuclear age (or the third) will produce its own vocabulary and assertions or continue to adopt the McNamara vision, any change will likely use these ideas as points for departure.

The discussion of strategic doctrine focused on certain key aspects of nuclear weapons:

1. *Weapons could be classified as either first- or second-strike weapons.* First-strike weapons were weapons that could not expect to survive an enemy attack. Their only sure role

in nuclear planning was therefore to strike first. The best way to ensure deterrence would be to have a large number of second-strike weapons. A nuclear arsenal of first-strike weapons, on the other hand, was a very dangerous one for deterrence, as the only doctrine that made sense was one of preventive war or preemption.

A weapon's status could change with time and advances in technology. Missiles buried in silos initially were second-strike weapons. However, as missile accuracy improved, and satellite reconnaissance pinpointed the location of all Soviet and American silo-based ICBMs, such weapons were very unlikely to survive a nuclear attack; they became first-strike weapons. On the other hand, a fleet of ballistic missile submarines, cruising silently deep beneath the surface of the ocean, would be—and still are—very difficult to destroy, and would therefore be quite effective as second-strike weapons. (See Table 5-2.)

2. *Nuclear weapons can be classified as counterforce and countervalue weapons.* Counterforce weapons are those best suited for the destruction of an enemy's military forces. Typically, counterforce weapons must be very accurate because military targets, particularly an enemy's strategic nuclear striking forces and their command and control facilities, are likely to be small in size and well-protected, buried in the earth or protected by concrete structures. Only a warhead detonated very close to such a target is likely to damage it significantly. In addition, a weapon intended to destroy counterforce targets must have a relatively brief flight time; otherwise an enemy would have sufficient time to launch its missiles or fly off its bombers.

Countervalue weapons are best suited for use against what an enemy values—a euphemism for an enemy's people, economic base, and all the networks that make a society. In this century, those values are predominantly found in urban areas, so countervalue weapons are essentially weapons targeted against cities. Such weapons can be relatively inaccurate and their flight time is irrelevant. Cities do not move, and it makes little difference whether a multimegaton weapon with a destructive radius of twenty miles lands in the exact center of a city.

3. *Counterforce weapons are likely to be first-strike weapons; countervalue weapons would most likely be second-strike weapons.* Counterforce weapons thus strain deterrence, making it more delicate; countervalue weapons make deterrence more rugged.

4. *With different types of weapons, a nation can choose the targeting strategy that seems to offer the greatest security.* Each orientation retains the goal of deterring war-initiation by the opponent. Four basic orientations stand out:

Sunday punch

Flexible response

Assured destruction and the avoidance of war

Prevailing in a nuclear war

We need to examine each orientation, for they reflect the range of choices available to nuclear-armed states that wish to deter a nuclear attack on themselves or their allies. Arrayed in this order, they also describe the evolution in American thinking about nuclear weapons.

The *Sunday Punch* orientation prescribes that at the start of the nuclear war, all weapons will be brought to bear as quickly as possible on the opponent. This was the basic doctrine through the 1950s and was enshrined in the first SIOPs that so disturbed President Kennedy. Such a strategy could be both counterforce and countervalue, first- or second-strike, but in actuality, the American plan was essentially first-strike (preemption), countervalue. Fearing such a *Sunday Punch*, an enemy nation would be deterred from aggression.

The *Flexible Response* approach represented McNamara's first effort to provide the

TABLE 5-2   STRATEGIC IMPLICATIONS OF WEAPON CHARACTERISTICS

CHARACTERISTICS	MANNED BOMBER	MINUTEMAN II	POSEIDON	MINUTEMAN III WITH MIRV	MX	CRUISE	TRIDENT II
Survivability	Short run: low Inter.: mod. Long: low	Poor	Very high	Poor	Poor	High	Extremely high
Penetrability* Yield	Low High (4 Mt.)	High Moderate (1 to 2 Mt.)	Very high Low (400 Kt.)	Very high Moderate (1 Mt.)	Very high High (3.5 Mt.)	Fairly high Low (200 Kt.)	Very high High (5 Mt.)
Accuracy (MMD)**	Moderate (1,500 ft.)	Moderate (700–1,500 ft.)	Moderate (1,500 ft.)	Good (730 ft.)	Good (300 ft.)	Good (300 ft.)	Fairly good (425 ft.)
Command control	Good	Prelaunch: excellent Postlaunch: none	Fair or less	Prelaunch: excellent Postlaunch: none	Prelaunch: excellent Postlaunch: none	Good	Fair or less
Use: First strike/ second strike	Second strike	Second strike	Second strike	First or second strike	First strike	Second strike	In crisis: second strike Preemptive: first strike
Targeting	Countervalue (citybusting)	Countervalue	Countervalue	Countervalue or counterforce	Counterforce	Countervalue	Counterforce or countervalue
Effects on stability	Moderately stabilizing	Stabilizing	Very stabilizing	Slightly destabilizing	Strongly destabilizing	Stabilizing	Stabilizing and destabilizing

*Penetrability: Ability of weapon to penetrate enemies' defenses.

**MMD: Mean-miss distance: One-half of warheads will land within this distance of target.

140

National Command Authority (the president or his constitutional successor, abbreviated NCA) with more options to respond to provocation or aggression than the single one of the "Sunday punch."[46] Flexible response was an explicit counterforce strategy, predicated on "city avoidance." It sought a means of limiting damage to the United States.[47] The principal objective in the event of war would be "the destruction of the enemy's military forces, not of his civilian population." By striking only at military forces, avoiding civilian casualties while maintaining a reserve sufficient to destroy the adversary's cities, "we are giving a possible opponent the strongest possible incentive to refrain from striking our own cities."[48] Thus an enemy's population would be maintained as hostages to discourage an enemy from attacking the U.S. population, while at the same time demonstrating U.S. ability to destroy the enemy's cities if it wished; war would become a demonstration of capacity to hurt. War would be terminated by bargaining, with the United States having the upper hand—the enemy's nuclear weapons destroyed, its cities vulnerable to incineration. But if the enemy saw *in advance* that at any level of nuclear use that it might contemplate, the United States could destroy its remaining nuclear weapons and then threaten the enemy's cities with devastation, the enemy would be deterred from contemplating nuclear war.

Although a policy of flexible response/"city avoidance" was attractive to McNamara for a brief period of time, its problems quickly became apparent. "City avoidance" required a considerable counterforce capability. Such a large arsenal of highly accurate nuclear weapons must make an enemy extremely nervous, for if these weapons were launched in a bolt from the blue, they could destroy the enemy's nuclear weapons, leaving the enemy open to nuclear blackmail. An enemy now must consider preemption if there is any sign that a bolt from the blue is in the offing, or to launch its own bolt from the blue. Deterrence would become very fragile indeed.

Moreover, McNamara's analysts calculated that even a limited nuclear war, or one in which both sides deliberately refrained from striking the other's cities, would still entail loss of life on an unprecedented scale (from fallout in nearby cities or downwind from military targets and from near misses), thereby making the effect practically indistinguishable from an unlimited nuclear exchange. And finally, as the Soviet Union increased the survivability of its retaliatory forces by protecting its ICBMs in concrete underground silos and by dispersing its missiles in submarines at sea, McNamara's analysts realized counterforce strategy would do little to protect the United States against intolerable damage.

These second thoughts led to what would become the principal nuclear strategy for the next twenty years, *Assured Destruction* and the avoidance of war. After less than two years in office, McNamara insisted that the basic objective of U.S. strategic military forces was "to deter a deliberate nuclear attack upon the United States or its allies by maintaining at all times a clear and unmistakable ability to inflict an unacceptable degree of damage upon any aggressor, or combination of aggressors—even after absorbing a surprise first strike."[49] That ability would assure the destruction of the opponent; as we discussed earlier, McNamara felt that assured destruction would be reached when surviving American forces could "destroy 20 percent to 33 percent of the Soviet population and 50 percent to 75 percent of the industrial capacity."[50]

MacNamara's view at the time, confirmed by subsequent Soviet actions, was that once the Soviets reached a similar assured destruction capability—creating the condition of *Mutual Assured Destruction* (MAD)—and adopted the strategic view that the only nuclear capability that mattered was the ability to assure the destruction of an enemy's society in a retaliatory second strike, both sides would have adopted a symmetrical military doctrine that would not be threatening. MAD did not call for preemption in order to work, nor encourage the deployment of first-strike weapons, and would make for a very effective mutual deterrence. *The only use then that nuclear weapons would have would be to deter an attack.*

WAR FIGHTING AND THE EVOLUTION OF SOVIET AND AMERICAN DOCTRINE

Would the Soviet doctrinal evolution carry them as well to a mutual assured destruction position? Is that likely to be the trajectory for all states who have the resources to fund a relatively large and sophisticated nuclear arsenal? Recall that one needs a survivable second-strike capability of sufficient size to put a large portion of an enemy's society at risk. Secretary McNamara, pressed by the Air Force for 10,000 missiles, was able to get acquiescence that a force of about 1000 ICBMS, 600 strategic bombers, and 600 submarine-launched ballistic missiles would be an assured destruction force. That was probably in excess of what was needed, but it was impossible to say by how much. Let us assume that for physically large, populous states such as the United States and the Soviet Union (or today's Russia), these are still reasonable figures.

It would take the Soviet Union until the middle of the 1970s to match the U.S. nuclear delivery capability. In the meantime, their doctrine lagged behind, remaining more firmly rooted in war-fighting—that is, preparing to use nuclear weapons to defeat the opponent and prevail, no matter what the opponent chose to do. A war-fighting orientation puts a premium on preemption, which remained the preferred Soviet use of nuclear weapons. And when it became clear that the Soviet Union could achieve parity in nuclear weapons, the war-fighting orientation, it was feared, would encourage an attempt to achieve superiority over the United States in nuclear weapons. In this view of deterrence, having more and better nuclear weapons and delivery systems seemed to be what was needed to deter war and, if deterrence failed, to prevail in a nuclear war.

Thus Soviet doctrine in practice furnished the fourth strategic doctrine, differing significantly from the MAD doctrine, *achieving superiority in order to win a nuclear war and thus deter an opponent for beginning such a war*, called in the shorthand of the nuclear age, a *prevailing strategy*.

As time went on, however, Soviet political leadership increasingly gravitated toward the view that nuclear weapons existed to preserve the peace. Communist Party Secretary Leonid Brezhnev declared emphatically that "it is dangerous madness ... to count on victory in a nuclear war." "I will add," the General Secretary said in an interview, "that only he who has decided to commit suicide can start a nuclear war in the hope of emerging victorious from it. Whatever strength the attacker may have and whatever means of starting a nuclear war he may choose, he will not achieve his aims. Retaliation is unavoidable. That is our essential point of view."[51] Brezhnev understood that the Soviet Union should seek "equal security" rather than superiority. The Soviets were therefore coming to recognize MAD.

The ambiguity in Soviet nuclear doctrine was matched in 1981 when Ronald Reagan came to office in the United States. The new administration set the mutual assured destruction doctrine aside, asserting that a war-fighting doctrine was more effective means of deterring nuclear war. The critics of assured destruction had long asserted that assured destruction was not a credible threat as it represented a suicide pact. These critics contended that, in a crisis, an adversary simply would not believe that the United States would launch a full-scale retaliatory attack against the adversary's society, particularly if the provocation was less than a full-scale attack against the U.S. homeland. The U.S. leaders would realize that this would mean the destruction of U.S. society by the adversary's surviving nuclear forces. According to these critics, an adversary would "nibble away" at U.S. interests while holding the U.S. cities and population hostage to countervalue full-scale strikes.

While the Reagan administration mounted a full-scale assault on the idea of deterrence through assured destruction, earlier political leaders had already modified the McNamara formulation. Since the first SIOP went into effect in 1960, there has been a continuing effort to make nuclear weapons more "useable." These efforts have been driven by the twin, and often incompatible, goals of increasing the credibility of deterrence by making possible small discrete strikes and of limiting damage to the United States by increasing the capacity to destroy military resources as a hedge against the failure of deterrence. Such reformulations reflected four basic factors influencing American nuclear planning:

1. To some, it seemed unreasonable to devote nuclear weapons almost completely to the task of preventing a massive attack against the United States. McNamara's original flexible response doctrine was more appropriate. Secretary of Defense James Schlesinger in 1974, for instance, while keeping assured destruction as the bedrock of American policy, approved changes in targeting doctrine for U.S. nuclear forces, codified in National Security Decision Memorandum 242 (NSDM-242), to make possible a range of nuclear options, including smaller strikes, which would be essentially counterforce rather than countervalue, that is, targeted against an enemy's nuclear forces rather than an enemy's civilian population. Schlesinger hoped that such options would allow the United States to attempt to limit damage in case of a less than total attack.

2. There is a chronic pressure to have nuclear weapons help achieve foreign policy goals, a point we will consider in the next chapter. Schlesinger's goal was to restore the sense of uncertainty in Soviet leaders that McNamara had sought to eliminate. To deter the Soviet Union from provocative acts, Schlesinger wished the Soviet leaders to be uncertain whether the United States would respond to a provocation with a limited use of nuclear weapons. McNamara, conversely, had sought to assure the Soviet Union that the United States would not use nuclear weapons except in response to a nuclear attack on the American homeland or Western Europe. He wished to reduce Soviet fears of a U.S. surprise attack and thus reduce the risk of a Soviet preemptive attack. This tension between flexible response and assured destruction is likely to continue, leading to variations in nuclear doctrine across time and will certainly plague newly arrived nuclear states as they work toward defining their own doctrines for the use of their own nuclear weapons.

3. As new nuclear states emerge, the nuclear threat they manifest toward the United States (or Russia) is not massive damage to the homeland, but injury to American interests abroad. How can such threats be deterred with nuclear weapons? Is threatening to destroy those societies a credible threat, or does the United States need the ability to use (and to threaten to use) limited nuclear strikes? Schlesinger felt that with flexible response the United States would be better able to deal with such contingencies "as accidental acts, the escalation of conventional conflicts, a challenge to a nuclear test of wills by ill-informed or cornered and desperate leaders involving the nuclear equivalent of shots across the bow."

4. A nuclear power's allies look to that power's nuclear arsenal for their own protection. The fear that a U.S. president would back down in a confrontation not involving an attack on the American homeland, rather than risk a nuclear exchange, was especially worrisome to the U.S. European allies. They feared that in a showdown with the Soviet Union the president of the United States "would not trade Chicago for Paris" and would let Europe fall to a Russian invasion rather than risk a full-scale nuclear attack on the American homeland. This problem of *extended deterrence* (using the threat of nuclear retaliation to deter an attack on one's allies as well as deterring an attack on the homeland) vexed U.S. relations with the NATO countries (and, in 1961–1962, Soviet relations with Cuba). The NATO allies responded in a predictable manner: Some wanted an increase in the number of U.S. troops and U.S. nuclear weapons stationed in Europe. The troops' role was not so much to block a Soviet advance into Western Europe but to be a tripwire to force the United States to employ its nuclear arsenal if Western Europe were invaded.[52] Others (Britain and France) sought to maintain an independent nuclear retaliatory capability.

Flexible response strategies rest on the assumption that nuclear war can be controlled. But can a nuclear war remain limited, not escalating to the point of a massive destruction of each other's cities? This is a question of *intrawar deterrence*. The proponents of intrawar deterrence contend that as long as both sides refrained from attacking their adversary's population, the threat of an attack on the enemy's cities would deter the enemy from attacking one's own cities, even while nuclear weapons are being used on the battlefield or against counter-force targets deep within a country. To the advocates of intrawar deterrence, deterrence does not end when the first bomb goes off.[53] Nuclear war, in this view, was controllable, limitable, and most important, could be ended short of full-scale exchange destroying both societies. It might even end with some political advantage to one of the combatants.

If this were possible, a nuclear-armed state needed to be ready to wage nuclear war. Without that readiness, its opponent might be tempted to stage limited nuclear strikes (or massive conventional attacks) to impose its will upon the state (or its allies), knowing that the state would not dare escalate to attacks on cities because that would be suicide. Thus, from this perspective, deterrence rested upon a state's ability to convince a would-be aggressor that no matter what level of war it chose, the state could match or even defeat the aggressor at that level, without having to escalate to a higher level of nuclear use.

The culmination of this strategic thinking came in the Reagan-Bush SIOPs, but as we have said, there has been an evolving attempt to have both assured destruction and flexible response as options, and to have both serve the cause of deterrence. Planners were guided by a series of presidential directives signed by Presidents Nixon, Carter, and Reagan, and by Nuclear Weapons Employment Policy documents (NUWEP) signed by their respective secretaries of defense. Nixon in 1974 directed the development of a capacity to conduct "selected nuclear operations," including the waging of regional wars. He authorized the creation of a Strategic Reserve Force of weapons to be withheld from an initial nuclear exchange.

In 1980 President Carter approved Presidential Directive 59, which set as the center of U.S. policy a *countervailing strategy*, defined as a strategy that denied an enemy the possibility of winning a nuclear war.[54] The key to successfully denying victory to the enemy according to PD-59 would be the destruction of the Soviet political leadership's control of the Soviet Union and the Soviet military leadership's control of its military forces. Thus PD-59 directed the U.S. armed forces to prepare for fighting a prolonged but limited nuclear war, targeting what "the Soviet leadership values most—its military forces and its own ability to maintain control after a war starts."[55] The ability to fight an all-out war would be maintained by a "secure strategic reserve"—invulnerable missiles that would be withheld in the early stages of the war. Implicit in this is the assumption that the threat of use of this "secure strategic reserve" against Soviet cities would deter the Soviet Union from attacking U.S. cities. The resulting SIOP added 5,000 leadership targets to the National Strategic Targeting Data Base (NSTDB), which had doubled in the preceding five years from 25,000 targets to 50,000.

In 1981 President Reagan signed National Security Decision Directive 13, which set the goal of "prevailing" in a protracted nuclear war of up to 180 days. This assumed that the Soviet Union would only be deterred if they feared that war would be lost, rather than just stalemated, as Carter's countervailing strategy implied. In the succeeding eight years, the SIOP went through six revisions in response to almost yearly NUWEPs promulgated by Secretary of Defense Weinberger, which gave a much greater emphasis to destroying the Soviet political and military command and control system and to attacking the new Soviet capabilities including mobile missile and command systems. President Reagan described the policy guiding these changes by saying that "Our targeting policy ... places at risk those political entities the Soviet leadership values most: the mechanisms for ensuring survival of the Communist Party and its leadership cadres, and for retention of the Party's control over the Soviet and Soviet Bloc peoples."[56]

This directive remained in force through the Bush presidency, increasingly out of touch with the political realities of the early 1990s. At a time when Soviet control over their former Warsaw Pact client states had disappeared and the Soviet leadership was seeking a reduction in arms expenditures and a normalization of relations with the United States, a SIOP that threatened that leadership and set the very expensive and probably unobtainable goals of locating and destroying mobile Soviet weapons and Soviet leadership seemed "not only wasteful but dangerously destabilizing because it increases the incentive to strike first."[57]

CRITICS OF FLEXIBLE RESPONSE/WAR WAGING

The war-waging orientation claimed that assured destruction alone was inadequate. It might deter an all-out attack, but it was insufficient to deter less extensive nuclear use; indeed, it might encourage such use. (President Reagan also argued that it was immoral, a point we examine in Chapter 9.) But a war-waging doctrine had its severe critics as well. These points were central to their analysis:

- Nuclear war could not be controlled. Once nuclear weapons start exploding, escalation to total war was extremely likely.
- If a nation's leaders believed nuclear war could be controlled, those leaders would be more likely to resort to nuclear weapons.
- A war-fighting doctrine has to emphasize counterforce weapons, raising fears in the rival's mind that the state would attempt a bolt from the blue, or, at the least, preemption in times of crisis, or, short of this, fears that the state might use its first-strike capability to coerce its rival.
- There would be pressure to forget that the primary objective of nuclear strategy was to avoid wars, not to fight them.

To the critics, the war-fighting doctrine jeopardized deterrence, thus increasing the peril for the nuclear nations and the world. McGeorge Bundy (who had been President Kennedy's assistant for national security affairs) speaking in reference to those who seriously considered fighting a nuclear war asserted:

> They can assume that the loss of dozens of great cities is somehow a real choice for sane men. They are in an unreal world. In the real world of real political leaders—whether here or in the Soviet Union—a decision that would bring even one hydrogen bomb on one city of one's own country would be recognized in advance as a catastrophic blunder; ten bombs on ten cities would be a disaster beyond history; and a hundred bombs on a hundred cities are unthinkable. Yet this unthinkable level of human incineration is the least that could be expected by either side in response to any first strike in the next ten years, no matter what happens to weapons systems in the meantime.[58]

The *experience* of the first nuclear age is, unfortunately, very ambiguous. Neither the established nuclear nations nor the new nuclear aspirant have final answers to two critical questions:

1. *Does deterrence actually work?* We have no empirical evidence that any nuclear nation from the beginning of the nuclear era through the dissolution of the Soviet Union seriously contemplated using nuclear weapons against another nuclear state, but stayed its hand for fear of the second-strike retaliation it would receive. If there was never a test of deterrence, we cannot conclude that it does work.
2. *If deterrence does work, what makes it work?* Is it a strategic doctrine that emphasizes assured destruction, or one that emphasizes flexible response/war-fighting? If the latter, is a *denial* capability (that is, a capability to deny an enemy any benefit from an attack) sufficient, or must one strive for a *winning* capability? Is it a countervailing or a prevailing strategy? The variation in the doctrines of the two major nuclear powers across time makes it difficult to know what would work best.

TECHNOLOGY'S IMPACT ON DOCTRINE

We have emphasized to this point that the debate over doctrine is a function of the powerfulness of the weapons, an acceptance—at least in a general way—that nuclear wars are not to be fought, and an uncertainty about how to make deterrence work. That is, the changes in doctrine reflected the attempt to devise ideas that could make sense out of the unfathomable, ideas that could provide some coherence to public policy. At the same time politics can play a crucial role. Kennedy early recognized the power of the perceived "missile gap" after Sputnik as an issue with which to defeat the Republicans; Reagan and the Republicans in turn wanted a political issue with which to defeat the Carter administration; Khrushchev sought an edge against Malenkov in the struggle for power in the Soviet Communist party. Organizational interests and perspectives also encourage doctrinal change, as in McNamara's attempt to head off an Air Force request for thousands of missiles.

Also driving doctrinal change—and playing a role in changing ideas, politics, and organizational interests—is the technology of the weapons and delivery systems. For instance, in the early years of the Kennedy administration, nuclear weapons could only be aimed effectively against cities, rather than military (counterforce) targets. Deterrence based on assured destruction better reflected the technological capability of the time.

But very quickly, technological advances made precise counterforce strikes technically possible. The increasing *accuracy* of missiles made possible relatively precise attacks on military targets: missile sites, factories producing weapons, transportation nodes, and buildings in which leaders might be working. For example, accuracy improved from an average-miss distance of 3,000 feet for the Titan missile first deployed in 1963 to less than 400 feet average-miss distance of the MX first deployed in 1986.[59] As accuracy improved, warheads shrunk in size—both in physical size and in explosive power. Increasing accuracy made ever-smaller-yield warheads able to achieve the same destructive effect against enemy military targets, thus reducing the amount of "collateral damage"—the American euphemism for the destruction of civilian population. For instance, reducing the average-miss distance by 50 percent from 4,000 to 2,000 feet decreased by ten times the explosive power needed to destroy a hardened target such as a missile silo.[60] For another example, the Titan missile carried a warhead with a yield of 9 megatons when deployed in 1963 (incidentally weighing over 8,000 pounds); the warheads on the Minuteman III and the MX/Peacekeeper, the only ground-based ICBMs currently deployed by the United States, carry warheads with yields between 300 and 475 kilotons, weighing less than 800 pounds each.[61] (The Minuteman III carries three warheads on each missile; the MX can carry up to twelve warheads per missile but by agreement carry fewer.)

Strategic accuracy demands, however, precise knowledge of the location of distant targets. Moreover, the task of fighting a nuclear war was made more difficult by the increase in the portion of an opponent's strategic force that was mobile missiles and mobile command and control facilities. Considerable effort was expended to develop sensors to locate these mobile forces, including the Stealth successors to the U-2 and SR-71 reconnaissance aircraft and a new series of signal intelligence, photographic, and radar-imaging reconnaissance satellites. One of these, the KH-12, reportedly has a resolution of under three inches, good enough to "read license plates" from space, and, in theory, can get real-time pictures of any spot on earth within twenty minutes of the transmission of the order.[62] Even with these, however, considerable doubt remained as to whether locating and destroying mobile targets during a nuclear exchange is achievable. Satellites would have to bear a major burden in locating these targets, and satellites are much better suited for the task for which they were designed, strategic reconnaissance in peacetime, rather than for tactical reconnaissance during a nuclear exchange. Satellites are vulnerable to attack themselves, and their communications are even more vulnerable. Although much progress was made in automating the retargeting of strategic weapons, greatly improving the ability of the National Command Authority to respond to changing conditions during a crisis, only manned bombers are truly retargetable in flight, and their ability to survive in defended airspace, given the commitment of the Soviet government to air defense, was questionable, as was their ability to locate mobile missiles and command facilities.

Most important of these technological developments was the multiple independently targetable reentry vehicle system (MIRV). Initially, each ballistic missile carried only one warhead and one reentry vehicle (the container that protects and carries the warhead from launch to target). In the 1960s when both the United States and the Soviet Union began work on various antiballistic missile defenses (ABM), missile designers looked at ways to counter these defenses. Their solution was to increase the number of warheads on each missile (see Figure 5-3 on page 148) to overwhelm the defense systems by the weight of numbers and to aim each warhead at a separate target

FIGURE 5-3
Three MIRV warheads and protective nosecone. *U.S. Air Force*

so each warhead would have to be attacked separately by the defense system. (Each warhead and its reentry vehicle separates from its launch vehicle soon after launch, long before the vehicle comes in range of the enemy's defenses; see Figure 5-4.) Even after both the United States and the Soviet Union discontinued work on ABM defenses, the deployment of MIRV went ahead, with deployment of U.S. MIRVed missiles beginning in 1970. The United States eventually deployed 550 three-warhead Minuteman III missiles (out of 1,000 Minuteman missiles); the submarine-launched Poseidon (successor to the Polaris missile) carried carry ten or more warheads, while the currently deployed Trident missile carries five warheads.[63]

MIRV provided ICBMs the *counterforce capability* they previously lacked just at the time that Secretary McNamara was leading doctrine away from an emphasis on counterforce weapons.[64] At least two warheads are required to destroy an enemy ICBM, given the uncertainty of each warhead striking its target. As long as each missile had only one warhead, the side that initiated a counterforce attack would use up all of its missiles before its adversary's force of ICBMs was destroyed, given rough parity in the number of missiles deployed by each combatant. However, with multiple warheads, one missile could destroy more than one enemy missile, raising again the specter of a disarming first strike, at least as far as fixed-based ICBMs were concerned. At the very least, MIRV seemed to spell the end of basing ICBMs in fixed silos and led to a proliferation of proposals for mobile ground-launched ICBMs. None of these schemes— ICBMs on moving railroad cars, on trucks, in cargo aircraft parked on the ends of runways—were ever deployed by the United States.

The possibility of maintaining a "secure strategic reserve" was considerably improved by the other major technological innovation of the 1970s—the cruise missile,

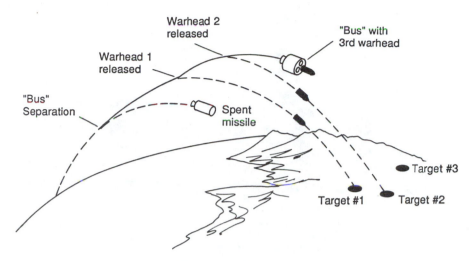

FIGURE 5-4   MIRV FLIGHT PATTERNS

a turbo-fan jet-powered, pilotless aircraft capable of carrying nuclear weapons. A revival of the German World War II V-1 weapon, advances in computer technology made it possible for an on-board computer to match the radar profile of the terrain it is flying over with radar images stored in its memory, determine the actual location of the missile, and make any course corrections needed.[65] Small in size (roughly twenty feet long), relatively cheap, and easily carried to within 1,500 miles of the target by aircraft, surface ships, and submarines, cruise missiles in large numbers could overwhelm any defense system. (See Figure 5-5 below and Figure 5-6 on page 150.)

FIGURE 5-5
Air-launched cruise missile dropped from a B-52. *Department of Defense*

FIGURE 5-6
A sea-launched cruise missile begins its flight after being launched from a submarine's torpedo tube. *U.S. Navy*

These technological advances are probably beyond the reach of new nuclear nations in the next twenty-five years, but there is in principle no reason why nations cannot acquire such sophistication with nuclear delivery systems if they put their resources to the effort. Many of these technological breakthroughs were byproducts of advances in computer technology, making computers smaller, more powerful and more rugged, as well as in aeronautics. And such advances are steadily becoming more sophisticated, cheaper, and more readily available. Also, there are no scarcity of states willing to sell delivery systems to other states. Russia, China's original supplier of arms, has resumed sales to China, selling complete submarines as well as ground attack aircraft.[66] India continues to purchase ground attack aircraft from Russia while it is developing its own ground attack aircraft and intermediate-range ballistic missiles, while Pakistan is purchasing ground attack aircraft and submarines from France.[67] Although arms sales to Iraq remain embargoed, Iran continues to be of concern: "Russia is reported to have supplied Iran with SS-6 cruise missile related equipment.... Iran is also believed to have acquired technology from North Korea for the *Scud*-derivative *Nodong* surface to surface missile."[68]

DEFENSE AGAINST MISSILES

In contrast with these all too successful technologies, the other technological path in the nuclear realm—the attempt to create defenses against nuclear warheads delivered by missiles—continues to elude success. In a speech broadcast on March 23, 1983, President Reagan surprised most of the country and some of his own advisors with these closing words:

> Let me share with you a vision of the future which offers hope. It is that we embark on a program to counter the awesome Soviet missile threat with measures that are defensive.... What if free people could live secure in the knowledge that their security

did not rest upon the threat of instant U.S. retaliation to deter a Soviet attack, that we could intercept and destroy strategic ballistic missiles before they reach our own soil or that of our allies.... I call upon the scientific community in our country, those who gave us nuclear weapons, to turn their great talents now to the cause of mankind and world peace, to give us the means of rendering these nuclear weapons impotent and obsolete.

Although officially called the Strategic Defense Initiative (SDI), the press quickly dubbed the president's plan "Star Wars" after the 1977 George Lucas science fiction movie, because it depended on the development of advanced technology such as satellite battle stations using particle beams and lasers to fight a defensive war in space.

Recall that Secretary McNamara's analysts had estimated that 200 Soviet warheads detonating in the United States would kill 50 million Americans. Given that there were some 10,000 ballistic warheads in the Soviet strategic arsenal at that time, a defense would have to destroy at least 98 percent of the warheads in a Soviet all-out strike to limit damage significantly to the United States. There are formidable obstacles to an effective ballistic missile defense: the short time during which the missiles are vulnerable to attack, the long distances across which the attacks must be made, the ruggedness of the warheads, and the thousands of warheads and decoys an attacker could send against the United States. To have any prospect of success at all would require a layered defense in which different methods would be used to attack incoming missiles at different stages of their flight.

All these layers would require a large, complex, and robust battle management system, which would have the task of coordinating and controlling the entire defensive system. It would consist of a system of sensing satellites, ground and satellite communication links, and computers, whose task it would be to track and identify targets, decide on optimum ways of meeting the attack, assign defensive weapons to particular targets, detect hits and misses, and reassign targets that had been missed.

The critics of SDI challenged the feasibility of an effective defense against ballistic missiles on a number of grounds. First, a number of the necessary technologies, such as particle beam weapons and directed energy weapons powered by nuclear explosives, do not yet exist and may not ever prove to be workable. The system could not be tested under realistic conditions (a large-scale surprise attack) and would have to work perfectly the first time it was needed. Second, countermeasures to missile defenses are readily available, less technically demanding, and much less expensive than the missile defenses themselves. For example, lasers, the most promising weapon for attacks during the initial stage, can easily be countered by giving the missile a reflective coating or causing the launch vehicle to rotate as it ascends so the laser could not remain focused on one spot.[69] Finally, the missile defenses rely on satellites, communications, and multiple computers linked together, which are all quite vulnerable to attack.

Ironically, while missile defenses would not be able to protect the population of the United States, they would be of some effectiveness in protecting missile sites. To complete the irony, while SDI would provide little protection against a first strike, particularly a surprise attack, it would be most effective in reducing the damage the United States would sustain from a retaliatory second strike, as all the components of the defensive system could be optimally positioned, fully manned, and prepared. Most important, the missile defenses would be contending with only the "ragged response" of the few missiles that survived the U.S. first strike, rather than the enemy's full arsenal launched in a single coordinated attack. Therefore, deployment of a ballistic missile defense would increase an enemy's fears that the United States was preparing for a preventive war or the unfettered use of nuclear coercion. These fears might lead an enemy to launch its own preemptive strike. Even worse, if the United States were to begin to deploy a defense in advance of an adversary, the enemy might feel that it had no alternative but to launch a preemptive strike before the U.S. missile defenses were operational. Thus, SDI, instead of making life in the United States more secure, might precipitate the very attack it is meant to defend against.

By 1987, even the scientists working on SDI had come to admit that the dream of a perfect shield against missiles was unobtainable, as they realized that the exotic technologies needed—nuclear-powered space-based laser guns, for example—were going to require decades to develop and might prove never to be practicable. By 1990, in light of this growing realization and the rapid dissolution of the Soviet military establishment, SDI's goals had become more modest: to protect the United States against up to 200 ICBMs or SLBMs and to protect deployed U.S. troops against theater or tactical missiles. The project had been renamed GPALS, Global Protection against Limited Strikes. Even so, the U.S. Congress has continued to set unobtainable target dates: first 1996, then 1997, then 2002, now 2003, for deployment of ground-based national missile defenses with testing and deployment of space-based missile defenses to follow soon thereafter. Most ominous, this ambitious agenda requires substantial changes to the Anti-Ballistic Missile Treaty, long a centerpiece of U.S./Soviet arms control.[70]

THE END OF THE FIRST NUCLEAR ERA

Mikhail Gorbachev's elevation to general secretary of the Soviet Union in 1985 ultimately led to a torrent of change in the Soviet Union and in its foreign relations. In six dramatic years, the Soviet Union moved to democratize itself, first by allowing open debate about the economy and society, and then, forced by growing public pressures and Gorbachev's evolving thinking, by permitting the organization of political parties that could challenge the dominance of Gorbachev's own Communist Party. The Soviet Union renounced a right to control the political destinies of Eastern Europe, and permitted Communist parties to fall from power there, even in East Germany, which allowed for the reunification of the two Germanies—something that previous Soviet leaders feared would imperil the Soviet Union. A right-wing coup attempt in Moscow in August 1991, aided by portions of the military, failed, but it led to the end of the Soviet Union, as leaders of the sixteen republics that constituted the Soviet state rode a tide of nationalism to create their own states; the Communist Party was discredited by the coup attempt, and power passed into the hands of others. Gorbachev found himself without political meaning, for the Soviet Union no longer existed and the Soviet Communist Party had no power. This, then, may have been the ultimate triumph of nuclear weapons: to allow Russia to see its national security safeguarded, even if its security shield of communist regimes and armies in Eastern Europe disappeared. And for the Soviet state to collapse peacefully.

Russia, led by Boris Yeltsin, was the major state that emerged from the breakup of the Soviet Union. It inherited the bulk of the Soviet nuclear arsenal, but tactical nuclear weapons could be found with Soviet forces throughout the former Soviet Union, and the new states of Belarus (formerly Byelorussia), Ukraine, and Kazakhstan had ICBMs located within their territories. The old Soviet military establishment, particularly the components dedicated to the nuclear arsenal, remained more or less cohesive and responsive to the top military command, which was dominated by ethnic Russians and responsive to the new Russian state. After protracted negotiations (aided by support from the United States), all Soviet nuclear weapons outside Russia were either returned to Russian territory or destroyed.

During the Cold War, some analysts had questioned the ability of the Soviet Union to sustain a military effort on the scale they had since World War II—the economic historian Paul Kennedy had asserted, for instance, in 1987 that the Soviet Union simply lacked the resource base to maintain a global military presence.[71] The fundamental premise of the American strategy of containment, the basis of U.S. strategy vis-à-vis the Soviet Union beginning with NSC-68, the Truman Doctrine, and Eisenhower's *New Look*, a strategy for the long haul of the Cold War, was that all the noncommunist world had to do was contain the spread of communism, discourage Soviet adventurism, and avoid direct confrontation while the historical processes of moderation would eventually produce a Russian state that could join the world community of nations.

However, when the breakup of the Soviet Union did come, it came with startling rapidity. Thus,

> In the space of 25 months [Nov 1989 thru Dec 1991], without a shot fired in anger, America's military security environment had been turned inside out. Gone was the 45 year threat of a massive Soviet/Warsaw Pact blitzkrieg across the divided Europe. Gone were the Soviet nuclear missiles stationed in Europe. Pledged to be gone were the nuclear arsenals inherited from the former Soviet Union by Ukraine, Belarus and Kazakhstan. In short, having been robbed of it[s] only significant military competitor, at the end of 1991 the United States stood alone with the world's most powerful military force but without an adversary worthy of the name.[72]

The U.S. response from 1985 onward to this revolutionary transformation of the Soviet bloc was interesting. Ronald Reagan had gone from the ideological Cold Warrior (pointing to an evil empire with which no one could or really should do business) to a president interested in reaching agreements with Gorbachev. George Bush, also a longtime Cold Warrior, displayed a general caution in response to the collapse of Soviet/communist power, treating Russia with respect. President Clinton expended considerable effort to maintain the viability of Russia as a political and economic unit, including substantial U.S. financial aid. In a sense, the United States passed the test of a nuclear relationship: to bring about political change equal to the consequence of war but without war and without a climactic nuclear confrontation. Since then, the United States has taken great pains to safeguard the existence of the longtime opponent—another novelty of a nuclear age. We can't be certain, but we certainly suspect that the opponent's possession of nuclear weapons played a decisive role

THE NEW NUCLEAR ORDER

At the dawn of the nuclear age, all commentators assumed that any industrial nation could, if it wished, build its own nuclear arsenal, so Bernard Brodie and the rest assumed that the future would be one in which every state with any independent industrial plant would also have a nuclear arsenal. But that has not happened, for a number of reasons discussed in Chapter 7. There are, however, a number of states that either have declared they do have nuclear arsenals or are presumed to have, or could quickly have nuclear arsenals of various sizes and mixes of weapons. In the remainder of this chapter, we will take a look at these states, what we know about their arsenals, and the doctrines they have developed for use of their weapons.

In the following discussion, we will use these three categories: *declared nuclear states, opaque nuclear states,* and *aspiring states.*[73] The problem with the last two categories is that they depend on judgments based on declarations of leaders and on appraisals of activities within another country. But leaders do change and states have been very successful in hiding nuclear weapons development. The world learned a salutary lesson after the 1991 Persian Gulf War when it was startled to uncover the scope of the Iraqi nuclear weapon program that had made substantial progress both through external acquisitions and by developing indigenous capabilities.[74]

Declared states are those that have declared they possess nuclear devices and have demonstrated that fact by detonating devices under the guise of tests. It is also useful to divide declared states into three subcategories: *first tier* states that have sufficient nuclear weapons and a global delivery system that can cause massive, widespread damage if it chooses to wage nuclear war, *second tier* states that can cause significant regional damage and *newly arrived nuclear states* that have quite limited arsenals and problematic delivery capability.

FIRST TIER

Clearly occupied by the United States and Russian; these two states do still possess sufficiently large arsenals to effectively destroy civilization on the planet and possibly destroy all life above the level of insects, despite the heartening progress in arms reduction and confidence building measures of recent years. (It has been estimated that even after all the START build-down goals have been reached, the Russian arsenal will contain about three times as much destructive capacity as all the rest of the world's arsenal combined, the United States excluded.)[75] Therefore, as long as these arsenals exist, the fate of all humankind rests on the ability of the leadership of both countries to manage these arsenals.

The collapse of the Soviet Union as an adversary accelerated a process of reducing the nuclear weapons in the arsenals of the United States and Russia. Under a series of agreements called START, both sides have slowly been decreasing their arsenals; in Chapter 8, we will examine the process in greater detail. Russian progress in reducing strategic warheads since the dissolution of the Soviet Union has been substantial (See Table 5-3) although progress has been slower in the U.S. build-down. And, most encouraging, all former Soviet warheads have been returned to Russia.

This has been matched with a reduction in U.S expenditures for defense:

In 1985, America appropriated about $400 billion for the Department of Defense (in constant, fiscal year 1997 dollars), which constituted 28 percent of our national budget and 7 percent of our Gross National Product. We had more than 2.2 million men and women under arms, with about 500,000 overseas, 1.1 million in the Reserve forces, and 1.1 million civilians in the employment of the Department of Defense. Defense companies employed 3.7 million more and about $120 billion of our budget went to procurement contracts....

Since 1985, America has responded to the vast global changes by reducing its defense budget by some 38 percent, its force structure by 33 percent, and its procurement programs by 63 percent. Today, the budget of the Department of Defense is $250 billion, 15 percent of our national budget, and an estimated 3.2 percent of our Gross National Product.[76]

TABLE 5-3   PROGRESS IN NUCLEAR ARMS REDUCTION

DEPLOYED STRATEGIC WARHEADS

RUSSIAN

	September 1987	January 1999
ICBMS	6,612	3,590
SLBMs	2,804	2,424
Bombers	855	564
Total	10,271	6,578

UNITED STATES

	September 1987	January 1999
ICBMS	2,458	2,451
SLBMs	5,760	3,776
Bombers	2,353	1,731
Total	10,563	7,958

Source: U.S. Arms Control and Disarmament Agency. START I aggregate numbers of strategic offensive arms (as of January 1, 1999, as compiled from individual data submissions of the parties). April 1, 1999. Available at: www.acda.gov/factsheet/wmd/nuclear/start1/startagg.hmm.

As part of this reduction, the U.S. defense establishment reexamined the role of strategic nuclear weapons and the number and mix of weapons, their mode of deployment, and their command, control, and custody. On September 18, 1994, President Clinton approved *The Nuclear Posture Review*, which set the following goals for the U.S. nuclear arsenal:

- 14 Trident submarines each with 24 D-5 missiles, each with 5 warheads. (1,680 total SLBM warheads)
- 450/500 Minuteman III ICBMs with single warheads
- 20 B-2s with gravity bombs
- 66 B-52 Bombers carrying air-launched cruise missiles (AGM-86B) and advanced cruise missiles (AGM-129)

The posture review reaffirmed the U.S. commitment to the Triad but did take the U.S. strategic bombers off day-to-day alert. As a confidence building measure, the *Posture Review* stipulated that all ICBMs and SLBMs would be detargeted, but given improvements in dynamic retargeting capability in recent years, this may be more cosmetic than substantive. To improve control of U.S. nuclear devices, Permissive Action Links (PALs) were ordered installed on all U.S. nuclear weapons by 1997.

The effect of all this was to reduce U.S. strategic warheads by 59 percent and nonstrategic warheads by 90 percent. No nuclear weapons were to be in the custody of U.S. ground forces, nuclear warheads were no longer deployed on surface ships, and a number of development programs were terminated (e.g., the rail garrison scheme).

In May 1997 the U.S. Department of Defense published its first Quadrennial Review (QDR) of U.S. defense posture. This review, mandated by Congress, sought to chart the course of U.S. defense policy for the next eight years. In response to this review, President Clinton issued a Presidential Decision Directive in November 1997, providing a new approach to American strategic policy, the first change in presidential guidance for nuclear weapons employment since 1981. In Secretary Cohen's words,

> Nuclear weapons play a smaller role in the U.S. security posture today than they have at any point during the second half of the 20th century, but … nuclear weapons are still needed as a hedge against an uncertain future, as a guarantee of U.S. security commitments to allies, and as a disincentive to those who would contemplate developing or otherwise acquiring their own nuclear weapons. Accordingly, the United States will maintain survivable strategic nuclear forces of sufficient size and diversity to deter any hostile foreign leadership with access to nuclear weapons.

The new directive provides a large measure of continuity with previous nuclear weapons employment guidance, including in particular the following three principles:

- Deterrence is predicated on ensuring that potential adversaries accept that any use of nuclear weapons against the United States or its allies would not succeed.
- A wide range of nuclear retaliatory options will continue to be planned to ensure the United States is not left with an all-or-nothing response.
- The United States will not rely on a launch-on-warning nuclear retaliation strategy (although an adversary could never be sure the United States would not launch a counterattack before the adversary's nuclear weapons arrived).[77]

SECOND TIER

The United Kingdom (Great Britain), France, and the Peoples' Republic of China have all demonstrated, through repeated public testing and repeated public declarations, that they all three have manufactured nuclear weapons and their delivery systems and that they intend to maintain their nuclear arsenals into the indefinite future.

United Kingdom   Although the United Kingdom's nuclear development program predates that of the United States, during World War II all British research efforts were merged with the U.S. Manhattan project and for some years after WW II, the U.K. relied on U.S. missiles based in Great Britain under "dual-key control" for its strategic defense. Even as Britain has developed its indigenous capacity to build weapons, it has continued to rely on the United States, for instance acquiring Plutonium, Uranium-235, and Tritium from the United States,[78] performing all its nuclear testing since 1962 at the U.S. test site in Nevada,[79] and even purchasing from the United States the missiles for its strategic submarines.[80] Its strategic nuclear retaliatory capacity will be entirely submarine-launched ballistic missiles on either three or four submarines equipped with 16 U.S. Trident missiles each, replacing earlier Polaris missile-carrying submarines over the next several years. Britain's stated policy is to maintain a total strategic retaliatory capacity of 192 warheads with at least one boat at sea at all times—a fierce debate continues as to whether that requires two, three, or four submarines. Britain has also maintained a "sub-strategic" capability in gravity nuclear bombs that can be carried by 72 Tornado strike aircraft whose declared purpose is to deliver "an unmistakable message of our willingness to defend our vital interest to the utmost" according to the British Secretary of State for Defense.[81]

The critical question regarding Britain's nuclear forces is their relation both to NATO and to the European Union. Britain has "subscribed" its principal nuclear forces to NATO "except where Her Majesty's Government may decide that supreme national interests are at stake"—that is, when it would matter. It is difficult to think that use of strategic nuclear forces would even be considered in any case less than one involving "supreme national interests."[82]

France   France's effort to build an independent nuclear capability has been dated to 1954, and in 1960 France tested their first nuclear device and in 1968 their first thermonuclear device. French delivery systems mirrored the Triad: air-dropped weapons, land-based ballistic missiles, and submarine-launched ballistic missiles, as well as battlefield weapons. Although France has retreated from battlefield weapons, it has still retained eighteen silo-launched missiles as well as air-launched missiles, but both as a backup to its principal retaliatory force, submarine-launched ballistic missiles that currently carry a total of 384 warheads. Like the United Kingdom, France continues to debate exactly how many submarines are needed to maintain a credible deterrent at sea but has embarked on a program to build four new ballistic missile submarines and has been developing an air-launched cruise missile similar to the U.S. Tomahawk.

France's stated targeting policy has been *tous azimuts* targeting—that is targeting not one specific enemy, permitting political and operational flexibility. Its principal justification for its nuclear arsenal is to maintain military independence so it can independently deter invasions of France or threats to its vital national interests. To that end, the size of the arsenal, in French thinking, is independent of any military balance but is determined by "sufficiency," that is the "capacity to inflict unacceptable damage on any aggressor."[83] This, of course, is a direct response to the fundamental critique of extended deterrence—that in a crisis the United States will not risk retaliation against U.S. cities to defend European cities—in de Gaulle's words the United States will not risk Chicago for Paris.

China   China is the most difficult to talk about with any certainty. Although no longer as impenetrable a society as formerly, in some ways its future is the most difficult to predict. China launched its nuclear program in 1954 with Soviet assistance, including a research reactor. Following the withdrawal of all Soviet aid in 1959, China's indigenous efforts culminated in a successful test in 1964. Although China's delivery systems development also benefited from transfers of Soviet material and from Soviet training, it is clear that Soviet aid only hastened Chinese development that would have gone on in any case. As early as 1966, China was targeting U.S. bases in Japan with both missiles and nuclear-armed bombers. Soviet cities were targeted beginning in 1971 and in 1978 Chinese missiles could reach Eastern Europe, all of the Soviet Union and India, but not Western Europe. China's first intercontinental ballistic missiles were only deployed in 1981 but most tellingly, only four to seven missiles were deployed.[84] And most interestingly, contrary to the practice of the other nuclear powers, China has not yet deployed multiple warhead missiles. And, given the size of China's military establishment, the total number of warheads remains modest—only 233 to 284 strategic warheads and at most about 150 tactical and theater weapons, a strategic arsenal only a little more than one-half of France.[85]

ISSUES OF SECOND TIER NUCLEAR NATIONS

Modernization   All three second tier nations have committed considerable resources to modernizing their arsenals, particularly their delivery systems. The rhetoric used to justify modernization by all three is the need to make their deterrent capacity

more robust, that is more survivable. The principal means of increasing survivability are
to increase the range of their delivery vehicles and decrease reliance on land-based and
even air-based delivery systems, which after all are ultimately land-based. The United
Kingdom has replaced its earlier Polaris and Poseidon submarine-based missiles with the
U.S.-made Trident missile with a range of 12,000 km, and France has replaced its gravity bombs with short-range airborne missiles.[86] France has announced its intention of
destroying its last remaining silo-based strategic missiles and the British government has
announced its intention of destroying its remaining air-delivered nuclear weapons.
China is also committed to moving its arsenal to mobile basing but given its relative
lack of success and the length of time the projects have been under development it is
difficult to speculate about them. After thirty years of work, China has only one ballistic missile submarine operational with only twelve missiles and is building a second
boat now.[87]

Testing   Most troubling, France defied world opinion to continue testing nuclear
weapons through 1996, long after the rest of the world's nuclear powers had agreed to
a moratorium, and China has tested a nuclear device as recently as October 1993. As
Britain no longer has any facility to test outside of the United States, Britain has had
no choice but to follow U.S. policy regarding a moratorium on testing.

Possible Uses   In light of the previous discussion, some inferences can be drawn
about possible uses of the second tier's nuclear arsenals. China's declared policy is that
the only purpose of its nuclear arsenal is to prevent blackmail by the nuclear states and,
given the short range of its delivery systems, it is clear that state about which they
were concerned was the Soviet Union. Also, given the small size of its arsenal and the
absence of multiple-warhead missiles, China's claim that it has no nuclear war-fighting pretensions is credible; in other words, it can be argued that China has built an arsenal sufficient to deter attack or intimidation but not large enough to threaten either
superpower. However, their arsenal can be read another way. While China may have
no global ambitions, its arsenal is well-suited to establish regional hegemony, that is
to dominate the Pacific Rim and Indian subcontinent, including, most important to
the United States, Japan.
    Although France claims that its arsenal is to protect it from threats all around the
horizon, in fact the relatively short range of its delivery systems suggest that its only use
was to deter the Soviet Union from an irresponsible act in Europe, and its extensive use
of multiple warheads can be justified as needed to give weight to its deterrence. Even
though it is the third largest nuclear power in terms of numbers of warheads, its arsenal
is still only one-seventeenth the size of the U.S. arsenal and a fourteenth the size of Russia's, even after the sizeable build-down of START I. Therefore, France's claim that its
nuclear weapons are only to deter, not to threaten, has some credence. British nuclear
weapons, although longer range, are so few in number that they too can not be thought
to represent an offensive threat to either of the two first nuclear powers. The long range
of their submarine-based missiles is needed to provide their only two operational submarines with a larger deployment area, not to enable them to threaten other countries.
However, the British government has stated their intention of deploying both strategic
warheads of about 100 kiloton yield and smaller tactical warheads on their submarines,
providing the government with the capability of using nuclear weapons both for the
final warning, the "nuclear shot across the bow" and in regional conflicts, such as their
Falklands War, where other nuclear powers might use tactical delivery systems.

NEWLY ARRIVED NUCLEAR STATES

India   India has acknowledged building and testing a nuclear device, has a visible missile program but did not acknowledge making nuclear weapons until the spring of 1998. However, given India's substantial nuclear industry and strong technical base, the assumption is that India possesses, or could quickly assemble from fissile material on hand, at least 80 weapons. There are questions whether the weapons India has or could build would be small enough and sufficiently rugged to mount as a missile warhead, but the India Air Force has sufficient aircraft to deliver nuclear weapons to a battle site on India's borders, to enemy troops massing on its borders or to any Pakistan city, or into China's border regions.

Pakistan   U.S. aid to Pakistan was suspended in 1990 because Pakistan would not confirm that it had not built nuclear weapons, although it did not test a nuclear device until after India declared itself a nuclear state in the spring of 1998. The general assumption is that Pakistan has fissile material for fifteen to twenty-five Hiroshima-style uranium fission bombs. (It must be kept in mind that confidence in the uranium bomb was so high in the Manhattan project in 1945 that the Hiroshima bomb was not tested before it was first used against Japan—the early test was of an implosion plutonium bomb.) Although Pakistan has been developing guided missiles with Chinese assistance, there is doubt that Pakistan's weapons would be small enough or robust enough to be delivered by missiles. However, the Pakistan Air Force does have aircraft capable of delivering weapons to targets in India, including many of India's major cities.

Opaque or Presumptive Nuclear States   These are defined as states for which evidence exists that they have designed and built nuclear weapons but whose governments deny that they actually have weapons. These are states who live in conditions of constant military tension, who have reasonable fears for their continued national existence, and in the case of Israel have enemies who even deny the right of the state to exist. In the past, this category has included some Latin American nations and South Africa, although both Brazil and South Africa have declared that they have abandoned their efforts to build nuclear weapons.

Israel   Israel is generally assumed, in spite of ambiguously worded denials, to have a sizeable and sophisticated nuclear arsenal; estimates range from a minimum of 100 weapons[88] to as many as 200, although these weapons may in fact be stored not fully assembled, putting Israel a "turn of a screwdriver" away from an actual weapon. Given Israel's considerable scientific and technical infrastructure, the absence of testing is not evidence of an absence of weapons. In fact, Israel's deliberately ambiguous statements about possible nuclear weapons and its handling of several security leaks in its nuclear program suggest that this ambiguity is part of a carefully studied policy to remind its enemies that it could have "a bomb in the basement." Israel has missiles capable of reaching the entire Middle East and even possibly into Russia and has a sizeable and very effective Air Force that can also deliver weapons.

Possible Uses of These Weapons   Pakistan/India and Israel are both instructive cases of the uses of nuclear weapons to ensure national survival. It has been argued that the Soviet Union/China/India/Pakistan are in effect a single system: a cascade of states that acquired nuclear weapons out of fear of another adversary state who they feared would use nuclear weapons to abridge what they saw as their sovereignty. We have seen that Stalin had little interest in nuclear weapons until the United States had them and then ordered a crash program to acquire them, and we have seen clear evidence that fear of nuclear blackmail by the Soviet Union drove China's nuclear program. It can be argued that the exact choice of weapons and delivery system by China clearly indicates a felt need to deter the Soviet Union. So too, it has been argued that India's acquisition of nuclear weapons was in direct response to China's acquisition of nuclear weapons. India's program did not begin until after China's invasion of Tibet, the acquisition of a common border with China, and the Indian Army's poor showing in the border clashes with the Chinese Army. It can be contended that the principal purpose of the Indian nuclear arsenal is to deter a Chinese invasion of India—a modest number of weapons with only limited range delivery systems, sufficient to impede an invasion but not enough weapons or long enough range to threaten China itself. Unfortunately, the same characteristics also describe an arsenal intended to threaten or even annihilate Pakistan—a smaller country much closer to India. This recognition has prompted Pakistan to develop its own capability but at quite some cost. As distances are short, sophisticated and long range delivery systems are not needed nor are large numbers of weapons needed to deter India from invading Pakistan or even from using nuclear weapons against Pakistan.

Israel presents a more complex case: It can be variously argued that the Israeli arsenal is intended for battlefield use only. Given the paucity of information about the mix of weapons in their inventory, that question is unanswerable. It can also be argued that the Israeli weapons, by threatening the capital cities of its enemies, serve to deter a large-scale invasion of Israel that might threaten its continued existence. It can also be argued that their arsenal is a "poison pill"—a warning that if the Israeli state is destroyed, no one will profit but that the entire Near East will be indefinitely uninhabitable. Also, the real target of Israeli deterrence could have been the Soviet Union—just as President Kennedy warned the Soviet Union during the Cuban missile crisis that the United States would hold the Soviet Union accountable for Castro's actions, saying that he would regard any missile coming from Cuba as if it were coming from the Soviet Union. Similarly, the Israeli arsenal could have been intended to warn the Soviet Union that they must keep limits on their clients in the Middle East.[89]

Robustness of Deterrence   What all this speaks to is the robustness of deterrence. Referring back to Bernard Brodie, the nuclear bomb is so very powerful—its destructive capacity is so great—that any credible hint backed by the most circumstantial of evidence (e.g., indigenous nuclear industry, acquisition of a nuclear reactor from abroad, evidence of successful clandestine efforts to obtain nuclear material whether fissile or not, importation of technology that could be diverted to production of nuclear weapons) is sufficient to deter potential enemies. Conversely, the bomb is so very powerful that even the suspicion that an enemy has, or may obtain, nuclear weapons, is powerful incentive for a state to commit considerable resources, sometimes quite scarce resources, to efforts to build nuclear weapons, or at least to make its enemies uncertain whether the state has nuclear weapons. Thus the number of states who have consciously chosen to remain ambiguous about their nuclear arsenals belies earlier arguments that deterrence is very fragile and requires exact symmetry in arsenals lest an adversary seize a momentary numerical advantage to launch a disarming first strike. In the case of the Soviet Union/China/India/Pakistan cascade each state does have the potential to destroy a sizeable portion of the arsenal of the next state down the chain, but apparently each state feels that their enemy could not be certain of destroying all their nuclear weapons and the few remaining weapons would be sufficient to inflict unacceptable damage on their enemy.

How concerned should the United States be about the nuclear arsenals of these states, which after all amount in sum to no more than a small fraction of the remaining U.S. and Russian arsenals, even after the most optimistic of START III build-down goals are met? We are not suggesting that any of the states discussed here would ever consider a direct threat against the United States—their arsenals are all far too small and their delivery systems far too unsophisticated: short-ranged, unreliable, and with small payloads in nuclear terms. There are the cynics who contend that current concerns over second-tier states arsenals and the possible proliferation of nuclear weapons to other states are driven principally by bureaucratic imperatives: that organizations that have grown up to counter a specific threat, such as Soviet adventurism, must now search for another threat to protect the country from, lest we all recognize that these organizations no longer have a purpose and should be closed down, much as the March of Dimes had to discover children with birth defects to aid after polio vaccine was invented. It is true that the principal concern over nuclear proliferation during the years of U.S.-Soviet confrontation was the risk of *catalytic war*, that is, that the use of a nuclear weapon by a client state, even if not directly authorized by the United States or the Soviet Union, would precipitate a full-scale exchange between the two superpowers. Now, however, with the lessened tension, such uncontrolled escalation is much less likely.

However, nuclear weapons in the hands of any other state does lessen the freedom of action the United States has in dealing with threats to U.S. interests and does heighten the risk of aggression in regional conflicts, possibly involving states the United States has pledged to protect. As the clearest case, would the United States have been able to act as determinedly against Iraq following their invasion of Kuwait if Iraq or Iran had even a small nuclear arsenal or even a credible nuclear threat? Would the United States have dared to concentrate troops on the ground and commit major warships as freely as they did? Would Iraq have been able to deter U.S. allies in the Middle East, such as Saudi Arabia, from supporting the invasion of Iraq? Would that not have destabilized the entire Middle East, a region recognized as vital to the U.S. interests, and caused U.S. allies there and in other regions to question their commitment to the United States as the United States showed its inability to stand behind its treaty obligations?[90]

States with Nuclear Aspirations   These are the states that are most troublesome to the world community; the two leading examples today are Iraq and North Korea. In spite of considerable world attention and considerable world effort expended in counterproliferation efforts, both states refuse to unambiguously renounce any nuclear ambition and agree to the safeguards that would reassure the rest of the world. It can be argued in the case of Iraq that this in part is political posturing—that defying world opinion is a fundamental part of Saddam Hussein's hold on the faction that maintains him in power and that to accept the abrogation of sovereignty that the United Nations demands would fatally weaken his hold on his party. Nonetheless, both regimes continue to pay substantial prices for their intransigence.

The counter-proliferation community was startled to see after the Persian Gulf War in 1991 how much progress Iraq had made in its clandestine effort toward building nuclear weapons using a mix of imported and indigenous technology, and how difficult it was to identify and destroy nuclear facilities even when unlimited force was used. Although the allies had identified only two Iraqi nuclear installations to attack, UN inspectors after the war discovered over twenty Iraqi nuclear weapons facilities, and 1,000 hours of allied air strikes left much of the Iraqi nuclear infrastructure untouched.[91] These discoveries upset the conventional wisdom of previous counter-proliferation efforts, forcing a recognition that states' clandestine efforts would not necessarily use the most efficient technologies for fissile production but rather those that are easiest to obtain and easiest to conceal, even if less efficient.

Although North Korea has had a small Soviet-supplied research reactor since 1965, in 1985 U.S. reconnaissance satellites discovered the construction of a second and larger reactor well-suited for the production of plutonium for weapons. Then, through the 1980s, U.S. intelligence discovered North Korea was building a plutonium reprocessing facility, conducting high explosive tests required to build implosion-style plutonium weapons, and erecting a third, giant reactor that could produce enough plutonium for several nuclear weapons every year.[92] In the fall of 1994, the United States and North Korea reached an agreement; in exchange for a U.S. promise not to use nuclear weapons against North Korea, North Korea promised to stop work on their new reactors and reprocessing plant and not construct any new nuclear facilities.[93] Questions still remain, however, about whether North Korea will abide by the terms of the agreement:[94] They have refused to permit inspection of a construction site discovered in the summer of 1998 that the United States fears could be a new nuclear reactor.[95] The North Korean effort, however, has been derided recently with arguments that a country that can not provide socks for its fighter pilots can not be much feared as a potential nuclear power. But the U.S. concern over North Korea is dramatic testimony to the power of the bomb: that even the least likely threat is sufficient to prompt the most vigorous counter-proliferation effort by the most powerful nation on the planet, the United States.

THE THREAT OF FORMER SOVIET FISSILE MATERIAL

An axiom of counter-proliferation efforts had been that the technology to construct a nuclear device is within reach of most of the world. The basic concepts of nuclear weapons are simple and well known. While the sophisticated thermonuclear weapons built by the United States and the Soviet Union require very advanced technology, the simple gun-type uranium device used untested at Hiroshima could be easily constructed.[96] The basic information needed to design a simple fission weapon is available in the open literature and the parts needed could be easily acquired from commercial sources.[97] A very simple gun-type weapon need not weigh more than 600–700 pounds or exceed six feet in length.[98]

The principal constraint on the spread of nuclear weapons up until now was the production of fissile material to fuel the nuclear device. Either enriching uranium to weapons-grade, that is, sufficient to fuel a nuclear explosive, or creating plutonium are very demanding technologically and require a considerable industrial infrastructure, an infrastructure not easily hidden. So up until now, the world has been reasonably secure in the knowledge that an effort by a nonnuclear state to acquire nuclear weapons could be conducted neither quickly nor secretly—the required industrial activity could be easily detected and would require sufficient time for the world community to mobilize against what it felt to be an irresponsible state acquiring nuclear weapons. Witness the difficulty Iraq has had with its nuclear program and the effectiveness of the world effort to frustrate Saddam Hussein's nuclear ambitions.

With the breakup of the Soviet Union, however, a new and very troubling prospect has arisen: former Soviet fissile material under very uncertain custody. With former Soviet fissile materials at risk for diversion, it would be possible for a state to acquire at least a limited nuclear capability clandestinely and with no warning. And even more chilling, up until now, no group less than a state could reasonably aspire to nuclear weapons so if any weapons or fissile material were passed to a terrorist group, as Libya passed conventional explosives to state-sponsored terrorist groups acting as a front, the state would clearly be held accountable for any use made of the weapons. Now, however, it would be possible for state-sponsored terrorists to detonate a device with former Soviet fissile material while the sponsoring state successfully denies responsibility. Thus an essential accountability of a state for its responsible use of nuclear weapons has been eroded.

With the dissolution of the Soviet Union, the authoritarian control that state exercised over every part of Soviet society has ended—control over travel within and in and out of the Soviet Union, control over much internal and all external communication, and intrusive surveillance of all industry. This gave the Soviet Union unquestioned control of weapons-useable nuclear materials and nuclear weapons, giving the Soviet Union the best record on inadvertent or unauthorized nuclear proliferation—a record the West could not emulate. Now, however, with the revolution that has swept through Russia—a revolution as fundamental and profound as that following the French Revolution in 1789—it has been alleged that "nothing valuable can be secure from loss, theft, or sale.... As a result, over the past three years, trickles of weapons-usable fissile material have begun seeping out of the former Soviet Union. The current trickle could well be a harbinger of things to come. A burgeoning flow, or even a catastrophic flood, of nuclear weapons material, or perhaps even of weapons themselves, has become a distinct danger given the conditions in which nuclear assets are held in Russia."[99]

The amount of fissile material at risk is staggering: only 10 to 25 kilograms (22 to 55 lbs.) of fissile material are sufficient to make Hiroshima-scale weapons with a yield of over 10 kilotons, and there are some 1,200 metric tons of weapons-usable fissile material under the control of the Russian Ministry of Defense, the Minatom design and production agency, and the various users of weapons-grade fissile material in Russia such as naval reactors and research reactors. Of all the former Soviet institutions, the military has shown the most stability, so the risk of theft of a weapon itself is fairly low, but what is most at risk is the fissile material removed from dismantled tactical and nuclear warheads and in the custody of Minatom. Between 1986 and 1992, some 12,000 to 13,000 weapons were dismantled as tactical and theater weapons were returned from Eastern Europe, the Baltic Republics and Mongolia, and 12,000 to 13,000 other nuclear weapons were consolidated into Russian storage facilities. START I and START II require dismantling some 15,000 to 20,000 additional weapons.[100] Dismantling has been underway since 1992 at the rate of about 2,000 weapons per year.

This dismantling has far exceeded secure storage available in Russia and stressed the Russian accounting system for keeping track of fissile material. Two examples suffice: When the United States retrieved 600 kilograms of weapons-grade Highly Enriched Uranium (HEU) left behind in Kazakhstan with the breakup of the Soviet Union, 24 kilograms more HEU was retrieved by the United States than Soviet records said were there—enough fissile material for two simple bombs.[101] Another example: Some 30 metric tons of plutonium were found to be stored in an old warehouse with glass windows and a padlock on the door.[102] Evidence abounds that attempts have been made to smuggle former Soviet fissile material out of Russia: Six smuggling attempts were detected from 1992 through 1994 and it is difficult not to assume that more attempts are successful than are detected. And one can only assume that if economic and political conditions continue to worsen in Russia, the risk of leakage of former Soviet fissile material will increase.

SUMMARY

From the perspective of our review of almost a half century of experience with nuclear weapons, we can now return to the four questions each state has had to answer:

1. Does the state need nuclear weapons in peacetime?
2. If it does, how many and what kinds?
3. What plans should be made for the use of nuclear weapons in the event of war?
4. What use do nuclear weapons have in peacetime?

These four questions have been answered differently by each nuclear state: the United States, the Soviet Union, the United Kingdom, France, China, India, Pakistan, and most likely Israel have decided that they do need nuclear weapons in peacetime. During the Cold War, the United States and the Soviet Union also decided they needed a large number of weapons and a large variety of weapons, ranging from nuclear artillery shells for battlefield use, only a little more powerful than conventional munitions, to multiwarhead intercontinental ballistic missiles. Other states, however, decided that limited nuclear arsenals would suit their purposes or were constrained by resource limitations.

However, the debate continues as intensely as it did twenty-five years ago as to how many and what kinds of weapons should be in the U.S. and Russian arsenals. We saw that McNamara found the only use for nuclear weapons was to deter their use. In the words of Bernard Brodie, "Thus far the chief purpose of our military establishment has been to win wars. From now on its chief purpose must be to avert them. It can have almost no other useful purpose."[103] It follows that their only use in the event of war is as instruments of retaliation, and therefore the principal requirement for the U.S. strategic forces is that they be able to survive any attack an enemy might consider making. Elaborate strategies for fighting a nuclear war are therefore not necessary.

The key, then, becomes the retaliatory *capability* of a nation and a nation's *will* to deliver such retaliation. We can imagine a situation in which the leadership of a nation just struck by a massive first-strike might not see any sense in retaliation. Or it may be the case that there is no national leadership left to order the retaliation. Thus the will to retaliate is critical, but without capability to retaliate, all the will in the world is meaningless.

Some states, such as the United States, have taken pains to make public the size and power of the country's strategic nuclear forces and the measures taken to ensure their ability to survive an attack. The final irony of the nuclear age would be for an attacker to initiate a nuclear exchange that caused the destruction of its own society because it was unaware that the adversary had forces of such strength and survivability that the attack had no prospect for success.

However, there is no shortage of advocates who contend that nuclear weapons do have a role in both war and peace. They contend that the U.S. strategic forces must be continually "modernized" (a euphemism for increasing their counterforce capability) to demonstrate that the United States will not be intimidated. They say that only by being able to fight a limited nuclear war, beginning with counterforce attacks on military targets, can the United States deter Russia, China, or some other potential adversary from initiating such a war.

This strategy, a countervailing strategy, answers the last three questions quite differently than does McNamara's strategy of assured destruction. A countervailing strategy requires a large strategic arsenal, containing a large number of quite potent counterforce weapons as well as a very survivable strategic reserve. It requires preparation for a variety of actual strategies for waging war, including a strategy for a protracted but limited nuclear war. And finally, this doctrine says that nuclear weapons must deter not only a full-scale strike against the United States and its allies, but they must also demonstrate U.S. resolve to the world.

It may be that deterrence and flexible response/war fighting are the twin poles that every nuclear nation's doctrine will oscillate between as each new nuclear nation retraces the same route that the United States and the Soviet Union traversed in the Cold War. Or it could be that France, China, and Israel point to the future: an arsenal of about 200 weapons, just enough to inflict unacceptable damage to an attacker yet too small to tempt preemption.

What, however, is the state of the world today? The United States and the Russian Republic both have the ability, regardless of any damage that could be inflicted on their strategic nuclear forces by an attacker, to destroy that attacker's society. Mutual assured destruction therefore is a fact of life today, not a doctrine. If as Clausewitz said, "war is a continuation of political activity by other means" and that "when communities go to war … the occasion is always due to some political objective," what political objective can be attained through nuclear war? Does nuclear war, which would result in the destruction of any state that engages in it, have any purpose?

We have seen that, regardless of an administration's policies, the military services are very influential in determining what weapons are actually procured and what operational plans are actually in place for their use. We have also seen that administrations are very much constrained by the weapons that are at hand during a crisis; this is particularly so for nuclear weapons, because nuclear war would be too brief to allow new weapons to be built. It has been suggested that regardless of the declared doctrine of any administration, there continue to be only two possible wartime uses of nuclear weapons that the U.S. military regards at all seriously: preemption and retaliation. One critic, for instance, citing a 1982 report by the Committee on Governmental Operations of the U.S. House of Representatives, points out that the Air Force Finance Center's computers have uninterruptable power supplies, while the computers at the North American Aerospace Defense Center do not. After a nuclear attack on the United States, Air Force personnel would still get their paychecks, but the Strategic Air Command would not be able to coordinate a precise counterstrike.[104] SAC clearly was not planning to fight a protracted nuclear war. Despite a decade and a half of movement on the part of successive administrations toward a doctrine of nuclear war fighting, codified in 1980 in PD-59, in 1985 another exhaustive study of command and control of nuclear forces concluded that "the direction of forces is not and cannot be nearly as central, flexible, or precise as the nuclear strategy of the

Reagan administration requires."[105] This suggests once again that administrations come and go, but organizational preferences prevail.

This does not mean, unfortunately, that we have the luxury of ignoring an administration's doctrines. After all, doctrine is declared policy, and declared policy sends signals to potential enemies as to how the administration intends to act in a crisis. Thus a war-fighting doctrine, particularly a war-fighting doctrine that specifically targets the enemy's leadership, could panic an enemy into a preemptive strike against the United States, even though the United States could not actually fight a protracted nuclear war.

NOTES

1. Stephen I. Schwartz, *Atomic Audit: The Costs and Consequences of U.S. Nuclear Weapons since 1940* (Washington, D.C.: Brookings Institution Press, 1998), p. 222.
2. Eric Schmitt, "U.S. Curtails 24-Hour Duty of Its Flying Command Post," *New York Times*, July 28, 1990, p. 6.
3. Schwartz, *Atomic Audit*, p. 207.
4. Daniel Ford, *The Button: The Pentagon's Strategic Command and Control System* (New York: Simon & Schuster, 1985), p. 148; and Ashton B. Carter, ed., *Managing Nuclear Operations* (Washington, D.C.: The Brookings Institution, 1987), p. 52.
5. *Nuclear Posture Review*, March 1993.
6. Schwartz, *Atomic Audit*, p. 225.
7. *Avoiding Nuclear Anarchy: Containing the Threat of Loose Russian Nuclear Weapons and Fissile Material*, CSIA Studies in International Security No. 12 (Cambridge, MA: MIT Press, 1996), p. 178.
8. *Atomic Audit*, pp. 264–265.
9. *Military Capacity and the Risk of War: China, India, Pakistan and Iran* (Oxford, Stockholm: International Peace Research Institute, Oxford University Press, 1997), pp. 16, 234.
10. Walter A. McDougall, *The Heavens and the Earth: A Political History of the Space Age* (New York: Basic Books, 1985), pp. 141–156.
11. Fred Kaplan, *Wizards of Armageddon* (New York: Simon & Schuster, 1983), pp. 161–162.
12. Desmond Ball, *Politics and Force Levels: The Strategic Missile Program of the Kennedy Administration* (Berkeley, CA: University of California Press, 1980), p. 9.
13. Kaplan, *Wizards of Armageddon*, pp. 44, 269; and Sagan, "SIOP-62: The Nuclear War Plan Briefing to President Kennedy," *International Security* 12 (summer 1987): 44, 48.
14. Kaplan, *Wizards of Armageddon*, p. 135.
15. Edmund Beard, *Developing the ICBM: A Study in Bureaucratic Politics* (New York: Columbia University Press, 1976), p. 220.
16. Ibid., p. 219.
17. Ibid., p. 6.
18. "Until late 1953, and despite the existence of contrary evidence and opinion, a general emphasis on manned bomber systems ... with a slow conservative approach to ballistic missiles persisted within the Air Force. Contrary opinions were disregarded, contrary evidence dismissed. Men who had always flown and relied upon bombers found it hard, indeed almost impossible, to sense the revolutionary implications of ballistic missiles." Beard, *Developing the ICBM*, p. 8. "Long range missiles might not be emphasized by the Air Force but no one else was going to build them either if the Air Force could help it." Beard, *Developing the ICBM*, p. 167.
19. Ibid., pp. 11, 222.
20. Ibid., p. 6. "The strategic bombardment function was still the most important in the Air Force. The chosen means to accomplish the mission remained the manned bomber fleet and would continue to do so with the future deployment of the B-52. Long range surface

missiles were not important within the relevant future of the Air Force. It was important, however, that other services not develop such weapons which could then compete with the Air Force responsibility and the chosen Air Force vehicle." Ibid., p. 105.

21. "The Secretary's Message," *Quadrennial Defense Review* (May 1997): 1.

22. U.S. President, *Public Papers of the Presidents of the United States: Dwight D. Eisenhower, 1960–61* (Washington, D.C.: U.S. Government Printing Office, 1961), p. 1038.

23. Dwight D. Eisenhower, *Waging Peace, 1956–1961* (Garden City, NY: Doubleday & Company, 1965), p. 615.

24. "The B-1 bomber presents a dramatic case of a weapon that was acquired in spite of determined opposition over a period of 30 years. It was opposed by four of the seven presidents, who considered that the day of the manned strategic bomber had passed, yet still more than $29 billion was spent to acquire this successor to the B-52. The economic and political rewards were enormous—during the seven years of the construction of 100 B-1 bombers an average of 40,000 workers in 48 states were employed by 5,200 companies in building the aircraft and its components. During the peak production year, 1986, 60,000 workers were employed, and the B-1 accounted for two-thirds of the income of the principal contractor, Rockwell International." Nick Kotz, *Wild Blue Yonder, Money, Politics and the B-1 Bomber* (New York: Pantheon Books, 1988), pp. 8, 222–223.

25. David Holloway, *Soviet Union and the Arms Race* (New Haven, CT: Yale University Press, 1983), p. 43.

26. Holloway, *Soviet Union and the Arms Race*, p. 43.

27. Peter J. Roman, *Eisenhower and the Missile Gap* (Ithaca, NY: Cornell University Press, 1995), pp. 140–141.

28. Sagan, "SIOP-63," p. 26.

29. McDougall, *The Heavens and Earth*, p. 329.

30. Ball, *Politics and Force Levels*, pp. 50, 56.

31. Ibid., p. 52.

32. Author's experience.

33. See Eric Arnett, ed., *Military Capacity and the Risk of War* (Oxford: Oxford University Press, 1977).

34. Steve Fetter, "Ballistic Missiles and Weapons of Mass Destruction," *International Security* 16, no. 1 (summer 1991): 19.

35. Albert Wohlstetter, "The Delicate Balance of Terror," *Foreign Affairs* 37 (January 1959): 211–234.

36. Fetter, "Ballistic Missiles and Weapons of Mass Destruction," p. 19.

37. Alain C. Enthoven and K. Wayne Smith, *How Much Is Enough: Shaping the Defense Program, 1961–1969* (New York: Harper & Row, 1971), p. 174.

38. Ibid., p. 175.

39. Kaplan, *Wizards of Armageddon*, p. 320.

40. Arthur M. Schlesinger, *A Thousand Days: John F. Kennedy in the White House* (Boston, MA: Houghton Mifflin, 1995), p. 388.

41. Kaplan, *Wizards of Armageddon*, pp. 263–270; David Allen Rosenberg, "The Origins of Overkill: Nuclear Weapons and American Strategy, 1945–1986," *International Security* 7 (spring 1983): 64–66; and Scott D. Sagan, "SIOP-62," pp. 22–51.

42. McDougall, *The Heavens and Earth*, p. 328.

43. Enthoven and Smith, *How Much Is Enough*, p. 207.

44. Nigel Calder, *Nuclear Nightmares: An Investigation into Possible Wars* (Hammondsworth, England: Penguin Books, 1979), p. 1.

45. Calder, *Nuclear Nightmares*, p. 10.

46. The policy of flexible response also included a substantial increase in the U.S. conventional military forces in order to deter Soviet aggression without risking a nuclear exchange.

47. "Damage limitation" as a concept had a more specific meaning: If the U.S. second-strike retaliatory force had counterforce weapons that were capable of destroying any of the

enemy's weapons that were not used in his initial strike, the damage to the United States could be reduced in the event of a nuclear exchange. In the scenario McNamara envisioned, the Soviet Union might launch a limited nuclear attack on the United States, withholding some missiles for subsequent attacks if the United States did not accede to its demands. To limit damage to the United States in the Soviet follow-on attacks, McNamara would use counterforce weapons to destroy the remaining Soviet missiles.

48. Robert S. McNamara, "Defense Arrangements of the North Atlantic Community," *Department of State Bulletin* 47, no. 1202 (July 9, 1962): 67.
49. Alain C. Enthoven and K. Wayne Smith, *How Much Is Enough*, p. 174.
50. Ibid.
51. Interview in *Pravda*, October 21, 1981, quoted in Dan Strode and Rebecca Strode, "Diplomacy and Defense in Soviet National Security Policy," *International Security* 8 (fall 1983): 91.
52. Lawrence Freedman, *Evolution of Nuclear Strategy*, 2d ed. (New York: St. Martin's Press, 1989), p. 90.
53. In the lexicon of nuclear strategy, "warfighting means the use of nuclear weapons for well-defined military purposes, as opposed to crude punishment with unbridled attacks on cities." Calder, *Nuclear Nightmare*, p. 18.
54. Gregg Herken, *Counsels of War* (New York: Knopf, 1985), p. 301.
55. Freedman, *Evolution of Nuclear Strategy*, p. 393.
56. Ronald Reagan, *National Security Strategy of the United States* (Washington, D.C., January 1988).
57. Frank von Hippel, Roald Sagdeyev, William G. Miller, and Robert S. McNamara, "How to Avoid Accidental Nuclear War," *Bulletin of the Atomic Scientists* 46, no. 5 (June 1990): 36.
58. McGeorge Bundy, "To Cap the Volcano," *Foreign Affairs* 48 (October 1969): 10.
59. Schwartz, *Atomic Audit*, p. 149.
60. Enthoven and Smith, *How Much Is Enough*, p. 181.
61. Thomas B. Cochran, William M. Arkin, and Milton M. Hoenig, *Nuclear Weapons Databook, Vol. 1: U.S. Nuclear Forces and Capabilities* (Cambridge, MA: Ballinger Publishing Co., 1984), pp. 55, 75, 122.
62. William E. Burrows, *Deep Black: Space Espionage and National Security* (New York: Random House, 1986), pp. 248, 307.
63. Ted Greenwood, *Making the MIRV: A Study of Defense Decision Making* (Cambridge, MA: Ballinger, 1975), pp. 8–11.
64. Kaplan, *Wizards of Armageddon*, p. 364.
65. Richard K. Betts, ed., *Cruise Missiles: Technology, Strategy, Politics* (Washington, D.C.: The Brookings Institution, 1981), pp. 34–45.
66. Duk-Ki Kim, "Cooperative Maritime Security in Northeast Asia," *Naval War College Review* (Washington) 52, no. 1 (winter 1999): 53–77.
67. *The Military Balance, 1997/98* (London: International Institute for Strategic Studies, 1997), pp. 150–151.
68. Ibid., pp. 118–119.
69. Jeff Hecht, *Beam Weapons: The Next Arms Race* (New York: Plenum Press, 1984), p. 177.
70. Schwartz, *Atomic Audit*, pp. 290–294.
71. Paul M. Kennedy, *The Rise and Fall of Great Powers: Economic Change and Military Conflict From 1500 to 2000* (New York: Random House, 1987).
72. *The Quadrennial Defense Review: A Sense of Deja Vu.* www.cdi.org
73. Bruce D. Larkin, *Nuclear Designs: Great Britain, France and China in the Global Governance of Nuclear Arms* (New Brunswick, NJ: Transaction Publishers, 1996).
74. Richard Kokoski, *Technology and the Proliferation of Nuclear Weapons* (New York: Oxford University Press, 1995), p. 1.
75. Larkin, *Nuclear Designs*, p. 9.

76. "The Secretary's Message," *Quadrennial Defense Review* (May 1997): 1.
77. U.S. Secretary of Defense, *Annual Report to the President and the Congress, 1998.* Chapter 5.
78. Larkin, *Nuclear Designs*, p. 165.
79. Ibid., p. 85.
80. Ibid., p. 32.
81. Ibid., p. 38.
82. Ibid., p. 39.
83. Ibid., p. 38.
84. Center for Defense Information, "Current World Nuclear Arsenals." October 15, 1997.
85. *SIPRI Yearbook 1998: Armaments, Disarmament, and International Security* (Oxford, Eng.: Oxford University Press, 1998), p. 442.
86. Larkin, *Nuclear Designs*, p. 323.
87. *SIPRI Yearbook 1998*, p. 442.
88. *The Military Balance 1997/98*, p. 127.
89. Seymour M. Hersh, *The Samson Option: Israel's Nuclear Arsenal and American Foreign Policy* (New York: Random House, © 1991).
90. Michael J. Mazaar, *North Korea and the Bomb: A Case Study in Nonproliferation* (New York: St. Martin's Press, 1995), p. 6.
91. Devin T. Hagerty "Nuclear Deterrence in South Asia," *International Security* 20, no. 3 (winter 1995): 84.
92. Michael J. Mazarr "Going Just a Little Nuclear: Nonproliferation Lessons from North Korea," *International Security* 20, no. 2 (fall 1995): 94.
93. Mazarr, *North Korea and the Bomb*, p. 173.
94. Ibid., p. 173.
95. Philip Shenon, "North Korean Nuclear Arms Pact Reported Near Breakdown," *New York Times*, December 6, 1998, p. 16.
96. Graham Allison et al., *Avoiding Nuclear Anarchy: Containing the Threat of Loose Russian Nuclear Weapons and Fissile Material*, CSIA Studies in International Security No. 12 (Cambridge, MA: MIT Press, 1996), p. 56.
97. Ibid., p. 58.
98. Ibid., p. 57.
99. Ibid., p. 2.
100. Ibid., pp. 179–180.
101. Ibid., p. 188.
102. Ibid., p. 191.
103. Bernard Brodie, ed., *The Absolute Weapon: Atomic Power and World Order* (New York: Harcourt, Brace and Company, 1946), p. 76.
104. Ford, *The Button*, pp. 80–81.
105. Bruce G. Blair, *Strategic Command and Control: Redefining the Nuclear Threat* (Washington, D.C.: The Brookings Institution, 1985), p. 65.

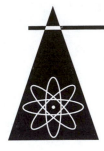

6

NUCLEAR RIVALS
AND NUCLEAR RELATIONS

Imagine that you are with President Kennedy on the day he learns that the Soviet Union is constructing nuclear missile sites in Cuba. His advisors seem convinced that the United States has no choice but to respond in some way, but Kennedy keeps groping to understand the Soviet action. Why would the Soviet Union take such a provocative action after the president's repeated public and private warnings that the United States would not tolerate Soviet nuclear weapons in Cuba?

Robert Kennedy—the president's brother and closest advisor—is speaking. While we cannot give you the Boston accents nor the styles of delivery, we can give you exactly what the people at the table said and how they said it, as their words were being secretly recorded.[1] Try reading the following excerpt aloud, taking the role of each person. It is an education in how leaders actually responded to a nuclear rival in a crisis.

ROBERT KENNEDY: Mr. President, while we're considering this problem tonight [at a follow-up meeting], I think that we should also consider what, uh, Cuba's going to be a year from now, or two years from now. Assume that we go in and knock these sites out. Uh, I don't know what's gonna stop them from saying, "We're gonna build the sites six months from now, bring 'em in...."

CHAIRMAN OF THE JOINT CHIEFS MAXWELL TAYLOR: Nothing permanent about it.

ROBERT KENNEDY: Uh, ... where are we six months from now? Or that we're in any better position, or aren't we in worse position if we go in and knock 'em out and say, uh, "Don't do it." Uh, I mean, obviously they're gonna *have* to do it then.

SECRETARY OF DEFENSE ROBERT MCNAMARA: You have to put a blockade in following any limited action.

ROBERT KENNEDY: Then we're gonna have to sink Russian ships. Then we're gonna have to sink Russian submarines. Now whether it wouldn't be, uh, the argument, if you're going to get into it at all, uh, whether we should just get into it and get it over with and say that, uh, take our losses, and if we're gonna.... If he wants to get into a war over *this*, uh ... Hell, if it's war that's gonna come on this thing, or if he sticks those kinds of missiles in, it's after the warning, and he's gonna, and he's gonna get into a war for, six months from now or a year from now, so....

MCNAMARA: Mr. President, this is why I think tonight we ought to put on paper the alternative plans and the probable, possible consequences thereof in a way that State and Defense [Departments] could agree on, even if we, uh, disagree and put in both views. Because the consequences of these actions have *not* been thought through clearly. The one that the attorney general [Robert Kennedy] just mentioned is illustrative of that.

PRESIDENT KENNEDY: If the, uh, it doesn't increase very much their strategic strength, why is it, uh, ... can any Russian expert tell us why they.... After all Khrushchev demonstrated a sense of caution [about] Berlin; he's been cautious, I mean, he hasn't been, uh....

UNIDENTIFIED SPEAKER: Several possibilities, Mr. President. One of them is that he has given us word now that he's coming over in November to, to the UN. If, he may be proceeding on the assumption, and this lack of a sense of *apparent* urgency would seem to support this, that this *isn't* going to be discovered at the moment and that, uh, when he comes over, this is something he can do, a ploy. That here is Cuba armed against the United States, or possibly use it to try to trade something in Berlin, saying he'll disarm Cuba if, uh, if we'll, uh, yield some of our interests in Berlin and some arrangement for it. I mean, that this is a, it's a trading ploy.

NATIONAL SECURITY ADVISOR MCGEORGE BUNDY: I would think one thing that I would still cling to is that he's not likely to give Fidel Castro nuclear warheads. I don't believe that has happened or is likely to happen.

PRESIDENT KENNEDY: Why does he put these in there though?

Why, indeed, would the Soviet Union put those nuclear weapons in Cuba? Did it mean, as Robert Kennedy wondered, that the Soviets had decided on war with the United States? Or were they willing to risk war to get their way? Would the United States have to risk nuclear war to deal with the missiles? The Cuban missile crisis captures the central question of this chapter: How do nuclear armed states behave toward each other? It is also a central question for our nuclear future.

In previous chapters, we looked at particular aspects of nuclear behavior: how states made decisions to use (or not use) nuclear weapons, how they fashioned doctrines for their use in times of war, and, as the idea of deterrence gained currency, how they fashioned doctrines to *prevent* the use of those weapons. In this chapter, we look at ways in which the nuclear age has affected basic relations among states. We concentrate on how states might seek to exploit their nuclear weapons to advance their national interests. Taking such actions increases the likelihood of use, and thus poses great peril to the states involved and to bystanders.

To look at the threatening aspects of nuclear international relations, we use three types of inquiry. First, we examine two specific crises in which nuclear weapons were important elements. Then we move to a cataloging of ways in which nuclear weapons have become parts of the foreign policy practices of nuclear weapons states—and how states without nuclear weapons have tried to cope with their nuclear-armed allies and adversaries. Our third level explores a model of relations between states, seeking to identify the role of nuclear weapons in a more general way. We illustrate this model by looking at the Soviet-American Cold War.

In each inquiry we examine the past as a way to review how nuclear weapons have been a part of world politics since 1945, but also to see if the past provides any predictions about the future. At the same time, we explore some ways in which a post-Cold War world might have changed the nuclear equation. Can we discern possible futures that are not predictable from looking at the past? Are predictions from the Cold War past applicable in the post-Cold War future? In each inquiry, we will see time and time again one basic element of the predicament: The promotion of national interest has encouraged states to bring nuclear weapons into their relations with other states, but in so doing they often increase the risk to their own survival, which is not in their national interest. Making nuclear weapons a part of world politics may seem inherently self-defeating. But one might well ask, once nuclear weapons appeared in August 1945, is it not the case that nuclear weapons are, wanted or unwanted, forever bound up in the international relations of many states? It is to this question that we turn first.

THE NUCLEAR SHADOW

We might imagine that nuclear weapons, because of their power, would dramatically affect the thinking and behavior of the leaders of nuclear weapons states, and, as well, the thinking and behavior of nonnuclear states having to deal with nuclear-armed states. We call this effect *the nuclear shadow*—the changes that the very existence of nuclear weapons have wrought on relations between states. There are clear indications of the shadow. The American president was and is accompanied by a military officer carrying a briefcase known as "the football"; it contains the information needed by the president to launch American nuclear weapons. The Russian president has a similar arrangement.[2]

The football is a daily reminder of the inescapable shadow—a burdensome reminder. Lyndon Johnson recalled his last moments in office:

> I heard Richard Nixon conclude his oath of office with the words "so help me God." To me, they were welcome words. I remember ... [a thought] running through my mind: ... that I would not have to face the decision any more of taking any step, in the Middle East or elsewhere, that might lead to world conflagration—the nightmare of my having to be the man who pressed the button to start World War III was passing.[3]

But to say that nuclear weapons cast a shadow does not take us very far into understanding the future. *How* have they affected world politics? We need to know how dark that shadow is and what features it has. Again, we might imagine that nuclear weapons would change everything in dramatic ways. Several days after the bomb was dropped on Hiroshima, journalist Theodore White interviewed General Douglas MacArthur, who had conducted a spectacularly successful series of offensives against the Japanese. MacArthur had just been briefed on the bomb.

> "White," he said, "White, do you know what this means?... Men like me are obsolete," he said, pacing back and forth. "There will be no more wars, White, no more wars."[4]

That, indeed, would be a profound impact, for it would eliminate one of the key features of traditional international relations: the waging of war to advance or protect the interests of the state. Has that been the case? Clearly, there has been no post-1945 nuclear war, nor has there been any war between the major powers. The fact that the two Cold War rivals, the United States and the Soviet Union, were able to keep "the long peace"[5] between themselves since 1945 made their relationship very unusual. Historically, most top rivals went to war against each other during such a time period. Was this peace a result of the nuclear shadow? Did nuclear weapons keep the peace or were other factors more important? There is no clear answer.[6]

There is, of course, the comforting belief that the long peace was a result of nuclear deterrence—that deterrence worked. If that were the case, then nuclear weapons would have cast a dark, sharp shadow. One way to demonstrate that deterrence has in fact worked is to find a case in which one nuclear-armed state actually contemplated waging war against another nuclear-armed state, but did not do so because it believed the costs would be unacceptable. There is no evidence that the top leadership of either the United States or the Soviet Union had an interest in waging war against the other. Therefore, it is probably better to say that nuclear deterrence has *never been meaningfully tested*. Thus, this part of the shadow also remains relatively unknown to us.

If we cannot say for sure that nuclear weapons kept the great powers from waging war against each other, perhaps we can suggest that the shadow's impact has been to make states more cautious in their foreign policies. Significant foreign policy blunders might lead to a nuclear confrontation and then to nuclear use. Therefore, it would seem reasonable to imagine that states became more risk-adverse in the nuclear world, making the world safer for all. Unfortunately, the evidence to support this claim is mixed.

In some cases, nuclear weapons did become a part of the considerations of decision makers, making them less willing to take actions if there was a risk of a nuclear war. In its Vietnam decision making, for instance, the U.S. government took great pains to avoid any action that might suck nuclear-armed China into the war. Some participants in the deliberations saw nuclear shadows. If the Chinese intervened in the Vietnam war and created a stalemate as they did in the Korean war, these participants reasoned,

> we should certainly expect mounting [American public] pressure for the use of at least tactical nuclear weapons.... [But using nuclear weapons] would upset the fragile balance of terror on which much of the world has come to depend for the maintenance of peace. Whether or not the Soviet Union actually used nuclear weapons against other nations, the very fact that we had provided a justification for their use would create a new wave of fear.... While no one can be certain, the best judgment is that the Soviet Union could not sit by and let nuclear weapons be used against China.[7]

Evoking the nuclear risk did bring about restraint in some ways—the United States worked diligently to prevent its actions in Vietnam from propelling the Chinese into the war. At the same time, however, the nuclear issue did not prevent the United States from undertaking its massive military intervention in the Vietnam war. Indeed, in some ways, the existence of nuclear weapons and nuclear deterrence made intervention in Vietnam seem necessary. American policymakers were convinced that deterrence rested on the belief that the United States would respond to an attack on itself or its allies by striking the Soviet Union. Was such a threat credible? American leaders were concerned that if the United States did not keep its word in each and every circumstance when it was costly to do so, then nuclear deterrence would be undermined. The Johnson administration, for example, took this view regarding Vietnam. In facing the question in the summer of 1965 of whether to commit ground forces to the war in Vietnam, Lyndon Johnson saw this aspect of the shadow:

> [Secretary of State] Dean Rusk expressed one worry that was much on my mind. It lay at the heart of our Vietnam policy. "If the Communist world finds out that we will not pursue our commitments to the end," he said, "I don't know where they will stay their hand."
> I felt sure they would *not* stay their hand. If we ran out on Southeast Asia, I could see trouble ahead in every part of the globe—not just in Asia but in the Middle East

and in Europe, in Africa and in Latin America. I was convinced that our retreat from this challenge would open the path to World War III.[8]

Moreover, if nuclear weapons induced restraint, then we might expect there to be no planned confrontations between the United States and the Soviet Union or with their allies. That historically was not the case, as we shall see in the Berlin and Cuban case studies that we discuss later. Nor did the existence of nuclear weapons prevent active consideration of the use of such weapons against others, as we saw in Chapter 2. Finally, in some cases, the existence of nuclear weapons might have forced states to take riskier actions against an opponent. For instance, the People's Republic of China in the winter of 1950–1951 felt so threatened by American military successes in the Korean War that it felt obliged to enter the war against the Americans, even though the latter was nuclear-armed and the Chinese were not. Indeed, some states may feel that they must take risky actions when confronting a powerful nuclear-armed state in order to demonstrate that they will not be blackmailed by nuclear weapons. Nikita Khrushchev expressed the point this way: "[T]he fear of a nuclear war … can paralyze that country's defenses. And if a country's defenses are paralyzed, then war is really inevitable: The enemy is sure to sense your fright and try to take advantage of it. I always operated on the principle that I should be clearly against war but never frightened of it."[9]

The nuclear shadow thus seems to have different consequences. Under some conditions, a nuclear-weapons state might be less willing to take risky actions in world politics because of nuclear weapons, but under other conditions, having nuclear weapons may make the state feel more confident in taking risky actions, believing that its opponent will be cowed into acquiescence because the opponent fears nuclear war. Under other conditions, the state may feel more impelled to take risky actions in order to shore up its credibility. Indeed, it may choose the most risky action of all: to use nuclear weapons. These responses might apply to a nonnuclear weapons state as well when confronting a nuclear-armed state.

In order to specify the conditions under which nuclear weapons might lead to riskier or more cautious world politics (and thus begin to gain a handle on our nuclear future), we turn now to two specific crises between the United States and the Soviet Union: the Cuban missile crisis and the several Berlin crises. In all these crises, the Soviet Union found it necessary or desirable to escalate an issue to the point of a clear challenge to Western interests, and it did so from a general posture of strategic nuclear inferiority to the United States. That is to say, nuclear superiority did not prevent challenges to the more powerful state, and, as we shall see, the peaceful resolution of those challenges was not guaranteed by the existence of nuclear weapons. The nuclear shadow played itself out in complex ways.

THE CUBAN MISSILE CRISIS

In October 1962, an American spy plane detected the construction of Soviet missile sites in Cuba.[10] Intelligence officers estimated that the Soviets would soon have 20–24 medium-range missiles carrying up to a 3 megaton warhead with a range of 1,200 miles ready to fire, and 4–12 intermediate-range missiles (5 megaton warheads) with a range of 2,500 miles ready in two to four weeks.[11] The shorter range missiles could reach Washington D.C.; the longer-range missiles, the United States east of the Rockies. We know that the American response and subsequent Soviet actions would bring the world to the brink of war—the closest the two rivals ever came during the Cold War. Because nuclear weapons were at the heart of the crisis, and because President Kennedy had pledged a full retaliatory response on the Soviet Union if a single missile were launched from Cuba, any hostilities that emerged held a real risk of escalation across the nuclear threshold. How was it that, in the nuclear age, two states would push or permit their relations to reach this point?

For Khrushchev and the Soviet leadership, the motivations for deployment were diverse. In 1961, the Kennedy administration had publicly announced that the strategic advantage (in terms of ICBMs and strategic bombers) was decidedly in the Americans' favor.[12] Khrushchev may not have been convinced that the Americans planned a preemptive strike, but he apparently feared that the United States would attempt to exploit the imbalance politically (as the trumpeting of American superiority seemed to foreshadow). Exploitation would take the form of blackmailing the Soviet Union into acquiescing to American demands, backed implicitly by a nuclear threat. Moreover, the American public posture of supremacy might persuade the decolonizing third world that the Soviet Union could not be a reliable ally. Soviet missile deployment in Cuba would thus help correct the strategic imbalance and serve notice that the Soviet Union did not intend to be blackmailed.

Secondly, some Soviet leaders—Khrushchev in particular—were angered that the United States had deployed its shorter range nuclear missiles in Italy and Turkey over the protests of the Soviet Union. Meeting with Marshal Malinovsky in the Crimea in the spring of 1962,

> Malinovsky drew Khrushchev's attention to the installation of American missiles just over the horizon of the Black Sea in Turkey. He told Khrushchev that the American missiles in Turkey could strike the Soviet Union in ten minutes, whereas Soviet missiles needed twenty-five minutes to hit the United States. Khrushchev then mused on whether the Soviet Union shouldn't do the same thing in Cuba, just over the horizon from the United States. The Americans, after all, had not asked Soviet permission.[13]

Soviet deployment to Cuba, mirroring the American deployment of missiles to its allies, would remind the United States that the Soviet Union expected to be treated as a leading power (a vision of itself that Khrushchev had enunciated during the 1950s). What the United States did, the Soviet Union could do as well.

Finally, deployment would, Khrushchev hoped, protect the Castro government from American attack. Castro had declared Cuba to be part of the socialist camp. The Soviet Union, engaged in a bitter war of words with the Chinese about the quality of its leadership of the socialist camp, could not risk the destruction of Castro by the United States. The Americans had made one abortive attempt in April 1961 at the Bay of Pigs, but had chosen to rely on CIA-trained and CIA-paid Cuban exiles to overthrow Castro. The Soviets calculated that the next American attempt would be with American military forces. (The American military had in fact begun an extensive series of preparations and training exercises for the invasion of Cuba; the Kennedy administration, however, had withheld a decision to undertake such an invasion.) Soviet missiles in Cuba would create the Soviet version of extended deterrence—the threat to use nuclear weapons in retaliation for an attack on Cuba would keep such an attack from happening.

Soviet motives, understandable in themselves and on balance defensive in nature, were what we might expect of a nuclear-armed state, particularly one on the short end of an asymmetrical relationship: trying to maintain a credible second-strike capability, to provide extended deterrence to an ally, and to engage tit-for-tat in missile deployment outside the home country. The motives, however, collided with American beliefs and politics.

The covert construction of the missile bases coincided with a major, overt Soviet conventional arms buildup in Cuba to show Soviet leadership of the socialist camp, to placate an anxious Fidel Castro, and to bolster deterrence against another American attempt to remove Castro. These overt actions challenged the century-old American belief (symbolized by the Monroe Doctrine) that no hostile power should have any influence in the Caribbean—certainly not a Communist power. As the fall of 1962 was a Congressional election year, President Kennedy found himself under intense pressure "to do something about Cuba." In particular, some Republicans alleged that there were nuclear weapons in Cuba. The president publicly (and privately) warned the Soviet Union that serious consequences would follow if the Soviet Union installed offensive weapons in Cuba. Khrushchev (already having made the decision to deploy) repeatedly assured Kennedy that the Soviet Union would not deploy offensive arms in Cuba. Lacking a sensitivity to the beliefs and politics of the United States (either before or after the decision to deploy), actions reasonable from the Soviet perspective would create a fearsome crisis.

The Soviets compounded the crisis by apparently not considering what might go wrong in a complex operation to transport and erect missiles clandestinely in an area saturated by American military assets. It is likely that the Soviet government assumed that the Americans would not learn of the missiles until the Soviet government revealed them, and the Americans would then respond in ways that would promote Soviet goals (such as acquiescing in the existence of such missiles). Such fatuous assumptions are not unusual in the making of foreign policy. But as we shall see, one of the hallmarks of the American administration's decision making was to think carefully about what the Soviet responses might be to its actions. That care, however, was counter-balanced by a hasty rush to decide on an appropriate response.

Kennedy was both puzzled and angered by the Soviet action. They had lied to him, and Kennedy was convinced that domestic politics gave him no option but to respond forcefully to the challenge. As we saw from the conversation quoted at the start of the chapter, he could not fathom the Soviet motivations, but in his eyes—and in those of many of his advisors—the Soviet Union was acting aggressively.

For someone, on the other hand, like Secretary of Defense Robert McNamara, who was beginning to formulate how deterrence worked, the deployment of these nuclear weapons capable of reaching the United States did not change the fact of deterrence, nor the fact that Soviet parity with the United States was bound to happen at some point (even if the Cuban missiles did not in fact redress the imbalance of strategic nuclear forces then in the American favor). McNamara suggested that, in terms of the nuclear world, the United States did not need to respond to the Soviet deployment of missiles to Cuba.

Such an argument carried no weight with the president or most of his advisors. Doing nothing would be political suicide, and seemed out of character with how the United States (or any great power) should respond when challenged so dramatically in its own sphere of influence. Moreover, the surreptitious mode of discovery (a U-2 overflight) and the estimate that the Soviets were just days from having operational sites encouraged policymakers to believe that they had to act quickly in light of what seemed to be an extremely aggressive Soviet move. The American leadership rushed past President Kennedy's critical question about what Soviet motivations might be, and Kennedy did not insist that it be answered. Thus the American government deprived itself of thinking about other possible Soviet motivations (e.g., that the Soviets were reacting defensively) or that this was the moment when it might be possible to work for some mutually acceptable understanding about security in a nuclear world—which, after all, was essentially what McNamara's thinking about deterrence implied. Instead, on discovery of the missile sites, Kennedy and his advisors made the hasty decision that the goal was to get the missiles out of Cuba.

The question then became a relatively narrow one: how to bring about the removal of the missiles. Three options suggested themselves: (1) a diplomatic protest and demand for their removal, (2) an air strike to destroy the missiles unilaterally, and (3) a blockade of Cuba. As we saw in the transcript at the beginning of the chapter, McNamara pointed out how important it was to explore any option carefully. His argument reflected two forces at work: (1) a recognition that when nuclear weapons were concerned, decision makers had to understand their options thoroughly, and (2) bureaucratic infighting. McNamara was opposed to an air strike, but the Joint Chiefs of Staff (subordinate to McNamara) were vigorous proponents of the idea, and worse, to McNamara's thinking, the president had quickly gravitated to the air strike option. Insisting on a careful canvas of the options is a time-honored way of exposing the problems in other people's preferred options and building a case for one's own. Without contending points of view within the leadership, a careful examination of the options may go by the boards, especially when the leaders feel under pressure to make a quick decision.

Indeed, it is likely that if the American government had felt compelled to make a quick decision (if, for instance, they had discovered the missile sites a week or two later when many of the missiles would have become operational), the air strike option would likely have carried the day. And, given the military's insistence that a successful air strike would have to be preceded by an extensive attack on Cuban airfields and Soviet installations in Cuba, especially the surface-to-air missile sites defending the missile bases, Soviet and Cuban casualties would have been extensive.

As it happened, the extent of the air strike was, in President Kennedy's mind, the basic question to be considered on the first day the missiles were discovered. As he said:

> I don't think we've got much time on these missiles. They may be.... So it may be that we just have to. We can't wait 2 weeks while we're getting ready to roll. Maybe we just have to take them out, and continue our other preparations if we decide to do that. That may be where we end up.
>
> I think we ought to, beginning right now, be preparing to. Because that's what we're going to do *anyway*. We're going to take out these missiles. The questions will be whether, what I would describe as number two, which would be a general air strike. That we're not ready to say, but we should be in preparation for it. The third is the general invasion. At least we're going to do number one. So it seems to me that we don't have to wait very long. We ought to be making *those* preparations.[14]

Note that connected to the air strike option was the option of a massive invasion of Cuba, most strongly advocated by the American military. We now know that in addition to the nuclear missiles in Cuba, there were *tactical* nuclear weapons in Cuba—weapons under the control of the commanders of Soviet combat units in

Cuba. While Moscow refused to give its commanders the authority to use those weapons on their own volition during the crisis, who knows what might have happened if an American invasion appeared in the offing. Imagine the shock to American leaders to learn that American troops coming ashore in Cuba had been attacked with Hiroshima-sized weapons, creating massive casualties. What then? It would not have been a missile leaving Cuba that had done the damage, but President Kennedy's promise of retaliation might have created inescapable pressure for some form of nuclear response. And then what?

We know, of course, that neither the air strike nor the invasion occurred. Rather, the United States imposed a maritime blockade of Cuba, prohibiting the passage of any ships suspected of carrying further offensive weapons to Cuba. The administration hoped that the blockade would communicate the seriousness with which the United States was backing its demand that the Soviet Union withdraw the missiles, and would allow for a later escalation if that became necessary. For the moment, however, the air strike was on hold, the result of effective lobbying by McNamara and Robert Kennedy. There was a risk, nonetheless, that Soviet and American warships would confront each other on the high seas.

It is commonly thought that this blockade forced the Soviets to withdraw their missiles, thus ending the crisis. This is not the case. The blockade, in fact, failed. The Soviets sped up construction, rushing to bring the sites to an operational status. Khrushchev denounced the blockade as illegal and declared it unacceptable that the United States should try to tell Cuba and the USSR, two sovereign nations, what they could and could not do. The Soviets decided not to challenge the blockade, but for several tense days, there was the prospect of some kind of crisis at sea. An American warship attempting to board a Soviet freighter being escorted by a Soviet submarine might be the spark that pushed the two into direct hostilities.

As the crisis mounted, both sides did work behind the scenes to explore the terms for a diplomatic settlement of the crisis. Such efforts ran into a serious roadblock. Kennedy was willing to pledge not to invade Cuba if the Soviets withdrew the missiles, but he balked at the Soviet demand that the United States withdraw its missiles from Italy and Turkey. Those missiles, Kennedy said, were tangential to the crisis, which in the American view centered on unacceptable Soviet behavior in Cuba. The blockade could not by itself force the withdrawal of the missiles; lifting the blockade would not meet the Soviet demand for a parallel withdrawal of American missiles. A new impasse had developed.

The crisis ended because of two American actions. First, the United States bluntly but privately warned the Soviets that unless there were a diplomatic settlement that secured the withdrawal of the missiles, the United States would invade Cuba within two days. Second, Kennedy agreed that while the United States could not formally agree to swap the missiles in Cuba for its missiles in Italy and Turkey, it would arrange for their withdrawal in the near future. This threat and concession brought Soviet agreement, thus ending the missile crisis.

Ironically, at the end of the crisis, the American government stood poised to execute the air strike and invasion options that it had first considered, then set aside. There is every indication that Kennedy would have followed through with his threat. We can therefore say that the United States and the USSR were two days away from some possible form of nuclear use, most likely by Russian commanders in Cuba and an American response. History would have been harsh in its judgment of the Soviets and

Americans if that had happened. And history would have taken a quite different turn if these events had come to pass.

THE LESSONS OF THE CUBAN MISSILE CRISIS

As it was, the American government would not learn for decades that tactical nuclear weapons were in Cuba, and history judged the handling of the crisis as a remarkable display of crisis management by two nuclear powers. In the immediate aftermath of the crisis, various "lessons" emerged. These lessons suggest that, at least for the two participants, a nuclear crisis is an important learning experience. Both Soviet and American leaders appear to have concluded that a nuclear-armed state cannot act provocatively with its nuclear weapons, especially in ways that change the status quo. Secondly, each now had an incentive to find ways to avoid such confrontations in the future. That conclusion helped accelerate the agenda for arms control and for codifying the "rules of the road" for the two states (which we discuss in Chapter 8). On the other hand, the Soviets came to believe that the lack of nuclear parity with the United States forced them into making concessions to the United States. "Never again," Soviet leaders declared, would they be forced to negotiate on such unequal terms; they redoubled their efforts to match the American arsenal. The American leadership concluded that the U.S. nuclear and conventional strength mattered. The threat to invade Cuba was a real one because the United States had overwhelming conventional superiority in the region.

Thus, events of the past can affect the future, and will continue to do so as long as the memory of the past remains (even though it may be a false memory). But whose future do such events affect? The future relationship between the United States and the USSR was clearly affected. But what about the nuclear futures of the states that observed the crisis? For instance, the Chinese Communists, in their critique of Soviet behavior during the crisis, denounced the Soviet deployment as unacceptably provocative and Soviet acceptance of the settlement terms as unacceptably craven. But did the crisis affect Chinese behavior when China became a nuclear power? More generally, what and when do others learn the lessons of a nuclear crisis? We advance four basic propositions:

1. Learning by others will occur if there is a *clear success* by one of the participants that changes the status quo in its favor at minimal cost. The lesson is that provocative nuclear behavior pays off. There was no such success in the Cuban missile crisis. The American "success" was in restoring the status quo, and paying a price to do so.

   Will learning occur for others if there is a *failure*? That is, did others learn from the Cuban missile crisis not to employ nuclear weapons to change or support a change in the status quo? There has been no comparable crisis staged by others since 1962. Does the absence of such behavior mean that such learning did, in fact, occur? We are as skeptical of such a claim as we are of the claim that the absence of a superpower war meant that deterrence worked.

   On the other hand, we suspect that failures do not create lessons of restraint in the minds of other actors. Perversely, what others might learn from failure is to avoid the mistakes of the participants when challenging the status quo. Indeed, observers might be encouraged to challenge the status quo precisely because they believe they have discovered the "correct" way to use nuclear weapons to bring about—and make permanent—a change in the status quo. We find no evidence, however, of such learning by others.

2. Learning will occur if others see the situation as generally applicable to themselves. To the degree, therefore, that others saw the crisis as a clash of two particular ideologies, or a pattern of behavior of superpowers (a class of states then populated by only the United States and the USSR), they may have not seen the crisis as offering them any guidance. We suspect that for reasons such as these, the Cuban missile crisis offered few lessons for others.

3. When some actors learn lessons from the nuclear crises of others, there is no guarantee that the lessons learned will be those of the participants, or that all observers will draw the same conclusions. Some observers of the Cuban missile crisis might have concluded, for instance, that it may be impossible to bring about a successful change of the nuclear status quo clandestinely, while others might conclude that more attention to details (the Soviets, for instance, did not camouflage the missile sites they were building in Cuba) will produce success.

4. Finally, once learning occurs, if it is not incorporated into the routines of governmental and military bureaucracies, the lessons are likely to fade as time goes on. Education is, of course, the device by which societies try to perpetuate lessons, particularly among the political elites (and you can look on this book and your reading of it as part of the process). But its lessons, too, degrade over time (or become reworked into new conclusions, which may have startlingly different consequences).

Irrespective of the lessons the participants or observers might or might not have learned, what does the Cuban missile crisis suggest to us about the world's nuclear future? Although this anticipates a discussion to follow, we can suggest that at some point in an adversarial nuclear relationship the following will occur:

- One of the states will take similar actions to restore the nuclear balance, extend deterrence, or make a claim to have the same rights and privileges that its opponent has.
- One of the states will take an action that it sees as reasonable (such as deployment of missiles to Cuba) while the other will see the action as an enormous provocation.
- The subsequent crisis interactions of the two states will feature threats made with nuclear weapons.
- Luck will play a large role in determining whether nuclear use occurs.

THE BERLIN CRISES AND LESSONS

The Cuban missile crisis lasted two weeks. Berlin was a decade-long friction point.[15] There, American and Soviet interests clashed, and their military forces were a stone's throw away from each other. The defeat of Nazi Germany in 1945 had led to the division of Germany into four occupation zones (for the British and French as well as the Soviets and Americans). Berlin, surrounded by the Soviet occupation zone, was likewise divided, and the Western powers were guaranteed the right of transit across the Soviet zone to their sectors of Berlin.

The war-time allies soon found themselves in disagreement about how Germany might be reunited and given some degree of autonomy. The Soviets wanted to ensure that Germany remained weak, never again to threaten the Soviet Union. The United States wanted to allow a modest rebuilding of a united Germany so as to end the burden of the United States having to sustain its occupation zone economically. The Soviets and the West could not agree on the terms of the economic reintegration and renewal. The United States, France, and Britain decided to go it alone, beginning with a currency reform in their zones. As we saw in Chapter 4, Stalin reacted by imposing a land blockade on Berlin in June 1948; it was a warning to the Western powers that they needed Soviet approval to change the status quo in Germany.

The Soviet blockade was a military as well as a political challenge. The Allies sent supplies and personnel by land to garrison their sectors of Berlin; their military convoys were being blockaded as well. President Truman and his advisors discussed the option of sending an armed convoy to test the blockade, with orders to fire back if fired upon. The option seemed to be high risk, for if fighting began, the large Soviet armies surrounding Berlin would quickly overrun the three Western zones, and it would likely take a world war to restore the status quo if that happened. There appeared to be no nuclear option available—using nuclear weapons to raise the blockade seemed preposterous, and the threat to use such weapons to do so was not a credible threat. Truman did approve the sending of a squadron of B-29s to Britain as an open reminder to the Soviets of the American nuclear monopoly and to make it clear that the United States would not be driven from Berlin. These B-29s, however, had not been configured to drop the bomb, nor were their crews trained to do so (although it is not clear whether Soviet intelligence was able to make this discrimination). The key question remained, how could the Western powers sustain themselves in their sectors, and sustain the Berliners as well, for depopulated Western sectors would undermine the reason for the West's insistence on being in Berlin. Moreover, as an early test of Western determination in the rapidly evolving Cold War, Berlin came to have a general political meaning for Washington.

Determined not to be driven from Berlin, but unwilling to challenge the blockade directly, the administration settled on an airlift of supplies to Berlin. The effort proved successful, with civilian supplies (food and coal) being delivered as well as military goods. The Soviets occasionally harassed the aircraft delivering the supplies, and threatened to use the air corridors for live ammunition target practice by Soviet fighter planes. But Stalin chose not to escalate the crisis to the point of open hostilities and after a year of around-the-clock air deliveries, Stalin ended the blockade. Western efforts to integrate their zones and then create a new West German state went ahead unimpeded.

Two things stand out about the first Berlin crisis. First, the Soviet Union was willing to take a highly provocative step, even when the United States alone had nuclear weapons. Thus, the existence of nuclear weapons did not prevent the putatively weaker state from vigorously defending its interests. It may be, however, that the American nuclear monopoly circumscribed the range of actions open to Stalin; the land blockade was a creative example of power politics, but may have represented the limit beyond which Stalin dared not push.

Second, nuclear weapons offered little for the Americans in dealing with the blockade. The "winning weapon" had no ability itself to restore the status quo. The American government needed to find a creative option of its own, one that would deal with the blockade on its own terms, yet not escalate the crisis by armed action. Indeed, the key to controlling any crisis, yet at the same time maintaining one's interests, is to discover an option that lies between the opponent's action and the outbreak of violence. The airlift did that. Nuclear weapons could not do this, except as a threat, and in this case (and many others), such a threat would not be credible.

Nuclear weapons probably did, however, encourage the Soviets, now presumably look-ing for their own creative option between the American airlift and the initiation of hostilities, to "see" little space open to them, leading them to end the blockade.

The search for creative options and the pressure that nuclear weapons create were at work in the Cuban missile crisis as well. The option of blockading Cuba positioned itself between the Soviet deployment of missiles and the option of beginning hostili-ties (which an air strike represented). The Soviet response of speeding up construction was an option that found a space between the American blockade and the opening of hostilities (such as attacking American ships on the high seas). Kennedy found little space available to the United States. He made a concession on the American missiles in Turkey, but had to warn the Soviets that the United States would initiate hostilities (the attack on Cuba) if there were no agreement on terms acceptable to the United States. That threat was credible because of an overwhelming American conventional capability in the Caribbean, backed by a clear strategic nuclear advantage.

The second Berlin crisis began in 1959 with Nikita Khrushchev's speech demanding that the United States, France, and Britain withdraw their troops from Berlin and ter-minate their occupation rights in the city. The West judged this as a preliminary step toward the incorporation of West Berlin into East Germany, a politically unacceptable outcome. The Soviets set a six-month deadline for compliance. If the West failed to do so, the Soviets warned, they would turn over control of the access routes to Berlin to the East German government. This, too, was unacceptable to the United States, as it would force the United States to deal with the German Communist state that the Unit-ed States refused to recognize. The East Germans, not party to any agreement about ac-cess, could disrupt access as they saw fit. (Washington expected them to see fit to do so in order to force recognition.) Although Khrushchev continued to extend the dead-line, he kept alive Soviet demands and threats throughout 1960 and 1961. One con-sequence of Soviet pressure was that many East Germans, fearing that free passage between the sectors in Berlin would end, began fleeing to the West through the West-ern sectors of Berlin. By mid-1961, East Germany faced a domestic political crisis as the trickle of its fleeing citizens turned into a flood.

The American position was that Berlin had to remain free, that the United States would not be forced out of the city or deprived of the right of access, but that it would talk about the issues. The new Kennedy administration, fearing that a new blockade of the western sectors was in the offing, looked at its options. NATO's contingency plan "called for sending a small military force down the Autobahn to Berlin and, if resisted, moving to the nuclear response envisioned in MC 14/2": "a massive nuclear response to any sustained Soviet attack, whether or not the Soviets used similar weapons."[16] As we saw in the last chapter, such thinking was obviously at odds with the administration's evolving notion of flexible response. A search for a different set of options began. Kennedy, however, grew increasingly concerned that the Soviets would misjudge his willingness to defend the status quo. The Cuban crisis was still in the future and at the June 1961 summit with Khrushchev, even Kennedy concluded that he had failed to im-press the Soviet leader about his resoluteness.

Apparently convinced that something had to be done, and estimating that there was one chance in five of nuclear use because of Berlin, Kennedy decided on a major build-up of conventional military strength and preparations for the reinforcement of American forces in Europe. In announcing his decision at the end of July 1961, Kennedy reiterated that the United States would not be driven from Berlin. Privately he told his advisors that the United States would use military force only if West Berlin were directly threatened.

During this time, Khrushchev had tried to increase pressure to force a settlement on his terms. As a nuclear power (and still basking in the prestige of Sputnik), Khrushchev experimented with nuclear threat-making to reinforce the pressure. In early July 1961, he warned the British ambassador, Frank Roberts, that "six H-bombs would be enough to annihilate the British Isles and nine would take care of France." Roberts later recalled that when Khrushchev

> mentioned the atom bombs I felt I had to respond and said, "You're right, we're a very small island, so it would not take many bombs to destroy us, but we can bomb all your 20 major cities" and he said "… oh, yes … that's right…."[17]

Khrushchev reacted in a similar manner when he learned of Kennedy's speech announcing the defense buildup and reiteration of American rights in Berlin. Emotion as well as calculation probably led him to tell an American diplomat that the speech was a preliminary declaration of war on the USSR, and to threaten to drop a 100 megaton bomb on the United States and completely destroy its European allies. This war of nuclear nerves probably did not work in Khrushchev's favor; if anything, it probably encouraged the Americans to redouble their efforts to secure their Berlin position.

As it happened, a local event came to control the crisis: the growing flood of East Germans fleeing into West Berlin. On August 13th, the East Germans erected barriers to impede flight, and then sealed off the Western sectors with a wall. While movement by Germans was now tightly controlled (and the refugee exodus ended), the East Germans did not deny Western military officials access to East Berlin nor did they interfere with access to West Berlin by West Germans or the three Western powers.

Washington, however, was increasingly jittery; the wall seemed another step to bringing about an unacceptable change in the status quo. Kennedy sent a small reinforcement across Eastern Germany to Berlin to demonstrate that the West would insist on maintaining access, and Vice President Lyndon Johnson went to West Berlin to reassure anxious Berliners that the United States would not abandon the city. But what were the options if another blockade were imposed? American tanks faced Soviet tanks across the checkpoints, the openings in the wall where controlled entry and exit took place. A mistake on the line might have led to an exchange of tank fire.

In October, the Kennedy administration finally reached agreement with itself on what it would do if the blockade occurred. Dubbed "Poodle Blanket," the United States prepared for four stages of escalation.

> In case one response failed, we would go to the next and then the next, and so on. The first three phases involved pressures through diplomatic channels, economic embargoes, maritime harassment, and UN action, followed by or in combination with NATO mobilization and then conventional military measures, such as sending armed convoy probes down the Autobahn…. Phase four called for the escalating use of nuclear weapons.[18]

Phase four remained contentious and probably not developed. One of the plan's formulators, Paul Nitze, urged President Kennedy to consider by-passing tactical or demonstration uses of nuclear weapons in favor of a strategic strike on the Soviet Union. If it were to be nuclear war, he argued, better for the United States to strike first. (Pentagon planners had estimated that a first strike on the USSR would limit U.S. casualties to 2–3 million, but as shorter-range Soviet missiles could not be immediately attacked, European casualties were likely to be in the "low tens of millions."[19]) Kennedy apparently remained noncommittal—and probably quite worried.

As it happened, the Soviets chose not to escalate the issue and the crisis evolved into business as usual. The demands remained, exploratory talks could find no agreement, but the crisis did not worsen. Then came the Cuban missiles—which some saw as a backdoor attempt to force a Soviet-dictated solution to the Berlin issue (a view illustrated by the unidentified person quoted in the transcript that begins this chapter). But after Cuba, the Berlin crisis melted, enough so that by 1971, the United States had agreed to recognize East Germany and the status of West Berlin was accepted by all the parties.

What lessons did the Berlin crises seem to suggest regarding the relations between nuclear armed states and the role of nuclear weapons? Unlike the Cuban crisis, nuclear weapons were not directly part of the crisis, but were not far away. Khrushchev's crude warnings about nuclear attacks on Britain and the United States seem in retrospect to be the fulminations of a leader who cannot find an "easy" solution to the political problem that he wanted to solve (in this case, settling the status of Berlin). Nuclear weapons bandied about as threats seemed to have no immediate payoff, although in Western capitals Khrushchev was gaining a reputation as a reckless bully, a reputation that might have been of some benefit. One might want to make concessions to reckless opponents.

Could nuclear threat-making work? The key then, as it is now, is how to force the other side to accept the loss of something such as a city in order to avoid a much greater cost, such as a nuclear war. This is nuclear compellence, a form of blackmail diplomacy, itself a familiar pattern in world politics. Adolf Hitler had created indelible memories of the practice in the immediate prenuclear era when he successfully proposed that Britain and France accept the loss of treaty provisions that demilitarized Germany or of Czechoslovak territory in order to avoid being thrown into another world war. On the surface, adding nuclear weapons to the threat would seem compelling—here, surely, was a war to be avoided at all costs. But the extreme costs of nuclear war meant that its threat was less credible. If the Soviet Union gained Berlin, but triggered a nuclear exchange in doing so, its gain would likely be overshadowed by the costs. And if those costs were highly probable from the start of the crisis, no one would think the Soviets would really insist on having Berlin.

In the second Berlin crisis, Khrushchev sought to win the concession by bluffing—he had no interest in paying the costs entailed in a nuclear exchange, but he did want to solve the Berlin problem. The West dared not assume that he was, in fact, bluffing. Its hope—and the hope of all states facing nuclear blackmail—was that a counter-threat of nuclear punishment would be so palpable that nothing could be gained that would be worth the cost. And because the nuclear defender of the status quo need do nothing but make clear that there will be such punishment if force is used to change the status quo, it would seem to have a dominant position. As long as the defender could credibly threaten nuclear retaliation, it could stalemate the attempt at nuclear blackmail.

Was that, then, the major lesson of the second Berlin crisis? Does a nuclear-backed status quo hold the upper hand? Deterrence and extended deterrence rest on this premise. The issue is one of credibility. The threat to unleash World War III if the homeland of nuclear power were attacked or if one of its major allies suffered such an attack is reasonably credible. But was the threat to defend lesser positions (like West

Berlin) with nuclear weapons credible enough to stay the hand of a state interested in challenging the status quo? One could, of course, attempt to bolster that credibility by publicly putting one's prestige on the line, or by placing one's forces in the line of fire. And one might count on the fact that since 1945, there has been a general disapproval of changes in the status quo that do not meet the approval of the individuals involved. But the more seemingly removed the point of contention from the interests of the state attempting to preserve the status quo, the more incredible the nuclear threat to defend the status quo.

The state seeking to change the status quo cannot overlook the point that blackmail diplomacy is confrontational. In that confrontation, local events might spark an uncontrollable escalation (imagine a nervous tank commander firing a round at an opposing tank at a Berlin checkpoint). The internal politics within the opposing government might produce a decision that now was the time to settle everything. Thus, one lesson of the Berlin crisis might be that if the supporter of the status quo is nuclear-armed, a direct, clear challenge to the status quo is too risky. The trick, then, would be to change the status quo in a way that catches the supporters of the status quo by surprise, and forces them to make the agonizing decision—do we use force (and hence run the risk of suffering nuclear retaliation) to restore the status quo? The surreptitious introduction of missiles into Cuba is what Khrushchev learned from the Berlin crisis. To Kennedy, however, the Soviet move was unsettling in the extreme. At the start of this chapter he was asking in a tone of bewilderment if anyone could tell him why the Soviets would attempt to put missiles in Cuba. "After all," the president said, "Khrushchev demonstrated a sense of caution" when it came to Berlin.

GENERAL PATTERNS OF NUCLEAR BEHAVIOR

To this point, we have concentrated on two crises in which nuclear weapons played an important role. We now want to expand our consideration of nuclear weapons in international relations by postulating a number of individual practices that have emerged historically and by assessing their probable occurrence in the future. Then we want to speculate on possible new patterns of nuclear relations that might emerge in the post-Cold War world, the world of the twenty-first century and the second nuclear era.

The historical practices illustrate three basic points that we expect will continue:

1. Nations will struggle to find ways to integrate nuclear weapons into their foreign policies. After all, the military establishment of a nation and its ability to wage war by utilizing the weapons in its inventories have traditionally underpinned every state's foreign policy. Having this most devastating weapon in the nation's arsenal raises the question: How does the nation exploit this awesome weapon in its peacetime foreign policy?

2. No nuclear nation to date can claim that it has found the route to success in making nuclear weapons a meaningful and potent part of its foreign policy practices. As we shall see later, specific behaviors have produced intermittent success and no small degree of failure. Thus, as the twenty-first century begins, no nuclear nation, old or new, can be sure that it has found a way to utilize the nuclear weapons in its arsenal to promote its foreign policy interests, and do so in a way that produces success at low risk to itself.

3. To the degree that states accept the idea that nuclear weapons exist *not to be used*, either in war or peace, their only relevance continues to be as a deterrent against

a nuclear attack or to constrain provocative or risky behavior by others. Moreover, nuclear weapons can be *self-deterring*, making oneself more cautious in the world. To the degree these realizations take hold, there will be an "emerging international norm that nuclear weapons should play no role in normal international politics."[20]

When presented in this fashion, the third premise emerges as the result of a basically unsuccessful search for ways to make such weapons a part of a state's foreign policy. That, we believe, accords with the historical reality of the two superpowers in the first nuclear age, and suggests a learning process based on trial and error. We suspect that young nuclear weapons states will experiment as suggested by the first proposition, and even more mature states will do so as the occasion arises (President Bush's threat of nuclear retaliation if Iraq used chemical or biological weapons against United Nations forces in the prewar confrontation in the Gulf is suggestive). Thus, we might expect the patterns we delineate in the text that follows to be with us in the future—not necessarily in great number, but with enough frequency to produce periodic crises in which nuclear weapons are a centerpiece (as in the Cuban missile crisis) or clearly delineated in the shadows (as in the Berlin crises).

These, then, are the patterns that we think most noteworthy for the future. Recall that we are not talking about the actual use of nuclear weapons to attack an opponent. Rather, these are the patterns of *brandishing* nuclear weapons to achieve political ends. In most cases, the actor has no desire to actually use the weapons.

PATTERN 1

Pattern 1 is brandishing nuclear weapons as a declaration of status. The *existence* of nuclear weapons in a nation's arsenal is an announcement of a special status in world politics—that a nation has the resources and incentives to acquire the most deadly of weapons. Possession is often accompanied by *displays* of the weapon, which are a form of request or demand to be treated as a major player in world politics, and to have the nation's policy preferences accorded greater attention than might otherwise be the case. At one extreme, a state may attempt to "hav[e] this weapon ostentatiously on our hip"[21] (as Secretary of War Stimson accused Secretary of State Byrnes of doing) in the hope that it would encourage one's rivals to be more accommodating. Soviet displays of its military hardware during the annual May Day parades were a carefully orchestrated effort to create prestige for the Soviet Union.

As we have seen, some states have become opaque proliferators. Opacity does allow the acquisition of some of the status as a nuclear weapons state, and presumably enhances an ability to have one's interests treated more carefully by one's neighbors and by the great powers. Opacity, however, does not permit the demonstration of an ability to detonate such weapons. We are not referring to the ability to cause an explosion; successful detonation is relatively easily achieved (recall the untested Hiroshima bomb) and so most observers credit an opaque proliferator with that capability. What is more in doubt is the *political* capability. For some political reason a nation has felt unable to detonate the device. That reticence may be enough to undermine the careful respect that detonation provides the overt nuclear-weapons states, for it suggests that in a crisis, the opaque proliferator will continue to be politically constrained.

We might expect that, at some point, opaque proliferators may find it necessary to demonstrate their political capacity to detonate a nuclear weapon. Particularly in a crisis—especially one where a nation's leadership may fear that others doubt its political capacity to use nuclear weapons—fears for the success of deterrence may lead the opaque proliferator to provide such a demonstration. Unfortunately, a demonstration of political will during a crisis may be singularly inappropriate for it may be misread by the other side in a dramatically different way, sending the crisis into an irreversible military clash.

PATTERN 2

Pattern 2 is brandishing nuclear weapons to signal that one's vital interests are engaged or that one is resolute and cannot be driven from one's position. Brandishing nuclear weapons has been a way in which states have indicated commitment to a particular position. We saw this with Khrushchev's waving of nuclear destruction in Ambassador Roberts's face during the Berlin Crisis of 1961. (This was not the first time that Khrushchev had done this. In 1956, when Britain and France had attacked Egypt, Khrushchev had spoken of "a rain of rockets" on the two powers if their aggression did not cease.) The classic cases of American signaling can be found in 1953 and 1954. In 1953, the Eisenhower administration quietly told the Chinese that unless they agreed to the American terms for an armistice in Korea, the United States would begin atomic warfare against Chinese forces in Korea. Secretary of State John Foster Dulles followed up a year later with the publicly declared threat of "massive retaliation" for future Communist aggression. While partially intended for military deterrence, massive retaliation had a strong political element here as well, as Dulles sought to make clear that preserving the political status quo against Communist inroads was of vital importance to the United States. Dulles's approach has been called "nuclear brinksmanship": taking states to the brink of war by threatening to use nuclear weapons if the status quo were disturbed. While subsequent secretaries of state wanted to preserve the status quo (it was a part of American policy for much of the Cold War), none chose to wave nuclear weapons as a signal.

Signaling also became connected to specific incidents, the last major example occurring in 1973 during the October War in the Middle East, when the United States increased its nuclear alert status (something that the Soviets would immediately detect) in order to warn the Soviet Union that the United States would not tolerate the dispatch of Soviet combat forces to the region. Indeed, displaying American nuclear weapons delivery systems in nonroutine ways to the Soviets has long been a part of American foreign policy. The dispatch of B-29s to Britain during the first Berlin crisis is illustrative.

Signaling is meant to remind the other of the importance of the stakes that are involved. It can also be meant to achieve *political deterrence*: to prevent an action by others that would damage the interests of the nation, such as the appearance of Soviet troops in the Middle East. It can also be meant to achieve *political compellence*: to force others to accept a change that they would find damaging to their interests. If Khrushchev had intended, for instance, to reveal the undetected missiles in Cuba and then demand a change in the status of Berlin, he would be counting on the presence of the nuclear weapons to compel the West to rethink its posture in Berlin. (If the missiles were to be *offered in exchange* for Berlin, the display of nuclear weapons would be as a bargaining chip, which we discuss later.)

Finally, signaling might be undertaken as a means of communicating something like toughness. For instance, the Kennedy administration decided in the summer of 1961 to deploy the short-range missiles to Turkey in spite of advice not to, because this was a way of demonstrating toughness after the Vienna summit with the Soviets.

Historically, signaling has been erratic in its effects. It is not clear whether the signal actually works. The American "bomb on the hip" did not clearly force Stalin to behave differently. Roberts's reply to Khrushchev suggests that one can treat the signal as a bluff, and call it with a counter-threat ("you might destroy Britain, but we'll destroy your 20 major cities"—which in 1961 would have put millions of Soviet citizens at risk.) In the October 1973 war between Israel and the Syrian-Egyptian coalition, according to a Soviet insider, the Soviet leadership was puzzled and angered by the American nuclear alert, for it seemed to fly in the face of American pledges to cooperate with the Soviet Union in resolving the conflict and seemed to be a case of rash overreaction on the part of President Nixon. Instead of countering with signals of their own, Leonid Brezhnev led the Soviet policymakers in the opposite direction: "What about not responding at all to the American nuclear alert?" he proposed. "Nixon is too nervous—let's cool him down."[22] Or the signal may provoke an undesirable response—Khrushchev reacted to the American deployment of missiles to Turkey with the deployment of Soviet missiles to Cuba.

Coupled with the erratic effect is the "cheapening" of the signal. If nuclear weapons are brandished repeatedly around issues that make it difficult to see *why* a nation's interests were so engaged as to warrant a nuclear threat, brandishing nuclear weapons loses its political punch. In 1956, for instance, while it was clear that the Soviet Union very much wanted to bolster its developing relationship with Egypt, it seemed quite doubtful that it was willing to have Moscow and Leningrad die to protect Cairo. Indeed, some commentators noted that the threat came only after the United States had declared its opposition to the Anglo-French operation, thus condemning the operation to failure. Khrushchev's "rocket rattling" took on an aura of bluff and bluster, rather than commitment.

After the Khrushchev era, nuclear signaling became a more restrained practice, and it has virtually disappeared at this point in time. However, we expect the traditional nuclear states as well as the new ones that emerge to continue to see it as a useful device. We would point out that signaling can be misread by the other side; in particular, it might be seen as the preparation for a nuclear attack, which would give those states whose strategy emphasizes preemption the incentive to begin a nuclear war—the very last thing a signaler wants.

PATTERN 3

Pattern 3 is brandishing nuclear weapons as a bargaining chip. The willingness to trade nuclear weapons for political concessions elsewhere is a relatively unknown phenomena. One version does appear in arms control negotiations, where a state might deploy or threaten to deploy a particular weapons system in order to get the other side to make a concession to prevent the deployment. Such brandishing, however, seems to be part and parcel of the deliberations about nuclear weapons. The American view that Soviet missiles in Cuba might be the opening of a deal regarding Berlin was just an American hypothesis. If the crisis had been prolonged (without American military intervention), it is possible that the two sides might have explored a political solution that traded missiles, say, for recognition of the East German state and its right to control access to Berlin.

The patterns that we have just discussed are those between states in some form of conflict. There are also two patterns that emerge when states are in amicable relations with each other.

PATTERN 4

Pattern 4 is a state brandishing nuclear weapons, which prompts its allies to restrain such behavior. Attempting to extract influence with nuclear weapons does raise the risk of nuclear war; a state's allies may see themselves in jeopardy because their nuclear-armed ally might provoke a nuclear exchange that targets them as well. Thus, brandishing nuclear weapons may send out shock waves through the nation's alliance. In 1950, when President Truman incautiously told a news conference that "nuclear weapons were always under consideration" in the Korean conflict, an extremely worried Prime Minister Clement Atlee hurriedly flew to Washington to register Britain's concern about Truman's statement. As it was, Truman was reacting defensively to a Korean situation turning sour—the Chinese had just intervened—and wanted to appear to the American public that he was considering all the options. He was not, in fact, considering nuclear weapons. That, however, was not known to the British, who feared that brandishing the weapons might bring the Soviets into the conflict, which then might escalate to Soviet attacks on Europe.

PATTERN 5

Pattern 5 concerns using nuclear weapons to bolster an alliance relationship. Beyond brandishing nuclear weapons at opponents, nuclear-armed states have also used nuclear weapons to firm up alliances with others. We have seen how states have fashioned extended deterrence—a pledge to defend an ally even at the risk of having one's cities destroyed by a nuclear opponent. Military alliances have always posed the risk of loss, but such nuclear pledges are dramatic in the level of loss the deterring state seems willing to run to protect an ally—so much so that some allies have felt such pledges lacked credibility, driving the French in particular to seek their own nuclear deterrent.

Beyond the pledges of future performance are the alliance-maintaining functions of cooperative endeavors to construct nuclear weapons. The Americans and British cooperated in the research to produce the first nuclear weapons during World War II (but once the war ended, the United States broke off all cooperation in the production of the bomb). The Soviet Union faced a more serious problem with its Chinese ally. In 1957, the Soviets tried to persuade the Chinese to forego a nuclear program. Here is how Mao Zedong, the Chinese leader, reacted:

> Mikoyan told me, too, that the Soviet bombs were enough for both our countries. "The Soviet nuclear umbrella can cover us all." But the Soviet Union wants to control us. That's why they don't want us to have the bomb. The fact is they can never control us. The Soviet Union is worried that we don't listen to them. They're afraid we might provoke the United States. But we're not afraid of getting into trouble with other countries. I will definitely develop the atom bomb. You can count on it. Nobody should try to restrict us.[23]

The Soviet Union agreed to aid the Chinese in constructing their nuclear weapons (aid, after all, can be a form of control as well as support), and then broke off the assistance as growing political antagonisms divided the two countries. The American government tried more successfully to cement the NATO alliance by allowing, for instance, its German ally to possess American nuclear weapons—weapons rendered inoperable by Permissive Action Links (PALs) until an American officer armed the weapon.

In peacetime, then, nuclear weapons have been called upon to serve a number of purposes, and we can expect brandishing to continue in the future. But we cannot overlook a basic point: The existence of nuclear weapons has not kept a state out of war with others or prevented a challenge to its interests. This holds true for the superpowers as well as others. Syria and Egypt decided to initiate war on Israel in October 1973 in spite of Israel's status as an opaque proliferator. They chose to run the risk that either Israel had no deliverable weapon, or would not react to their assault with nuclear weapons if it had them. The Chinese chose to enter the Korean War in November/December 1950 in spite of the clear nuclear weapons capability of the United States and its demonstrated willingness to use them against others.

Nuclear Relations in a Cold War

The period from 1947 to 1990 marks a period in world history known as the Cold War, a period characterized by the intense rivalry between the United States and the Soviet Union, a rivalry that had a nuclear dimension. What relationship did nuclear weapons have to the Cold War? In particular, did nuclear weapons cause the Cold War?

Our basic answer is that nuclear weapons played a role in the cold war (and in its ending), but the relationship is complex. The complexity begins with the very term "cold war." We think it useful to say that cold wars are a type of relationship that can exist between states, with the historic Cold War being just one prominent example. A *cold war* is a relationship between two or more states in which (1) the leadership of each state *believes* that another state in the relationship has extremely hostile intentions against its own state and that the other state contemplates waging war to accomplish those intentions, but (2) *in reality* no state's leadership desires war with the other.

Thus, cold wars are "a mistake." They need not have happened, and might not have happened if the states in the relationship had a correct appreciation of the intentions of the other.

This is *not* to say that with a correct appreciation there would be no conflicts between the two. States can be in conflict, and often are over many issues. The key question is whether each believes that the other has truly injurious intentions and will wage war against it to secure those goals. Nor is this to deny that, from time to time, states *do* seek to destroy other states (Hitler's goal vis-à-vis the Soviet Union) or to shatter their power (Hitler's goal vis-à-vis France and England) by waging war. Nor, finally, is it to deny that goals can change: At some point the leadership may conclude that they now do wish to wage war to advance their goals. But a cold war is, first and foremost, a product of mistaken assumptions that another intends to wage war.

In a cold war system, even though neither state intends war, there is a constant *threat of war*. The threat is partially created by the perception of the other state's hostile intentions: "They intend to attack us!" To keep war from happening, we make threats and brandish our weapons. And, as the other side only seems to understand the language of force, our foreign policy takes on strong military overtones. The other state, which finds itself in serious conflict with us, in turn sees our threats and our brandishing of weapons as ample proof of our hostile intentions, and it responds with threats of its own. Those reactive threats convince us that we were right in judging them willing to attack us.

In the historic Cold War, both sides came to see the other as having injurious intentions. George Kennan, an American diplomat in Moscow in 1946, presented an assessment that captured the Truman administration's thinking. The Soviet regime, he argued, had "learned to seek security only in patient but deadly struggle for total destruction of rival power, never in compacts and compromises with it."[24] Soviet thinking ran in similar veins. Nikita Khrushchev, drawing on his ingrained Marxist perspective, recalled that at the end of the war, it was "difficult to judge what the intentions of the Allies were," but he surmised that "they wanted to take advantage of the results of the war and impose their will not only on their enemy, Germany, but on their ally, the USSR, as well."[25] In this environment of suspicion, nuclear weapons played a role—they made the opponent look more terrifying, but they are terrifying precisely because of the assumption of very hostile intentions. The United States and Britain, on the other hand, possess nuclear weapons, but those weapons do not incite fear vis-à-vis the other.

Cold wars do inherently increase the risk of nuclear use, for they make war begun by the other seem quite likely. We saw in the last two chapters how the emergence of Soviet and American military doctrine reflected the belief that their opponent stood ready to deliver a nuclear attack (or the American fear that the Soviets stood ready to invade Western Europe with conventional arms, which would force the United States into a nuclear response). Both sides prepared *preemptive* strategies that were based on the premise that if we suspected the other was now readying an attack, we would strike first. Chapter 2 pointed to a number of near-use decisions predicated on the assumption of the other's intense hostility.

But no dire nuclear event occurred in the historic Cold War and the United States and the Soviet Union were able to keep the peace between them. Was that because nuclear weapons made war so perilous, or is it that cold wars will generally remain cold because of the *nature* of a cold war, thus making the type of weapons the nations possess essentially irrelevant? We begin our analysis by first arguing that cold wars can turn hot. In 1941, for example, the Japanese decided to convert their five-year-old cold war with the United States into a hot one. Both had looked on the other as having hostile intentions (they had radically different views of acceptable foreign policy in the western Pacific region), and both had come to the conclusion that the other intended to wage war at a propitious time. At immediate issue was a growing Japanese military presence in French Indo-China. The Japanese were using the French colony as another avenue of attack against China and they now seemed poised to use the colony as a springboard to attack British colonies in South East Asia.

The United States engineered an international oil embargo against Japan in the summer of 1941 to force the Japanese to end the expansion into French Indo-China. For the Japanese, the embargo was tantamount to an act of war as Japan lacked oil; the embargo threatened to bring Japan's economy and military machine to a halt. Japan's answer was to attack Pearl Harbor and unleash war against American, British, and Dutch forces in South East Asia. In effect, the Japanese staged a preemptive attack on the United States before the American embargo could mortally damage Japan. (The initial defeat of the American and British forces allowed Japan to seize the oil-rich Dutch East Indies as well as the rest of the region.)

Ironically, the last thing that President Roosevelt wanted was a war with Japan; he and the British felt that all attention had to be directed toward the defeat of Germany.

The oil embargo was designed to deter further Japanese aggression in the region. Thus we have a cold war turning hot precisely because there was an attempt at deterrence! But no matter the reason, cold wars have the potential to eventuate in hot war.

It is, of course, possible for cold wars to turn hot by accident. As we saw in Chapter 2, there were several routes by which a nuclear war might begin even when both states did not really want war. A cold war can encourage states to have hair-triggers for their nuclear systems and create extensive intelligence operations to discover if it is *tomorrow* that the opponent intends to unleash its attack. Those probes to gather warning information are often intrusive and might be read as the prelude to an attack. During the Cuban missile crisis, the American routine monitoring of the atmosphere for radioactive particles, now coupled with having the intelligence aircraft approach the Soviet Union over the north pole—the flight path for American bombers—momentarily panicked the Soviet leadership.

Cold wars can also end peacefully, as the historic Cold War did. Are peaceful endings of cold wars inherently possible irrespective of the weapons that states possess? We suggest that they are. Cold wars can "dissolve" through the *mutual* recognition that the other state does *not have the hostile intentions ascribed to it*. Indeed, both parties in a cold war—neither of which plans to wage war on the other—may be very desirous of communicating that fact to the other. In the fall of 1948, for instance, as the Cold War was deepening, President Truman decided to take the highly unusual step of asking the chief justice of the Supreme Court, Fred Vinson, to talk to Stalin "man-to-man."

> I asked Vinson to point out to Stalin that the folly and tragedy of another war would amount to an act of national suicide and that no sane leader of any major power could ever again even contemplate war except in defense. Surely the next war—an atomic war—was as unthinkable as it was abhorrent.[26]

Truman diagnosed the problem as one of perceptions:

> The Russians simply did not understand—or *would* not—our peaceful intentions and our genuine desire to co-operate through the United Nations toward the establishment of a climate of peace; that we did not want to force and had no intention of forcing our way of life upon them or anyone else....[27]

Similarly, immediately after Stalin's death in 1954, his successor as head of the Soviet Communist Party, Georgi Malenkov, sought to reassure the West of the Soviet Union's peaceful intentions. "At present," he declared, "there is no litigious or unsolved question which could not be settled by peaceful means on the basis of mutual agreement of the countries involved. This concerns our relations with all states, including the United States of America."[28]

These efforts to correct the perception of the other side are inherent in a cold-war situation. *If* they occur at the right time and in the right context, they may begin to undermine the belief that the other intends to attack. Further cooperative actions, now possible because of the lessened fear, may reinforce and deepen this new perception to the point that both sides mutually recognize that the other does not intend to wage war, and thus end the cold war. The historic Cold War ended in this way, with both states coming to see in the late 1980s and early 1990s that neither intended war.

In fact, both states had edged toward this mutual recognition earlier in the late 1960s and early 1970s, a period that came to be called détente, a term that captures the essence of a waning cold war as it means a relaxation of tensions. But then both states rediscovered reasons to be fearful of the intentions of the other, and the Cold War waxed again. We expect any cold war to show this fluctuation across time (indicated in Figure 6-1) as leaders come closer to the truth about their rival's intentions (a waning of the cold war), but then perceive that the other's willingness to wage war had not really abated (a waxing of the cold war, as occurred in the last years of the 1970s and early 1980s).

What causes a cold war to wax and wane? Cold wars wax for two central reasons. First, it is very difficult to sustain efforts to persuade the other side that one does not have deadly intentions. Consider what happened to Truman's and Malenkov's efforts. In Truman's case, he found that his secretary of state strongly opposed the Vinson trip, and when the proposed trip leaked to the press, it was caught up in the whirlwind of a presidential election year, with Truman's Republican opponents accusing him of promoting a disastrous policy of appeasement. Vinson stayed home. Thus, internal disagreement and domestic politics can stifle cooperative gestures.

The Malenkov case reflects how difficult it is at times to change the ingrained mind-set of the other side. In the mid-1950s the Soviets made a number of cooperative gestures. The American secretary of state, John Foster Dulles, believed as a matter of faith that the Soviets had very hostile intentions. When the Soviets made a concession, Dulles interpreted the action in one of two ways: (1) this was a trick to lull the United States into complacency while the Soviets prepared the *coup de gras*, or (2) the Soviets made a concession because they were momentarily weak.[29] In neither case did the concession signal that the Soviets might *not* have hostile intentions.

And note this problem. If your opponent drew the conclusion that you made a concession because you *were* weak, your opponent *might act to exploit your presumed weakness*. You would then face a severe, unnecessary, and self-created challenge to your own survival. This is how Malenkov chose to interpret Dulles's responses to his offer to reach mutual agreement regarding their conflict. To Malenkov, the American leadership seemed

> ... to regard the Soviet Union's efforts to safeguard peace among nations, its concern to lessen international tensions, as manifestations of weakness. It is precisely this

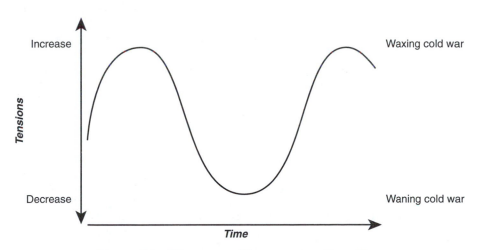

FIGURE 6-1   WAXING AND WANING OF THE COLD WAR

preposterous assumption that explains the flagrantly unreasonable approach in certain U.S. circles to the settlement of international issues, and their policy of pressure and indiscriminate adventurism.[30]

In a cold war environment, leaders need to be very cautious about appearing weak, as
that might trigger the attack they fear.

The second reason a cold war can wax is that, even when the two states have taken
some significant steps to communicate their true intentions to the other side, the normal processes of world politics intervene. Major powers, especially those with global interests or pretensions, will periodically find themselves in conflict over various issues
because they see their interests in quite different lights. This is a remarkably consistent
feature of world politics. In 1979, for instance, the Soviet Union felt compelled to intervene in Afghanistan to support a Marxist government that showed no signs of being
able to maintain either itself in power or peace within Afghanistan. The Soviet Union—
like most powerful states—sought to preserve peace on its frontiers, and do so through
a friendly government. The United States rejected this intervention as being against
the accepted rules of international relations, and worried that the Soviet Union was
using détente as a smokescreen behind which to pursue goals quite injurious to American interests. Or alternatively, even if the Soviet Union did not currently have such
goals, it would be so emboldened by a success in Afghanistan that it might seek to
adopt more injurious ones. Would the Soviet invasion, the Carter administration wondered, be a preliminary step to bring the oil-producing states of the Persian Gulf under
Moscow's influence, an outcome deemed unacceptable to American security interests?
The Soviet action and American response pushed an already troubled détente into a
period of a waxing cold war.

When a cold war waxes among nuclear powers, or between a nuclear and nonnuclear state, we might imagine that dangerous nuclear events are more likely, and because
of the power of such weapons, the participants in a cold war will have greater incentives to communicate their true, peaceful intentions. At the same time, however, the
fear of appearing weak will make them cautious. The resulting mix of confrontation and
accommodation in each state's approach to its rival may help nudge both toward détente, and then out of a cold war, but it is just as likely that such actions would lead to
a waxing cold war, one that threatens to break through to hot war.

During the 1950s and early 1960s, the United States and Soviet Union were on a
collision course, as evidenced by the Berlin and Cuban crises. In fact, the crises of 1961
and 1962 proved to be the point at which both sides came to realize that their cold war
could turn excruciatingly hot. President Kennedy, for instance, estimated that during
the Cuban missile crisis the likelihood of nuclear war was as high as fifty-fifty within
ten years.[31] The existence of nuclear weapons probably performed one clear function:
They made starkly vivid the kinds of costs that a state would pay if it engaged in war
with its nuclear-armed rival. Thus we could suggest that nuclear weapons have (a)
forced decision makers to be more sensitive about the possibility that crises might escalate across the war threshold, and (b) made the prospect of such war quite unpalatable. That would argue that there will come a point in the waxing of a cold war where
a crisis leads both sides to purposefully de-escalate the cold war, and in so doing, give
themselves the opportunity to discover that they are not mortal enemies. But—and it
is a terrifying "but"—the deescalation comes *after* the crisis, a crisis that, if Kennedy was
right, could easily have gone in the other direction.

Were there other factors that might have contributed to the ability of the two states to pull back from the brink in 1962, and then have constrained the waxing of the cold war as conflict resurfaced? To the degree that these factors were unique to the Soviet-American relationship, they might well not be available as constraints working in other cold wars, such as the one that has characterized Indo-Pakistani relations for more than three decades (and produced one major war in 1971). These three factors suggest themselves:

1. A *long-term perspective* Both American and Soviet leaderships assumed that time was on their side. Marxist-Leninist doctrine told Soviet leaders that the future belonged to the proletariat. As capitalism was an archaic economic system that would fail, capitalist states would be replaced by proletarian states who by definition would live in peace with their neighbors. Less formal American thinking saw authoritarian regimes as archaic, believing that in the future the wishes of the people would be increasingly influential, and people generally wanted peace. Hence, denied success by a policy of containment, the Soviet regime would "mellow," transforming itself into a more traditional, status-quo-orientated state. The key for both states was to get through the transition period successfully—and that meant avoiding war. The waxing of the cold war was undesirable. Other leaderships, without long-term visions about the likely success of their desires, may be far less concerned about an escalating cold war. Indeed, if not welcoming the escalation, they may accept it as inevitable.

2. A *recent experience with the cost of war* The costs of war for Russia/USSR in this century have been horrendous, not only in terms of lives lost in combat, but of massive civilian deaths and dislocation, as well as having foreign armies in occupation of vast stretches of territory. The Soviet leadership understood that cost vividly. Gerald Ford, for instance, recalled a conversation he had with Leonid Brezhnev in 1974:

   > And that's when the strangest thing happened. Brezhnev reached over and grabbed my left hand with his right hand. He began telling me how much his people had suffered during World War II. "I do not want to inflict that upon my people again," he said.[32]

   American costs of war paled by comparison, but Americans fought two major wars during the Cold War (with roughly 100,000 deaths for both), and the public came to see them as of dubious value in promoting American interests.

3. A *reluctance to move toward the goal of destroying the other* A chronic temptation in a cold war would be for the leadership to say, "As the other side wishes to wage war against us, let us deal with this threat by removing it." Recall Bobby Kennedy's comment at the beginning of this chapter: If the Soviets intend war over Cuba, perhaps "we should just get into it and get it over with." Nuclear weapons would make a direct and overpowering attack possible, but mutual assured destruction— or even more modest levels of retaliation—would give any leader pause. Neither nation's leadership contemplated such action That left only two other lines of attack available: to "roll back" the opponent from the positions of influence or control that it exercised in the world, or to weaken the economy of the opponent so that its leadership would have trouble governing at home and exercising influence abroad. Both sides experimented with roll-back, but were extremely cautious, usually avoiding direct challenges by relying on proxies such as local Vietnamese communists or Afghan anti-Marxist guerrillas. Given that the American economy was the stronger of the two and had more ties with other economies, periodic American attempts to organize economic boycotts of the Soviet Union did have some effect. Moreover, the Reagan administration would claim, after the

fact, that its vast rearmament program was a conscious design to force the Soviet Union into a spending race that would ultimately break the inefficient Soviet economy and pave the way for its democratization and breakup. What is important is that these attempts were sporadic during the Cold War and involved very uncertain means; they never crystallized into an ongoing program that would reinforce a Cato-like declamation, "Carthage/the USSR must be destroyed," and in that way make crossing the threshold to nuclear war much more likely.

THE END OF THE COLD WAR AND THE RUSSIAN FUTURE

As we have seen, the possession of nuclear weapons did not prevent nuclear rivals from exhibiting provocative behavior toward each other, nor did nuclear weapons prevent their possessors from having to wage debilitating conventional wars (the United States in Korea and Vietnam, the Soviet Union in Afghanistan). Indeed, in these instances, the possession of nuclear weapons failed to cow the "weaker" party into submission. In addition, nuclear parity with the United States probably encouraged a more ambitious Soviet foreign policy—or, at least, nuclear parity encouraged the Soviets to think that the United States would accord them equal privileges as a world (i.e., nuclear) power. Some of the key conflicts in the Cold War were in good measure struggles to claim the rights of being a world power.

But it is also likely that nuclear weapons induced some caution on the part of others, if not for the presence of the weapons themselves, then because they are *reflections* of the over-all power of the possessor, a power that extends beyond the weapons themselves. For example, when Stalin ordered Greek communists and their Yugoslav supporters to end the insurgency in Greece in the late 1940s, he angrily told the Greeks, "What do you think, that Great Britain and the United States—the United States, the most powerful state in the world—will permit you to break their line of communication in the Mediterranean! Nonsense!"[33] Such power encouraged, at the least, a more careful calculation of risks.

Beyond the sometimes erratic prestige power that nuclear weapons both created and mirrored, the possession of nuclear weapons in sufficient number made one fact clear: The possessor of deliverable nuclear weapons could not be forced to surrender as Japan was in 1945 at a cost its opponents would be willing to pay. Thus, while the possession of nuclear weapons could not guarantee the achievement of foreign policy goals to change the status quo, they could come close to ensuring the survival of the possessor—as long as nuclear weapons were not used. This is one profound aspect of the nuclear predicament: Nuclear weapons offered a kind of security undreamed of by the leaders of nations in earlier times, but only so long as nuclear weapons were not used—a very precarious security indeed.

The key question then became, how could one manage the relations between nuclear states so that, with the likely clash of interests that inhere in the relations between sovereign states, those clashes would not push a cold war across the nuclear threshold? One could try to isolate the other side, to keep its contacts with others minimized and the area of the world under its direct control or influence constricted. American policy basically took this approach, and gave the generic label to the only reasonable, long-term policy available to either side in a nuclear cold war: *containment*. But containment is difficult and costly and dangerous, for containment meant that one had to be willing to wage local wars where the other side seemed poised to spill beyond its area of control. The American wars in Korea and Vietnam epitomize the price and the frustration of a containment policy.

In the long run, with a rival that one cannot defeat in war but that is too dangerous to ignore, both sides will be impelled to seek some form of understanding with the other, and that will necessitate negotiations with the other. One logical place to negotiate is about nuclear weapons themselves, a topic we address directly in Chapters 7 and 8. In addition, after the near fatal collisions of the Berlin and Cuban crises, it became apparent that nuclear rivals should negotiate an understanding of how nuclear powers can relate to each other to minimize the potential of conflict (a point we also explore in Chapter 8). Those negotiations, which were part of the Cold War and will, we suspect, emerge in future cold wars, help impel the trajectory of the relations in a cold war first toward détente, and then possibly into the discovery that neither side wants war, which ends the reasons for a cold war.

Thus, over time, in a nuclear relationship there will be a constant pressure to move toward policies that accommodate the other side. Accommodation is likely because one cannot manage conflict successfully by insisting that one's own side always wins while the other side always loses. Bargaining with the other side to manage conflict means accepting, to one degree or another, *the other's definition of its security and prestige interests*. The historic Cold War ended during the last four years of the Reagan administration as both sides accepted the idea that they needed to provide *mutual security* and *mutual prestige*.

When the Soviet Union began to disintegrate, first Bush and then Clinton tried to ensure the continuing survival of the Russian state. Of course, by the early 1990s, Russia had a different economy and political system. And, of course, no one wanted to have the Russian government lose control over its nuclear weapons. But the point is that Soviet and then Russian leadership felt secure enough to allow the peaceful collapse of its alliance system and the state created by the Communists seventy years earlier. The United States, in contrast to the military victory over Japan and Germany a half-century earlier, took pains not to appear to be dictating the conditions of peace in the post-Cold War world.

But the future of nuclear relations over the next twenty-five years will still depend on the future of Russia. In the early 1990s, the Russian government and people embraced democracy and a version of a free-market economy. By the end of the decade, the democratic experiment persisted, but the Russian economy foundered, bringing wide-scale dissatisfaction and no little privation. It became easy to blame the West for the problems (the new economy seemed a Western rather than a Russian idea, and Western pressures for continued economic reforms smacked of gross interference), and the new democracy gave ultra-nationalists both a platform and a share of power as coalition politics churned up new governments. The expansion of NATO to include Poland, the Czech Republic, and Hungary moves NATO to the borders of the former Soviet Union and keeps alive two crucial questions: Is the military purpose of NATO to contain Russia, and will the former states of the Soviet Union such as Belarus and Ukraine be admitted? Russian nationalists—particularly those harboring dreams of one day reuniting the former Soviet Union—have seen NATO's expansion, along with the attempt to westernize the Russian economy, as a plot to injure Russian interests. The potential for a backlash against the West has been an ever-present backdrop to Russian politics.

For the most part, however, the Russian government cooperated with the West on international issues, or at least it did not attempt to block Western efforts. It found ways to reach an understanding with China, its most powerful contiguous neighbor. But it insisted on having its views heard and its interests heeded. Nuclear weapons have been important in this regard. As one American official involved in monitoring the Russian arsenal has said, "The Russians acknowledge in the open press and face to face that their ticket to the big time, their ability to sit at the big people's table, rides on the fact that they still have this nuclear capability. And that is, very frankly, their only claim to superpower status."[34] Russia is likely to hang on to its arsenal for its ability to solicit Western concern, and because in an uncertain world, it provides security and the potential for leverage with its nonnuclear neighbors. Those are realities that are likely to motivate any nuclear state.

The Russian state, however, faces a continuing series of foreign policy challenges and temptations: (1) It has ethnic Russians living outside its borders (for instance, in Ukraine, Moldova, and Kazakhstan) that create irredentist pressures; (2) it has internal factions that call for an annexationist policy toward "the near abroad"—those states such as the Baltic Republics and Ukraine—that were once part of the Soviet Union; and (3) a large proportion of its population lives with the historical memory "that their Motherland was, virtually overnight, deprived of its name, its flag, nearly half of its territory, its defining ideology, its governing structure, and its protective alliance."[35]

The future American relationship with Russia has the potential for serious conflict, as the United States is a plausible villain to explain Russian ills, and as the American government will likely promote its long-standing goal of, in President Clinton's words, "a Europe that is united, democratic, and secure for the first time since the rise of nation states on the European continent."[36] Such a Europe has no room for Russian expansion (except by the agreement of those affected, and most of the successor states have expressed clear opposition to reincorporation into a Russian dominated state). At same time, Strobe Talbott, the deputy secretary of state in the Clinton administration, warned that there is

> a tendency among some commentators and political figures in the West to see only the darkest side of the picture and therefore to propose a return to the old policy of containing or quarantining Russia. That would be a mistake, every bit as dangerous as those that the Russians themselves are currently making [regarding their economy]. If we were to write Russia off and brace ourselves for a new cold war, our pessimism could become self-fulfilling. Russia will make its own choices and often its own mistakes, but it will make both in no small measure in response to us.[37]

The possibility for a revived cold war is real but at the moment modest. If it were to occur, the issues would be more complex and fraught with nuclear danger. For example, Russian attempts to control or influence the near-abroad states (just out of security concerns, never mind whatever expansionist goals its leaders may have) are sure to be resisted, and two avenues for those threatened states suggest themselves: to seek protection from NATO with its access to nuclear-armed member states, or to develop indigenous nuclear weapons. Indeed, even peaceful Russian attempts to incorporate near-abroad states by mutual agreement may drive antagonistic near-abroad states into seeking similar guarantees for their security for fear that any integration would encourage Russia to bring pressure on them. Moreover, the Russian leadership is likely to be composed of individuals who have only modest experience with international relations and who may be tempted to re-open the question that Khrushchev wrestled with: How might nuclear weapons be used in peacetime to advance Soviet foreign policy interests?

As troublesome as it might appear, this future might still be manageable, but what would happen if a society loses control over its nuclear arsenal? The collapse of the Soviet Union into constituent republics threatened to produce a wide-scale proliferation and dubious new systems of command and control over the weapons. As it happened, a command structure dominated by the Russian state continued to exercise control over the arsenal, although the leadership of various republics apparently considered how they might bring actual control over the weapons into their hands. Subsequently, all weapons were returned to Russia. But what if the Russian state begins to disintegrate, or the military becomes factionalized enough so that various military organizations become sources of autonomous command and control? Where the weapons do not seem to be under effective centralized control, and where there is growing fear that a local commander may "do something foolish" against the United States or other Western or Chinese interests, will there be an incentive to preempt? What will stay the hand of the United States from using its nuclear arsenal to destroy *all* existing Russian facilities—in the belief that this would be the least risky and most acceptable action to take?

THE FIVE CRISIS POINTS OF THE NUCLEAR FUTURE

The Russian future is one of five crisis points that we point to as areas that you should be monitoring across the next quarter-century. A crisis point exists when states have yet to settle into a particular pattern of conduct. Such a pattern tends to make the inevitable conflicts between sovereign states seem expected and thus, to some degree, manageable, especially without recourse to nuclear weapons. Crisis points, on the other hand, reflect the fact that a significant, unexpected, and undesirable change has occurred in a relationship. The ever-present nuclear shadow in such circumstances makes some form of the nuclear option—from brandishing weapons to actual use—seem appropriate or necessary.

Of course, new crisis points are likely to emerge in world politics in the next twenty-five years as world politics is constantly changing. But we have strong reason to expect these five—which are the carry-overs of the twentieth century—to be with us for some time into the next:

1. *The Russian future* (discussed previously)
2. India-Pakistan These two states have had a long history of conflict, beginning with their violent creation in 1948 and carried forward by wars in 1965 and 1971. In the latter, India abetted the secession of East Pakistan, which became Bangladesh. The disputed province of Kashmir is a constant source of tension, as is a more pervasive ethnic tension between Muslims and Hindus. The crisis point is that both nations have become openly nuclear weapons states and are in a new environment in which they have no experience.
3. *The two Koreas* Neither North nor South Korea has reconciled itself to the division of Korea (a division that is the last of such legacies from World War II). In a fundamental sense, both political systems desire the destruction of the other, but outside the northern attempt in the summer of 1950 to bring about reunification by war, neither side has been willing to use force, although these two states have the most militarized border in the world (with American forces on the ground in the south). The new element in this world is the north's moves to add nuclear weapons to its arsenal and to cope with an economic system that is in collapse

and has no external support. The north has alternated between bellicosity toward the south and its American ally, and an expressed willingness to reach some kind of accommodation (including nuclear weapons, a point we take up in Chapter 8). The south's economic miracle was battered by the Asian recession of the late 1990s, but as long as relative prosperity continues in the south, its political leadership can hope that economic collapse will shatter the Communist control of the north. But that collapse and the political strains it is likely to produce may be the impetus to war.

4. *Missile technology* As we noted in the last chapter, in the long run missiles are likely to be the delivery system of choice for new nuclear weapons states. The momentum of technology will, over the next twenty-five years, provide those states with the capability to deploy long-range missiles, ranges that encompass the major powers, possibly including the United States, but certainly China, Russia, and Europe. Historically, these "weak" states have had to cope with the presence of threatening major powers on their periphery, as the major power could deploy its naval, air, and ground power adjacent to the weak state and threaten the territory of the weak state with no fear of meaningful retaliation against its homeland. Long-range nuclear missiles change that equation, and in so doing create a new context for world politics.[38] North Korea, for instance, has been expanding the range of its missiles; how likely will it be that the United States would challenge a second invasion of the south, one that comes with a clear northern warning that American cities are at risk if the United States resists on the ground? What might a major power do to prevent such a circumstance?

5. *Nuclear weapons in the hands of less-than-state actors* The nuclear future may find a group having a nuclear device, a group willing to use it as terrorists do to cause havoc or to extort concessions as the price of staying their hand. Such an occurrence would create a new situation. In the past, the victim of a nuclear explosion—especially if it were a nuclear armed state—would be expected to deliver horrendous retaliation against the state that had caused the explosion, because a nation has a physical existence in its territory and in its human-made artifacts such as cities. Terrorists, on the other hand, have no physical expression and they usually live among the innocents. How would the victim of nuclear terrorism cope with this kind of crisis? How could it hope to deter such an attack without something vital to threaten as a target of its retaliation? It may be, of course, that the victim might suspect that the terrorist group is connected to existing states. Would the victim rightly or wrong wreck vengeance on those states as well? And if a weak state were the victim, how would the more powerful react? Could they afford to let one act of nuclear terrorism go unpunished?

SUMMARY

Our nuclear past—the first nuclear age—has included the development and use of nuclear weapons, the creation of strategies for their use in war, and the eventual perception that their power makes them effective for nothing but deterrence. At the same time, nuclear weapons states attempted to fit their nuclear weapons into their foreign policy. If they could not be used in war, could they be exploited diplomatically to achieve one's objectives? Could they be used to protect the status quo, even in the face of nuclear threat?

The answer to those questions has been ambiguous. Nuclear weapons did seem to confer prestige, a prestige that might have made the accomplishment of a state's foreign policy objectives easier. Other states may have been willing to make concessions precisely because their opponent had nuclear weapons. But even *that* shadow was, in fact, hard to discern. Some states (such as North Korea and its Chinese allies, or Vietnam) chose to wage wars against a nuclear United States, forcing the latter to accept a military draw and a defeat. What did become clear was that attempts to brandish weapons (including an attempt to deploy them abroad) could create severe crises or exacerbate existing crises. Indeed, crisis was a way of testing deterrence, but it was a test that the United States and the USSR chose not to undertake again after the Cuban missile crisis.

The historical Cold War was coterminous with the existence of nuclear weapons, and those weapons have tended to obscure the fact that the United States—and to a lesser degree, the Soviet Union—had emerged from the Second World War in positions of predominance that had nothing to do with nuclear weapons. The United States spanned the globe, projecting its power everywhere, and would have done so without nuclear weapons. Soviet power, its ability to enforce the communization of Eastern Europe, and its ideological connections with burgeoning communist movements in Asia and the rest of the world provided the Soviet Union with a continental reach—and that predated the emergence of Soviet nuclear weapons. These two states, the most powerful after the war, found themselves in conflict for manifold reasons, only one of which was the nuclear issue.

Was a cold war a relatively safe environment in which to begin to construct nuclear relations? In a sense it was, because neither side wanted to wage war against the other, thus enforcing some restraint. At the same time, a cold war made each side intensely suspicious of the actions of the other. The system would be crisis prone, and thus constantly threaten to push the relationship across the nuclear threshold. But crisis became the opportunity and encouragement to manage the relationship to reduce tensions—to produce détente and thereby create the opportunity to end the cold war. In sum, the Cold War offered a mixed experience. And that indeterminacy about how and why things worked the way they did makes predictions about our nuclear future that much more uncertain.

Our nuclear *present*—the first years of the second nuclear age—is, we suspect, the lull between the storms of the past and those of the future, wherein new nuclear states emerge and mature, and all states return to the question of how nuclear power translates into diplomatic power. The nuclear *future* therefore is likely to be a renewed test of our abilities as a species. As we have hypothesized, there is a relatively good possibility (two to three chances out of ten) that there will be a use of nuclear weapons in the next twenty-five years. Such a use may well grow out of an attempt to exploit nuclear weapons for their political effect, an attempt that goes dangerously awry.

In a perverse way, nuclear weapons are critical for survival, not so much because they guarantee the peace (we cannot say for sure that they do), but because they threaten the future (and *that* we can be sure of). The first fifty years of the nuclear era has provided precious little guidance for what we need to consider for our particular future. There are, however, two interrelated areas that have had an important bearing on that future with which we have had some experience in the first nuclear age: nuclear proliferation and controlling nuclear weapons. We turn to those considerations in the next two chapters. But for the moment we are left with the sobering conclusion that at the start of the twenty-first century, we still do not have an answer to a central question of world politics: In a nuclear world, what role can force play, especially force that includes nuclear weapons? Einstein urged us to change our way of thinking about the world. Our predicament deepens when we see that a rich nuclear past may not help us much in seeing the world anew.

NOTES

1. Transcript of White House meeting, October 16, 1962, 11:50 A.M.–12:57 P.M. We have edited the transcript slightly, to remove interjections and the like that broke into conversations. The ellipses that appear are the original pauses of the speaker. Human speech is most definitely not like a movie script! The published version (which has edited the transcript even more) can be found in *The Kennedy Tapes: Inside the White House during the Cuban Missile Crisis*, ed. Ernest R. May and Philip D. Zelikow (Cambridge, MA: Belknap Press, 1997), pp. 99–100.
2. Bruce W. Nelan, "Nuclear Disarray," *Time*, May 19, 1997, p. 46.
3. Lyndon B. Johnson, *The Vantage Point: Perspectives on the Presidency, 1963–1969* (New York: Holt, Rinehart, and Winston, 1971), p. 566.
4. Theodore H. White, *In Search of History* (New York: Warner Books, 1978), p. 296.
5. John Lewis Gaddis, *The Long Peace* (New York: Oxford University Press, 1987); John Mueller, *Retreat from Doomsday: The Obsolescence of Major War* (New York: Basic Books, 1989).
6. See, among others, John Lewis Gaddis, *We Now Know: Rethinking Cold War History* (New York: Oxford University Press, 1997); Walter LeFeber, *America, Russia, and the Cold War, 1945–1992*, 7th ed. (New York: McGraw-Hill, 1993); and Ronald Powaski, *The Cold War* (New York: Oxford University Press, 1998).
7. Memo by George Ball, October 1965; quoted in Deborah Shapley, *Promise and Power: The Life and Times of Robert McNamara* (Boston, MA: Little, Brown, 1993), p. 312.
8. Johnson, *Vantage Point*, pp. 147–148.
9. Nikita Khrushchev, *Khrushchev Remembers*, trans. and ed. by Strobe Talbott (Boston, MA: Little, Brown, 1970), p. 518.
10. On the missile crisis, see, among others, Graham Allison, *The Essence of Decision* (New York: HarperCollins, 1971); James G. Blight and David Welch, *On the Brink: Americans and Soviets Reexamine the Cuban Missile Crisis*, 2nd ed. (New York: Noonday, 1990); Aleksandr Fursenko and Timothy Naftali, *"One Hell of a Gamble": Khrushchev, Castro, and Kennedy, 1958–1964* (New York: Norton, 1997); Roger Hilsman, *The Cuban Missile Crisis* (Westport, CT: Praeger, 1996); and Mark J. White, *The Cuban Missile Crisis* (London: Macmillan, 1996).
11. Top secret memorandum of 27 October, 1962, reported in Raymond Garthoff, *Reflections on the Cuban Missile Crisis*, rev. ed. (Washington, D.C.: The Brookings Institution, 1989), pp. 202–203.
12. At the time of the crisis, the United States estimated that the Soviets had 60–75 ICBMs, no submarine-launched missiles deployed along American shores, and 155 bombers capable of reaching the United States, but not deployed in significant numbers to do so. The United States had 172 ICBMs, 112 SLBMs, and 1,450 strategic bombers. In fact, the Soviets had only 25–45 ICBMs. In either case, the strategic balance was drastically in the Americans' favor. Garthoff, *Reflections*, pp. 206–208.
13. Garhoff, *Reflections*, p. 12.
14. Meeting of Tuesday, October 16, 11:50 A.M.; *The Kennedy Tapes*, pp. 71–72.
15. For the first Berlin crisis, see Avi Shlaim, *The United States and the Berlin Blockade, 1948–1949* (Berkeley, CA: University of California, 1983); Jean Smith, *The Defense of Berlin* (Baltimore, MD: Johns Hopkins, 1963); and Lucius Clay, *Decision in Germany* (Garden City, NY: Doubleday, 1950); for the second, see Vladislav Zubok and Constantine Pleshakov, *Inside the Kremlin's Cold War* (Cambridge, MA: Harvard, 1996); and Michael Beschloss, *The Crisis Years: Kennedy and Khrushchev* (New York: HarperCollins, 1991).
16. Paul Nitze, *From Hiroshima to Glasnost: At the Center of Decision* (New York: Grove Weidenfeld, 1989), pp. 197, 195.

17. Seminar transcript appearing in John P. S. Gearson, "British Policy and the Berlin Wall Crisis, 1958–61," *Contemporary Record* 6 (summer 1992): 172.
18. Nitze, *From Hiroshima*, pp. 203–204.
19. Gearson, "British Policy," p. 125.
20. Frans Berkhout, Oleg Bukharin, Harold Feiveson, and Martin Miller, "A Cutoff in the Production of Fissile Material," *International Security* 19 (winter 1994/95): 168.
21. Quoted by Bundy, *Danger and Survival*, p. 138.
22. Victor L. Israelyan, *Inside the Kremlin during the Yom Kippur War* (University Park, PA: Pennsylvania State University Press, 1995), pp. 182–183. Ironically, Nixon did not order the alert; Henry Kissinger had while the president slept!
23. Quoted in Li Zhisui, *The Private Life of Chairman Mao* (New York: Random House, 1994), pp. 206–207.
24. Kennan telegram of February 22, 1946; *Foreign Relations of the United States 1946*, Vol. VI (Washington, D.C.: U.S. Government Printing Office, 1969), p. 699.
25. Khrushchev, *Khrushchev Remembers*, pp. 223–224.
26. Harry S. Truman, *Memoirs*, Vol. 2, *Years of Trial and Hope* (Garden City, NY: Doubleday, 1956), p. 215.
27. Ibid., p. 214.
28. Malenkov speech of March 15, 1953; *Documents on International Affairs 1953* (London: Oxford University Press, 1956), pp. 12–13.
29. Ole Holsti, "Cognitive Dynamics and Images of the Enemy: Dulles and Russia," in D. Finlay, O. Holsti, and R. Fagen, *Enemies in Politics* (Chicago, IL: Rand McNally, 1967), pp. 25–96.
30. Malenkov speech of August 8, 1953; *Documents 1953*, p. 29.
31. Quoted by Arthur M. Schlesinger, Jr., *A Thousand Days* (Boston, MA: Houghton Mifflin, 1965), p. 802.
32. Gerald Ford, *A Time to Heal* (New York: Harper & Row and Reader's Digest, 1979), p. 218.
33. Meeting with East European leaders, February 1948, quoted by Milovan Djilas, *Conversations with Stalin* (New York: Harcourt, Brace and World, 1962), p. 182.
34. Vice Admiral Dennis A. Jones, quoted by James Brooke, "Former Cold Warrior Has a New Mission: Nuclear Cuts," *New York Times*, January 8, 1997, p. A12.
35. Deputy Secretary of State Strobe Talbott, "Dealing with Russia in a Time of Troubles," *The Economist* 349 (November 21–27, 1998): 55.
36. Quoted by James Bennet, "Clinton's Wide Web," *New York Times*, May 1, 1998, p. A10.
37. Talbott, "Dealing with Russia," p. 56.
38. For one speculation, see Paul Bracken, "America's Maginot Line," *Atlantic Monthly* 282 (November 1998): 85-93. Seymour Hersh has argued that Israel had a similar strategy: to threaten the Soviet Union with nuclear attack if it did not restrain its Arab allies; *The Sampson Option* (New York: Random House, 1991).

7

THE EXPANSION OF THE NUCLEAR WORLD: NUCLEAR PROLIFERATION AND TERRORISM

In 1993, South African President F. W. de Klerk announced that his nation had dismantled the six or seven nuclear weapons it had built in the 1980s and was signing the Nuclear Non-Proliferation Treaty, thereby allowing international inspections of its nuclear facilities.[1] The South African case shows that nuclear proliferation is a reversible process. Nuclear proliferation, our concern in this chapter, is the most serious nuclear problem in the post-Cold War era. South Africa is, so far as we know, the first state with nuclear weapons to have given them up.

The South African case may give us some hope that the problem posed by nuclear proliferation can be overcome. But there are reasons not to be so sanguine. One is that India and Pakistan each openly joined the nuclear club by conducting a series of nuclear tests in May of 1998. Another is that South Africa is so far the only nation to have given up its nuclear weapons, and there are factors involved in the South African decision that are unique and unlikely to be repeated elsewhere. The South African decision was made by its White minority government in the process of transition from its policy of racial apartheid to Black majority rule, and it is likely that the government was motivated by its desire not to have the weapons fall into the hands of the Black majority. Thus, the South African case may not indicate a solution to the problem of nuclear proliferation is at hand.

Nuclear proliferation is the process by which nations without nuclear weapons acquire them. The traditional nuclear powers, the United States, Russia, Britain, France, and China, were at one point nuclear proliferators.[2] Israel, India, and Pakistan are all more recent nuclear proliferators. What is the problem of nuclear proliferation?[3] Part of it concerns nuclear deterrence and its effectiveness. Many believe that nuclear deterrence works, that it can provide a reliable form of military security. After all, the argument goes, nuclear deterrence allowed the United States and the former Soviet Union to avoid a hot war during the turbulent decades of the Cold War. We consider the soundness of this argument elsewhere. But here we ask a different question. If nuclear deterrence is effective, for whom is it effective? Would nuclear deterrence provide security for any state? Or does it work only for some states? If nuclear proliferation is a serious problem, it must be that acquiring nuclear weapons at least sometimes fails to provide reliable military security.

But the effectiveness of nuclear deterrence is not the only factor to consider in determining the dangerousness of nuclear proliferation. Nor is it the only factor to consider in explaining why states might seek to acquire nuclear weapons. States seek nuclear weapons for a variety of reasons beyond the desire for security through nuclear deterrence. Nuclear weapons are often seen as international status symbols, and states may seek them for this reason. Related to this motivation, nuclear weapons may be sought by a state to assert its independence and sovereignty. These factors, likely involved in the 1998 decision by India and Pakistan to test nuclear weapons and, much earlier, in the decisions of Great Britain and France to become nuclear powers, make nuclear proliferation more likely to occur, because they lead states to seek the weapons even if not convinced that the weapons would enhance their military security. More ominously, states may seek nuclear weapons because they desire to use them against military opponents, or to intimidate their neighbors, that is, for compellence rather than mere deterrence. These factors, perhaps involved in Iraq's efforts to acquire the weapons (efforts at least temporarily interrupted by the Persian Gulf War), make proliferation more dangerous, because they make the weapons more likely to be used.

One of the central questions of this chapter is: Why is nuclear proliferation dangerous and how dangerous is it? This is addressed shortly. But first we consider the politics of nuclear proliferation—how nuclear proliferation occurs and why. Only when we understand this can we appreciate how likely it is to occur. Later we take up the question of what policies should be adopted to decrease the likelihood of further nuclear proliferation. Finally we consider a different form of nuclear proliferation, one where the potential proliferator is not a nation-state. This is the problem of nuclear terrorism.

THE POLITICS OF NUCLEAR PROLIFERATION

Recall that the nuclear predicament rests on the following three facts: (1) Humans will always have the knowledge that nuclear weapons can be built; (2) independent, sovereign nation-states will be the principal actors in world politics for some time to come; and (3) many of these states have the resources necessary to construct nuclear weapons and, for those with the resources, the weapons are not difficult to make. To these three facts, we should add a fourth: (4) With the end of the Cold War, there are new opportunities and perhaps new motivations for nonnuclear states to acquire nuclear weapons. How may we expect these facts to play themselves out in terms of the proliferation of nuclear weapons? How likely is it that the number of states with nuclear weapons will increase considerably in the future?

There are two factors involved in the likelihood of nuclear proliferation. Mitchell Reiss notes:

> Nuclear proliferation is a function of two variables: technological capability and political motivation. Both must be present for a country to acquire nuclear weapons. The capability without the motivation is innocuous. The motivation without the capability is futile.[4]

But Reiss's first factor, technological capability, should be understood more broadly as the *opportunity* to acquire the weapons. Opportunity is primarily a function of the technological capability to build the weapons, but it also includes, especially with the end of the Cold War, the possibility of a state's acquiring nuclear weapons on the international black market, or stealing them. The issue of the technological capability involved in nuclear proliferation was discussed in Chapters 3 and 5. In this chapter we expand on that discussion by bringing into consideration other dimensions of the factor of opportunity, as well as discussing the second factor, that of political motivation. One of the most interesting and important facts about the history of proliferation is that, expectations to the contrary, it has progressed slowly. In 1963, President Kennedy stated: "[P]ersonally I am haunted by the feeling that by 1970, unless we are successful, there may be ten nuclear powers instead of four, and by 1975, fifteen or twenty."[5] But such fears about proliferation were not realized. Rather than accelerating, the pace of nuclear proliferation has actually slowed. Consider cases of tested nuclear devices. Counting decades since 1945, the first decade saw three states demonstrate a nuclear explosion (the United States, the Soviet Union, and Great Britain), while the second saw two (France and China), and the third decade, only one (India). No state did in the fourth or fifth decades. But there has been one state to test so far in the sixth decade, namely, Pakistan, in response to additional tests by India. This suggests that the rate of proliferation may again accelerate. The important fact is that many states with the technological capability have not proliferated (states such as Japan, Canada, and many European nations, including Germany), which means that they lacked the political motivation. Either they did not believe that nuclear deterrence would work for them or, if they did, there were countervailing pressures determining their overall lack of motivation to acquire nuclear weapons.

But the pace of proliferation suggested by the number of nations testing nuclear weapons is misleading. The nuclear properties of matter are now so well known, and computers are so powerful, that it is no longer necessary to actually test a device in order to have confidence that it will explode as designed.[6] As we saw in Chapter 3, both the gun assembly and implosion designs worked the first times they were tried by the United States, and that was done in an era of relative ignorance of nuclear properties and during the infancy of computers. The clearest case of proliferation without (as far as we know) testing is Israel, which is reported to have assembled a large number of nuclear devices. Mordechai Vanunu, a former Israeli nuclear technician, told the *London Times* that Israel has 100 to 200 fission weapons and is in the process of developing weapons that make use of fusion. Some analysts credit Israel with material for some 100 nuclear devices, based on estimates of the potential plutonium production rate of the Dimona nuclear reactor.

But there have been some cases where the move toward proliferation has been arrested.[7] The case of South Africa was mentioned earlier. Two other cases are Brazil and Argentina. In 1991, these nations signed a pair of agreements by which each sought to assure the other, and the rest of the world, that it was not developing nuclear weapons.[8] One of these agreements was with the International Atomic Energy Agency, which allowed international inspections of the nuclear facilities of the two nations. In 1991, both nations had recently adopted democratic, civilian governance after a period of repressive military rule and mutual military rivalry, a period in which there was fear that each side was trying to outrace the other to be the first to have the bomb. This suggests that the process of democratization may be effective in reducing the likelihood of proliferation, although this may be countered by the observation that three of the five principle nuclear powers were democracies (as were India and Israel) when they developed their weapons.

Then there is a very different kind of antiproliferation success story in the case of Iraq. When Iraq was defeated in the 1991 Persian Gulf War, a very intrusive weapons inspection regime was established, conducted by the international community, authorized by the United Nations (Security Council Resolution 715), and accepted by Iraq as part of the terms of the cease fire. The inspectors uncovered a vast program for the development of nuclear weapons. Iraq had "pursued a range of technologies, built an impressive collection of buildings at many sites, and purchased hundreds of thousands of pieces of special equipment and hundreds of tons of specialty materials from abroad."[9] It is estimated that had the program not been interrupted by the Iraqi defeat, a bomb would have been produced by 1996. Prior to the war Iraq had been subject to international inspections as part of what was required of it as a signatory of the Nuclear Non-Proliferation Treaty, but these inspections had proved inadequate to uncover the nuclear weapons program then underway. As the intensive post-war inspection regime is relaxed, it may be difficult to keep Iraq from resuming its program. The success in stopping proliferation in the case of Iraq was a fluke, and it should be a source of concern rather than celebration. It clearly shows that the normal efforts to avoid nuclear proliferation are inadequate to stop a state like Iraq that is determined to acquire a bomb.

What is the rate of proliferation likely to be in the future? There are several factors suggesting that the rate may increase. Perhaps the most significant is the Indian and Pakistani series of nuclear tests. But there are other background factors of importance. First, the advance of technology has made the production of nuclear weapons easier. An indication of this is that reliable nuclear weapons can now be made without the need for test explosions. Another factor is the accelerating growth of global economic integration, which makes it easier for a state determined to acquire nuclear weapons to obtain the industrial technology to make this possible. The Iraqi case is a prime example of this. But, the most important factor making an increase in nuclear proliferation more likely in the future is the breakup of the Soviet Union and the end of the Cold War.

The end of the Cold War has changed the proliferation problem in significant ways.[10] For one, it has turned the Soviet nuclear threat into a nuclear proliferation threat. The breakup of the Soviet Union caused the dispersal of the Soviet arsenal. Soviet weapons were left in several of the break-away states, such as the Ukraine and Kazakhstan.[11] This problem, however, has been largely overcome by successful efforts to get these states to return their weapons to Russia. There is also the possibility that Soviet nuclear material will find its way to third countries.[12] This is the so-called "loose nukes" problem. Due largely to financial problems following the breakup of the Soviet Union, Russia, as discussed in Chapter 5, has not been able to afford to maintain tight security on its nuclear materials, raising the risk of their being stolen, and it has not been able to afford adequately to pay its military personnel, raising the risk that they will seek to sell nuclear materials on the black market.

But there is an important political factor as well. Another, and more lasting, way in which the end of the Cold War has effected the proliferation problem is that the steep decline of Soviet/Russian power has lead to stronger incentives, and weaker disincentives, for nonnuclear states to acquire nuclear weapons. As one commentator notes: "Former Soviet clients may at once be more desperate (lacking a superpower patron) and more autonomous (lacking a superpower to restrain them)."[13] This decline in Soviet/Russian power is complemented by a decline, though much less steep, in the power of the United States, as economic power has become as important as military power. These shifts in power have had several important consequences, among which are the following: (1) a probable prolonged period of serious economic dislocation and ethnic and political unrest in the Former Soviet Union and Eastern Europe; (2) the relative increase in power of Western Europe and East Asia, especially China and Japan; (3) the end of the certainties of the Cold War, such as the alliance systems and the tendency of regional conflicts to be subsumed under the East-West conflict, which has left states to define anew their interests and relations with others; and (4) a shift from the bipolar world of the Cold War to a multipolar world order. India's decision to test in 1998 may show some of these factors at work. For example, one reason for these tests may have been that India felt isolated by the loss of its former alliance with the Soviet Union. In any case, many expect these changes to further increase tendencies toward proliferation.[14]

One important feature of contemporary nuclear proliferation, partly related to the changes discussed previously, is the difficulty we now have answering the question: Who has the bomb? There is now no sharp line, as there was thirty years ago, between being and not being a nuclear state. This is in part a matter of our lacking information about the capabilities of possible proliferators, but also partly a matter of our not knowing how to classify states, even based on full information about their capabilities. There are two reasons for this difficulty in line-drawing, one technological and one political. Technologically, it is not now a difficult matter for a state to approach the production of a nuclear weapon, but deliberately stop short of final assembly, to be "a screwdriver away."[15] Acquiring nuclear weapons is more appropriately thought of not as reaching a plateau, but ascending a staircase.[16] The question is, at what step on the stair does a state become a nuclear state? It used to be thought that a necessary and sufficient condition for being a nuclear state was the successful testing of a weapon. Indeed, this definition is enshrined in the Non-Proliferation Treaty (to be discussed later).[17] But, as we have seen, a state can be confident that it has a reliable weapon without testing.

The political reason for the difficulty in "drawing a line" is that sometimes proliferators find it attractive not to reveal their possession of the weapons. This phenomenon, made possible by there being no need to test, has been referred to as "opaque proliferation." As discussed in Chapter 3, it refers to situations in which states possess nuclear weapons but do not make this known by declaration or demonstration. This form of proliferation has also been referred to as "part-way proliferation" and has been characterized as "a tactic for having it both ways; for making use of some of the deterrent power of nuclear armaments without driving neighboring countries into the nuclear business or incurring whatever sanctions the international community can impose for a breach of the nuclear rules."[18] Given its technological feasibility and its political appeal, opaque proliferation may be one form that proliferation takes in the future, posing additional difficulties for our theoretical understanding of proliferation.

Let us look more carefully at the question of political motivation for proliferation, and do this by bringing into the discussion three perspectives from which to view international relations, namely, realism, liberalism, and institutionalism. Realists tend to be pessimists about the course of international relations, liberals tend to be optimists, and institutionalists tend to be somewhere in between. The application of this three-way scheme in discussing the post-Cold War world has been developed by Jack Snyder and Thomas Risse-Kappan.[19]

Realists often take the view that peace and stability in the world are only possible when strong bipolar political and military balances prevail. According to this view, the stability of the superpower confrontation of the Cold War was further strengthened by the existence of powerful nuclear arsenals integrated into the armed forces of both sides, thus ensuring that any war between the superpowers would inevitably be a nuclear war, and therefore unthinkable. On this view, the dissolution of the Soviet Union, the possible withdrawal of U.S. forces from overseas, the rise of new power centers such as the European Union and a united Germany, and the independence of the Eastern European nations are all seen as threats to peace and stability. Take Germany as an example. A realist might argue that a united Germany may bring on a new era of German domination. At its most basic level, this fear has to do with borders. Considerable territory was taken from Germany to punish it for starting World War II and as a hedge against World War III. With a reunified Germany dominating the continent, and with the United States following the Soviet Union in taking its military forces out, who will stop Germany if it invokes a statute of limitations on World War II and demands restoration to its former boundaries? No one can be absolutely certain that Germany ten or twenty years from now will not dismiss any pledge it has made to honor current borders. Germany's demanding restoration of its former borders may be especially likely if it perceives instability, ethnic conflicts, economic unrest, or the presence of political or economic vacuums in Eastern Europe that could be filled by its expansion.

What does the realist perspective have to say about how likely it is that nonnuclear states will have the political motivation to acquire nuclear weapons? The question is whether the changes in the international system after the Cold War will move leaders to see their national interest in new ways, encouraging them to consider proliferation where they had not considered it before. Given the instability that realists see as characteristic of the post-Cold War era, they would regard it as likely that such a change in perception will occur, leading to a higher likelihood of proliferation. For example, John Mearsheimer, writing just before the demise of the Soviet Union, in an argument that applies to Russian power as it did to Soviet power, argued:

> The Germans are not likely to be willing to rely on the Poles or the Czechs to provide their forward defense against a possible direct Soviet conventional attack on their homeland. Nor are the Germans likely to trust the Soviet Union to refrain for all time from nuclear blackmail against a non-nuclear Germany. Hence they will eventually look to nuclear weapons as the surest means of security, just as NATO has done. The small states of Eastern Europe will also have strong incentives to acquire nuclear weapons. Without them they would be open to nuclear blackmail by the Soviet Union, or by Germany if proliferation stopped there. Even if those major powers did not have nuclear arsenals, no Eastern European state could match German or Soviet conventional strength.[20]

In contrast, liberals assume that the Cold War world has been replaced by an entirely new environment in which the mutual threat has disappeared, not only between the two superpowers, but also between the two blocs. The potential for greater political cooperation has reemerged along with a renewed interest in mutual security arrangements that protect the territorial integrity and sovereignty of all parties. Perhaps most important, anti-Communism and anti-Westernism can no longer be used effectively to mobilize voters or significant groups in the two societies. With the downfall of both authoritarian governments and communist economic systems, the main source of conflict is being removed and we are therefore justified in being optimistic about the world's future. Furthermore, the increased importance of social welfare and the satisfaction of consumer demands in the capitalist world render war increasingly counterproductive to nations' long-term interests, as does increasing economic interdependence and the internationalization of corporations. Thus the democratization of Eastern Europe and of Russia reduces the threat of war and should usher in an age of peace and mutual cooperation not unlike the relations that exist between the United States, Canada, and Great Britain. There will be a growing realization of the expanding economic benefits of cooperation, as free trade increases. Military power will no longer be seen as the most important measure of power in world politics. Where military power remains important, conventional military force will be seen as more useful than nuclear force, in part because military challenges will more often be internal threats to national unity rather than external threats to national security.

As a result, a liberal would likely argue that the realist fear of increased proliferation is based on an outmoded view of world politics. We are moving, the liberal might say, away from Cold War behavior, perhaps even away from the traditional behavior of nation-states, as the growing integration of the European Union attests. There is no reason to assume that nations will blindly follow the practices of the past, especially as the nuclear weapons states have made some movement toward the elimination of their own nuclear arsenals. Democratic governments, freed from a fear of external threat, may find it more difficult to persuade themselves and their citizens to undertake costly nuclear weapons programs, especially where popular antinuclear movements are strong, as they are in Germany and Japan. Indeed, democratic governments may be more willing to erect internal barriers to proliferation. As we saw earlier, the trend toward democracy worked against proliferation in the cases of Brazil and Argentina.

The third perspective, institutionalism, lies between realism and liberalism. Like liberals, institutionalists recognize and appreciate the potential to be realized in the democratization and liberalization of Eastern Europe and other parts of the world. But institutionalists are like realists in their recognition that the disappearance of one source of antagonisms may simply open the way for other conflicts of interest that could lead to war. Their source of optimism is the development over the last thirty years of various international institutions, agreements, and arrangements by which the world has been able safely to navigate even the extremes of the Cold War. These mechanisms of détente include West Germany's *Ost Politik* begun in 1969, the Helsinki accords of the Conference on Security and Cooperation in Europe (CSCE) in 1975, the Stockholm agreement on confidence-building measures of 1986, the Intermediate Nuclear Forces agreement and the START treaties (to be discussed in Chapter 8), and the Nuclear Non-Proliferation Treaty (to be discussed later in this chapter). The European Union and the United Nations are yet other institutional mechanisms through which cooperation has replaced competition. Recent years have seen the United Nations playing an increasingly effective role in world affairs. UN forces have provided effective buffers in a number of armed disputes, and several thorny international problems have been settled or managed under the UN's auspices. In addition, NATO has taken on the role of peacekeeper in Bosnia and has used force to seek to reverse "ethnic cleansing" in Kosovo. Mutual security is the key idea for institutionalists, who see both institutions already in place that can be strengthened and other institutions that can be created, by which nations can guarantee their mutual security and work out their disagreements.

When speculating on the likelihood of proliferation, the institutionalists are likely to focus on both the dangers and opportunities of the new international environment. They would seek to create agreements like the one between Argentina and Brazil, but also build on some of the institutions established in the past. In Europe, they might see the reduced influence of Russia and the partial disengagement of the United States as leading various European nations to seek new ways to guarantee their national survival, perhaps leading to further proliferation, either individually as in the case of Germany, or collectively as in the idea of the "Euro-Bomb," a nuclear arsenal held collectively by the European Community.[21] But, against this tendency, the institutionalist would point out that the United States and Russia will remain important in Europe. The growth of Russian-American cooperation and collaboration—in partnership with an integrating Europe—may create many opportunities for the negotiation of mutually acceptable security agreements (although the expansion of NATO to nations in Eastern Europe and its role in the former Yugoslavia may dampen the prospects for this cooperation). The institutionalist recognizes that nations will, in the short run, have conflicting nuclear interests. The key for the institutionalist is to build constraints against further proliferation, or failing that, to channel proliferation into a less destabilizing path.

Of course, events may occur that would make the international situation much worse. For example, there may be serious economic dislocations experienced during the transition to market economies, resulting in the return of authoritarian governments to Eastern Europe or Russia. Such governments may rediscover the "external threat" and make nuclear weapons a priority matter. Or, democratic governments in this region (or elsewhere) might be swept by intense nationalistic sentiments and images of themselves as great powers, which may make nuclear weapons attractive, at least as symbols. None of the three perspectives can rule out the possibility of such events, but they differ in how they would react to that possibility. The liberal might say that while these things are possible, if we spend our energies worrying about them we will not put our full effort into making the most of the opportunities, such as ensuring that the economic transition works by providing economic aid. Besides, the history of our time is that democracies do not wage war on other democracies. Enhancing the prospects for democracy in Eastern Europe will lead those nations away from an interest in the weapons of war that could be used against their democratic neighbors.

The realist might say that basic prudence requires us to concentrate on what might go wrong, for in a nuclear world things "going wrong" would be catastrophic. Some nations will experience economic calamity and blind nationalism, which may lead to proliferation. Moreover, the current international situation makes such an eventuality much more worrisome. Instead of the bipolar arrangement characteristic of the Cold War, where the world was politically divided between the United States and the Soviet Union, we now have a multipolar system, one with more than two centers of power, which is inherently less stable and therefore more dangerous. Instead of just one potential threat to a nation's security (the other bloc), there now are multiple threats. Conflicts multiply in a disorganized fashion, as particular issues emerge in the relationships with several different nations. Thus, the realist would conclude that it would be dangerous to do anything other than preparing for the eventuality of proliferation. We should devote our energies along two lines. First, we should continue to emphasize the role of nuclear deterrence, because nuclear weapons will always be with us. Second, we should create coalitions or alliances that can balance power, thus reducing the prospects of war between nations, more of which will likely have nuclear arms in the future.

The institutionalist, like the realist, would see a high likelihood of things going wrong and the consequent strong tendency toward nuclear proliferation. Thus, the institutionalist would disagree with the liberal view that we should not put our energies into preparing for that eventuality. But, unlike the realist, the institutionalist would argue that the strong tendencies toward proliferation need not lead to a great increase in the actual rate of proliferation. Institutional mechanisms can be put in place that can limit the extent of actual proliferation. The chief mechanism in this effort has been the Nuclear Non-Proliferation Treaty (NPT), which was negotiated in 1967 and renewed in 1995 for an indefinite period. In the long run, the chief institutional mechanism may be some kind of international authority that, unlike the current United Nations, has real power to provide security for states threatened with aggression. We will discuss the prospects for such an institution in Chapter 11.

We have seen three perspectives on the likelihood of nuclear proliferation. Which is closest to the truth? What is the likelihood of an increase in the rate of nuclear proliferation in the future? It seems clear that the opportunities for nuclear proliferation are increasing and that the technological capability of building the weapons is becoming more widespread. But for proliferation to occur, the motivation to proliferate must be present as well. What do the three perspectives tell us about the motivation for proliferation in the future? The liberal assumes it will not be high, while the institutionalist and the realist assume that it will be high, though the latter two differ on whether this increased motivation need lead to actual proliferation.

There are arguments that can be made for each of the perspectives, and it is not an easy matter to judge which is closest to the truth. There is a certain attraction in the institutionalist position, in the way it recognizes both the strengths and weaknesses in the other two perspectives. According to the institutionalist, the liberal is wrong in holding that there will not be strong tendencies toward increased proliferation, but the realist is wrong in believing that these tendencies will necessarily result in increased proliferation. Moreover, the liberal is likely wrong in viewing the end of the Cold War as bringing about an international climate in which cooperative tendencies will have a strong upper hand over competitive tendencies. The realist has the better view in this regard: The end of the Cold War does not undo human history. The international situation is likely to produce a variety of crises among a diverse set of actors, and security and stability will difficult to achieve. On the other hand, the realist is likely wrong in believing that a worsened climate must lead to increased proliferation. Institutional arrangements, primarily the NPT, have kept the rate of proliferation low, despite earlier expectations to the contrary, which suggests that the tendency toward future proliferation, even though greater, can be successfully countered by strengthening and augmenting those arrangements.

But one should, on the one hand, be aware of the risks in siding with the institutionalist against the liberal. There are, as the liberal believes, real reasons to think that the international situation after the Cold War may be different in fundamental ways from what it has been since the formation of the current nation-state system in the seventeenth century. The extent of the spread of democracy and the greater role of economics in international relations are new factors that may, as the liberal believes, profoundly lessen the likelihood of military hostility and competitiveness. As the case of Japan in the 1980s illustrates, economic prowess can be as much a source of international power as can military prowess. Growing international economic integration and interdependence can only accelerate this tendency. The problem is that the adoption of the realist assumption (which the institutionalist shares) that military competitiveness will continue to play a dominating role may become a self-fulfilling prophecy. If we act as if military competitiveness will continue to dominate, it may do so despite the factors that could fundamentally change the international situation in a positive way. Put another way, the institutions the institutionalist seeks to promote may be corrupted by the assumptions and fears that the institutionalist shares with the realist. On the other hand, there are risks to the institutionalist's rejection of the realist assumption that increased proliferation is likely inevitable. If that proliferation occurs despite our institution-building efforts, we may be caught without an adequate military response of the sort the realist recommends. More seriously, we may mistakenly and unwisely believe that institutions can prevent the use of the weapons.

But though we are uncertain about the choice of perspective, believing that none of the three has an overwhelming case in its favor, the following argument could still be made. We need to make two kinds of choices. Between the liberal assumption that the post-Cold War world will be fundamentally different and the realist assumption that it will not, it is prudent to choose the latter, given the consequences of being mistaken. For, if we mistakenly adopt the liberal assumption, we will be unprepared for the proliferation and the military instability that will result, and the results could be catastrophic. If we mistakenly adopt the realist assumption, we may miss an opportunity to increase peace and prosperity in the world, but we would be less likely to face the potential catastrophe of military instability. Better here to choose a path that would avoid the greater evil. Between the realist assumption that the increasing tendencies toward proliferation will almost inevitably result in greatly increased proliferation and the institutionalist assumption that they need not so result, it is prudent to choose the latter. The reason is that, if we act on the assumption that proliferation will occur, our primary efforts will not be focused on preventing it, so that it is more likely actually to occur. If it does occur, it will be a great source of danger, despite whatever efforts we might make as realists to minimize that danger. Better to try, through institutional mechanisms, to ensure that the increased potential toward proliferation is not actualized. Moreover, if the liberal is right about the nature of the new world order, its positive effects cannot be realized without much effort, and at least some of that effort will have to be institution-building of the sort the institutionalist recommends.

But there is an important caveat to note about this discussion of the three perspectives. Little has been said explicitly about what may motivate states to seek to acquire nuclear weapons. The underlying assumption has been that states may seek to acquire the weapons if they believe that doing so is in their defensive interests. The three perspectives then differ over whether states are likely to have such a belief and, if so, what should be done to weaken the belief or to ensure that it does not lead to actual proliferation. But, as we mentioned earlier in the chapter, states may be motivated to acquire nuclear weapons for reasons other than the desire to deter potential adversaries. One possibility is that they may be motivated to seek the weapons to use them for aggressive purposes, whether by firing them against an opponent or by making the threat to do so (compellence). The perspectives would have something to say about aggressive motives, as they do about defensive motives, but factoring in aggressive motives would complicate the discussion a great deal. The prior question, which we simply raise and do not attempt to resolve, is whether human beings and human society are so constituted that nations are as likely to act aggressively as defensively in their relations with others. How much of an anomaly was Nazi Germany? More to the point, how much of an anomaly is Iraq under Saddam Hussein, which has sought to acquire nuclear weapons apparently for aggressive purposes?

Another possibility is raised by India's decision to conduct nuclear tests in May 1998 (see Figure 7-1). On the one hand, the Indian government gave the defense justification: India needed a demonstrable nuclear capacity, beyond the nuclear ambiguity created by its 1974 test, in order to counter the nuclear capacity of China. A senior advisor to the Indian prime minister, who made the decision to test, defended that decision by claiming that in South Asia there was "a huge gap, a vacuum" in the geographical domain of nuclear deterrence that India felt the need to fill.[22] India felt that while the United States would protect Japan from China's nuclear threat, no one would protect India from this threat. India had to act to protect itself. As one commentator noted, there was a "pointed contrast between India's sense of isolation and insecurity, and the American nuclear umbrella that protects Japan, Western Europe, and many of the countries that lined up against India's test."[23] Showing the difficulty with the liberal assumption that the basis for state action changed with the end of the Cold War, the senior advisor went on to observe: "The United States of America then proposed a new thesis, that the principal dynamic or relations would be trade and commerce. The United States assumed everyone thought the same."[24]

On the other hand, India apparently had other motives as well. The Indian prime minister, Atal Bihari Vajpayee, proclaimed that with the nuclear tests, India had taken "its rightful place in the international community."[25] India thinks of itself as a great nation, but believed that it was not being recognized as such because, unlike other great nations, it did not have a developed nuclear arsenal. The initial overwhelming and enthusiastic support of everyday Indians for the government's decision to test suggests that feelings of national pride and self-respect played a major role in the decision. In

Figure 7-1
The Indian nuclear tests in 1998 had strong popular support. *Reuters/Sunil Malhotra/Archive Photos*

addition, the prime minister, the first leader of India from the strongly nationalist Bharatiya Janata Party, clearly had domestic political reasons to test, not only out of his nationalist desire to demonstrate India's greatness, but also out of the need to do something to support the shaky minority government over which he presided.

Our conclusion is that the world will likely face in the future not only increasing opportunities for proliferation but increasing motivations on the part of nations to proliferate as well, whether those motivations are exclusively defensive or also partly nationalistic or aggressive. In other words, unless we take serious action, there will almost certainly be further proliferation. The world can act effectively to minimize the extent to which this increased potential for proliferation will lead to actual proliferation by focusing on various institutional mechanisms of international cooperation, such as the NPT. Before discussing what antiproliferation policy should be, however, we should consider more carefully what has been assumed in the discussion so far, namely, that nuclear proliferation is inevitably a bad thing.

HOW DANGEROUS IS NUCLEAR PROLIFERATION?

Conventional wisdom holds that nuclear proliferation makes the world a more dangerous place, that it undermines rather than enhances security. Nuclear proliferation increases the risk of war (and the level of destructiveness of war). Indeed, this increased danger is assumed whenever nuclear proliferation is labeled a "problem," as it normally is. Nuclear proliferation may well be dangerous, but the matter deserves examination.

At first glance, there seems to be a contradiction in the conventional wisdom, because it normally combines the view that proliferation is dangerous with the view that the possession of nuclear weapons by the superpowers made the Cold War world less dangerous. It is odd, notes Kenneth Waltz, that "a happy nuclear past leads many to expect an unhappy nuclear future."[26] The apparent contradiction is that the conventional view seems to answer both yes and no to the question whether nuclear deterrence works: Nuclear deterrence worked in the case of the United States and the former Soviet Union, it maintained the Cold War peace; but it will not work in the case of would-be proliferators, whose nuclear weapons would increase the risk of war. There are ways to respond to this claim of contradiction, but let us begin by considering a view that takes the contradiction as real. This is the view, in contrast with the conventional wisdom, that nuclear proliferation would make the world less dangerous.

Those who believe that the spread of nuclear weapons would have beneficial effects on security argue from both theory and history.[27] They argue that the view that proliferation would be dangerous "flies in the face of the inherent logic of nuclear deterrence, as well as the history of the Cold War."[28] The argument that proliferation would not be dangerous is put most strongly by Kenneth Waltz.[29] Speaking from history, he argues that the long Cold War peace among the major powers must be attributable largely to nuclear deterrence, since that factor distinguished the era from earlier historical periods when great-power wars were more frequent. If nuclear deterrence worked for the superpowers, it should work for others.

Waltz's theoretical argument seeks to explain how nuclear deterrence works, thus showing how it makes things less dangerous. The signal features of nuclear weapons are their tremendous destructive capability and the near impossibility of a state's defending itself against their use by an opponent. Any state with a modest number of nuclear weapons can threaten to inflict "unacceptable damage" against an opponent. As a result, "the presence of nuclear weapons makes states exceedingly cautious." Being certain of an opponent's ability to destroy it with nuclear weapons, a state would be much less likely to start a war or to act in ways that might lead to war. This caution would characterize any state facing a nuclear-armed foe. Thus, when both sides have nuclear weapons, war would be less likely. Waltz concludes: "Nuclear weapons, responsibly used, make wars hard to start. Nations that have nuclear weapons have strong incentives to use them responsibly. These statements hold for small as for big nuclear powers."[30] The theoretical conclusion bolsters the historical point, explaining why in fact the Cold War was the long peace, and strengthens the expectation that the same effects would be found in the case of would-be proliferators.

Most of those who believe that proliferation is dangerous grant the claim that nuclear deterrence worked in producing the long peace, but seek to avoid the contradiction by citing a number of differences between the Cold War superpowers and the would-be proliferators that show how nuclear deterrence, while it worked for the superpowers, would not work for would-be proliferators. Joseph Nye argues that the claim that nuclear deterrence works well

> assumes governments with stable command and control systems, the absence of serious civil wars, the absence of strong destabilizing motivations such as irredentist passions, and discipline over the temptation for preemptive strikes during the early stages when new nuclear weapons capabilities are soft and vulnerable. Such assumptions are unrealistic in many parts of the world.[31]

The difference between the superpowers and would-be proliferators regarding these factors and others suggests that would-be proliferators are not only more likely than were the superpowers to get themselves into a deliberate nuclear war, but they are also more likely to get into an accidental nuclear war.[32] The risk of inadvertent or unauthorized use is greater. As a result, the lessened danger that nuclear weapons brought about during the Cold War would not hold in the case of would-be proliferators.

Consider one specific case, that of India and Pakistan. These states became recent nuclear proliferators, conducting a series of nuclear tests in 1998.[33] There are three important ways in which the relations of these two states differ from the Cold War relations between the United States and the Soviet Union. First, India and Pakistan share a long and disputed border, while the superpowers did not. Second, the two have had three wars between them in their history, whereas the superpowers had never been at war with each other (in fact, they were allies in World War II). Third, the superpowers had developed a robust system of command and control of their nuclear weapons, while India and Pakistan have not. These differences seem to make nuclear war between India and Pakistan much more likely than it was between the United States and the Soviet Union. In fact, it is reported that "every time the Pentagon has conducted a war game between a nuclear-armed India and Pakistan, the result is a nuclear exchange, something that does not happen between … Russia and the United States."[34]

Waltz, in response, examines a number of the differences that are said to distinguish would-be proliferators from the superpowers. In general, he argues that the prospect of nuclear destruction is so powerful an influence on behavior that it would induce caution even in the face of these differences.

To think further about this issue, we should distinguish the differences that are technological from those that are political. The technological differences concern the safety and security of nuclear weapons and the systems for their command and control.

The superpowers had sophisticated systems to prevent the use of the weapons accidentally or without authorization and to make the weapons systems invulnerable to destruction by a preemptive or preventive attack. Would-be proliferators, in general, would not. But the current nuclear states largely have it within their power to correct for this problem by providing assistance to proliferators in constructing nuclear systems.[35] For example, the United States could provide a proliferator with arming technology that avoids unauthorized use (what are called "permissive action links").

What about the political differences, "the absence of those patterns of behavior and modes of thought that produced prudence in the Soviet-American relationship"? Do they by themselves make proliferation dangerous? Do would-be proliferators lack the capacity for prudence characteristic of the superpowers? A positive answer, John Weltman argues, "would assume that the capacity for political rationality is a narrow, culturally based attribute."[36] This point is emphasized by Waltz, who argues that the kind of rationality needed to make nuclear deterrence work is simply the human tendency to act cautiously in the face of extreme danger. "Many Westerners who write fearfully about a future in which Third World countries have nuclear weapons seem to view their people in the once familiar imperial manner as 'lesser breeds without the law.'"[37]

How is this disagreement over the dangerousness of nuclear proliferation to be resolved? The critics of proliferation argue that would-be proliferators are less likely to act rationally than the superpowers in their handling of nuclear weapons. What determines how rationally a state acts? The degree of rationality of a state's actions is not only a function of what individual leaders choose to do, but also of the organizations through which they act. This point is developed by Scott Sagan, who discusses the characteristics of military organizations and their implications for nuclear danger.[38]

Sagan approaches the problem from general observations about the nature of organizations, especially military organizations. Regarding military policy, often "the biases, routines, and parochial interests of powerful military organizations, not the 'objective' interests of the state, can determine state behavior."[39] You might remember here the anecdote from Chapter 4 about General LeMay's assertion that he would make the decision to launch a first strike against the Soviet Union. There are two main reasons that organizations do not act rationally. First, the rationality of their behavior is bounded by the routines and standard operating procedures they adopt. Second, the process by which their conflicting goals determines their behavior is highly political, resulting in behavior that is, from an outside perspective, often "systematically stupid."[40] Thus, given the influence of the military in the governments of most would-be proliferators, proliferation can be expected to create new dangers. This argument gives strong support to the conventional view that nuclear proliferation is dangerous.

But this argument proves both too much and too little. It proves too much because, like the proverbial sword, it cuts two ways. It applies not only to would-be proliferators, but also to the older nuclear states themselves. Large organizations characterize the modern nation-state. Organizational factors influence the actions of the nuclear states as they influence the actions of would-be proliferators, even though civilian control may be firmer for the nuclear states. The sins attributed to the military in the last paragraph can apply to any large organization. Here the critics of proliferation can appeal to Cold War history. First, as discussed in Chapter 2, there were a number of occasions when the United States came close to using nuclear weapons.[41] Second, in the view of the those like Waltz who believe that proliferation is largely benign, nuclear deterrence works because the parties to the relationship have the capacity to destroy each other, the condition of mutual assured destruction, and this policy is best maintained by relatively small nuclear forces that avoid "war-fighting" weapons and doctrines that threaten the nuclear weapons of the other side. But, as we saw in Chapter 5, the superpowers did not follow this script. Instead, they assumed that "deterrence required much larger forces than the minimum deterrence requirement," and they "opted for precisely the war-fighting nuclear doctrines that are regarded as unnecessary, inappropriate and destabilizing by most deterrence theorists."[42]

These historical points suggest that the organizational characteristics discussed by Sagan determined superpower nuclear policy. From this perspective, the Cold War history that supporters of proliferation had counted in their favor seems to tell a different tale. As these critics of proliferation see it, the Cold War was a time of nuclear danger, not nuclear safety. The long peace of the Cold War was more a matter of luck than of the effectiveness of nuclear deterrence. The implication is that nuclear proliferation is dangerous, whether in the past, in the case of the current nuclear powers, or in the future. Nuclear proliferation is dangerous because nuclear deterrence is a dangerous policy, whoever is its practitioner. The proper argument, from this perspective, is not that proliferation would be dangerous *because* would-be proliferators are different from the established nuclear powers, as most critics of proliferation maintain. Nor is it that proliferation would not be dangerous because nuclear deterrence was not dangerous for the superpowers, as defenders of proliferation such as Waltz maintain. The proper argument is that proliferation would be dangerous just as nuclear deterrence was dangerous for the superpowers.

On the other hand, the argument proves too little because of its broad-brush character. It is not attuned to the particularities of individual cases. Though the possession of nuclear weapons may tend to be dangerous, it will be more dangerous in some cases than in others. One cannot apply the general point about dangerousness without looking at the details of the particular cases. For example, it can make a great difference whether the proliferator is the first of a pair of military opponents to acquire nuclear weapons or the second, because a one-sided nuclear relationship can be much more dangerous than a two-sided relationship of mutual assured destruction. The fact that one must look at the details of the particular case is recognized by all of the participants in the debate. Those sanguine about proliferation, such as Waltz, acknowledge that proliferation would be dangerous were it to occur too rapidly, while those critical of proliferation admit that proliferation might in some cases even have beneficial effects outweighing the dangers.[43] But the general point is that nuclear weapons tend to increase danger and lessen security, even if there are in some cases factors that mitigate or even outweigh that tendency. Nuclear proliferation is dangerous because it increases the likelihood of nuclear use.

ANTIPROLIFERATION POLICY

Given that nuclear proliferation is dangerous, and given that the potential for proliferation is and will continue to be greater in the post-Cold War world, the question now is what policies would reduce the chances that proliferation will occur? In other words, what kind of antiproliferation policy should be adopted? In answering this question, we will want to give special attention to the kinds of antiproliferation efforts recommended by the institutionalist. There are three kinds of antiproliferation policy.

States may seek to prevent proliferation: (1) through achieving the consent of the would-be proliferator not to acquire the weapons; (2) through denying the would-be proliferator the necessary means of acquiring the weapons; or (3) through coercively preventing the would-be proliferator from acquiring the weapons. These are policies of cooperative antiproliferation, denial antiproliferation, and coercive antiproliferation. In contrast with cooperative antiproliferation policy, both denial and coercive antiproliferation policies are noncooperative in the sense that they seek to stop a would-be proliferator against its will. Consider first the noncooperative forms, denial and coercive antiproliferation policy.

Denial antiproliferation policy seeks to thwart proliferation by restricting access to necessary ingredients of the bomb-making process (nuclear fuel, technology, or knowledge). An example of this is the Nuclear Suppliers Group, a group of industrialized states that has agreed to limit nonnuclear states' access to the nuclear-related technology its members command.[44] The kinds of technologies in question are principally those associated with enrichment at the front end of the fuel cycle and reprocessing at the back end. This arrangement works only imperfectly inasmuch as the guidelines are ambiguous and nuclear-export interest groups in the various states try to influence and even evade the various prohibitions. In addition to mutual arrangements such as this, nuclear states have adopted their own individual forms of denial antiproliferation policy. The U.S. Congress passed the Nuclear Non-Proliferation Act in 1978 that denies foreign aid to any country that attempts to construct a nuclear explosive.

But denial, the effort "to keep the genie in a few bottles," is, whether in its mutual or individual forms, largely ineffective and difficult to implement, in part because it is in conflict with other interests shaping national policy. But, more important, it runs up against the economic and technological factors mentioned earlier.[45] "Technology is no longer a barrier to weapons proliferation, but merely a hurdle," because "technological progress and the dissemination of knowledge make building nuclear weapons a more manageable task now."[46] Advances in technology, and its global dissemination, mean that proliferation can no longer be stopped solely by an attempt to restrict technological access. Moreover, as one commentator argues, such an attempt "amounts to treating the symptoms while ignoring the disease." "Over the long run, the 'cure' for the problem of nuclear proliferation lies ultimately with the reduction of national nuclear propensities."[47]

It is precisely with national nuclear propensities that coercive antiproliferation policy seeks to deal. The point is to stop proliferation not by denying access to the means of bomb-making, but by making threats that influence the choices of a would-be proliferator, threats that work on its fear or dislike of the threatened punishment, and thereby alter its propensities. The point is to deter proliferation.[48] The mildest form of coercive antiproliferation is the threat of economic sanctions. But economic sanctions in general do not seem to be very effective, and they would be least effective in the most problematic cases where nuclear ambitions go along with economic isolation, such as in the case of North Korea.

The other main kind of coercive measure involves the threat of military force, primarily the threat of the destruction of nuclear facilities. Some have proposed the idea that nuclear states should be willing to fight proliferation through more vigorous measures such as these. (Destruction of nuclear facilities could be considered a different form of denial.) They recommend moving from a "passive" policy of nonproliferation to an "active" policy of "counterproliferation."[49] The model for counterproliferation was set by the Israeli raid on the Iraqi nuclear reactor at Osirak in 1981, but it is as old as the Allied efforts to thwart Germany's development of the bomb in World War II. The United States has considered adding a counterproliferation dimension to its antiproliferation policy.[50] But antiproliferation policy pursued through military force suffers from serious difficulties. One problem is that using force against nuclear facilities "may precipitate ecological disasters and nuclear war," with the destruction and the deaths of millions of innocent people that this would entail.[51] Another problem is that such force is likely to be ineffective, even counterproductive. The Israeli bombing of the Iraqi nuclear facility seems to have strengthened Iraqi determination to acquire a bomb, and the extensive Iraqi nuclear facilities discovered to have survived the Persian Gulf War show how ineffective the intensive bombing campaign of that war was in their elimination.[52]

Consider, then, cooperative antiproliferation. It is here that we find the kinds of solutions proposed by the institutionalists, solutions based on a cooperative international order. Cooperative antiproliferation is achieved by striking a bargain through offering a would-be proliferator positive consideration for eschewing the nuclear option.[53] The switch from noncooperative to cooperative forms of antiproliferation policy is a switch from seeking a military or a technical solution to the proliferation problem to seeking a political solution.[54] It involves states working together, accommodating each other, in contrast with a situation in which some states seek to impose their wills on others. As such, it seems to promise a more effective antiproliferation policy.

What are the terms of the trade? The would-be proliferator promises to eschew nuclear weapons, but what consideration is offered in return to induce its cooperation? One kind of consideration, one that was apparently quite effective in limiting proliferation during the Cold War, is nuclear security guarantees, that is, promises by nuclear states to protect nonnuclear states against nuclear threats. By offering nuclear security guarantees, nuclear states extend a "nuclear umbrella" over the nonnuclear states they promise to protect. Such guarantees are a policy of *extended deterrence*. Nuclear security guarantees can be effective because they respond to a main motive nonnuclear states have in acquiring nuclear weapons, namely, concerns about their own security. A state that receives nuclear security guarantees can have nuclear deterrence work for it without having to go to the trouble of acquiring the weapons for itself. In other words, security guarantees would obviate what is called the self-help character of the international system. The international system leaves it to each state to look after itself, to help itself, to provide for its own protection. Security guarantees modify this system through some states accepting responsibility for the protection of others.

During the Cold War, the nuclear security guarantees provided by the United States to West Germany (through the NATO alliance) and to Japan are thought to have kept these states from becoming proliferators. Speaking of the superpowers, one commentator remarks on "the key role played by their alliance guarantees in stemming proliferation."[55] Indeed, as another notes, all of the second-generation proliferators had "special security problems unmet by the Cold War alliance system."[56] As we discussed earlier in this chapter, one of the strongest motivations India had for its 1998 nuclear tests was its fear of being outside of any alliance system that could have provided a measure of nuclear protection. Without such protection, India felt it had to go it alone and develop its own nuclear capacity.

But there are serious difficulties with a policy of nuclear security guarantees as a solution to the problem of proliferation. One is that the states most requiring security guarantees to induce their consent to nonacquisition are often those that the nuclear states are, for other reasons, reluctant or even loath to protect.[57] Other difficulties are that security guarantees are expensive for nuclear states to undertake and that providers of security guarantees risk getting dragged into a war, even a nuclear war, of which they would not otherwise be a part. But, more important, the policy may be counter-productive or self-defeating in the long run, because of an aspect of the policy that would encourage rather than discourage proliferation. For example, for the United States to provide wide-spread security guarantees, it would have to support an ex-panded military establishment, despite the end of the Cold War, and be free in its use of military power abroad. The United States would have to "interfere and regulate the security equations in problematic regions."[58] It would have to adopt what Hedley Bull calls a "high posture," as opposed to a "low posture."[59] This aspect of a policy of security guarantees could encourage proliferation, emphasizing to would-be prolifera-tors the importance of nuclear weapons by providing them with an example of how well nuclear deterrence is thought to work, and of how valuable and effective the nu-clear states take nuclear threats to be. As one commentator notes: "The more one emphasizes the success of deterrence in a world of insecurity, the more alluring the deterrence system is bound to appear."[60]

This is the dilemma of antiproliferation through security guarantees: The more a nuclear state bolsters its military capability to provide more effective and extensive se-curity guarantees to discourage proliferation, the more it encourages proliferation by pro-viding a vivid example of the benefits of nuclear weapons. Security guarantees seem simultaneously to discourage and encourage proliferation. The dilemma, of course, works the other way round as well. If nuclear states adopt a low posture, this would dis-courage nuclear proliferation by denying to would-be proliferators evidence of the util-ity of proliferation. But it would, of course, also encourage proliferation. For example, the more the United States downplays the importance of nuclear weapons in its own policy, "the more it also degrades the extended U.S. nuclear guarantee, which might over the long run contribute to decisions in Berlin and Tokyo to acquire a nuclear weapons capability."[61] The dilemma is that whatever military policy the nuclear states adopt, high posture or low, the positive effects on proliferation seem stymied by the negative effects. Security guarantees seem self-stultifying.

The question then is whether there are forms of cooperative antiproliferation that avoid the difficulties of security guarantees. Indeed there are, and they are interna-tional institutions, precisely those forms of antiproliferation policy recommended by the institutionalists. The premier institution of this sort is the Nuclear Non-Proliferation Treaty (NPT). The NPT works on the same problem as security guarantees, namely, the motivation states have to acquire nuclear weapons in order to protect themselves against the nuclear weapons of their opponents. Security guarantees address this problem by ex-tending nuclear deterrence from nuclear states to nonnuclear states. The NPT does this by seeking to ensure nonnuclear states that their opponents will not acquire nu-clear weapons. In other words, the NPT does this by seeking to establish a *nonprolifer-ation norm*, that is, a rule against proliferation that a state can generally expect its military opponents to abide by. It may be that the NPT does not address the problem as directly or as effectively as security guarantees do, but the NPT may not have the drawback of also encouraging proliferation. We will first discuss the structure and his-tory of the NPT, and then discuss its role in establishing a nonproliferation norm.

Negotiations leading to the NPT were sponsored by the United States, Great

Britain, and the USSR in the mid-1960s. The resulting treaty was signed by 62 nations and ratified by the United States in 1970. Since then other nations have become signatories, bringing the total number to 178. A number of important states refused to sign at the time, states such as France, China, India, Pakistan, Argentina, Brazil, and South Africa, though some of these have subsequently signed. The world's nuclear weapons states, as declared in the treaty, were the United States, the Soviet Union, Great Britain, France, and China.

Several different interests were seen as served by the treaty. First, the nuclear nations sought to protect their nuclear monopoly and to promote the interests of their nuclear-power export industries without exposing themselves to the danger of nuclear weapons in the hands of yet other nations. Second, the developing nations sought to ensure themselves access to the peaceful uses of nuclear technology. Third, the nonnuclear states, developed and developing, sought to rein in the nuclear arms race being pursued by the nuclear states. These goals are evident in the treaty's ten articles. Articles I and II forbid the transfer of nuclear weapons devices and technologies from nuclear states to nonnuclear states, and Article IV explicitly exempts nuclear power technologies from this ban. Article III obligates nonnuclear states to submit all of their nuclear facilities to inspection and monitoring by the International Atomic Energy Agency (IAEA). Article VI commits all signatories to work toward universal nuclear disarmament (clearly directed at the nuclear states), and Article VII permits the establishment of regional nuclear-free zones. Article VIII establishes procedures for amending the treaty and mandates treaty review conferences every five years. Article IX offers treaty membership to any state that accepts IAEA safeguards, and Article X provides that a state may withdraw at any time after giving three months' notice. Article X further provides for a review conference after twenty-five years to determine whether or not the treaty should be continued indefinitely. This conference, which occurred in 1995, will be discussed later.

What are the strengths and weaknesses of this treaty? The treaty has been unexpectedly successful in restraining other nations from producing, testing, and stockpiling nuclear weapons. This supports the view of the institutionalists that institutions can be effective in restraining proliferation. Since the treaty was negotiated, only two states (India and Pakistan) have tested a nuclear weapon, and only one other state (it is thought) currently has a nuclear weapons capacity (Israel). When the treaty was signed no one expected that there would be so few nuclear states thirty years later. This undoubtedly reflects the fact that most nations recognize that it is in their interests to eschew nuclear weapons as long as an effective mechanism exists to deny them to their adversaries. The NPT appears to satisfy this need for the majority of states. This attests to the effectiveness of the NPT in establishing a nonproliferation norm.

The treaty's principal shortcoming has been its failure to prevent what is called *vertical proliferation*. The proliferation we have been discussing in this chapter is *horizontal proliferation*. Vertical proliferation, in contrast, is the accumulation of nuclear weapons by the nuclear states. Article VI of the NPT committed the nuclear states to engage in a process leading to nuclear disarmament, but since 1970 there has been a huge increase in the size of their nuclear arsenals. What is most important, the NPT failed to halt the nuclear arms race between the two nuclear superpowers. Despite some progress in recent years in reducing the size of the nuclear arsenals of the United States and USSR/Russia under the START treaty regime (to be discussed in the next chapter), these arsenals remain larger than they were in 1970. The long-term viability of the treaty may depend on correcting this glaring weakness that grows out of its fundamentally discriminatory nature. It appears, in practice, to ratify a world in which five states are privileged to have nuclear weapons, while the rest of the world is deemed unfit to possess them.

The discriminatory aspect of the treaty and the failure of the nuclear states to comply with Article VI (points emphasized by India) were key issues in the 1995 conference in New York to renew the treaty. At that conference were 175 of the 178 signatories of the treaty.[62] Most, of course, were nonnuclear states, many of which were unhappy with the lack of compliance on the part of the nuclear states. But the nonnuclear states that were critical of the nuclear states for failure to take seriously their responsibilities under Article VI worked not for scrapping the treaty, but rather renewing it in a qualified form. They argued for two kinds of qualifications. First, they wanted the treaty to be extended, not indefinitely, but for a series of twenty-five-year periods conditional on certain goals being met, in order better to hold the nuclear states to their disarmament commitments. Second, they proposed that a series of additional conditions be incorporated into the treaty, conditions such as commitments to a comprehensive test ban treaty, to universality for the treaty (bringing the undeclared nuclear states into the process), to the elimination of stockpiles of weapons grade fissile material, and so forth.

The nuclear states opposed both of these kinds of qualifications on the treaty. Each side got part of what it wanted. The nuclear states got an indefinite extension of the treaty. The nonnuclear states got a commitment to the conditions they had sought in a series of twenty "principles and objectives." The principles and objectives, however, were not part of the formal treaty, but were a separate document, and thus are regarded not as legally binding, but only as "politically binding." The nonnuclear states also got a strengthened review process in the form of substantive review conferences to be held every five years. Clearly, though the nuclear states achieved their objective of a renewal of the treaty, their lack of willingness to treat seriously their disarmament obligations under the treaty, if it continues, will cause serious problems with the effectiveness of the treaty and its ability to curtail proliferation.

In any case, one may attribute the success of the NPT to date in constraining horizontal proliferation to its having created a nonproliferation norm, a rule, largely adhered to, that states without nuclear weapons will not acquire them. There are several reasons that the NPT has succeeded in this way. First, having signed the treaty, a nonnuclear state sees itself as under a legal obligation to refrain from proliferation, even should it see proliferation as in its interest. Second, and perhaps more important, because a state views other states as likely to adhere to the treaty, it has reason to believe that if it does fulfill its obligation under the treaty, it will not be taken advantage of by its opponents acquiring nuclear weapons. This belief is strengthened by the work of the International Atomic Energy Agency, whose monitoring activities help to reassure nonnuclear states that other nonnuclear states (in particular, their military opponents) are not cheating on their treaty obligations. Thus, a nonnuclear state is likely to adhere to its obligation under the treaty both because it accepts the obligation it has undertaken by signing the treaty and because it believes that its opponent, accepting the same obligation, will not take advantage of its restraint by acquiring nuclear weapons. Third, states recognize that their violation of the treaty would likely lead to violations by others, making them all worse off.[63] The result is a general expectation that nonnuclear states will not proliferate, an expectation that is self-reinforcing in that it increases the tendency of states to adhere to the treaty. This expectation undergirds the nonproliferation norm that the NPT has created. The exceptions prove the rule. Israel, India, and Pakistan did not sign the treaty and proceeded to develop a nuclear capability. But in their case, the treaty could not guarantee their security. India felt under nuclear threat from China, and Pakistan from India, and Israel, though it was not under nuclear threat, was under conventional military threat of complete destruction.

While the NPT was successful in its first twenty-five years, the question arises as to whether it will be successful in its next twenty-five. One reason for doubt on this score, discussed earlier, is the increased potential for proliferation at the end of the Cold War. Given the new international situation, the norm may not hold, though the institutionalist would argue that the treaty can be made to succeed even in the new environment. This leads to a second reason for doubt. Perhaps the treaty could succeed if all parties adhered to their commitments under it, but, given the unwillingness of the nuclear states to take Article VI seriously, the treaty may fail. To help in our thinking about this matter, it is useful to draw a distinction between a nonproliferation norm and a *nonnuclear norm*. A nonnuclear norm includes a nonproliferation norm, but is broader. A nonnuclear norm requires that nuclear states, as well as nonnuclear states, adopt a negative attitude toward their own (actual or potential) nuclear weapons. Under a nonnuclear norm, the nuclear states would move toward *deacquisition* of their nuclear weapons as the nonnuclear states would continue a policy of nonacquisition. The language of the NPT supports not simply a nonproliferation norm, but a nonnuclear norm as well. Article VI commits the nuclear-state signatories "to pursue negotiations in good faith on effective measures relating to cessation of the nuclear arms race at an early date and to nuclear disarmament." The treaty clearly sets forth the idea of a nuclear-free world. This was a basic part of the "deal" that won the consent to the treaty on the part of the nonnuclear states. But the deal has not been kept. The success of the treaty in constraining horizontal proliferation contrasts with its failure to halt vertical proliferation.

The disarmament requirement of Article VI has been treated by the nuclear states as, at best, a distant goal, one that they need not make deliberate progress toward fulfilling. As a result, one commentator argues, the treaty has become "an instrument to legalize nuclear arsenals and unlimited [vertical] proliferation."[64] This raises the issue of discriminatory treatment. The nuclear states have ignored their obligations under the treaty, or have treated these obligations so as to allow a more or less permanent division between the nuclear haves and the have-nots. The nuclear have-nots are discriminated against because they are denied a form of military protection that is allowed to the nuclear states. Joseph Nye recognizes this issue as "the central dilemma in nonproliferation policy," but he argues that the discriminatory treatment may be justifiable. Nye argues that if the nuclear have-nots understood the nature of the nuclear danger, they would agree to accept their status as second-class citizens in the nuclear world.[65] According to Nye: "If they were informed that, in current circumstances, efforts to create either [a world of many more nuclear states or a world of no nuclear states] might significantly increase the risk of nuclear war, they may well, under certain conditions, accept nuclear inequality." Elsewhere, he argues that, "some inequality in weaponry is acceptable to most states because the alternative anarchic equality is more dangerous."[66]

Crucial to Nye's argument is the claim that the risk of nuclear war would be greater, were the nuclear states to disarm themselves of nuclear weapons. Why does he believe that this is true? The matter comes, again, to the notion of security guarantees. Nye argues that security guarantees play a role in avoiding proliferation, so that the nuclear states' "Article VI obligations cannot be interpreted as simple disarmament." He is thus led to speak of "the degree of discrimination that is inherent in the nonproliferation regime."[67] In a similar vein, another commentator argues that the assumption of nuclear disarmament is part of "the flawed conceptual foundations of the NPT."[68] The flaw is the failure to recognize the necessary role of nuclear security guarantees in avoiding proliferation, a failure to appreciate that nuclear disarmament would increase incentives for proliferation. Were the nuclear states to disarm, states that are now content to remain nonnuclear under security guarantees from the nuclear states would acquire the weapons, making the world more dangerous. This position assumes that an attempt to interpret the NPT strictly, as supporting a nonnuclear norm, would destroy the treaty's ability to support even a nonproliferation norm. As Nye puts it, nonproliferation efforts are threatened "by those who pursue a broader anti-nuclear agenda and assert it as proliferation policy."[69]

The position argued for by Nye and others is then, in effect, that a nonnuclear norm is impossible to establish, because a necessary part of that norm, namely, a nonproliferation norm, cannot be established without security guarantees, which of course require that the nuclear states retain their nuclear weapons. A nonproliferation norm, as embodied in the NPT, is not an alternative to security guarantees as a form of cooperative antiproliferation because, according to this line of thinking, a successful nonproliferation norm requires security guarantees. But then the objection raised earlier to security guarantees, the dilemma of antiproliferation, comes again to the fore. The dilemma is that security guarantees are self-stultifying, because they encourage as well as discourage proliferation. If this is true, then the discriminatory way the nuclear states have conducted themselves under the NPT will eventually compromise the treaty's effectiveness. If this dilemma holds, we should be pessimistic about the long-term prospects for constraining proliferation, for the implication is that the antiproliferation effort cannot succeed without security guarantees and cannot succeed with them.

Does the dilemma hold? There are two horns to the dilemma: (1) that nuclear security guarantees are necessary to avoid proliferation; and (2) that nuclear security guarantees will encourage proliferation in the long run. The dilemma, with its pessimistic implications regarding our nuclear future, holds only if both (1) and (2) are true. Nye and many others would reject the dilemma by claiming that (2) is false. But the results of the NPT renewal conference suggest that (2) is true. The pressure that the nonnuclear states put on the nuclear states to live up to their Article VI commitments suggests that nonnuclear states will not forever tolerate a situation in which they are not allowed nuclear weapons while the nuclear states refuse to give theirs up. If (2) is true, the only option to escape the pessimistic conclusion is to argue that (1) is false. (1) amounts to the claim that a successful nonnuclear norm is impossible to achieve, that the world cannot rid itself of nuclear weapons. This is a deep and controversial issue. We will discuss it in the last chapter. But for now, left hovering in the air is the pessimistic conclusion that the dilemma might hold, that it is unlikely that proliferation can in the long run be avoided. In other words, a world of a small number of nuclear states may be unstable, in the sense that nuclear weapons, once they exist, will eventually spread widely. If this conclusion is true, we would be forced to abandon the institutionalist perspective argued for earlier and to adopt the realist perspective. If so, and if nuclear proliferation is as dangerous as it seems to be, the temporary respite in the nuclear danger following the end of the Cold War should bring us little satisfaction, only an opportunity to prepare for the nuclear danger sure to return.

NUCLEAR TERRORISM

The nuclear world could extend in another way. While nuclear proliferation is the extension of nuclear weapons to states that did not previously possess them, nuclear weapons may in the future also spread to nonstate groups, to terrorist groups. This is potentially a very serious problem. Speaking in part of the risk of nuclear terrorism, a group of writers suggested recently that, despite the common perception that the end of the Cold War has lessened our nuclear danger, "the risk of a nuclear detonation on American soil has increased."[70] There is frequent speculation in the media, and in popular works of fiction, about the possibility of nuclear terrorism. We speculated in Chapter 1 about what could have happened had the bombers of the World Trade Center in New York or the Federal Building in Oklahoma City been in possession of nuclear weapons.[71] What are the prospects for nuclear terrorism?

First, a word on what nuclear terrorism is. By nuclear terrorism, we mean the possession of one or more nuclear weapons and their use, through either detonation or threat of detonation, by a group of individuals acting independently of a state and seeking through the use or threat of violence to achieve political ends. Three points should be made about this definition. First, terrorism might involve a nuclear dimension other than the use or threatened use of nuclear weapons. Terrorists might, for example, attempt to seize nuclear power facilities, attempt to hold for ransom a nuclear weapon or nuclear material, seek to contaminate some area with radioactive material, or even seek to perpetrate a nuclear hoax. Some of these other activities would be much easier to do than to obtain or construct a weapon.[72] In our discussions, we will focus attention on terrorism that involves the use or threatened use of a real nuclear weapon. Second, to say that the group of individuals in question is independent of a state does not imply that they are not receiving assistance from or coordinating their activities with some state. Thus, there may be such a thing as state-sponsored nuclear terrorism. Third, the nonstate groups that might do such things are called terrorist groups because they often, though not always, employ violence in a terroristic way, that is, in a way that is meant to put innocent civilians at risk. Thus, nuclear terrorism is so-called because the groups using the nuclear weapons are called terrorist groups. But there is a case to be made that *any* use or threatened use of nuclear weapons involves terrorism, putting at risk innocent civilians, whether the actors are states or nonstate groups.[73] The argument for this conclusion will be discussed in Chapter 9 when we consider the moral issues raised by nuclear weapons.

As with nuclear proliferation, the prospects for nuclear terrorism must be assessed in two dimensions: opportunity and motivation. One question is whether terrorists would have the opportunity to acquire and use nuclear weapons, and another is whether they would have the motivation to do so. The question of opportunity, whether terrorists would likely be able to acquire nuclear weapons, was addressed in Chapter 5. As we saw there, the main factor effecting such opportunity at the end of the Cold War (a factor also in the case of nuclear proliferation) is the dissolution of the Soviet Union, an event that has created the real possibility of nuclear materials or perhaps even complete nuclear weapons finding their way from Russian stockpiles into the black market where they would be available to terrorist groups as well as states bent on proliferation. The opportunities for terrorist groups to go nuclear are now greater. If the terrorist group is state-sponsored, it would be even easier.

In any case, the concern here is the question of motivation. Unless terrorist groups have the motivation to use nuclear weapons, any increased opportunity they have to do so should not be a source of concern. Many discussions of nuclear terrorism effectively ignore this fact, simply assuming that if terrorists had the opportunity to acquire nuclear weapons, they would do so.[74] But this assumption needs to be examined. The question of motivation is in many ways more difficult than the question of opportunity. As one commentator notes, "We are in the paradoxical position of having a clearer understanding of the interior of the atom than we do of the interior of the mind of the terrorist."[75]

There are some factors that suggest that terrorists are not likely to use nuclear weapons. First, there is the nuclear taboo. Nuclear weapons have not been detonated to destroy humans since 1945, by either states or nonstate groups, and this long period of nonuse may have established a taboo against their use. While it is possible that this lack of use may have been due, in the case of nonstate groups, more to the absence of opportunity than to the absence of motivation, the fact that the weapons have not been used for so long may make it less likely that a terrorist group, even with the opportunity, would now choose to use them. On the other hand, this point cuts the other way as well. There is clearly no taboo against the threat to use nuclear weapons, since such threats have been a constant in world politics since 1945, and use may follow threat.

Second, given the fragility of the infrastructure of urban industrial societies, if terrorists were motivated to destroy a large number of innocent lives, there are certainly easier (though perhaps less effective) ways for them to do this than to use nuclear weapons. For example, city water supplies could be poisoned or deadly organisms could be released in crowded areas.[76] The fact that such things have not happened (with the exception of the 1996 effort of the Hom Shinriki religious cult to disperse deadly nerve gas in the Tokyo subways) suggests that terrorists have not, in general, been motivated to kill large numbers of people. The third point is related to the second. If terrorists are motivated to escalate the harmful effects of their operations, there remain many stages of escalation, so to speak, short of the use of nuclear weapons. As Konrad Kellen notes:

> Terrorists still have so many ways of escalating, so many more means of violence, and so many more lucrative targets that they can escalate a long way without engaging in nuclear terrorism. The temptation to go nuclear, for terrorists as well as for nations, probably will arise only when all other means are exhausted.[77]

But we must examine the issue more carefully. When considering the potential motivations of terrorists to go nuclear, there are two questions that have to be examined. First, would going nuclear be rational for terrorists? Second, are terrorists likely to act rationally regarding such a choice? Let us consider these questions in turn. Would it be rational for terrorists to use nuclear weapons? An act is rational only relative to the goals and assumptions of the actor. So, to ask whether nuclear terrorism is rational for a terrorist group is to ask whether it is rational relative to its goals and assumptions. Normally, a terrorist group has goals and assumptions different from those of the ordinary person. Still, there is some reason to think that nuclear use would not be rational for the terrorist, even from the terrorist's point of view. For one thing, the main concern of terrorists seems to be to make their grievances known, not just to kill people. Brian Jenkins notes: "Simply killing a lot of people has seldom been a terrorist objective.... Terrorists want a lot of people *watching*, not a lot of people *dead*." He bolsters this point by observing that many terrorists are morally opposed to indiscriminate violence, given that "they regard a government as their opponent, not the people," and they do not want to alienate the people.[78]

There are other reasons to think that nuclear terrorism would be irrational from the terrorist's perspective. The cohesion of a terrorist group is of great importance to the group, and the use of nuclear weapons risks the loss of that cohesion. Given the revulsion some in the group might feel toward such an act, the decision to use nuclear weapons might shatter the group.[79] Moreover, terrorists might well discover the same truth that states have discovered, namely, that nuclear weapons are too powerful. For the question arises: What demands could nuclear terrorists make that would correspond in magnitude to what they threaten, demands that they could be assured that the state would carry out, given the temporary nature of the nuclear threat they would pose?[80] It is important to note, however, that the main reason that the use of nuclear weapons is not rational for states may not apply in the case of terrorists. The threat of nuclear retaliation, generally effective against states, is unlikely to be effective in the case of terrorist groups. Because they control no territory, they cannot be targeted with nuclear weapons.

Then there is the second question: Is it likely that terrorists would act rationally when choosing whether or not to go nuclear? This question of the psychology of terrorists is explored by Jerrold Post. He argues that even though terrorists in the main do not suffer from profound distortions in their thought processes that would make their actions irrational, they are nonetheless likely to suffer from "a pattern of psycho-social vulnerabilities that renders [them] particularly susceptible to the powerful influences of group and organizational dynamics."[81] Post's point is that there are certain personality characteristics that lead people to join terrorist groups and that these characteristics, along with the isolated nature of the group itself, predispose the group to make decisions that might not be what most of its members would individually regard as appropriate or rational. "There is a tendency for individual judgment to be suspended so that conforming behavior results."[82]

Unfortunately, the recent direction of terrorist activity supports this pessimistic perspective. Consider the terror bombing of the federal building in Oklahoma City in 1995. The convicted bomber, Timothy McVeigh, was opposed to the government, not the people, but this did not dissuade him from engaging in indiscriminate violence. He might well have used a nuclear weapon against the building had he had one. Moreover, this case illustrates another aspect of contemporary terrorism. There is no reason to expect that McVeigh, had he avoided immediate capture, would have claimed responsibility for the blast. Terrorists have more frequently in the past decade or two avoided claiming responsibility for their terrorists acts. This is troubling because it suggests that they are acting irrationally. Assuming that the purpose of a terrorist group is to promote a cause, identifying itself as the perpetrator of its acts in order to call attention to its grievances would seem to be a necessary part of any rational strategy it might adopt. An obvious explanation for this is that terrorist groups are often acting out of blind emotion, such as an overwhelming desire for vengeance against their enemies. Another explanation is that the terrorists are in fact acting rationally, but with a different goal than we have assumed. Their goal may be not to call attention to their grievances in order to get them attended to, but rather to spread indiscriminate chaos in the expectation, or at least the hope, that this will cause the political system to collapse. In either case, terrorists would likely have the motivation to go nuclear.

We conclude that the motivation of terrorist groups to use nuclear weapons is probably fairly high. If terrorists are not acting rationally, and there is some evidence for this, their motivation would probably lead them to cause as much destruction as possible. If, on the other hand, terrorists are acting rationally, their goal may be to create chaos rather than to call attention to their grievances, in which case they would also probably seek to cause as much destruction as possible. Nuclear weapons would be the implement of choice in either case.

Moreover, even if this is wrong and terrorists are not strongly motivated to use nuclear weapons, there are still good reasons to conclude that we should take the prospects of nuclear terrorism very seriously. First, even if terrorists are not strongly motivated to use nuclear weapons, they still may be motivated to threaten to use the weapons.[83] The factors discussed previously that would make nuclear use irrational for terrorists do not come into play as strongly, if at all, if use is only threatened, and, regarding the perceived rationality of nuclear threats, terrorists can, as mentioned before, model their behavior on the nuclear states that find nuclear threats a useful instrument of statecraft. But the prospect of a terrorist nuclear threat should be taken almost as seriously as the prospects of deliberate terrorist use of nuclear weapons. For it is easy to imagine such a threat getting out of hand and eventuating in nuclear use. For example, the authorities might refuse to give in to the terrorists' demands, which could well lead, in the escalatory dynamic of such situations, to the detonation of the weapon; or, efforts by the military to find and neutralize the weapon could easily lead to its being detonated, in desperation or accidentally.

The second reason that the prospect of nuclear terrorism should be taken very seriously, even if terrorists were not strongly motivated to use nuclear weapons, is the simple fact that the stakes are so high. To appeal to an analogy, given the potentially catastrophic nature of cancer, it would irresponsible for a physician not to recommend exploratory surgery for a patient who had symptoms suggesting the real possibility of cancer, even if the probability were low. Similarly, we should take serious precautions to avoid nuclear terrorism, even if terrorists were not strongly motivated to use nuclear weapons. For even so, as Karl-Heinz Kamp points out: "The cost of nuclear terrorism is grave enough to deserve continuing attention."[84] If the motivation of terrorists to use nuclear weapons is strong, as we believe, all the more reason to take serious precautions.

What precautions should we take against the risk of nuclear terrorism? Here there is a close relationship between the two targets of antiproliferation policy: states, as discussed earlier in the chapter, and terrorist groups. First, stopping states from acquiring nuclear weapons will help stop terrorist groups from acquiring them. As Thomas Schelling notes: "The best way to keep [nuclear] weapons and weapons-material out of the hands of nongovernmental entities is to keep them out of the hands of national governments."[85] Second, precautions to keep nuclear weapons from proliferating to terrorist groups are of the same general sort as precautions against the more familiar kind of nuclear proliferation involving states. Our antiproliferation efforts directed against nonstate groups, like those directed against states, can be based on coercion, denial, and/or cooperation. In terms of coercion, authorities can engage in on-going intelligence activities to attempt to learn of any efforts on the part of terrorist groups to acquire nuclear weapons, coupled with the availability of military-type rapid response teams, such as the Nuclear Emergency Search Teams maintained by the U.S. Department of Energy,[86] to thwart any such effort. In terms of denial, authorities can make efforts to keep nuclear weapons and the materials needed to construct them out of the hands of terrorist groups. Cooperative antiproliferation takes a different form in the case of nonstate groups. In the case of cooperative efforts to stop proliferation by states, one seeks to negotiate with those states to convince them in one way or another that acquiring nuclear weapons is not in their interest. To seek to stop terrorist groups from using nuclear weapons, the cooperation that is appropriate does not involve working with the terrorist groups themselves, but rather working with the people whose grievances the terrorist group claim to represent, and with their governments, to reduce the injustices that give rise to those grievances.

SUMMARY

Nuclear proliferation has become a central focus of attention with the end of the Cold War. Currently there are seven acknowledged nuclear states (the United States, Russia, Great Britain, France, China, India, and Pakistan) and at least one additional nuclear state (Israel). But the number of nuclear states could grow in the future. Not only is there now greater opportunity for nonnuclear states to acquire nuclear weapons, but also nonnuclear states likely now have greater motivation to acquire the weapons. This is due primarily to the dissolution of the Soviet Union at the end of the Cold War and the greater uncertainty this has interjected into international relations. But, despite the greater tendency toward nuclear proliferation, there is no inevitability about this. We should be able to devise institutions at the international level that can constrain that tendency.

How dangerous is nuclear proliferation? The conventional wisdom is that it is very dangerous. But against this, some argue that, since nuclear deterrence worked for the superpowers during the Cold War, there is no reason to think it would not work for other nations, so nuclear proliferation is not to be feared. Defenders of the conventional wisdom respond that this is based on a bad analogy. The superpowers differ from likely nuclear proliferators in ways (e.g., in the degree of their political stability) that make nuclear weapons in the superpower's hands much safer. But one can argue that the main danger from nuclear possession lies in the errors and mistakes characteristic of the organizations that must exist to watch over and service the nuclear arsenals. In this view, the danger of nuclear proliferation is, in fact, the danger of nuclear possession, and it applies to the nuclear states as well as to the nonnuclear states.

Given the dangerousness of nuclear proliferation, what policies should be adopted to attempt to constrain it? There are three kinds of antiproliferation policy. We can seek to coerce nonnuclear states into not acquiring the weapons; we can seek to deny them the wherewithal to build the weapons; or we can work cooperatively with them to seek their agreement not to acquire nuclear weapons. Coercion is unlikely to be effective. Denial is widely practiced, but its ability to constrain proliferation is limited. Only cooperation promises an effective antiproliferation policy. One widely practiced form of cooperative antiproliferation policy is the offering by nuclear states of nuclear security guarantees to nonnuclear states. But there are limits to the effectiveness of nuclear security guarantees. An alternative approach that has met with some success is the institution of a nonproliferation norm through the adoption of the Nuclear Nonproliferation Treaty. But there is reason to doubt that this treaty can be successful in containing nuclear proliferation in the long run unless the nuclear states take seriously their nuclear disarmament obligations under the treaty. In other words, the nonproliferation norm must ultimately be supplanted by a nonnuclear norm.

Finally, there is the issue of nuclear terrorism. Like states, terrorists now have greater opportunity to acquire nuclear weapons. Again the main question is motivation. Are terrorists likely to choose to go the nuclear path? It is reasonable to conclude that terrorist groups would have a strong motivation to go nuclear, whether that motivation is rational or irrational. Even if the motivation is not strong, the stakes are so high that the risk of nuclear terrorism must be taken seriously. Here the efforts to thwart nuclear terrorism joins with the efforts to avoid nuclear proliferation. The more effective antiproliferation efforts are, the less likely that terrorists will be able to acquire nuclear weapons or the materials needed to make them.

In the second nuclear age, the risks of nuclear proliferation and nuclear terrorism are significant. If little or nothing is done, it is likely that proliferation will increase and that terrorist groups will acquire nuclear weapons, both of which would greatly increase the likelihood that the weapons will be used. But we need not accept this eventuality. We can seek to make the second nuclear age not an age in which the spread of nuclear weapons increases, but an age in which the spread decreases, where nonnuclear states and terrorist groups do not acquire the weapons, and where the nuclear states begin to follow the example, set by South Africa, of weapons abandonment.

NOTES

1. David Albright, "South Africa Comes Clean," *The Bulletin of the Atomic Scientists* 49, no. 4 (May 1993): 3–5.
2. When the Soviet Union broke up, some of its nuclear weapons, both strategic and tactical, remained in the hands of some of the newly created states. But in the years since, through a laborious process of negotiation and inducement, the new states have returned all of these weapons to Russia.
3. Portions of this chapter are adopted from Steven Lee, "Nuclear Proliferation and Nuclear Entitlement," *Ethics and International Affairs* 9 (1995): 101–131. The material from that article has been used by permission of the journal.
4. Mitchell Reiss, *Without the Bomb* (New York: Columbia University Press, 1988), p. 247.
5. Ibid., p. 16.
6. See Theodore Taylor, "Nuclear Tests and Nuclear Weapons," in *Opaque Nuclear Proliferation*, ed. Benjamin Frankel (London: Frank Cass, 1991), pp. 175–190.
7. For a discussion of why some nonproliferating states have not gone nuclear, see Mitchell Reiss, *Bridled Ambition: Why Countries Constrain Their Nuclear Capabilities* (Washington, D.C.: Woodrow Wilson Center Press, 1995).
8. Jean Krasno, "Brazil, Argentina Make It Official," *The Bulletin of the Atomic Scientists* 48, no. 3 (April 1992): 10–11.
9. David Albright and Robert Kelley, "Has Iraq Come Clean at Last?" *The Bulletin of the Atomic Scientists* 51, no. 6 (November/December 1995): 60.
10. Some of the novel features of proliferation in the 1990s are discussed by John Simpson, "Nuclear Non-Proliferation in the Post Cold War Era," *International Affairs* 70, no. 1 (1994): 17–39.
11. Scott Sagan, "The Perils of Proliferation," *International Security* 18, no. 4 (spring 1994): 68–69.
12. There have been stories about plutonium being smuggled out of the states of the former Soviet Union and put on the black market. See, for example, William Broad, "A Smuggling

Boom Brings Calls for Tighter Nuclear Safeguards," *New York Times*, August 21, 1994; and Gary Milhollin, "Plutonium Plunder," *Boston Globe*, September 4, 1994.

13. Robert Jervis, "The Future of World Politics: Will It Resemble the Past?" *International Security* 16, no. 3: 63.

14. See, for example, Benjamin Frankel, "The Brooding Shadow: Systemic Incentives and Nuclear Weapons Proliferation," in *The Proliferation Puzzle*, ed. Zachary Davis and Benjamin Frankel (London: Frank Cass, 1993), p. 37.

15. Despite being a signatory of the Non-Proliferation Treaty, Sweden has been reported to be preserving a capacity developed thirty years ago to produce nuclear weapons on short notice. Steve Coll, "Sweden Preserving Key Elements of an Atom Bomb Project," *Boston Globe*, November 25, 1994.

16. Joseph Nye, "Maintaining a Nonproliferation Regime," in *Nuclear Proliferation: Breaking the Chain*, ed. George Quester (Madison, WI: University of Wisconsin Press, 1981), p. 33.

17. According to Article IX of the NPT, "a nuclear-weapon State is one which has manufactured and exploded a nuclear weapon or other nuclear explosive device prior to January 1, 1967." www.acda.gov/treaties/npt1.htm

18. For a discussion of opaque proliferation, see Avner Cohen and Benjamin Frankel, "Opaque Nuclear Proliferation," in Frankel, *Opaque Nuclear Proliferation*. "Part-way proliferation" is discussed by Michael Mandelbaum, *The Nuclear Future* (Ithaca, NY: Cornell University Press, 1983), p. 93.

19. Jack Snyder, "Avoiding Anarchy in Europe," *International Security* 14 (spring 1990): 5–41; and Thomas Risse-Kappan, "Predicting the New Europe," *Bulletin of the Atomic Scientists* (October 1990): 25.

20. John Mearsheimer, "Why We Will Soon Miss the Cold War," *The Atlantic* 266 (August 1990): 41–42.

21. Mark Hibbs, "Tomorrow, a Euro-Bomb?" *The Bulletin of the Atomic Scientists* 52, no. 1 (January/February 1996).

22. Jaswant Singh, quoted in Barbara Crossette, "Why India Thinks Atomic Equation Has Changed," *New York Times*, June 15, 1998, p. A6.

23. John Burns, "India Charts a Pariah's Path to Glory," *New York Times*, May 17, 1998, section 4, pp. 1, 4.

24. Singh quoted in Crossette.

25. Vajpayee, quoted in Steven Weisman, "Nuclear Fear and Narcissism Shake South Asia," *New York Times*, May 31, 1998, sec. 4, p. 16.

26. Kenneth Waltz, "The Spread of Nuclear Weapons: More May Be Better," *Adelphia Paper No. 171* (London: International Institute for Strategic Studies, 1981), pp. 3–4.

27. Sagan, "Perils of Proliferation," p. 67.

28. John Mearsheimer, "The Case for a Ukrainian Nuclear Deterrent," *International Security* 18, no. 4 (spring 1994): 57.

29. Waltz, "The Spread of Nuclear Weapons."

30. Ibid., pp. 5, 17, 30.

31. Joseph Nye, "Maintaining a Nonproliferation Regime," p. 32.

32. Lewis Dunn, "What Difference Will It Make?" in *The Nuclear Arms Race Debated*, ed. Herbert Levine and David Carlton (New York: McGraw-Hill, 1986), pp. 330–331. On the general risks of accidental nuclear war, see Scott Sagan, *The Limits of Safety: Organizations, Accidents, and Nuclear Weapons* (Princeton, NJ: Princeton University Press, 1993); and Bruce Blair, *The Logic of Accidental Nuclear War* (Washington, D.C.: Brookings Institution, 1993).

33. India conducted a nuclear weapons test in 1974, as we mentioned, but prior to 1998 was thought to have had no nuclear arsenal.

34. Steven Erlanger, "India's Arms Race Isn't Safe Like the Cold War," *New York Times*, July 12, 1998, sec. 4, p. 18, citing Joseph Cirincione, director of the Non-Proliferation Project at the Carnegie Endowment for International Peace.

35. John Weltman, "Nuclear Devolution and World Order," *World Politics* 32 (January 1980): 189.

36. Weltman, "Nuclear Devolution," p. 189.
37. Waltz, "Spread of Nuclear Weapons," p. 11.
38. Sagan, "Perils of Proliferation."
39. Ibid., p. 68.
40. Ibid., pp. 71–72.
41. Ibid., pp. 96–97.
42. Ibid., p. 86; and Steven Miller, "The Case against a Ukrainian Nuclear Deterrent," *Foreign Affairs* 72 (summer 1993): 71.
43. See, for example, Waltz, "Spread of Nuclear Weapons," p. 26; and Lewis Dunn, "What Difference Will It Make?" p. 335.
44. Simpson, "Nuclear Non-Proliferation," pp. 25–26.
45. Betts, "Paranoids, Pygmies, Pariahs and Nonproliferation," *Foreign Policy* 26 (spring 1977): 157.
46. Frankel, "Brooding Shadow," p. 39.
47. Stephen Meyer, *The Dynamics of Nuclear Proliferation* (Chicago, IL: University of Chicago Press, 1984), p. 165.
48. Sergie Kortunov, "Nonproliferation and Counterproliferation: The Role of BMD," *Comparative Strategy* 13: 138.
49. See Ibid.," p. 138.
50. Avner Cohen, "The Lessons of Osirak and the American Counterproliferation Debate," in *The Counterproliferation Dilemma*, ed. Mitchell Reiss.
51. Simpson, "Nuclear Non-Proliferation," p. 38.
52. Richard Betts, "Paranoids, Pygmies, Pariahs and Nonproliferation Revisited," in *Proliferation Puzzle*, ed. Davis and Frankel, p. 122; and Cohen, "The Lessons of Osirak."
53. An example of this is a 1994 agreement reached between the United States and North Korea whereby North Korea agreed "to freeze and gradually dismantle its nuclear weapons development program." "Clinton Approves a Plan to Give Aid to North Koreans," *New York Times*, October 19, 1994. See also, Leon Sigal, "Rethinking Nuclear Diplomacy: The Bold Premises of the North Korea Deal," *New York Times*, November 8, 1994.
54. Simpson, "Nuclear Non-Proliferation," p. 19.
55. Nye, "NPT," p. 128.
56. Cohen, "The Lessons of Osirak."
57. Betts, "Paranoids," p. 165.
58. Betts, "Paranoids, Revisited," p. 100. In addition, see Frankel, "Brooding Shadow."
59. Hedley Bull, "The Role of the Nuclear Powers in the Management of Nuclear Proliferation," in *Arms Race Debated*, ed. Levine and Carlton, p. 368.
60. Barrie Paskins, "Proliferation and the Nature of Deterrence," in *Dangers of Deterrence*, ed. Nigel Blake and Kay Pole (London: Routledge & Kegan Paul, 1983), p. 128.
61. Brad Roberts, "From Nonproliferation to Antiproliferation," *International Security* 18, no. 1 (summer 1993): 172.
62. See William Epstein, "Indefinite Extension—with Increased Accountability," *The Bulletin of the Atomic Scientists* 51, no. 4 (July/August 1995): 27–30. The treaty itself is reprinted in many places, including the reference in note 17.
63. This is, by the way, similar to the logic that is said to make nuclear deterrence effective at avoiding nuclear war: "Just as each superpower is deterred from using the bomb by the fear that the other will do so in return, so lesser countries may be deterred from getting [the bomb] by the fear that rivals will get it also." Mandelbaum, *The Nuclear Future*, p. 92 (emphasis omitted).
64. K. Subrahmanyam, "Regional Conflicts and Nuclear Fears," in *The Nuclear Arms Race Debated*, ed. Levine and Carlton, p. 348.
65. Nye, "Maintaining a Nonproliferation Regime"; and "NPT."
66. Nye, "Maintaining a Nonproliferation Regime," p. 36.
67. Nye, "NPT," p. 128; and "Maintaining a Nonproliferation Regime," p. 36.

68. Frankel, "Brooding Shadow," p. 61. See also Betts, "Paranoids."
69. Nye, "Maintaining a Nonproliferation Regime," p. 16.
70. Graham T. Allison et al., *Avoiding Nuclear Anarchy* (Cambridge, MA: The MIT Press, 1996), p. 3 (italics removed).
71. See also, Allison, *Avoiding Nuclear Anarchy*, p. 1.
72. Brian Jenkins, "Is Nuclear Terrorism Plausible?" in *Nuclear Terrorism: Defining the Threat*, ed. Paul Leventhal and Yonah Alexander (Washington, D.C.: Pergamon-Brassey's, 1986), p. 26.
73. Thomas Schelling, *Choice and Consequence* (Cambridge, MA: Harvard University Press, 1984), p. 315.
74. The work *Avoiding Nuclear Anarchy* by Graham Allison et al. is in this category.
75. Jerrold Post, "Prospects for Nuclear Terrorism: Psychological Motivation and Constraints," in *Preventing Nuclear Terrorism*, ed. Paul Leventhal and Yonah Alexander (Lexington, MA: Lexington Books, 1987), p. 91.
76. Karl-Heinz Kamp, "An Overrated Nightmare," *The Bulletin of the Atomic Scientists* 52, no. 4 (July/August 1996): 32.
77. Konrad Kellen, "The Potential for Nuclear Terrorism: A Discussion," in *Preventing Nuclear Terrorism*, ed. Leventhal and Alexander, p. 117.
78. Jenkins, "Is Nuclear Terrorism Plausible?" pp. 28, 29, 30.
79. Ibid., p. 30.
80. Ibid., p. 32; Kamp, "An Overrated Nightmare," p. 32; and Kellen, "The Potential for Nuclear Terrorism," p. 122.
81. Post, "Prospects for Nuclear Terrorism," p. 93.
82. Ibid., p. 101.
83. Ibid., p. 102.
84. Kamp, "An Overrated Nightmare," p. 34.
85. Schelling, *Choice and Consequence*, p. 325.
86. Kamp, "An Overrated Nightmare," p. 34.

8

CONTROLLING
THE NUCLEAR FUTURE

On May 22, 1972, President Richard Nixon flew to Moscow to complete a strate-gic arms limitation treaty (SALT) with the Soviets. Most of the treaty had been worked out in a complicated process over three years. Both sides had sent delegations to Helsinki, Finland, to negotiate the details, but the real channel for bargaining was in Washington, where Special Assistant for National Security Affairs Henry Kissinger met privately with Soviet Ambassador Anatoly Dobrynin. Indeed, it appeared to some observers that Kissinger treated the head of the American delegation in Helsinki "with contempt"[1] and viewed the delegation itself as narrow-minded bureaucrats who could not make the necessary compromises to get an agreement. The Kissinger "back chan-nel" had produced the main outlines of a mutual agreement to limit the number of mis-siles, but there were still contentious details that Nixon and his Soviet counterpart, Leonid Brezhnev, chairman of the Soviet Communist Party, would have to resolve if there were to be an agreement.

Those final negotiations in Moscow illustrated the difficulty and the possibility of controlling nuclear weapons. Significant agreements such as SALT seem to de-pend on a host of factors, some quite obvious, such as balance of power between the two states, and others that are less obvious, such as the power relations between in-dividuals in the same government. At Moscow, it may have depended on who was in the room. Agreements emerged in an intangible but real atmosphere of respect and empathy for the person across the table—and an ability to engage in banter. Nixon noted the following:

> There is no question that the Russian leaders do not have as much of an inferiority com-plex as was the case in Khrushchev's period. They do not have to brag about everything in Russia being better than anything anywhere else in the world. But they still crave to be respected as equals, and on this point I think we made a good impression.[2]

And a key Nixon speechwriter tells this story:

> Brezhnev and Nixon found common ground in making Kissinger the butt of jokes, a role Henry enjoys when conducted by the heads of superpowers. "Our people have

instructions to settle SALT," said Brezhnev, over a brandy. "If not, it has to be Dr. Kissinger's fault." The President, with some zest, suggested: "We'll send him to Siberia— would you take him?" Brezhnev roared at this kind of sinister good humor.... After a half-dozen vodka toasts, the Russians pretended to argue the wisdom of getting Kissinger drunk. Since he had to negotiate that night when he returned to the Kremlin, would he be a pushover if drunk, or would he get belligerent? Lots of laughs."[3]

Negotiations could be tense, however, for both delegations had to secure what each considered acceptable terms, not only in light of their own estimates of their security interests, but also in terms of what could be sold to influential groups at home. The American Joint Chiefs of Staff, for instance, warned that they might have to disavow support for the emerging terms, even when they had previously accepted them. An enraged Nixon declared to his advisors, "The hell with the political consequences. We are going to make an agreement on *our* terms regardless of the political consequences if the Pentagon won't go along."[4] But at the same time, he told Kissinger to hold out for the American bottom line, even if it meant refusing to reach an agreement that both the United States and Soviet Union had already announced would be forthcoming.

Attempts to control the nuclear world always engender an intense internal debate about how to do it, and how much others can be trusted, and what will—or will not— promote a nation's security. Part of the debate is fueled by the hopes and fears of various organizations and individuals within a government who see important implications for their power and careers, the role they will play—or not play—in the future, and whether any change increases or decreases their claim on the national budget. In 1972, American State Department officials and the American armed services scrutinized arms control proposals carefully, both to weigh the impact on the nation's security and on their organizational fortunes.

And at the same time, any attempt to control the nuclear world occurs when other issues and events that are seemingly unrelated to the matter at hand intrude. For example, in April 1972—just before the Moscow summit—the North Vietnamese had launched a major offensive into South Vietnam. Nixon had ordered a mining of North Vietnam's key port of Haiphong, thereby endangering Soviet ships and escalating the war against a Soviet ally. The Soviet leadership agreed to go ahead with the Moscow summit; it looked weak in the eyes of communist militants. At a three-hour private meeting with Nixon and Kissinger, Brezhnev and other top Soviet leaders denounced American actions as "barbaric" and "just like the Nazis." Was any hope for arms control unraveling before the president's eyes?[5]

Nixon listened quietly to the harangue. If he had responded with an equally acrimonious criticism of Soviet foreign policy, the summit might have ended there and then. On the other hand, Nixon was sensitive to what he took to be threats, for he, like most leaders, did not wish to appear weak when dealing with other states. When Premier Aleksei Kosygin warned, "There may come a critical moment for the North Vietnamese when they will not refuse to let in forces of other countries to act on their side," Nixon retorted, "That threat doesn't frighten us a bit, but go ahead and make it." Kosygin did not back down. "Don't think you are right in thinking what we say is a threat and what you say is not a threat. This is an *analysis* of what may happen, and that is much more serious than a threat."[6] The need to appear tough on an unrelated issue might easily have lead to a rejection of compromises on the arms control treaty.

In spite of Soviet anger and worry over U.S. policy in Vietnam, the Soviet leadership still wanted an agreement on nuclear weapons. And in spite of what Nixon considered to be the unhelpful Soviet position on Vietnam, he, too, wanted an agreement. The political leadership of both states prevailed. In 1972, as we shall see, they found a mutually acceptable way to exercise control over an aspect of the nuclear world.

This chapter is based on the premise that we, too, must exercise some control over our nuclear future, but it also acknowledges that controlling the nuclear future is difficult. It begins the last section of this book, which has two central questions: What *should* we do to create the kind of nuclear future that we desire, and, secondly, what are we *capable* of doing? To answer these two questions, we begin with an examination of the techniques for control that emerged during the first nuclear era.

CONTROLLING THE FUTURE

In some ways, it is fatuous to think that we can control the future, be it nuclear or otherwise. There is a temptation, in looking back at the Cold War period, to assume that its peaceful outcome was the result of calculated choices, that those choices inevitably made the future we are now in. Choices (and the failure to choose) do, indeed, make the future, but the question for us is, How much can we foresee the consequences of our choices? During the Cold War, concerned individuals made choices that they hoped would not ruin the planet and yet would preserve their nation's interest. They had to do so with a calculus that often seemed reasonable in its own terms (recall the Soviet decision to place missiles in Cuba), but that was clearly dangerous when it intersected with choices made by others.

The problem for us lies in trying to decide how *particular* choices are likely to shape *particular* futures. As we saw in the last chapter, it is difficult to be sure. Will proliferation increase the risk of nuclear use because young nuclear powers are more prone to consider use and because the possibility of inadvertent use will multiply, or as Kenneth Waltz argued, will the power of nuclear weapons force all who wield such power to be quite restrained? We simply cannot know for sure exactly how choices will turn out. On the other hand, we can make informed guesses about how particular choices might move us closer to or further away from a particular future that we would like to achieve (or avoid).

For the moment, let us imagine three possible futures for the next twenty-five years, roughly matching the three perspectives we introduced in Chapter 7:

- *Future 1: The realist perspective.* The number of nuclear states grows; such states brandish their weapons and there are periodic crises between nuclear weapons states; there are several uses of nuclear weapons against opponents. We do not imagine that such use is extensive in terms of numbers of weapons or area attacked, but use does occur.
- *Future 2: The institutionalist perspective, and generally descriptive of the world today.* There is slight to no growth in numbers of nuclear states and there is a continuing pressure on the existing nuclear states to reduce their arsenals; a growing set of international agreements and informal understandings constrain nuclear weapons behavior; there are managed crises that, while they might involve nuclear threats, rarely come to the point of decisions about nuclear use.
- *Future 3: The liberal perspective.* There is a decrease in the number of nuclear states and a reduction in the size of nuclear arsenals, with a general commitment

to universal nuclear disarmament. Conflicts are resolved or managed without recourse to—or calculations of—nuclear threat. Not only is there no nuclear use,
nuclear use is, in John Mueller's terms, "subrationally unthinkable"[7]: Policymakers
no longer even think of nuclear weapons as an option in dealing with a conflict.

Our basic question is: What kinds of actions make these futures more or less likely? We hypothesize that a number of conditions and actions taken during the Cold
War did increase the likelihood that we today would live in Future 2. They did not
make that outcome inevitable. We need only recall the near-use decisions the American government made, particularly when confronting the Chinese, to sense how differently today might have been if even one of those uses had occurred. In our look at
choices that shape the future, we focus on two broad elements: (1) the *conditions* in
which nuclear states relate to each other and to nonnuclear states, and (2) *the explicit
attempts to control nuclear weapons and nuclear relations.*

The ability to shape the future will depend in part upon the kind of relationship
that nuclear-armed states are in, for the nature of the relationship will make some futures more or less likely, and some conscious efforts to create a particular future more
or less likely to succeed. The first nuclear era was a condition of a cold war. Recall that
we defined a cold war as a relationship between two or more states in which (1) the
leadership of each state believes that another state in the relationship has extremely
hostile intentions against one's own state and that the other state contemplates waging war to accomplish those intentions, but (2) in reality no state's leadership desires
war with the others. The fear of war initiated by the other side makes the world seem
a dangerous place.

A cold war thus fosters two opposing impulses: to show one's ability to wage war
in order to deter it, and to show one's willingness to negotiate with the other in order
to see if peaceful coexistence is possible. We saw in Chapter 6 that these two impulses
led to a periodic waxing and waning of the historic Cold War. While the frightfulness
of nuclear weapons was not enough to ensure peaceful coexistence, they did encourage
a very specific kind of dialogue with the opponent, a dialogue that may help change perceptions about the other. That dialogue has been called "arms control."[8]

ARMS CONTROL IN THE COLD WAR

Arms control itself refers to agreements limiting the quantity or capability of weapons.
Disarmament, a form of arms control, envisions the abolition of the weapons (reducing the quantity and quality to zero). An interest in arms control did not begin with nuclear weapons. For instance, in 1921 the major naval powers agreed to put limits on the
number and size of the capital ships in their navies. Some forms of arms control are
imposed on the losers of a war. Britain and France forced a defeated Germany to sign
a treaty in 1919 that limited the German army to 100,000 men and denied Germany
the right to deploy war planes or submarines. After World War II, the United States
forced the Japanese to adopt a constitution forbidding the creation of a military establishment. And at the end of the Gulf War, the American-led coalition insisted that Iraq
give up its nuclear, chemical, and biological warfare programs.

Outside of the relatively infrequent victor-imposed arms control (or disarmament),
arms control rests on mutual agreement. That is, states must agree to be bound by a set
of limitations. If a state refuses to sign such an agreement, it is not bound by the treaty's

provisions. Moreover, the continued compliance with any agreement rests on the willingness of the signatories to adhere to the agreement (or on the power and willingness of some of the signatories to coerce the compliance of others). As nations can back out of agreements, many agreements contain escape clauses that legalize the renunciation of a treaty. For instance, the Nuclear Test Ban Treaty of 1963 stipulated that "each Party shall in exercising its national sovereignty have the right to withdraw from the Treaty if it decides that extraordinary events, related to the subject matter of this Treaty, have jeopardized the supreme interests of its country."[9]

The escape clause makes clear that arms control is expected to serve a nation's national interests. Hence, a nation's definition of a desirable agreement has usually been that which is most congenial to its position in the arms race. Typically, states have attempted to restrain the other side more than themselves. This parochial outlook on nuclear arms control has been driven by four forces: (1) Weapons makers and nuclear research laboratories have been very reluctant to have restraints put on promising weapons; over time, they have developed close ties with influential members of the political elite who share their reluctance; (2) conservative political leaders have usually been able to mobilize support for cautious approaches. The fear that others might "break out" of an agreement and put one's nation at risk has continually led to pressures for insurance in the form of weapons or technologies that are not constrained significantly by an arms control agreement; (3) arms control represents a diminishing of state sovereignty: The state's ability to do what it wishes within its own borders, particularly for its own defense, is constrained. In periods of heightened nationalism, arms control can take on the appearance of an attempt by foreigners to interfere with that sovereignty; (4) finally, the image of nuclear weapons as a war-winning weapon creates pressures to maintain them in the inventory "just in case."

Historically, nuclear arms control became a concern as the Manhattan Project entered its last stages. American leaders recognized that the American monopoly could not last. As we have pointed out, the real secret of nuclear weapons was that they could be built; that secret would end the moment the bomb detonated over Hiroshima. It seemed better to seek some form of control when there was little risk to American security and when the American voice would dominate the negotiations.

Interestingly, both the United States and the Soviet Union initially adopted the position that nuclear weapons should not be possessed by states. The Americans proposed that an international agency control all aspects of atomic energy, from the mining of uranium to fissioning the atom. Should a nation attempt to evade the controls, the international community would force that state back into compliance. The very threat of these sanctions, it was thought, would help deter violations. The Baruch plan, presented in June 1946 by a special American negotiator, Bernard Baruch, called for the destruction of nuclear weapons and the creation of this international agency to control the peaceful development of nuclear energy.

Debate on the merits of the proposal was overshadowed by disagreement on how and when to abolish the existing American weapons. Truman had told Baruch that "we should not under any circumstances throw away our gun until we are sure the rest of the world can't arm against us."[10] Until there was an effective international control agency, the United States would keep, build, and continue to test its weapons. The Soviet position reversed the sequence. The United States would destroy all of its nuclear weapons. Then the nations would decide on a system of control. The Soviets wanted unilateral American disarmament; Truman was not about to drop the gun.

The Baruch plan and the Soviet counterproposal came to naught. Neither side could find the formula to bridge the gap between the two positions. Neither side found it possible to abandon the goal of the abolition of nuclear weapons and to try for something less ambitious. And as long as the Soviet Union had to negotiate from a position of serious inferiority (recall that it was a nonnuclear state until the fall of 1949), little progress was likely. Equally important, as the Cold War heated up it seemed foolish to both sides to give up the very weapon one might need to preserve the peace or to defeat the other if it came to a showdown.

The Cold War, however, did not still the efforts to achieve some form of control over nuclear weapons. The Soviet leadership regularly called for nuclear disarmament—the removal of all nuclear weapons from a nation's inventory. Such proposals may have reflected a deeply held view of what needed to be done in a nuclear world, but the Soviet leadership was well aware of the propaganda advantage of such a position, and for a weaker nuclear power (as the Soviet Union was during the 1950s), nuclear disarmament promoted its security goals. But there was a cost to demanding nuclear disarmament. Arkady Shevchenko, a Soviet diplomat, was dismayed in 1959 to learn that Soviet leader Nikita Khrushchev was going to insist that Soviet negotiators keep "general and complete disarmament" as the goal. He felt that partial measures such as a nuclear test ban were feasible, but the all-encompassing Khrushchev program was unrealistic as a bargaining goal and would retard achievement of the more realistic partial measures.[11]

Gradually the two states' perspectives on arms control began to converge; in the short run, they would try to reach agreement on particular aspects of nuclear weapons and the then-burgeoning arms race. Several partial measures were accepted during the Cold War, and have continued in the post-Cold War world. They have helped shape the nuclear future and will continue to do so, as long as nations find arms control in their interest. But as those measures are but partial, their incompleteness stands as an ever-present reminder that the nuclear nations are not willing to contemplate giving up their weapons. They, and many other nonnuclear states, have, however, agreed to some important constraints on their nuclear weapons. Those constraints can be called an *international regime*—a set of expectations that many states have about how they should behave. We turn now to the major kinds of measures of control.

ARMS CONTROL MEASURES

We have divided our analysis into three types of control measures: those undertaken by a number of states (*multilateral control* efforts), those undertaken essentially by two states (*bilateral* efforts), and those undertaken by one state (*unilateral* efforts). These divisions are somewhat artificial. Multilateral agreements such as the partial nuclear test ban and the nuclear nonproliferation treaty did involve dozens of states, but they were created by the two nuclear giants who saw such agreements as enhancing their security and prestige and would have been meaningless without their signatures. Moreover, they, like the bilateral agreements between the two, emerged in a period when the Cold War was waning. The two superpowers felt that they could take modest risks to show a conciliatory side to the other, and when that seemed to pay off, they felt encouraged to made additional efforts to control the nuclear arms race between them. Thus, in the first nuclear age, the arms control agenda has revolved around the interests of the United States and the Soviet Union, and the pace of arms control has been determined by the state of the relations between the two. Nonetheless, all states have displayed an interest in controlling nuclear weapons.

MULTILATERAL EFFORTS TO CONTROL NUCLEAR WEAPONS

Controls on the Testing of Nuclear Weapons   Banning the testing of nuclear devices has had support for decades. Some see it as a means to retard or prevent proliferation. Others see it as a means to prevent the addition of more sophisticated nuclear warheads to the world's arsenals, based on the presumption that nations would be loath to build and stockpile weapons whose design had not been confirmed as effective. Such hopes have been undermined by the experience of Israel (which apparently feels comfortable with a stockpile of untested weapons) and India and Pakistan, who chose not to sign the treaty and would openly become nuclear weapons states in 1998 by testing their weapons.

A more realistic hope in the early nuclear era was that a test ban would reduce the level of radioactive fallout that was spreading around the world from atmospheric testing by the four nuclear weapons states. By the late 1950s fallout had become a political issue, threatening public health not only within the states conducting the tests but around the world. In 1963, the United States, the Soviet Union, and ultimately more than 120 other states signed the Partial Test-Ban Treaty that prohibited testing in the atmosphere, in outer space, and under water. Notable holdouts included China, Cuba, France, North Korea, and Vietnam.

While the agreement reduced atmospheric radioactivity (in spite of the fact that states such as China were not signatories and would test their weapons aboveground), the treaty allowed the arms race to go on underground. The average number of underground tests per year after 1963 exceeded the average number of total tests prior to the test ban (although the yields were smaller).[12] The ban was partial for two central reasons. First, no nuclear nation wanted to forgo all opportunities to test nuclear weapons. Progress toward lighter warheads was deemed important (and would be necessary if MIRVed systems were to be developed). Second, there were limitations on verification. Recall that treaties are upheld only as long as the signatories agree to abide by them. The nagging fear is that one side will cheat while the other remains in compliance. Such cheating might, in some cases, produce such a nuclear advantage that it would make a first strike very tempting.

The insistence on verification is thus said to be a hedge against nuclear war. Both the United States and the Soviet Union could monitor atmospheric and underwater detonations because increased radiation would show up in the world's atmosphere and be detectable. Underground testing, however, could not be detected reliably with the technology then available. To get around the technological limitation, the United States insisted on on-site inspections. The Soviets had as early as 1956 accepted the principle of on-site inspection, but the two sides could not work out the details to effect a compromise.

To an important degree, therefore, a willingness to agree to arms control depends upon verification capabilities. Conversely, for those opposed to a particular measure of arms control, challenging the reliability of verification has been a time-honored means to kill an arms control proposal. Clearly, one can never be 100 percent certain that verification will work, even when there is on-site inspection. The chronic difficulty that United Nations inspectors had in policing Iraq's de-nuclearization makes the point vividly.

The technology of verification, however, has continued to become more sophisticated (e.g., seismic monitoring has become more sensitive and precise), while at the same time the number of states that have the resources to go nuclear has also increased. These factors, coupled with reduced suspicions of the United States and Russia toward each other, helped spur a renewed push for a Comprehensive Test Ban Treaty (CTB). Such a treaty was signed in September 1996, obligating its signatories "not to carry out any nuclear weapon test explosion or any other nuclear explosion." It set up an organization and procedure for monitoring state compliance and dealing with issues as they emerged. But it made the treaty's entry into force dependent upon acceptance (ratification) by forty-four specific nations—those nations with nuclear reactors (and hence, all the nuclear weapons states). Those states include India, Pakistan, and North Korea. The big five announced that in the interim they would not test nuclear weapons, and that seems to be holding, but India and Pakistan tested in 1998— and faced with a hostile response by many nations, made pledges to sign the CTB under certain conditions.

But just as the ability to continue underground testing was the "escape hatch" that allowed nuclear weapons states to sign the Partial Test Ban Treaty, so too does the CTB have similar escape hatches. Each signatory, "in exercising its national sovereignty, [has] the right to withdraw from this Treaty if it decides that extraordinary events related to the subject matter of this Treaty have jeopardized its supreme interests."[13] A number of states indicated the conditions that would trigger withdrawal. For instance, apparently the Clinton administration said that such a condition would emerge if its stockpile of warheads could not be judged safe and reliable without testing.[14] In addition, modern technology may make nuclear testing relatively unnecessary. The historical experience of nuclear weapons states is that they usually get the design right for implosion devices and that a gun-type device really need not be tested, as the Americans correctly assumed in 1945. Nuclear weapons designers have concluded that computer simulations of a weapon's detonation can take the place of actual testing. And technological advances constantly threaten to undermine the restraints. Recall from our discussion in Chapter 3 that a fusion (hydrogen) bomb needs a fission explosion to occur first in order to trigger the fusion. Testing fusion devices of this type is not allowed by the CTB, but the treaty does permit testing of "pure fusion" explosions created by lasers or particle beams. Such testing may lead to the production of cheap, safe energy for peaceful purposes—and to a new type of nuclear weapon whose detonation system has been tested.

The bottom line, then, on test bans is that they do help constrain the technologies the treaty covers, making it more difficult for a state to go nuclear or enhance its existing nuclear arsenal. They do favor the technologically advanced states whose scientific establishment can work effectively in the narrow realms of inquiry and experiment left open by the agreement. They cover only those states who agree to be bound to the terms of the treaty. States can desert the treaty if they feel there is a significant advantage in doing so, or if there is a compelling necessity—which is likely to emerge if a state feels its security is jeopardized.

Preventing the Proliferation of Nuclear Weapons   In the last chapter, we described three types of antiproliferation policies (denial, coercive, and cooperative) designed to prevent an increase in the number of nuclear weapons states. The principal multilateral control device has been the Non-Proliferation Treaty (NPT) of 1968, a form of cooperative antiproliferation. The nonnuclear signatories agreed not to receive such weapons from others or manufacture nuclear weapons themselves, and accepted a form of monitoring by the International Atomic Energy Agency (IAEA) to prevent diversion of nuclear fuel from electrical energy generating nuclear plants to a nuclear weapons program. These signatories thus accepted a form of nuclear disarmament for themselves. Those with nuclear weapons agreed not to transfer such weapons to another state or to provide assistance in manufacturing such weapons. The latter also agreed to negotiate in good faith for nuclear disarmament for themselves. Thus, the NPT pointed to a goal of a denuclearized world. In a fundamental sense, then, the signatories agreed to seek the third of the three futures we have identified, though in practice the NPT was firmly rooted in the second future.

The NPT has proved to be the most widely accepted nuclear arms control agreement, ultimately getting more than 170 adherents. The holdouts were generally the states that had long been suspected of having a nuclear weapons program (as we saw in Chapter 3): Argentina, Brazil, Chile (a rival of Argentina and Brazil, but with no known program), Cuba, India, Israel, and Pakistan; or states that had been accused of supplying weapons technology (China, which became a signatory in 1992); or made a practice of demonstrating its independence from the two superpowers (France, also a 1992 signatory). Some states accepted the treaty, but with reservations. Germany, for instance, conditioned its adherence to nonproliferation upon NATO's ensuring its security.

The NPT also stipulated review conferences every five years after the treaty entered into force to evaluate adherence to the treaty, and a general conference after twenty-five years to decide whether to make the treaty permanent. The general conference met in April–May 1995.[15] Many states, most notably India, criticized the existing nuclear powers for making little progress toward their pledged goal of general nuclear disarmament. The Arab states sought to pressure Israel into signing the NPT, thus bringing about its denuclearization, as an opaque proliferator is technically a nation without nuclear weapons. These two groups of states threatened to block making the treaty permanent. A clear majority (including the existing nuclear powers) wanted permanency, but they did not want to force a vote that would clearly divide the conference and thus appear to rupture the general belief that proliferation was undesirable. The compromise was that the 175 delegations "understood" that the treaty was permanent, that all nations would be urged to sign the NPT, and that at future five-year review conferences, a key issue would be nuclear disarmament by the existing nuclear weapons states.

Between NPT's entry into force in 1970 and the 1995 conference, there had been other disquieting events in addition to the lack of commitment by the nuclear weapons states to nuclear disarmament. Iraq, which had signed the treaty in 1969 and reached an agreement with the International Atomic Energy Agency to prevent diversion of nuclear fuels, had clearly gone ahead with a nuclear weapons program. Iran, a 1970 signatory with similar IAEA safeguards, may be pursuing a nuclear weapons program today. And North Korea, a 1985 signatory with IAEA safeguards, has publicly threatened to go nuclear.

On balance, the NPT has probably made it more difficult but not impossible for states to go nuclear. It has continued to reinforce the image that nuclear weapons are undesirable and general nuclear disarmament is a goal worth seeking, thus creating a significant international regime backed by commitments to particular actions. But there are always loose threads (like Iraq or North Korea) that threaten to unravel the tapestry. Can an NPT regime withstand the strain of one or several new states going nuclear? India and Pakistan's open proliferation in 1998 raised that possibility, but they were not signatories, and both encountered a wave of opposition, some of it in the form of economic sanctions from the United States. Would that be enough to keep other states from being tempted to defect from their treaty commitments? One might suggest that the global economic recession that began in 1998 might encourage some would-be proliferators to adhere to the nonproliferation regime in order to prevent further damage to their economies resulting from economic sanctions. On the other hand, economic distress might revive intensely nationalistic politics within various societies, and those politics may impel more states to consider joining the nuclear club. Moreover, some future successful use of nuclear weapons may cause states to stampede toward nuclearization, if for no other reason than to protect themselves from others who might be tempted to use such weapons. In the end, then, the permanence and effectiveness of the nonproliferation regime over the next twenty-five years will depend on how secure the world's nations feel.

Agreements Prohibiting the Threat of Nuclear Use   A third way in which states have sought to control nuclear weapons is to create agreements that would *ban the threat of nuclear use*. Some states have traditionally proclaimed a "no first use" policy, in which they declare that they would not be the first to use nuclear weapons. The Soviet Union, for instance, routinely made such pledges—but at the same time seemed willing to engage in nuclear threat-making. The United States (and its NATO allies), on the other hand, made first use of nuclear weapons a central part of their doctrine for the defense of Western Europe; and the United States, particularly during the 1950s, made open nuclear threats against its opponents, particularly the Chinese. The issue of nuclear threats became a part of the negotiations for the Non-Proliferation Treaty. The nonnuclear weapons states (NNWS) demanded that there be guarantees against the use or threatened use of nuclear weapons against them. "The Soviet Union had included a non-use pledge in its original Draft Treaty. Britain and the United States opposed the restriction on the use of weapons and instead offered a 'positive' assurance of action through the United Nations in the event of a nuclear threat against a NNWS."[16] The no-first-use provision was kept out of the treaty, but eventually the United States and Britain felt compelled to issue a "negative security assurance." For instance, the British government declared in 1978, "Britain undertakes not to use or to threaten to use nuclear weapons against such states [who are members of the NPT or other binding agreements not to acquire nuclear weapons] except in the case of an attack on the United Kingdom, its dependent territories, its Armed Forces or its Allies by such a state in association with a nuclear weapons state."[17]

BILATERAL AGREEMENTS TO CONTROL NUCLEAR WEAPONS

The second major form of arms control has been the efforts by two nuclear states to reach mutual agreements concerning their weapons. While the principal participants have been the United States and the Soviet Union (and its successor, Russia), the early atomic age saw a promising step taken by Britain and the United States. In July 1943 President Roosevelt and Prime Minister Churchill agreed that the two states "will never use this agency against each other … [and] we will not use it against third parties without each other's consent."[18] Four years later, the United States and Britain agreed to give up the veto power each had over the other's use of the weapon. In practice, each remained solicitous about the other's views regarding nuclear use, but neither was interested in having to have its arsenal so directly controlled by the other again.

The Cold War did not allow a comparable situation for the United States and the Soviet Union, but they did, nonetheless, take a series of steps to reach mutual controls on their nuclear weapons. The principal results have been SALT and START. A Strategic Arms Limitation Treaty (SALT I) was first signed in 1972, with a follow-up (SALT II) in 1979. Both SALT agreements emerged in the waning of the Cold War. The United States judged that it had enough nuclear weapons to make deterrence work (hence building more made no sense economically, especially with the defense budget strained by the Vietnam war). The Soviet Union had successfully overcome the strategic inferiority that it had lived with since the start of the first nuclear age. Indeed, with the United States not building more missiles, the Soviet Union was forging ahead. SALT I capped the number of strategic missiles that both sides could have: 1710 ICBMs and SLBMs for the United States, 2358 for the Soviet Union. In a separate agreement, both sides agreed to limit the deployment of an antiballistic missile system to two sites (the ABM treaty).

Because such agreements have to be negotiated within the government as much as with the rival, they will have significant weaknesses as methods of control. In SALT I, for instance, Nixon accepted fewer ICBMs and SLBMs than the Soviets as the price to get the Soviet Union to stop building. Such numerical inferiority would have been opposed by the American Air Force and Navy had it not been for the fact that SALT I purposefully left the number of nuclear warheads unconstrained. With multiple independent re-entry vehicle (MIRV) technology about to come on line, Nixon could argue that launcher numbers did not really matter if more than one warhead could be put on each missile, and a good proportion of the missile force was in invulnerable submarines.

MIRV helped sell SALT I in the United States, but created a whole new problem for arms control. First, how destabilizing was a growing number of warheads? No one knew, but as we saw in Chapter 5, a plethora of accurate warheads created images of a first-strike capability (and possibly the temptation to launch such a strike). Secondly, how does one verify the number of warheads in a sealed nosecone of a missile? Verification was possible with SALT I, because spy satellites watched the construction of missile bases in both countries and the construction of submarines capable of carrying SLBMs. Thus caps on the number of missiles could be effectively verified. What would it take to verify any further arms control?

SALT II increased the coverage of the treaty. Strategic bombers were now included, but the ceiling for all strategic delivery systems was increased to 2400 for both sides (with a symbolic reduction to take place in three years to 2250). A maximum of 1320 systems could be MIRVed. Verification could determine which particular systems were tested in a MIRVed configuration and that became the "counting rule"; if tested as a MIRVed system, all such deployments would be counted as MIRVed. Still missing, however, was a limit on the number of warheads; the temptation would be to put more on each missile.

SALT II was concluded at the point when the Cold War began to wax again. President Carter did not dare submit it to the Senate for ratification, but both sides pledged to adhere to the agreement—a posture that both nations kept even during the Reagan reorientation of the nuclear doctrine and foreign policy. Thus at the bilateral level as well, the nuclear regime that favored control over nuclear weapons continued. At the same time, signing arms control agreements helped energize a growing network of individuals and organizations within various nations who made arms control their life's work.

START, as the name implies, sought to reduce the number of strategic warheads, and to get rid of weapons systems that seemed dangerous because they had all the characteristics of first-strike weapons.[19] The Reagan administration, for instance, initially proposed that START set ceilings of a total of 850 ICBMs and SLBMs with no more than 5,000 warheads, of which only 2,500 could be on ICBMs. ICBM accuracy made them first-strike weapons. The Soviets had invested heavily in their ICBM force, which made it, in American eyes, dangerous. The Soviets rejected the American proposal as one-sided; with three-quarters of their warheads on ICBMs (6,000 in all), the Soviets would have to make radical changes in their force structure to meet the new ceilings, while the American triad could much more easily accommodate the changes. Reagan's announcement of the effort to create a ballistic missile defense ("Star Wars") created even greater animosity. Not only would it challenge the ABM treaty, but American technology might be the first to produce such a system, making an American first strike possible: An initial American surprise attack would destroy much of the Soviet ICBM force, allowing the Star Wars defense to defeat a ragged Soviet retaliatory strike. Then the Soviet Union would be forced to capitulate to avoid having its cities incinerated by the remaining American nuclear force.

By the end of the decade, however, both Reagan and Mikhail Gorbachev came to accept the idea of a long-term goal of de-nuclearization, with a shorter-term goal of significant reductions in strategic delivery systems to 1,600 systems with 6,000 warheads. The American insistence on development of Star Wars led to an impasse with START, but in December 1987 both sides agreed to eliminate, over a period of three years, all land-based missiles with ranges between 300 and 3,400 miles (the Intermediate-Range Nuclear Forces agreement). As the momentous changes occurred in Eastern Europe (but before the disintegration of the USSR and the end of Communist party control), Bush and Gorbachev were able to reach agreement in July 1991 on a START treaty (now called START I), setting ceilings at 1,600 systems with 6,000 warheads. When ratification was completed in December, 1994, it began a seven-year period of stepped reductions and close monitoring by both sides of the dismantling and destruction of the delivery systems. The process was complicated by the breakup of the Soviet Union, as Belarus, Ukraine, and Kazakhstan inherited portions of the Soviet nuclear arsenal. They ultimately reached agreements with Washington and Moscow, ending their temporary status as nuclear powers.

The signing of the START I treaty in 1991 led the United States and the new Russian state to consider the next step of de-MIRVing the ICBM forces of both sides and further reducing the number of strategic warheads. In January 1993, George Bush and Russian President Boris Yeltsin signed START II, which set a warhead ceiling of 3,500 by the year 2003 and prohibited MIRVed ICBMs. The American Senate ratified the treaty in January 1996, but the Russian Parliament stalled. The growing opposition to President Yeltsin pushed the treaty into the swirl of domestic politics. Russian critics also claimed that Russian security was at stake. The United States was continuing its efforts to create a missile defense system, now ostensibly oriented to protect local ("theater") assets rather than the nation as a whole. It was promoting the expansion of

NATO, which in 1998 had accepted Poland, the Czech Republic, and Hungary as new members. And, in the eyes of these critics, START II was one-sided. Russia would give up its modern MIRVed ICBM force, while the powerful and accurate MIRVed SLBMs would remain in the U.S. arsenal; the decay of the Russian navy meant that it had fewer equivalent weapons.

By the end of the 1990s, it was unclear if there would be further formal agreements to continue the reduction of the nuclear arsenals, although both countries' leaders pledged to continue the process. American planners sought to maintain great flexibility in planning their force structure to cover a wide range of post-Cold War contingencies (including a return to conflictual relations with Russia), a flexibility that would be curtailed by further START reductions. Financial exigencies in Russia constantly pressed Russia to reduce the size of its arsenal; therefore, in Russian eyes a new START that reduced the American arsenal as well was attractive. The nuclear weapons bureaucracies in both states do not, however, seem willing to drop below the 1,000 delivery system level. At the same time, the Non-Proliferation Treaty's call for nuclear disarmament will create political pressures for a continued series of ever-lower ceilings. We can expect, in the next twenty-five years, a series of clashes between these conflicting demands. As things now stand, the claims that nuclear weapons provide security will have the edge in the domestic debate, which will be interpreted by many signatories of the NPT to mean that these two states will not, in practice, meet their treaty commitments to nuclear disarmament. That in turn may speed proliferation.

Will other pairs of nuclear weapons states seek some form of bilateral control in the next twenty-five years? We think that relatively unlikely for the following reason. During the Cold War, the United States and the Soviet Union were far and away the two most powerful nuclear weapons states (a condition that has not changed radically in the second nuclear era). The weaker nuclear powers, even in alliance with one of the two superpowers, did not affect the nuclear equation between the United States and the USSR, even when the two states began to reduce their arsenals. For instance, in the 1990s, the nuclear balance was roughly as shown in Table 8-1.[20]

Now add into the picture India, with some 100 total warheads, and Pakistan, with 30. Suppose these two states decide that it would be important to prevent an arms race by agreeing to put a cap on the total number of nuclear weapons. What cap might they select? Suppose they consider 100, which constrains India but permits Pakistan to build 70. That might be reasonable from the perspective of those two states in isolation. But India has a strategic concern about China. To set a ceiling at 100 means that India

TABLE 8-1   THE NUCLEAR BALANCE IN THE 1990S

	DELIVERY SYSTEMS*	WARHEADS AVAILABLE IN STOCKPILE*
United States	1085	7139
Russia	1308	7249
Britain	128	260
France	133	449
China	275	275

*Strategic (intercontinental) systems for the United States and Russia; all nontactical systems for Britain, France, and China.

would unilaterally accept a decided inferiority with China (at least 3:1 for more-than-tactical systems). This interconnectedness between nuclear weapons states suggests that it will be difficult for nations to negotiate purely bilateral agreements. To deal with those difficulties, states will most likely have to engage in multilateral negotiations. Drawing China into the picture, however, means that China must not only think about the relationship with India, but also with the United States and Russia if it were to agree to some limitation on its weapons. (And if, in the near future, Japan or Vietnam were to become nuclear weapons states—or appear likely to become such—China's thinking would have a new set of risks to contemplate.) Thus, we would predict that any negotiations regarding arms control with states other than the United States and Russia will have to be multilateral, and that such negotiations are likely to be very complicated. We should also point out that, as the weapons levels for the United States and Russia drop, they too might become more concerned about how smaller arsenals will stand in relationship to the now not-so-weak other nuclear powers. This complexity suggests that negotiated levels are unlikely in the next twenty-five years among these states.

Unilateral Efforts to Control Nuclear Weapons

In addition to multilateral or bilateral agreements, a state can pursue a variety of tactics to discourage proliferation or control the nuclear weapons of others by initiating actions in which its nuclear arsenal is not involved. In some cases, the action is punitive. In the last chapter, we pointed to the coercive efforts such as unilateral strikes against a nation's nuclear facilities (as in the Israeli raid against the Iraqi reactor in 1981). A far more common tactic is to threaten economic sanctions if a state undertakes a nuclear weapons program. American legislative acts, for instance, mandate such sanctions, and they were applied most recently after the 1998 tests by India and Pakistan. But such sanctions have had a checkered history. For instance, in 1979 the Carter administration placed economic sanctions on Pakistan in the face of evidence that it was attempting to build a bomb. The Reagan and Bush administrations reversed the decision when they needed Pakistan as the staging area for aid to the Afghan rebels fighting the Russians in Afghanistan. Both administrations chose to ignore clear evidence of the Pakistani program and extensive Chinese aid, and both certified, as American law required, that Pakistan was not building nuclear weapons. As Milt Bearden, a senior CIA official in Pakistan from 1986 to 1989, said, "Reagan and Bush said it ain't a bomb until they turn the last screw and paint B-O-M-B on the side."[21] This tension created by competing policy interests is echoed in other ways. The 1994 American law, for example, which prohibits commercial or financial transactions or foreign aid with a proliferator, permits the continued export of American farm products, partially on the argument that to refuse to make food available harms the people of the proliferating nation, and partly because the American farm bloc exercises power in the Congress.

Threatening to sanction would-be proliferators unilaterally may at times be a means of exercising control over the future. In December 1995, for example, American spy satellites noticed activity in an area suspected of being a possible test site for Indian nuclear weapons. The American government quietly pressed India not to test, and India did not. That success, however, had the following consequences. When the nationalist Bharatiya Janata Party came to power in March 1998, it decided to test its weapons in order to show that the new government, "unlike previous regimes, will not give in to international pressure."[22] Moreover, it successfully disguised its preparations so that international pressure prior to the test would be avoided. Most discouragingly, while both India and Pakistan have sought ways to ease the sanctions imposed after the 1998 tests, neither seems likely to give up its nuclear weapons in exchange for lifting the sanctions.

In place of sanctions, the United States from time to time has offered "bribes" to keep a nation from going nuclear or to exercise some form of control over its nuclear weapons. For instance, with the decline in the Russian government's ability to control its nuclear weapons and the continued economic chaos in Russia (which makes black-market sales of nuclear materials attractive and which creates incentives for those skilled in developing nuclear weapons to offer their services to other states or groups), the United States has stepped in with cash. The United States is buying up weapons-grade Russian uranium and helping to pay for programs that convert Russian weapons scientists into scientists engaged in nonmilitary endeavors. In the winter of 1998–1999, the United States became increasingly concerned that Russian guards at nuclear facilities would succumb to economic pressures (many were not being paid). As the overseer of the American program in Russia, American Secretary of Energy Bill Richardson wrote the following:

> But the question of [paying] operating expenses, such as guard salaries, is troubling. The United States has never paid such expenses in the past, considering them Russia's responsibility. Nonetheless, we are looking for ways to help individual [nuclear] sites cope by providing winter clothing for some guards and subsidizing commissaries to ensure that guards are fed while on duty.[23]

The use of monetary incentives (and a healthy dose of punitive threats) has emerged even more dramatically in an American, Japanese, and South Korean effort to head off the North Korean nuclear weapons program. After torturous negotiations,[24] North Korea in 1994 agreed to end activities that seemed to move toward the development of fissile materials in return for an American, Japanese, and South Korean pledge to supply North Korea with light-water (non-plutonium-producing) nuclear reactors for the generation of electrical energy and to pay for fuel oil to meet North Korea's energy needs while North Korea decommissioned its plutonium-producing reactors and awaited completion of the light-water reactors. The agreement constantly threatened to unravel. Economic and political turmoil in North Korea encouraged the government to maintain a belligerent stance toward the outside world (and the forty-year hostility between north and south would provide a continual set of irritants). In the summer of 1998, North Korea announced a partial suspension of the agreement because the United States was late with the oil deliveries (the Congress held up funding), the Americans suspected the North was constructing a new nuclear weapons facility, and continued northern testing of long-range missiles led the Japanese to threaten to withdraw from the agreement. Squabbling between Japan, the United States, and South Korea also was delaying the reactor construction. It remains to be seen if the three can successfully purchase the de-nuclearization of the Korean peninsula.

A third unilateral effort to exercise some form of control over the nuclear future comes with declaring an end to certain types of nuclear activities. For instance, during the Cold War (and more recently in the period before the Comprehensive Test Ban enters into force), states declared unilateral moratoria against further nuclear testing—but usually coupled the moratorium with a demand that the other states stop testing as well. Such moratoria often were declared at the end of an extensive set of nuclear tests, and served a propaganda purpose rather than an exercise in either self-restraint or to encourage reciprocal actions by the other side. More positively, states have terminated aspects of nuclear programs on their own. We saw in Chapter 5, for instance, that the United States unilaterally froze the number of missiles in its inventory when it reached a particular level. Moreover, the smaller nuclear powers have kept a relatively stable nuclear establishment without creating agreements with others to do so.

NUCLEAR RULES OF THE ROAD

Arms control has been one path to controlling the nuclear future. Arms control, taken to the level of nuclear disarmament as established in the Non-Proliferation Treaty, would qualitatively change the nature of the nuclear predicament, but would not end it. Nuclear weapons can be "re-invented" relatively quickly by states with the components of nuclear weapons available to them. While we expect the nuclear regime controlling nuclear weapons to continue and deepen over the next twenty-five years, if things continue as they are, we do not expect to find a nuclear-disarmed planet.

Arms control is not the only means of shaping the nuclear future. Indeed, the future might be quite dangerous if we rely on arms control alone to reduce the likelihood of nuclear use, for arms control always seems to have an after-the-fact quality to it. Arms control begins with the fact that nuclear weapons exist, and asks, what do we do now? Recall that this was Secretary of War Stimson's concern when he spoke to the newly sworn in Harry Truman (Chapter 2). Stimson did not oppose using the bomb; he wanted the president to consider what could be done to control it *after* it had been used.

Control of the nuclear future, therefore, must also rest on an effort to *reshape international politics* to reduce the likelihood of use, and, ultimately, to reduce the attractiveness of nuclear weapons. There are two key questions here. The first concerns the here-and-now: Can nations prevent the emergence of situations where nuclear weapons might be brought into play—as either threat mechanisms or as weapons to be used? In other words, can they fashion *the rules of the road* that decrease the likelihood of a collision? The second question looks to a more extended future, possibly one where nuclear disarmament emerges: Can nations find ways to ensure both their security and the achievement of their national interests without reliance on weapons of mass destruction? In other words, can they fashion *processes of international politics* that obviate the need for nuclear weapons in their arsenals? In this chapter, we examine the rules of the road that might emerge in the next twenty-five years. In the concluding chapter, we take up the much more daunting question of a new process for world politics.

In the twentieth century, as war became more total and therefore more costly (as we pointed out in Chapter 4), states have been greatly interested in creating rules of the road to avoid the collision of total war. The question was no longer, "Should rules govern the relations between states?" but "Just what rules should be set, and who would do the setting?" Would they be set, for instance, by a powerful state acting unilaterally, crafting the rules to prevent collisions by all the drivers, yet having those rules accommodate its own interests? For example, the powerful state might say, "I may drive where I please. You will drive on the right-hand side of the road, but when you see me, you must pull off the road." Such a rule might serve my interests as an average driver—having everyone drive on the right will reduce the chances of being in a collision, and pulling off now and then when the powerful state comes along might be a small price to pay for the orderly behavior of others. But it might not serve the interests of others; they, too, might feel it desirable, perhaps even imperative, that they drive anywhere they please.

As the most powerful state in the aftermath of World War II, the United States did attempt to set the rules, rules that it felt were both appropriate and accepted by the other states in the coalition that had just destroyed Germany and Japan. The American vision, enshrined in the United Nations Charter, set this basic rule: Aggression was forbidden; war could only be waged in self-defense. Members of the UN and nonmembers alike were to "refrain in their international relations from the threat or use of force against the territorial integrity or political independence of any state," and were, instead, to "settle their international disputes by peaceful means in such a manner that international peace and security, and justice, are not endangered."[25]

This basic rule challenged the traditional practices of world politics, as waging war was a right traditionally accorded to sovereign, independent states. It would be wrong to suggest that American power and persuasiveness were alone responsible for the fact that this rule has won general acceptance in the international community. The carnage of two world wars, the threat of nuclear weapons, the organization of the world into two powerful blocs and a loose coalition of unaligned but weak states, and American power all worked together to create an environment that persuaded or coerced states to adjust their interests to fit the "no aggression" rule. When a state chose not to accept the rule, as Iraq did not in 1990, it found an international community united against it, and powerful states (led by the United States) willing to pay the price to enforce the rule.

It is likely that in the next twenty-five years, enough states will support this rule so that the national ambitions of most states will remain modest, security fears will be tempered by the knowledge of community support for the territorial integrity and political independence of the states of the international community, and as a consequence, nuclear weapons are not likely to come into play as weapons to challenge the geographic or political existence of another state. That would seem to suggest a pacific future no matter what happens with arms control. But, regrettably, there are two basic problems.

First, there are likely to be sets of circumstances in the next twenty-five years that lead one or several states to have immoderate ambitions, or to fear that community aid in defense against aggression might be too little and too late, or to fear that a nuclear-armed opponent might be planning a nuclear attack (a common, but incorrect, Soviet and American fear for much of the Cold War). The case of Iraq in 1990 is instructive in this regard.[26] From the Iraqi perspective, the war against Kuwait was not inappropriate behavior. Iraq had a long historic claim to Kuwait, which had detached itself from the Ottoman empire under the protection of the British navy at the end of the eighteenth century. In 1990, the Iraqi government faced an economic crisis that threatened to undermine the regime. It was attempting to rebuild a society devastated by eight years of debilitating war with Iran. The Kuwaitis had loaned Iraq the funds to wage war, but insisted on being repaid. Iraq wanted the loan forgiven, arguing that the war it fought alone also protected the Kuwaiti regime from the Islamic revolutionaries in Teheran. Additionally, Iraq depended upon oil sales to rebuild its society, but found that the Kuwaitis were flooding the oil markets in contravention of their agreed-upon oil quota, thus driving oil prices—and Iraqi revenues—downward. One need not enter the ambitions of Saddam Hussein into this mix to understand why the conquest of Kuwait might appeal to any Iraqi government. We can expect that in the next twenty-five years, other states will be driven to undertake what the rest of the community considers to be behavior forbidden by the no-aggression rule.

The second problem with a prediction of a peaceful future based on adherence to the rule of no aggression is the problem that the United States soon discovered in the post-World War II period. The rule did not address the fundamental issue of the second half of the twentieth century: How were oppressed peoples to achieve their freedom, and what role could outsiders play in that struggle? The search for liberation could mean violence (those in control sometimes resisted the sought-for change) and solicitation of outside support (insurrectionists were often weak and thus desirous of outside aid, but the government in control was often weak as well, and also interested in finding outside support). Given the diversity of outside states and their histories and interests, it was inevitable that some outsiders would become involved.

As the Cold War emerged, the United States began to see the situation as one in which Communist states used local proxies to wage a kind of war that got around the United Nations prohibition against war or the threat of war. The Cold War emerged at a time of—and was fueled by—struggles by peoples in the colonized world to liberate themselves from their European overlords. To the United States and other European powers, if Vietnamese communists, for instance, abetted by the Russians or Chinese, were able to seize the French colony of Indo-China, was this not the same as if Chinese forces crossed the border and seized the colony? The latter would be a naked act of aggression, and prohibited by the Charter. But what happened if political change came from within the society? The American government, increasingly committed to resisting the expansion of Communist influence, often equated the expansion of that influence with conventional aggression. Indeed, the two major post-1945 wars the United States fought (Korea and Vietnam) were predicated on the assumption that attempts by Korean and Vietnamese communists to reunite their countries were acts of aggression forbidden by the UN Charter.

In the American view, there needed to be a new rule that prohibited such "indirect aggression." The American government fashioned one. One of its earliest expressions came to be called the Truman Doctrine. Truman declared to Congress:

> One of the primary objectives of the foreign policy of the United States is the creation of conditions in which we and other nations will be able to work out a way of life free from coercion.... I believe that it must be the policy of the United States to support free peoples who are resisting attempted subjugation by armed minorities or by outside pressure.... The world is not static, and the status quo is not sacred. But we cannot allow changes in the status quo in violation of the Charter of the United Nations by such methods as subversion, or by such subterfuges as political infiltration.[27]

A good part of the historical Cold War can be read as the attempt by the United States to impose this new rule on others. For the United States, internal change had to come essentially through peaceful means and reflect the will of the majority.[28] Others would find the rule unacceptable. And as long as the Soviet Union or China was willing to render support to those who opposed the rule, the United States would find itself challenged by major opponents and always in risk of a collision.

Moreover, as Soviet and Chinese power grew, weaker states that had cast off their British or French colonial overlords (often peacefully, it should be noted) came to see the USSR and China as needed counterweights to the United States or its French or British allies. Having such a counterweight also made it possible for weaker states such as Egypt to consider challenging the basic rule of no aggression embodied in the UN Charter. Egypt, for instance, found a Soviet connection useful to ward off British threats and to serve as a cover for threatening Israel. The United States, often linked to the local opponent (in this case Israel), now found that a local conflict might drag the Soviet Union or China and the United States into the confrontation, creating the threat of a nuclear war at the superpower level. Hence there was a need for a set of rules overseeing this part of international relations as well, for a superpower collision arising from local circumstances seemed quite likely.

The Cuban missile crisis marked the intersection where the collision almost occurred. Fidel Castro claimed the right of Cubans to determine their own future. After initially accepting Castro, the United States concluded that an armed minority had seized the Cuban state. And no matter how popular Castro might be, Communist control of Cuba was unacceptable. Moreover, Castro's intimate connections with the Soviet Union—the necessary counterweight to American power as well as a reflection of an ideological compatibility—violated a long-standing American rule that the entrance of a European power into the region was unacceptable (the Monroe Doctrine). The Soviet Union, on the other hand, claimed the right to aid any sovereign nation in meeting its security needs, and, as we saw in Chapter 6, if the Americans could place nuclear missiles in Turkey, they could hardly object if the USSR did the same in Cuba (one rule applied to all).

The near collision in Cuba (along with the crises in Vietnam and the Middle East) encouraged both states to see if they could reach a mutually acceptable set of rules of the road for at least their bilateral relations. By 1972, they had agreed on the "Basic Principles of Relations," signed by Nixon and Brezhnev at the SALT summit in Moscow. The new rules adopted the Soviet formulation of "peaceful coexistence" that Malenkov and Khrushchev had promoted nearly twenty years earlier. Relations were to be based on "the principles of sovereignty, equality, non-interference in internal affairs, and mutual advantage." Furthermore, both sides pledged to "exercise restraint in their mutual relations, and will be prepared to negotiate and settle differences by peaceful means." They acknowledged "that efforts to obtain unilateral advantage at the expense of the other, directly or indirectly, are inconsistent with these objectives." They pledged to "avoid military confrontations" and "to do everything in their power so that conflicts or situations will not arise which would serve to increase international tension."[29]

Now, it is the case that both sides soon thereafter concluded that the other was not completely adhering to this agreement, and as the Cold War waxed once again in the late 1970s, the agreement was set aside, *but it was not renounced*. Indeed, both sides accepted the rules but viewed the other as transgressing them, and saw its own actions as generally acceptable under the rules. Most alleged violations occurred in the Third World. It was different in Europe, the place where a most deadly conflict might occur between the two heavily armed alliance systems. Both sides were able to begin and sustain a dialogue about security in Europe under the aegis of the Conference on Security and Cooperation in Europe that met periodically to reach agreements on the avoidance of provocative actions in that region (as well as to deal with such issues as human rights). At the Helsinki conference in 1975, for instance, NATO and the Soviet bloc states agreed to give twenty-one day voluntary advance notice of military maneuvers along frontiers if more than 25,000 troops were involved. This would prevent the other side from panicking when they suddenly observed large-scale military movements. Eleven years later at Stockholm they agreed to an obligatory 42-day advance notice for anything involving 13,000 troops. While the Reagan administration initially chose to see such agreements as foolish, believing that the Soviet Union could never be trusted to adhere to such rules, it did not deny that rules could be important for safeguarding the future.

This experience with both acknowledging the necessity of nuclear rules of the road and the difficulty in crafting them does point to several important lessons for the future:

1. Rules can be one method of achieving some control of the nuclear future.
2. Rules may not work, but if there is to be any hope for their working, the rules must be negotiated between states who treat each other as equals.
3. States will perceive the need for rules when relations are most tense, and be less concerned when the threat declines.

Looking to the near-term future, we do not expect states collectively to invest much time in trying to craft additional rules of the nuclear road beyond the basic rule in the United Nations Charter: States cannot make unilateral changes in the international status quo by force. That rule (and the status of the United Nations as the enforcer of that rule) was revalidated in 1990–1991 when it was invoked and upheld in the face of Iraq's seizure of Kuwait. The major nuclear actors do not see a need to do more, as there are no tensions currently that would raise concerns about their nuclear relationships. It is most likely that the next round of rule-making, if it is to occur, will come among states such as India and Pakistan. As they are overt nuclear weapons states, they must decide if they can afford to leave their relationship to day-to-day improvisation, or if they need to agree on rules that clarify what each expects of the other, and thereby give warning that certain actions will be quite provocative. Agreeing on rules is a difficult process, forcing the states to weigh the costs of the negotiation (including objections voiced by internal opponents to the government) against the potential loss in the absence of such rules. If the Cold War is any guide, success in fashioning such rules will come fifteen to twenty years after the emergence of the nuclear relationship, and will be spurred by a crisis in which nuclear weapons figure prominently. On the other hand, the superpowers and their European partners did create a model that others might emulate.

OTHER MECHANISMS FOR CONTROLLING THE NUCLEAR FUTURE

During the Cold War, other institutions and regimes emerged that, while not directly concerned with creating rules of the road for nuclear-armed states, did offer possibilities for reducing the likelihood of clashes between nuclear powers or between nuclear-armed and conventionally-armed states. The United Nations, for instance, was a standing organization that worked out mechanisms for dealing with the threat of war. The Charter gives the Security Council (composed of the five major nuclear weapons states as permanent members plus ten elected members) the power to consider any threat to world peace and to authorize a response by the organization. The organization has a modestly successful track record in dealing with the conventional forms of aggression that were outlawed by the Charter. It has occasionally been able to intervene with modest success in internal conflicts that threatened to pull in outside powers. It has been less willing or able to deal with "unconventional" aggression.

Regional organizations such as the Organization of African Unity or ASEAN (the Association of Southeast Asian Nations) have attempted to create mechanisms similar to those of the United Nations whereby nations in conflict can communicate and noninvolved members of the organization can bring collective pressure to bear on the parties in conflict. Such organizations, again, have had modest but important successes to point to. In addition, some regional military alliances such as NATO created institutionalized forums for the coordination of security policies that served multiple purposes. NATO, for example, had three purposes: (1) to keep the United States involved in European politics, (2) to control German power, and (3) to deter aggression by the Soviet Union or one of its European allies. Each of these purposes served to maintain the no-aggression rule (albeit at a cost—the Soviet Union saw NATO as a means to wage aggressive war, or as a means to compel the Soviet Union and its allies to act in certain ways in order to avoid war). With the end of the Cold War, NATO has agreed to the expansion of its membership (first for Poland, the Czech Republic, and Hungary, and possibly other Eastern European states later); new members are obligated to accept alliance rules. As expansion has been seen by Russia as a security threat, NATO has attempted to reassure Russia of its pacific intentions by creating ties with the Russian state and its military establishment in a formalized structure called Partnership for Peace. This alliance system thus continues its effort to coordinate state behaviors in line with rules designed to reduce conflicts within its membership as well as outside.

Other formats have emerged over time to allow some form of consultation among political leaders. The wartime conferences between Roosevelt, Churchill, and Stalin became part of the process of world politics as alliance leaders came to meet periodically. The tensions of the Cold War initially ended such conferences between the now rival nations, but the same tensions impelled the leadership to go to the "summit"—the first being held in Geneva, Switzerland in 1955. Summit conferences have become a standard practice among rival states since that time and have, as we saw in the opening pages of this chapter, become important devices by which the rules of the road can be worked out. Indeed, summit conferences among the major powers (such as the G-7 economic summits) have become routine. Even when rules are not created, summit meetings provide a means of establishing common perspectives and expectations. In addition, summits are a means of displaying the attendees as equal in stature and of validating the claim that the interests of the attendees deserve consideration. This latter function was quite important for the Soviet Union. As Nixon noted (at the start of this chapter), the Soviet Union sought confirmation that it was a great power and that its interests would be considered.

To the degree that summits are places where confirmation of status and the validity of others' interests occur, they can function as substitutes for explicit rule-making. To the degree that they raise unmet expectations, they pose some risk. And they can produce other undesirable results. The summit conferences between Hitler and British Prime Minister Chamberlain in 1938 became synonymous with disastrous appeasement, and the Vienna summit between Kennedy and Khrushchev in 1961 led the former to think that he did not appear tough enough, and the latter to assume that he could press harder. The Cuban missile crisis probably played itself out the way it did in part because of the "lessons" of the 1961 summit conference.

The Historic Cold War Revisited: Lessons for the Future

Our experience with the control of nuclear weapons, the creation of rules of the road, and the shaping of international institutions and practices such as summit conferences has come essentially from a cold war environment and bears the impress of the context. One might say that, on balance, humans did quite well in securing a reasonable nuclear future in that context. Was a cold war the *optimal condition* to produce the acceptance of and procedures for both nuclear arms control and rule-creation? Can these approaches maintain their momentum in the post-Cold War era? Or, in the second nuclear age, will these established procedures generally atrophy and must we all rediscover or invent anew the means to shape the nuclear future?

Before we turn to these questions, it is well to keep in mind that the historic Cold War had several particular features that likely made a relatively peaceful future possible. Recognizing those features does give us a means of assessing our current predicament (and serves, secondly, as a warning that a return to either a global or regional cold war environment may no longer promote a desirable future). We examine four particularities of the historic Cold War.

1. *The historic Cold War emerged relatively unexpectedly.* There was no long history of animosity between the Soviet Union and the United States. Indeed, they were war-time allies for the four years prior to Hiroshima, seeing themselves engaged in a deadly struggle against a common enemy (first Germany, then Japan) and thus having an incentive to cooperate. The absence of an extensive history of hostility would allow each side to think that some understanding with the other might be possible (one is reluctant to consider agreements with a historic enemy), and even in the depths of the cold war, there were enough people in the governments of both states that were willing to take the risk to find out if some cooperative effort for control were possible. We suspect that in the future, particularly for the younger nuclear weapons states such as India and Pakistan, a nuclear relationship is likely to come out of a long-standing hostility, making control of the future much more difficult.

2. *The historic Cold War emerged gradually.* The view that the other state might contemplate war did not emerge overnight, but across a two- to five-year period. There was no dramatic challenge that caused high levels of fear to grip the leadership. To be sure, there were crises in which war was possible, but the crisis itself was over a local issue (like access to Berlin), not the survival of the two states. Even during many of the frictions of the early Cold War, there was the feeling that things could be made right—that the other side could be educated about one's peaceful intentions, as Truman's instructions to Vinson indicated.

3. *In the historic Cold War there was no event that made it permanent.* The waning of the Cold War—which periodically led to periods called "détente"—was made possible because there was no event that made permanent the image of an opponent as one with intentions of attacking. For the United States, the nearest "permanentizing" event was the Korean War of 1950–1953; the American leadership concluded that the Soviet Union would be willing to use military force to promote its interests. But even here, the Soviet Union and the United States did not clash directly in the Korean War. The war ended in a bloody stalemate that created a great deal of bitterness in the United States, but that bitterness was directed toward the other communist power, the People's Republic of China, which had intervened in the war and had snatched victory from the United States. The *Chinese-American* cold war was made more permanent by this event, and it is important to recall that when the American leadership contemplated using nuclear

weapons, China was almost invariably the target. The Cuban missile crisis threatened to become such an event for the United States and Soviet Union, and we saw how close the race was between peace and war. In its outcome, it had just the reverse effect: It persuaded both sides that they had to make clear their intentions toward the other.

4. *In the historic Cold War, the cold war ended before the collapse of the Soviet Union.* From 1989 to 1992 three critical events occurred: (1) The Soviet Union gave up its control over Eastern Europe; (2) The Soviet Communist Party abandoned its insistence on being the only political force in the USSR and then accepted its loss of power to other political forces; (3) The Soviet Union peacefully fragmented into its constituent republics, leaving a weakened Russia and a surrounding belt of weak states, some in serious conflict with the Russian state. These three things would have been highly improbable if the Soviet leadership (and people) felt that the United States harbored intentions of attacking the Soviet Union. The gradual return to a détente-like condition in the last four years of the Reagan administration allowed Mikhail Gorbachev to accelerate his reforms and denied his internal opposition the most powerful rallying cry that Soviet leaders had ever developed: "If we weaken ourselves, the West will destroy us."

RIVALRIES IN THE TWENTY-FIRST CENTURY

As we cannot count on the next major rivalry involving nuclear-armed states to take on the characteristics of a cold war, we want now to try our hand at imaging alternative futures. These are futures where war is quite probable, to which we now add the possession of nuclear weapons by one or several parties. We also need to consider the possibility that other nuclear-armed states will be dragged into other conflicts. Large powers may, as they have in times past, become captives of the actions and interests of their smaller allies. The Gulf War of 1990–1991 is one example of this phenomenon: A conflict between Iraq and Kuwait escalated to the point that three nuclear weapons states (the United States, Britain, and France) felt compelled to enter the conflict, another (Russia) supported the intervention, and yet another (Israel) stood poised to become involved in the fighting.

The astute reader will notice that our scenarios of the future are, for the most part, images of the past, which raises a fundamental question: In trying to see into the nuclear future, are we forever going to be limited by our awareness of the past? Nonetheless, the past is often our springboard to imagining the future, and will serve us relatively well. Here, then, are three key patterns of rivalry that we may observe in the future and the likely difficulties they will pose for control of the nuclear future.

TYPE I CONFLICT: A COLD WAR

Just so we do not lose sight of a cold war as a type of conflict we may encounter in the future, we will call it a *type I conflict*, to which we would apply the preceding observations.

TYPE II CONFLICT: IRREDENTISM AND EMPIRE BUILDING

World War II is the century's classic case of wars of conquest unleashed by major powers (in this case Germany, Japan, and Italy) to recover land historically claimed by the nation or to build a new empire on the lands of others. Imagine, for a moment, a

Hitler in command of nuclear-armed Germany—or, for a paler shadow of the issue, a Saddam Hussein in command of Iraq armed with nuclear weapons. Would such a leader use nuclear weapons in the pursuit of those ambitions? Would other nuclear-armed states have responded with nuclear weapons? How can nuclear relations be managed, and at what cost, when one confronts an irredentist or empire-building nuclear power?

There are no clear answers, for we have not dealt with such a world. We can offer the following observations, drawn from our interpretation of historical experience.

1. Hitler was cautious strategically and tactically. While he was willing to run the risk of war with major powers (Britain and France in particular), he calculated that by making the challenge to the status quo relatively modest at any point in time, he would minimize that risk. That strategy worked until the attack on Poland, which prompted an Anglo-French declaration of war (but no attack on Germany proper). Tactically, Hitler avoided such things as air attacks on urban centers until German cities had been struck by the British. And he chose not to use poison gas against Germany's battlefield opponents. Thus it is not clear that a nuclear-armed aggressor would choose to *initiate* nuclear war, but it is likely that such an aggressor would seek to exploit the umbrella that nuclear weapons might provide—to stage a quick, conventional assault on the status quo, and then threaten nuclear war if the nation's opponents attempted to reverse the change in the status quo.

2. Caught in an unexpected war, or an unexpectedly long war, an irredentist or empire-building leader may be tempted to use nuclear weapons (but, as we saw historically, that was the temptation of the democratic leadership of the United States as well). Such a leader may also see no option other than escalation to nuclear war because of the nature of his or her goals. Waging war to expand the state is often perceived as a do-or-die situation: Either the state expands or it will collapse. That perception leaves little room for compromise to end the war; hence, nuclear weapons may seem that much more attractive. (But, historically, the American leadership pledged to wage war against Germany and Japan until they surrendered unconditionally; that would make meaningful compromise difficult as well, paving the way to a temptation to use nuclear weapons.)

3. Facing an irredentist or empire-building state, we can expect the potential victims to become intensely interested in acquiring nuclear weapons (or acquiring committed allies who possessed such weapons), and in creating policies that made the use of nuclear weapons seem a sure thing if aggression occurred. Such states would likely mimic the behavior of the United States and the Soviet Union during the Cold War, as each assumed that the other had such aggressive goals, and their allies sought either nuclear weapons or a nuclear umbrella.

4. An interest in nuclear arms control and rules of the road would likely be erratic. Both the irredentist or empire-builder and their potential victims would be interested when either feared it was in a weaker position, or when one felt it could use the offer of arms control or rules of the road to fragment a coalition against it (as Hitler did in the 1930s when he offered a naval arms agreement with Britain—which, incidentally, he was covertly breaking when the agreement went into effect). Indeed, in the early to middle stage of the Cold War, both sides felt the other's interest in arms control or rules of the road—such as peaceful coexistence—was fueled by similar motivations. Unlike the Cold War, however, the nuclear relationship in this kind of conflict is likely to be one long series of very deadly threats. Here, then, would be the true test of deterrence.

Is it likely that states with irredentist or empire-building goals will emerge in the next twenty-five years, thus defining the second nuclear age? The answer is that irredentist goals currently exist. India and Pakistan, for instance, have been in chronic conflict over the Kashmir, a province currently held by India, but claimed by Pakistan—a claim supported by a goodly number of Kashmiris. At the present time, Pakistan is too weak to challenge India directly but has supported a low-level war of insurgency against the Indian presence. Will a nuclear arsenal embolden the Pakistanis? We do not think this likely in the short run, but the Indian fear that Pakistan might attempt a seizure of the province will keep tensions high, as would an escalating revolt by citizens of Kashmir against Indian control.

Empire-building, on the other hand, has become unacceptable in the international community. Political or military leaders with such intentions are likely to face difficulty in coming into positions of power within their own societies on such a platform, and are likely to find collective opposition from the international community if they do come to power. But that is not to deny the possibility. There are, for instance, political groups within Russia that call for a re-forming of the Soviet state, which would mean that more than a dozen currently independent states such as the Ukraine or Uzbekistan or Latvia may face a nuclear-armed Russia with empire-building ambitions.

TYPE III CONFLICT: TOP-DOG RIVALRIES

Some conflicts revolve around questions of prestige and standing in world politics: Who is the paramount power, and what rights and privileges does that confer on the most powerful? These conflicts take on patterns of rivalry and the threat of war, because war traditionally has been the only way to settle conclusively how much power states really have in relation to others. Rivalry and the threat of war often, in turn, necessitate alliances for security. But in those alliances, weaker states are often able to force the much more powerful alliance leader to act in dangerous ways.

The outbreak of World War I is the classic illustration of this type of conflict. By 1914, a rising Germany challenged British paramountcy, and growing Russian power created uncertainty about the future in the minds of the German leadership. But the war was the direct result of a weak German ally's effort to destroy a weak Russian ally. When Austria-Hungary declared war on Serbia, which Russia pledged to defend, Germany felt compelled to declare war on Russia and on France, Russia's ally. Britain felt compelled to honor its understanding with France, and declared war on Germany. The major powers thus felt it necessary to transform a local conflict between minor powers into a world war because prestige was on the line. Prestige (or reputation) has been important for states, for in the absence of war, it is what provides clout in world politics. States can effectively promote their interests abroad to the degree that others think them powerful and willing to use that power—that they have the reputation of being and acting like a great power.

How likely are such "reputation" conflicts in the future? Are they likely to fall into warfare, particularly nuclear war? We should point out that much of the armed conflicts waged by the superpowers in the Cold War did involve reputation issues. For instance, American involvement in Vietnam was predicated on the assumption that if the leader of the free world refused to defend a portion of the free world, its reputation would be severely damaged and other states would be willing to stage a series of challenges to American interests. While American decision-making regarding Vietnam did not involve nuclear weapons, its (successful) attempts to protect islands held by the Chinese Nationalists from attack by the People's Republic of China did involve consideration of nuclear weapons.

Ironically, the possession of nuclear weapons is one way of claiming the rights to prestige in the international system. In a prestige race, therefore, proliferation might become very attractive to nonnuclear states, as would having a sophisticated nuclear arsenal for the existing nuclear weapons states. On the other hand, arms control (especially bilateral measures) and negotiating the nuclear rules of the road are ways in which states recognize the power of others—they engage them in meaningful negotiations, thus acknowledging their status and the right to be consulted. The trick, however, is for those states traditionally accorded the status of a great or super power to be able to recognize the up-and-coming nuclear rival, and agree to readjust their thinking and patterns of behavior to accommodate the pretensions and interests of that rival. That can be hard to do in the best of circumstances (it is not easy to have to accept that one's national interests have to be scaled back in order to accommodate those of another); it is much more difficult when the rising state seems at odds with the traditional states in terms of, for instance, domestic political practices and ideology, or in terms of visions of how international relations should be organized. (These differences made it much more difficult for the United States to accord status to the rising Soviet Union after World War II.)

At the moment, there do not seem to be great pressures in the international system regarding reputation. Reputation conflicts often emerge when there is a dramatic rise in the power of one state that has been relatively low in the international pecking order. No rapid change in the global distribution of power seems imminent, and the one existing superpower, the United States, historically has been relatively restrained in the defense of its reputation. In the recent past, there was a thought that Japan might be the next global rival of the United States, and some authors hinted at a military conflict. The Asian financial crisis of the late 1990s and a booming American economy seemed to consign those predictions to the ashcan of history. To date, the western states have attempted to preserve Russia's status as a major power. The reputational disputes of the future are most likely to center on the United States, China, and an emerging European unity if they are to happen at all among the most powerful states. On the other hand, crises that involve reputations are more likely to be found in regional conflicts such as between India and Pakistan, or between the two Koreas, where both states tend to define their privileges in mirror terms: What the other expects, so too do we.

SUMMARY

The nuclear world is a dangerous world, if for no other reason than that the power of nuclear weapons is such that they can effectively obliterate life. But this is also a dangerous world because since their creation, leaders have actively considered using such weapons, constructed policies around the declared intention to use them under certain circumstances, and brandished them in confrontations with others. This is a dangerous world because other states or groups want—and some will continue to want—to join the nuclear club. And this is a dangerous world because as societies, we have had little practice with fitting nuclear weapons into peacetime diplomacy, and the experiences of dealing with nuclear crises are now just memories.

As long as there are sovereign states and as long as people define themselves as members of a particular group or nation distinct from others, there will be conflicts. State sovereignty and group or national identity are our current condition, and will be with us for some time into the future. Thus we must be prepared for conflicts in which one or both of the parties to the conflict are armed with nuclear weapons (or are making a concerted effort to acquire nuclear weapons).

Attempts to exercise some control over the nuclear future have taken a number of paths. As Chapters 4 and 5 pointed out, the emergence of a military doctrine of deterrence based on mutual assured destruction has become one form of control over nuclear weapons, as it builds on the premise that nuclear weapons exist not to be used. But such doctrinal controls cannot speak to the myriad ways in which the foreign interests and policies of states intersect and collide. For that, states seeking to prevent the use of nuclear weapons have sought more active or proactive means of control. They have devised rules of the road that at least point out how states are expected to act. They have created relatively binding commitments to control some aspects of their nuclear capabilities. They have generally endorsed the idea that nuclear weapons are to be, at some point, dispensed with.

But arms control and rules of the road and institutional arrangements do depend upon a willingness of states to abide by the agreements and norms that have been created. Granted, those norms and agreements will create pressures that will maintain some control over nuclear weapons in the future, and in that way, control is a self-fulfilling prophesy. But with more than two dozen states currently possessing or capable of possessing nuclear weapons, and with the shocks that emerge in world politics, and with the pressures that arise in domestic politics, there is no guarantee that across the next twenty-five years the current agreements regarding nuclear weapons, be they treaties or the unwritten norms of behavior, will hold.

A relatively optimistic view of the future would be that we will emerge from the next twenty-five years at the same point at which we are now at the end of the Cold War. That is, our future may be *Future 2*, with slight to no growth in the number of nuclear states and continuing pressures on the existing nuclear states to reduce their arsenals; a growing set of international agreements and informal understandings that constrain nuclear weapons behavior; and managed crises that, while they might involve nuclear threats, rarely come to the point of nuclear use. In Chapter 2 we speculated that the odds of some form of nuclear use are from .2 to .3 for the next twenty-five years. Conversely, the odds are much better that there will be *no* nuclear use—thus conforming to this relatively optimistic view. But there is the nagging worry. Our historical experience has been in a Cold War environment in which two superpowers confronted each other and, to one degree or another, had organized many of the powerful states in the world into two rival coalitions. Now we are in a different international environment and a new nuclear age. The risk of nuclear use is still there, and the forms of controlling the nuclear world are still young and relatively untested. Perhaps what we need now is the encouragement to rethink what we should be doing to exercise some control over our nuclear future. What might we do differently? How might we think differently? Those are the basic questions to which we now turn.

NOTES

1. William Safire, *Before the Fall: An Inside View of the Pre-Watergate White House* (Garden City, NY: Doubleday, 1975), p. 449.
2. Diary entry, Richard Nixon, *RN: The Memoirs of Richard Nixon* (New York: Grossett & Dunlap, 1978), p. 619.
3. Safire, *Before the Fall*, p. 449.
4. Nixon, *RN*, p. 615.
5. Safire, *Before the Fall*, p. 448.
6. Nixon, *RN*, p. 613.
7. John Mueller, *Retreat from Doomsday: The Obsolescence of Major War* (New York: Basic Books, 1989).
8. For general works, see Bruce Russett and Fred Chernoff, *Arms Control and the Arms Race* (San Francisco, CA: Freeman, 1985); and Duncan Clarke, *Politics of Arms Control* (New York: Free Press, 1979).
9. *United States Treaties and Other International Agreements*, Vol. 14, part 2, 1963 (Washington, D.C.: U. S. Government Printing Office, 1964), p. 1319.
10. Harry Truman, *Memoirs: Years of Trial and Hope* (New York: Signet, 1965), p. 25.
11. Arkady Shevchenko, *Breaking with Moscow* (New York: Knopf, 1985), pp. 86–92, 101–102.
12. For data on testing, see William Epstein, "A Critical Time for Nuclear Nonproliferation," *Scientific American* 253 (August 1985): 38.
13. For the text of the treaty, see *SIPRI Yearbook 1997* (Oxford, Eng.: Oxford University Press, 1997), pp. 414–431; the escape clause appears on p. 430.
14. Jonathan Weisman, "Who's Minding the Store," *The Bulletin of the Atomic Scientists* 53 (July/August 1997): 37.
15. For a review, see John Simpson, "The Nuclear Non-Proliferation Regime after the NPT Review and Extension Conference," *Stockholm International Peace Research Institute, SIPRI Yearbook 1996: Armaments, Disarmament, and International Security* (Oxford, Eng.: Oxford University Press, 1996), pp. 561–609.
16. Joseph Gallacher, "Article VII, The Treaty of Tlatelolco and Colonial Warfare in the 20th Century," *Arms Control* 5, no. 3 (1984): 75–76.
17. Ibid., p. 76.
18. Quebec Agreement, quoted in McGeorge Bundy, *Danger and Survival* (New York: Random House, 1988), p. 110.
19. The yearbooks of the Stockholm International Peace Research Institute (SIPRI) are excellent sources for tracking arms control agreements and implementation. We have drawn on Shannon Kile and Eric Arnett, "Nuclear Arms Control," *SIPRI Yearbook 1996* (Oxford, Eng.: Oxford University Press, 1996), pp. 611–655.
20. Appendix 11A, in *SIPRI Yearbook 1997* (Oxford, Eng.: Oxford University Press, 1997), pp. 394–401.
21. Tim Weiner, "U.S. and China Helped Pakistan Build Its Bomb," *New York Times*, June 1, 1998, p. A6.
22. B J Party president, Kushabhau Thakre, quoted in *New York Times*, May 12, 1998.
23. Bill Richardson, "Fallout from Russia's Woes," *Finger Lakes Times*, December 29, 1998, p. 9.
24. See Leon V. Sigal, *Disarming Strangers: Nuclear Diplomacy with North Korea* (Princeton, NJ: Princeton University Press, 1998).
25. United Nations Charter, Chapter 1, Article 2, sections 4, 3. United Nations, *Yearbook of the United Nations 1995*, Vol. 49 (The Hague: Martinus Nijhoff, 1995), p. 1525.
26. See Lawrence Freedman and Efraim Karsh, *The Gulf Conflict 1990–1991* (Princeton, NJ: Princeton University Press, 1993).

27. Harry Truman, Special Message to the Congress on Greece and Turkey, March 12, 1947; *Public Papers of the Presidents: Harry Truman 1947* (Washington, D.C.: United States Government Printing Office, 1963), pp. 176–177.
28. This is not to say that the United States accepted its own rule when it proved bothersome. In Cuba, for instance, Castro came to power in a popular revolution (ironically, supported by a number of American officials) and probably had the support of a majority of Cubans for years. Yet within two years of his accession to power, the United States was planning to wage a war of indirect aggression against his regime. Rule-makers often initially want to be able to drive anywhere they choose, while insisting that others keep to one side. In Chile, a Marxist, Salvador Allende, came to power in free elections; the Nixon administration could not accept the outcome and sought ways to topple him.
29. Agreement of May 29, 1972; *Public Papers of the Presidents: Richard Nixon 1972*, p. 633.

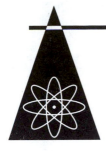

9

NUCLEAR WEAPONS
AND MORALITY

In December of 1994, the General Assembly of the United Nations requested that the International Court of Justice, also known as the World Court, issue a ruling on the question of whether "the threat or use of nuclear weapons in any circumstance [is] permitted under international law." On July 8, 1996, the court delivered its ruling. In that ruling, the court maintained "that the threat or use of nuclear weapons would generally be contrary to the rules of international law applicable in armed conflict, and in particular the principles and rules of humanitarian law." This was an historic opinion. For the first time an authoritative body had ruled that the possession of nuclear weapons merely for the sake of deterrence was generally contrary to the requirements of international law.

As a result of its view that the use and threatened use of nuclear weapons is generally illegal, the Court found that the nuclear nations have "an obligation to pursue in good faith and bring to a conclusion negotiations leading to nuclear disarmament in all its aspects under strict and effective international control."[1] The obligation of nuclear states to pursue nuclear disarmament need not be based on any treaty commitment they have individually made. It is inherent in their membership in the international community, in virtue of which they are bound by international law.

Law and morality have always been closely linked. Law often closely follows morality and is usually designed to give force to the important moral values of a community. The same is the case for international law. There are moral norms that are regarded as applying to the relationship among nations across the globe, expressing the moral values of the human community. These norms are the basis of much of international law. Thus, this World Court ruling has important implications for understanding how morality applies to nuclear weapons. The Court asserted that its ruling is based on "the principles and rules of humanitarian law," in particular, on one of "the cardinal principles contained in the texts constituting the fabric of humanitarian law [which] is aimed at the protection of the civilian population and civilian objects and establishes the distinction between combatants and non-combatants."[2] As we shall see, this principle of international humanitarian law is also one of the fundamental principles on which we must assess the morality of nuclear weapons.

264

But the Court's judgment that the use and threatened use of nuclear weapons are contrary to international law was not unqualified. The Court asserted:

> In view of the current state of international law, and of the elements of fact at its disposal, the Court cannot conclude definitively whether the threat or use of nuclear weapons would be lawful or unlawful in an extreme circumstance of self-defense, in which the very survival of a State would be at stake.[3]

In this qualification, the Court said that it could not determine whether or not nuclear threat or use under such extreme circumstances would be legally justified, which is different from asserting that it would be so justified. Nevertheless, this qualification is an important one, and it reflects a similar area of doubt in the moral assessment of nuclear weapons. This area of doubt in both the legal and the moral assessment of nuclear weapons is one of the most troubling and difficult features in the discussion of nuclear weapons. As Richard Falk puts it, the Court's conclusion "most accurately reflects the complex and contradictory mixture of normative elements including the tension between the logic of prohibiting all weaponry of mass destruction and the logic of self-defense."[4] The moral assessment, as well as the legal assessment, of nuclear weapons often leads to paradoxical results. Indeed, it gives rise to what we will call the paradox of nuclear weapons.

The morality of nuclear weapons has from time to time become an important part of the public debate over military policy. One such time was the mid-1980s, partly in response to an extraordinary document. In May 1983, the National Conference of Catholic Bishops issued their controversial and long-awaited pastoral letter on nuclear weapons, *The Challenge of Peace: God's Promise and Our Response*. The bishops had debated the issues through two earlier drafts and had heard expert testimony from a wide variety of witnesses, including high-level representatives of the administration of then-president Ronald Reagan. The letter focused on the morality of nuclear weapons policy, and, because of the attention it received, it introduced moral issues into the public debate about nuclear weapons to an extent unprecedented since 1945. The bishops asserted: "In the nuclear arsenals of the United States or the Soviet Union alone, there exists a capacity to do something no other age could imagine: We can threaten the entire planet." This is close to a passage from the World Court opinion, in which the Court asserts that nuclear weapons "have the potential to destroy all civilization and the entire ecosystem of the planet."[5] As a result of their potential to destroy the planet, the bishops continue: "Nuclear weapons ... raise new moral questions. No previously conceived moral position escapes the fundamental confrontation posed by contemporary nuclear strategy."[6]

In this chapter our attention shifts from the physical, military, and political realities of the nuclear predicament to its moral dimension.[7] As the bishops claim, nuclear weapons have raised new moral problems for our understanding of war. This must be counted as one of the changes that, as Einstein suggested, has yet to be fully reflected in our ways of thinking. The purpose of this chapter is to understand the nature of this change, Its purpose also is to consider whether or not the end of the Cold War has affected the moral issues raised by nuclear weapons.

Our world was altered forever on August 6, 1945, when the atomic bomb exploded on Hiroshima. This change was, in part, a moral change. Speaking of Hiroshima, Fred Cook asserted: "The ruthless employment of that power to obliterate 80,000 men, women and children in one blinding flash meant that all considerations of morality, all moral restraint, had now become archaic concepts." The bombing meant "that naked force had been enthroned over the world as never before."[8] Have nuclear weapons made morality obsolete, as Cook suggests? Do moral restraints no longer apply to war when nuclear weapons are involved? Is this the moral change that nuclear weapons have rendered? To answer these questions, we must consider, first, what morality has to say about war in general, and second, in the light of this, what special moral problems nuclear war and nuclear weapons pose. In this, we will be following the moral tradition appealed to by the Catholic bishops, known as just-war theory. But, third, we must also ask how things may have changed in the moral assessment of nuclear weapons with the end of the Cold War. The bishops wrote their pastoral letter at a time of high Cold War tension between the United States and the Soviet Union. Do the moral principles on which they based their conclusions still have the same implications in the very different international environment in which we now find ourselves?

MORALITY AND WAR

We have seen in earlier chapters the tremendous increase in destructive power introduced into war by nuclear weapons, from the actual destruction caused to Hiroshima and Nagasaki to the much greater destructive potential of present nuclear arsenals. We got a glimpse of what the world might be like if this potential were to be actualized in a nuclear war. The first question we must ask is: What does morality have to say about war?

There are three possible responses to this question. The first answer is that, due to the violence that war entails, all war is morally unacceptable. This is the position known as pacifism. Second, some people regard war as an inevitable and necessary feature of the international political order and view morality as irrelevant or inapplicable to war. This is the position known as realism. Third, a position between pacifism and realism is that some wars and some military activities are morally acceptable and others are not. This position is known historically as just-war theory.

Just-war theory differs from both pacifism and realism in that it makes moral distinctions *within* war. Pacifism regards all activity in war as morally unacceptable, while realism regards no activity in war as morally unacceptable, or simply makes no moral judgments of any kind about such activity. Thus neither of these positions distinguishes morally acceptable from morally unacceptable activities in war. But just-war theory does. Just-war theory is the approach to the morality of military matters traditional in Western culture.

Before we can examine the morality of war, however, we should briefly discuss morality itself. Morality concerns rules for the guidance of human actions, especially those actions involving our relations with other people. Morality prescribes how individuals and groups of individuals (such as nations) ought to behave. When individuals or groups act morally, they act in a way that takes account of the interests of others. If individuals or groups act from self-interest, the interests of others are not foremost in their consideration, and they are said to act prudentially rather than morally.

Morality and prudence sometimes provide conflicting guidance for our actions. For example, someone who finds lost money normally has a moral obligation to return it, if possible, even though keeping it would usually be in the finder's self-interest. Such conflict arises for nations as well. For example, while there have been strong moral objections expressed to the bombing of Hiroshima, the bombing is also said to have been in the self-interest of the United States because it saved the lives of American troops. Morality and prudence do not always conflict, but when they do, moral behavior will require sacrifice of self-interest. This becomes crucial when considering the actions of nations at war, where a great deal is at stake, perhaps even the nation's very survival. Nations could not be expected to behave morally if this would require a great sacrifice of self-interest, such as putting their very existence as a state at risk. As we shall see, just-war theory traditionally has not required such great sacrifice of national self-interest, but nuclear weapons seem to change this.

Another feature of the rules of morality is their claim to apply universally. This is especially important when considering the morality of war. War often involves a clash between people of different cultures, and different cultures can disagree about what is morally right or wrong. Because of this diversity of moral views, it may seem that morality is not universal, rather that it is relative to particular cultures. This would make talk about the morality of war often pointless. But the fact of cultural diversity does not show that morality is not universal. When people from different cultures argue about what is morally right or wrong, they appeal to universal moral principles in an attempt to persuade the others to adopt their own moral view. If morality were culturally relative rather than universal, then arguing about moral views would be as pointless as arguing about which flavor of ice cream tastes best. The preferences for different flavors of ice cream, unlike moral claims, are clearly a matter of cultural and individual taste.

Just-war theory seeks to provide a basis for judging the correctness of claims about the morality of war by appeal to universal moral standards. Because it argues for (that is, provides reasons for) the moral claims it makes, it treats morality as distinguishing between right and wrong, even in cases where cultures would differ on such claims. In any case, there is, as a matter of fact, nearly universal general agreement among the nations of the world about what conduct in war is right or wrong. Nearly all nations have expressed support for the international laws of war, the law that was appealed to by the World Court in its ruling about the legality of nuclear weapons. To say that nations have expressed support for these laws is, of course, not to say that they have consistently abided by them.

Returning to the question of what morality has to say about war, we should note an important difference between aggressive and defensive wars. If a war is morally justified, it must be a defensive war. The war fought by the Allies against Nazi Germany, for example, is a clear case of a morally justified war, in part, because it was a defensive war. The war by Nazi Germany against the Allies, being an act of aggression, was not morally justified. To help understand more clearly the moral basis for defensive wars, we will consider an analogous, small-scale use of violence: individual self-defense.

What is the morality of an individual's act of self-defense? The ordinary or "common-sense" view would seem to be this. First, it is morally acceptable to use violence self-defensively, only if there is no other way to stop the attack, such as by talking the attacker out of attacking or by calling for the aid of a nearby police officer. Second, it is not morally acceptable to use more violence than is needed to stop the attack. For example, if the person can stop the attack by temporarily disabling the attacker, it would be morally unacceptable to kill the attacker instead. Third, it is not morally acceptable to use significantly more violence in stopping the attack than the attacker threatens to inflict. In other words, defensive violence should be at most roughly in proportion to the violence it is seeking to avoid. For example, it would be morally unacceptable to shoot an attacker who threatened one with only a punch in the nose.

Finally, it is morally acceptable to use violence only against the person who is attacking, even if using violence against someone else would help to stop the attacker. For example, even if seriously injuring the attacker's child would stop the attack, this would be morally unacceptable, since the child is not responsible for the attack.

This discussion of individual self-defense brings out important points relevant to an understanding of national self-defense, which is at the heart of the morality of war. First, it indicates the three central questions of just-war theory.

- *Question 1*. When is it morally acceptable to use military violence?
- *Question 2*. How much military violence is it morally acceptable to use?
- *Question 3*. Against whom is it morally acceptable to use military violence?

Second, it suggests answers to these questions:

- *Answer 1*. It is morally acceptable to use military violence only for defensive purposes and only when there is no alternative method of stopping the aggression.
- *Answer 2*. It is morally acceptable to use military violence only to the extent needed to stop the aggression and only in an amount at most proportional to the violence the aggressor threatens to inflict.
- *Answer 3*. It is morally acceptable to use military violence only against those who are taking part in the aggression.

These are, in rough form, the answers to the three questions offered by just-war theory.

Just-war theory has its traditional source as a doctrine of Christian moral thinking, but in its development it has become increasingly secularized, so as to represent Western culture more generally. Through the spread of international law, which in large measure reflects the rules of just-war theory, it has come to be a universal expression of our understanding of the morality of war.

Just-war theory is often traced back to the early Christian theologian and philosopher Augustine. Augustine wrote after Christianity had been accepted by Rome, and he thus faced the question whether Christians should participate in wars in the defense of Rome. For Augustine, war is acceptable in Christian terms, if it is necessary to stop aggression against innocent persons. Here is Augustine's view, in the words of the Catholic bishops:

> Faced with the fact of attack on the innocent, the presumption that we do no harm, even to our enemy, yielded to the command of love understood as the need to restrain an enemy who would injure the innocent.[9]

We can draw from Augustine's view partial answers to Q1 and Q2. First, it is the defensive purposes of war that make it morally acceptable, as indicated in A1. Second, the amount of violence used should be only that necessary to restrain the aggression (that is, one should do the least harm possible), as indicated in A2. In addition, we see here the notion of the innocent person, which is central to just-war theory.

While the roots of just-war theory are religious, it has major secular components from the military and the legal spheres.[10] One of the military contributions to just-war theory, bearing on A3, is the idea of the honor of the military professional, which goes back to the days of knights and the chivalric code. It was the job of the knight to do battle against other knights, and so it would be unprofessional for a knight to attack anyone other than a knight. Today, the rules of just-war theory are often part of the codes of military honor officially acknowledged by the armed forces in many nations.[11] The legal contribution to just-war theory has come through the development of international law, where a major concern is to limit the violence of war. For example, the rules of war laid down by the Geneva Conventions have sought to define certain classes of persons (such as medical personnel) as noncombatants, that is, as not acceptable objects of attack. This is part of humanitarian law to which the World Court appealed in its ruling.

The moral rules of the just-war tradition are of two kinds.[12] First, there are rules concerning when it is morally acceptable for a nation to go to war. These rules, which address Q1, are known as rules of *jus ad bellum*, morality *of* war. It is morally acceptable to go to war, only if the following conditions are met. The war must have a just cause (e.g., to stop another nation's attack on innocent persons), and it must be fought with the intention of serving that cause. Going to war must be a last resort, all peaceful avenues for resolving the dispute having been exhausted. Both these points are included in A1. In addition, there must be a real chance of success, and the war must be declared by those with the legal authority to do so.

Second, there are rules concerning how much violence may be used in war and whom the violence may be directed against. These address Q2 and Q3, and are the rules of *jus in bello*, morality *in* war. Since these rules concern how a war should be fought, not whether it should be fought, they are the rules relevant to the moral acceptability of the use of nuclear weapons in war. The rules regarding how much violence may be used are based on what is called the *principle of proportionality*, and those regarding whom the violence may be directed against are based on what is called the *principle of discrimination*.

The principle of proportionality follows A2. The amount of violence employed in war should be the least necessary to achieve the just objective of the war (stopping aggression). In addition, the amount of violence should be at most proportionate to that objective. A minor aggression would not justify massive military force in response. Although "proportionality" may suggest mathematical exactitude, this is clearly a difficult moral principle to apply and cannot be based on precise calculations. The principle of proportionality applies both to the war as a whole and to individual battles or military actions within the war. The basic idea is this: The violence employed in war should not be gratuitous, nor should it be excessive in relation to the end the war seeks to achieve. An example of a policy that threatened violence not in accord with the principle of proportionality is the 1950s U.S. nuclear policy of massive retaliation, discussed in Chapter 4.

According to the principle of discrimination, violence should be employed in a way that discriminates between combatants and noncombatants. Specifically, violence is not to be directed against noncombatants, those not engaged in fighting the war. (This principle is sometimes known as the principle of noncombatant immunity.) A noncombatant should not be attacked, because he or she is *innocent* of involvement in the aggression that justifies the military response. This notion of innocence is central to the principle of discrimination. This principle follows the idea in A3 that defensive violence may be used only against the attacker or, more broadly, against those who are participating in or directly contributing to the aggression. This would include the enemy's military personnel and also, perhaps, those who are supplying the means of making war, such as munitions workers. But obviously many people in the society would be innocent of direct involvement in the aggression, and it would not be morally acceptable to attack them. A nation at war should not only minimize the number of persons it kills (following the principle of proportionality), but it should attempt to ensure that it does not kill certain kinds of persons (noncombatants) at all. The principle of discrimination explains why the bombing of Hiroshima was not morally acceptable even though it may have saved lives overall: Most of those killed were innocent noncombatants.

Two further points need to be made about the principle of discrimination. First, some critics of just-war theory have challenged the applicability of this principle on the grounds that in modern war there are no innocent persons, since the entire population is involved in support of the war effort. Defenders of just-war theory respond in this way. While it is true that in modern war a much higher percentage of the population may be involved than generally was the case prior to the introduction of mass citizen armies into war, it is simply false that there are no longer uninvolved persons.[13] For example, young children are surely innocent. There may be a legitimate question about precisely where to draw the line between the innocent and the noninnocent, but it cannot be doubted that there is a line to be drawn.

The second point is an important qualification of the principle of discrimination. If all killings of noncombatants were morally unacceptable, virtually all major military actions would be ruled out. Since few such actions can avoid the risk that noncombatants will be killed, very little use of military force would be allowed. But the principle of discrimination rules out only *intentional* killings of noncombatants. If a battle is planned so that attacks are directed only against combatants and efforts are made to minimize the number of others injured or killed, any noncombatant deaths occurring would not be intentional and the battle would be morally acceptable in terms of the principle of discrimination. (But these noncombatant deaths would still need to be considered in applying the principle of proportionality.) This shows the importance for just-war theory of judging an action in terms of its intention.

Since Augustine, just-war theory has witnessed profound changes in the ways of warfare. Two of the most important are the great nineteenth century revolutions in warfare discussed in Chapter 4, the introduction of the citizen soldier and the industrialization of war. One might expect these changes to have a major impact on the way military leaders would regard the rules of just-war theory. But consider the effect of the introduction of the citizen soldier. Prior to the French Republic's *levee en masse*, the principle of discrimination had the support of military thinkers because it was required by the professional code of the knight. With the passing of knighthood this rationale was lost. But another arose to take its place.[14] Military discipline became a serious problem with the citizen soldier, and to maintain it, soldiers had to be forbidden to engage in acts of plunder, and hence forbidden to attack noncombatants. In this way, military support for the principle of discrimination survived the introduction of the citizen soldier. The rules of just-war theory have remained relevant to military leaders despite the major changes in warfare, because the leaders continued to have reason to respect them, or at least have not found them to be an unacceptable restraint on their activity. To say that the rules of just-war theory remain relevant is to say that military leaders can in general adhere to the rules without sacrificing too much in the way of national self-interest. In other words, military policies respecting just-war principles have traditionally been not too greatly at variance with doing what is prudent for the nation.

This issue of the relevance of just-war theory raises the question of realism. Realism, as mentioned earlier, is the position that morality does not apply to war. Realism may be expressed by the cliche "all is fair" in war. The claim that all is fair in war implies that no action in war is morally unacceptable.[15] If nothing one could do in war is morally unacceptable, then morality places no limits on war. Realism was repudiated by the judgments against the Nazi leaders at the international war-crimes tribunal at Nuremberg. Despite this, realists argue that nations are different from individuals, in that the moral limits that apply to the actions of individuals do not apply to the actions of nations. Also, realists argue that because nations at war often ignore moral limits, moral limits do not apply in war.

The defender of just-war theory would respond to this as follows. The first of these arguments assumes that the differences between an individual and a state entail moral limits applying to one but not to the other. But the actions of nations are the actions of individuals done in the name of the state. So if moral limits apply to actions of individuals, they should apply to the actions of nations as well. The second argument assumes that if nations ignore the rules, the rules do not apply to them. This does not follow. If certain people consistently break the law, for example, the law still applies to them. Otherwise, we could not say that they had broken the law. One does not make moral rules inapplicable to one's actions by ignoring them, or it would be impossible to act immorally.

But realism remains a popular view. Its popularity is not hard to understand. First, many people view morality as an external imposition on the activity of war, that is, as an attempt by someone on the outside (the moralist) to interfere with the legitimate business of military leaders in protecting their nation. But this is a mistaken way to view the relation between war and morality. The moral rules of just-war theory are recognized, accepted, and generally practiced by military leaders. They are not an external imposition on the military.

The second explanation for the popularity of realism may be the belief that if a nation respects moral limits it will put itself at a great disadvantage in war, perhaps risking its very survival. As mentioned earlier, many believe that morality and prudence conflict sharply in war. But this belief is false to the extent that just-war theory is relevant. If military leaders do not view the rules of just-war theory as a significant restraint on the military activity they see as necessary for the defense of the nation, then respecting these rules would not put them at a great disadvantage in relation to their opponents. It follows that just-war theory is relevant and this argument for realism is mistaken. The same holds for the morality of individual self-defense: Respecting the moral limits would not normally place those under attack at a significant disadvantage in defending themselves. But the relevance of just-war theory in the past does not guarantee its continuing relevance in the face of the other major change in modern warfare, the industrialization of war and the advanced technology it has brought, especially nuclear weapons. We must now consider whether just-war theory remains relevant in the face of nuclear technology.

THE MORALITY OF NUCLEAR WAR

Would the use of nuclear weapons in war ever be consistent with the limits set by just-war theory? Would the use of nuclear weapons in war accord with the principles of discrimination and proportionality? We will consider first the principle of discrimination, and to do this we should recall the idea of total war discussed in Chapter 4.

Total war is war in which the opponent's whole society, not just its military forces, becomes a target for attack. Total war violates the principle of discrimination, for a society is composed in large measure of noncombatants. Advances in technology over the past century, especially the development of aerial bombing, have made total war possible. Aerial bombing allows a nation to attack the heartland and civilian economy of the opponent without having to defeat its army on the battlefield. In addition, aerial bombing has historically been much less accurate than artillery bombardment, increasing the likelihood that noncombatants would be killed.

World War II was total war even prior to Hiroshima. Great sections of German and Japanese cities such as Dresden, Hamburg, and Tokyo were deliberately destroyed with fire bombs. The principle of discrimination was disregarded, as John Ford argued in his 1944 essay critical of the Allied policy of bombing cities:

> For in practice, though one may adhere verbally to the distinction between innocent and guilty, the obliteration of great sections of cities, including whole districts of workers' residences, means the abandonment of this distinction as an effective moral norm.[16]

Ford argues that such bombing violates the principle (or abandons it "as an effective moral norm"), even if one tries to maintain the principle in a formal sense by claiming that the intention was the destruction of the economy supporting the military effort, not the killing of noncombatants.

The conclusion is that it is morally unacceptable for a nation to use its bombs in a way that kills large numbers of noncombatants. Instead, bombs must be used only against military targets, in a way that avoids killing a large number of noncombatants. Because nonnuclear bombs can be used in a discriminate way, by aiming them at places away from noncombatants, their use in war is sometimes morally acceptable.

But nuclear bombs are different. Using them even against military targets does not, in general, avoid killing large numbers of noncombatants. Nuclear explosions, unlike nonnuclear explosions, produce windborne radioactive debris (fallout), which can kill people at great distances from the site of the blast. As the World Court said in its ruling, the use of nuclear weapons "cannot be contained in either time or space."[17] This makes it likely that a large number of noncombatants will be killed, no matter where the weapon is aimed. This means, following Ford's observation, that virtually any use of nuclear weapons would involve the abandonment of the principle of discrimination. The claim that nuclear weapons can be used with a discriminate intention represents only a verbal adherence to the distinction between the innocent and the noninnocent. Any use of nuclear weapons would almost certainly be an indiscriminate use.[18] Thus, the principle of discrimination prohibits virtually all uses of nuclear weapons in war.

How does the use of nuclear weapons fare in terms of the principle of proportionality? Nuclear weapons are so destructive that their use in any numbers in a war would cause catastrophic harm. Such terrible destruction would be disproportionate to whatever goals the war was fought to achieve, including the halting of aggression. The U.S. Catholic bishops assert: "To destroy civilization as we know it by waging a total war as today it could be waged would be a monstrously disproportionate response to aggression on the part of any nation."[19] In the case of two nuclear nations, the destruction could, of course, be reciprocal, for the use of nuclear weapons by one side against the other could lead to retaliation in kind. In the resulting demise of the society that initiated the nuclear attack, whatever objective it had sought would obviously be lost. This is disproportionality of means to ends with a vengeance!

There are two objections that could be made to these arguments. Against the argument that use of nuclear weapons would violate the principle of discrimination, the objection would be that a nuclear weapon exploded in the air creates little fallout and that some more advanced nuclear weapons (such as the neutron bomb) are so "clean" (low in fallout) that the use of such weapons on an isolated military target would do little or no harm to innocent persons. Against the argument concerning proportionality, the objection would be that use of a low number of small nuclear weapons (such as tactical nuclear weapons) would not necessarily result in an amount of destruction disproportionate to the military objective sought. Thus, a nuclear war fought against military targets with a few nuclear weapons might not violate the principles of discrimination and proportionality. The assumption is, of course, that such a war could be kept limited, that escalation would not occur.

To be persuasive, these objections must show that there is a significant probability, not a mere possibility, that a nuclear war would remain sufficiently limited. If there is a serious risk of nuclear escalation from the use of a small number of nuclear weapons, then the harm to be expected is more than the principles can permit. Even those who believe that nuclear war between major nuclear powers might be kept limited, however, do not believe that we could ever be very certain in some particular case that it would be. Given the number of nuclear weapons that exist, there is a serious possibility that any use of nuclear weapons between major nuclear powers would escalate into a large-scale nuclear war. Thus, any use of a nuclear weapon between such nations risks more than just-war theory can allow.

One other potential consequence of nuclear war between major nuclear powers must be considered. A large-scale nuclear war would have serious nonlocal effects beyond fallout. For example, there is a real possibility that such a war would deplete the upper-atmospheric layer of ozone that protects the earth from the sun's ultra-violet radiation to such an extent that lethal levels of this energy might get through, or that it would raise so much smoke and dust into the atmosphere that the sun would be blotted out for months, leading to a devastating "nuclear winter."[20] This could conceivably lead to extinction of the human species—what Jonathan Schell calls "the second death."[21] The possibility of human extinction, or "omnicide," as it is sometimes called, puts nuclear war potentially in much more serious violation of the principle of proportionality. Human extinction would not only represent the greatest level of harm to those currently alive, but also destroy the possibility of future generations. Nuclear war would then not merely destroy much of human value; it would destroy everything of human value. This possibility shows, again, the unprecedented moral import of nuclear weapons.

The previous discussion, in particular the response to the two objections, has focused on the possibility of nuclear war between major nuclear powers, such as the United States and the former Soviet Union, where a large number of nuclear weapons could be used. But with the end of the Cold War, this kind of nuclear war seems less and less likely. Much more likely now are nuclear wars involving nuclear proliferators, wars between new nuclear powers, such as India and Pakistan. Such wars would be inevitably limited, limited not necessarily by restraint, but by the small number of nuclear weapons available to the combatants. If a nuclear war could be limited, even if only by the exhausting of the combatants' nuclear arsenals, then perhaps it would not violate the principles of discrimination and proportionality. This line of thinking suggests that there could be some nuclear wars that are morally acceptable.

But wars between nuclear proliferators would not be morally acceptable. Nuclear wars involving such states would almost certainly not be limited enough to be in accord with the principles of discrimination and proportionality. The reason is that new nuclear powers are unlikely to have the advanced technology to make small nuclear weapons and deliver them accurately. The weapons nuclear proliferators develop are likely to be large and crude, and these states will have no accurate means to deliver them. Any use of such weapons would almost certainly involve so much destruction as to violate the principles of discrimination and proportionality. By the time a nuclear proliferator develops small, accurately deliverable weapons, it very likely will have a large arsenal, and hence be a major nuclear power, whose use of a small weapon would seriously risk indiscriminate escalation. This course of nuclear development, in which the first weapons developed are large and inaccurate, is that followed by the United States and the former Soviet Union, and there is no reason to think, despite technological advances in the meantime, that the nuclear development of new nuclear states would be different.[22]

There is one other point to be made about the effects of the use of nuclear weapons by nuclear proliferators. While the small arsenals involved guarantee that only a few weapons would be used in a particular war, it is possible that such a war would lead to a relaxation of the restraints on the use of nuclear weapons by other powers, leading to future nuclear wars that themselves would be morally unacceptable. Thus, even if a nuclear war between new nuclear states could be limited enough to be morally acceptable, such a war would be morally unacceptable because it seriously risks bringing about, by example, other nuclear wars. In other words, a war between new nuclear states could not itself escalate to a large-scale nuclear war, due to their limited arsenals, but it could "escalate" to nuclear wars between other states. On the other hand, such a war could, as we have suggested elsewhere, have the opposite effect, hardening attitudes against nuclear use and making a larger nuclear war less likely. In any case, the chance that such a war could make a major nuclear war more likely provides another reason to regard nuclear wars involving new nuclear states as morally unacceptable.

The conclusion is that any use of nuclear weapons in war is morally unacceptable. The use of conventional (nonnuclear) weapons in war is sometimes morally acceptable, but the use of nuclear weapons is never so. Nuclear weapons are morally different. This seems to confirm Fred Cook's observation earlier in this chapter that, in the face of nuclear war, morality itself becomes an archaic concept. Because the use of nuclear weapons is never morally acceptable, nuclear war cannot be waged within moral limits. Morality is obsolete to those waging nuclear war, because it can provide no guidance for their actions. It can only tell them not to wage war at all. Just-war theory has, in effect, lost its intermediate position between realism and pacifism. As far as nuclear weapons are concerned, just-war theory joins hands with pacifism in finding moral grounds for ruling out war altogether. Thus, just-war theory implies "nuclear pacifism."

Just-war theory, then, seems to have lost its relevance, its usefulness as a guide to military leaders. Military leaders must now ignore just-war theory, or they cannot wage nuclear war at all. For the sake of the nation they are sworn to protect, if national self-interest requires the use of nuclear weapons, they must be willing to ignore the just-war rules. Thus, morality and national self-interest (or prudence) may be in deep conflict.

The apparent irrelevance of just-war theory has been brought about by the second of the revolutions in modern warfare, the industrialization of war. As the world has, over the past century, moved toward total war through the application of technological innovation to weapons, the relevance of just-war theory has been steadily eroding. But still the theory retained some hold, since the new weapons prior to 1945 did not make discriminate and proportionate war impossible, only less likely. Nuclear weapons finally make such war practically impossible, and thus are a fatal blow to the relevance of just-war theory. With this new level of destructiveness, no military goal can be achieved in a discriminate or proportionate manner, or achieved at all, insofar as nuclear war threatens an end to civilized life.

But we should not give up so easily on the relevance of morality in the nuclear age. For nuclear weapons have a use other than their use in war. After Nagasaki, they have been used, fortunately, not to wage war, but to deter war. By threatening nuclear war, the policy of nuclear deterrence seeks to ensure that there will not be a nuclear war. If just-war theory permits nuclear deterrence, which is the main military reason for having nuclear weapons, then it will continue to be relevant to military leaders. Thus the relevance of just-war theory in the nuclear age turns, finally, on whether nuclear deterrence is morally acceptable.

THE MORALITY OF NUCLEAR DETERRENCE

Nuclear deterrence seems, morally speaking, to be a totally different matter than nuclear war, for nuclear war would cause catastrophic destruction while nuclear deterrence, if it works, causes none at all. Nuclear deterrence is, moreover, designed largely to avoid nuclear war. For these reasons, nuclear deterrence seems to be a morally acceptable policy. Yet, the World Court in its ruling found both nuclear threat and nuclear use unacceptable. Nuclear deterrence is a subject of great moral controversy.

Nuclear deterrence is a policy by which a nation threatens to attack its opponent with nuclear weapons if the opponent engages in aggression. Different forms of nuclear deterrence policy are distinguished in part by the nature of the nuclear attack that is threatened and the kind of aggression to which a response is threatened. But all have in common the threat to use nuclear weapons. We must assume, further, that this threat involves a real intention to use the weapons, if aggression occurs, and is not a mere bluff. Sometimes, of course, threats are bluffs, but if a nation's threat to use nuclear weapons were a bluff, the risk would be too great that the opponent would discover it to be a bluff and would no longer be deterred. Credibility is crucial for an effective deterrence policy, and a policy of bluff would not be credible. Nuclear deterrence, therefore, involves an intention to use nuclear weapons. In the light of our conclusion that their use in war is morally unacceptable, the question becomes, is it morally acceptable to intend to do what would be morally unacceptable to do (that is, retaliate with nuclear weapons)?

For many contemporary thinkers in the just-war tradition, the answer to this question is clearly no. For example, one commentator argues:

> If an action is wrong no matter what the circumstances, it is wrong to intend to do it in any, no matter how carefully limited and specified, circumstances. If exploding nuclear weapons is morally wrong in any circumstances, it is morally wrong to intend exploding them in any, no matter how carefully circumscribed the conditions.[23]

If the exploding of nuclear weapons is morally unacceptable, the intention to explode them is as well. The importance given to intention in just-war theory is the basis of this line of argument. As we saw earlier, the intention to attack noncombatants is what violates the principle of discrimination. The theory holds that such an intention by itself, even in the absence of the act, is morally unacceptable. Accepting our earlier conclusion that it is morally unacceptable to use nuclear weapons in war, the conclusion that these thinkers are led to is that a policy of nuclear deterrence is morally unacceptable as well. In this view, because nuclear weapons are aimed at civilians, the threat to use them, not merely the use of them, is an act of terrorism. All nuclear states are terrorist states.[24] In contrast to this view, some thinkers in the just-war tradition have argued that nuclear deterrence is morally acceptable, but they usually do so on the basis of the claim, contrary to our earlier argument, that some uses of nuclear weapons in war are morally acceptable as well.[25]

But the U.S. Catholic bishops in their pastoral letter took a different line. The bishops appear to hold both that the use of nuclear weapons is morally unacceptable and that nuclear deterrence is morally acceptable.[26] They endorsed the basic just-war principle that "no *use* of nuclear weapons which would violate the principles of discrimination or proportionality may be *intended* in a strategy of deterrence."[27] At the same time they regarded the nuclear attack intended in U.S. policy of nuclear deterrence of the former Soviet Union to be at least "morally disproportionate."[28]

The bishops did not, however, draw the apparent conclusion that nuclear deterrence is morally unacceptable. They argued for "a strictly conditioned moral acceptance of nuclear deterrence."[29] The condition is that nuclear deterrence must not be seen as a permanent solution, but as an interim step on the way to disarmament. Their position is in some ways similar to, though more lenient than, that of the World Court in its 1996 ruling on nuclear weapons discussed earlier. Both the bishops and the Court found the threat to use nuclear weapons to be severely problematic from a moral or legal perspective, but both qualified this negative judgment, the Court by admitting that the threat might be legally justified in cases where a nation's survival was at stake, and the bishops by acknowledging that the threat was conditionally morally acceptable. Moreover, the condition that the bishops put on the moral acceptability of deterrence is a condition also endorsed by the Court, namely, that nuclear states had an obligation to pursue nuclear disarmament.

Critics of the bishops' letter have called attention to the apparent inconsistency between the strictures of their just-war position and their conditional acceptance of nuclear deterrence. Why were the bishops led to accept deterrence despite its seeming to be at odds with the just-war position? They were clearly impressed with what deterrence seems to be able to achieve. Following Pope John Paul II, they argued: "The moral duty today is to prevent nuclear war from ever occurring and to protect and preserve those key values of justice, freedom and independence which are necessary for personal dignity and national integrity."[30] Nuclear deterrence, they believed, is the only policy that can achieve this until alternative arrangements for keeping the peace are found. Apparently this made nuclear deterrence morally acceptable to the bishops despite their recognition that, contrary to the requirements of just-war theory, nuclear deterrence involves an intention to do what is morally unacceptable.

The bishops' position goes beyond what just-war theory should endorse. The bishops appear to place more emphasis on the results or consequences of a nuclear deterrence policy, consequences that bear on the interest of nations in their own survival, and less emphasis on the nature of deterrent intentions in relation to the principles of discrimination and proportionality. Several writers on the morality of nuclear deterrence have explicitly adopted this alternative moral view.[31] In the view of these writers (and perhaps the bishops), abandoning nuclear deterrence would have grave consequences in terms of national survival, and concern to avoid these consequences should override the just-war principles. Abandoning nuclear deterrence would open a nation to a nuclear attack or aggression through nuclear blackmail. Concern with this morally supersedes the concern about the intention to do what is morally unacceptable, emphasized by just-war theory. Their conclusion is that nuclear deterrence is acceptable, even if only conditionally.

Both the bishops' conclusion and the World Court ruling represent the paradoxical nature of nuclear weapons. The traditional moral perspective on military matters, as well as the closely connected legal traditions of international humanitarian law, seem clearly to condemn nuclear deterrence. But nuclear deterrence, as it was practiced in the Cold War by the superpowers, seemed uniquely able to avoid nuclear war, as well as nonnuclear aggression. When a nation is facing a military opponent armed with nuclear weapons, as the World Court's ruling suggests, nuclear deterrence seems to be a policy necessary for its very survival. Given the importance of survival, we could say that the apparent role of nuclear threats in achieving it makes the policy of nuclear deterrence necessary. At the same time, the moral unacceptability of nuclear threats in terms of the just-war principles of discrimination and proportionality seem to make nuclear deterrence morally impossible, something that is not morally acceptable under any conditions. This is the *paradox of nuclear weapons*: Nuclear deterrence seems at once both necessary and morally impossible, necessary in terms of national survival but nevertheless morally unacceptable in any form. The way in which the bishops and the Court qualified their moral and legal condemnation of nuclear deterrence is a recognition of this paradox.

This paradox arose for the first time with the advent of nuclear weapons. While just-war principles have ruled out a few other kinds of weapons (such as chemical weapons), there have been no other kinds of weapons whose use threatened the survival of other nations. Thus, only in the case of nuclear weapons does the conflict that is at the heart of the paradox arise. To say that the paradox exists for nuclear weapons is to say that just-war theory is irrelevant in the nuclear age. Thus the claim about nuclear weapons making just-war theory irrelevant is confirmed in the case of nuclear deterrence.

Has this paradox survived the end of the Cold War? Before we consider this question, we should note that there is reason to question the paradox, even in its Cold War context. The reason is not because nuclear deterrence is, despite the previous argument, morally acceptable. The paradox depends on two claims: that nuclear deterrence is morally unacceptable and that it is necessary for a nation's survival. It is the latter claim that can be questioned. The claim that nuclear deterrence may be necessary for a nation's survival depends on the assumption that nuclear deterrence *works*, that it succeeds in avoiding nuclear war as well as other forms of aggression. This assumption is open to challenge.

How well did nuclear deterrence work during the Cold War? This is a difficult question to answer. We might argue that deterrence worked well by pointing out that there was not a nuclear war, or any war, between the United States and the Soviet Union during the forty-five years of the Cold War. But there may be other factors that explain this absence of war. In other words, there might not have been a war even if the United States had not had a nuclear deterrent. If you point out to someone wearing elephant repellent in New York City that such measures are unnecessary since there are no elephants there, the response could be, "See how well it's working!" Just as we cannot conclude from the absence of elephants that the repellent worked, we cannot conclude from the absence of war that nuclear deterrence worked. The question whether nuclear deterrence deters war is somewhat like the controversial question whether capital punishment deters murder, except that in the case of capital punishment, there is a much greater amount of historical evidence on which to base an answer.

The question is one of risks and probabilities. There is no policy that would have made war between the superpowers impossible. The question is whether nuclear deterrence made war between them less likely than it otherwise would have been. There are some ways in which nuclear deterrence may have lessened the risk of war, such as by decreasing the likelihood of deliberate aggression by one superpower against the other, but there are also some ways in which nuclear deterrence may have increased the risk of war. It created the risk of accidental nuclear war and encouraged suspicion and mistrust, which may have increased the risk of war from miscalculation. The question whether nuclear deterrence works requires a balancing of these various considerations.

One important point to note is that the answer to the question of whether nuclear deterrence worked depends on whether deterrence could have been achieved without the nuclear threat, and this depends, in part, on how much deterrence was needed between the superpowers. A severe form of deterrence like nuclear deterrence might not be needed, and hence would not work, in a situation where little deterrence was needed. When the nation being threatened has little inclination to aggress against the threatener, conventional military deterrence might be enough to do the job very well. But if the nation being threatened has a strong tendency to engage in aggression, that form of deterrence might not work very well. For example, if motorists have little inclination to speed, a law stipulating only minor fines for speeding might work well, whereas, if motorists have a strong inclination to speed, much tougher penalties might be necessary. How much deterrence was needed in the relations between the United States and the Soviet Union? This is a controversial question, and much of the debate over Cold War nuclear weapons policy discussed earlier turns on the different perceptions of strategists about the answer. Some saw the Soviet Union as strongly inclined to aggression and needing a great deal of deterrence, while others saw it as only weakly inclined to aggression and not needing much to deter it. But, whatever amount of deterrence was needed between the Cold War superpowers, our situation going into the twenty-first century is quite different, and it is this we must now explore.

NUCLEAR ETHICS AFTER THE COLD WAR

The main impact of the end of the Cold War on nuclear ethics is that the paradox of nuclear weapons, as represented by the nuclear standoff between the United States and the Soviet Union, seems to have disappeared. At the same time, the problem of nuclear proliferation has increased greatly in importance. In this section, we consider whether the paradox has truly disappeared and discuss the moral issues raised by nuclear proliferation.

The paradox of nuclear weapons, as it existed during the Cold War, was that nuclear deterrence, though morally impossible (because it involved threats against innocent civilians), was necessary (because it reasonably seemed to be the only way available to each side to ensure its survival in the light of the threats of the other). The end of the Cold War has made nuclear deterrence between the superpowers no longer necessary. Because these nations are no longer military opponents, neither has to practice nuclear deterrence in order to protect itself from the other. Thus the paradox disappears for them. Nuclear deterrence remains morally unacceptable, but it is not now necessary for their survival. The disappearance of the paradox, however, may be only temporary. The United States and Russia could find themselves as military opponents again in the future. For example, some commentators argue that the 1998 expansion of NATO may bring extreme nationalists to power in Russia, setting the stage for a new cold war.

What does morality have to say about nuclear proliferation? There are two kinds of moral questions that nuclear proliferation raises. First, is proliferation itself morally acceptable? Is it morally acceptable for a nation without nuclear weapons to acquire them? Second, what is morally acceptable for one nation to do to attempt to stop another nation from acquiring nuclear weapons? The current nuclear powers (and some nonnuclear powers) have adopted policies seeking to halt nuclear proliferation. What are the moral limits of those antiproliferation policies?

If a nonnuclear nation acquires nuclear weapons, it may seek to use them against an opponent or to practice deterrence with them. We have already seen that the use of nuclear weapons is not morally acceptable, whether by a nuclear superpower or by a new nuclear proliferator. Thus it is not morally acceptable for a state to acquire nuclear weapons in order to use them. What about deterrence? The earlier argument applies here as well. Nuclear deterrence is not morally acceptable, whether by a nuclear superpower or a newly nuclear state, because it is morally wrong to threaten to do what it would be morally wrong to do. If it is morally wrong for any state to use nuclear weapons, as it is, it is morally wrong for any state to practice nuclear deterrence. Hence, it is morally wrong for any state to acquire nuclear weapons. Nuclear proliferation is not morally acceptable.

Notice an important implication of this argument. All nuclear states were at one time proliferators. If it is morally wrong for a nonnuclear state to acquire nuclear weapons, it is, by parity of reasoning, morally wrong, other things being equal, for a nuclear state to retain its nuclear weapons. Other things being equal, the moral obligation for nonacquisition of nuclear weapons on the part of nonnuclear states corresponds to a moral obligation for *deacquisition* of nuclear weapons on the part of nuclear states. This is also implied by the conclusion we arrived at earlier, namely, that it is not morally acceptable for the nuclear states to practice nuclear deterrence. If it is morally wrong for them to practice nuclear deterrence, then they have an obligation not to practice it, which means getting rid of the weapons.

But, this is where the paradox of nuclear weapons comes back in. During the Cold War, nuclear deterrence was seen as necessary for the survival of the superpowers. As a result, the moral obligation they had to abandon nuclear weapons was set against the apparent need to possess nuclear weapons for their own survival. But the same argument applies to many nuclear proliferators, actual or potential. Their national survival may be threatened by nuclear weapons already in the hands of opponents. Thus, the nuclear weapons program of Nazi Germany threatened the United States, U.S. nuclear weapons threatened the Soviet Union, Soviet bombs threatened China, Chinese bombs threatened India, and Indian bombs threatened Pakistan. So, the paradox applies to new nuclear proliferators as well, and their obligation not to acquire nuclear weapons is set against the apparent risk to their survival if they do not.

Let us turn now to the question of what moral limits there are on antiproliferation policies. What is one nation morally permitted to do to stop another nation from acquiring nuclear weapons? One central moral issue, discussed in Chapter 7, is that of discriminatory treatment. If a nuclear state seeks to stop a nonnuclear state from acquiring nuclear weapons, it looks like the nuclear state is guilty of discriminatory treatment, in the sense that it seeks to deny the other state a privilege (the possession of nuclear weapons) that it refuses to deny itself. If the nuclear states are entitled to nuclear weapons, why not the nonnuclear states? Conversely, if the nonnuclear states are not entitled to nuclear weapons, the same should be the case for the nuclear states. The argument is that a world in which some nations are allowed to have nuclear weapons and some are not is a world in which the nuclear "haves" engage in discriminatory treatment of the nuclear "have-nots."

Indian leaders and academics have often made this argument, that the nonproliferation regime is discriminatory against the nuclear have-nots. India has given this as one of its reasons for refusing to sign the Nuclear Non-Proliferation Treaty.[32] India has also used this argument to justify its 1998 series of nuclear tests. In fact, the perceived discriminatory treatment explains an apparent inconsistency in India's pronouncements regarding nuclear weapons. India has long argued that the nuclear powers should disarm themselves of nuclear weapons, while asserting its own right to develop nuclear weapons. This seems like a contradiction, but it may not be. Both of these recommendations (that the nuclear powers should disarm and that India has the right to acquire nuclear weapons) are ways of avoiding the discriminatory situation: Either no nation should have nuclear weapons or every state should have the right to acquire them.

In any case, the discriminatory treatment argument implies that it is morally unacceptable for a nuclear nation to seek to stop a nonnuclear nation from acquiring nuclear weapons. But we have to be more careful about how this argument applies. Recall from the discussion in Chapter 7 that there are three kinds of antiproliferation policy: coercion, denial, and cooperation. In seeking to stop another nation from acquiring nuclear weapons, one nation can either *coerce* the other not to acquire nuclear weapons (e.g., through force or threat of force), *deny* the other some knowledge or material necessary for building a bomb, or seek to acquire the other nation's *cooperation* in not proliferating. The discriminatory treatment argument seems clearly to apply if the nuclear nation is using coercion and denial to stop proliferation, for then it is seeking to stop the other from acquiring nuclear weapons. But it seems not to apply if the nuclear nation's antiproliferation policy is cooperative, for then the potential proliferator is voluntarily refraining from acquiring nuclear weapons. From a moral perspective, a concern for discriminatory treatment seems to rule out coercion and denial as acceptable forms of antiproliferation policy. So, to the objections to these forms of policy discussed in Chapter 7, we can now add this moral objection. The conclusion is that the only form of antiproliferation policy likely to be morally acceptable is a cooperative one.

The most promising kind of cooperative antiproliferation policy is international treaties or agreements, especially the Nuclear Non-Proliferation Treaty (NPT). Here we discuss the NPT from a moral perspective. If the nonnuclear nations agree in signing the NPT not to acquire nuclear weapons, it is not a case of discriminatory treatment to hold them to that agreement.[33] But just as the nonnuclear signatories of the NPT should be held to their legal obligations under that treaty, so should the nuclear signatories. The nuclear nations, under Article VI of the treaty, agreed "to pursue negotiations in good faith on effective measures relating to cessation of the nuclear arms race at an early date and to nuclear disarmament."[34] They have not lived up to their commitments under the treaty. Nuclear disarmament is a goal of the nuclear nations in name only; they give every indication of expecting to hang on to their nuclear weapons indefinitely. Thus, the NPT has become discriminatory in the way it is applied. The nuclear nations are using the treaty as a means to keep others from acquiring nuclear weapons while hanging onto their own. If states are regarded as *legal* equals in international relations, then it is wrong for some of them not to be allowed to practice a form of military defense (such as nuclear deterrence) that others are allowed to practice. If the nuclear states use force or other forms of coercion to keep a nonnuclear state nonnuclear, then they are treating that state unfairly.

The conclusion is that the antiproliferation policies currently practiced by the nuclear nations, whether based on coercion, denial, or cooperation, are instances of discriminatory treatment and, therefore, morally unacceptable. The only way for the nuclear nations to pursue an antiproliferation policy that did not involve such treatment would be for them to adhere to their commitments under Article VI of the NPT and vigorously pursue nuclear disarmament. As we discussed in Chapter 7, this could be accomplished by efforts to establish a nonnuclear norm, that is, a general expectation that no nation would ever use or threaten the use of nuclear weapons against another nation.

This moral requirement of antiproliferation policy, that the nuclear nations seek to halt proliferation by seriously pursuing their own disarmament, is, as it turns out, identical with the moral obligation they have in regard to their own nuclear weapons apart from their antiproliferation policies. Moreover, now that the end of the Cold War has at least temporarily ended the paradox of nuclear weapons for the main nuclear powers, their moral obligations are not contradicted by their requirements for survival. In fulfillment of their moral obligations, the two principal nuclear nations, the United States and Russia, should lead an international effort toward global nuclear disarmament. By doing so, they can allow the other nuclear nations to disarm as well by removing the paradox of nuclear weapons as it affects them and thereby create a different, more positive and hopeful third nuclear age. If all nuclear nations together disarm themselves of nuclear weapons, no one of them would have its survival at risk from nuclear weapons in the hands of an opponent.

Of course, there are no guarantees that disarmament would last. After all nations had disarmed, nuclear weapons might be reintroduced by one nation or another, in which case the paradox of nuclear weapons might reemerge and prudence might dictate that other nations rearm as well. The fact that the paradox, even when absent, can always return is another way of describing the nuclear predicament. In the second nuclear age and in the third, the predicament will be with us as it was in the first. The hope, as we discuss in Chapter 11, is that once nations have disarmed, they could strengthen international relations so as to make the possibility of rearmament less and less likely.

The argument for abandoning nuclear deterrence is now much stronger than it was during the Cold War. Even if nuclear deterrence has worked in the past, in the sense that it avoided a war between the United States and the Soviet Union that otherwise would have occurred, it now may no longer be needed, just as speeding laws would no longer be needed if motorists become disinclined to speed. But, while there may be little harm in leaving speeding laws on the books when they are no longer needed, there may be a great deal of harm, in terms of the risk of their accidental use, in leaving nuclear weapons in place when they are no longer needed. Moreover, if the paradox of nuclear weapons returns for the major nuclear nations in the future, due to the emergence of a new Cold War, the chance we now have for nuclear disarmament will have been lost. There is now a window of opportunity to accomplish disarmament, though it may be a narrow one. The moral imperative for the nuclear nations beyond the Cold War is to move with all deliberate speed beyond nuclear deterrence. The practicality of nuclear disarmament is an issue we take up in Chapter 11.

SUMMARY

Just-war theory is the traditional approach to the morality of military matters, but this theory has been seriously undermined in the nuclear age. While this theory has previously allowed a significant range of military activity, as far as nuclear weapons go, it allows none. According to the theory, not only is nuclear war morally unacceptable, but so is nuclear deterrence. In the moral realm, nuclear weapons have changed everything except our way of thinking: We continue to assume nuclear weapons are legitimate military implements, when in terms of the traditions of military morality they are not. Nuclear weapons have made traditional military morality obsolete and irrelevant. In the words of Michael Walzer:

> Nuclear weapons explode the theory of just-war. They are the first of mankind's technological innovations that are simply not encompassable within the familiar moral world.[35]

The traditional relevance of just-war theory in the prenuclear era lay in the fact that it maintained an intermediate position between realism and pacifism. The advent of nuclear weapons has caused it to lose this middle position. As far as nuclear weapons are concerned, just-war theory has joined ranks with pacifism in prohibiting the use of military force, even for deterrence. This represents a sharp break between morality and prudence, a break represented by the paradox of nuclear weapons.

Military leaders see as their purpose to protect their nation's interests, that is, to act in the prudential interest of the nation, using whatever military means are at hand. Any moral theory that precludes the use of the military means at hand when a nation's survival is at stake, as just-war theory does in the case of nuclear weapons, will be ignored and treated as irrelevant. Military leaders now seem forced to choose between morality and prudence, and they will choose prudence. In the prenuclear era, the choice between morality and prudence was not generally forced, because just-war theory allowed the use of military force. Military leaders could carry out their prudential task while satisfying moral requirements, even though they often ignored these requirements. This profound reordering of the relation between force and moral right is another way in which nuclear weapons have fundamentally changed our world.

The end of the Cold War has pushed the paradox into the background for the superpowers. But the paradox of nuclear weapons may arise again for them, because they may again face each other as military opponents. The potential for the paradox is inherent in the existence of nuclear weapons, and these weapons cannot be disinvented. Moreover, even now the paradox is actual, not merely potential, for other states, and some of these states have become or may soon become the next generation of nuclear proliferators. The moral imperative of our time, while the old nuclear powers are not at the moment facing the paradox, is for these powers, especially the United States, to lead the world toward ending the need to practice nuclear deterrence. In Chapter 11, we consider how this might be done.

In the next chapter we discuss the impact that nuclear weapons have had on contemporary society and culture. Because we live in a democracy, we are at least partly responsible for governmental policies. If U.S. nuclear weapons policy is at odds with what morality requires, we share in the responsibility for this. The choices our society faces are not just choices for military and political leaders, but for all of us. Each of us must choose how to act in the face of the moral implications of the nuclear predicament. Citizens of the nuclear nations are the agents of the predicament as well as its victims. Working toward its solution is incumbent on us all. What are the social and cultural implications of this shared responsibility? The next chapter explores what effects our general failure or unwillingness to recognize this responsibility has had on our society and culture. In Chapter 11, we ask what we should do.

NOTES

1. The quotations in these two paragraphs are taken from Mike Moore, "World Court Says Mostly No to Nuclear Weapons"; and Peter Weiss, "And Now, Abolition," both in *The Bulletin of the Atomic Scientists* (September/October 1996): 39, 41, 43.
2. Quoted in Moore, "World Court," p. 41.
3. Ibid., p. 41.
4. Richard Falk, "Nuclear Weapons, International Law and the World Court: A Historic Encounter," *The American Journal of International Law* 91 (1997): 70.
5. Quoted in Moore, "World Court," p. 41.
6. The passages in this paragraph from the Catholic Bishops are in U.S. Catholic Bishops, *The Challenge of Peace* (Washington, D.C.: U.S. Catholic Conference, 1983), p. 39.
7. A number of important books discussing morality and nuclear weapons appeared in the 1980s. Among these are: Douglas Lackey, *Moral Principles and Nuclear Weapons* (Totowa, NJ: Rowman & Allenheld, 1984); Douglas MacLean, ed., *The Security Gamble* (Totowa, NJ: Rowman & Allenheld, 1984); Russell Hardin et al., eds., *Nuclear Deterrence—Ethics and Strategy* (Chicago, IL: University of Chicago Press, 1985); Michael Fox and Leo Groarke, eds., *Nuclear War—Philosophical Perspectives* (New York: Peter Lang, 1985); Avner Cohen and Steven Lee, eds., *Nuclear Weapons and the Future of Humanity* (Totowa, NJ: Rowman and Allanheld, 1986); James Child, *Nuclear War—the Moral Dimension* (New Brunswick, NJ: Transaction Books, 1986); Joseph Nye, *Nuclear Ethics* (New York: Free Press, 1986); and John Finnis, Joseph Boyle, and Germain Grisez, *Nuclear Deterrence, Morality and Realism* (Oxford: Oxford University Press, 1987). See also, Steven Lee, *Morality, Prudence, and Nuclear Weapons* (Cambridge: Cambridge University Press, 1993).
8. Fred J. Cook, "The Enthronement of Naked Force," in *The Atomic Bomb: The Great Decision*, ed. Paul Baker (New York: Holt, Rinehart, and Winston, 1968), p. 75.
9. Bishops, *Challenge of Peace*, p. 26.
10. For a brief discussion of these two influences, see James Turner Johnson, *Can Modern War Be Just?* (New Haven, CT: Yale University Press, 1984), pp. 5–7.
11. For example, some of the rules are contained in the U.S. Department of the Army, *The Law of Land Warfare*, Field Manual (FM) 27-10 (July 1956).
12. For a discussion of *jus ad bellum* and *jus in bello*, see U.S. Catholic Bishops, *Challenge of Peace*, pp. 26–34; and William O'Brien, *The Conduct of Just and Limited War* (New York: Praeger, 1981), pp. 13–70.

13. For an excellent argument to this effect, see John C. Ford, "The Morality of Obliteration Bombing," in *War and Morality*, ed. Richard Wasserstrom (Belmont, CA: Wadsworth, 1970), pp. 15–41.

14. James Turner Johnson, *Just War Tradition and the Restraint of War* (Princeton, NJ: Princeton University Press, 1981), pp. 188–189.

15. For a valuable discussion of realism, see Richard Wasserstrom, "On the Morality of War: A Preliminary Inquiry," in *War and Morality*, ed. Richard Wasserstrom, pp. 78–85.

16. Ford, "Morality of Obliteration Bombing," p. 39.

17. Quoted in Moore, "World Court," p. 41.

18. This is a controversial claim. For an argument that nuclear war could satisfy the principle of discrimination, see Paul Ramsey, *The Just War* (New York: Scribner and Sons, 1968).

19. U.S. Catholic Bishops, *Challenge of Peace*, p. 33.

20. See Paul Ehrlich et al., *The Cold and the Dark* (New York: Norton, 1984).

21. Jonathan Schell, *The Fate of the Earth* (New York: Avon Books, 1982), section II.

22. Israel may pose an exception to this claim, given reports that have filtered out about the nature of its nuclear arsenal.

23. R. A. Markus, "Conscience and Deterrence," in *Nuclear Weapons: A Catholic Response*, ed. Walter Stein (New York: Sheed and Ward, 1961), pp. 71–72.

24. Thomas Schelling, *Choice and Consequence* (Cambridge, MA: Harvard University Press), p. 315.

25. For example, see Ramsey, *Just War*.

26. Bishops, *Challenge of Peace*, pp. 46–62.

27. Ibid., p. iii.

28. Ibid., p. 58.

29. Ibid., p. 58.

30. Ibid., p. 55. For an excellent critical discussion of the bishops' letter, see Susan Okin, "Taking the Bishops Seriously," *World Politics* 36, no. 4 (summer 1984): 527–554.

31. See, for example, Michael Walzer, *Just and Unjust Wars* (New York: Basic Books, 1977), Chap. 17; and Gregory Kavka, "Some Paradoxes of Nuclear Deterrence," *Journal of Philosophy* 75 (1978): 285–302.

32. See, for example, K. Subrahmanyam, "Regional Conflicts and Nuclear Fears," in *The Nuclear Arms Race Debated*, ed. Herbert Levine and David Carlton (New York: McGraw-Hill, 1986).

33. Of course, if the nuclear states have applied coercion to get some nonnuclear states to sign the NPT, this argument would not apply to those nonnuclear states. On the issue of the moral status of the discriminatory treatment, see the discussion of Joseph Nye's argument in Chapter 7, at the text around note 65.

34. www.acda.gov/treaties/npt1.htm

35. Michael Walzer, *Just and Unjust Wars* (New York: Basic Books, 1977), p. 282.

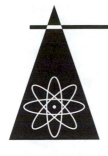

10

LIVING IN THE NUCLEAR AGE: THE SOCIAL AND CULTURAL IMPACT OF NUCLEAR WEAPONS

Hiroshima is a watershed event that has permanently altered our scientific, technological, political, and military landscapes. It has not, however, been widely perceived to have had a comparable impact on our perceptions of self, reality, history, future, and faith. This is not surprising, for often the more important a human event, the more its significance eludes us. Precisely because of its dimensions, the meaning of Hiroshima is difficult to penetrate. The awesome nature of the technology of destruction itself and the resulting psychic "numbing," has inhibited our ability to comprehend the transformations that have occurred. Human beings master new technical skills quickly but are slow to interpret the effect that new technologies have on their nature, their changing values, and their ways of thinking and behaving.

This is particularly true in the post-Cold War period. Since the fall of the Berlin Wall in 1989, we have almost managed to forget that this is the Nuclear Age, an age that had been characterized by apocalyptic anxiety. For most of the last five decades, the nightmare of a fiery end seemed real. Now the nuclear threat is precisely the one we find least prominent and difficult to comprehend. Nuclear weapons have been with us for so long, we don't really think about them anymore. But there is a danger in this. The more familiar they are, the less dangerous they seem, the less able we are to appreciate the horrific damage they can inflict and the impact they continue to have on society and politics.

It is difficult to recapture the sense of nuclear anxiety that ran through the years of nuclear brinksmanship. It might seem, in the light of the collapse of the Iron Curtain and the subsequent dismantling of the Soviet Union in December 1991, as if a new era of optimism has overtaken the nuclear fears of the Cold War. Indeed, there are genuinely hopeful possibilities in our new situation. However, as we have demonstrated, there are reasons to be cautious. We should not equate dramatic changes in the political configuration of the superpowers with the needed changes in the deep cultural and psychological structures of our world. Although the tension of the Cold War between Russia and the United States has eased, we should not forget that each possesses more than 10,000 nuclear warheads, often under less control than in the past. The danger of nuclear proliferation seems greater; the weapons may soon be in the hands of reckless leaders or terrorist groups. Since Nagasaki, nuclear weapons have never been used in a war, but they have nearly been used on a number of occasions, as we pointed out in earlier chapters. We can hardly put permanent faith in the mixture of restraint and good fortune that has prevailed. The events of recent years cannot yet be counted as genuinely utopian. We have to resist the tendency to believe that nothing needs fundamental changing. A closer examination of the situation has revealed that we still face dangers and that, in fact, we still are anxious about the dangers. The threat of nuclear destruction has receded in our imaginations, replaced by a less focused, less specific anxiety. We have traded one threat for a panoply of others. We now find ourselves afflicted by what existential philosophers call angst: the nonspecific worry, the pervasive fear of the ill-at-ease. And there are good reasons: Cities around the world are crumbling, dangerous gaps are opening up between rich and poor; population and consumption are growing without heed to the gradual and inevitable decline of nonrenewable resources. There may be a merging, therefore, of nuclear fear with fear of other serious threats, such as environmental destruction and global warming.

In any case, the threat of nuclear weapons can be an important warning that functions to draw our attention to the tribalistic and technobureaucratic patterns of dehumanization at work in our emerging postmodern world. By closing ourselves off from the human costs of the devastating weapons, by not thinking about them, we are more able to do the same in relation to other experiences of collective suffering (e.g., the 1990s genocides in Bosnia and Rwanda). The habit of denial, of numbing, becomes a way of coping with large human disasters, even if we are not primarily responsible for them. However altered in its expression, the fear of the future initiated by Hiroshima remains.

We therefore believe, with journalist Roger Rosenblatt, that even when the implications of the event are not obvious, "Hiroshima survives in the mind, which broods, denies, forgets and eventually must deal with what it saw.... What the people saw after Hiroshima was a fearful vision of the future."[1] It is in this spirit that the young French Algerian Albert Camus wrote a prescient essay in 1946: "We can sum it up in a single phrase: Mechanized civilization has just achieved the last degree of savagery.... Already it is hard enough to breathe in this tortured world. But now we are being offered a new form of anguish, which may well be final...."[2] Camus, like Einstein, understood something of history and something of the nature of the transformation created by Hiroshima. It is that vision and transformation we will be discussing later, in terms of the effect nuclear weapons have had on how Americans define their sense of self-worth and ability to control their own lives; their behavior in the social and political arenas; their willingness conceptually and politically to confront the nuclear dangers; and their relationship to such "ultimate" questions as death, immortality, and eschatological hopes for the future. As the journalist Robert Manoff commented: "Nuclear weapons have not and never will be an inert presence in American life. Merely by existing they have already set off chain reactions throughout American society and within every one of its institutions."[3]

At first glance, in the light of the physical and social destruction that would occur if nuclear weapons are ever used again, it seems trivial to concern ourselves with the effects of living under the shadow of the bomb. On second thought, however, a better understanding of how people cope with an unprecedented threat may bring us closer to the heart of the predicament, since it is people who design and build nuclear weapons, who plan strategies and doctrines for their use, and who will either live or die with them.[4]

NUCLEAR DENIAL

The point we would like to stress is the overriding significance, in varying degrees, for each generation after Hiroshima of this threat of historical extinction. Some have responded by being attracted to the weapons; still others, maybe the majority, suffer from an inability to properly confront and deal with their ubiquitous threat—a phenomenon that Robert Jay Lifton calls "psychic numbing." Daniel Lang observed in the *New Yorker* as early as 1946 that many Americans were coping with the atomic threat "by simply refusing to think about it."[5] People try to avoid facing the nuclear danger through several mechanisms. Some simply blot the idea from their consciousness in an extreme form of defensive avoidance. A significant percentage of patients informed that they have cancer, for example, refuse to accept this information as true. The simplest type of defensive avoidance is not exposing oneself to the threatening information—refusing to visit a doctor when one recognizes danger signs—choosing not to read or think about nuclear weapons. The presence of this behavioral tendency is supported by a 1963 public opinion poll that indicated that people who are most anxious about a nuclear holocaust are often the most badly informed about the weapons.[6]

Others practice displacement activities—they engage in endeavors that are far removed from the life-threatening situation. They immerse themselves in family, work, physical activity, and so on, thereby facilitating the repression of the very real danger that exists. Most people, in fact, simply go about their business as usual as if these weapons did not threaten life itself. However many nuclear weapons exist, however big, powerful and accurate they are, life goes on. A high-level intellectualization of this tendency may be deterrence theory itself and those who advocate its implementation in policy. Credible and potent deterrence as an end to the threat of nuclear war may, in fact, be partially a method to rationalize not thinking about nuclear weapons—a way to avoid or obscure their danger. Others take the position that precisely because nuclear weapons are so horrible, they never will be used, or they resign themselves to the belief that nothing can be done to significantly lessen the danger. Still others fall back on a reliance on history: No nuclear weapons have been used in war since 1945. Here history ironically conspires to inhibit the possibility of meaningfully confronting these weapons and recognizing them as fundamentally different from conventional ones. Because the weapons are so horrible and unreal and because, except for the survivors of Hiroshima and Nagasaki, no one has actually experienced the effects of a nuclear explosion and few have even witnessed one, nuclear weapons are particularly difficult to deal with.

THE DOMESTICATION OF NUCLEAR LANGUAGE

Consequently, we domesticate these weapons and we normalize them in the language that we use. Rather than speak about their deadly power, we render them trivial and benign. We have learned to live with the unthinkable and not to think about it. An expression, "to nuke," has become part of the English language. A popular computer game is entitled, "Duke Nukem." This tendency was explicit in the naming of the two atomic bombs dropped on Japan—the first, "Little Boy," suggesting an innocent little child, the second, "Fat Man," after Winston Churchill. Secretary of War Henry Stimson referred to the weapon in his diary as "the thing," "the dire," "the awful," or "the secret." At Los Alamos, the code name for the bomb was the "Gadget." The Pentagon's atomic-war plans in the early years after Hiroshima bore such code names as Pincher, Broiler, Grabber, and Sizzle. By sanitizing the language of nuclear weapons, we have etherized ourselves to their lethal implications.

Many have pointed to the anesthetizing quality of the language of nuclear weapons, often referred to as "nukespeak."[7] We need to recall here the power of language, that language affects thinking and meaning, and that meaning provides an interpretive frame for reality. Just as there are no uninterpreted facts, there is no unmanipulated language. And we are trapped by the very language that we use. Such words as superiority, inferiority, margin of safety, victory, defeat, and defense make sense when we speak about conventional weapons, but they may have little relevance in the nuclear world. The word "defense" is itself powerfully ironic. At almost the very moment in 1947 when the name of the War Department was changed to the Department of Defense, America lost the capacity to truly defend itself. Today, when there are still thousands of nuclear weapons in the world, it is questionable whether they defend in the traditional sense, in the sense of warding off danger.[8] Yet we use such beguiling metaphors as "nuclear shields," and many people still advocate for missile "defense" systems. Since our perception of reality is largely shaped by the language we use to describe it, using the language of conventional weapons creates the false impression that nuclear weapons are simply bigger and therefore better than conventional ones.

In nukespeak, we find terms like nuclear yield, peacekeeper, surgical strike, city busting, escalation dominance, hardware, delivery systems, reentry vehicles, buses, window of vulnerability, and window of opportunity.[9] Suffering is rendered invisible by sterile words like "megadeaths"; nuclear war is called a "nuclear exchange." Bombs are called "thermonuclear devices." The neutron bomb is called an "enhanced radiation instrument." People are referred to as a nation's "values." Targeting them is referred to as "countervalue targeting." Deployment of weapons to kill people is called "defense." The euphemisms are either emptied of fear or are implicitly reassuring, referring to familiar activities and evoking images that suggest protection and stability, such as umbrella, window, and hardware. In them we find nothing about millions of people incinerated or vaporized, nothing about millions of corpses. Rather, the weapons come to seem ordinary and manageable. Thus the language used to describe them reinforces and contributes to our ability to repress the anxiety produced by the weapons.

People are psychologically resilient enough to come to terms with almost anything. But such adaptation is achieved at a price. The inner knowledge on the part of the post-Hiroshima generations that human beings are capable of initiating a nuclear holocaust creates an undercurrent of anxiety and an uncertainty about human continuity. "Our tragedy," William Faulkner said in his 1950 Nobel Prize address, "is a general and universal fear so long sustained by now that we can even bear it. There are no longer problems of the spirit. There is only the question: When will I be blown up?"[10] To lose the future means to lose the past as well and may be associated with the growing sense of profound historical dislocation—with the decline or disintegration of formerly vital symbols of stability and continuity associated with family, religion, community, and nation. As journalist and critic Dwight MacDonald commented: "Now that we confront the actual, scientific possibility of The End being written to human history and at a not so distant date, the concept of the future, so powerful an element in traditional ... thought, loses for us its validity."[11] Consequently, there has been a retreat among the "nuclear-haunted" generations to the narrowest sliver of the present, to the "illusory" protection of self-interest. On the surface, most people simply go about business as usual as if the threat of technological annihilation did not exist. However, if one probes deeper, one finds evidence that beneath the apathy and repression there resides a pervasive anxiety.[12]

Ever since Hiroshima, the bomb has been a presence and a factor in social, cultural, and intellectual life, even when people have attempted to accommodate themselves to it or to avoid it. In fact, in the years immediately after Hiroshima, the public seemed not to want to deal with the threat of the bomb directly and preferred instead to immerse itself in a culture that supplied numerous diversions and consumer pleasures. To the extent that popular culture dealt with the threat, it did so indirectly through the genre of science fiction films with titles like The *H-Man*, *The Blob*, *It*, and *Them*; the revival of *King Kong*; *The Invasion of the Body Snatchers*; dozens of English-dubbed movies produced in Japan about radioactive monsters from the deep; and Nevil Shute's 1957 best seller, *On the Beach*, subsequently made into a film. Sublimated nuclear warnings and fears were also present in other less popular films like *Killers from Space*, *The Beast from 20,000 Fathoms*, and *The Beginning of the End*. In more recent years there were films like the new version of *Godzilla*, *Broken Arrow*, *Peacemaker*, *Crimson Tide*, and even *Armageddon*, in which nuclear weapons were used to save the world from a meteor about to collide with the earth.

There was also a tendency to trivialize the bomb. Within days of the Hiroshima bombing, bars were selling "Atomic Cocktails," department stores were running "Atomic Sales," tasteless jokes were making the rounds concerning the Japanese suffering from "Atomic Ache," songs were being recorded with titles like "Atom Polka," and MGM was promoting an actress as "The Anatomic Bomb." In 1946 the General Mills Corporation offered an "Atomic 'Bomb' Ring" for 15 cents and a Kix cereal box top. Some 750,000 children ordered rings that year.[13]

Yet there were some more direct and serious confrontations. The 1950s were also the time of bomb shelters and "duck-and-cover" instructions to schoolchildren. Tom Lehrer was singing in 1958 "We Will All Go Together When We Go," and Robert Lowell was about to write "Fall 1961," a powerful poem about extinction in nuclear war. The major reaction of the era, however, was to look at the threat with a sidelong glance. People were too close to the initial shock of this horrendous technology of war to deal with it in any other way. As one cultural observer noted in those early years, attempts to make light of the bomb or to avoid serious consideration of its impact were caused by "paralyzing fear."[14]

In the 1960s and 1970s, however, individuals began reacting to the bomb in more explicit ways. The behavior of this particular post-Hiroshima generation was distinctive in ways that suggest roots in nuclear-induced anxieties. These decades, when many of those born in the late 1940s and 1950s reached maturity, were rebellious ones. People questioned authority and challenged sacred institutions and policies—be they related to government, foreign policy, universities, or civil rights. This kind of activity has a plausible connection to the nuclear fear and may in fact be in large part a logical reaction to it. It may be interpreted as a protest against the absurdity of annihilation by a generation devoid of assurance of living on eternally as a species and angry at the "establishment" for passing on this rather hopeless legacy.[15] The 1962 Port Huron Statement, the founding document of the New Left group Students for a Democratic Society (SDS), for example, reflected this sentiment. "Our work is guided by the sense that we may be the last generation in the experiment with living."[16]

Similarly, many members of this generation chose to turn their backs on their class interests and rejected materialism, the conventional family, organized religion, the accepted social and cultural mores of society, and preferred instead a more "natural" life in rural and urban communes, in the joys of vegetarianism and holistic healing, organic farming, and so on. More contemporary versions of this utopian tendency are found among "survivalist" groups who are preparing for the "event" so that they can somehow survive it, and among those who advocate space colonization as a method of ensuring biological survival. Those who "opt" out may be seeking survival in a return to nature, in mystical traditions, in a commitment to communalism, in a revival of nineteenth-century rugged individualism, or in space travel; but they all agree on the fundamental rejection of and desire to escape from the harsh realities of what appears to be a self-destructive world.[17] The mass suicide of dozens of "Heaven's Gate" followers in 1997 in California may have been an extreme example of this tendency.

Others were so deeply disturbed by the world they were about to inherit that they responded with cynicism and mockery. Some observers as early as 1945–1946 anticipated an era in the near future of hedonistic self-indulgence caused by nuclear-induced anxiety.[18] A striking pattern of behavior that emerged in the 1960s and 1970s, for example, was a dramatic rejection of the social and sexual mores of society. During those decades there was a great preoccupation with intensified forms of experience via drugs, sex, rock music, meditation, dance, religion, and even politics. During times of crisis and anxiety, people tend to gravitate toward physical and immediate pleasures.[19] Consequently, some form of hedonism may also be a plausible reaction to the threat of nuclear holocaust. When existence itself is threatened, people seek to do more with or to their bodies, to stretch the possibilities of human pleasure. The nuclear generation that came of age in the 1960s and 1970s had about it a sense of urgency, both to produce political and social change and to cram all the personal pleasure and experience possible into what might be a short lifetime.[20] A very large number of people regarded the future as so deeply terrible that it hardly warranted planning for and they preferred to concern themselves with more immediate, gratifying, and manageable pleasures. As one young person reflected: "It's terrifying to think that the world may not be here in a half-hour, but I'm still going to live for now." Or, as another remarked: "Sometimes when I think that there may be no future at all, I feel just like letting myself go. Why wait?"[21]

There are obviously other plausible explanations for this behavior: For example, student protests are a recurrent feature of social history. The unpopular Vietnam war and military draft were further inducements to political activism. Changes in sexual mores may have been as much due to advances in birth control technology as anything else. Attitudes toward work and career are affected by economic considerations and demographic realities. The levels of anxiety and apathy were intensified by the very size of the baby boom generation that faced stiff competition in an America of shrinking economic opportunities. Apathy and alienation may have been caused as much by the revelations concerning World War II death camps, the assassinations of the Kennedys and Martin Luther King, and Watergate as by the nuclear threat.[22]

Nevertheless, we maintain that one important factor contributing to the behavior of that generation was their nuclear-induced anxiety. As Erich Fromm has argued, one can appropriately speak of the nuclear generation as being composed of new types of persons who turn away from life and transform all life into objects, including themselves. "Sexuality becomes a technical skill"; love is equated with genital stimulation;

radio personalities promote the virtues of "good sex"; "joy, the expression of intense aliveness, is replaced by 'fun' or 'excitement'; and whatever love and tenderness man has is directed toward machines and gadgets. The world becomes a sum of lifeless artifacts," from artificial food to artificial hearts. Life has become technique.[23]

The complex psychological link between atomic destruction and Eros raises some interesting possibilities. The first postwar atomic test in 1946 in the Bikini atoll in the North Pacific led a French fashion designer to name his new revealing bathing suit the "bikini." Dr. Helen Caldicott has underscored the phallic symbolism of the bomb and missiles in terms of "missile envy." Elongated missiles, erupting and ejecting their warheads are phallic symbols. Even some of the names associated with these weapons are laden with psychosexual allusions; missile erector, thrust, deep penetration, soft laydown.[24] There may be a perverse identification with the bomb on the societal level, an anticipation of oblivion experienced as ecstasy, as a cosmic orgasm, related to the objectification of immediate and intense sensory pleasures on the individual level. Even our omnicidal weapons have become objects of psychosexual adoration. We see this nuclear high portrayed in the 1964 Stanley Kubrick film *Dr. Strangelove: Or, How I Learned to Stop Worrying and Love the Bomb*, in which a pilot straddles the bomb on its way to its target while uttering a wild Texas yodel.

If Fromm is correct, why is this the case? It may be because of the profound threat posed by nuclear weapons, the threat of meaninglessness, of an absurd mass death caused by a horribly nondiscriminating weapon. Long-term, substantial, and authentic commitments of an emotional and social nature are problematic risks under the best of circumstances; in an unstable, unpredictable world that may end, they carry such risks or show so few promises of dividends that many people find commitments and social conventions increasingly difficult to accept. They prefer to direct their libidinous energies to objects that can be manipulated, controlled, interchanged, and collected. In a world characterized by impermanence, people seem to revert to the false security and pleasure provided by "stuff," to the "haven" of the cluttered room.

They may also revert to self-inflicted pain. The phenomenon of extreme body decoration—the tattooing, piercing, scarring, and branding that borders on self-mutilation and that is increasingly popular in the 1990s, is itself an expression of uncertainty. Body piercing fashion has been marked by a kind of escalation, a sort of ring race. Highly visible contravention of the social rules reveal a new and more subtle lesson about cultural unease. In a strange way, these trends can be seen as attempts to get the body back, a way of coping with anxiety, an attempt at getting cultural insecurity under control. The decline of straightforward anxiety into this extreme anxiety is the movement of a culture that has lost faith in its promise of security. To decorate the physical body, especially in painful ways, is to reclaim its natural reality. The statement is simple: I exist; I am in pain; therefore I am material; I am alive. Here body mutilation, a self-conscious toying with primitiveness, is a political act. It marks a rejection of modernity, a rejection of the increasing meaninglessness of life. It is a symptom of the multilayered forms that anxiety about the future now often takes.[25]

This tendency to objectify pleasure and pain is depicted with great force in Dan DeLillo's panoramic 1997 novel, *Underworld*. In this 827-page work, DeLillo's wake for the Cold War, the discontinuity of American cultural life is primarily caused by nuclear weapons. Everything changed in 1945 when the power of the atom was unleashed, and fear was institutionalized five years later when the Soviet Union began to achieve rough parity. Cosmic might was now being wielded by mortal hands and by the state. The prologue of the novel is called "The Triumph of Death." In the end, the bombs did not go off and death didn't triumph. It just ruled the social and psychological landscape for fifty years. Nick Shay, the protagonist of the novel, works for a company called Waste Containment, a powerful and suggestive metaphor for life in the postnuclear age. We live with and must process, like Nick, the sludge, the excreta, the junk of the nuclear age. There is human waste that can be disposed of. But then there is nuclear waste that never goes away, that threatens our health, our existence. In the epilogue, Shay visits the Museum of Mishapens in Semipolatinsk, the test site of five hundred nuclear explosions. He sees fetuses preserved in Heinz pickle jars. "There is the two-headed specimen. There is the normal head that is located … perched on the right shoulder."[26] All our better feelings took a beating during these decades, according to DeLillo. An ambient mortal fear constrained us. Love, even parental love, got harder to do.

THE PSYCHOLOGICAL IMPACT OF NUCLEAR WEAPONS

There certainly are other causes contributing to this behavior, including the anomie pervasive in a sprawling, urbanized, technological society without the familiar supports provided by family, community, religion, and shared values. Yet the central anxiety derives from the sense that all forms of human connection are perhaps pointless because they are subject to a sudden, total end. The psychological consequences of this atmosphere of futurelessness are just beginning to reveal themselves. What are the implications for childhood development, personality formation, individual values, expectations, and self-projection? What are the effects on the family structure? What is the impact on cultural values and social mores?[27]

Studies have indicated "the ubiquitous presence of the bomb at some level of people's minds."[28] Michael Carey, a psychoanalytic researcher, conducted a research project in the early and mid-1970s to determine what impact the nuclear air-raid drills of the 1950s and other aspects of nuclear weapons had on people of his generation. He found that many of his subjects described a general feeling of death anxiety that manifested itself in frequent dreaming about nuclear catastrophe. Others described extended periods of avoidance or the feeling that nothing is permanent, that nothing can be depended on, that life is absurd,[29] as Bob Dylan mused in his 1963 song, "Talkin' World War III Blues."[30] Similarly, the 1980 Rock Music Sound Book listed over forty songs that have as their theme imminent nuclear disaster with titles like "So Long Mom," "We Will All Go Together When We Go," "Political Science," "The End," "Eve of Destruction," "Judgement Day," "A Hard Rain's Gonna Fall," "Waiting for the End of the World," and "I'm Scared."[31] Nuclear fear has been a prominent theme in the songs of rock groups like Van Halen, Iron Maiden and the Sex Pistols. After years of neglect, movies and television began in the 1980s to be drawn to the themes of how a nuclear conflict might begin (War Games), and its impact on specific communities ranging from Sheffield, England (Threads), to Kansas City (The Day After), to northern California (Testament).[32]

A 1982 Gallup Poll reported that some 47 percent of the respondents believed that nuclear war is likely within five years, and about half of those felt that they would not survive such a war.[33] Below the sense of fatalism and acceptance—it's going to happen anyway so why worry about it—that seems to characterize the response of so many

Americans is a deep-seated apprehension and numbing fear. In fact, growing up in a social environment that seems to tolerate and ignore the nuclear threat tends to foster those patterns of personality development that can lead to a sense of cynical resignation and apathy. The opposite of love is not hate, as writer Elie Wiesel has often reflected, it is indifference.

For children and adolescents, optimism about a livable future largely depends on the sense of security provided by the adult world. Eric Erikson has emphasized the importance for the child of gaining a sense of basic trust early in life. Without it, one's self-confidence and creativity can be damaged. Without this sense of security, the perception of the self as competent, as an active agent who can change reality, may be underdeveloped.[34]

Again, DeLillo in *Underworld*, has a schoolteacher in the 1950s (a nun) issue dog tags to her class. "Then Sister told them to place their dog tags out above their shirts and blouses so she could see them.... The tags were designed to help rescue workers identify children who were lost, missing, injured, maimed, mutilated, unconscious or dead in the hours following the onset of atomic war.... She said, 'Woe betide the child who is ... wearing someone else's tag'"[35] Nuclear war never happened during the Cold War, but a generation of children "ducked and covered" hoping to be shielded from the end of the world. Notwithstanding the absurdity of the exercise, they could not be shielded from the sense that life was not secure and that it was pervaded by an unknowable terror.

A study performed by a special task force of the American Psychiatric Association by Drs. John Mack and William Beardslee between 1978 and 1981 and similar studies conducted by the *Houston Post*, the *Boston Globe*, and other scholars demonstrated a consistent apprehension among children and adolescents, an alarm about what nuclear war might do to all of us.[36] What comes through is their sense of powerlessness, of the insecurity of life, but also an anger and frustration directed at the adult world that created this situation. Collectively, these young people indicate that the nuclear threat is too terrible to contemplate; when they do think about it they feel angry and helpless. They learn to cope either by living for the present, by persuading themselves that nuclear war will never happen, or that, if it does, they will be on the winning side, by putting hope in bomb shelters or missile defense initiatives and, probably, most of the time, by repressing the fear. Some representative comments are indicative of their feelings. An eleven-year-old girl commented: "I don't know, I feel there's a nuclear war going on inside me. It's terrible."[37] One seventeen-year-old young woman said: "As for a career, it seems like it is a waste to go to college and to build up a career and then get blown up someday."[38] Another said: "Mommy, I don't think I'll ever have a baby."[39] Finally a nine-year old remarked: "I sometimes think that I'd rather be dead because then I could go up to heaven and I wouldn't have to worry about all this stuff about nuclear war."[40]

The implications of such studies have become the subject of some disagreement. Robert Coles, a Harvard University child psychiatrist, believes that the children who were most affected by the nuclear threat tended to be from middle- and upperclass families whose parents are themselves involved in the nuclear freeze or disarmament movements. Working-class children, by and large, were not emotionally touched by this fear. Class, for Coles, seems to be a primary determinant in how children sort themselves out on the issue.[41] For the majority of American children, poverty and inequality seem to be more pressing concerns.

Obviously, the nuclear threat does not exist in a vacuum. It coexists with a wide range of other factors that affect psychological and emotional development. Yet, because of its extraordinary nature, it seems likely, and there is growing evidence to support the claim, that at least among large segments of the population, it has contributed to, if not substantially accounted for, much of what is psychologically troubling to many people on the societal level—feelings of dislocation, unidentified dangers, insecurity, aimlessness, and loneliness. The threat of nuclear war may be a possible contributor to the increase in family disruption, drug abuse, heightened loneliness, and despair, and behaviors such as body mutilation. Parental authority may be weakened since children sense that parents cannot fulfill their primary responsibility, that of providing security. Because the permanence of any relationship is thrown into question, the institution of the family itself may be threatened. There may be a greater reluctance to marry and to bring children into the world. There is also some evidence that the nuclear shadow has altered normal economic planning. Several studies have shown that the fear of nuclear war has diminished people's willingness to save for future use. The image of futurelessness may also be contributing to the high divorce rates and the decision of many people to avoid long-term commitments by living together. As writer and biologist Lewis Thomas reflected: "What I cannot imagine, what I cannot put up with ... is what it must be like to be young. How do the young stand it? How can they keep their sanity? If I were very young, sixteen or seventeen years old, I think I would begin perhaps very slowly and imperceptively to go crazy."[42]

THE BOMB AND THE CULTURAL IMAGINATION

Literature provides further evidence for the presence of a debilitating alienation felt by many in contemporary society. It is through literature and poetry and what might be called "high-cultural" reflections that people strive to express, often in new comparisons and metaphors, things beyond the sphere of easy perception and observation. This is especially true when language tries to lead to where our senses and our intellect find it hard to follow. Humans can speak only in metaphor of the infinite and the unfathomable. If people wish to describe the indescribable, they can often only do so by "poetry." Even science, when it reaches its deepest fundamentals, is forced to use the symbols and metaphors of "poetry." It is the intellectuals, writers, and poets among us who have the fine-tuned sensibilities to perceive and articulate what many of the rest of us are only beginning to feel and understand.

In E. L. Doctorow's novel, *The Book of Daniel*, these themes of alienation, despair, and meaninglessness are brilliantly explored. The novel is a thinly fictionalized version of the Ethel and Julius Rosenberg spy case of the late 1940s and early 1950s. The defendants and their two coconspirators were alleged to have been participants in a plot aimed at obtaining national defense information for the Soviet Union. But the crux of the matter was the accusation that the Rosenbergs had stolen the secrets of the atomic bomb and passed them on to the Soviet Union. From the moment of their arrests until their executions on June 19, 1953, in the electric chair at Sing Sing Prison, they proclaimed their innocence. They were the only Americans in U.S. history ever executed for espionage by judgment of a civil court. This was also the first double execution of a husband and wife in American history. The peculiarities and poignancy of the case have inspired not only numerous histories, but also poems, plays, novels, television documentaries, and a major motion picture based on Doctorow's powerful novel. It still speaks to us of great contemporary concerns: the abuse of secrecy by governmental agencies, the inability of national leaders to properly confront the realities of nuclear weaponry, and the hysteria of the Cold War years.

Doctorow incorporates the Rosenberg story into a larger family drama: that of a son searching to determine the truth about his parents and through this quest finally coming to terms with their values and legacy; and that of a daughter who is psychologically crushed by their fate, a victim of the hysteria created by the nuclear fear. Rage and meaninglessness are at the heart of *Daniel*, a book about children whose parents were convicted and executed for conspiracy to commit atomic espionage. The rage exists both on the personal level, since the two children obviously feel greatly aggrieved, and on a broader political plane. While the book avoids explicit evidence as to the guilt or innocence of the executed couple, it expresses enormous outrage over their fate. The double execution of the Rosenbergs that *The Book of Daniel* powerfully depicts cannot be understood outside of the context of Cold War hysteria, blacklisting, McCarthyism, Red-baiting, and anti-Semitism that characterized this period of American history. The political and psychological travail of the children serves as an analogue for an entire generation of post-Hiroshima youths searching for meaning within absurdity.

Meaninglessness and absurdity of different sorts have become almost stereotyped characterizations of twentieth-century life, central themes in modern art, politics, and theater. In what other age would Franz Kafka's haunting characters, unaware of place and identity, metamorphosized into grotesque, alienated insects, have been so celebrated? The possibility of nuclear holocaust makes us doubt that anything we create will last. We find examples of what Lifton calls the "new ephemeralism" in the literary works of Norman Mailer, the poetry of Alan Ginsberg, the novels of Günter Grass, Kurt Vonnegut, Ken Kesey, Thomas Pynchon, Joseph Heller, and William Burroughs—even the unlikely connection of a pseudo-kabbalistic mysticism and nuclear dread in a novel by Chaim Potok entitled *The Book of Lights*.[43] The theme of waste, particularly nuclear waste, provides the landscape for Delillo's *Underworld*, a novel of betrayal and innocence abused. Poets have applied themselves to the theme of living in the nuclear age perhaps more imaginatively and consistently than filmmakers and fiction writers. They can attempt to get at the meaning of nuclear weapons in a more creative, imagistic fashion. Many well-known poets such as Robert Penn Warren, Marc Kaminsky, Campbell McGrath, Philip Levine, and Denise Levertov have focused on the issue. McGrath in "Nagasaki, Uncle Walt, the Eschatology of America's Century," examined how the atomic bombings had affected his entire generation. He noted that young people had "invested so much in World War III it seems a shame to miss it."[44] In the visual arts, as Lifton has pointed out, "we find increasing acceleration in shifts in styles and movements ... from pop art ... to kinetic art, to minimalist, to conceptual art, to photorealism."[45] Furthermore, there are artists who directly grapple with the themes of destruction and impermanence. Some conceptual artists, like Peter Hutchinson, who placed works under water, designed art out of perishable materials that were meant to gradually disintegrate as if to underscore the ephemeral nature of contemporary civilization. In a world that could witness the destruction of a city in seconds or, in the view of some, could countenance the deterioration of traditional democratic freedoms in the United States during the Rosenberg case, and other episodes since, there are no permanent values, no permanent institutions.

DEATH AND DYING

Even the security or sense of purpose provided by the anticipation of a meaningful death has been seriously undermined. The prospect of nuclear war poses a basic challenge to what has been one of humanity's most universal problems—the attempt to come to terms with death and dying. Death is anticipated as a severance of connection—or severance from the inner sense of organic relationship to nature and particularly to the people most necessary to feelings of continuity and relatedness. Death therefore threatens to bring about that which is most intolerable: total severance, total nothingness.[46]

Existentialist philosopher Martin Heidegger and others have pointed out that people understand themselves largely in terms of the deaths they anticipate. If, for example, an individual is a devout theist who believes in reward and punishment and life after death, that person will understand and presumably live his or her life differently than an individual who is a committed secularist. Their philosophies of life are different because their views of death are different.[47]

Individual death is not the only death that affects the way people live. Since humans are social beings who define themselves naturally as parts of families, societies, kinship groups, religions, nations, and humanity as a whole, how they view themselves will depend largely on whether they anticipate the continuing existence of these social entities. In the prenuclear age, the individual obviously dies, but the social unit, the nation, the family, the species, was understood as outliving death.[48]

But in the nuclear age, we must anticipate nuclear death as a collective experience, what Norman Cousins called "irrational death"—death of a new kind, a nondiscriminating death without warning, death en masse. While all deaths are individual, in the mass deaths of the twentieth century, be they at Auschwitz or at Hiroshima and Nagasaki, the individual is lost in a faceless, mindless, random destruction. Writer Norman Mailer described the transformation as follows:

> For the first time in civilized history, perhaps for the first time in all history, we have been forced to live with the suppressed knowledge that the smallest facets of our personality or the most minor projections of our ideas … might be doomed to die as a cipher in some vast statistical operation in which our teeth would be counted, and our hair would be saved, but our death itself unknown, unhonored and unrewarded, a death which could not follow with dignity as a possible consequence to serious actions we have chosen, but rather a death in a gas chamber or a radioactive city; and so … in the midst of civilization … our psyche was subjected itself to the intolerable anxiety that death being causeless, life was causeless as well, and time deprived of cause and effect had come to a stop.[49]

If the type of death we anticipate is important because it affects how we view ourselves in the world, then the pervasive fear of nuclear annihilation does not necessarily tell us anything about death per se, but rather it reveals something about the perception humans have of their place and worth in the world.[50]

Nuclear weapons challenge a basic belief in the importance of the individual. They challenge possibly the most central tenet of the Judeo-Christian world view: Each individual is unique and important and created in the image of God. If you save one life it is like saving the entire world, the Talmud teaches. "God so loved the world that He gave His only begotten son," John says. Now, we are haunted with the image of human beings as objects, as matter, to be burned, radiated, turned into ashes or vapor. In the nuclear age, vaporization has replaced organic decay as the metaphor of death. When the bomb fell on Hiroshima, people not only witnessed a weapon of unprecedented destructive power; they saw one more proof of their insignificance. What meaning can one's individual life have when all human life might vanish at any time? We live in a world of "virile weapons and impotent men," the French historian Raymond Aron wrote in 1983, a world that has engendered feelings of powerlessness and profound meaninglessness; a world where humans find themselves severed from virtually all their notions of connection and worth, including their struggle to maintain symbolic paths to immortality. And this is not a trivial matter. The need for symbolic immortality, as psychiatrist Robert Jay Lifton has argued, seems to be basic to humans. It "… can be expressed biologically … by living on through one's community, nation, race, species; theologically, in the notion of life after death or in the spiritual conquest of death; creatively, through one's work, books, poems, paintings and influences large and small, that exist beyond one's death; or through identification with eternal, cyclical nature.…"[51] In each case, the individual contributes to something of value that survives him. Death is not the end.

Nuclear weapons, however, challenge these notions of symbolic immortality and connectedness because they threaten not only biological death but also ontological death, what Jonathan Schell refers to as the "second death"—a rendering into nothingness of that which constitutes the world and human relatedness to it, including memory, history, the sense of individuality, and belief in the inevitability of progress. Nuclear weapons, unlike all other weapons, even the incredibly destructive chemical and biological weapons, have the power to turn everything into nothing. In a nuclear war-ravaged world, as Schell has powerfully argued, we cannot imagine the survival of nations, culture, works, or innocence, and even the idea of an afterlife may not be sufficiently convincing to quell the anxieties of total severance.[52]

Joyce Maynard, in *Looking Back: A Chronicle of Growing Up in the Sixties*, wrote that "what especially alarmed me about the bomb … was the possibility of total obliteration. All traces of me would be destroyed. There would be no grave and if there were, no one left to visit it."[53] Woody Allen, whose humor is so obsessed with death, put it another way: "Eternal nothingness is O.K. as long as you are dressed for it." The devastation of nuclear war, of course, belies the notion that one can be ready and "dressed" for immortality. Yet, despite doubts, many are still inclined to want to believe in an afterlife. Again, Allen: "I don't believe in an afterlife, although I am bringing a change of underwear just in case."[54] A nuclear holocaust would make this hedging of one's theological bets quite ineffective. Even the immortality symbolized by nature, as Schell has argued, would be threatened by the destruction of a nuclear war. Writer Lewis Thomas expressed the pathos experienced by the fear of omnicide as follows: "I cannot listen to Mahler's Ninth Symphony with anything like the old melancholy mixed with high pleasure I used to take from the music. Now … I cannot listen to the last movement … without the door-smashing intrusion of a huge new thought: death everywhere, the dying of everything, the end of humanity.…"[55]

NUCLEARISM

Pathos, however, has not been the only response to this anticipation of the "death of death." Some have perversely identified with these weapons of mass destruction. Lifton refers to this phenomenon as "nuclearism," "the passionate embrace of nuclear weapons as a solution to [human] anxieties, especially anxieties concerning the weapons them-selves...."[56] The fact that nuclear death threatens the profound meaning of life itself may in part account for the attraction some feel for these weapons and their use, for this serves as a way of denying the very anxiety they experience. Most people fear death, and some deal with this fear by actually toying with death as a way of gaining power or control over their mortality. On a trivial level, video games enable players to vaporize planets and stars. A rock group calls itself the B-52s. The Grateful Dead until the death of its leader Jerry Garcia on August 9, 1995, the fiftieth anniversary of the Nagasaki bomb, remained a persistent cultural artifact of the 1960s.

This counterphobic mechanism may indeed also be operating in many of the sci-entists, engineers, nuclear planners, and theorists who make up the nuclear "priest-hood." They and all who are attracted to these weapons, in one of the ultimate human ironies, may seek in the technology of nuclear destruction a source of power, of life.[57] At the root of this tendency is the struggle to achieve power by controlling death. As anthropologist Ernest Becker argued in *The Denial of Death*, there is a tendency of want-ing to kill in order to affirm one's own life. By killing an enemy we have symbolically killed death, we have attempted to forestall our own deaths.[58] It may also have some-thing to do with the fetishizing and worship of technology that seems peculiar to recent times. Technology, the systematic study (*logos*) and exercise of skill (*teknai*), has been with us as long as we have used tools. We have not always believed, however, that we could destroy the world using the tools we have invented, or that we could usher in new forms of consciousness through the virtual realities of cyberspace we developed. Now our tools seem tools no longer. We do not use technology; it uses us, it stands over us, sometimes threatening, sometimes seductively beckoning.

There is nothing about nuclear necrophilia, however, that suggests deliberate evil. Those who are attracted to nuclear weapons and even nuclear war may be influenced by the powerful urge to avoid evil, to avoid anxiety, as Becker pointed out in *Escape from Evil*: "Men cause evil by wanting heroically to triumph over it, because man is a fright-ened animal ... who will not admit his own insignificance, that he cannot perpetuate himself and his group forever...."[59] So if we accept Lifton's concept of "nuclearism," and the notion that it has little to do with evil, then we may also have to accept that it is humanity's genius or character that propels it to the possible ultimate misfortune. As Erich Fromm argues in *On Disobedience* and *The Heart of Man*, "the fundamental choice for humans, inasmuch as they seek fulfillment, is to choose either acts of creation or acts of destruction, either to love or to kill." "Only part of us is sane," Rebecca West writes, "only part of us loves pleasure and the longer day of happiness, wants to live to our nineties and die in peace.... The other half of us is nearly mad. It ... loves pain and its darker night despair, and wants to die in a catastrophe that will set life back to its beginnings and leave nothing of our house save its blackened foundations."[60]

This life-denying tendency has also found expression among certain fundamentalist Christian groups who, in their literal reading of biblical imagery, equate nuclear holo-caust with Armageddon and seem to welcome the event as a confirmation of their view of human sinfulness and as a necessary "cleansing."[61] They infuse new meaning in such biblical passages as "the heavens shall pass away with a great noise, and the elements shall melt with fervent heat, the earth also and the works that are therein shall be burned up."[62] They construct a loose tie between religious end-of-the-world imagery and nuclear threat. In that way they do precisely what other religious thinking cannot do: provide an immortality system that includes nuclear disaster as a vehicle for the end of human history and the beginning of a new spiritual era. In an age of ultimate weapons capable of annihilating the human race, apocalyptic fantasies are understandable, but they are exceedingly dangerous. Apocalyptic belief is a way of overcoming what Mircea Eliade calls the "terror of history" and is the result of a desperate search for order.[63] It must be comfortable and reassuring to believe that one's future and that of the world will be taken care of by God in a flash near the end of time as part of a divine plan. A 1980 Jehovah's Witnesses circular said, for example, "that ... the approach of Armageddon should not be a cause for fear, but for real hope! Why? Because Armageddon is God's way to cleanse the earth of all wickedness, paving the way for a bright, prosperous new order!"[64] There is a connection, as well, between nuclear threat and the worldwide spread of fundamentalism. Fundamentalism in general, including its political forms, stems from the loss, or fear of loss, of fundamentals. Nuclear weapons fueled that fear. The problem with all apocalypticism, however, is that no one has to plan for the future because God has already determined the final battleground and knows who the enemies will be in that cosmic conflict. It doesn't matter what the peacemakers do, it doesn't matter how many START treaties come about between Russia and the United States. The die is already cast and we simply have to play our appropriate roles. This is theological determinism with a vengeance because it denies the possibility of human agency. It must be distinguished from older images of the "end of days." "Terrifying as these may be, they are part of a world view or cosmology—man is acted upon by a higher power ... who destroys only for spiritual purposes (such as achieving 'the kingdom of God'). That is a far cry from man's destruction of himself with his own tools, and to no purpose."[65]

This impulse to make the weapons themselves objects of pseudo-religious adoration and anticipation may be the ultimate idolatry. The prophets of monotheism did not denounce pagan religions as idolatrous because of the worship of several gods, but rather because people spent their energies and intellects on building objects and then worshiped these objects as idols, as gods. The ultimate idolatry, and hence the ultimate alienation, may be nuclearism because it is the weapons themselves, objects of human creativity that still stand over and threaten the future of the species itself, that inflame mutual distrust and that have become our nemesis, more than any ideological differences between nations.

NUCLEAR NORMALITY: LIVING WITH NUCLEAR PEACE

What may have emerged in the post-Cold War period is a species of nuclear normality, a sense of relief—the idea that we are now living in a world that has seen or will soon be able to see reduction of the likelihood of nuclear war to an "acceptable" level, even though the threat has not been removed totally. What may emerge is a "new realism," the notion that our best hope for the future lies in living with the weapons in this new era of nuclear peace. That will be seen as appropriate "realism." Imagining that we could be involved in actively shaping history will run up against our sense of powerlessness and normality. "That's the best that we can hope for," may emerge as the new refrain. Finding the will and imagination to think about a world without nuclear weapons; to develop effective disarmament solutions; to control proliferation; to find creative ways to implement a rational world order, may remain difficult to generate because there is no longer a recognized "evil empire" threatening our collective well-being.

That may be the ironic situation we are in. As the immediate dangers recede somewhat, it becomes even more difficult to think oneself through the unthinkable. We may become complacent, victimized by this sense of nuclear normality and susceptible to the false illusion of security that seems to be extant. This feeling of nuclear normality perpetuates the illusion that we can, in fact, expect to live with nuclear weapons. It is bound up with popular culture in the West, with video games and movies that have helped condition the public to imagine nuclear war as a high-tech game played by computers with minimal human risk and involvement. Language again conspires to obscure the uniqueness of nuclear weapons. We speak today of "weapons of mass destruction"—the triumvirate of nuclear, chemical, and biological weapons. This terminology creates a generalized notion of danger but does not encourage specific reflections on the unique characteristics of these technologies. Nuclear weapons really should stand alone. Chemical and biological weapons do not threaten the end of history, the "second death" that Schell talks about. The term, weapons of mass destruction, represents a way of taming weapons by renaming them. The language obscures and muffles the reality. This new sense of nuclear normality, combined with the seduction of "realism" may convince us that the greater degree of security we are enjoying in the short term is, in fact, real security. We may, therefore, be more unwilling to take the kinds of political and military risks that would lead us to a nuclear-free world. If we are lulled into complacency by nuclear normality we may miss a critical opportunity to fundamentally address the predicament; we may miss what the Greeks referred to as a Kairos moment, one so crucial because it has a profound effect on all that follows.

SUMMARY

In this posture of "living with the bomb," then, we encounter various combinations of normality, resignation, numbing, cynicism, and even anticipation—along with large numbers of people, most of them well-intentioned, going about tasks that may contribute to a potential nuclear catastrophe. Whatever can be said for or against our time, it is burdened with a knowledge that otherwise rational people have carried out the extermination of entire populations if it suited their purpose; that professionals with pride in their professions lent their expertise to mass murder; that students and professors continued to learn and teach; and that many good citizens, far from raising a wild cry of outrage, accepted these policies as an eminently sensible means of waging a war or establishing socialism in one country, or eliminating a superfluous population."[66] Polls show that Americans have generally supported nuclear weapons developments and even first use of the weapons. According to Gallup surveys, a majority supported using the atomic bomb in Korea in 1951 after China entered the conflict; in Vietnam in 1954 when the French were surrounded; and against China in 1955 during the first Quemoy-Matsu crisis. During the 1980s with antinuclear sentiment rising, polls showed overwhelming support for a no-first-use pledge—but a later survey found a near majority backing use of the bomb against Iraq in 1991.[67]

Nuclear arsenals, meanwhile, remain in place. Although the United States and Russia have agreed to destroy thousands of warheads, each will retain nine thousand of the newest and most accurate variety even after the next round of arms cuts. Russia remains disturbingly unstable, proliferation is a growing problem, and in America there are constant calls for spending more on future weapons technology and missile defense.

Just as the Hiroshima and Nagasaki decisions were prefigured in the fire bombings of Hamburg, Dresden, and Tokyo, in the policy of unconditional surrender, and in laboratories in Chicago and New Mexico, we are preparing today for the crises of tomorrow. Yet, there are choices to be made. The Deuteronomist implored: "I have set before you life and death, blessing and cursing: therefore choose life, that both you and your seed may live."[68]

How can we confirm this notion of human agency? How can we break out of the syndrome of numbing and resignation that is at least partially caused by living in a world with nuclear weapons? How can we recognize that we are all to some degree affected by these weapons, whether we know it or not, whether we want to admit it or not? We believe that intellectual and emotional engagement are required to help provide the will and intentionality necessary to break through the barriers impeding action. That is why this chapter takes the form that it does. It attempts to capture and evoke the essence of what it means to live in the nuclear age. At times the prose may be emotional, metaphorical, angry, and startling, very different from the style of the other chapters. This was done because we are struggling to somehow touch the well-springs of the issue; to stimulate our own and our readers' consciousness in order to reveal the true impact and significance of the nuclear danger. We did so as well because this "literary" approach expresses what we feel as informed observers of the nuclear predicament and as ordinary citizens who want to learn not only how to live with the predicament but also how to begin to solve it.

There may, in fact, be an ironic advantage to living in the nuclear age. If we can reorient "our ways of thinking" the Hiroshima experience can help us avoid war. The paradox is a fundamental one: The existence of weapons that threaten the globe and its history with destruction, may also, however indirectly, be a stimulus to forestalling the catastrophe, if their meaning can be grasped. The ubiquitous specter of the bomb, as we have seen, intrudes to some degree in our work, our play, our capacities to love and nurture, in our public and private lives, in our very ability to deal effectively with nuclear weapons. The problem is compounded by the difficulty most people have in appreciating how malignant the bomb actually is. We ask you, the reader, to consider how this tendency may be operating in your own life. Yet, confront we must. As the ancient rabbis advised, "It is not incumbent upon us to finish the task; neither are we free to exempt ourselves from it."[69] Chapter 11 will suggest some ways we can begin this work.

NOTES

1. Roger Rosenblatt, Witness: The World since Hiroshima (Boston, MA: Little, Brown and Co., 1985), pp. 4–5.
2. Albert Camus, "Combat," 8 August 1945 (Gallimard, 1950): 109–110.
3. Robert Karl Manoff, "The Media: Nuclear Security vs. Democracy," Bulletin of the Atomic Scientists (January 1984): 29.
4. See Sibylle Escalona, "Growing Up with the Threat of Nuclear War: Some Indirect Effects on Personality Development," American Journal of Orthopsychiatry 52, no. 4 (October 1982): 600.
5. Quoted in Paul Boyer, By the Bomb's Early Light (New York: Pantheon Books, 1985), p. 282.
6. Jerome D. Frank, Sanity and Survival in the Nuclear Age (New York: Random House, 1967), pp. 30–33.

7. Stephen Hilgartner, Richard C. Bell, and Rory O'Connor, *Nukespeak* (New York: Penguin Books, 1983); Lifton, *Indefensible Weapons*, pp. 106–107; and Paul Chilton, "Nukespeak," *Undercurrents* 48 (1982): 12.
8. See Richard Barnet, "Fantasy, Reality, and the Arms Race," *American Journal of Orthopsychiatry* 52, no. 4 (October 1982).
9. Hilgartner, Bell, and O'Connor, *Nukespeak*.
10. Ibid., p. 251.
11. Ibid., p. 236.
12. See Robert Jay Lifton, *Indefensible Weapons* (New York: Basic Books, 1982); and *In A Dark Time* (Cambridge, MA: Harvard University Press, 1984).
13. See Boyer, *By the Bomb's Early Light*, pp. 10–12.
14. Ibid., p. 12.
15. Michael Mandelbaum, *The Nuclear Revolution* (New York: Cambridge University Press, 1981), pp. 207–229.
16. Quoted in Lifton, *Boundaries* (New York: Random House, 1967), p. 96.
17. See Christopher Lasch, *The Minimal Self: Psychic Survival in Troubled Times* (New York: W. W. Norton, 1984).
18. See Boyer, *By the Bomb's Early Light*, pp. 281–282.
19. See Mandelbaum, *The Nuclear Revolution*; and Lifton, *Indefensible Weapons*.
20. Ibid.
21. Quoted in Milton Schwebel, "Effects of the Nuclear War Threat on Children and Teenagers: Implications for Professionals," *American Journal of Orthopsychiatry* 52, no. 4 (October 1982): 611.
22. See Mandelbaum, *The Nuclear Revolution*.
23. Erich Fromm, *The Anatomy of Human Destruction* (New York: Holt, Rinehart and Winston, 1974), pp. 350–351.
24. Dr. Helen Caldicott, *Missile Envy* (New York: Bantam Books, 1984).
25. Mark Kingwell, *Dreams of Millennium: Report from a Culture on the Brink* (Boston, MA: Faber and Faber, 1996), pp. 182–186.
26. Don DeLillo, *Underworld* (New York: Scribner, 1997), p. 466.
27. See Richard Barnet, "Fantasy, Reality, and the Arms Race," *American Journal of Orthopsychiatry* 52, no. 4 (October 1982): 582.
28. Lifton, *Indefensible Weapons*, p. 47
29. Ibid., pp. 48–49.
30. Bob Dylan, "Talkin' World War III Blues," quoted in Lifton, *In a Dark Time*, p. 87.
31. Ibid.
32. See Boyer, p. 361.
33. Quoted in Barnet, "Fantasy, Reality and the Arms Race," p. 583.
34. See Sibylle Escalona, "Growing Up with the Threat of Nuclear War"; and Lifton, *Indefensible Weapons*.
35. DeLillo, *Underworld*, p. 717.
36. John Mack, "The Perception of U.S.-Soviet Intentions and Other Psychological Dimensions of the Nuclear Arms Race," *American Journal of Orthopsychiatry* 52, no. 4 (October 1982): 590–599; *Houston Post* (December 13–15, 1981); *Boston Globe* (October 29, 1981); *New York Times* (May 27, 1982); P. L. Blackwell and J. C. Gessner, "Fear and Trembling: An Inquiry into Adolescent Perceptions of Living in the Nuclear Age," *Youth and Society* 15 (1983): 237–255; B. M. Kramer, S. M. Kelich, and M. A. Milburn, "Attitudes Toward Nuclear Weapons and Nuclear War: 1945–1982," *Journal of Social Issues* 39 (1983): 7–24; A. Rapoport, "Preparation for Nuclear War: The Final Madness," *American Journal of Orthopsychiatry* 54 (1984): 524–529; Susan Hargraves, "The Nuclear Anxieties of Youth," *Peace Research* 18 (1986): 46–64; and J. Thompson, *Psychological Aspects of Nuclear War* (Chichester, Eng.: John Wiley, 1985).
37. Reprinted in Lifton, *In a Dark Time*, p. 89.

38. Quoted in Caldicott, *Missile Envy*, p. 335.
39. Ibid., p. 336.
40. Quoted in Lifton, *In a Dark Time*, p. 89.
41. Robert Coles, "Children and the Bomb," *New York Times Magazine*, December 8, 1985, pp. 44, 46, 48, 50, 54, 61–62.
42. Joel Slemrod, "Savings and Fear of Nuclear War," *Journal of Conflict Resolution* 30 (September 1986): 403–419; Bruce Russett and Miles Lackey, "In the Shadow of the Cloud," *Political Science Quarterly* 102 (summer 1987): 259–272; and Lewis Thomas, *Late Night Thoughts on Listening to Mahler's Ninth Symphony* (New York: Viking Penguin, 1983), p. 168.
43. Lifton, *Indefensible Weapons*, p. 77.
44. Robert Jay Lifton and Greg Mitchell, *Hiroshima in America* (New York: G. P. Putnam's Sons, 1995), pp. 380–381.
45. Lifton, *Indefensible Weapons*, pp. 71–72.
46. See Robert Jay Lifton, *Boundaries* (New York: Random House, 1967); and *The Broken Connection* (New York: Simon & Schuster, 1979).
47. David Weinberger, "A Phenomenology of Nuclear Weapons," *Philosophy and Social Criticism* 10, no. 3/4 (1984): 98–99.
48. Ibid., p. 101.
49. Norman Mailer, *Advertisements for Myself* (New York: G. P. Putnam's Sons, 1959), p. 338.
50. Weinberger, pp. 102–105.
51. Robert Jay Lifton, *Home from the War* (New York: Simon & Schuster, 1973), p. 25.
52. Jonathan Schell, *The Fate of the Earth* (New York: Avon Books, 1982).
53. Joyce Maynard, *Looking Back: A Chronicle of Growing Up in the Sixties* (New York: Doubleday & Co., 1973), p. 13.
54. Woody Allen, *Getting Even* (New York: Warner, 1972), p. 31.
55. Thomas, *Late Night Thoughts*, p. 167.
56. Lifton, *Boundaries*, pp. 26–27.
57. See Robert Jay Lifton and Richard Falk, *Indefensible Weapons* (New York: Basic Books, 1982).
58. Ernest Becker, *The Denial of Death* (New York: The Free Press, 1973).
59. Quoted in Louis René Beres, "Vain Hopes and a Fool's Fancy: Understanding U.S. Nuclear Strategy," *Philosophy and Social Criticism* 10, no. 3/4 (1984): 46.
60. Rebecca West, *Black Lamb and Grey Falcon* (New York: Viking Press, 1982), p. 1102.
61. See Lifton, *The Broken Connection*, pp. 339–343.
62. 2 Peter 3:10b, KJV.
63. Mircea Eliade, *Cosmos and History* (New York: Harper, 1959).
64. Quoted in Lifton, *In a Dark Time*, p. 66.
65. Lifton, *The Broken Connection*, p. 335.
66. See Richard Rubenstein, *The Age of Triage* (Boston, MA: Beacon Press, 1983); *The Cunning of History* (New York: Harper & Row, 1975); Irving Horowitz, *Genocide: State Power and Mass Murder* (New Brunswick, NJ: Transaction Books, 1976); Robert Jay Lifton, *Death in Life* (New York: Random House, 1967); and Ronald Aronson, *The Dialectics of Disaster* (London: Verso, 1983). The connection between culture and mass death is examined in some of the following: Jules Henry, *Culture against Man* (New York: Vintage Books, 1965); Ernest Becker, *Escape from Evil* (New York: The Free Press, 1975); George Steiner, *Language and Silence* (New York: Atheneum, 1967); and Isidor Wallimann and Michael Dobkowski, eds., *Genocide and the Modern Age* (New York: Greenwood Press, 1987).
67. Lifton and Mitchell, *Hiroshima in America*, p. 305.
68. Deuteronomy 30:19b, KJV.
69. Pirkei Avos 2:16.

11

SOLUTIONS TO THE NUCLEAR PREDICAMENT

In December 1996, fifty-eight retired generals and admirals from seventeen nations, including many from Russia and the United States, issued a statement supporting the abolition of nuclear weapons:

> We military professionals who have devoted our lives to the national security of our countries and our peoples, are convinced that the continuing existence of nuclear weapons in the armories of nuclear powers, and the ever-present threat of acquisition of these weapons by others, constitute a peril to global peace and security and to the safety and survival of the people we are dedicated to protect.... [Nuclear weapons] represent a clear and present danger to the very existence of humanity.... That threat has now receded, but not forever—unless nuclear weapons are eliminated.

Their statement continues: "Long-term international nuclear policy must be based on the declared principle of continuous, complete, and irrevocable elimination of nuclear weapons." This is their conclusion:

> We have been presented with a challenge of the highest possible historic importance: the creation of a nuclear-weapons-free world. The end of the Cold War makes it possible. The dangers of proliferation, terrorism, and a new nuclear arms race render it necessary. We must not fail to seize the opportunity. There is no alternative.[1]

What is most significant about this strong endorsement of the abolition of nuclear weapons is not the novelty of the recommended policy. Complete nuclear disarmament is a policy that had been recommended by many people before, going back at least to Albert Einstein in the immediate postwar period. What is unprecedented about this recommendation is the recommenders. Never before has such a large and prominent group of former military leaders, most of whom had been in charge of nuclear weapons themselves, called for nuclear abolition. Their endorsement of complete nuclear disarmament carries special weight. With this statement, the endorsement of the abolitionist position moved from the theoretical preserve of academics and visionaries, where it had largely resided before, to the practical world of hard-headed military leaders. The end of the Cold War seems to have opened up the minds of many to the virtues of complete nuclear disarmament.

The question before us is: What is the solution to the nuclear predicament? One of the alternative solutions is the abolition of nuclear weapons, but there are other possible solutions to consider as well. This question of solutions has both a theoretical and a practical side. On the theoretical side, there are two issues. First, what would it mean to solve the nuclear predicament? Is the nuclear predicament something that has a solution, and, if so, what would a solution look like? Second, if there is a solution, what is it? Is it abolition or some other policy? Switching to the practical side, the issue is how we should go about achieving whatever solution seems to be the best. As it will turn out, however, the theoretical and practical dimensions of the question cannot be separated.

We can get a preliminary idea of the difficulty in determining what the solution to the nuclear predicament is by considering an instructive episode in the history of the Cold War, an episode in which the abolition of nuclear weapons was seriously considered at the highest levels of policymaking. This is the extraordinary superpower summit meeting at Reykjavik, Iceland, in October 1986.

At that meeting, then President Reagan of the United States and then General Secretary Gorbachev of the Soviet Union were set to discuss proposals for a new nuclear arms agreement. Most observers expected another meeting like the numerous summits and arms control-negotiating sessions that had gone before, in which the proposals offered were small steps designed simply to slow the future growth of nuclear arsenals, not to reduce them. Many observers had become disillusioned by this lack of boldness, coming to believe that the arms control process was unlikely to lead to a solution to the nuclear predicament. But the discussion at Reykjavik did not follow the pattern of previous arms-control meetings. To the surprise of nearly everyone and the shock of many, Reagan and Gorbachev entertained proposals that would have not only reduced existing nuclear arsenals by roughly 50 percent in five years, but completely eliminated them in ten years. In the end, however, a deal escaped the participants. Gorbachev wanted to include in the agreement a ban on the Strategic Defense Initiative, the U.S. program to develop defenses against nuclear missiles, and Reagan refused.

Those opposed to the revolutionary proposals discussed at Reykjavik were relieved that the agreement failed.[2] Part of their concern may be expressed through the notion of crisis stability, discussed in Chapter 5. When there is crisis stability, war is less likely because each side is certain that if it launched a nuclear attack, no matter how successful, the other side would have enough nuclear weapons left to destroy it in retaliation. According to the critics of the Reykjavik proposals, the process of mutual disarmament would decrease crisis stability, for when each side had reduced its arsenals to a small number of weapons, a nuclear attack by one side might not leave the other side with enough weapons to guarantee retaliation. In a crisis, this would create a great risk that one side, fearing that the other side might be about to strike, would launch a preemptive attack. In addition, when there are few or no nuclear weapons, cheating on an agreement can yield a much more significant advantage. In the view of the critics, the process of complete nuclear disarmament would make nuclear war more rather than less likely.

This opposition to the Reykjavik proposal reveals something that may not have been evident earlier. Before Reykjavik, it might have seemed that the problem with the nuclear predicament was not so much determining *what* the best solution is, but rather getting the nuclear powers to put what was obviously the best solution into effect. Most people would probably have agreed that the solution was nuclear disarmament. The main problem was seen to be the infeasibility of implementing that solution. In other words, prior to Reykjavik, the main stumbling block to a solution to the nuclear predicament seemed more practical than theoretical. But Reykjavik, though it ended without agreement, showed that nuclear disarmament might be practically possible after all, since Reagan and Gorbachev appeared to have come close to agreeing to it. At the same time, the objections to the Reykjavik proposal challenged the belief that nuclear disarmament is the best solution. Nuclear disarmament may not be a solution at all. It may itself be more dangerous than continued possession of the weapons. Solving the nuclear predicament suddenly seemed not as simple a matter as many had thought.

The changes in international politics brought about by the end of the Cold War have made the problems first revealed by Reykjavik all the more evident. The end of the Cold War made proposals for nuclear disarmament more mainstream, thus making disarmament a more likely prospect. The statement of the military leaders discussed earlier is only one example of this. Michael Mazarr notes that during the Cold War

> the concept of disarmament provided one of the clear litmus tests of an analyst's ideological stance—and to some, his or her sanity as well. Those who broached the idea … thereby defined themselves as members of what was viewed as an unserious and irrelevant fringe of the Washington policy community.

But calls for disarmament are now being taken much more seriously. "As with so many national security issues in the United States, the end of the Cold War has fractured old consensuses and called into question well-established ideologies and belief systems."[3] As nuclear weapons have changed our way of thinking about military matters, the end of the Cold War has changed our way of thinking about nuclear weapons.

But, precisely because the practical obstacles to nuclear disarmament have become less formidable, the theoretical difficulties have come more to the fore. It may now be possible, as it was not during the Cold War, to pursue a policy of complete nuclear disarmament with some hope of success. So, we must carefully assess the theoretical question of whether or not abolition is the best solution.

All of this makes clear once again that our situation is a predicament. Part of the nuclear predicament is that nuclear weapons create great danger for our civilization and for billions of the earth's inhabitants. This is why nuclear disarmament may seem to be the obvious solution. If nuclear weapons create the problem, then the solution must be to rid ourselves of them. We must get beyond nuclear deterrence. But the other part of our situation, which makes it a predicament, is that we have nuclear weapons in order to avoid certain dangers. The main purpose of nuclear deterrence, after all, is to avoid nuclear war. So getting rid of the weapons may make our situation more dangerous. There is danger on all sides.

Reykjavik raises another issue. While both Reagan and Gorbachev professed a desire to rid the world of nuclear weapons, the disagreement that ended the summit in failure represents a fundamental difference about the practical side of the question—how nuclear disarmament should be achieved. To put it roughly, Gorbachev saw disarmament as something that could be achieved through agreements alone, whereas Reagan saw disarmament as a process that required the development of a technology that can provide defenses against nuclear weapons. This difference is reflected in an exchange that Reagan and Gorbachev were reported to have had at one point in their meeting: Gorbachev asked why Reagan felt the need to build defenses if, as their agreement would stipulate, nuclear weapons would be eliminated, to which Reagan responded by asking why, if there would be no nuclear weapons, Gorbachev cared whether or not the United States built defenses. The question is whether a nation can protect itself from nuclear danger largely through its own efforts, as Reagan thought the United States could through the development of missile defenses, or whether it is the restraint of other nations, secured through international agreements, that is the foundation of protection from the nuclear danger, as Gorbachev believed.

In the earlier chapters of this book, we sought to understand various aspects of the nuclear predicament. The ultimate purpose of such an understanding must be to take action to lessen the dangers. This chapter examines the factors that need to be considered in this effort. We analyze and evaluate three possible solutions to the nuclear predicament. In addition to abolition, we consider the solution of continued reliance on nuclear deterrence, which is what the critics of the Reykjavik supported, and the solution of developing technology to protect a nation from nuclear attack, which was Reagan's vision.

Our task in this chapter is also to seek to reunite the concerns of prudence and morality, which, as we argued in Chapter 9, nuclear weapons seem to have sundered. This split between morality and prudence is itself one of the expressions of the fact that our situation is a predicament. So, in considering a solution to the predicament, we might also seek to overcome this split, the paradox of nuclear weapons. Any proposed solution to the nuclear predicament should be evaluated in moral terms, as well as in strategic and security terms. Retired U.S. General George Butler, one of the leaders in the group of military officers issuing the statement favoring abolition, in speaking of the abolition proposal, observed that the United States has a responsibility in "dealing with the conflicted *moral* legacy of the Cold War," that we must "work painfully back through the tangled *moral* web of this frightful 50-year gauntlet."[4]

The ultimate purpose of our discussion in this book must be to determine what we ought to do. If there ever was an area of study in which the purpose of understanding is action, the study of the nuclear predicament is it. Thus, we devote this chapter at the end of the text to solutions. But it is important to consider not only what we should do collectively to solve the nuclear predicament, but also what we can do individually to promote this collective effort. The nuclear predicament is an area in which individuals have felt especially helpless and powerless to effect any change. But any collective solution can occur only through individual actions. So, we consider at the end what an individual can do.

Some people would regard the entire discussion in this chapter as unnecessary. They would take the view that, with the end of the Cold War, we need not worry about nuclear weapons any more. The danger posed by nuclear weapons during the Cold War is now past. The nuclear predicament has come to an end. What solved the predicament was the great historical change of the dissolution of the Soviet Union and the consequent end of the superpower rivalry. This kind of view we called in the last chapter nuclear normality, the attitude that with the end of the East-West confrontation, we need no longer worry about nuclear weapons.

On the contrary, *the end of the Cold War does not end the nuclear predicament.* The predicament may now be less visible, but it remains. With it remains our reason to be concerned. Indeed, rather than solving the nuclear predicament, the end of the Cold

War reveals its depth. The conflict between the United States and the Soviet Union is the main form that the nuclear predicament has taken in our historical experience. This is why the end of that conflict has seemed to some to herald the end of the predicament. But, though the Cold War was the occasion for the emergence of the nuclear predicament, the predicament transcends that historical episode. The 1998 nuclear tests by India and Pakistan clearly demonstrate this. Nuclear weapons continue to exist, as do conflicts between sovereign states. The nuclear predicament, in its most general form, is based on the existence of nuclear weapons in the hands of sovereign states with conflicting interests. The end of the Cold War has not altered this feature of international relations.

Not only does the nuclear predicament remain, but, as we earlier argued, it may now be a greater source of danger than it was during the Cold War. The second nuclear age in which we currently live may be more dangerous than the first nuclear age. The current world order is less stable, and is likely to remain so for some time. As we saw in Chapter 7, increased nuclear proliferation may result, making nuclear use more likely. We predicted in Chapter 2 that the likelihood of nuclear use over the next twenty-five years is 20 to 30 percent, and nuclear use would likely usher in a third nuclear age of even greater danger. While a future nuclear war is more likely to be regional than global, representing a lesser level of catastrophe, this does not minimize the danger. Not only would a regional nuclear war be a major human catastrophe in its own right, but such a war could lead to a larger nuclear war later, by its example and its breaking of the nuclear taboo. In addition, nuclear terrorism now is a greater risk. Given these unfortunate possibilities, it would not be surprising if, in another generation, we look back on the Cold War, perhaps nostalgically, as a period of great international stability and comfortable predictability.

Given that our nuclear danger may well be greater than it was during the Cold War, our task becomes more urgent at the same time as our will, sapped by perceptions of nuclear normality, may have weakened. The third nuclear age is ours to shape. Inaction will likely result in that age being ushered in by nuclear use and an even greater level of danger. But concerted action, informed by a clear understanding of our situation, can lead to a very different third nuclear age, one in which the nuclear danger has faded.

Albert Einstein warned at the dawn of the nuclear age that nuclear weapons had changed everything except our way of thinking. As a result, he feared that catastrophe lay ahead. The end of the Cold War has lessened the *immediate* risk of catastrophe, but it has not eliminated that risk. How must our thinking change in order to eliminate the risk?

This reference to Einstein's warning brings us back to the point at which the book began. Einstein was one of the first to recognize the nuclear predicament because he was one of the first to be caught in it. As we saw earlier, his letter to President Roosevelt initiated the effort to build the bomb. Leo Szilard's request that Einstein send this letter placed Einstein in the earliest manifestation of the nuclear predicament. As a pacifist, Einstein was certainly strongly opposed to the creation of such a terrible weapon of war. Yet, he was led to sign the letter by the deep fear, which he shared with many of the refugees from fascism who would work on the Manhattan Project, that Nazi Germany might get the bomb first. Einstein may have recognized the need for nuclear deterrence, reasoning in this way: Such a weapon must never be used, and to ensure that it will not be used, the Allies must acquire the bomb in order to deter its possible use by Germany in the event that Germany develops it as well. After the war, Einstein proposed his own solution to the nuclear predicament, involving his view on how our thinking must change. We consider his solution later. But more fundamentally, Einstein provides us with the framework within which our search for a solution must be understood. The purpose of this chapter is to investigate how our thinking must change if we are to have the best chance of averting the catastrophe he feared.

We begin in the next section by considering two questions. Is a solution to the nuclear predicament possible? What would a solution look like? In subsequent sections, we consider three possible solutions to the nuclear predicament, including the abolition of nuclear weapons. Finally, in the last section, we consider what an individual can do.

IS THERE A SOLUTION TO THE NUCLEAR PREDICAMENT?

What would count as a solution to the nuclear predicament? The first step to finding a solution is to determine what a solution must achieve. The nuclear predicament is a problem because it is a situation of great danger. Even if the likelihood of nuclear war is low, the unprecedented catastrophe it could lead to makes the danger great. It is a predicament because there is danger on all sides. The danger seems inescapable. A solution to the nuclear predicament would allow us to escape the danger. That is what a solution would look like.

A *complete* solution to the nuclear predicament would eliminate the possibility of nuclear war. Danger seems to exist on all sides because there appears to be no policy that would eliminate the possibility of nuclear war. Indeed, we cannot eliminate the possibility of nuclear war. It is a truism that nuclear weapons cannot be "disinvented." Even if all nuclear weapons were dismantled, we would still know how to rebuild them, and we will always have this knowledge. The knowledge of how to make nuclear weapons cannot be forgotten or unlearned.[5] Thus, the possibility of nuclear war will exist forever. In 1900 nuclear war was impossible, so there was no nuclear predicament. But, as a civilization, we can never return to 1900.[6] We lost our nuclear innocence in 1945, and innocence once lost cannot be recovered.

Nuclear war cannot be made impossible. If a solution to the nuclear predicament requires that nuclear war be made impossible, as we have been assuming, the nuclear predicament has no solution. The nuclear predicament, in this sense, will be with us forever. But, if we understand a solution in a somewhat different way, it may not be impossible. Here are two alternative ideas for what would count as a solution:

1. The nuclear predicament would be solved when the possibility of nuclear war had been reduced to zero.
2. The nuclear predicament would be solved when the likelihood of nuclear war had been virtually eliminated, that is, reduced to near zero.

In sense 1, the nuclear predicament has no solution. What about sense 2? If we take our goal to be the virtual elimination of the likelihood of nuclear war, and count the achievement of that goal as a solution, a solution might be possible. The virtual elimination of the likelihood of nuclear war would mean a reduction in the probability of nuclear war to a figure of practical insignificance. For example, while it is, strictly speaking, possible that Britain and the United States will next year wage a nuclear war against each other, the likelihood of this happening is so small that we treat it for all practical purposes as zero. Thus, in sense 2, the nuclear predicament between Britain and the United States has been solved.

Consider this analogy. People often speak of "the human predicament." One of the many things this can mean is the following. On the one hand, human beings are seriously at risk if they live by themselves, apart from a human social group, because, unlike Robinson Crusoe, they need the help of others to survive. On the other hand, human beings are seriously at risk if they live in proximity to others who may attack and harm them. Humans are at risk whether they live apart from or together with others. There is danger on all sides. Is there a solution to this predicament? There is no solution, if we mean a solution that completely eliminates the risks of these dangers to humans. (This would correspond to sense 1.) But there is a solution, if we mean a solution (corresponding to sense 2) that reduces the likelihood of these harms to near zero. That solution is just and effective government, as well as a set of norms that promote comity among people.[7] When humans live under such a government and set of norms, they do not face the risks they would living apart, and the risks of aggression by others is reduced to near zero by the state's enforcement of laws guaranteeing the physical security of all citizens.

But we need to say more about what should count as a solution. The nuclear predicament, like the human predicament, can have no *permanent* solution. In the case of the human predicament, governments can become unjust and ineffective, and norms can break down. In the case of the nuclear predicament, while it is hardly possible to imagine the United States and Britain having a nuclear war next year, it is possible to imagine their having a nuclear war sometime in the distant future. If nuclear weapons had existed in 1812, the two nations might have had a nuclear war. (Of course, as a defender of nuclear deterrence would point out, if the two nations had had nuclear weapons in 1812, war might have been deterred.) We can imagine Britain and the United States becoming military antagonists in the future, making nuclear war between them a real possibility. What this shows is that any solution to the nuclear predicament cannot be permanent. Thus, if a solution is to be possible, it must be understood in a third sense:

3. The nuclear predicament would be solved when the likelihood of nuclear war had been virtually eliminated for an extended period of time (for the long-term).

It is in this sense that we will understand what a solution to the nuclear predicament would be, for only in this sense is a solution possible. Even in this sense, however, a solution will certainly be difficult to achieve. The question we must address is what policy approach is most likely to bring about such a solution.

Many proposals have been put forth for solving the nuclear predicament. Most of these proposals are complex and they conflict with and overlap each other in complicated ways, making it difficult to sort them. Without doing too much violence to their complexity, however, we may roughly divide them into three groups, representing three general approaches to solving the nuclear predicament. These three approaches are technological obviation, minimum deterrence, and nuclear abolition. Technological obviation is the approach that recommends letting technology solve the nuclear predicament. Minimum deterrence is the approach that argues that our best chance of virtually eliminating the risk of nuclear war is to retain nuclear arsenals and practice nuclear deterrence, but with relatively small arsenals. Nuclear abolition, the policy recommended by the military leaders, is the approach that maintains that our best chance of solving the nuclear predicament is to eliminate nuclear weapons.

Before considering each of these three approaches in some detail, note one respect in which they differ. An approach to solving the nuclear predicament can rely either on nations acting individually or on nations acting together. In fact, any approach involves both of these elements, but different approaches emphasize one more than the other. Technological obviation relies primarily on nations acting individually, developing the technology that would greatly reduce the risk of or the harm from nuclear attack. Nuclear abolition, on the other hand, relies primarily on nations acting together. The only way nuclear disarmament could be safely accomplished is for it to be done mutually. The third approach, minimum deterrence involves a more even mixture of nations acting independently and nations acting together. Another way to describe this difference is to say that technological obviation is primarily unilateral and relies primarily on technology, while nuclear abolition is primarily multilateral and relies primarily on politics, with minimum deterrence being both unilateral and multilateral, relying strongly on both technology and politics. We will consider the interplay of these factors as we discuss the three approaches to a solution.

TECHNOLOGICAL OBVIATION

The nuclear revolution is a revolution in military technology. It is interesting to look at the nuclear revolution in the context of the history of such revolutions. One way to look at that history is to see it as a constant struggle for dominance between offensive capabilities and defensive capabilities. Some technological developments give the advantage to offensive forces in combat and some give the advantage to defensive forces. For example, the machine gun and barbed wire of World War I gave the dominance to the defense, resulting in trench warfare and vast slaughter, while the tank and other technologies of World War II restored a more even balance between the two.

The nuclear revolution gave much greater advantage to the offense. When nuclear warheads are sent to their targets by ballistic missiles, there is little or no way to defend against them. The nuclear predicament is closely tied to the fact that nuclear weapons have created a situation of overwhelming offense dominance. But maybe this situation of offense dominance created by nuclear weapons is, like the situations of offense dominance in the past, a temporary one. Perhaps technology can provide a solution to the nuclear predicament. Technology got us into this fix; perhaps it can get us out. Perhaps there is a technological revolution in our future that will turn the tables and establish a situation of defense dominance. Perhaps some future technology will overcome the impact of nuclear weapons the way the tank overcame the influence of barbed wire and the machine gun. This would be a solution through technological obviation.

The technology that might solve the nuclear predicament by establishing defense dominance would be effective ballistic missile defenses (BMD). The nuclear predicament is tied to the existence of the mutual capacity for assured destruction between nuclear opponents, and what allows this condition to continue is the inability of either side to intercept more than a small number of the ballistic-missile warheads that the other side might launch. If one side (or both sides) could develop the capacity whereby the warheads of the other side could be effectively intercepted, the other side would no longer have an assured destruction capacity against it. This could end the nuclear predicament. But to achieve this, the BMD capacity would have to be extremely effective. Nuclear weapons establish offense dominance not simply because the ballistic missiles by which they are delivered are very hard to intercept, but because the weapons are so tremendously destructive. The capacity for assured destruction lies not simply in the difficulty of intercepting ballistic missile warheads, but in the fact that only a small number of nuclear weapons, delivered, for example, against the largest dozen cities of a nation, could effectively destroy that society. To solve the nuclear predicament, a BMD capacity would have to be near perfect—it would have to ensure that almost no nuclear weapons could get through.

Compare nuclear weapons with conventional bombs, such as were used extensively in World War II. There could be an effective defense against such bombs not only because they were delivered by airplanes, which were much easier than ballistic missile warheads to shoot down, but because a nation could survive some of the bombers getting through and dropping their bombs. For the defenses to be effective they did not have to be perfect. London survived the blitz. But with nuclear weapons, if even a few get through the nation is lost.

Through much of the Cold War there was military research on missile defenses, most prominently in the 1980s when then president Ronald Reagan inaugurated the Strategic Defense Initiative (SDI), popularly known as "Star Wars." We discussed this in Chapter 5. Given the need for a very high intercept rate, the SDI developed the idea of a layered defense. One layer would intercept some of the newly launched missiles from weapons platforms in the earth's orbit, using, for example, chemical lasers. Another layer would intercept some of the warheads that got through the first layer as they flew above the atmosphere heading for their targets. A third, ground-based layer would intercept most of the remaining warheads as they descended on their targets through the atmosphere. If each layer would achieve ninety percent effectiveness, only one warhead in a thousand would make it through to its target. This would, perhaps, be close enough to perfection to bring about defense dominance and a technological solution to the nuclear predicament.

But this is an impossibly ambitious goal, for several reasons. First, the technological demands are simply too daunting. In the research to date there has been some limited success in developing defensive systems that "can hit a bullet with a bullet" (the analogy used to show the difficulty of destroying a ballistic missile warhead) under ideal test conditions. But such a capacity is far short of the near-perfection necessary. Moreover, there are inexpensive countermeasures that the opponent could take (such as deploying decoy warheads) that would greatly reduce the effectiveness of any defensive system. Second, there are alternative means of delivering nuclear warheads, such as cruise missiles, and near-perfect defensive measures would have to be developed against them as well. Third, even if near-perfection could be achieved, the defenses might, ironically, make nuclear destruction more rather than less likely. The reason is that perfection could not be expected to last. The other side would be working on ways to beat the defenses, and such ways would probably be found. When the defenses were no longer perfect, the danger of nuclear war might be great. The military balance might be temporarily so out of kilter that in a crisis fears of the other side's attacking first might lead one side to launch a preemptive attack. In other words, perfect defenses could lead to a situation of great crisis instability.

Defenders of the idea of missile defenses would respond that this is too pessimistic an assessment. They would argue that the characteristics of technological revolutions are, by their very nature, unforeseeable. We cannot flatly claim that an effective BMD capability is impossible. Such a claim would be like the claims of those in the past that it was impossible that humans would ever fly or visit the moon. There are reasons to view this analogy as a weak one. In other words, the basis for the claim that an effective BMD capacity is impossible is much stronger than the basis of the nineteenth-century claim that humans would never fly in a heavier-than-air craft. But even so, the basic point of the defenders of BMD is surely a correct one. No one can now say with reliability that humans will never develop an effective BMD capacity. The technological future cannot be foreclosed in this way. But, we can reliably say that the prospects for an effective BMD capacity, given the destructive power of nuclear weapons, are dim, at best. Nuclear weapons establish an overwhelming offense dominance. For practical purposes, for the foreseeable future, there is no technological fix for the nuclear predicament.

But many supporters of missile defenses are more limited in their expectations about what a BMD capacity would achieve. For example, one of the main arguments since the end of the Cold War for the deployment of such a capacity has been that it could avoid nuclear destruction in the cases of an accidental launch of a nuclear missile by a major nuclear power or the deliberate launch of a nuclear missile by a "rogue" state or a terrorist group. This concern has been fueled by the increasing proliferation not only of nuclear weapons, but of ballistic missile technology. But a BMD capacity that would achieve these ends, however desirable it might be in its own right, would not be a solution to the nuclear predicament. For such a BMD capacity would not by itself do much to reduce the damage from a nuclear war between major nuclear powers. In fact, a BMD capacity might increase the risk of such a war, thereby increasing our nuclear danger.

This discussion leads us to consider another objective that proponents argue a BMD capacity could achieve. According to this view, missile defenses would not solve the nuclear predicament by putting an end to the other side's capacity of assured destruction, but they might at least lessen our nuclear danger by making nuclear deterrence between major nuclear powers more effective. If a BMD capacity would make nuclear deterrence much more effective, this might reduce the risk of nuclear catastrophe, and hence count as a partial solution to the nuclear predicament. But would a BMD capacity make deterrence more effective?

The kind of deterrence strategy that missile defenses would enhance is countervailing strategy (see Chapter 5), or, in its more extreme version, prevailing strategy. This strategy relies on counterforce capability, and it is because missile defenses are a form of counterforce, a way of destroying the other side's forces, that they would make countervailing strategy more effective. Countervailing (or prevailing) strategy requires that a nation have the capacity to match (or exceed) its opponent at any potential level of nuclear conflict. This strategy envisions the possibility of limited nuclear wars, that is, nuclear wars using only a small portion of existing arsenals, fought against military targets only, sparing cities. This would provide a better deterrent, the strategy's proponents claim, because nuclear threats would then be more credible. If side A had the ability to match or exceed side B at any potential level of nuclear conflict, side B would be more certain that side A would respond militarily to side B's aggression, and hence would be better deterred. The ability of A to keep a nuclear war limited would, in the eyes of B, make A more likely to offer a nuclear response. In contrast, without counterforce capability, the only response A would have available would be countervalue nuclear retaliation, and B might then doubt that A would make a nuclear response to limited aggression. Missile defenses would increase this advantage of countervailing strategy by creating a better counterforce capability.

But, we argue, countervailing strategy is not effective at reducing the likelihood of nuclear catastrophe.[8] First, the advantages it claims in terms of greater credibility of nuclear threats are largely illusory. These advantages depend on the possibility of limited nuclear war. The threat of a limited, counterforce response is more credible than the threat of a countervalue response only if the limited response would result in a limited war. But it is unlikely (as we argued in Chapter 9) that a nuclear war would remain limited. So we cannot count on its remaining limited, and, because we cannot, the threat of a limited counterforce response would have little more credibility than the threat of a countervalue response. Either response is likely in the end to amount to the same thing. Second, there are major dangers in a strategy that relies on a threat that a nuclear response to aggression is more likely. This strategy could lead to crisis instability, and so make war more likely. Counterforce weapons are useful in a first strike because they can destroy the opponent's means of retaliation. If side A had a countervailing strategy, side B might, in a crisis, come to believe that A was about to strike first, since there would be a military advantage from its doing so. This might lead B, in desperation, to launch a preemptive attack in order to deny A this advantage. In this way a countervailing strategy would increase the likelihood of nuclear war.

There is one final idea that should be discussed under the category of technological obviation. Advancing military technology may allow offensive conventional weapons to replace nuclear weapons. The idea is that "smart" conventional weapons could be developed with the explosive power and accuracy needed to achieve all of the military purposes for which nuclear weapons might be used. The cruise missile is a good example of how technology is moving in this direction. A conventionally armed cruise missile, given its accuracy, can now achieve many of the military purposes that only a nuclear warhead could have achieved twenty years ago. Paul Nitze asserts: "From a policy perspective, there should be a conscious decision by the government to pursue the conversion of our strategic deterrent from nuclear to conventional weapons."[9] If conventional deterrence replaced nuclear deterrence, this might eliminate the nuclear danger.

But conventional weapons, no matter how effective, could not completely replace nuclear weapons. The military purposes for which conventional weapons could replace nuclear weapons are counterforce purposes. The countervalue dimension of nuclear weapons would remain. Nuclear weapons would still pose the threat of destruction of the opponent's society, and the opponent would therefore still need to threaten such destruction in response. Conventional deterrence can never replace that aspect of nuclear deterrence. We still must ask the question, as we do in the next section, whether or not some form of nuclear deterrence could be the solution to the nuclear predicament.

Thus, technological obviation provides no solution to the nuclear predicament. Missile defenses cannot eliminate the nuclear threat directly, and, if pursued as a way to enhance nuclear deterrence, they would likely increase our nuclear danger. Likewise, conventional deterrence cannot replace nuclear deterrence. The conclusion is that, though technology got us into the mess we are in, it cannot get us out. There is no policy a nation can adopt by itself to remove the nuclear danger. If there is a solution to the nuclear predicament, it must rely, at least in part, on mutuality, on binding agreements between nuclear rivals. Next we consider whether a form of nuclear deterrence that relies on a high degree of mutuality is the solution.

MINIMUM DETERRENCE

The second approach to solving the nuclear predicament is to continue to practice nuclear deterrence, but nuclear deterrence of a specific kind, namely, *minimum deterrence*. Minimum deterrence involves a nuclear strategy that is distinct from countervailing or prevailing strategy. The goal of prevailing strategy, especially, is to overcome what are believed to be the strategic limitations inherent in the situation of mutual assured destruction (MAD). But, as we have argued, this strategy cannot overcome MAD.

The appropriate nuclear strategy, one that could be a solution to the nuclear predicament, is one that appreciates, as countervailing/prevailing strategy does not, the implications of the condition of mutual assured destruction. This strategy, minimum deterrence, is discussed in Chapter 5.[10] It requires small nuclear arsenals of invulnerable warheads, because only a relatively small number of nuclear weapons is needed to guarantee the assured destruction of one's opponent. In addition, this smaller number of warheads would lessen the opponent's fears of a first strike, thereby lessening the risk of nuclear war. This, of course, is crucial if this strategy is to reduce the risk of war close to zero, so that it could achieve a solution to the nuclear predicament.

The virtue of minimum deterrence is that it provides crisis stability. This is what makes it different from all other forms of military strategy. Minimum deterrence eschews both the traditional notion of trying to achieve military advantage over the opponent and the traditional military goals of seeking to destroy the opponent's weapons and to defend one's own territory. It seeks military parity with, rather than military superiority over, the opponent. It recognizes the break in the traditional connection between having more weapons and having greater security, realizing that, beyond a certain point at least, the more weapons a nation has, the less secure it is. It recognizes that one's own security lies in one's opponent's feeling secure.

The appeal of countervailing/prevailing strategy arises from a failure to acknowledge that nuclear weapons require such a change in our way of thinking. Proponents of this strategy sometimes believe that they have reduced minimum deterrence to absurdity by pointing out that, according to this policy, protecting weapons is good, while protecting people is bad, and threatening people is good, while threatening weapons is bad. But this sounds absurd only in terms of traditional ways of military thinking. When one recognizes the implications of the condition of mutual assured destruction, it is clear that as long as there continue to be nuclear weapons in the hands of antagonistic powers, minimum deterrence is the best policy to guide their deployment.

An analogy may help to explain why nuclear war is more likely under countervailing/prevailing strategy than under minimum deterrence. Imagine two mortal enemies coming upon each other in a corridor, each with loaded gun in hand. If they are poor shots, each would have a strong reason not to fire first. A poor shot may leave a wounded opponent, who is able then to return the fire. On the other hand, if both are good shots (like the Lone Ranger, able to shoot a gun out of his opponent's hand), each has a strong reason to fire first. A good shot would be able with a single shot to kill or to disarm the opponent, leaving the opponent unable to return the fire. So one or the other is likely to shoot first, either to remove the opponent as a source of danger or out of fear that the opponent is about to shoot first. Nations practicing minimum deterrence are like the poor shots, while those practicing countervailing strategy are like the good shots. Minimum deterrence is much more likely to avoid gunplay.

But the argument that minimum deterrence could be a solution to the nuclear predicament lies not simply in the claim that it would be a safer form of nuclear deterrence than countervailing or prevailing strategies. It lies rather in the claim that nuclear weapons are fundamentally different and that only minimum deterrence recognizes and takes advantage of this difference. The difference is, to put it roughly, that nuclear weapons can put an end to war among nations that possess them. But nuclear weapons can do this job only if they are deployed under a strategy that recognizes this difference and seeks to take advantage of it, as minimum deterrence does. Nuclear weapons are very dangerous, but their potential destructiveness makes it possible to avoid war, and so guarantees that the potential destructiveness is never made actual. This is another nuclear paradox. With these weapons, safety can be, in Churchill's apt phrase, "the sturdy child of terror." But only so long as a strategy of minimum deterrence is employed.

The claim that nuclear weapons are different in the sense that they can be used (under a strategy of minimum deterrence) to ensure the avoidance of war is based, in part, on their ability to create what is called "the crystal-ball effect."[11] Because it is known that a large-scale nuclear war would be far more destructive than any war in history, the catastrophic results would be clearly foreseen by any leader in a position to start such a war. This provides a great clarity of foresight. Leaders of the nuclear nations can see, as if in a crystal ball, that utter devastation would be visited upon their nations should they choose the path of war. This is new. Prior to 1945, wars were both longer and less destructive than a nuclear war would be. This meant that leaders were not likely to be able to foresee that war would inevitably lead to their nation's destruction. They could not foresee this both because such destruction was less likely to be the result and because the length of war made it hard to anticipate what the final result would be. A good example of this is World War I, where the belligerents foresaw in 1914 a quick and relatively painless victory for themselves.

In the past, nations often deliberately chose policies leading to war because their leaders believed that they could win the war and that the nation would benefit as a result. Nuclear weapons do not as readily allow such a belief when the relationship between the nations in question is one of mutual assured destruction. When such a relationship holds, as it did between the United States and the Soviet Union, the crystal-ball effect creates a much stronger motivation on the part of leaders to choose war-avoiding policies. Minimum deterrence ensures that the crystal-ball effect will hold.

It is due to the central role of the crystal-ball effect in avoiding war that most advocates of minimum deterrence are opposed to ballistic missile defenses and are strong supporters of the antiballistic missile treaty of 1972.[12] The fear is that if a nation had an effective BMD capacity, it might come to believe that it would not be destroyed in a war, and its opponent might come to fear that its opponent had such a belief. The crystal ball would thus be shattered and crisis stability would be lost.

Two other points should be made about minimum deterrence. First, the strategy implies no precise number of weapons that should be held. The only requirement in terms of numbers is that they should be low enough that crisis stability is not disturbed. Second, minimum deterrence should not be seen as a solution that can successfully be adopted by one side only. Countervailing or prevailing strategies are seen in this way because they are competitive strategies in which a nation tries constantly to match or exceed the counterforce capability of its opponent. But minimum deterrence is largely a cooperative strategy, combining the technical elements of invulnerable weapons systems and the political elements of arms reductions and other forms of military cooperation.

How could minimum deterrence be achieved? Primarily through the cooperative method of arms control. One proposal is put forth by Jonathan Dean, who discusses three progressively more stringent forms of minimum deterrence, arguing for the most stringent form.[13] Under the first form, the United States and Russia would push beyond the START II treaty and reduce their nuclear warheads to 2,000 each. Under the second form, they would reduce to 1,000 warheads each and be joined in a weapons control regime by the other nuclear weapons states. Under the third form, the five declared nuclear weapons states would reduce their nuclear holdings to 200 warheads each, and the undeclared nuclear weapons states would be put under controls as well. Most of the remaining warheads would be "separated from their launchers and placed in deep, secure storage on the territory of the owner state under international monitoring."[14] The first two forms could be understood as steps to take to get to the third form. This proposal makes clear the important role of international cooperation and agreements in implementing a minimum deterrence strategy.

But, given the virtues in reducing the number of nuclear weapons involved in implementing a minimum deterrence strategy, why not go further, all the way to zero? If nuclear arms reductions are good, it seems to stand to reason that the more reductions the better. Why not adopt the advice of the former military leaders discussed at the beginning of the chapter? The advocates of minimum deterrence would respond that reducing to zero would be too much of a good thing. Like adopting a countervailing or a prevailing strategy, going to zero would undermine the crystal-ball effect and thus forsake crisis stability. According to Michael Quinlan, it is "the existence of nuclear weapons [that] can bring with it valuable crisis stability." He continues:

> Abolishing actual nuclear weapons does not remove nuclear risk. Might reduced awareness of that risk weaken the deterrence of war itself? Might adventurist leaders gamble more readily? Might they hope to complete a coup before an adversary could rebuild a nuclear option?[15]

Nuclear weapons can guarantee the avoidance of war under a minimum deterrence strategy. But these weapons might encourage thoughts of war either if they are thought of as weapons in the traditional sense (prevailing or countervailing strategy) or if they are all dismantled. How would advocates of the abolition of nuclear weapons respond to this argument?

THE ABOLITION OF NUCLEAR WEAPONS

If nuclear weapons did not exist, they could not be used. This suggests that a solution to the nuclear predicament lies, as the generals and admirals cited at the beginning of the chapter claim, in the elimination of nuclear weapons: complete and universal nuclear disarmament. As we saw in Chapter 4, one of the questions that leaders had to answer at the dawn of the nuclear age, at the end of World War II, was whether or not nuclear weapons should be built and stockpiled in times of peace. The answer chosen was, of course, that nuclear weapons should be part of the military arsenal in times of peace, and out of this choice developed the doctrine of nuclear deterrence. But now, in the second nuclear age, we face this question again. Many see nuclear disarmament as the natural result of the end of the Cold War. Jonathan Schell writes:

> The abolition of nuclear arms—to cite a chapter of American history—would be to the end of the cold war what the Constitutional Convention was to the War of Independence. The end of the cold war was a liberation. Abolition is the act of foundation toward which the liberation points as its natural consequence and completion.[16]

But before considering the argument that can be made for nuclear disarmament, we need to consider exactly what nuclear disarmament is. As Michael Mazaar notes: "The question of nuclear-weapon capability is one of degree, not an either/or proposition; no major industrial power will ever have 'zero' nuclear-weapon capability."[17] To take one example of the uncertainty attached to the idea of nuclear disarmament, there is, as mentioned in Chapter 7, the concept of "being a screwdriver away" from having a functioning nuclear weapon. In other words, a nation may have no nuclear weapons fully assembled, but have components that could be assembled into a functioning warhead in a short time. Would such a nation be said to be disarmed of nuclear weapons? There is no definite answer. It is a matter of how we define "nuclear disarmament." The end state of nuclear disarmament means, at a minimum, having no functioning nuclear weapon, but does it also mean being more than a screwdriver away from a functioning weapon? There is a continuum from a nation's having or being very close to having (being a screwdriver away from) a functioning nuclear weapon to a nation's being very far away from having a functioning nuclear weapon. As Jonathan Schell has noted, this can be thought of in terms of the amount of time it would take a nation to construct a functioning nuclear weapon, should it choose to do so.[18] The kind of policy one recommends in advocating the abolition of nuclear weapons will depend on what definition one adopts, where one draws the line on that continuum between being disarmed and armed of nuclear weapons.

We will consider two different definitions of the end state of nuclear disarmament, leading to two different policies of abolishing nuclear weapons, and discuss the different arguments that could be made for each of them. We will call these policies *Disarmament I* and *Disarmament II*. The definitions will be very rough, but will serve our purposes anyway.

- *Disarmament I*. A former nuclear power has disarmed itself of its nuclear weapons when it has no functioning weapons, even though it may have extensive nuclear capability and be close to having functioning weapons, for example, being only a screwdriver away.
- *Disarmament II*. A former nuclear power is disarmed only when it is very far away from having a functioning nuclear weapon, that is, only when it has little existing nuclear capability.

When a nation is disarmed of its nuclear weapons, in the sense of Disarmament I, it has merely eliminated these weapons, but when it is disarmed of nuclear weapons in the second sense, both its nuclear weapons and most of its nuclear capacity have been eliminated. A practical condition for Disarmament II, as we shall see, is that nuclear weapons have been *delegitimated*.

Consider first Disarmament I. If all the nations of the world were to divest themselves of their nuclear weapons in this sense, many of them would presumably retain the capacity to rebuild their weapons relatively quickly. A nation that retained this quick-rebuild capacity would have what is called a "virtual nuclear arsenal."[19] Being perhaps only a screwdriver away from a functioning nuclear weapon, such a nation would have a nuclear arsenal *in effect*, though no fully assembled weapons.[20] The most important point to recognize is that *a nation with a virtual nuclear arsenal could still be practicing nuclear deterrence*! Because it could rebuild its weapons in short order, it could make nuclear threats against its opponents even in the absence of assembled weapons. In Jonathan Schell's apt phrase, a nation with a virtual nuclear arsenal could practice "weaponless [nuclear] deterrence."[21] The abolition of nuclear weapons, in the sense of Disarmament I, does not by itself move us beyond nuclear deterrence. Because the knowledge of how to build nuclear weapons is forever ours and because the technology for building them is part of any advanced industrial society, eliminating nuclear weapons will not by itself eliminate the threat of nuclear destruction. The nuclear predicament lies not in the weapons themselves, but in our knowledge of the laws of physics and our advanced industrial infrastructure that makes their production possible.

So the question is whether we are more likely to find a solution to the nuclear predicament in minimum deterrence or in Disarmament I (weaponless deterrence). The first issue to examine is whether it is minimum deterrence or weaponless deterrence that leads to a lower risk of nuclear catastrophe. As we have seen, the argument in favor of minimum deterrence lies in the role of the crystal-ball effect in producing the crisis stability that greatly reduces the likelihood of war. But it seems that the end of the Cold War may have weakened the impact of the crystal-ball effect in avoiding nuclear war. The effect depends on nuclear nations being in a MAD relationship, and with the increasing risks of nuclear proliferation (see Chapter 7), there are likely in the future to be pairs of nuclear opponents, such as India and Pakistan, who do not have enough protected nuclear weapons to be in a MAD relationship. In addition, given a growing number of nuclear nations, a one-way nuclear war (a war between a nuclear power and a nonnuclear power) would become more likely.[22] Increasing the likelihood of these possibilities even more is that the constraints imposed on the actions of the lesser nuclear nations by the bipolar division of the world between East and West has faded with the end of the Cold War. Lesser nuclear nations contemplating the use of nuclear weapons need not now be so worried about how the great powers would react to such behavior.

Although the kinds of nuclear wars discussed in the last paragraph would not amount to the global catastrophe that a superpower nuclear war during the Cold War would have been, they would be catastrophe enough. Moreover, there is another danger. Such a war could result in victory for the side that used (or first used) nuclear weapons (as it did for the United States against Japan). Were a nation in the future to appear to gain victory from its use of nuclear weapons, this would make future nuclear use much more likely. The lesson other nations would draw would *not* be the one that the superpowers had come to accept, that nuclear use between them would be disastrous, but rather that nuclear weapons can provide a military advantage in war. If this lesson were widely accepted, it would not only make nuclear use by existing nuclear powers more likely, but it would lead to an increase in the proliferation of nuclear weapons. Nonnuclear nations would want nuclear weapons not only for the military advantage they would seem to provide, but also to counter the military advantage they may believe their opponents to be seeking through these weapons.

But this argument against minimum deterrence based on the cloudiness of the post-Cold War crystal ball does not necessarily show that Disarmament I would be more effective at avoiding war than minimum deterrence. Weaponless deterrence also depends on the crystal-ball effect. Under weaponless deterrence, what is supposed to keep nations from rebuilding and then using their nuclear weapons is the same perception that is supposed to keep them from using their nuclear weapons under minimum deterrence, namely, their ability to foresee in the crystal ball the utter catastrophe that would likely result. But the crystal ball seems even cloudier under Disarmament I than under minimum deterrence. This is implied by the argument against the abolition of nuclear weapons rehearsed at the end of the last section. Because leaders might believe under weaponless deterrence that they could secretly rebuild their nuclear weapons and use them to destroy the ability of their opponent to rebuild and retaliate, the crystal ball does not yield the clear perception of catastrophe that it does under minimum deterrence. In other words, crisis stability is weaker under weaponless deterrence than it is under minimum deterrence.

How do proponents of the abolition of nuclear weapons respond to this argument? The main response is that, while under minimum deterrence "the risk of accidental or unauthorized use would decline dramatically," it would "not disappear altogether."[23] The risk of accidental or inadvertent nuclear war has always been a serious problem for nuclear deterrence. Minimum deterrence would reduce this risk, in comparison with more aggressive forms of nuclear strategy, but it would not eliminate the risk, for the weapons would still be there to be accidentally used. Nuclear disarmament, on the other hand, would eliminate this risk, because there would be no weapons to be accidentally used. So, in comparing minimum deterrence and Disarmament I on the scale of safety, we must decide whether the greater crisis instability of Disarmament I or the greater risk of accidental nuclear war under minimum deterrence is a more important consideration. This would be a very difficult judgment to make, the least of the reasons being that it is an apples-and-oranges kind of comparison.

But there is a larger point to be made.[24] Because there are strong objections to both minimum deterrence and Disarmament I, it may well be that whichever of them turned out to be safer, *neither of them would be safe enough to count as a solution to the nuclear predicament*. The risk of nuclear catastrophe is simply too great under either approach. Neither approach can reduce that risk to the level of insignificance, as required if there is to be a genuine solution to the nuclear predicament.

We should turn then to consider Disarmament II. We would do well to begin this discussion by pondering an observation by Salvador de Madariaga:

> The trouble with disarmament was (and still is) that the problem of war is tackled upside down and at the wrong end.... Nations don't distrust each other because they are armed; they are armed because they distrust each other. And therefore to want disarmament before a minimum of common agreement on fundamentals is as absurd as to want people to go undressed in winter. Let the weather be warm, and they will undress readily enough without committees to tell them so.[25]

This insightful remark brings us back to the matter of international cooperation.

Disarmament II would depend much more than either minimum deterrence or Disarmament I on such cooperation. Disarmament I does depend on greater international cooperation than minimum deterrence because the former could be implemented only through an agreement among nations to abandon, not merely reduce, their nuclear weapons. But this cooperation does not go far enough. Under Disarmament I, nations would still feel the need to practice nuclear deterrence, in the form of weaponless deterrence, to keep their opponents from aggression. Only when the level of cooperation were much greater, would trust be high enough that nations would feel sufficiently confident in the friendly intentions of other nations to abandon most of their nuclear capacity and achieve a state of Disarmament II. The clothes would be shed only when the weather had sufficiently warmed. More important, only when trust was that great, irrespective of the weapons, would there be any hope of the risk of nuclear catastrophe falling to a level of insignificance, as required of a genuine solution to the nuclear predicament. If there is a solution to the nuclear predicament, it must be political. But is such a solution possible? Can nations ever achieve the level of cooperation necessary to bring about Disarmament II?

One way to approach this question is to consider what other goals would need to be achieved in order to reduce the risk of nuclear catastrophe to a level of insignificance, and then to ask whether or not it is possible for those other goals to be achieved. There are two such goals worth our attention. The first is avoiding conventional war. The second, related goal is guaranteeing that nations will not interfere with the legitimate interests of other nations. These subsidiary goals must be part of a solution to the nuclear predicament because of their relation to the main goal—the avoidance of nuclear war.

Conventional war must be avoided because, so long as it remains a significant possibility, nuclear war will remain a significant possibility as well. Nuclear disarmament could not by itself guarantee that a conventional war would remain conventional, because the weapons could be rebuilt. In a conventional war under Disarmament I, both sides would be greatly tempted to rebuild their nuclear weapons, the losing side in order to turn defeat into victory and the winning side in order to deny the losing side this advantage.

But the need to avoid conventional war creates one of the most difficult problems facing the search for a solution: the incompatibility between the goals sought. The goal of avoiding conventional war may be incompatible with the goal of avoiding nuclear war. For nuclear deterrence deters conventional wars as well as nuclear wars. Nuclear states are afraid of engaging in any kind of military conflict with other nuclear states out of fear that the conflict could escalate into nuclear war. This is the logic behind the U.S. Cold War policy of first use of nuclear weapons in Europe, discussed in Chapter 4. The threat to use nuclear weapons against conventional aggression is meant to deter that aggression. Efforts to lessen the likelihood of nuclear war would also lessen this element of fear and so make conventional war more likely. But conventional war can lead to nuclear war. There is a paradox here. The less likely one makes nuclear war, the more likely one makes conventional war; but the more likely one makes conventional war, the more likely one makes nuclear war.

Consider now the second subsidiary goal: guaranteeing that nations will not interfere with the legitimate interests of other nations. Here there seems to be an incompatibility of goals as well. For in order to ensure noninterference, nations acquire military forces, conventional and nuclear, and practice deterrence. So interference is avoided by armaments, but armaments create the possibility of such interference, since they can be used for aggression as well as defense. To try to ensure noninterference with its interests, a nation creates the material basis for war. This incompatibility is at the heart of the nuclear predicament. For the nuclear predicament is a situation in which efforts to achieve national security through nuclear deterrence end up threatening national survival through the risk of nuclear catastrophe. These efforts seem self-defeating, since they pose the serious risk of destroying the nation whose interests they are designed to serve. It seems impossible for a nation both to ensure the avoidance of nuclear ruin and to guarantee that its legitimate interests will not be interfered with.

But these incompatibilities among goals exist only in an international climate in which there is insufficient trust and cooperation among nations. These incompatibilities assume a background of international hostility and mistrust. They exist only in cold weather, not warm. If there were sufficient trust and cooperation, nations would not feel the need to deploy military forces and practice deterrence to protect their interests. When conflicts of interest arose, the expectation would be that they would be settled peacefully. Consider one small example of how cooperation among nations can avoid conflicts of interest leading to war. In pursuit of economic prosperity, many nations might seek to mine the resources of the deep oceans. If nations simply try to compete with each other in staking out areas of the ocean containing valuable minerals, this might lead to war. But if all nations agree in advance on some scheme of dividing up ocean plots or profits from ocean mining, then the conflict would be handled cooperatively and war would be unlikely to result. The basis for the cooperative resolution of this kind of conflict has been established by the Law of the Sea Treaty.

What is needed is a scheme of international cooperation, including effective means by which conflicts can be resolved without the use of military force, that is sufficiently deep to remove the fear of aggression. Moreover, the scheme of cooperation would have to involve all nations, not simply the nuclear powers, since conflict anywhere on the globe that is not cooperatively resolved creates risks of nuclear war, due to the possibility of the nuclear powers' being dragged into the fray. When we speak of the peace that nuclear deterrence is said to have brought to the world since 1945, we often forget the continuous series of bloody military conflicts that have occurred between or within other nations (or between a nuclear and a nonnuclear nation). We must put a stop to all such bloodshed not only because of the great human suffering it represents, but also because a solution to the nuclear predicament itself requires this. Nuclear weapons have created a situation in which security for one requires security for all, not just among nuclear powers, but among all nations.

There are two kinds of cooperative, nonviolent conflict resolution among nations. First, the nations in conflict may themselves negotiate a resolution of that conflict, either through a formal or an informal negotiating process. This may be called *direct cooperation*. Second, the nations may have previously created or accepted an institutional arrangement, the purpose of which is peacefully to resolve conflicts between them. This may be called *indirect cooperation* because the nations may not agree with the particular resolution, but are bound to accept it because they are cooperating in a common institutional framework that has dictated that resolution. For example, if two neighbors are in conflict over their property line, a cooperative resolution might come directly through negotiations between them or indirectly through the legal system of that community, which the neighbors have voluntarily joined (say, by freely choosing to move to the community).

Though force or threat of force need not come into play with direct cooperation, it can come into play with indirect cooperation. In the latter case, nations initially agree voluntarily to accept the authority of the institution for conflict resolution, but part of that agreement may be to allow the institution to use force or threat of force against them if they do not voluntarily accept the institution's peaceful resolution of particular conflicts in which they are involved. In a legal system, the police back the courts.

How might it come about that nations could, either directly or indirectly, cooperatively resolve their conflicts? This is a question of what would constitute a *cooperative world order*.[26] One possibility is that nations might have such good relations with each other that all conflicts between them are, as a matter of course, resolved through direct cooperation. Consider, again, the case of the United States and Britain. They do not require an independent institutional framework to resolve their conflicts because it is simply unimaginable that their conflicts could ever lead them to war. The political, economic, and cultural ties between the United States and Britain are now so close that no leader of either nation would ever seriously consider using force against the other. War would risk too much. So when conflicts arise between them, pushing things to the point of force is never a real option. A resolution is formally negotiated or arrived at through informal give and take.

In the case of nations whose relations are not close, direct cooperative resolution of conflicts can sometimes be achieved, but not always counted on. When relations are not close, it is not unthinkable that the nations could seek to resolve a conflict between them with force. In the case of such nations, only indirect cooperation can guarantee no war. What is called for are independent institutions for resolving their conflicts, supranational institutions with authority over these nations and an ability to enforce their decisions, a form of federation of nations or world government. This is the solution to the nuclear predicament advocated by Einstein. After the war Einstein worked hard with his fellow scientists and with the public at large, seeking to bring about recognition of the need for a world government. This was the situation as he saw it:

> So long as there are sovereign nations possessing great power, war is inevitable. That is not to say when it will come, but only that it is sure to come. That was true before the atomic bomb was made. What has been changed is the destructiveness of war.[27]

This was Einstein's solution:

> Mankind can only gain protection against the danger of unimaginable destruction and wanton annihilation if a supranational organization has alone the authority to produce and possess these weapons.[28]

The nations of the world could voluntarily create supranational institutions with the power to enforce resolutions of conflicts. As a token of such police power, Einstein suggests the world institution may need the authority to possess nuclear weapons, an authority denied to its member nations. Thus, under this kind of scheme of Disarmament II, only individual nations would be disarmed of nuclear weapons, not the world authority.

There are two obvious problems with such a vision of a world authority. First, it is probably quite infeasible. Nations would likely never agree to a world government with real police power, because it would involve such an extensive interference with their valued independence and sovereignty. Nor is fear of such an international authority unjustified, since its great power would be open to abuse. The authority might even become tyrannical. So, it is hard to imagine that the nations of the world would ever voluntarily submit to the authority of a world government with true police power. Second, even assuming it were feasible, if the authority possessed nuclear weapons, it would not even provide a solution to the nuclear predicament, since it may practice nuclear deterrence and possibly use its nuclear weapons.

But consider the possibility of a weaker form of world authority, one that could provide an effective means of conflict resolution among nations, but would not involve extensive police power, and, especially, would not possess nuclear weapons. If such an authority came into being, it might represent a form of cooperation among nations that would lead to a level of international trust sufficient to bring about Disarmament II and constitute a genuine solution to the nuclear predicament. Under this form of world authority, nations would not be forced to surrender their nuclear weapons because of nuclear threats from the authority, but would, over time, give up their weapons and their nuclear capability through negotiation because the need for the weapons would no longer be felt.

But is there reason to think that achieving this form of world authority is any more feasible than achieving the world authority with extensive police power? Perhaps it is feasible, if we conceive of its coming about in a different way. Instead of nations deliberately surrendering their sovereignty at the founding convention of a world government, they might slowly and only half consciously surrender their sovereignty by acquiescing in the development of rules of international law. Even now, without the central enforcement mechanism necessary for a true world government, international law does sometimes serve as an effective mechanism of control over the behavior of nations and for resolving disputes among them. This is due, in part, to the fact that other nations can "punish" violators of international law by applying various kinds of sanctions, especially economic sanctions, and this, in conjunction with growing economic interdependence, makes compliance with international law generally in the national self-interest.

This could lead to the gradual empowering of a central authority to enforce a resolution of conflicts, as suggested by Stephen Toulmin.

> [G]reater interdependence makes it increasingly disadvantageous for states to act as "outlaws," even in advance of formal machinery for the enforcement of international law.... [A]s Vico and the Epicureans both foresaw, the pragmatic demands of the actual situation may nonetheless lead to the progressive crystallization of supranational institutions and constraints, without any need for the sovereign nations involved to agree explicitly on any formal treaty or contract.[29]

Toulmin suggests an analogy. When humans discovered how to use fire, its destructive potential in the hands of one's enemies must have seemed as frightening as nuclear energy in the hands of our enemies seems to us. But fire was brought under community control. What brought the technology of fire under human control was a legal invention: the concept of "arson." The use of fire was safely naturalized into human life through the development of new institutions and public attitudes, by which the misuse of fire was stigmatized as antihuman and punished as a crime.[30]

A cooperative world order of the sort here envisioned would, over time, allow Disarmament II to come into being. It would be the warm weather that would lead the nations to remove their defensive coats of their own volition. This could bring about a true solution to the nuclear predicament, a reduction in the risk of nuclear catastrophe to a level of insignificance. As we suggested earlier, however, it is not primarily the abandonment of the nuclear capacity that would reduce the risk to this level, but rather the cooperative world order itself. The relationship is this: The reduction of the risk to a level of insignificance, brought about by the cooperative world order, would lead to the abandonment of the nuclear capability. It is the extensive network of international political institutions, and the deep level of trust that they could in time engender, that would lead to the reduction of the risk of nuclear catastrophe. The nuclear capacity itself would be abandoned almost as a side effect. It is not the abolition of nuclear weapons, by itself, that would solve the nuclear predicament.

Earlier, we mentioned that a condition for Disarmament II is that nuclear weapons be delegitimated. This shows, finally, how a solution to the nuclear predicament would close the gap that nuclear weapons have created between morality and prudence. The people of the world have always looked upon nuclear weapons with a degree of horror— a recognition of the terrible moral price we collectively pay for having them in our midst. But once these weapons had come into being, and the other side had them too, it seemed necessary in terms of security or prudence to keep them. But, were a sufficiently cooperative world order to come into existence, so that the risk of nuclear catastrophe would be reduced to a level of insignificance, the weapons would no longer be seen to have that prudential value. There would no longer be the conflict between the moral horror the weapons engender in us and our belief that we had to have them for our security. Thus we would look upon the weapons only with horror, and the conflict between morality and prudence caused by them would be removed. Possession of the weapons would no longer be seen as legitimate. Once the prudential need for the weapons was removed, they would be seen as lacking legitimacy, as delegitimated, and this perception would hasten their abandonment.

In the end, is a solution to the nuclear predicament possible? There is a solution only if the kind of cooperative world order discussed earlier could come into being. There are reasons to think that it could come into being, but whether it will, no one, of course, can say. If it cannot come into being, or simply does not, we will be stuck in the nuclear predicament for as far as we can see into the future. This raises the question: If the nuclear predicament cannot be solved, what kind of nuclear policy should we adopt? Should we opt instead for technical obviation or minimum deterrence?

There might be a conflict here. We should attempt to achieve a cooperative world order, for only this would solve the nuclear predicament, even though we do not know at this point whether or not it can be achieved. If it cannot be achieved, we should adopt the least risky alternative policy. The potential conflict is that our attempts to establish a cooperative world order might lead us in a direction away from the least risky alternative policy. Fortunately, this is not the case. As we have seen, minimum deterrence is a less risky policy than countervailing or prevailing strategy. Moreover, moving toward a minimum deterrence strategy, that is, reducing the number of nuclear weapons so that any deterrence relationship would be one of minimum deterrence, is also what would move us toward a cooperative order, if one is possible. The reason is that minimum deterrence requires much more international cooperation than do the other strategies. Not only would nations learn better to work with each other, but they would come to realize through experience that getting rid of nuclear weapons does not degrade their security. Thus, working toward minimum deterrence is the beginning of, and moves us further toward, a cooperative world order. As a result, our recommendation for the immediate future is that we work toward a policy of minimum deterrence. If this effort shows the feasibility of a cooperative world order, we are well on our way. If it does not, we at least will have arrived at the safest nuclear policy we can achieve.

Unless and until the nuclear predicament is solved, and until we know whether or not the policy that would solve it can succeed, we will have to choose nuclear policies in terms of their relative safety, in the light of the knowledge that the risk of nuclear catastrophe will remain significant whatever we do. We have argued that the nuclear policy we should now choose is minimum deterrence, not only because it is the safest alternative to the abolition of nuclear weapons under a cooperative world order, but because it is a necessary first step toward that true solution. So, the near-term choice of minimum deterrence need not blunt our purpose in seeking a true solution to the predicament. Minimum deterrence is the policy for the second nuclear age, not only because it is itself the best in the near-term, in our current less than cooperative world order, but because it is the best way to seek to bring about the conditions that could lead to a third nuclear age in which the nuclear danger is reduced to near-zero.

WHAT CAN AN INDIVIDUAL DO?

Once you have come to a conclusion about an approach that offers a genuine solution to the nuclear predicament, or, short of a genuine solution, one that promises the safest nuclear policy, what can you do as an individual to help bring about that approach or policy? This is where prospects may look especially daunting. It may seem that a single individual, far from the corridors of power, can do little to move the world in the right direction. But the stakes are so high that an effort that has only a small impact in the overall scheme of things is still of great importance.

There are certain impediments that stand in the way of a collective will to adopt the best approach or policy, and the main role of an individual in lessening the nuclear danger is to work to overcome them. There are two kinds of impediments: (1) ignorance and a lack of understanding of the nature of the nuclear predicament and (2) harmful attitudes of certain sorts. These impediments exist within individuals, in their ways of thinking, so working to overcome them often requires working on ourselves as well as on others. The bomb may have affected us in ways that interfere with effective thinking about a solution, as our discussion in the last chapter suggests. Or, on the contrary, the bomb may *not* have affected our thinking in ways that it should have if we are to think well about avoiding its dangers, as Einstein's famous remark suggests. Either way, the thinking of individuals is a major impediment to achieving a solution.

The first kind of impediment is ignorance or a lack of understanding. There is, of course, a great deal of plain ignorance about nuclear weapons and nuclear weapons policy. But even among those with some knowledge, there is a widespread lack of understanding of the nature of the nuclear predicament. This is not surprising. Our ways of thinking about the world often lag significantly behind changes in the world. So it is not unexpected that the changes wrought by nuclear weapons have yet to be fully reflected in our understanding. Nuclear weapons have overturned basic military truths accepted for centuries, and our thinking has had little more than half a century to adjust. Among the beliefs that must be abandoned when nuclear weapons are involved is that the use of weapons can serve military purposes, that the more weapons a nation has, the more militarily secure it is, and that a nation can make itself militarily secure by making its opponent militarily insecure. The condition of mutual assured destruction falsifies these beliefs. In addition, and perhaps more important, there is the belief that the end of the Cold War has removed the nuclear danger and solved the nuclear predicament.

The second type of impediment, harmful attitudes, is primarily a matter of feelings, but feelings that are associated with or supported by certain beliefs. Some of these attitudes, such as patriotism and nationalism, involve strong positive feelings toward one's own nation. Patriotism and nationalism are associated with the belief that one's own nation is special. These positive feelings are often beneficial, for example, when they promote the social cohesion needed for a nation to function effectively. But at times they are harmful, since they can result in the glorification of one's own nation at the expense of other nations and in policies that encroach on the legitimate interests of other nations. Patriotic zeal has been a cause of many wars. Because they are feelings, moreover, they are difficult to control or shut off at the point at which their effects become harmful.

Other attitudes, such as national chauvinism and xenophobia, are almost always harmful in their effects. These attitudes are associated with the belief not merely that one's nation or culture is special, but also that other nations or cultures are inferior or evil. National chauvinism goes beyond patriotism to include strong negative feelings toward other nations. Such feelings can lead one nation to disregard the rights and concerns of other nations. Xenophobia, fear of what is foreign, can lead to the mistaken belief that other nations are out to get us and will do everything in their power to destroy us. This sort of paranoid misperception clearly can lead to policies that increase the risk of war. For example, xenophobic misperceptions of the aggressiveness of the other side's intentions helped to drive the arms race during the Cold War. Such attitudes are a major stumbling block to the kind of cooperative world order needed to solve the predicament.

But two words of caution are in order. First, it may not be possible to overcome these impediments completely. For example, some would argue that negative attitudes, such as xenophobia, are so ingrained in the human mind-set that no amount of education could completely remove them. Second, even if all of the impediments could be completely removed, this would not guarantee the adoption of the best nuclear policy. The reason, as we hope the discussion in the book has made abundantly clear, is that there is ample room for reasonable disagreement about what nuclear policies we ought to adopt.

This point suggests a third impediment. Because nuclear weapons issues are so complicated, and because the stakes are so high, another impediment to a solution is the belief that the answers are easy. What we must do, in addition to removing misunderstanding and working on avoiding harmful attitudes, is to promote in ourselves and others a recognition of the need to think critically about nuclear policy, to appreciate and tolerate the complexity of the issues, and not to be uncomfortable with the uncertainty that the complexity engenders. Above all, perhaps, the inherent difficulty and complexity of the issues implies that we should be tolerant of the views and arguments of others. This is surely an area where a genuine public debate is necessary.

The need for a genuine public debate over nuclear weapons issues leads naturally to the issue of collective decision making. So far we have been discussing impediments in individuals, impediments such as lack of understanding, harmful attitudes, and uncritical thinking processes. But nuclear policy is the result of a political process.

Individual beliefs about lessening the nuclear danger must be translated into national and international policy. So, in addition to the education that is required to remove the impediments, we also need political action.[31]

Political action would be necessary, even if there were no impediments in the decision-making process, for the understanding and openness in attitude among individuals must be democratically translated into effective policy. Moreover, political activity is itself an important part of the educational process. But political activity divorced from the educational effort to remove the impediments is not sufficient, and can in fact be counterproductive. If people have little understanding of the nuclear predicament, little inclination to think critically about it, or the sorts of harmful attitudes discussed earlier, democratic decisions can increase rather than decrease the nuclear danger. This is the reason some people argue that the public should not be trusted and that nuclear policy should not be democratically decided. Instead, they argue, nuclear policy should be determined by policy elites, who are thought to be wiser than the public in such matters. But democratic decisions are likely to be bad decisions only to the extent that the impediments are widespread among the public, and the policy elites may operate under impediments of their own.[32] Thus, education and democratic political action remain the avenues we should pursue.

Success in these endeavors is not guaranteed, but it is possible. The likelihood of nuclear war is not independent of the action we take, individually and collectively. Reducing the risk of nuclear catastrophe, perhaps even solving the nuclear predicament, should not be seen as a utopian dream. The task is formidable, but the prize is great. Not only can we secure our civilization from destruction, but in doing so, we may be able to bring about a world in which all war, not just nuclear war, is a thing of the past. Such may be the fruit of the change in our ways of thinking needed to solve the nuclear predicament.

NOTES

1. International Generals and Admirals, "Statement on Nuclear Weapons," reprinted in *Washington Quarterly* 20, no. 3 (summer 1997): 125–130. Quotations are from pp. 125, 126, 127.
2. For a discussion of Reykjavik developing the kind of criticism discussed here, see James Schlesinger, "Reykjavik and Revelations: A Turn of the Tide," *Foreign Affairs* 65, no. 3 (1987): 426–446.
3. Michael Mazarr, "Introduction," special issue on nuclear arms control, *Washington Quarterly* 20, no. 3 (summer 1997): 82.
4. George Lee Butler, "The General's Bombshell: Phasing Out the U.S. Nuclear Arsenal," *Washington Quarterly* 20, no. 3 (summer 1997): 133, 134 (emphasis added).
5. This is argued by a number of writers, including Jonathan Schell, in *The Fate of the Earth* (New York: Avon Books, 1983).
6. Except through our inadequate computer software on January 1, 2000, the Y2K problem.
7. See our discussion of norms in international relations in Chapter 7.
8. For a good discussion and critique of countervailing strategy, see Robert Jervis, *The Illogic of American Nuclear Strategy* (Ithaca, NY: Cornell University Press, 1984).
9. Paul Nitze, "Is It Time to Junk Our Nukes?" *Washington Quarterly* 20, no. 3 (summer 1997): 99.
10. Such a strategy is also discussed, for example, in H. A. Feiveson et al., "Reducing U.S. and Soviet Nuclear Arsenals," *Bulletin of the Atomic Scientists* (August 1985): 144–150.

11. See The Harvard Nuclear Study Group, *Living with Nuclear Weapons* (New York: Bantam, 1983): 43–44.
12. Some of those opposed to BMD would permit theater missile defenses (TMD). BMD are primarily strategic defenses, designed to protect a nation's homeland, whereas TMD are for the local protection of troops on the battlefield. Thus, TMD by themselves would not undermine the crystal-ball effect, though some are concerned that a TMD capacity could be too easily converted into a BMD capacity.
13. Jonathan Dean, "The Road Beyond START: How Far Should We Go?" consultation paper (Washington, D.C.: The Atlantic Council of the United States, 1997).
14. Ibid., p. 19.
15. Michael Quinlan, "The Future of Nuclear Weapons in World Affairs," *Washington Quarterly* 20, no. 3 (summer 1997): 139.
16. Jonathan Schell, "The Gift of Time," *The Nation*, February 2, 1998, p. 16.
17. Michael Mazaar, "Virtual Nuclear Arsenals," *Survival* 37, no. 3 (autumn 1995): 23.
18. Jonathan Schell, *The Abolition* (New York: Alfred Knopf, 1984).
19. Mazaar, "Virtual Nuclear Arsenals."
20. In a fuller discussion of the idea of being close to having a functioning nuclear weapon, we should consider as part of this idea the role of a delivery vehicle for the weapon. If a nation had a fully assembled nuclear weapon in a laboratory somewhere but could not move it anywhere, it would not have a nuclear arsenal in the sense that it could not use or credibly threaten anyone with the weapon. But, for the sake of simplicity, we will not examine this aspect of the issue.
21. Schell, *The Abolition*.
22. The only nuclear war to have occurred was such a war, the one between the United States and Japan.
23. Michael Mazaar, "Virtual Nuclear Arsenals," p. 13.
24. For an elaboration of this argument, see Steven Lee, *Morality, Prudence, and Nuclear Weapons* (Cambridge, Eng.: Cambridge University Press, 1993), especially Chapter 7.
25. Salvador de Madariaga, quoted in Quinlan, "The Future of Nuclear Weapons," p. 141.
26. There is a large literature on world order studies. One classic example is Richard Falk, *A Study of Future Worlds* (New York: Free Press, 1975).
27. Albert Einstein, *Ideas and Opinions* (New York: Bonanza Books, 1954), p. 118.
28. Ibid., p. 150.
29. Stephen Toulmin, "The Limits of Allegiance in a Nuclear Age," in *Nuclear Weapons and the Future of Humanity*, ed. A. Cohen and S. Lee (Totowa, NJ: Rowman and Allanheld, 1986), p. 365.
30. Ibid., p. 365.
31. Two books from the Cold War era discussing education and political action in the area of nuclear weapons are Belle Zars, Beth Wilson, and Ariel Phillips, *Education and the Threat of Nuclear War* (Cambridge, MA: Harvard Education Review, 1985); and David Barish and Judith Lipton, *Stop Nuclear War—A Handbook* (New York: Grove Press, 1982).
32. For example, they may speak for groups that have an interest in promoting weapons production or an interest in promoting their own economic well-being at the expense of other nations, which may lead them toward decisions that would undermine a cooperative world order.

GLOSSARY

ABM Antiballistic Missile; a missile designed to destroy incoming warheads.

ABM Treaty Treaty signed in 1972 restricting the testing and deployment of ABMs; currently in force.

Alpha Particle The He-4 nucleus consisting of two protons and two neutrons.

Appeasement Offering real concessions in return for an opponent's pledge to behave in a particular way in the future.

Arms Control Agreements to stabilize the qualitative and quantitative arms race; may involve reductions in force levels or restraints on the development, testing, and deployment of weapons.

Arms Race An upward-spiraling competition between two or more nations, each trying to equal or exceed the number and quality of weapons held by an opponent.

Arms-Race Stability A military situation in which an arms race is unlikely to arise, because neither side believes that building new weapons would provide it with a significant military advantage, or help it overcome a significant military disadvantage.

Assured Destruction The strategic doctrine first promulgated by Secretary of Defense McNamara in which the United States sought "to deter a deliberate nuclear attack upon the United States or its allies by maintaining at all times a clear and unmistakable ability to inflict an unacceptable degree of damage upon any aggressor … even after absorbing a surprise first strike."

Atomic Number (Z) The number of protons in the nucleus of an atom; also equal to the number of electrons.

Atomic Weight (A) The sum of the number of protons and neutrons in an atom's nucleus; very close to the actual weight of the atom.

Beta Rays Electrons; may have an electrical charge of either +e or −e.

Blitzkrieg "Lightning war"; the use of motorized and armored units along with airpower to break through enemy defenses quickly, isolate enemy units, and defeat them piecemeal.

BMD Ballistic Missile Defense; a variety of systems capable of destroying enemy missiles or warheads after their launch.

Bolt from the Blue An unexpected attack launched by one nation against another.

CBW Chemical and Biological Weapons.

Cold War The intense rivalry between the United States and Soviet Union following World War II in which war was a possibility but was not deliberately sought by either nation.

Collateral Damage   The inadvertent destruction of civilian population adjacent to military targets.

Combatant   A person serving in the military forces of a nation at war or otherwise closely involved in the nation's war-making activity (such as a munitions worker).

Command, Control, Communication, and Intelligence (C³I)   The systems required to obtain timely intelligence, maintain reliable communications during crisis, and direct and control a nation's armed forces in a war.

Compellence   Getting another nation to make some concession under threat of punishment if it fails to do so.

Confidence Building   Measures designed to reassure an opponent that its rival does not intend a sudden use of force.

Containment   Any policy attempting to restrict the expansion or influence of another nation; usually associated with U.S. foreign policy toward the Soviet Union since the late 1940s.

Conventional Forces   The nonnuclear component of a nation's military establishment.

Coulomb Force   The force of attraction or repulsion between electrical charges.

Counterforce Weapons   Weapons best suited for the destruction of an enemy's military forces.

Countervalue Weapons   Weapons best suited for use against what an enemy values, a euphemism for an enemy's industry, recovery capability, and population.

Crisis Stability   A military situation in which war is unlikely to arise in a crisis because neither side would achieve an advantage from striking first, and so neither side has much reason to fear that the other side would strike first.

Critical Mass   The mass of fissionable material required to produce a self-sustaining fission reaction.

Cruise Missile   An air-breathing, computer-guided pilotless aircraft that can carry nuclear weapons.

CTBT   Comprehensive Test Ban Treaty; 1996 treaty prohibiting all nuclear weapons testing; the treaty is not in force, as all forty-four nuclear-weapons-capable states must sign and ratify the treaty, which has yet to occur.

Decapitation   The elimination of an adversary's top command in order to immobilize the adversary's nuclear forces.

Decoupling   The termination of a nation's willingness to use nuclear weapons for the defense of its allies.

Détente   Generally, a policy of seeking better, more cooperative relations between two nations; specifically, the Nixon administration's policy toward the Soviet Union.

Deterrence   Persuading another nation by threat of military retaliation not to engage in aggression, especially the launching of a nuclear attack.

Disarmament   Traditionally, the elimination of the materiel of war possessed by a nation.

Disarming First Strike   A nuclear attack that attempts to destroy a large enough portion of an enemy's nuclear arsenal to forestall nuclear retaliation by the enemy.

Electron Volt (eV)   A unit of energy appropriate for measuring the energies of electrons in atoms and molecules.

Extended Deterrence   Use of the threat of nuclear retaliation to deter an attack on one's allies as well as on one's homeland.

Fallout   Radioactive particles carried by the wind away from the site of a nuclear explosion, posing a threat to living organisms.

First Strike   The initiation of war by a nuclear strike against an opponent.

First Use   A declared policy of being willing to use nuclear weapons if conventional war breaks out.

Flexible Response   A doctrine proposed by Secretary of Defense McNamara under which the U.S. leadership would have a variety of options with which to respond to provocation or aggression, other than the single one of launching a massive nuclear strike.

Forward-Based Systems   A nation's nuclear delivery systems (such as aircraft) located outside the nation's borders near an opponent nation.

Gamma Ray   Electromagnetic radiation (or "light") with frequencies much higher than that of the visible and ultraviolet spectrum.

Geosynchronous Satellites   Satellites that orbit the earth once a day, thereby remaining over a fixed spot on the earth's surface.

Ground Zero   That land or water area above which a nuclear weapon detonates.

Half-Life   The amount of time it takes for half of a sample of a radioactive isotope to decay to its more stable element; the more unstable the isotope, the shorter the half-life.

Hibakusha   The Japanese term for the surviving victims of the atomic explosions over Hiroshima and Nagasaki.

Horizontal Proliferation   What is traditionally understood by the term *proliferation*, namely, the acquisition of nuclear weapons by states not already possessing them.

ICBM   Intercontinental Ballistic Missile.

INF Treaty   1987 treaty between the United States and the USSR abolishing all intermediate and short-range missiles (300–3,500 miles).

Isotope   A term used to differentiate between atoms of an element whose masses differ from one another because their nuclei contain different numbers of neutrons.

JCS   Joint Chiefs of Staff; the commanding officers of each of the U.S. military services plus a chairman, who serve as the principal military advisors to the U.S. government.

Jus Ad Bellum   That part of just-war theory concerning the conditions under which it is morally acceptable for a nation to go to war.

Jus In Bello   That part of just-war theory concerning the conditions under which it is morally acceptable for a nation to use force in the midst of war.

Just-War Theory   The traditional set of standards for judging the morality of military activity, largely recognized by military authorities themselves and embodied in international law.

Kiloton (Kt)   A convenient unit of energy for measuring the prompt energy yield of nuclear explosions; equal to energy released by the explosion of one thousand tons of TNT.

Linkage   Making decisions about arms control or nuclear policy based on nonnuclear actions by one's opponent such as intervention in the Third World or human rights practices.

MAD   Mutual Assured Destruction.

Manhattan Project   The code-name for the U.S. project to build atomic weapons in World War II.

Massive Retaliation   A doctrine in the mid-1950s under which the United States threatened to retaliate instantly by means and at places of its own choosing for a variety of actions by communist states.

Megaton (Mt)   A convenient unit of energy for measuring the prompt energy yield of a nuclear explosion; equal to the energy released by the explosion of one million tons of TNT.

Minimum Deterrence   A nuclear weapons policy that involves the deployment of relatively small numbers of deliverable nuclear warheads, invulnerable to a first strike and lacking an extensive counterforce capability.

Minuteman   A U.S. solid-fueled ICBM deployed in underground silos.

MIRV   Multiple Independently Targeted Reentry Vehicle; separate nuclear warheads mounted on one missile, each capable of being directed at a different target.

Multiplication Factor (k)   A parameter describing the growth or decay in the number of free neutrons in fissionable material. If k is greater than one, the fission reaction will grow exponentially.

Mutual Assured Destruction   The condition under which each of two nations has the ability to destroy the other even after receiving a surprise attack.

MX   A very accurate U.S. ICBM with ten warheads.

National Command Authority   The president of the United States and the Secretary of Defense or their successors, who have the authority to order the use of nuclear weapons.

National Security Council (NSC)   Established in 1947 as the formal advisory body to the president on major national security issues.

National Technical Means A collective name for monitoring capabilities such as satellites used to verify arms control agreements.

NATO North Atlantic Treaty Organization; a mutual security alliance between the United States and the major powers of Western Europe.

Noncombatant A person who is not a combatant and, according to just-war theory, is therefore not a morally acceptable object of attack in wartime.

NPT Non-Proliferation Treaty; 1968 treaty obligating signatories not to provide or facilitate acquisition of nuclear weapons, nor to become a nuclear-weapons state.

Nuclear Fission A process in which a large unstable nucleus breaks up into two smaller nuclei; it may occur spontaneously or be induced by an incident neutron.

Nuclear Fusion A process in which two nuclei are brought close enough together so that the strong nuclear force can act to fuse them into a single new nucleus.

Nuclear Pacifism The doctrine that the use of nuclear force or the threat of its use is morally unacceptable in any form.

Nuclear Terrorism The use or threatened use of nuclear weapons by a group acting partly or completely independently of any state and seeking to achieve political ends through such use or threatened use.

Nuclear Winter A theory that hypothesizes that the spreading blanket of darkness from dust and smoke and other debris generated by numerous nuclear explosions could cause world temperatures to plummet.

Nucleon A generic name for protons and neutrons.

Nunn-Lugar U.S. program to provide financial and technical aid to former Soviet republics in dismantling and safeguarding their nuclear arsenals and nuclear weapons infrastructure.

Omnicide The destruction of all human life; the extinction of the human species.

Opaque Proliferation A situation in which a state acquires nuclear weapons but refuses to acknowledge that it has the nuclear weapons and does not test them.

Pacifism The doctrine that the use of force, or the threat of its use, against other persons is morally unacceptable.

PAL Permissive Action Link; devices on U.S. nuclear weapons that require the use of a unique code to arm the weapons.

Peaceful Coexistence Soviet term for peaceful relations but with continued ideological and economic competition.

Point Defense A defensive system designed to protect a very small target area against missile attack.

Poseidon A U.S. solid-fueled SLBM carrying ten or more warheads.

Politburo The top decision-making group of the Soviet Communist Party and, until recently, of the USSR.

Positron An electron with a charge of +e.

Preemptive Attack An attack launched against an opponent who has given indications that it is preparing to attack.

Preventive War A war initiated without provocation out of fear that some day the enemy might have sufficient power to threaten a nation's security.

Principle of Discrimination That part of just-war theory that requires that force be directed only against combatants; sometimes called the principle of noncombatant immunity.

Principle of Proportionality That part of just-war theory that requires that the amount of force used, either in particular military engagements or in a war overall, not exceed what is proportionate to the military objective.

Proliferation The acquisition of nuclear weapons technology and capability by nonnuclear nations.

Quantum State A particular configuration assumed by an electron in an atom; it is described by a function that gives the probability of finding the electron at different points about the nucleus.

Radioisotope An isotope that is radioactive.

Realism   The doctrine that morality is irrelevant or inapplicable in international relations, especially regarding war.

SAC   Strategic Air Command; the U.S. Air Force command with responsibility for strategic bombers and ICBMs.

SALT   Strategic Arms Limitation Talks/Treaty; arms control negotiations that produced two treaties (SALT I and II). The first, signed in 1972, fixed the number of Soviet and American ICBM and SLBM launchers. The second—signed in 1979, never ratified by the United States, but generally adhered to—limited missiles, bombers, and MIRV deployments.

SDI   Strategic Defense Initiative ("Star Wars"); a proposed system to destroy attacking missiles or warheads.

Second Strike   A nuclear attack launched by a nation after it is struck by a nuclear first strike.

SIOP   Single Integrated Operational Plan; the U.S. government's plan for the use of nuclear weapons in case of war.

SLBM   Submarine-Launched Ballistic Missile; such missiles are launched when the submarine is submerged.

START   Strategic Arms Reduction Talks/Treaties; two treaties (1991, 1993) reducing U.S. and Soviet/Russian strategic delivery systems and nuclear warheads over roughly a fifteen-year period, and banning MIRVs on ICBMs. Both the United States and Russia ratified START I; Russia has not ratified START II. START III talks are underway.

Star Wars   Popular name for SDI (Strategic Defense Initiative).

Strong Nuclear Force   A force that exists between neutrons and protons when they are close together.

Survivability   The degree to which a strategic weapons system can survive an enemy attack and still be available for retaliation.

Tactical Nuclear Weapons   Small nuclear weapons intended for battlefield use.

Technological Obviation   An approach to solving the nuclear predicament that seeks to solve the predicament largely through the development of weapons technology, especially defenses against nuclear missiles.

Thermonuclear Weapon   Weapons whose force is derived at least in part from nuclear fusion, releasing great energy.

TMD   Theater Missile Defense; weapons designed to destroy incoming warheads that had been launched by an enemy's battlefield or theater delivery systems.

Total War   A war with the aim of complete destruction of the enemy nation, in which all possible means are employed without restraint; noncombatants may become objects of direct attack on a large scale.

Triad   The U.S. reliance on ICBMs, SLBMs, and bombers as its strategic delivery systems.

Trident D-5   A long-range U.S. SLBM with very accurate warheads.

Trinity   Code-name for the first nuclear device detonated on July 6, 1945, at Alamogordo, New Mexico.

Verification   The process of determining if a nation is in compliance with its treaty obligations; often performed by satellites.

Vertical Proliferation   An increase in the number of nuclear weapons held by states that already possess nuclear weapons.

WMD   Weapon(s) of Mass Destruction; chemical, biological, or nuclear weapons capable of extensive devastation.

Worst-Case Analysis   A military planning tool that assumes that the enemy will take the most damaging course of action possible.

INDEX